Villas, Sanctuaries and Settlement in the Romano-British Countryside

Villas, Sanctuaries and Settlement in the Romano-British Countryside

New Perspectives and Controversies

Edited by

Martin Henig, Grahame Soffe,
Kate Adcock and Anthony King

Archaeopress Roman Archaeology 95

Archaeopress Publishing Ltd
Summertown Pavilion
18-24 Middle Way
Summertown
Oxford OX2 7LG
www.archaeopress.com

ISBN 978-1-80327-380-8
ISBN 978-1-80327-381-5 (e-Pdf)

THE ASSOCIATION
FOR ROMAN
ARCHAEOLOGY

This volume has been financially supported by a generous subvention from the Association for Roman Archaeology.

This book is available direct from Archaeopress or from our website www.archaeopress.com

Contents

List of Figures

NB All figures are originated by the author or their associated project team, except where indicated at the end of each caption in the relevant chapter. Copyright information and attributions are given in brackets at the end of captions not originated by the author/project.

Cover

Front: Winter view of the Chedworth Roman buildings, looking south-east from above the 'Capitol'. (Copyright Luigi J. Thompson) See Figure 9.16.
Back: Cut-away reconstruction of the 'deep room' and house church at Lullingstone Roman villa, c. AD 380. (Painting by Peter Dunn/Richard Lea. Copyright English Heritage Archive) See Chapter 15.

Roman villas in Britain and beyond

Where, when and what for? Coin use in the Romano-British countryside

Villa mosaics and archaeology

The Roman villas of the Lower Nene Valley and the *Praetorium* at Castor

Piddington, Northamptonshire: wealthy private farm or imperial property?

Whitley Grange villa, Shropshire: a hunting lodge and its landscape

Moor Park, Hertfordshire: two evaluations of an excavation of the 1950s

Great Witcombe, Gloucestershire: a reinterpretation of the site as a temple rather than a villa

Chedworth, Gloucestershire: a question of interpretation

Acroterial decoration and *cantharus* fountains

The stones with Chi-Rho inscriptions at Chedworth

The St Laurence School villa, Bradford on Avon, Wiltshire

Dinnington and Yarford: two villas in south and west Somerset

The Ashtead Roman villa and tileworks

Lullingstone Roman villa

Clinging to Britannia's hemline: continuity and discontinuity in villa estates, boundaries and historic land use on the islands of *Vectis* and *Tanatis*

Where did Sidonius Apollinaris live?

From Roman villa to medieval village at the Mola di Monte Gelato, Lazio, Italy

List of Tables

Roman villas in Britain and beyond

Clinging to Britannia's hemline: continuity and discontinuity in villa estates, boundaries and historic land use on the islands of *Vectis* and *Tanatis*

List of Contributors

KATE ADCOCK
Hon. Editor, Association for Roman Archaeology.
aranews2@gmail.com

ANTHONY BEESON
Late Hon. Archivist, Association for Roman Archaeology.

MARTIN BIDDLE
Emeritus Fellow of Hertford College, University of Oxford OX1 3BW.
martin.biddle@hertford.ox.ac.uk

DAVID BIRD
Former Head of Heritage Conservation,
Surrey County Council.
davidgeorgebird@ntlworld.com

JOHN COLLIS
Professor Emeritus, Department of Archaeology, University of Sheffield.
j.r.collis@sheffield.ac.uk

MARK CORNEY
Independent Archaeological Consultant and Researcher.
Faulkland, Somerset.
mark.redpig@btinternet.com

STEPHEN R. COSH
Stephen R Cosh, DLitt, FSA. Archaeological writer and illustrator. Vice chairman of ASPROM (Association for the Study and Preservation of Roman Mosaics).
stephencosh675@btinternet.com

ROY and DIANA FRIENDSHIP-TAYLOR
Directors of Piddington Villa Museum and Excavation Project.
dianaf-t@hotmail.com

CHRISTINA GRANDE
Former Senior Lecturer in Classical art and architecture, University of Winchester.

MARTIN HENIG
Visiting Professor, Institute of Archaeology, University College London. Research Adviser to the Association for Roman Archaeology. Wolfson College, University of Oxford, OX2 6UD
martin.henig@wolfson.ox.ac.uk or;
School of Archaeology, 36 Beaumont Street, Oxford, OX1 2PG
martin.henig@arch.ox.ac.uk

ANTHONY KING
Hon. President, Association for Roman Archaeology. Professor Emeritus of Roman Archaeology, School of History and Archaeology, University of Winchester, Winchester SO22 4NR.
tony.king@winchester.ac.uk

VICTORIA LEITCH
Hon. Researcher, University of Durham. Publications Manager, British Institute for Libyan and North African Studies.
victoriamleitch@gmail.com

DAVID RIDER
Field Archaeologist, physical and virtual model-maker and horologist.
davidirider2@gmail.com

GRAHAME SOFFE
Editor and Hon. Chairman, Association for Roman Archaeology, Former Archaeological Investigator, Royal Commission on Historical Monuments (England) and Lecturer in Archaeology.
saxbysoffe@aol.com

DAVID TOMALIN
Visiting Professor, Centre for Maritime Archaeology, University of Southampton. Former County Archaeologist for the Isle of Wight. Trustee of the Vectis Archaeological Trust.

STEPHEN G UPEX
Former Professor of Landscape Archaeology, University of Brunei; Tutor, Institute of Continuing Education, University of Cambridge; 25 Church Street, Warmington, Peterborough PE8 6TE.
stephenupex@hotmail.com or
stephen.upex@tutor.ice.cam.ac.uk

BRYN WALTERS
Founding Director of the Association for Roman Archaeology.

PHILIPPA WALTON
Lecturer in Roman Archaeology, University of Reading.
p.j.walton@reading.ac.uk

ROGER WHITE
Former Senior Lecturer in Roman Archaeology, University of Birmingham.
rhw2109@gmail.com

PATRICIA WITTS
Patricia Witts, PhD. Author and specialist in Roman mosaics.
pat.witts42@gmail.com

1

Roman villas in Britain and beyond

New discoveries and new interpretations of their role in culture, religion and landscape

Martin Henig, Anthony King and Grahame Soffe

The genesis of this volume was a conference held in the Stevenson Lecture Theatre at the British Museum, 13-14 June 2009, jointly organised by the Association for Roman Archaeology (ARA) and the British Museum's Departments of Prehistory and Europe, and Portable Antiquities and Treasure (Soffe 2009, 73; Walters and Soffe 2009). It followed a similar event by the ARA in the 1990s that resulted in the publication of the volume *Architecture in Roman Britain* (Johnson and Haynes 1996) which contained several papers on villas, and can be seen as the basis on which the initiative for the current volume was founded.

The rationale for the 2009 conference was to challenge the traditional focus on villas as agricultural establishments, following the emphasis by Rivet on a definition of a villa as 'a farm which is integrated into the social and economic organisation of the Roman world' (1969, 177). Economic interpretations have tended to dominate villa studies in Britain, especially in the 1980s and 1990s (e.g. Branigan and Miles 1988), together with socio-economic interpretation of villa plans (e.g. Smith 1997). There had been suggestions, however, that other lines of interpretation could be equally important, notably in the article by Graham Webster (1983; 1991, 95-111) on Chedworth and its possible role as a sanctuary rather than a villa. By the 1990s, the move away from strictly economic interpretations had become more marked, as surveyed in two brief but influential papers by Webster (1993; 1995). Other villas were put forward by Webster as potentially religious shrines rather than purely villas, notably Great Witcombe, Gloucestershire, Box, Wiltshire and Gadebridge, Hertfordshire. Of these, Great Witcombe is the subject of re-evaluation in this volume (Walters and Rider; Beeson), together with new findings concerning Chedworth itself (Walters and Rider; Beeson; Cosh, all in this volume), while Box has been considered elsewhere, including the possibility of a sanctuary to the west of the main building (Corney 2012, 68-73). Gadebridge has been the subject of further excavation since Webster's papers, but the report did not take up the suggestion of a religious reinterpretation (Neal 2001, 124).

In preparation for the conference, speakers were asked to present in-depth interpretations that might lead in new directions, for instance villas with unusual origins, with unconventional architecture, or with topographical locations that might challenge an agricultural purpose. Did some of the villas, both newly discovered and very well-known, have architectural elements that could lead to their being interpreted as something else altogether, such as a religious sanctuary? Were some villas primarily leisure retreats, without a clear agricultural function? Finally, how far did the chronological sequence at a villa indicate changes in usage?

Most of the speakers who delivered papers at the conference are represented in this volume, with the exception of a small number who published their research elsewhere. It has taken far longer than we had hoped and anticipated to collect and edit these papers, and we apologise to those contributors who sent in their contributions on time. Others were held up by new research, or the evidence presented gave rise to new papers or appendices being commissioned. The result is we hope a far better book than it would have been, though inevitably in a work of this sort more questions have been raised than answered. All the papers were fully revised in 2020/21.

As this introduction was reaching its final draft, news of an important mosaic acquisition came through, concerning the sumptuous villa at Dewlish, Dorset (Hewitt *et al.* 2021; Randall 2021). A panel from one of the mosaics, dating from the second half of the fourth century (Fig. 1.1; Cosh and Neal 2005, 74-86, mosaic 164.8) had been lifted at the time of the excavation in the 1970s, and kept in Dewlish House until sold at auction in 2020. It was afterwards sold to a foreign buyer, and was set to leave the country, unless an equivalent to the valuation of £135,000 could be raised. Following a vigorous campaign, it was successfully acquired for Dorset County Museum in Dorchester (where other portions of the mosaic are displayed) thanks to grants from several charitable organisations, including the

Figure 1.1 The 'Leopard Mosaic', from Dewlish villa, Dorset. This was recently acquired for Dorset County Museum from private owners, after a fund-raising campaign. (Photo courtesy of Dorset County Museum and Anthony Beeson)

Association for Roman Archaeology. This is the only almost completely surviving figural panel from the site and depicts a leopard leaping upon the back of an antelope. Highly naturalistic, it seems to be influenced by similar scenes of animal conflict from North Africa, though the general style of the mosaic and others from the villa shows it was the work of a regional Durnovarian workshop. The mosaics and wall-paintings from villas in Roman Britain had artistic merit equivalent to those of Mediterranean villas, especially during the fourth century.

Museums such as the one at Dorchester have a vital role to play in promoting our understanding of Roman villas, and also in preserving the Roman past for public display (Dawson 2021). Only a modest number of villa-type sites in Britain have mosaics and structural remains *in situ*, and still visible to the public. These include Chedworth, Great Witcombe, Brading and Lullingstone, all discussed in this volume, although several others, amongst them Fishbourne and Bignor, both in West Sussex, Rockbourne, Hampshire, Newport, Isle of Wight, Littlecote, Wiltshire, Crofton, Greater London, and North Leigh, Oxfordshire,

may also be visited (cf. Allen and Bryan 2020). The Association for Roman Archaeology has links with many of these sites, and membership of the ARA offers a discount or free entry into the vast majority of them (see *ARA News* 43, 2020, for further information).

Changing interpretations

This volume appears to be the first collection of papers on the villas of Roman Britain since Malcolm Todd's *Studies in the Romano-British villa*, published as long ago as 1978, although of course a great deal of work has been done over the past 45 years. Very important studies, including those by Ernest Black (1987), Keith Branigan and David Miles (1988), Richard Hingley (1989), T. F. C. Blagg (1990; 2002), Eleanor Scott (1993), Roy Friendship-Taylor, ed. (1997), J. T. Smith (1997), Pat Witts (2000), John Manley (2000), David Tomalin (2006) and Barry Cunliffe (2008; 2013a), have vastly increased our knowledge, while the great corpus of *Roman Mosaics in Britain* by David Neal and Stephen Cosh (Neal and Cosh 2002; 2009; Cosh and Neal 2005; 2010) has not only provided a comprehensive listing of villa mosaics mostly of fourth-century date but

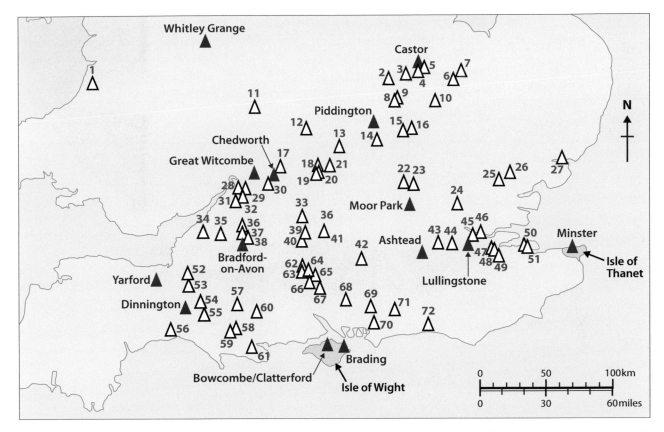

Key to numbers: **1** Abermagwr; **2** Stanion; **3** Cotterstock; **4** Haddon; **5** Orton Hall Farm; **6** Chatteris; **7** Stonea; **8** Stanwick; **9** Redlands Farm; **10** Rectory Farm; **11** Bays Meadow; **12** Pillerton Priors; **13** Croughton; **14** Bancroft; **15** Marsh Leys; **16** Newnham; **17** Turkdean; **18** Shakenoak; **19** Stonesfield; **20** North Leigh; **21** Tackley; **22** Gadebridge; **23** Gorhambury; **24** Chigwell; **25** Great Holts Farm; **26** Rivenhall; **27** Little Oakley; **28** Frocester; **29** Woodchester; **30** Ditches; **31** Wortley; **32** Kingscote; **33** Alfred's Castle; **34** Gatcombe; **35** Keynsham; **36** Truckle Hill; **37** Box; **38** Atworth; **39** Littlecote; **40** Castle Copse; **41** Boxford; **42** North Warnborough; **43** Beddington; **44** Keston; **45** Darenth; **46** Northfleet; **47** Snodland; **48** Eccles; **49** The Mount, Maidstone; **50** Bax Farm; **51** Hog Brook; **52** Shapwick; **53** Low Ham; **54** Lufton; **55** Halstock; **56** Holcombe; **57** Hinton St Mary; **58** Druce Farm; **59** Dewlish; **60** Tarrant Hinton; **61** Bucknowle; **62** Thruxton; **63** Grateley South; **64** Dunkirt Barn; **65** Fullerton; **66** Houghton Down; **67** Sparsholt; **68** Meonstoke; **69** Batten Hanger; **70** Fishbourne; **71** Bignor; **72** Southwick.

Figure 1.2. Map of villas in Table 1.1, and of the villas that are the subject of papers in this volume (individually named).
NB, seven villas in Table 1.1, Aiskew (N Yorks), Beadlam (N Yorks), Eastfield (N Yorks), Ingleby Barwick (Teesside), Ketton (Rutland),
Lyde Green (S Gloucestershire), and Bratton Seymour (Somerset; cf. this volume, Fig. 13.1, no. 9) are not shown on this map.
(Map by Nicholas Hogben)

made many basic plans accessible (see also Cosh 2020). Sarah Scott's study of the art and architecture of these villas (Scott 2000) places them, or at least the richer villas of the Late Roman period, in their social context.

At a more specific level, individual villas have been published in significant numbers over the last four decades, both as substantial monographs, reports in journals or as more synoptic papers and volumes. A selection of these is given in Table 1.1 and on the map, Fig. 1.2, to illustrate the rich resource now available to students and researchers into Romano-British villas. It is very apparent from the number of reports, especially those of the twenty-first century, that much activity

has been undertaken on villas in Britain. An important contributory factor has been the use of modern geophysical survey methods, which have found new sites, such as Dinnington (this volume), or established the full plans of those already known, such as Low Ham, Somerset (Payne *et al.* 2019) or North Leigh, Oxfordshire (Creighton and Allen 2017). These techniques have fully proved their worth in increasing our understanding of villas, and are destined to be a major element in most field projects in the future. The older technology of aerial photography still yields important discoveries, however, such as the villa at Abermagwr, Ceredigion, discovered from the air during the drought of summer 2006 (Davies and Driver 2018).

3

Table 1.1. Select list of villa excavation reports and studies from Roman Britain, 1990-2020.

Site	County	Reference
Abermagwr	Ceredigion	Davies & Driver 2018
Aiskew	N Yorkshire	Shepherd 2021; Shepherd *et al.* 2022
Alfred's Castle	Oxfordshire	Gosden & Lock 2003
Ashtead	Surrey	Bird, this volume
Atworth	Wiltshire	Erskine & Ellis 2008
Bancroft	Buckinghamshire	Williams & Zeepvat 1994
Batten Hanger	W Sussex	Kenny *et al.* 2016
Bax Farm	Kent	Wilkinson 2011; n.d.
Bays Meadow	Worcestershire	Hurst 2006
Beadlam	N Yorkshire	Neal 1996a
Beddington	Surrey	Howell 2005
Bignor	W Sussex	Aldsworth & Rudling 1995; Rudling & Russell 2015
Bowcombe/Clatterford	Isle of Wight	Busby *et al.* 2001; Tomalin, this volume
Box	Wiltshire	Corney 2012
Boxford	Berkshire	Beeson *et al.* 2019; Dunbabin 2020
Bradford-on-Avon	Bath and NE Somerset	Corney, this volume
Brading	Isle of Wight	Hanworth 2004; Cunliffe 2013b; Tomalin, this volume
Bratton Seymour	Somerset	Hughes & Biddulph 2020; *The Newt in Somerset* 2021
Bucknowle	Dorset	Light & Ellis 2009
Castle Copse	Wiltshire	Hostetter & Howe 1997
Castor	Cambridgeshire	Upex 2011; this volume
Chatteris	Cambridgeshire	Evans 2003
Chedworth	Gloucestershire	Papworth 2021; Esmonde Cleary *et al.* 2022; Walters & Rider, this volume
Chignall	Essex	Clarke 1998
Cotterstock	Northamptonshire	Upex 2001
Croughton	Northamptonshire	Dawson 2008
Danebury Environs villas	Hampshire	Cunliffe 2008
Darenth	Kent	Black 1981; Beeson 2020
Dewlish	Dorset	Putnam 2007, 97-116; Hewitt *et al.* 2021; Randall 2021
Dinnington	Somerset	Croft 2009; King & Grande, this volume
Ditches	Gloucestershire	Trow *et al.* 2009
Druce Farm	Dorset	Ladle & Bithell 2016; Beeson 2016; Ladle 2022
Dunkirt Barn	Hampshire	Cunliffe & Poole 2008, Part 7
Eastfield	N Yorkshire	Beeson 2021
Eccles	Kent	Ratcliff 2018; Stoodley and Cosh 2021
Fishbourne	W Sussex	Cunliffe 1991; 1998; Cunliffe *et al* 1996; Manley 2000; Manley & Rudkin 2003; 2005; 2006
Frocester	Gloucestershire	Price 2000; 2010
Fullerton	Hampshire	Cunliffe & Poole 2008, Part 3
Gadebridge	Hertfordshire	Neal 2001

Site	County	Reference
Gatcombe	Somerset	Smisson & Groves 2014
Gorhambury	Hertfordshire	Neal et al. 1990
Grateley South	Hampshire	Cunliffe & Poole 2008, Part 2
Great Holts Farm	Essex	Germany 2003
Great Witcombe	Gloucestershire	Leach 1998; Holbrook 2003; Walters & Rider, this volume
Haddon	Peterborough	Hinman 2003
Halstock	Dorset	Lucas 1993; Cosh 2022
Hinton St Mary	Dorset	Putnam 2007, 88-9; *Mosaic* 40, 2013, whole issue
Hog Brook, Faversham	Kent	Wilkinson 2009
Holcombe	Devon	Walters 1996
Houghton Down	Hampshire	Cunliffe & Poole 2008, Part 1
Ingleby Barwick	Teesside	Willis & Carne 2013
Keston	Kent	Philp *et al.* 1999
Ketton	Rutland	Henig 2022a; *ARA News* 47 & 48, 2022; Thomas *et al.* 2022
Keynsham	Bath and NE Somerset	Russell 1985; Walters 1996; 2015
Kingscote	Gloucestershire	Timby 1998
Littlecote	Berkshire	Phillips 2022; Walters 1996; Anon 1994
Little Oakley	Essex	Barford 2002
Low Ham	Somerset	Croft 2009; Henig 2019; Payne *et al.* 2019
Lufton	Somerset	Walters 1996
Lullingstone	Kent	Henig 1997; Mackenzie 2019; Henig & Soffe, this volume
Lyde Green	Gloucestershire	Hobson & Newman 2021
Marsh Leys	Bedfordshire	Luke & Preece 2011
Meonstoke	Hampshire	King & Potter 1990; King 1996; 2020
Minster in Thanet	Kent	Perkins 2003; Perkins *et al.* 2004-19; Tomalin, this volume
Moor Park	Hertfordshire	Leitch & Biddle, this volume
Mount, The, Maidstone	Kent	Houliston 1999
Newnham	Bedfordshire	Ingham *et al.* 2016
Northfleet	Kent	Biddulph 2011
North Leigh	Oxfordshire	Ellis 1999; Wilson 2004; Creighton & Allen 2017
North Warnborough	Hampshire	Wallace 2018
Orton Hall Farm	Peterborough	Mackreth 1996
Piddington	Northamptonshire	Friendship-Taylor, this volume
Pillerton Priors	Warwickshire	Sabin 2003
Rectory Farm	Cambridgeshire	Green 2017, 43-5; Lyons 2019
Redlands Farm	Northamptonshire	Keevil 1996
Rivenhall	Essex	Rodwell & Rodwell 1993
Shakenoak	Oxfordshire	Brodribb *et al.* 2005
Shapwick	Somerset	Abdy *et al.* 2001
Snodland	Kent	Dawkes 2015
Southwick	W Sussex	Standing 2014

Site	County	Reference
Sparsholt	Hampshire	Johnston & Dicks 2014
Stanion	Northamptonshire	Tingle 2008
Stanwick	Northamptonshire	Neal 1989; 1996b, 38-43; Coombe *et al.* 2021
Stonea	Cambridgeshire	Jackson & Potter 1996; Malim 2005
Stonesfield	Oxfordshire	Freshwater *et al.* 2000
Surrey villas	Surrey	Bird 2017
Sussex villas	E & W Sussex	Rudling 1998
Tackley	Oxfordshire	Sánchez 2021
Tarrant Hinton	Dorset	Graham 2006
Thruxton	Hampshire	Henig & Soffe 1993; Cunliffe & Poole 2008, Part 4
Truckle Hill, North Wraxall	Wiltshire	Andrews *et al.* 2013; Andrews 2016
Turkdean	Gloucestershire	Holbrook 2004
Whitley Grange	Shropshire	White, this volume
Wilts villas	Wiltshire	Walters 2001
Woodchester	Gloucestershire	Walters 1996
Wortley	Gloucestershire	Wilson *et al.* 2014
Yarford	Somerset	Croft 2009; King & Grande, this volume

Research on the Romano-British countryside during the 1990s to 2010s has moved away from a focus on villas to an approach that can be regarded as more holistic and landscape orientated, such as the major project *New Visions of the Countryside of Roman Britain* that resulted in three influential volumes in the Britannia Monograph series (Smith *et al.* 2016; 2018; Allen *et al.* 2017). Other projects on similar lines (King 2004; Taylor 2007; Rippon *et al.* 2015; Millett *et al.* 2016, Part IV), also pushed the research direction towards agricultural exploitation, field systems, and integration of varying forms of rural settlement, as prefigured in the research agenda put forward by Webster (1995). This has been mirrored in other Roman provinces, too, notably northern Gaul and Germany (e. g. Roymans and Derks 2011; Habermehl 2014; Roymans *et al.* 2015; Reddé 2017/18). Nevertheless, villas are recognised as a specific form of ancient rural settlement, even if their definition can on occasion be problematic, and a recent volume on Mediterranean villas has highlighted their continuing importance as a focus of study (Marzano and Métraux 2018).

This volume draws on the recent landscape studies of Roman Britain, and has papers devoted to regional evaluations (Tomalin, Upex, this volume). It is, however, specifically concerned with a wide range of structures from the countryside of Roman Britain, which have all at one time or another been designated as Roman villas. They range from buildings of very modest size to country houses sometimes planned on a palatial scale and endowed with every luxury. Most of the medium sized and smaller houses were centres of agricultural production, and the wealth of the large estates would generally have depended on farming, doubtless from dependent, satellite tenant farms as in the case of the great estates of medieval and early modern times. However, some villas were industrial centres like Chesters, Woolaston, Gloucestershire, with its evidence for iron furnaces (Fulford and Allen 1992), Ashtead, Surrey (this volume) and the villa associated with a tile kiln at Crookhorn, Hampshire (Soffe, Nicholls and Moore 1989), while others both inland as well as on the coast, may have been based on pisciculture (fish farming), for example Shakenoak, Oxfordshire (Brodribb *et al.* 2005, 420-23, 553), or salt working, such as Bays Meadow, Droitwich (Hurst 2006). David Tomalin's paper in this volume discusses the significance of coastal villas and their links with maritime communications and exploitation (see also Tomalin 2006).

A significant theme in the volume is that it has become apparent that some buildings generally regarded as simple villas also had a religious aspect, where temples were contiguous to villas. This was almost certainly true of Chedworth, where several temples, one of very large size, a number of images of Diana as well as what appear to be two wings of rooms for presumably paying guests are suggestive of some sort of sanctuary. Is one to regard the main block of the building with its rich mosaics in corridors, bath-house and *triclinium* as a luxury country house like that at Woodchester or rather in the nature of the guest house like that at the sanctuary of Nodens in Lydney Park also in Gloucestershire? More certainly the 'villa' at Great Witcombe and the partially excavated building at Moor Park, Hertfordshire (this volume), represent water sanctuaries on the lines of those in Gaul such as Fontaines-Salées. Lullingstone, discussed in this volume, is enigmatic, with evidence for religious cult extending from a second century shrine of the nymphs presumably of the River Darent in the basement, to offerings made in the third century before two marble busts, and finally a house church in an upper room. Near to Lullingstone, the large villa at Darenth also has good evidence suggesting a water cult was practised at this site, which may have been as much a public building as a private villa (Beeson 2020; Black 1981). Cult activity at villa sites may have originated in the Iron Age, as seen in the horse and foal burials under a mid/late Roman hexagonal building at Meonstoke, Hampshire (King 2020). The hexagonal building is an unusual architectural form for Roman Britain (King 2023) and was almost certainly a shrine adjacent to an aisled building, and probably part of a villa estate.

In the late Roman period, there is evidence for pagan religious rites in a triconch building beside the main villa and beside a stream at Littlecote (Walters 1996; Anon 1994) and in a room attached to the aisled villa at Thruxton, Hampshire (Henig and Soffe 1993; Cunliffe and Poole 2008, vol. 2, part 4). Apart from Lullingstone, Christianity was also present in Hinton St Mary, Dorset, as revealed by the well-known mosaic apparently depicting a bust of Christ set against a Chi-Rho, and at Frampton also in Dorset with a Chi-Rho in mosaic on the cord of the apse in its largest room (see a range of papers with references in *Mosaic* 40, 2013).

Whether luxury houses, working farms, centres of industry or religious sanctuaries, all the buildings discussed were components in a flourishing countryside, so in order to understand them it is important to consider the rural economy as several contributors have attempted to do. In this context, the early establishment of villas during the first century along the south coast, especially in West Sussex (Rudling 1998) or in Kent (e.g. Eccles; Stoodley and Cosh 2021), represents precocious building of Roman-style dwellings within a landscape that was still largely Iron Age in its economy and society. The inspiration for this is likely to have come from villa building activity in northern Gaul, where Iron Age to Roman sequences demonstrate continuity in agriculture and social organisation, integrated with the newly introduced Roman building techniques (see Agache 1978; King 1990, 92-5; Roymans and Derks 2011).

When villas are mentioned the arts, especially those of the architect and architectural sculptor and the mosaicist inevitably come to mind. With regard to the latter, the figural mosaics of fourth-century Britain are remarkable for their concentration on their owner's *paideia* in preference to, for example, amphitheatre scenes, often displaying an erudite knowledge of mythology. They range from the Greek and Roman epics, as in the mosaic depicting scenes from the denouement of the Iliad, showing Achilles dragging Hector's corpse behind his chariot and including a scene, very rare on mosaic, of the weighing of Hector's body, from a villa near Ketton, Rutland (Henig 2022a; Thomas *et al.* 2002; *Association for Roman Archaeology News* 47 and 48, 2022), and the Vergilian mosaics depicting Dido and Aeneas from the bath-house at Low Ham, Somerset (Henig 2019; 2022a), to representations of myths drawn from Ovid's *Metamorphoses* and Hyginus' *Fabulae* (Henig 2022b). These include Apollo and Daphne at Dinnington (King and Grande, this volume), the myths of Hercules and Antaeus in a sculpture at Dinnington (*ibid.*) and a mosaic at Bramdean, Hampshire, and no less than five mosaics figuring Bellerophon at Hinton St Mary and Frampton in Dorset, Croughton, Northamptonshire, Lullingstone, Kent and now Boxford, Berkshire. At the last site in this list, however, the main subject was concerned with Pelops, very rare indeed on mosaics. The villa at Lullingstone contains a two-line poem which indicates knowledge of both Ovid and Virgil while the scenes on the Boxford mosaic and others probably derive from Hyginus (Beeson *et al.* 2019; see Henig 2019; Dunbabin 2020). Architecture and architectural ornament, as well as imported marbles from the richer villas are indicative of far-flung contacts (Blagg 2002). However, architectural plans and artistic styles also point to the villas of Britain being in many ways distinctive and locally conceived.

To place the buildings that form the main subject of this volume into context we have thought it good to include a couple of papers on villas in Gaul, where Ausonius and Sidonius Apollinaris provide valuable evidence for villas in Late Antiquity (Collis, this volume), as well as Italy, where the villa at Mola di Monte Gelato demonstrates how a villa became first a farmstead in the late Roman period, and then a focus for a dispersed village in the early middle ages (King, this volume). This is a sequence seen at many villa sites, amplified in the case of Monte Gelato by the presence of an early Christian church from the fourth century AD within the villa buildings.

Acknowledgements

We owe our very special thanks to Dr Sam Moorhead who made the venue at the British Museum available to us for the original conference, and for his continued support. Nicholas Hogben has also provided invaluable help during the editing process, in redrafting many of the maps and other illustrations. We must thank the Association for Roman Archaeology for their monetary support. Finally we are very grateful to David Davison of Archaeopress for facilitating the publication of this volume, and to Ben Heaney for his careful and attentive preparation, layout and design work.

Anthony Beeson 1948-2022

This volume was in the hands of the publisher when the editors heard of the sudden and very untimely death of one of our contributors, Anthony Beeson. He was a leading light in the Association for Roman Archaeology, and for many years had contributed prolifically to its periodical publications, *ARA, The Bulletin of the Association for Roman Archaeology* and *ARA News*, as well as being a mainstay of the many foreign and British study tours run by the Association. He also published extensively on villa mosaics in *Mosaic* and wrote acclaimed books on Roman gardens and mosaics in Roman Britain (Beeson 2019; 2022). Perhaps his most memorable achievements in relation to villas were 'rescuing' the Newton St Loe Orpheus pavement (Beeson and Henig 1997), campaigning to save the Dewlish mosaic from export (see above), and his interpretation of the Boxford mosaic (Beeson *et al.* 2019). His considerable interest in villas and their architecture is attested by his contribution to this volume.

References

Abdy, R., Brunning, R. and Webster, C. 2001 The discovery of a Roman villa at Shapwick and its Severan coin hoard of 9238 silver denarii. *Journal of Roman Archaeology* 14, 358-72.

Agache, R. 1978 *La Somme pré-romaine et romaine*. Société des antiquaires de Picardie, Amiens.

Aldsworth, F. and Rudling, D. 1995 Excavations at Bignor Roman villa, West Sussex 1985-90. *Sussex Archaeological Collections* 133, 103-88.

Allen, D. and Bryan, M. 2020 *Roman Britain and Where to Find It*. Amberley Publishing, Stroud.

Allen, M., Lodwick, L., Brindle, T., Fulford, M. and Smith, A. 2017 *New Visions of the Countryside of Roman Britain. Volume 2: The Rural Economy of Roman Britain*. Britannia Monograph 30, London.

Andrews, P. 2016 Truckle Hill, Wiltshire: bath-house and possible *nymphaea*, villa and the Late Iron Age setting. *ARA Bulletin of the Association for Roman Archaeology* 23, 24-31.

Andrews, P. *et multi alii* 2013 Two possible *nymphaea* at Truckle Hill, North Wraxall, Wiltshire. *Archaeological Journal* 170, 106-53.

Anon 1994 *Littlecote Roman Villa. Illustrated Guide*, Roman Research Marketing Ltd, Swindon.

Barford, P. M. 2002 *Excavations at Little Oakley, Essex, 1951-78: Roman villa and Saxon settlement*. East Anglian Archaeology 98, Chelmsford.

Beeson, A. 2016 The mosaics at the Roman villa at Druce Farm, Puddletown, Dorset. *Association for Roman Archaeology News* 23, 78-84.

Beeson, A. 2019 *Roman Gardens*. Stroud, Amberley Publishing.

Beeson, A. 2020 Newly discovered photographs record the 1895 excavation of Darenth Roman villa. *Association for Roman Archaeology News* 44, 46-9.

Beeson, A. 2021 An exceptional architectural complex at Eastfield, North Yorkshire. *Association for Roman Archaeology News* 45, 4-6.

Beeson, A. 2022 *Mosaics in Roman Britain*. Stroud, Amberley Publishing.

Beeson A. and Henig, M. 1997 Orpheus and the Newton St Loe mosaic pavement in Bristol City Museum. In L. Keen (ed), *'Almost the Richest City'. Bristol in the Middle Ages*, 1-8, pl. I-II. British Archaeological Association Conference Transactions XIX, Maney, Leeds.

Beeson, A., Nichol, M. and Appleton, J. 2019 *The Boxford Mosaic. A unique survivor from the Roman Age*. Countryside Books, Newbury.

Biddulph, E. 2011 Northfleet villa. In P. Andrews *et al.*, *Settling the Ebbsfleet Valley. High Speed 1 Excavations at Springhead and Northfleet, Kent. The Late Iron Age, Roman, Saxon, and Medieval landscapes. Volume 1: the sites*, 135-88, 213-30 (plus finds, etc. in Vols 2 and 3). Oxford Wessex Archaeology, Oxford.

Bird, D. 2017 Rural settlement in Roman-period Surrey. In D. Bird (ed.), *Agriculture and Industry in South-Eastern Roman Britain*, 111-33. Oxbow Books, Oxford

Black, E. 1981 The Roman villa at Darenth. *Archaeologia Cantiana* 97, 159-83.

Black, E. 1987 *The Roman Villas of South-East England*. British Archaeological Reports (BAR) British Series 171, Oxford.

Blagg, T. F. C. 1990 First-century Roman houses in Gaul and Britain. In T. F. C. Blagg and M. Millett (ed.), *The Early Roman Empire in the West*, 194-209. Oxbow Books, Oxford.

Blagg, T. F. C. 2002 *Roman Architectural Ornament in Britain*. British Archaeological Reports (BAR) British Series 329, Oxford.

Branigan, K. and Miles, D. 1988 (ed.) *The Economies of Romano-British Villas*. University of Sheffield Department of Archaeology and Prehistory, Sheffield.

Brodribb, A. C., Hands, A. R. and Walker, D. R. 2005 *The Roman Villa at Shakenoak Farm, Oxfordshire. Excavations 1960-1976.* British Archaeological Reports (BAR) British Series 395, Oxford.

Busby, P., De Moulins, D., Lyne, M., McPhillips, S. and Scaife, R. 2001 Excavations at Clatterford Roman villa, Isle of Wight. *Proceedings of the Hampshire Field Club & Archaeological Society* 56, 95-128 (*Hampshire Studies 2001*).

Clarke, C. P. 1998 *Excavations to the South of Chignall Roman Villa, Essex 1977-81.* East Anglian Archaeology 83, Chelmsford.

Coombe, P., Hayward, K. and Henig, M. 2021 The sculpted and architectural stonework from Stanwick Roman villa, Northamptonshire. *Britannia* 51, 227-75.

Corney, M. 2012 *The Roman Villa at Box.* Box Archaeological and Natural History Society, Salisbury.

Cosh, S. R. 2020 Mosaics and building projects. *Mosaic* 47, 5-15.

Cosh, S. R. 2022 The lost Medusa mosaic from Halstock, Dorset. *Proceedings of the Dorset Natural History & Archaeological Society* 143, 215-24.

Cosh, S. R. and Neal, D. S. 2005 *Roman Mosaics of Britain. Volume II South-West Britain.* Illuminata Publishers and Society of Antiquaries of London, London.

Cosh, S. R. and Neal, D. S. 2010 *Roman Mosaics of Britain. Volume IV Western Britain.* Society of Antiquaries of London, London.

Creighton, J. and Allen, M. 2017 A fluxgate gradiometry survey at North Leigh Roman villa, Oxfordshire, *Britannia* 48, 279-87.

Croft, B. 2009 (ed.), *Roman Mosaics in Somerset.* Somerset County Council Heritage Service, Taunton.

Cunliffe, B. W. 1991 Fishbourne revisited: the site in its context. *Journal of Roman Archaeology* 4, 160-9.

Cunliffe, B. W. 1998 *Fishbourne Roman Palace.* Tempus, Stroud.

Cunliffe, B. W. 2008 *The Danebury Environs Roman Programme. A Wessex Landscape during the Roman Era. Volume 1, Overview.* English Heritage and Oxford University School of Archaeology Monograph 70, Oxford.

Cunliffe, B. W. 2013a 'For men of rank ... basilicas': British aisled halls reconsidered. In H. Eckardt and S. Rippon (ed.) *Living and Working in the Roman World: Essays in Honour of Michael Fulford on his 65th Birthday.* 95-109. Journal of Roman Archaeology Supplementary Series 95, Portsmouth, RI.

Cunliffe, B. W. 2013b *The Roman Villa at Brading, Isle of Wight. The excavations of 2008-10.* Oxford University School of Archaeology Monograph 77, Oxford.

Cunliffe, B. W. and Poole, C. 2008 *The Danebury Environs Roman Programme. A Wessex Landscape during the Roman Era. Volume 2, Part 1, Houghton Down, Longstock, Hants,* 1997; Part 2, Grateley South, Grateley, Hants, 1998 and 1999; Part 3, Fullerton, Hants, 2000 and 2001; Part 4, Thruxton, Hants, 2002; Part 7, Dunkirt Barn, Abbotts Ann, Hants, 2005 and 2006. English Heritage and Oxford University School of Archaeology Monograph 71, Oxford.

Cunliffe, B. W., Down, A. and Rudkin, D. 1996 *Chichester Excavations IX. Excavations at Fishbourne, 1969-1988.* Chichester District Council, Chichester.

Davies, J. L. and Driver, T. G. 2018 The Romano-British villa at Abermagwr, Ceredigion: excavations 2010-15. *Archaeologia Cambrensis* 167, 143-219.

Dawkes, G. 2015 *Flavian and Later Buildings at Snodland Roman Villa. Excavations at Cantium Way, Snodland, Kent.* SpoilHeap Publications, Portslade.

Dawson, M. 2008 Excavation of the Roman Villa and Mosaic at Rowler Manor, Croughton, Northamptonshire. *Northamptonshire Archaeology* 35, 45-93.

Dawson, M. 2021 *Spectacle and Display: a modern history of Britain's Roman mosaic pavements.* Archaeopress Roman Archaeology 79, Oxford.

Dunbabin, K. M. 2020 The myths of Boxford: questions about the patron and the designer of the mosaic. *Journal of Roman Archaeology* 33, 763-8.

Ellis, P. 1999 North Leigh Roman villa, Oxfordshire: a report on excavation and recording in the 1970s. *Britannia* 30, 199-245.

Erskine, J. G. P. and Ellis, P. 2008 Excavations at Atworth Roman villa, Wiltshire 1970-1975. *Wiltshire Archaeological & Natural History Magazine* 101, 51-129.

Esmonde Cleary, S., Wood, J. and Durham, E. 2022 *Chedworth Roman Villa. Excavations and re-imaginings from the nineteenth to the twenty-first centuries.* Britannia Monograph 35, London.

Evans, C. 2003 Britons and Romans at Chatteris: investigations at Langwood Farm, Cambridgeshire. *Britannia* 34, 175-264.

Freshwater, T., Draper, J., Henig, M. and Hinds, S. 2000 From stone to textile: the Bacchus mosaic at Stonesfield, Oxon., and the Stonesfield embroidery. *Journal of the British Archaeological Association* 153, 1-29.

Friendship-Taylor, R. M. and D. E. 1997 (ed.), *From Round House to Roman Villa.* Upper Nene Archaeological Society, Northampton.

Fulford, M. G. and Allen, J. R. L. 1992 Iron-making at the Chesters villa, Woolaston, Gloucestershire: survey and excavation 1987-91. *Britannia* 23, 159-215.

Germany, M. 2003 *Excavations at Great Holts Farm, Boreham, Essex 1992-4.* East Anglian Archaeology 105, Chelmsford.

Gosden, C. and Lock, G. 2003 Becoming Roman on the Berkshire Downs: the evidence from Alfred's Castle. *Britannia* 34, 65-80.

Graham, A. 2006 *Barton Field, Tarrant Hinton, Dorset. Excavations 1968-1984.* Dorset Natural History and Archaeological Society Monograph 17, Dorchester.

Green, H. J. M. 2017 *Durovigutum. Roman Godmanchester.* Archaeopress, Oxford.

Habermehl, D. 2014 *Settling in a Changing World. Villa development in the northern provinces of the Roman Empire.* Amsterdam University Press, Amsterdam.

Hanworth, R. 2004 A possible name for a landowner at Brading villa. *Britannia* 35, 240-4.

Henig, M. 1997 The Lullingstone mosaic: art, religion and letters in a fourth-century villa. *Mosaic* 24, 4-7.

Henig, M. 2019 The Vergil mosaic from Low Ham villa, Somerset. *Association for Roman Archaeology News* 42, 29-30.

Henig, M. 2022a High culture in Roman Britain. Epics of Troy and Carthage. *Antiqvvs* Spring 2022, 27-32.

Henig, M. 2022b High culture in Roman Britain, The Myths of Ovid and Hyginus. *Antiqvvs* Summer 2022, 13-18.

Henig, M. and Soffe, G. 1993 The Thruxton Roman villa and its mosaic pavement. *Journal of the British Archaeological Association* 146, 1-28.

Hewitt, I., Putnam, M., Milward, J. and Monteith, J. 2021 *Dewlish Roman Villa, Dorset. Bill Putnam's excavations 1969-1979.* Dorset Natural History and Archaeological Society Monograph 25, Dorchester.

Hingley, R. 1989 *Rural Settlement in Roman Britain.* Seaby, London.

Hinman, M. 2003 *A Late Iron Age Farmstead and Romano-British Site at Haddon, Peterborough.* British Archaeological Reports (BAR) British Series 358, Oxford.

Hobson, M. S. and Newman, R. 2021 (ed.) *Lyde Green Roman Villa, Emersons Green, South Gloucestershire.* Archaeopress Roman Archaeology 85, Oxford.

Holbrook, N. 2003 Great Witcombe Roman villa, Gloucestershire: field surveys of its fabric and environs, 1999-2000. *Transactions of the Bristol & Gloucestershire Archaeological Society* 121, 179-200.

Holbrook, N. 2004 Turkdean Roman villa, Gloucestershire: archaeological investigations 1997-1998. *Britannia* 35, 39-76.

Hostetter, E. and Howe, T. 1997 *The Romano-British Villa at Castle Copse, Great Bedwyn.* Indiana University Press, Bloomington.

Houliston, M. 1999 Excavations at the Mount Roman villa, Maidstone, 1994. *Archaeologia Cantiana* 119, 71-172.

Howell, I. 2005 (ed.) *Prehistoric Landscape to Roman Villa. Excavations at Beddington, Surrey, 1981-7.* Museum of London Archaeology Service Monograph 26, London.

Hughes, V. and Biddulph, E. 2020 *Cattle Hill Roman Villa, Hadspen House, Bratton Seymour, Somerset. Archaeological Excavation Report.* Oxford Archaeology, Oxford.

Hurst, D. 2006 (ed.) *Roman Droitwich. Dodderhill fort, Bays Meadow villa, and roadside settlement.* Council for British Archaeology (CBA) Research Report 146, York.

Ingham, D., Oetgen, J. and Slowikowski, A. 2016 *Newnham: a Roman bath house and estate centre east of Bedford.* East Anglian Archaeology 158, Bedford.

Jackson, R. P. J. and Potter, T. W. 1996 *Excavations at Stonea, Cambridgeshire 1980-85.* British Museum Press, London.

Johnson, P. and Haynes, I. 1996 (ed.) *Architecture in Roman Britain*, Council for British Archaeology (CBA) Research Report 94, York.

Johnston, D. E. and Dicks, J. 2014 *Sparsholt Roman Villa, Hampshire. Excavations by David E. Johnston.* Hampshire Field Club and Archaeological Society Monograph 11, Bristol.

Keevil, G. D. 1996 The reconstruction of the Romano-British villa at Redlands Farm, Northamptonshire. In Johnson and Haynes 1996, 44-55.

Kenny, J., Lyne, M., Magilton, J. and Buckland, P. 2016 A Late Roman 'hall' at Batten Hanger, West Sussex. *Britannia* 47, 193-207.

King, A. C. 1990 *Roman Gaul and Germany.* British Museum Press, London.

King, A. C. 1996 The south-east façade of Meonstoke aisled building. In Johnson and Haynes 1996, 56-69.

King, A. C. 2004 Rural settlement in southern Britain: a regional survey. In M. Todd (ed), *A Companion to Roman Britain,* 349-70. Blackwell Publishing, Oxford.

King, A. C. 2020 Romano-Celtic temples in the landscape: Meonstoke, Hampshire, UK, a hexagonal shrine to Epona and a river deity on a villa estate. In R. Haeussler and G. F. Chiai (ed.), *Sacred Landscapes in Antiquity. Creation, manipulation, transformation,* 147-58. Oxbow Books, Oxford.

King, A. C. 2023 [in press] Hexagonal buildings, rooms and structures in Roman architecture. *ARA Bulletin of the Association for Roman Archaeology* 25, 61-72.

King, A. C. and Potter, T. W. 1990 A new domestic building façade from Roman Britain. *Journal of Roman Archaeology* 3, 195-204.

Ladle, L. 2022 *The Rise and Fall of Druce Farm Roman Villa (AD 60-650).* British Archaeological Reports (BAR) British Series 676, Oxford.

Ladle, L. and Bithell, J. 2016 Investigations at the Roman villa at Druce Farm, Puddletown, Dorset: an interim report. *Association for Roman Archaeology News* 23, 70-77.

Leach, P. 1998 *Great Witcombe Roman Villa, Gloucestershire. A report on excavations by Ernest Greenfield, 1960-1973.* British Archaeological Reports (BAR) British Series 266, Oxford (reprint 2016).

Light, T. and Ellis, P. 2009 *Bucknowle, a Roman Villa and its Antecedents: excavations 1976-1991.* Dorset Natural History and Archaeological Society Monograph 18, Dorchester.

Lucas, R. N. 1993 *The Romano-British Villa at Halstock, Dorset. Excavations 1967-85.* Dorset Natural History and Archaeological Society Monograph 13, Dorchester.

Luke, M. and Preece, T. 2011 *Farm and Forge: Late Iron Age/ Romano-British farmsteads at Marsh Leys, Kempston, Bedfordshire*. East Anglian Archaeology 138, Bedford.

Lyons, A. 2019 *Rectory Farm, Godmanchester, Cambridgeshire. Excavations 1988–95, Neolithic monument to Roman villa farm*. East Anglian Archaeology 170, Cambridge.

Mackenzie, C. K. 2019 *Culture and Society at Lullingstone Roman Villa*. Archaeopress, Oxford.

Mackreth, D. F. 1996 *Orton Hall Farm. A Roman and Early Anglo-Saxon farmstead*. East Anglian Archaeology 76, Manchester.

Malim, T. 2005 *Stonea and the Roman Fens*. Tempus, Stroud.

Manley, J. 2000 Measurement and metaphor: the design and meaning of building 3 at Fishbourne Roman Palace. *Sussex Archaeological Collections* 138, 103-113.

Manley, J. and Rudkin, D. 2003 Facing the Palace. Excavations in front of the Roman palace at Fishbourne (Sussex, UK) 1995-99. *Sussex Archaeological Collections* 141, *passim*.

Manley, J. and Rudkin, D. 2005 A pre-AD 43 ditch at Fishbourne Roman Palace, Chichester. *Britannia* 36, 55-99.

Manley, J. and Rudkin, D. 2006 More buildings facing the palace at Fishbourne. *Sussex Archaeological Collections* 144, 69-113.

Marzano, A. and Métraux, G. P. R. 2018 (ed.), *The Roman Villa in the Mediterranean Basin: Late Republic to Late Antiquity*. Cambridge University Press, Cambridge.

Millett, M., Revell, L. and Moore, A. 2016 (ed.) *The Oxford Handbook of Roman Britain*. Oxford University Press, Oxford.

Neal, D. S. 1989 The Stanwick villa, Northants: an interim report on the excavations of 1984-88. *Britannia* 20, 149-68.

Neal, D. S. 1996a *Excavations on the Roman Villa at Beadlam, Yorkshire*. Yorkshire Archaeological Report 2, Leeds.

Neal, D. S. 1996b Upper storeys in Romano-British villas. In Johnson and Haynes 1996, 33-43.

Neal, D. S. 2001 Gadebridge revisited: excavations on the Roman villa 2000. *Antiquaries Journal* 81, 109-29.

Neal, D. S. and Cosh, S. R. 2002 *Roman Mosaics of Britain. Volume I Northern Britain incorporating the Midlands and East Anglia*. Illuminata Publishers and Society of Antiquaries of London, London.

Neal, D. S. and Cosh, S. R. 2009 *Roman Mosaics of Britain. Volume III South-East Britain*. Society of Antiquaries of London, London.

Neal, D. S., Wardle, A. and Hunn, J. 1990 *Excavation of the Iron Age, Roman and Medieval Settlement at Gorhambury, St Albans*. English Heritage Archaeological Report 14, Swindon.

Papworth, M. 2021 The case for Chedworth villa. Exploring evidence for 5th-century occupation. *Current Archaeology* 373, 18-25.

Payne, A., Linford, N., Linford, P., Roberts, D. and Leech, R. 2019 Geophysical survey and excavation at Low Ham Roman villa. *Association for Roman Archaeology News* 42, 30-33.

Perkins, D. 2003 Minster Roman villa, Kent. *ARA Bulletin of the Association for Roman Archaeology* 14, 5-9, 17.

Perkins, D. *et multi alii* 2004-19 The Roman villa at Minster in Thanet. Part 1: introduction and report on the bath-house; Part 2: the Late Iron-Age, Roman and later coinage; Part 3: the corridor house, building 4; Part 4: the south-west buildings, 6A and 6B; Part 5: the main house, building l; Part 6: the villa enclosure, buildings 2 and 5; Part 7: building 7, a Late Roman kiln and post-built structures; Part 8: the pottery; Part 9: an architectural reconstruction; Part 10: the bone objects; Part 11: the glass; Part 12: quernstones and millstones. *Archaeologia Cantiana* 124, 25-49; 125, 203-28; 126, 115-33; 127, 261-96; 128, 309-34; 129, 333-58; 130, 315-32; 131, 231-76; 135, 189-208; 137, 1-16; 138, 89-103; 140, 1-12.

Phillips, B. 2022 *Littlecote, Wiltshire: Archaeological excavations in the Park*. Hobnob Press, Gloucester.

Philp, B., Parfitt, K., Willson, J. and Williams, W. 1999 *The Roman Villa at Keston, Kent. Second Report (Excavations 1967 and 1978-1990)*. Kent Archaeological Rescue Unit, Dover.

Price, E. 2000 *Frocester. A Romano-British settlement, its antecedents and sucessors. Volume 1: The Site; Volume 2: The Finds*. Gloucester and District Archaeological Research Group, Stonehouse.

Price, E. 2010 *Frocester. A Romano-British settlement, its antecedents and successors. Volume 3: Excavations 1995-2009*. Gloucester and District Archaeological Research Group, Stonehouse.

Putnam, B. 2007 *Roman Dorset*. Tempus, Stroud.

Randall, C. 2021 A leopard in Dorset: the Dewlish Roman villa. *British Archaeology* 181, 34-41.

Ratcliff, A. 2018 *What can we deduce about the ownership of Eccles Roman villa and its place in the social and economic development of the Medway valley and the civitas Cantiacorum?* MA Dissertation, University of Kent.

Reddé, M. 2017/18 (ed.) *Gallia Rustica 1 & 2. Les campagnes du nord-est de la Gaule, de la fin de l'âge du fer à l'antiquité tardive*. Ausonius Editions, Collection Mémoire 49 and 50, Pessac.

Rippon, S., Smart, C. and Pears, B. 2015 *The Fields of Britannia. Continuity and Change in the Late Roman and Early Medieval Landscape*. Oxford University Press, Oxford.

Rivet, A. L. F. 1969 Social and economic aspects. In A. L. F. Rivet (ed.), *The Roman Villa in Britain*. Routledge & Kegan Paul, London, 173-216.

Rodwell, W. and Rodwell, K. 1993 *Rivenhall: investigations of a Roman villa, church and village, 1950–77. Volume 2, specialist studies*. Council for British Archaeology (CBA) Research Report 80, York.

Roymans, N. and Derks, T. 2011 (ed.), *Villa Landscapes in the Roman North. Economy, culture and lifestyles*. Amsterdam University Press, Amsterdam.

Roymans, N., Derks, T. and Hiddink, H. 2015 *The Roman Villa of Hoogeloon and the Archaeology of the Periphery.* Amsterdam University Press, Amsterdam.

Rudling, D. 1998 The development of Roman villas in Sussex. *Sussex Archaeological Collections* 136, 41-65.

Rudling, D. and Russell, M. 2015 *Bignor Roman Villa.* History Press, Stroud.

Russell, J. 1985 The Keynsham Roman villa and its hexagonal triclinia. *Bristol and Avon Archaeology* 4, 6-12.

Sabin, D. 2003 Roman villa and mosaic at Pillerton Priors: an important discovery for Warwickshire. *ARA Bulletin of the Association for Roman Archaeology* 14, 3-4.

Sánchez, D. 2021 *A Roman Villa at Street Farm, Tackley, Oxfordshire.* Thames Valley Archaeological Services Monograph 41, Reading.

Scott, E. 1993 *A Gazetteer of Roman Villas in Britain.* Leicester University Archaeology Monographs 1, Leicester.

Scott, S. 2000 *Art and Society in Fourth-Century Britain. Villa Mosaics in Context.* Oxford University Committee for Archaeology Monograph 53, Oxford.

Shepherd, J. 2021 *Before Bedale. Archaeological excavations along the route of the Bedale, Aiskew and Leeming Bar Bypass.* Pre-Construct Archaeology Ltd, London.

Shepherd, J., Goode, A., Vance, S. and Proctor, J. 2022 *The Bedale Enclosure and Aiskew Villa. Archaeological investigations ahead of the Bedale, Aiskew and Leeming Bar Bypass (A684), North Yorkshire.* Pre-Construct Archaeology Monograph 25, London

Smisson, R. P. M. and Groves, P. 2014 Gatcombe Roman settlement: geophysical surveys 2009-2010. *Britannia* 45, 293-302, online supplementary material.

Smith, A., Allen, M., Brindle, T. and Fulford, M. 2016 *New Visions of the Countryside of Roman Britain. Volume 1: The Rural Settlement of Roman Britain.* Britannia Monograph 29, London.

Smith, A., Allen, M., Brindle, T. and Fulford, M. 2018 *New Visions of the Countryside of Roman Britain. Volume 3: Life and Death in the Countryside of Roman Britain.* Britannia Monograph 31, London.

Smith, J. T. 1997 *Roman Villas. A study in social structure.* Routledge, London (reprint 2011).

Soffe, G. 2011 ARA events in 2009-2010. *ARA Bulletin of the Association for Roman Archaeology* 20, 72-80.

Soffe, G., Nicholls, J. and Moore, G. 1989 The Roman tilery and aisled building at Crookhorn, Hants, Excavations,1974-5. *Proceedings of the Hampshire Field Club & Archaeological Society* 45, 43-112.

Standing, G. 2014 Southwick Roman villa, West Sussex: 'one of the lost treasures of Roman Britain'. *ARA Bulletin of the Association for Roman Archaeology* 22, 34-41.

Stoodley, N. and Cosh, S. R. 2021 *The Romano-British Villa and Anglo-Saxon Cemetery at Eccles, Kent. A summary of the excavations by Alex Detsicas with a consideration of the archaeological, historical and linguistic context.* Archaeopress, Oxford.

Taylor, J. 2007 *An Atlas of Roman Rural Settlement in England.* Council for British Archaeology (CBA) Research Report 151, York.

The Newt in Somerset 2021 *Villa Ventorum. A Roman estate reimagined.* The Newt in Somerset, Bruton.

Thomas, J., Beeson, A., Neal, D. and Kruschwitz, P. 2022 Greek myth in Roman Rutland. Unearthing scenes from the Trojan War. *Current Archaeology* 383, 14-17.

Timby, J. 1998 *Excavations at Kingscote and Wycomb, Gloucestershire. A Roman estate centre and small town in the Cotswolds with notes on related settlements.* Cotswold Archaeological Trust, Cirencester.

Tingle, M. 2008 Archaeological recording of a Roman Villa at Brigstock Road, Stanion, Northamptonshire (April-May 2002). *Northamptonshire Archaeology* 35, 95-136.

Todd, M. 1978 (ed.) *Studies in the Romano-British Villa.* Leicester University Press, Leicester.

Tomalin, D. 2006 Coastal villas, maritime villas: a perspective from southern Britain. *Journal of Maritime Archaeology* 1.1, 29-84.

Trow, S., James, S. and Moore, T. 2009 *Becoming Roman, Being Gallic, Staying British. Research and excavation at 'Ditches' hillfort and villa 1984-2006.* Oxbow Books, Oxford.

Upex, S. G. 2001 The Roman villa at Cotterstock, Northamptonshire. *Britannia* 32, 57-91.

Upex, S. G. 2011 The *Praetorium* of Edmund Artis: a summary of excavations and surveys of the palatial Roman structure at Castor, Cambridgeshire 1828-2010. *Britannia* 42, 23-112.

Wallace, L. M. 2018 Community and the creation of provincial identities: a re-interpretation of the Romano-British aisled building at North Warnborough. *Archaeological Journal* 175, 231-54.

Walters, B. 1996 Exotic structures in 4th-century Britain. In Johnson and Haynes 1996, 152-62.

Walters, B. 2001 A perspective on the social order of Roman villas in Wiltshire. In P. Ellis (ed.), *Roman Wiltshire and After. Papers in honour of Ken Annable,* 127-46. Wiltshire Archaeological and Natural History Society, Devizes.

Walters, B. 2015 The Keynsham Project 2015. *Association for Roman Archaeology News* 34, 34-7.

Walters, B. and Soffe, G. 2009 Roman villas in Britain. *Minerva* 2.5, 19-20.

Webster, G. 1983 The function of the Chedworth Roman 'villa'. *Transactions of the Bristol & Gloucestershire Archaeological Society* 101, 5-20; also in Webster 1991, 95-111.

Webster, G. 1991 *Archaeologist at Large.* Batsford, London.

Webster, G. 1993 What we don't know about Roman Britain, No. 2. *Roman Research News* 6, 6.

Webster, G. 1995 What we don't know about Roman Britain, No. 5, the Roman villa. *Roman Research News* 10, 3.

Wilkinson, P. 2009 *An Archaeological Investigation of the Roman Aisled Stone Building at Hog Brook, Deerton Street, Faversham, Kent 2004-5.* Kent Archaeological Field School, Faversham.

Wilkinson, P. 2011 An octagonal bath-house at Bax Farm, Teynham. *Journal of Roman Archaeology* 24, 407-22.

Wilkinson, P. n.d. *An Archaeological Investigation of the Roman Octagonal Bath-house at Bax Farm, Teynham, Kent 2006 & 2009.* Kent Archaeological Field School, Faversham.

Williams, R. J. and Zeepvat, R. J. 1994 *Bancroft. The Late Bronze Age and Iron Age settlements, Roman villa and temple-mausoleum.* Buckinghamshire Archaeological Society Monograph 7, Aylesbury.

Willis, S. and Carne, P. 2013 (ed.) *A Roman Villa on the Edge of Empire. Excavations at Ingleby Barwick, Stockton-on-Tees, 2003-4.* Council for British Archaeology (CBA) Research Report 170, York.

Wilson, D. R. 2004 The North Leigh Roman villa: its plan reviewed. *Britannia* 35, 77-113.

Wilson, D., Bagnall, A. and Taylor, B. 2014 *Report on the Excavation of a Romano-British Site in Wortley, South Gloucestershire.* British Archaeological Reports (BAR) British Series 591, Oxford.

Witts, P. 2000 Mosaics and room function: the evidence from some fourth-century Romano-British villas. *Britannia* 31, 291-324.

2

Where, when and what for?
Coin use in the Romano-British countryside

Philippa Walton

Introduction

The Portable Antiquities Scheme is one of the most significant recent innovations in British archaeology. Since 1997, it has created a database of more than 1,519,000 archaeological objects up until 2012, which have been offered for recording by members of the public. This database (http://finds.org.uk/database) provides an invaluable resource for those studying the material culture of England and Wales from prehistory to the post medieval period and numerous research projects have been undertaken which integrate its material (see Worrell *et al.* 2010). Roman coins represent the largest single category of object recorded by the PAS, accounting for nearly a fifth of all finds on the database.[1] The size of this dataset and its broad geographical spread allow patterns of coin use to be studied, not only at the level of the individual site, but also on a regional and provincial scale. This paper provides a brief overview of these patterns and suggests how they can be used to explore the geography, chronology and function of coinage in the Romano-British countryside.

The significance of the PAS dataset of Roman coins

Despite growing awareness that the majority of the population of Roman Britain lived in the countryside (Mattingly 2006, 365; Taylor 2001, 46; Millett 1990, 183ff), study of rural coin use has been limited, with most work concentrating on large excavation assemblages from urban, military and temple sites (Reece 1991; 1995). Where patterns of rural coin loss have been investigated, the focus has been on 'the villa' and 'the villa economy' (Branigan and Miles 1988) rather than on the range of site types which undoubtedly populated the ancient countryside (i.e. 'the village'; 'the farmstead'; 'the small town'; 'the shrine') but have not been excavated with the same frequency.[2] The PAS, with its records of

unstratified, metal-detected finds from arable areas, allow us to look beyond 'the villa' and to study rural coin loss in its broadest sense.

Where were Roman coins used?

The distribution of all Roman coin finds recorded by the PAS throughout England and Wales is shown in Fig. 2.1. Whilst this map demonstrates the hard work of the PAS between 1997 and 2011, it does give the somewhat misleading impression that coin use was widespread and almost uniform in intensity throughout the province. This is because it includes the find-spots of coins of all dates and of stray losses as well as larger groups.[3] Such losses do not so much indicate habitual coin use, as the presence of a few people, who happened to lose a few coins, over the 400-year period of Roman rule.

A more accurate picture of where coins were actually being used, can be gained by looking at the distribution of larger groups of coins or 'assemblages'. There is much debate as to what constitutes an 'assemblage' (Casey 1986, 89; Reece 1991) although here it has been defined as a group of twenty or more coins from any individual parish or site. In 2008, 457 parish assemblages in England were identified using PAS data, as well as a further 367 excavation assemblages, equating to a total of more than 220,000 coins.[4] Together, their distribution as illustrated in Fig. 2.2, represents the most comprehensive picture of where coins were actually used in Roman Britain.[5]

---

[1] On 04.04.12, 187,003 Roman coins had been recorded by the Portable Antiquities Scheme. This includes the 53,165 coin records from Wales collected by Cardiff University's Iron Age and Roman Coins from Wales project (Guest 2008). A further 184 Roman Provincial coins have also been recorded.

[2] This paper was written before the Roman Rural Settlement Project was undertaken. The project has brought together the excavated

evidence for the rural settlement of Roman Britain including artefactual and numismatic data to inform a comprehensive reassessment of the countryside throughout the province (see Smith et al. 2016; Allen et al. 2017; Smith et al. 2018).

[3] Anything from single finds to small groups of coins.

[4] Assemblages from Wales were excluded in order to avoid replication of the research being undertaken by Cardiff University's Iron Age and Roman Coins of Wales Project (see Guest 2008). By May 2011, the total number of PAS coin assemblages had risen to 909 (Moorhead and Walton 2011).

[5] Whilst the number of coins recorded may only represent a very small sample of the original coin population of Roman Britain, its absolute size makes it significant. The total original coin populations at the forts of Corbridge and Caerleon have been calculated on the basis of military pay rates. Using these calculations, it is estimated that 0.003% of the original coin population from Corbridge and 0.00000034% from Caerleon survive (Casey 1986, 84ff)

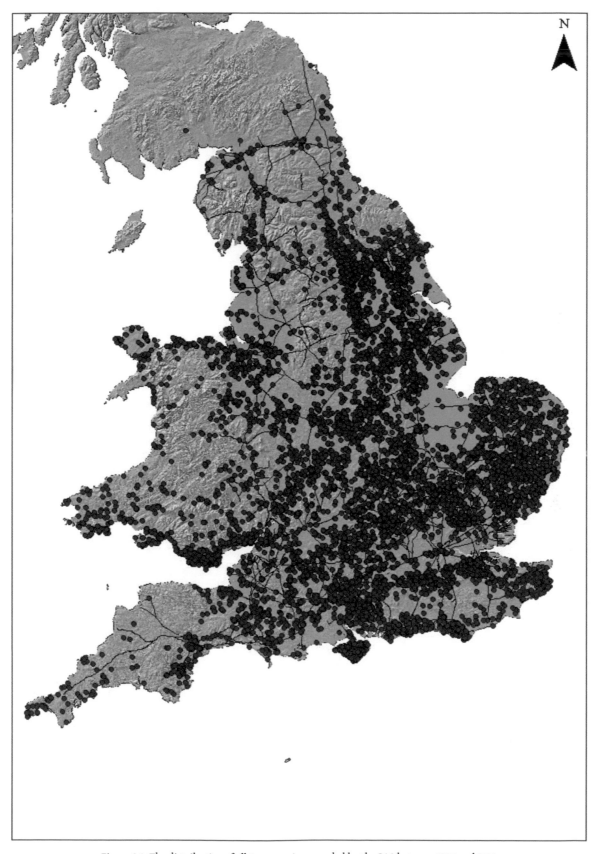

Figure 2.1. The distribution of all Roman coins recorded by the PAS between 1997 and 2011 (a dot can represent anything from a single coin to an assemblage of more than 1000).

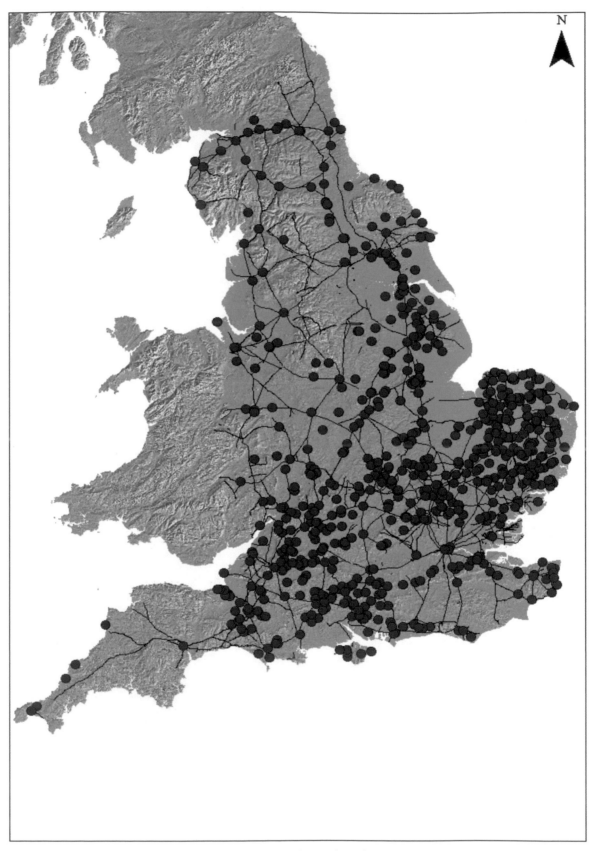

Figure 2.2. The distribution of site and parish assemblages.

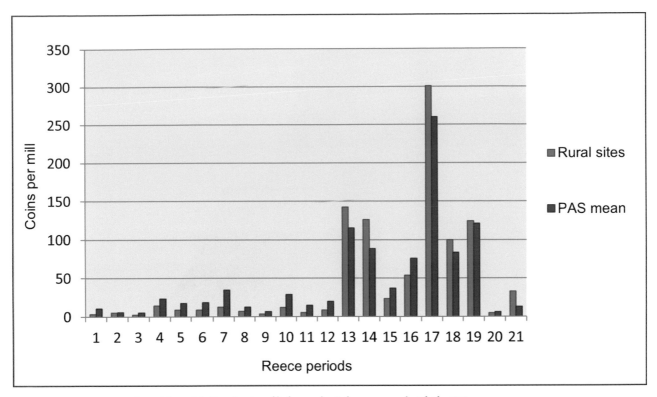

Figure 2.3. Bar-chart profile for rural coin loss compared with the PAS mean.

As with other types of Roman material culture, such as brooches and nail cleaners (McIntosh 2012; Eckardt and Crummy 2003), the distribution pattern of coin assemblages is not uniform throughout the province. There is, for example, a clear contrast between the abundance of assemblages in the south-east and their scarcity in the north west, where the majority are associated with military installations. These differences must, to some extent, reflect varying ancient population density, site function and different native attitudes to coinage. However, modern biases and constraints must also be taken into account and in some counties, such as Hampshire and Suffolk, it is difficult to determine whether the large numbers of assemblages are due to ancient economic factors or the intensity of modern metal detecting.

Whilst Fig. 2.2 outlines the geographical extent of coin use during the Roman period, it cannot illustrate nuances in the chronology and function of the sites represented by each assemblage. Excavated site assemblages are lumped together with PAS assemblages where for the most part, the function of the sites from which they come remain unknown. In order to look specifically at rural coin use, 'applied numismatic' techniques must be used to pick out sites with 'rural' coin profiles from a background of all sites.

When were Roman coins being used in rural areas?

The spread of coin use into the Romano-British countryside is generally agreed to be a late Roman phenomenon (Walker 1988, 304).[6] As a result, most rural sites exhibit similar coin profiles, regardless of their function as farmsteads, villas or nucleated settlements (Davies and Gregory 1991, 76; Reece 1988a, 106). These coin profiles are broadly characterised by low levels of first- to mid-third-century coinage, coupled with larger quantities of late third- and fourth-century coinage (Reece 1972; Reece 1988b; Reece 1995; Lockyear 2000, 403) and more specifically by a higher proportion of fourth-century *nummi* to late third-century radiates (Reece 1988a; Moorhead 2001, 90).

An investigation of the dataset reveals that 443 assemblages (equating to a total of 115,772 coins) exhibit this characteristic rural coin profile (Fig. 2.3).[7]

[6] A lack of coinage in the first to third centuries AD does not mean that the countryside operated outside the Romano-British economy. Indeed, other forms of Roman material culture such as pottery and jewellery appear in quantity at rural sites, where coinage does not. This attests to the continued use of alternative exchange mechanisms despite 'Romanisation'.
[7] The assemblages were identified as similar using DMax Cluster Analysis. For further discussion of this statistical technique and its application, see Walton 2012, 51.

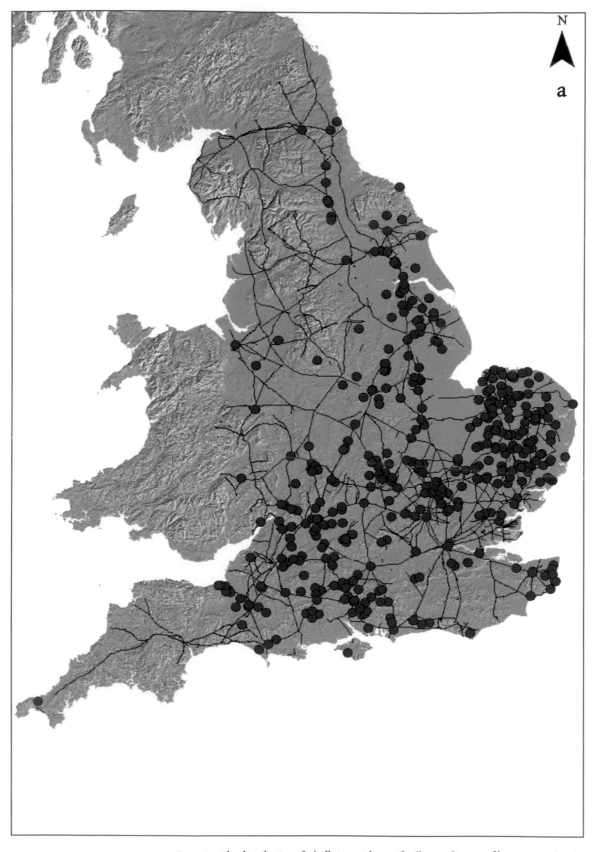

Figure 2.4. The distribution of, a) all sites with specifically 'rural' site profiles, compared with,

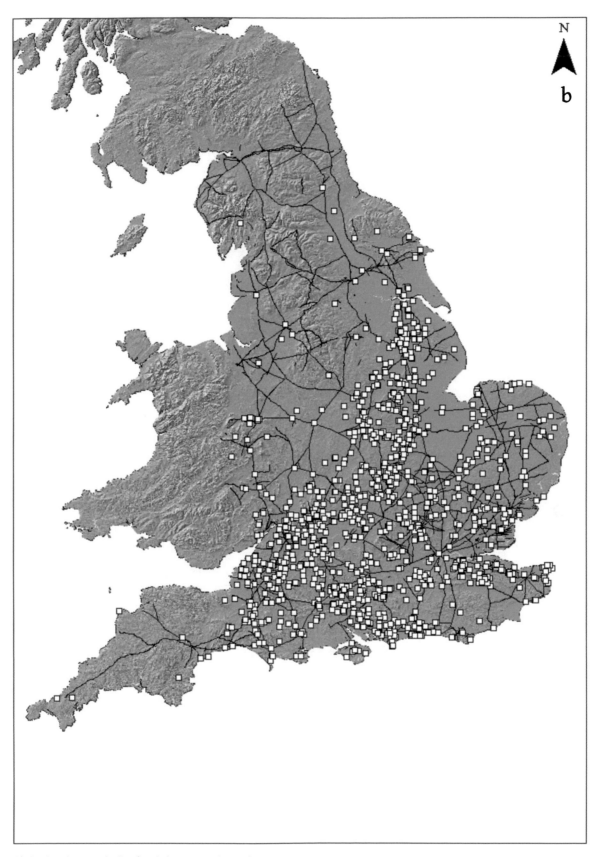

b) the distribution of villas (English Heritage dataset).

As Fig. 2.4a illustrates, their distribution pattern is, for the most part, restricted to southern, lowland Britain, and is strikingly similar to that of Roman villas (Fig. 2.4b). However, despite this similarity, it is clear that rural coin use is not exclusively associated with villas. Few PAS coins are likely to have been recovered from villas as most are Scheduled Monuments and numerous assemblages have been recorded in East Anglia, where few villas are known.

Fig. 2.4a outlines the widest extent of late Roman rural coin loss. However, this is not a static pattern and as the 4th century progresses, there is a clear decline in the number of sites using coins and a contraction in their geographical extent. Fig. 2.5 illustrates this decline.[8] Assemblages with above average[9] coin loss for the late third and early fourth century AD are located throughout the countryside, even away from major road networks. However, by the mid fourth century, there are fewer sites and there is a significant shrinkage in their distribution. By the end of the Roman period, assemblages are almost completely restricted to sites located on major communication and transport routes, particularly at nodal points such as cross-roads.[10]

How was coinage being used in rural areas?

It is relatively easy to trace the geographical extent of this short-lived horizon of prolific rural coin use. However, we can only speculate as to why it occurred. The traditional theory is that changes in the denominational composition of Roman coinage in the late third century AD resulting in a plentiful supply of low value coinage, accompanied by a boom in economic production and prosperity (Moorhead 2001a, 94ff) brought coinage within the reach of rural populations for the first time. Instead of functioning as a unit of taxation and a mechanism for paying the army and administration, it was embraced by the rural marketplace and used in everyday exchange (Millett 1990, 169; Esmonde Cleary 1989, 96; Mattingly 2006, 497; Reece 1988a, 102).

Whilst such a theory has much to recommend it, it is not the only plausible interpretation of the evidence.

The appearance of large quantities of coinage in rural areas in the early fourth century AD could reflect changes in the way the Roman administration exploited the countryside and its agricultural output.[11] Rather than reflecting widening participation in a monetary economy, this coinage could instead represent the pay of both officials and military units stationed throughout the countryside and tasked with extracting taxes in kind, such as the 'Annona militaris' (Moorhead 2001, 94ff). At a time when the Continent was suffering significant instability and the effects of barbarian invasion, it seems logical that the Roman authorities would have wanted to establish and maintain a stranglehold over Britain's agricultural resources (Moorhead and Stuttard 2012, 171ff). With this in mind, it is worth noting the similarity in the distribution pattern of rural sites with above average mid to late Roman coin loss and late Roman belt fittings (Laycock 2008, 115). These fittings have been interpreted as the insignia of civilian administrators and local militias (Leahy 2007).

Large volumes of fourth-century coinage and a peak in Valentinianic coin loss (AD 364 to 378) have already been noted to be characteristic of late Roman temple sites (Esmonde Cleary 1989, 95; Davies and Gregory 1991, 71; Moorhead 2001, 93). The PAS data continues to reinforce the relationship between prolific rural coin loss and religion. At sites such as Nether Wallop, Hampshire and Beedon, Berkshire, the coin assemblages are associated with objects with votive associations such as cut brooches and miniature objects, whilst at Tisbury, Wiltshire, a small proportion of the coins are mutilated or pierced with iron nails, probably indicating ritual activity.[12] It is therefore possible that when coinage did eventually reach the rural population at large, they had little economic use for it in the traditional sense. Instead, they offered it to the gods, as part of more numinous transactions.[13]

---

[8] The assemblages were divided into three sub-groups based on their chronology using DMax Cluster Analysis. For more detailed discussion, see Walton 2012, 103.

[9] In this instance, 'above average' coin loss is defined as a per mill figure which is greater than or equal to twice the PAS Mean for that period.

[10] Obviously, earlier fourth century coinage could continue to circulate throughout the fourth century AD, so we cannot rely on these distribution maps to provide a completely accurate view of the decline of coin circulation in late Roman Britain. However, it is interesting to note that the distribution pattern of Theodosian hoards is very similar to that of above average late Roman coin loss.

[11] The Panegyric of Constantius emphasises the full potential of Britain as an agricultural resource: 'Without doubt Britain...was a land that the state could ill afford to lose, so rich are its harvests, so countless the pasturelands in which it delights, so many the metals whose seams pervade it , so great the wealth which comes from its taxes, so many the harbours which encompass it, so great an area it covers...' (VIII,11.1.; Moorhead and Stuttard 2012, 172).

[12] 898 Roman coins from Beedon, Berkshire; 954 coins from Nether Wallop, Hampshire.

[13] This interpretation could also be applied to Roman coin hoards of the period, some of which may be votive deposits in a more contained form.

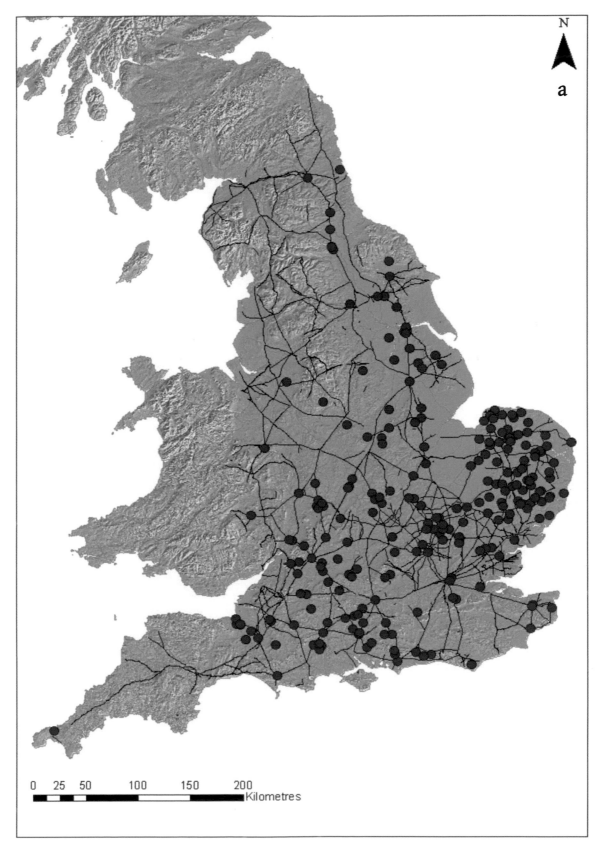

Figure 2.5. The decline of rural coin loss in the fourth century AD, a) late third to early fourth-century profiles.

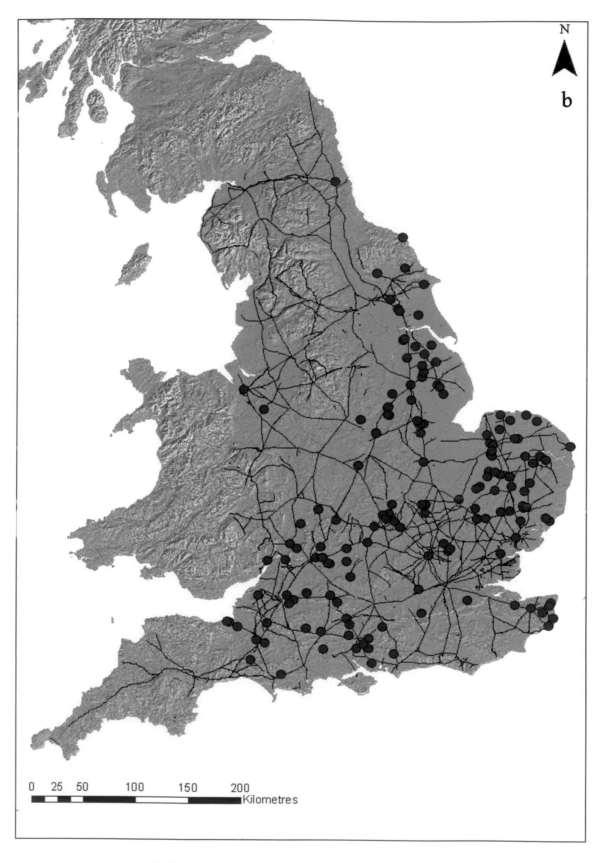

Figure 2.5. The decline of rural coin loss in the fourth century AD, b) mid fourth-century profiles.

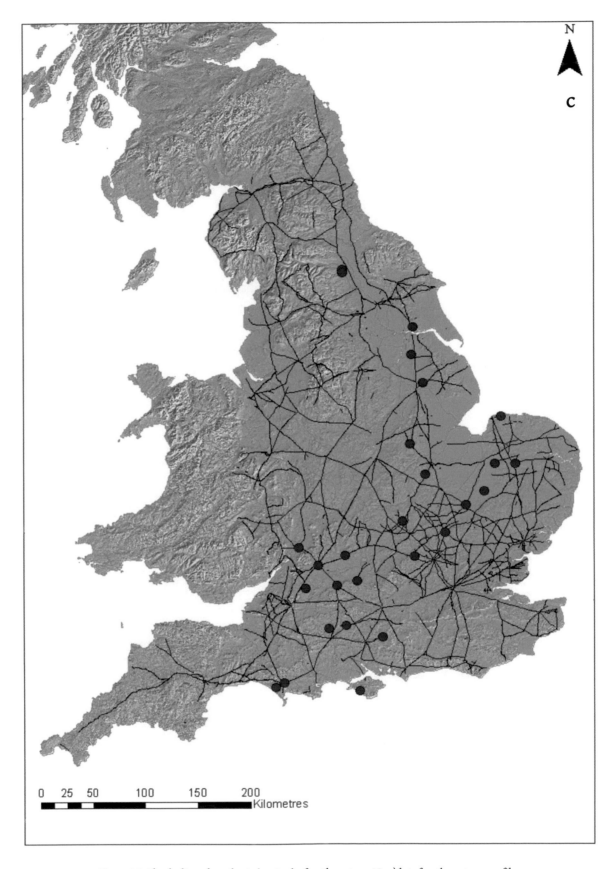

Figure 2.5. The decline of rural coin loss in the fourth century AD, c) late fourth-century profiles.

Conclusions

This paper has outlined the contribution that Portable Antiquities Scheme data can make to our understanding of rural coin use in Roman Britain. Emphasising the need to look beyond assemblages from villas, it has illustrated the limited extent and chronology of coin use in the countryside. Most importantly, it has suggested that a fundamental reinterpretation of the nature of Roman activity in the fourth century AD is necessary. Far from being a 'Golden Age' of prosperity for all, it is possible that the Roman authorities exploited Britain's resources, at the expense of the majority of the Romano-British population.

References

Allen, M., Lodwick, L., Brindle, T., Fulford, M. and Smith, A. 2017 *New Visions of the Countryside of Roman Britain. Volume 2: The Rural Economy of Roman Britain.* Britannia Monograph 30, London.

Branigan, K. and Miles, D. 1988 *The Economies of Romano-British villas.* Sheffield University Press, Sheffield.

Davies, J. A. and Gregory, T. 1991 Coinage from a *Civitas*: a survey of the Roman coins found in Norfolk and their contribution to the archaeology of the *Civitas Icenorum. Britannia* 22, 65-102.

Eckardt, H. and Crummy, N. 2003 Regional identities and technologies of the self: nail-cleaners in Roman Britain. *The Archaeological Journal* 160, 44-69.

Esmonde-Cleary, S. 1989 *The Ending of Roman Britain.* Batsford, London.

Guest, P. 2008 The early monetary history of Wales: identity, conquest and acculturation. *Britannia* 39, 35-58.

Laycock, S. 2008 *Britannia. The Failed State. Tribal Conflicts and the End of Roman Britain.* The History Press, Stroud.

Leahy, K. 2007 Soldiers and settlers in Britain, fourth to fifth century – revisited. In M. Henig and T. J. Smith (ed.), *Collectanea Antiqua: essays in memory of Sonia Chadwicke Hawkes,* 133-144. British Archaeological Reports (BAR) International Series 1673, Oxford.

Lockyear, K. 2000 Site finds in Roman Britain: a comparison of techniques. *Oxford Journal of Archaeology* 19.4, 397-423.

Mattingly, D. 2006 *An Imperial Possession: Britain in the Roman Empire.* Allen Lane, London.

Millett, M. 1990 *The Romanization of Britain. An essay in Archaeological Interpretation.* Cambridge University Press, Cambridge.

McIntosh, F. 2011 Regional brooch-types in Roman Britain: evidence from northern England. *Archaeologia Aeliana* 5th series, 40, 155-182.

Moorhead, T. S. N. 2001 Roman coin finds from Wiltshire. In P. Ellis (ed.), *Roman Wiltshire and After. Papers in honour of Ken Annable,* 85-105. Wiltshire Archaeological and Natural History Society, Devizes.

Moorhead, T. S. N. and Stuttard, D. 2012 *The Romans who shaped Britain.* Thames and Hudson, London.

Moorhead, T. S. N. and Walton, P. 2011 Roman coins recorded with the Portable Antiquities Scheme – a summary. *Britannia* 42, 432-437.

Reece, R. 1972 Roman coins found on fourteen sites in Britain. *Britannia* 3, 269-276.

Reece, R. 1988a Coins and villas. In Branigan and Miles 1988, 34-41.

Reece, R. 1988b *My Roman Britain.* Cotswold Studies, Cirencester.

Reece, R. 1995 Site-finds in Roman Britain. *Britannia* 26, 179-206.

Smith, A., Allen, M., Brindle, T. and Fulford, M. 2016 *New Visions of the Countryside of Roman Britain. Volume 1: The Rural Settlement of Roman Britain.* Britannia Monograph 29, London.

Smith, A., Allen, M., Brindle. T, Fulford, M., Lodwick, L. and Rohnbogner, A. 2018 *New Visions of the Countryside of Roman Britain. Volume 3: Life and Death in the Countryside of Roman Britain.* Britannia Monograph 31, London.

Walker, D. R. 1988 The Roman coins. In B. Cunliffe (ed.), *The Temple of Sulis Minerva at Bath. Vol. II. The Finds from the Sacred Spring.* Oxford University Committee for Archaeology Monograph 16, Oxford.

Walton, P. 2012 *Rethinking Roman Britain: coinage and archaeology.* Moneta Monograph 137. Moneta, Wetteren.

Worrell, S., Egan, G., Naylor, J., Leahy, K. and Lewis, M. 2010 *A Decade of Discovery. Proceedings of the Portable Antiquities Scheme Conference 2007.* British Archaeological Reports (BAR) British Series 520, Oxford.

3

Villa mosaics and archaeology

Patricia Witts

The discovery of a mosaic is a mixed blessing for an archaeologist. Inconveniently large and not portable, it immediately poses problems of preservation and conservation. Lifting is difficult, expensive and time-consuming, and then there is the question of what to do with the mosaic thereafter, but unless it is lifted it bars the way to potentially useful evidence lying beneath it. On the positive side, mosaics have their own inherent charm and provide eye-catching images to enliven excavation reports. They attract visitors and can be employed to decorate publicity material and souvenirs. In addition to these ephemeral benefits, however, a mosaic can often make a solid contribution to the archaeological interpretation of a site. The aim of this paper is to look closely at, and evaluate the reliability of, some aspects of that contribution.

Various papers in this volume reconsider the function of the establishments being discussed. For instance, the building at Lullingstone is not of the large size associated with villas and might instead have been a leisure retreat or hunting lodge, an interpretation also offered for the function of the building at Whitley Grange for similar reasons. The Great Witcombe villa is reinterpreted as a magnificent water shrine. In the first part of this paper, I consider whether there is anything about the mosaics – in particular their figured elements - that lends support to or might contradict such ideas. I also look closely at the mosaic from Bradford on Avon (Budbury), comparing and contrasting it with similar mosaics thought to have been laid by the same group of craftsmen, to see what such an exercise can tell us about the use of mosaics in Late Roman villas.

The second part of this paper is concerned with the topic of chronology. Archaeologists often look to mosaics to provide an indication of date, but caution is needed in using them in this way. The mosaic discovered at the Yarford villa poses an important question about the reliability of dating by style. Such dating can also lead to controversial results. A re-evaluation of the date of the Bacchus mosaic at *Verulamium* is a case in point and, while this pavement is from an urban site, it has implications for villa studies.

Mosaics and Function

My consideration of the likely function of a building in the context of its figured mosaics starts with a simple example. The Whitley Grange mosaic has a stylised representation of the head of Medusa at the centre of an otherwise geometric design (Fig. 3.1; this volume, Fig. 6.4; Cosh and Neal 2010, 310-313, Mosaic 480.1; Witts 2005, 94). There were a number of Romano-British mosaics with this subject. Those from Room 56 at Bignor (Neal and Cosh 2009, 511-513, Mosaic 396.11; Witts 2005, 94, fig. 40), Room N13 at Fishbourne (Neal and Cosh 2009, 551-553, Mosaic 403.45; Witts 2005, 94, fig. 41) and Room K at Keynsham (Cosh and Neal 2005, 235-237, Mosaic 204.5; Witts 2005, 96) were similar to Whitley Grange in depicting Medusa as the sole figured image at the centre of the pavement. Her long history and enduring popularity made her a suitable choice for a good-luck image that could be used in a variety of contexts.

If the main function of the Whitley Grange building was as a hunting lodge, a good-luck image would seem appropriate. It is notable, however, that in mosaics in which Medusa appears with other images, those images do not depict or have a connection with hunting. Instead, the most common link is with time. Medusa appears with Seasons in the mosaics from Room 12 at Brading (this volume, Figs 16.16-16.20) (Neal and Cosh 2009, 271-280, Mosaic 331.6; Witts 2005, 95, figs 9, 16), Room 33 at Bignor (Neal and Cosh 2009, 510, Mosaic 396.7; Witts 2005, 95, fig. 33), and from Toft Green in York (Neal and Cosh 2002, 373-375, Mosaic 149.5; Witts 2005, 95). She also featured in the centre of the lost Days of the Week mosaic from Bramdean (Neal and Cosh 2009, 166-167, Mosaic 308.1; Witts 2005, 95, col. pl. 10). Although the Cirencester Seasons mosaic juxtaposes a small head of Medusa with a hunting scene - she appears in a compartment adjacent to the depiction of Actaeon being attacked by his dogs as he turns into a stag - this combination of images is probably coincidental: the other three scenes adjoining the Medusa compartment do not depict or allude to a hunt (Cosh and Neal 2010, 110-113, Mosaic 421.46; Witts 2005, 96, fig. 34). Medusa is also shown in the Hunting Dogs mosaic from the same house (Cosh and Neal 2010,

Figure 3.1. Painting of the Whitley Grange mosaic by David Neal. (Copyright D. S. Neal)

107-110, Mosaic 421.45; Witts 2005, 96, fig. 42) but this pavement is thought to contain work of more than one period. The creation of the Medusa head might not have been contemporary with the central hunting scene but it demonstrates that this combination of images was regarded as acceptable.

If the Whitley Grange building was a hunting lodge, the subject of its mosaic was by no means inappropriate. However, given the strong link between Medusa and the Seasons elsewhere, it is more likely that the patron's interests lay in the yearly round. It might be safer to regard the Whitley Grange building as a country retreat for a proprietor concerned with the productivity of crops rather than as a base for hunting parties.

Lullingstone – Bellerophon and Europa

A similar concern with time can be seen in the Lullingstone mosaic, where the Seasonal imagery is explicit: busts of the Seasons surround a cushion-shaped compartment, peopled by dolphins and shells, in which Bellerophon, mounted on Pegasus, is shown in the act of slaying the Chimaera (this volume, Fig. 15.5) (Neal and Cosh 2009, 379-385, Mosaic 361.1; Witts 2005, 50, col. pl. 3; Witts 2016, 21, pl. (E)). Bellerophon's link with the Seasons is also attested in mosaics from other provinces. The fragmentary mosaic from Ravenna (Ghirardini 1916, 788-796; Carini 2007) is similar to the Lullingstone mosaic both in its subject matter and in the inclusion of an inscription, although the Lullingstone inscription refers not to Bellerophon but to the other figured scene. The extant inscription at Ravenna describes control of the Seasons: *Sum e quod autumnus, quod ver, quod bruma, quod estas alternis reparant ...* (I am [he] through whom autumn, spring, winter, and summer are in turn restored) (Ellis 1991, 125). The employment of inscriptions in Bellerophon mosaics is notable, with other examples in Britain being recorded from Frampton, where the inscription referred to the other imagery (Cosh and Neal 2005, 134-137, Mosaic 168.2; Witts 2005, 51, figs 10, 18) and Boxford, where the variety of inscriptions included one naming Bellerophon (Tomlin 2020, 474-475, Berkshire 5; see also Beeson 2019, esp. 36-43). Elsewhere, in mosaics from Malaga (Blazquez 1981, 77-78, Mosaic 53) and Ucero (Blazquez and Ortego 1983, 50-51, Mosaic 50), the wording was simpler but referred to Bellerophon.

The association with water indicated by the dolphins and shells at Lullingstone is recalled by the wave-pattern borders around the busts of the Ravenna Seasons. There are further similarities between the Lullingstone mosaic and other mosaics depicting Bellerophon. The Bellerophon mosaic from Nîmes (Aymard 1953, 249-259) not only had Seasons but also borders of swastika-meander, recalling the swastika-meander border at Lullingstone and the prominent swastikas in its chequerboard panel. The aquatic element of the Nîmes mosaic was provided by water birds and two small dolphins, while at Frampton the outer border was filled with dolphins and a head of Neptune. Below the Bellerophon compartment at Nîmes was a prominent *crater*, recalling the large vessel in the apse at Frampton and in the border at Boxford. The Bellerophon mosaic from Avenches (*ibid.* 260-261) included figures interpreted as Seasons or Winds, while the marine element was provided by small fish. The Avenches mosaic also depicted drinking vessels – in the

form of small cups rather than a crater – and hunting scenes. At Lullingstone the remains of a large *cantharus* adjoin the Bellerophon panel, while a cup is featured in one of the chequers. The Avenches hunting scenes are loosely paralleled by the scene in the Lullingstone apse which shows Europa being abducted by Jupiter in the guise of a bull: Aymard, writing about hunting scenes generally, and evidently before the discovery of the Lullingstone pavement had become known, made a similar link when he suggested that the conventional hunting scenes in the Lillebonne mosaic (Ling 1998, fig. 93) are complemented by 'la chasse amoureuse du dieu' (Aymard 1953, 266). Moreover, Bellerophon himself represents a specific heroic hunter (Toynbee 1955; Huskinson 1974; Pugliara 1996).

At first glance, the themes discussed above are common to Bellerophon mosaics and would have been appropriate for a villa, a hunting lodge or a country retreat. In themselves, they do not necessarily help us to distinguish between the different types of establishment. It is widely recognised that the Lullingstone apse was suitable for holding a dining couch – even if, in the absence of other grand apartments, the room might have served a variety of functions – and dining itself is an activity that no doubt took place in all three of the sorts of building being discussed. But there are other aspects of the Lullingstone mosaic, such as the orientation of the imagery, that can help us to be more precise.

A diner reclining in the apse would have seen the Europa panel, the inscription above it, and the Bellerophon scene from the correct direction. The prominent image of an almost-naked female in the apse, albeit in a well-known and often-depicted mythological scene, is a bold choice for a family villa and sits more plausibly with a private male retreat. The inscription reinforces this. While it is replete with classical allusion and has long been regarded as evidence of literacy, perhaps representing the sort of impromptu compositions that took place at dinner parties (Smith 1969, 90-91, n.6; Barrett 1978, 311), it is a light-hearted reference to male dalliance. Leader-Newby compares it with the inscription from Sperlonga (2007, 192, n. 36). The latter, while longer and carved in stone, is strikingly similar to the Lullingstone inscription in the structure of its opening. The Lullingstone wording - 'If jealous Juno ... she would ...' - has its complement at Sperlonga in the wording: 'If Mantua could resurrect its divine-poet priest, he, amazed at the tremendous work, would defer to the cave ...' (Squire 2007, 104). It is notable that the depiction of Jupiter conquering Europa at Lullingstone is shown in alignment with Bellerophon conquering the Chimaera amid Seasonal and aquatic imagery. If a proprietor, perhaps with landed and marine interests, wished to emphasise ideas of control and of maritime and agricultural prosperity in his country retreat, this combination of images would be highly appropriate. The unique chequerboard panel, perhaps a game-board as discussed but dismissed by Meates (1979, 79), adds to the aura of leisure pursuits. It reinforces the concept of the building as being primarily for relaxation rather than a conventional home.

The array of images at Lullingstone can be contrasted with those at Bignor, an establishment whose plan is that of a courtyard villa. The opulence of the mosaic decoration at Bignor, with its series of high-quality pavements, tends to obscure the fact that the iconography is remarkably straightforward. It is concerned not with a representation of power but with hospitality, beauty and good luck. For instance, in the inner part of Room 7 Ganymede is shown being abducted by Jupiter while a series of maenads surround a pool in the outer part of the room (Fig. 3.2; Neal and Cosh 2009, 498-503, Mosaic 396.3; Witts 2005, 118, fig. 57, col. pl. 4). The iconography of the two parts of the pavement reflects a simple and unified theme: the cup-bearer to the gods and the attendants of the god of wine. In Room 3, the bust of Venus adorns the apse of a room whose pavement features two sets of Cupids (Neal and Cosh 2009, 492-497, Mosaic 396.1; Witts 2005, 120, 139, fig. 58, col. pls 18, 22). The remaining figured mosaics show Medusa (Room 56), Seasons (Room 26) and Medusa and Seasons (Room 33) (Neal and Cosh 2009, 506-513, Mosaics 396.6, 396.7 and 396.11; Witts 2005, 94, 80, figs 40, 32 and 33). None of these presents any problem of identification nor is there a complex series of mythological scenes that might prompt reflection and conversation.

Three of the depictions of Bellerophon in Romano-British mosaics paired him with a powerful figure in another part of a bipartite or tripartite room: Jupiter, albeit in a light-hearted amorous scene, is featured in the apsidal part of the room at Lullingstone (Neal and Cosh 2009, 379-385, Mosaic 361.1; Witts 2005, 29-30, col. pl. 3); Bacchus decorated the mosaic in the outer part of Room B at Frampton (Cosh and Neal 2005, 134-137, Mosaic 168.2; Witts 2005, 113, fig. 18); and a bust with the Chi-Rho symbol was shown in the centre of the other part of the Hinton St Mary mosaic (Cosh and Neal 2005, 156-160, Mosaic 172.1; Witts 2005, 50-51, 60, fig. 14). It has often been noted that, in addition to the depiction of Bellerophon, these three mosaics are linked by apparently Christian connections: the Chi-Rho in the chord of the apse at Frampton and behind the bust at Hinton St Mary, the possible cryptogram in the Lullingstone inscription (Henig 1997, 2000; *contra* Ling 2007a, 78-79), and the wall-paintings found in another room at the same site. The theory about the Lullingstone cryptogram is not settled, the wall-paintings are thought to be later than the mosaic thus making the connection tenuous, and the significance of the Chi-Rho and the identity of the bust in the Hinton St Mary mosaic are still being debated (Pearce 2008). The image of Bellerophon is, however, readily recognisable and common to all.

The Frampton and Hinton St Mary mosaics are often compared to one another and clearly there are similarities in the choice and style of image; Henig also notes a general similarity to the Lullingstone mosaic (1997, 4). In terms of the iconography and the way in which the room may have been used, the connection between Frampton and Lullingstone is closer than that between Frampton and Hinton St Mary: the Frampton and Lullingstone mosaics both have love scenes, inscriptions, marine imagery, a prominent *cantharus*, and hunting scenes (reading the Lullingstone Europa scene as an amorous 'hunt'). The Hinton St Mary mosaic has no love interest, only the Chi-Rho by way of an inscription, a modest marine element in the form of the wave-pattern border and, although four small *canthari* occupy the spandrels around Bellerophon, no single prominent *cantharus*. Its hunting panels feature dogs and deer, whereas the two Frampton panels were more exotic: each contained a human figure respectively hunting a leopard and a stag (Witts 2016, 13, 17, 172, figs 5, 69).

The Frampton and Lullingstone mosaics are also close to one another in the way the imagery was viewed. At Lullingstone the viewer was intended to see the images after entering the room and while static within its innermost part, the apse. At Frampton, the cantharus and the Chi-Rho were viewed by someone approaching the apse, but the other images were all oriented to be seen from within the apse and on leaving the room: Bellerophon, the head of Neptune, and the inscription referring to Neptune faced the apse; Bacchus, Cupid and the inscription referring to Cupid were all seen as the viewer left (Witts 2000, 313; cf. Ling 2007b, 5). In other words, the focus was not on viewing the images as one entered but the emphasis was on what happened after one had arrived. The viewer would need time to consider the four corner scenes and the two inscriptions as well as the main images. Although little is known of the overall plan at Hinton St Mary, it is thought that Bellerophon was seen on entry but the bust with the Chi-Rho faced the opposite direction. The dynamic was completely different from Frampton and Lullingstone, a feeling reinforced by the placement of the hunting panels: those flanking Bellerophon faced inwards, creating a corridor effect, while in the inner part of the room they faced the walls and created a more spacious feel (Witts 2000, 309-

Figure 3.2. Bignor villa, Ganymede mosaic. (From Lysons 1817, pl. V)

312). Lysons, who excavated the site at Frampton in 1796, recorded that he had not come across buildings other than those in the L-shaped bank of earth he indicated on his plan (1813, 2 and pl. II). He commented that the other part of the meadow was level and occasionally subject to flooding. His doubts, later endorsed by Farrar (1956; see also Sparey-Green 1994), as to whether Frampton functioned as a villa reinforce the suggestion that the function of the Lullingstone building, whose main room operated in a similar way to Room B at Frampton, was also not that of a normal villa.

Great Witcombe and marine themes

Elsewhere in this volume, the Great Witcombe 'villa', built on a steep slope riddled with springs, is reinterpreted as a magnificent water shrine. At the southern end of the south-west wing was a bath suite decorated with mosaics, among them a figured pavement in Room 6 (the *frigidarium*) showing a variety of sea creatures (Cosh and Neal 2010, 160-161, Mosaic 433.2; Witts 2005, 97, fig. 43; Witts 2016, 59, 61-63, 68, 174, figs 150, 153, 165, 199, 226, 262-264, pl. (C)). While the subject was clearly appropriate decoration for a bath, this mosaic stands out for three reasons and lends support to the suggestion that this building was special. First, the figures are limited to sea creatures: there is no depiction of Neptune or other divine or human figures. This sets the Great Witcombe mosaic apart from some of the other mosaics that feature sea creatures. For instance, the remains of the splendid marine mosaic with a variety of sea beasts found at Gloucester House, Dyer Street, in Cirencester included a wheel thought to have been part of Neptune's chariot, a Nereid seated on a sea beast and several Cupids (Cosh and Neal 2010, 106, Mosaic 421.44; Witts 2005, 121, fig. 59; Witts 2016, 159-160, pl. (B)). The fragment of a marine mosaic found in the bath suite at the Dewlish villa (Cosh and Neal 2005, 84-85, Mosaic 164.13; Witts 2005, 121, col. pl. 16; Witts 2016, 166-167) also depicted a Cupid although this has since been lost. In both the Cirencester and Dewlish mosaics the large sea creatures are all swimming in the same direction, apparently as part of a marine *thiasos*, rather than adopting the different orientations of the Great Witcombe beasts. Secondly, the sheer variety of creatures in the Great Witcombe mosaic is notable. As well as dolphins, fish and shellfish, the pavement includes marine versions of a bull, goat and griffin. On the other hand, it does not depict any sea felines or sea horses although both of these are commonly found in other Romano-British marine mosaics. For instance, the Cirencester mosaic and a fragment from Bath (Cosh and Neal 2005, 189, Mosaic 188.6; Witts 2005, 97, fig. 44; Witts 2016, 58-59, 150, figs 135, 141) both include a sea horse

and a sea feline, while the Dewlish mosaic includes the latter and a fragmentary mosaic at Bromham (Cosh and Neal 2005, 331, Mosaic 235.1; Witts 2016, 59, 155, fig. 142) included the former. Finally, the Great Witcombe mosaic includes some unique representations: one creature has a long, thin pointed snout, another had a serrated feature (since lost) protruding from its head, and another has an elaborate tail. Even the dolphins have unusual tails, in one case particularly ornate.

Although marine themes are common in Romano-British mosaics, and especially so in baths, the factors discussed above demonstrate that the Great Witcombe mosaic was a special case. This tends to support the reinterpretation of the function of the site: it is unlikely that this scene, teeming with an array of varied and unusual sea creatures, was the floor of a domestic bath suite.

Bradford on Avon – dolphins and canthari

By contrast with the complexities of some of the figured mosaics discussed above, the iconography of the mosaic in the straight-sided apse at Bradford on Avon appears to be simple: a vessel conventionally described as a *cantharus* is flanked by a pair of dolphins, two large leaves and two small leaves (Fig. 3.3, this volume, Fig. 11.7; Cosh and Neal 2005, 328-330, Mosaic 234.1; Witts 2005, 101, col. pl. 1; Witts 2016, 62, 73, 152, figs 171-172). Dolphins and *canthari* were both exceptionally popular motifs for mosaics and often appeared in combination with one another, but the precise depiction at Bradford on Avon is the only one of its kind in a Romano-British mosaic. In some other mosaics, such as those from Pound Lane, Caerwent (Cosh and Neal 2010, 355-356, Mosaic 483.24; Witts 2016, 62, 73-74, 158, fig. 178), and Admiral's Walk, Cirencester (Cosh and Neal 2010, 81-82, Mosaic 421.8; Witts 2005, 102; Witts 2016, 62, 74, 164, fig. 182), the dolphins were in separate compartments from the *cantharus*. The separation was maintained, but in a different way, in the Fifehead Neville mosaic in which dolphins swam in a circular border around the centrally-placed *cantharus* (Cosh and Neal 2005, 125-126, Mosaic 167.1; Witts 2016, 62, 73, 169, fig. 190). The dolphins were also relegated to the border of the mosaic from Room B at Frampton, leaving the *cantharus* alone in the apse (Cosh and Neal 2005, 134-137, Mosaic 168.2; Witts 2005, 127-129, fig. 18; Witts 2016, 62, 74, 172, fig. 196). In the apse of the lost mosaic from Whatley, four segments, each with a *cantharus*, converged on a semicircle with a dolphin (Cosh and Neal 2005, 303-305, Mosaic 222.1; Witts 2005, 75, fig. 31; Witts 2016, 62, 73, 195-196, figs 215-216). Even in the mosaic from Room 2 at Brislington, which had stylistic similarities with the mosaics in the

Figure 3.3. Mosaic in apse at Bradford on Avon. (Photograph P. Witts, courtesy of M. Corney)

adjacent panel from Bradford on Avon, the dolphins appeared in rectangles at the edges of the mosaic and not with the *cantharus* in the centre (Barker 1901, pl. V; Cosh and Neal 2005, 43-44, Mosaic 153.2; Witts 2005, 102; Witts 2016, 62, 73, 155, figs 174-175).

In other mosaics, the dolphins were placed in the same compartment as the *cantharus* but they faced towards the vessel instead of swimming away from it as at Bradford on Avon. Examples are known from Rooms N8 and N20 at Fishbourne (Neal and Cosh 2009, 549-550, Mosaic 403.43; 542-543, Mosaic 403.34; Witts 2005, 97, fig. 47; Witts 2016, 62, 73, 169-170, figs 191-192) and the fragment found at Great Tew (Cosh and Neal 2010, 242-243, Mosaic 461.1; Witts 2016, 62, 73, 174, fig. 198). In mosaics where the dolphins and *cantharus* were in a prominent position, the dolphins were depicted as physically linked with the *cantharus*. For instance, the mosaics from Buildings IV.10 and XXVIII.3 at *Verulamium* showed the dolphins entwined in the *cantharus* handles (Neal and Cosh 2009, 332-333, Mosaic 348.26; 349-351, Mosaic 348.47; Witts 2005, 101, fig. 50; Witts 2016, 62, 73, 193-194, figs 213-214)

and at Downton they formed the handles themselves (Cosh and Neal 2005, 345, Mosaic 241.1; Witts 2005, 101, col. pl. 17; Witts 2016, 62, 73, 168, fig. 189). In the mosaic in Room 11 at Dewlish the dolphins were shown at the focal point of the apse, leaping out of the *cantharus* (Cosh and Neal 2005, 79-82, Mosaic 164.8; Witts 2016, 62, 73, 166, fig. 184). At Littlecote the dolphins were shown in the same panel as the *cantharus* but were separated from it by a pair of sea beasts that mirrored the conventional felines in the panel on the opposite side of this part of the room (Cosh and Neal 2005, 351-355, Mosaic 248.1; Witts 2005, 102, col. pl. 2; Witts 2016, 62, 73, 181-182, fig. 209). Along with the four symmetrically disposed shellfish they indicate the marine setting: they lack the importance of the Bradford on Avon dolphins.

Perhaps the closest parallel for the Bradford on Avon mosaic in iconographical terms is the small mosaic found in the irregularly shaped Room L at Keynsham but since destroyed (Cosh and Neal 2005, 237, Mosaic 204.6; Witts 2008, 8; Witts 2016, 62, 73, 178, fig. 204). One dolphin swam away from the *cantharus* while the other, no doubt constrained by the shape of the room, was shown vertically in relation to the vessel. A small heart-shaped leaf, recalling those at Bradford on Avon, filled a corner. The locations of the two mosaics were strikingly different: Room L at Keynsham seems to have served as an ante-chamber to the adjacent bipartite room designated by the excavators as Rooms J-K, whereas the Bradford on Avon apse lay at the innermost end of the room and formed the culmination of an impressive series of mosaic panels. Equally notable, however, is the similarity between motifs in the panel adjoining the Bradford on Avon apse and those in the mosaic in the adjacent Room J at Keynsham: a prominent and accomplished floral centrepiece, motifs with linked leaves, lozenges with swastikas, the use of curvilinear compartments and wave-pattern borders. Cosh and Neal note the swastika-lozenges and suggest that this could indicate an attribution to the same group of mosaicists (2005, 235 and 330).

Another distinctive feature of the Bradford on Avon mosaic is the form of triple-*calyx* urn decorating the corners of the panel adjoining the apse, resembling three lotus-like flowers growing one out of the other. This recalls the similar urns in the Brislington mosaic, although this had two rather than three *calices* and the stem of the upper flower was visible. The overall design of the Brislington mosaic, with four cushion-shapes, is matched by the design of the mosaic in the outer part of the room at Bradford on Avon. The Bradford on Avon, Keynsham and Brislington mosaics were all in the same geographical area and the close similarities between them makes it easy to assume that the same mosaicists might have worked on them. Cosh and Neal attribute all three mosaics to the putative South-western Group (*ibid.* 27-28).

Given the similarities between the mosaics, the differences between the sizes and shapes of the rooms they decorated is notable as is the disparity between the sizes of the establishments. The extent of the room at Bradford on Avon uncovered in the initial excavations was 4.5 x 5.2 m (c. 14 x 16 feet) (Corney 2003, 19), to which can now be added the dimensions of the outer part of the room, approximately doubling the size. Cosh and Neal do not give the overall dimensions but offer the following measurements: room with Panel A, in the outer part of the room, 6.10 x 5.90 m; room with Panel C, with the central flower, and Panel D, the apse, 4.40 x 5.08 m. It is unclear whether Panel B, the rectangular panel with three circles lying between Panels A and C, is included in these dimensions, but it is apparent that the overall size of the room is large (2005, 328). Room 2 at Brislington was approximately 18 feet square (Barker

1901, 13); Cosh and Neal give a metric measurement of 5.54 m square (2005, 43). The irregularly shaped Room L at Keynsham measured 11 feet 3 inches for the south wall, 11 feet for the east wall, 5 feet for the west wall and 12 feet 6 inches for the north-west wall (Bulleid and Horne 1926, 122); Cosh and Neal give the dimensions as 3.46 x 3.38 m tapering to 1.54 m (2005, 237).

Although the Keynsham room was by far the smallest of the three, it appears that the villa was the largest: for instance, the north corridor was 209 feet 6 inches (63.85 m) long and the west corridor was 202 feet 3 inches (61.65 m) long (Bulleid and Horne 1926, 113 and 124). Scaling from the published plan of the Brislington villa (Barker 1901, pl. 1), its overall size was in the order of 125 x 70 feet (c. 38 x 21 m). Unless there were other buildings in the area that had been destroyed or went unrecognised, it was much smaller. The overall size of the Bradford on Avon establishment is harder to assess since the full extent is not known. The main building containing the mosaic measured 38 x 18 m (118 x 56 feet). There was a second building of identical size lying some 30 m (over 90 feet) to its west and the main building also had two ranges to the south which were at least 60 m (188 feet) in length (Corney 2003, 11-12). Overall, therefore, its size might have been similar to the Keynsham villa but, on the basis of present knowledge, the extent and nature of its mosaics was far simpler. There are no complex mosaics with mythological scenes such as that found in Room W at Keynsham, and the dolphins chosen for what appears to have been the most prestigious room belong to the same theme as that used in a small ante-room at Keynsham.

What conclusions can be drawn from this comparative exercise? If the mosaics were indeed laid by the same group of craftsmen, as the stylistic similarities between some of the motifs suggest, it would seem that their patrons were diverse: the mosaicists could work on a palatial establishment such as Keynsham and also on a more modest house such as Brislington. On the other hand, as well as finding stylistic similarities it is equally easy to look for and find differences. For instance, if the dolphins are closely compared with one another, it is immediately apparent that they are drawn in markedly different ways. It seems likely that a different craftsman carried out the figure-work at each site. It is also evident that the Brislington dolphins are small and played a minor role in the design. The choice of subject matter was not governed by the nature or size of the room: dolphins could flank a *cantharus* in the smallest and least elaborate mosaic in a building as well as occupying the focal position in an apse. Analysis of motifs and figures can highlight many interesting points but does not always provide the clear and consistent pattern that an archaeologist might wish to have.

Chequers on mosaics

So far, I have referred to the similarities between the Bradford on Avon mosaic and others nearby, but we need to look further afield for parallels for a little-discussed feature. The mosaic in the inner part of the room is bordered by a series of dark and light squares. These are described by Cosh and Neal as 'a row of grey-brown and creamy-grey chequers contained within grey-brown triple fillets' (2005, 328 and 330). They are perhaps more interesting than the description evokes since chequers in a single row are rare. The Bradford on Avon squares recall the row of squares at the inner end of the Victorious Charioteer mosaic from Rudston (Neal and Cosh 2002, 358-362, Mosaic 143.7). These were more delicate than the Bradford on Avon squares, being outlined in red with small red centrepieces but, like Bradford on Avon, they were associated with an apse as they ran across the shallow apsidal end of the room. The whole of the decorated area of the Rudston mosaic was surrounded by a T-shaped border representing a wall. As the row of squares lay outside this border, it would seem that it did not need 'protecting' in the same way. Might the squares themselves have functioned as a protective device? The placement at Bradford on Avon is consistent with such an interpretation. The inner part of a room evidently deserved special protection. For instance, only the inner part of the room with the Brading Seasons mosaic was 'protected' by a T-shaped border similar to that at Rudston (Neal and Cosh 2009, figs 252-253; Witts 2005, fig. 16). Neither the Keynsham nor Brislington mosaics had any such borders although it is notable that a band of meander ran along at least one side of the Brislington mosaic, recalling the meander border (of a simpler type) around the outer part of the Bradford on Avon room.

The intriguing series of squares at Bradford on Avon is a reminder that, while some elements of mosaics may have been transmitted by the same mosaicists, or by direct contact between craftsmen or their putative pattern books, not all elements can easily be explained in this way. It is a salutary reminder that for all the fascination of detailed analysis of mosaics as artefacts, and for all the insights that we can gain through such a scientific type of approach, they cannot be neatly pigeon-holed.

Dating by Mosaics

Another reflection of the desire to understand mosaics by categorising them is the attention that has been paid to constructing a chronology. The discovery of the mosaic at the Yarford villa (this volume, Fig. 13.14), with its apparently second-century design featuring a style of *cantharus* used in fourth-century mosaics, poses a challenge to this, while Neal's redating of the mosaics found in Building XXVII,2 at *Verulamium*, an urban site but with implications for villa mosaics, challenges previously accepted views. This is therefore an appropriate time to review the topic and to highlight some of the difficulties inherent in using style as a guide to the date of a mosaic. My aim is not to undermine the broad concept of stylistic dating, for which there is ample and well-argued evidence, but to stress that it should be used with caution.

Using similarities between mosaics to assess their date requires a securely dated starting point but few Romano-British villa mosaics have been firmly and precisely dated by archaeological evidence (Smith 1969, 79-82; Cosh 2001; Neal and Cosh 2002, 32-33; Cosh and Neal 2005, 35). In his Empire-wide study of coins found beneath mosaics, Donderer lists only 85 examples of which twelve are from Romano-British sites (1984, esp. 183). In the absence of coins, stratified pottery finds can provide a broad indication of date but both coins and pottery can at best only indicate the earliest date for a mosaic. An element of subjectivity and interpretation is involved in assessing, for instance, the degree of wear on a coin and in taking an overall view based on all the dating evidence from a site and its phasing. Lockyear's general discussion of coin analysis highlights difficulties with coin-wear data (2007, esp. 215).

Where pieces of samian pottery have been used as *tesserae*, this provides useful information but again only indicates the earliest date for the mosaic. Ling (1997, 270) suggests that the presence in a mosaic of samian from a limited number of vessels might represent the acquisition by mosaicists of stock that had perhaps been broken in transport. If so, the mosaic could have been laid soon after the pottery had been made. On the other hand, a prestigious piece of samian ware could have been kept for many years as an antique before eventually breaking. In such a case, the pottery could show little sign of wear yet be used in a mosaic long after the original vessel had been made. Wallace (2006) has drawn attention to the longevity of samian and concludes that some second-century vessels may have survived into the fourth century. It would seem unwise to attach too much weight to samian *tesserae* as a precise aid to dating.

Despite the limitations and difficulties of external dating, it provides a starting point for a chronology and is more reliable than the internal evidence of a mosaic, where a style of dress or hair need not reflect the fashion contemporary with the mosaic (Scott 2000, 20). Such styles could even be a deliberate attempt to refer back to an earlier time with the intention of lending authority to an image. The Late Roman costume of the hunters in the genre scene from East Coker (Cosh and Neal 2005, 209-210, Mosaic 198.4; Witts 2005, 153, fig. 75) might plausibly reflect clothing worn at that period (Toynbee 1964, 239-240), but a full appreciation of dating arguments based on the hairstyle of the Hinton St Mary bust (Reece 1980) requires an understanding of imperial iconography.

Even without a securely fixed starting point, a stylistic approach can form the basis of a relative chronology. Smith's pioneering work on 'schools' of mosaicists has since been developed by others, with the latest thoughts being contained in the Corpus of Romano-British mosaics (Neal and Cosh 2002, 20-33; Cosh and Neal 2005, 21-35; Neal and Cosh 2009, 12-21, 24-26; Cosh and Neal 2010, 14-21; see also Ling 1997, 269-271). This work is rightly respected, but it is worth first setting it into context by touching upon some of the doubts and difficulties that have been expressed about the overall concept of stylistic dating.

Writing about Roman art in general terms and before Smith's theories had been published, Toynbee (1964, 4) drew attention to 'its lack of any regular and accurately predictable pattern of development – a state of affairs which often makes the dating on stylistic grounds alone … an extremely hazardous proceeding'. In her discussion of the problems of chronology in relation to mosaics, Dunbabin (1999, 3) refers to 'the dangers of stylistic dating' and comments that: 'A craft such as mosaic, which on the one hand is highly traditional, but on the other depends upon the very varying levels of skill of its practitioners, can be especially misleading.' However, she goes on to express a more favourable view of using ornamental patterns, especially within a narrow regional context, the study of which 'allows sequences to be established and relative chronologies proposed'. Reece has continued to sound a general warning note about the dangers of misusing stylistic dating (2007, 46-47).

Commenting specifically on Romano-British mosaics, Ling (1997, 270) has pointed out that 'a difference in quality or ambition … does not necessarily mean a difference in date; and conversely (and more important) a similarity of patterns is not by itself sufficient to indicate a closeness of date'. Ling does, however, accept that 'a fairly consistent picture has tended to emerge'. In place of Smith's 'schools', Ling prefers to see 'regional groupings of patterns, motifs, and subjects' representing 'a complex scenario of workshops and branch workshops, independent imitators, and itinerant jobbing craftsmen

working over a period of many years' (ibid. 265). He also draws attention to the dangers of equating style with repertory (ibid. 265-266), a point echoed by Scott (2000, 22) who notes that 'in the search for affinities it is easy to overlook any anomalies in the data'.

Even where similarities can be observed between different mosaics, it is rare for one mosaic to replicate another exactly. The question of whether mosaicists elaborated upon their source or, conversely, simplified it is a vexed one and expert opinion is divided. The order in which the Romano-British Orpheus mosaics were laid is a case in point (Smith 1969, 97-102; cf. Neal 1981, 19; Cosh and Neal 2010, 16), as is the debate about whether mosaicists came from Trier to make the Orpheus pavement at Woodchester, Gloucestershire – which contains an element that is very similar to a mosaic in the Palastplatz in Trier – or moved to Trier after constructing the Woodchester mosaic. Ling has summarised the arguments and concluded that the mosaicist or his pattern book travelled to Britain (1997, 268; contra Cosh and Neal 2010, 18, 31). Any attempt to fit mosaics into a rigid process of development or decline is unlikely to reflect a true picture. Mosaicists were individuals, albeit working within a traditional framework. At any given time, some craftsmen may have built upon their sources of inspiration while others may have misunderstood and detracted from it.

Yarford and mosaic chronology

The Yarford mosaic illustrates the difficulty of applying a coherent stylistic chronology since it has a second-century design with a fourth-century style of cantharus at the centre (King and Grande, this volume, Figs 13.14, 13.15; King 2005, 21-22; Neal and Cosh 2009, 17; Cosh and Neal 2010, 406-408, Mosaic 493.1). The building in which it was laid is thought by the excavator to have been constructed in the late third century, with the mosaic belonging to a phase of enlargement and embellishment in the early/mid-fourth century (King 2005, 21). If so, the mosaic cannot be a second-century survival into which the cantharus was inserted at a later period. In any event, there is nothing in the appearance of the mosaic apart from the mixture of styles to suggest that it might have been laid at more than one period.

If the fourth-century style of cantharus had not survived at Yarford and we had only been aware of the second-century scheme, what influence might this have had on the interpretation of the site as a whole and of its chronological sequences? The lesson of Yarford prompts us to reconsider whether other mosaics that have been dated on the basis of style alone have been assigned to the correct period. The Yarford mosaic does, however, appear to be an exception and there is no reason to think that the later re-use of an earlier scheme was widespread. The somewhat isolated position of Yarford on the extreme western edge of the area known to have had villas might account for the unusual choice. It would not be surprising for traditional, conservative ideas to linger in such a place and for there to have been a conscious desire to hark back to older times.

The intriguing question is what model was available for the Yarford mosaicist to follow. Was the older scheme so well known that it formed a natural part of the mosaicist's design vocabulary or was there an old pattern book in existence? In either case we might expect to know of other mosaics combining styles of two periods. Alternatively, the mosaicist could have seen a surviving second-century scheme elsewhere and used it as the inspiration for Yarford, but again it is likely that other examples would have been made. A further, and perhaps more feasible, possibility is that the patron could have been aware of the scheme, perhaps because he or she had a connection with an older property elsewhere that had a mosaic of this design, and wished to reproduce it as a demonstration of the connection.

In support of the idea that the patron was responsible for the Yarford scheme, it is notable that although it is attractive and effective it is also very simple. It is achieved by using different types of guilloche and lacks the varied series of motifs used elsewhere. For instance, it can be contrasted with the superficially similar mosaics from North Hill, Colchester (Neal and Cosh 2009, 97-99, Mosaic 291.15) and Building IV,1 at *Verulamium* (*ibid.* 320-321, Mosaic 348.17). They both have three concentric bands 'underlying' a nine-panelled scheme as at Yarford, but each band uses a different type of ornament. It is also striking that the Yarford *cantharus* is surrounded only by a wide border of guilloche, whereas the Colchester *cantharus*, for example, is set within a medallion which is then enclosed within a floral or foliate border. Overall, the Colchester and *Verulamium* mosaics are far richer; the Yarford mosaic, on the other hand, could have been created from minimal instructions, the Roman equivalent of a sketch on the back of an envelope.

The Bacchus mosaics at Verulamium and London Leadenhall Street

The hypothetical difficulty that could have been caused if the Yarford *cantharus* had not been present to indicate a late date in keeping with the archaeological indications, has a parallel in the issues raised by the Bacchus mosaic from Room 8/9 of Building XXVII,2 at *Verulamium* (Neal 2003, fig. 19.4; Neal and Cosh 2009, fig. 322; Cosh and Neal 2015, fig. 11). Frere's argument based on archaeological

evidence for the building suggested the continuation of urban life well into the fifth century (1983, 203-224; 2011, 263-270). However, Neal and Cosh offer a revised interpretation both of the evidence for the building and of the dating of the mosaics (Neal 2003; Neal and Cosh 2009, 343-347, Mosaic 348.42; Faulkner and Neal 2009; Cosh and Neal 2015, offering a more detailed discussion of the issues). In this paper I focus on the latter, looking in particular at the design and motifs but not at the subjective question of quality.

First, it is contended that the scheme of complex overall meander in the main panel is generally found in earlier pavements. Secondly, in the adjacent Panel B the rhomboids in the eight-lozenge star are dark grey/black, which it is argued are an earlier type: 'Later fourth-century examples would be expected to have coloured rhomboids filling the lozenges or with the rhomboids alternating in colour ... or with the rhomboids concentrically shaded' (Neal 2003, 198; Cosh and Neal 2015, 22). The third factor concerns the rectangular compartment bordering the eight-lozenge star. This has a lozenge with its acute angles terminating in *peltae*. A similar lozenge was found in the fragments of the border of the mosaic in Room 15/16 from the same house (Neal and Cosh 2009, 348, Mosaic 348.45; Cosh and Neal 2015, esp. figs 8 and 14). It is argued that parallels for these lozenges are not common although they are compared to the lozenges in the border of the Bacchus mosaic from Leadenhall Street, London (Neal and Cosh 2009, 422-425, Mosaic 370.56; Witts 2005, col. pl. 20; Witts 2012, figs 2-3; Cosh and Neal 2015, 23). Neal notes that the Leadenhall Street lozenges contain roundels of guilloche and draws attention to the fragment of such a roundel – although not within a lozenge - in the mosaic in Room 15/16 at *Verulamium*.

The Leadenhall Street mosaic was found in 1803 and there is no recorded dating evidence to give a secure starting point. Neal dates it stylistically to the third or perhaps the very early fourth century (2003, 200; see also Neal and Cosh 2009, 347, 422, 424-425; Cosh and Neal 2015, 20, 23). For the purposes of this paper, I express no view about the dating of this or the other mosaics being discussed, nor will I set out at length the detailed stylistic arguments which interested readers can find for themselves in the original works. Instead, I wish to use some aspects of the Leadenhall Street and *Verulamium* Bacchus mosaics to present a case-study. By considering certain motifs in depth, I hope to highlight some of the issues to be considered and difficulties to be addressed when comparing mosaics with one another. While the *Verulamium* pavement comes from an urban site, the questions that it raises apply equally to villas and many of the mosaics in the discussion that follows came from

Figure 3.4. Verulamium, Building XXVII,2, Room 8/9, Bacchus mosaic, detail. (Copyright School of Archaeology, University of Oxford)

rural sites. All dates given below are those cited by Neal and Cosh in their Corpus. I neither endorse nor disagree with those dates: in what follows, I take them at face value and simply employ them in the discussion.

Looking first at the two *Verulamium* mosaics, the *peltae* at the acute ends of the lozenges in Rooms 8/9 and 15/16 are drawn differently from one another, with the volutes of those in Room 8/9 terminating in solid circles. The contents of the two lozenges are also different. The guilloche roundel seen in the same border as the lozenge in Room 15/16 does not feature in the surviving remains of the mosaic in Room 8/9. It follows that there are a number of differences between these two mosaics even if they are contemporary. I note in passing that the volutes of the *peltae* in the Leadenhall Street mosaic are thicker than those in Room 15/16 at *Verulamium* but more delicate than those in Room 8/9. In other words, there are differences as well as similarities.

The first of the three factors said to count against a late date for the *Verulamium* Bacchus mosaic concerns the scheme of complex spaced swastika-meander. The various volumes of the Neal and Cosh Corpus contain several similar and arguably comparable schemes in

which the swastika-meander forms the overall scheme. One from South Street/Trinity Street in Dorchester is described as of uncertain date (Cosh and Neal 2005, 117-118, Mosaic 165.48). It resembles the *Verulamium* mosaic in that the meander is of latchkey type. Two of the squares between the meander survived and contained stylised flowers. The splendid geometric mosaic from Room 23 of House XIV,1 at Silchester is tentatively assigned to the second century (Neal and Cosh 2009, 210-211, Mosaic 321.40). It also features spaced swastika-meander albeit of a different type. Its dimensions are similar to those of the *Verulamium* mosaic. The decorative part of the Bacchus mosaic is stated to be 4.75 m square while the measurements of the Silchester panel are given as 4.92 m x 4.46 m, in each case with the addition of coarse outer borders. In the original excavation report, the Silchester measurements are given as 20 x 22 feet 6 inches for the room and 16 x 14 feet 6 inches for the mosaic (Hope and Fox 1896, 226). Both mosaics contained squares enclosing a variety of decoration but there are significant differences in the form taken by that decoration. In the Silchester mosaic it is almost entirely composed of simple geometric patterns, with *peltae* being used for the central square of the two sides of the room: a single *pelta* on the north side, and an arrangement of four *peltae* on the south side. The latter motif resembles the arrangement of four *peltae* in the Verulamium mosaic which had the addition of a small red concave-sided square in the centre. A much less accomplished panel in a mosaic from the Oulston villa, tentatively attributed by Neal and Cosh to the early fourth century, can also be noted. This had swastika-meander enclosing squares containing guilloche mats, an eight-lozenge star and swastika-*peltae*, the latter being an arrangement based on a guilloche knot to which four *peltae* are added (Neal and Cosh 2002, 348-350, Mosaic 141.1). Cosh and Neal (2015, 20) suggest that 'there is only one other certain example of [Room 8/9's] particular scheme of overall spaced latchkey-meander: from Fishbourne, dating to the late first century' (Neal and Cosh 2009, 533, Mosaic 403.7). In the Fishbourne mosaic, the surviving squares all contained linear motifs unlike those at *Verulamium*.

While it would seem that there is nothing here to contradict the argument that there are no late fourth-century parallels for this type of scheme, it is notable that these arguably similar mosaics are few and of widely different – and uncertain – date. They do not constitute evidence that the *Verulamium* mosaic *must* pre-date the late fourth century. Although at first glance very similar to the Silchester example, the *Verulamium* mosaic differs not only in the form of the meander but also in its polychromy and in containing, instead of geometric patterns, a variety of motifs employing curves – guilloche mats, flowers, a circular motif, and at least one *cantharus*. This suggests that perhaps the *Verulamium* mosaic was taking inspiration from, but building upon, a much earlier idea.

Turning to the rhomboids in the eight-lozenge star at *Verulamium*, it is notable that solidly-coloured rhomboids were found in a similar star in the Orpheus mosaic from the Newton St Loe villa, the only difference being the colour used: dark grey at *Verulamium* and red at Newton St Loe. The Newton St Loe mosaic is attributed to the second half of the fourth century (Cosh and Neal 2005, 274-278, Mosaic 209.2). It must be questionable whether the dark grey colouring of the Verulamium rhomboids is sufficient to place the mosaic at a different period.

The third factor said to be distinctive at *Verulamium* is the nature of the lozenges. Leaving aside for the moment the precise way in which they were drawn, it is notable that many Romano-British mosaics with lozenge borders come from villa sites that are considered to be late. They include the Winterton Orpheus mosaic attributed to c. AD 350 (Neal and Cosh 2002, 201-205, Mosaic 68.2; Witts 2005, col. pl. 12), the mosaic with nine busts from Brantingham described as mid-fourth century (Neal and Cosh 2002, 326-329, Mosaic 126.3), and two mosaics from

Newton St Loe – the geometric pavement from Room 1 and the Orpheus mosaic – to which a date in the second half of the fourth century is assigned (Cosh and Neal 2005, 274-278, Mosaics 209.1 and 209.2). The Brantingham mosaic is particularly notable as its lozenges contain a variety of circular motifs. Two of those motifs are close parallels for the motif in the lozenge in the mosaic in Room 8/9 at *Verulamium*. The latter comprised a small solid circle surrounded by the outline of a circle with a petal shape on either side. In the two Brantingham examples, the solid circle is replaced by a small cross. The basic motif recurs, although more prominently, in the lozenges flanking the Brading astronomer, where it takes the form of what Neal and Cosh describe as 'a circular band' and has a small concentric rather than solid circle in the centre (Neal and Cosh 2009, 276, fig. 253). The Brading mosaic is assigned to the mid-fourth century (*ibid.* 271).

Cosh and Neal (2015, 23) draw a distinction between the specific lozenge motif at *Verulamium* and rows of ordinary lozenges, which they describe as 'more commonplace and employed by at least two of the fourth-century mosaic groups in western and northern Britain'. They cite the Leadenhall Street mosaic as the only other example of this specific motif, where 'it also forms a border and incorporates an identical guilloche knot within a circle'.

As the Leadenhall Street mosaic has been used to advance the case for an earlier dating of the *Verulamium* mosaics it is worth considering it in more depth. Its most eye-catching feature is the representation of Bacchus reclining on a tigress, a depiction unparalleled in Romano-British mosaics and alluding to the Indian triumph of Bacchus (Neal and Cosh 2009, 422-425, Mosaic 370.56; Witts 2005, 112, col. pl. 20; Witts 2012, 18-20, figs 1-3; Witts 2016, 14, 183, fig. 37). Also notable is the vivid series of borders around the Bacchus medallion: ribbon, wave-pattern and awning. While wave-pattern is common elsewhere, the others are not, and it is instructive to seek parallels for them and to note their dates.

Mosaics from Great Casterton and Poultry, London, contained ribbon borders that were broadly similar to that in the Leadenhall Street mosaic. The Great Casterton mosaic is dated to the mid-fourth century (Neal and Cosh 2002, 82-83, Mosaic 23.2), while that from Poultry, of which only two small fragments survived, is dated to the early third century (Neal and Cosh 2009, 440, Mosaic 370.82). Examples of awning borders similar to that in the Leadenhall Street mosaic are found in mosaics at a number of rural sites: around the Orpheus medallion in the Horkstow mosaic (Neal and Cosh 2002, 148-157, Mosaic 53.1; Witts 2005, col. pl. 11), around Bellerophon and the Chimaera in the mosaic from Room B at Frampton (Cosh and Neal 2005, 134-137, Mosaic 168.2; Witts 2005, fig. 10), and around the splendid flower in the mosaic from Room J at Keynsham (Cosh and Neal 2005, 235-237, Mosaic 204.5). A fourth-century date is attributed to all three of these mosaics, with the mid-fourth century for the first two. Two further fourth-century examples, this time used as a rectilinear rather than circular border, come from the Royal United Hospital site in Bath (Cosh and Neal 2005, 192, Mosaic 188.14) and from the Combe St Nicholas villa (*ibid.* 200-201, Mosaic 195.4), respectively regarded as fourth-century and probably fourth-century. Only the mosaic from Bucklersbury in London (Neal and Cosh 2009, 444-446, Mosaic 370.88) and the Leadenhall Street mosaic are assigned to the third century ('probably' for Bucklersbury; 'possibly' for Leadenhall Street).

I conclude that there is nothing in the motifs and borders discussed above that compels us to accept a third-century, or even early fourth-century, date for a mosaic that employs similar motifs and borders. Indeed, it would seem that if the *Verulamium* Bacchus mosaic was of this date it would be anomalous as the bulk of the evidence would place it much later. There are also two other factors within the *Verulamium* mosaic that are suggestive of a late date, the bust itself and the circular motif in the compartment below it.

Frere has rebutted the earlier dating of the *Verulamium* mosaic (2010; 2011; see also with particular regard to the mosaic evidence, Witts 2011, summarising the arguments advanced here). In doing so, Frere draws attention to the busts in the spandrels of a mosaic from the Fullerton villa, a pavement ascribed by Neal and Cosh to the first half of the fourth century (2009, 173-175, Mosaic 311.3). The simple execution and three-quarters view are indeed similar. Other examples, mostly from villas, can also be cited: from Bratton Seymour (Cosh and Neal 2005, 196-197, Mosaic 191.1), Fifehead Neville (*ibid.* 127-128, Mosaic 167.2), Itchen Abbas (Neal and Cosh 2009, 182, Mosaic 316.3), Oulston (Neal and Cosh 2002, 348-350, Mosaic 141.1), Thenford (*ibid.* 261-262, Mosaic 102.1), Whittlebury (*ibid.* 264-265, Mosaic 104.1), Winterton (*ibid.* 199-200, Mosaic 68.1) and York (*ibid.* 376-377, Mosaic 149.9). These are all cases where the bust was, like that at *Verulamium*, the sole figured image at the centre of the mosaic. Other examples are the fragment depicting a bust from Lincoln (Neal and Cosh 2002, 170-171, Mosaic 55.15) and the nine busts in the Brantingham mosaic (*ibid.* 326-329, Mosaic 126.3). A particular characteristic of the *Verulamium* Bacchus is his sideways glance, and such a glance is also notable in a number of figures in the Venus mosaic from the Rudston

villa including Venus herself and the bust of Mercury (Neal and Cosh 2002, 353-356, Mosaic 143.2; Witts 2005, 122, 141, figs 60 and 73). Neal and Cosh attribute fourth-century dates to all of these mosaics, with those from Fifehead Neville and Whittlebury placed in the mid-fourth century, the two mosaics from Winterton assigned to c. AD 350, and the Thenford mosaic to AD 350-360. We can conclude from this that simply-drawn busts were common in the fourth century. Indeed, the presence of a single bust in an otherwise geometric mosaic seems to have been a fourth-century fashion.

The circular motif below Bacchus in the *Verulamium* mosaic is generally known from Neal's painting and consisted of 'a concave-sided octagon in a linear circle' which was originally divided radially into sixteen segments outlined in black (Neal and Cosh 2009, 346 and fig. 322(a)). A colour photograph taken at the time of excavation and published here for the first time (Fig. 3.4) shows that the segments appear to have been coloured grey and white – rather than yellow and white as Neal and Cosh state – alternating with red and white, and that the spaces between the octagon and the circle were grey rather than white as shown in Neal's painting. Neal and Cosh suggest that the motif could have been adapted from a scallop shell although they draw attention to a similar motif from the Grateley villa, also with sixteen segments, thought to have depicted a fan with a handle (Neal and Cosh 2009, 177-178, Mosaic 312.2). They attribute a date in the first half of the fourth century to the Grateley mosaic and the mid-fourth century to a mosaic with a similar motif found at Brantingham in 1941 but subsequently stolen (Neal and Cosh 2002, 325, Mosaic 126.1). The Brantingham motif had fewer divisions than that from Grateley and no handle. In both cases the motif was prominently located at the centre of the mosaic. Unlike the *Verulamium* motif, in each case the radial division associated with each concave 'scallop' had a solid colour, while the area outside the radial 'scallops' was left white rather than coloured as at *Verulamium*.

Closer parallels for the motif at *Verulamium* can be found in the mosaic discovered at the Lopen villa in 2001. A concave-sided octagon decorates the centre of one of the pairs of interlaced squares in Panel A, the larger of the two panels. It can be studied in the close-up photograph usefully included in the Corpus entry for this mosaic (Cosh and Neal 2005, 248-252, Mosaic 206.2, esp. 251, fig. 246). It differs from the *Verulamium* motif in minor respects: it is divided into eight segments, and its concave edges are enlivened by a band of red and white *tesserae*. It is, however, strikingly similar both with regard to its location within the mosaic – near to but not at the centre – and in the fact that each segment has more than one colour, creating a fluted effect. The smaller Panel B at Lopen has a similar motif but without the red and white edging. Neal and Cosh date the Lopen mosaic to the third quarter of the fourth century. The fragment discussed above with the ribbon border from Great Casterton, dated to the mid-fourth century, also had a circular motif (although not 'scalloped') divided into eight segments and with a red and white banded edge as in the example in Panel A at Lopen. The motifs in the Lopen mosaic are the closest parallels I have been able to find for the motif in the *Verulamium* mosaic. They provide further evidence suggestive of a late date for the latter.

In contesting Neal and Cosh's stylistic arguments regarding the date of the *Verulamium* Bacchus mosaic it is important to pay tribute to the work they have carried out. Without their efforts over many years recording the mosaics and bringing them to publication, the sort of comparative work undertaken for this paper could not feasibly have been undertaken. It is thanks to their commitment to the subject that we can take the discussion forward, broadening the search for parallels and being alert to differences as well as similarities. A stylistically based chronology is a useful guide, not a straitjacket.

As an important postscript to the topic of the dating of mosaics, recent evidence from the Chedworth Roman villa must be noted. Radiocarbon dating of materials excavated in the North Range suggests that a wall subdividing an earlier space to create Room 28 was built after AD 424, thereby giving a fifth-century date for the mosaic installed to fit that room (Papworth 2020; Papworth 2021). It provides the impetus for a future direction of Romano-British mosaic studies, reconsidering whether other mosaics might be later than previously thought.

Conclusion

In the two parts of this paper, I have attempted to extend and to challenge the use that can be made of mosaics as archaeological artefacts in villa studies. By widening our focus, we can assess whether there is anything unusual or interesting about the iconography, and that in turn can suggest whether there is anything unusual and interesting about the building. This approach does not lend itself to absolute proof, but it can build up a persuasive picture. Conversely, by narrowing our focus even more than usual and conducting a deeper analysis of the already well-analysed fields of style and chronology, we can have a better understanding of the

shortcomings of these approaches. Such shortcomings do not undermine the whole edifice but offer potential explanations when inconveniently unexpected results appear to arise. Mosaics were not just constructed by people who would, in any event, bring different skills, interests and experience, but often by a variety of people working together: the patron, the designer, the figure-specialist, the pattern-specialist, the master craftsman, the apprentice, the inept craftsman, and the competent worker who has been inadequately briefed, was trying to draw something unfamiliar, or who was just having a bad day. We do not know how many of these people worked on a given mosaic, nor who took the lead. In some cases, it is possible that one mosaicist carried out all the work and was given a fairly free remit, but in others it is likely that mosaics were, in effect, created 'by committee'. The inconvenient quirks that can result from this make it impossible to fit every mosaic into a neat classification. This conclusion might not assist the archaeologist who is keen to use a mosaic as evidence of date or of the work of a particular mosaic group, but archaeology is concerned with finding out about and understanding people, and mosaics are some of the best clues we can hope to find. It should not come as a surprise if we find that some of them defy the rules we have constructed.

References

Aymard, J. 1953 La mosaïque de Bellérophon à Nîmes. *Gallia* 11, 249-271.

Barker, W. R. 1901 *An Account of the Remains of a Roman Villa discovered at Brislington, Bristol, December, 1899.* City of Bristol Museum and Art Gallery, Bristol.

Barrett, A. A. 1978 Knowledge of the literary classics in Roman Britain. *Britannia* 9, 307-313.

Beeson, A. 2019 The Myths of the Mosaic: The Triumphs of Pelops and Bellerophon. In Anthony Beeson, Matt Nichol and Joy Appleton, *The Boxford Mosaic. A Unique Survivor from the Roman Age*, 31-77. Countryside Books, Newbury.

Blazquez, J. M. 1981 *Mosaicos Romanos de Cordoba, Jaen y Malaga.* Corpus de Mosaicos de España Fasciculo III, Madrid.

Blazquez, J. M. and Ortego, T. 1983 *Mosaicos Romanos de Soria.* Corpus de Mosaicos de España Fasciculo VI, Madrid.

Bulleid, A. and Horne, Dom E. 1926 The Roman house at Keynsham, Somerset. *Archaeologia* 75, 109-138.

Carini, A. 2007 Il mito di Bellerofonte: uno studio iconografico delle raffigurazioni musive nell'ambito della penisola Italica. In C. Angelelli and A. Paribeni (ed.), *AISCOM Atti del XII Colloquio dell'Associazione Italiana per lo Studio e la Conservazione del Mosaico*, 463-471. Tivoli.

Corney, M. 2003 *The Roman Villa at Bradford on Avon. The Investigations of 2002.* Bradford on Avon.

Cosh, S. R. 2001 Mosaics and the end of Roman Britain. *Mosaic* 28, 22-25.

Cosh, S. R. and Neal, D. S. 2005 *Roman Mosaics of Britain. Volume II South-West Britain.* Illuminata Publishers for the Society of Antiquaries of London, London.

Cosh, S. R. and Neal, D. S. 2010 *Roman Mosaics of Britain. Volume IV Western Britain.* The Society of Antiquaries of London, London.

Cosh, S. and Neal, D. 2015 The dating of Building 2, Insula XXVII, at Verulamium: a reassessment. *The Antiquaries Journal* 95, 1-26.

Donderer, M. 1984 Münzen als Bauopfer in römischen Privathäusern. *Bonner Jahrbücher* 184, 177-187.

Dunbabin, K. M. D. 1999 *Mosaics of the Greek and Roman World.* Cambridge University Press, Cambridge.

Ellis, S. P. 1991 Power, architecture, and decor: how the Late Roman aristocrat appeared to his guests. In E. K. Gazda (ed.), *Roman Art in the Private Sphere,* 117-134. University of Michigan Press, Ann Arbor.

Farrar, R. A. H. 1956 Archaeological fieldwork in Dorset in 1956: the 'Frampton Villa', Maiden Newton. *Proceedings of the Dorset Natural History and Archaeological Society* 78, 81-83.

Faulkner, N. and Neal, D. 2009 The end of Roman Verulamium. *Current Archaeology* 20.9 (237), 29-35.

Frere, S. S. 1983 *Verulamium Excavations II.* Reports of the Research Committee of the Society of Antiquaries of London 41, London.

Frere, S. S. 2010 Late Roman Verulamium. *Current Archaeology* 21.1 (241), 37-39.

Frere, S. S. 2011 The saga of Verulamium Building XXVII 2. *Britannia* 42, 263-270.

Ghirardini, G. 1916 Gli scavi del Palazzo di Teodorico a Ravenna. *Monumenti Antichi* 24, 737-838.

Henig, M. 1997 The Lullingstone mosaic: art, religion and letters in a fourth-century villa. *Mosaic* 24, 4-7.

Henig, M. 2000 The secret of the Lullingstone mosaic. *Kent Archaeological Review* 139, 196-197.

Hope, W. H. and Fox, G. E. 1896. Excavations on the site of the Roman city at Silchester, Hants, in 1895. *Archaeologia* 55.1, 215-256.

Huskinson, J. 1974 Some pagan mythological figures and their significance in Early Christian art. *Papers of the British School at Rome* 42, 68-97.

King, A. C. 2005 A mosaic in western Somerset: Yarford, Somerset, excavations 2003-5. *Mosaic* 32, 19-22.

Leader-Newby, R. 2007 Inscribed mosaics in the Late Roman Empire: perspectives from east and west. In Z. Newby and R. Leader-Newby (eds), *Art and Inscriptions in the Ancient World,* 179-199. Cambridge University Press, Cambridge.

Ling, R. 1997 Mosaics in Roman Britain: discoveries and research since 1945. *Britannia* 28, 259-295.

Ling, R. 1998 *Ancient Mosaics.* British Museum Press, London.

Ling, R. 2007a Inscriptions on Romano-British mosaics and wall-paintings. *Britannia* 38, 63-91.

Ling, R. 2007b The Bellerophon mosaic at Frampton: inscriptions and programmatic intent. *Mosaic* 34, 5-11.

Lockyear, K. 2007 Where do we go from here? Recording and analysing Roman coins from archaeological excavations. *Britannia* 38, 211-224.

Lysons, S. 1813 Account of a discovery of mosaic pavements near Frampton in Dorsetshire, in the years 1794 and 1796. In *Reliquiae Britannico-Romanae Volume* I.iii London.

Lysons, S. 1817 Remains of a Roman villa discovered at Bignor in Sussex. In *Reliquiae Britannico-Romanae Volume* III, London.

Meates, G. W. 1979 *The Roman Villa at Lullingstone, Kent. Volume I: the Site.* Monograph Series of the Kent Archaeological Society 1, Maidstone.

Neal, D. S. 1981 *Roman Mosaics in Britain.* Britannia Monograph 1, Gloucester.

Neal, D. S. 2003 Building 2, *Insula* XXVII from *Veralamium* [sic]: a reinterpretation of the evidence. In P. Wilson (ed.), *The Archaeology of Roman Towns. Studies in honour of John S Wacher,* 195-202. Oxbow Books, Oxford.

Neal, D. S. and Cosh, S. R. 2002 *Roman Mosaics of Britain. Volume I Northern Britain incorporating the Midlands and East Anglia.* Illuminata Publishers for the Society of Antiquaries of London, London.

Neal, D. S. and Cosh, S. R. 2009 *Roman Mosaics of Britain. Volume III South-East Britain.* The Society of Antiquaries of London, London.

Papworth, M. 2020 https://archaeologynationaltrustsw. wordpress.com/2020/10/06/the-5th-century-chedworth-mosaic/ (accessed 06.10.20)

Papworth, M. 2021 The case for Chedworth villa. Exploring evidence for 5th-century occupation. *Current Archaeology* Issue 373 (April 2021), 18-25.

Pearce, S. 2008 The Hinton St Mary mosaic pavement: Christ or emperor? *Britannia* 39, 193-218.

Pugliara, M. 1996 La fortuna del mito di Bellerofonte in età tardo-antica. *Rivista di Archeologia* 20, 83-100.

Reece, R. 1980 A date for Hinton St Mary? *Mosaic* 2, 21-22.

Reece, R. 2007 *The Later Roman Empire. An Archaeology AD 150-600.* Tempus, Stroud.

Scott, S. 2000 *Art and Society in Fourth-Century Britain. Villa Mosaics in Context.* Oxford University School of Archaeology Monograph 53, Oxford.

Smith, D. J. 1969 The mosaics. In A. L. F. Rivet (ed.), *The Roman Villa in Britain,* 71-125. Routledge & Kegan Paul, London.

Sparey-Green, C. 1994 The 'Frampton villa', Maiden Newton: a note on the monument and its context. *Proceedings of the Dorset Natural History and Archaeological Society* 116, 133-135.

Squire, M. 2007 The motto in the grotto: inscribing illustration and illustrating inscription at Sperlonga. In Z. Newby and R. Leader-Newby (eds), *Art and Inscriptions in the Ancient World*, 102-127. Cambridge University Press, Cambridge.

Tomlin, R. S. O. 2020 Roman Britain in 2019, III. Inscriptions. *Britannia* 51, 471-525.

Toynbee, J. M. C. 1955 Mosaïques au Bellérophon. *Gallia* 13, 91-97.

Toynbee, J. M. C. 1964 *Art in Britain under the Romans*. Clarendon Press, Oxford.

Wallace, C. 2006 Long-lived Samian? *Britannia* 37, 259-272.

Witts, P. 2000 Mosaics and room function: the evidence from some fourth-century Romano-British villas. *Britannia* 31, 291-324.

Witts, P. 2005 *Mosaics in Roman Britain. Stories in Stone.* Tempus, Stroud.

Witts, P. 2008 Unearthing the Keynsham mosaics – 'excavating' in archives II. *Mosaic* 35, 5-15.

Witts, P. 2011 Some brief comments on the stylistic dating of mosaics with particular reference to Verulamium Building XXVII 2. *Britannia* 42, 270-274.

Witts, P. 2012 Bacchus in London – 'excavating' in archives VI. *Mosaic* 39, 18-24.

Witts, P. 2016 *A Mosaic Menagerie. Creatures of land, sea and sky in Romano-British Mosaics.* BAR British Series 625, Oxford.

4

The Roman villas of the Lower Nene Valley
and the *Praetorium* at Castor

Stephen G. Upex

The Roman villas of the Lower Nene Valley, which comprises the area between the Fen Edge around Peterborough and the middle reaches of the river system above Oundle (Fig. 4.1), have been studied in only a passing way over the past few decades, largely because there has been little new excavation on any of the major villa sites within the region. Only one site at Walton, within the urban area of Greater Peterborough, has been excavated in recent years and the full publication of this site will make a very significant contribution to our knowledge (Pickstone 2012). However, there have been publications on some of the lesser sites, which proved to be more farmsteads than fully developed villas, such as that at Haddon, Orton Hall Farm and Barnwell

(Hinman 2003; French 1994; Mackreth 1996; Upex 2015) but by-and-large any comments on the organisation, geographical distributions or the functions of major villa sites has had to rely on early excavation accounts which prove to be either unreliable (see for example Apethorpe in *VCH* 1902, 191-2, pl. 19, 20; RCHM(E) 1975, 8-10) or the work of early antiquaries, principal of whom was Edmund Artis who published an account of the area in a series of plates in 1828 (Artis 1828). General reviews of the Roman villas of the area have been made by Wild (1974; 1978) and more recently by Upex (2008; 2011) but significant developments in our understanding of the villas of the area still wait for the results of future large scale scientific excavation.

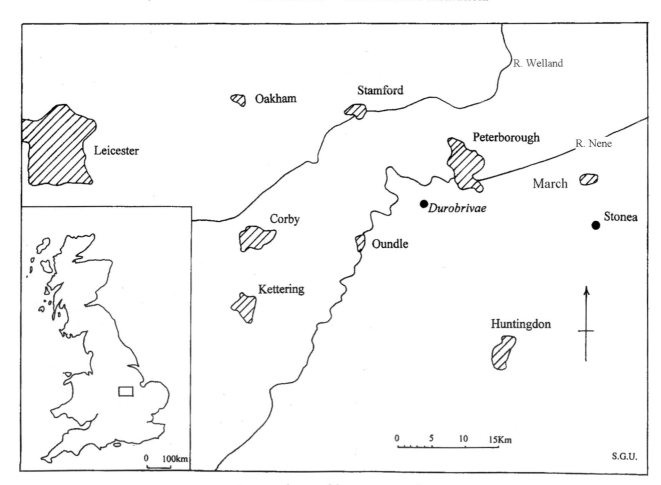

Figure 4.1. The area of the Lower Nene Valley.

Edmund Artis and more recent research in the Lower Nene Valley

The work of Edmund Artis still forms the core of detail in our understanding of the area. Artis was active during the early nineteenth century and published a summary of his work in a series of plates in 1828 (Artis 1828) showing the outlines of various sites either in fairly accurate plans or illustrative views (Fig. 4.2) which exhibit a certain amount of artistic licence. Artis only concentrated on the major villa sites where mosaic floors, wall plaster and heating systems were located – although he did have an amazing understanding of the workings of some of the industrial production sites within the area concerned with metalworking and pottery production. However, he appears not to have carried out any work on lesser farmsteads or native sites and the production of the 1828 volume was more a visual summary of the spectacular in order to attract subscribers rather than a detailed written account of his overall understanding of the Roman archaeology of the area. Artis' introductory map (his Plate 1) of the distribution of sites within the area still forms the basis, admittedly with later additions made by air photography and small-scale modern excavations, of any modern view of Roman sites within the area.

The more recent contributions to our understanding of the major villas in the area come from the support of the Nene Valley Archaeological Trust (NVAT) which, during the period 1980-2000, sponsored a series of surveys of local sites resulting in a plan of the major villa at Cotterstock (Upex 2001) and the discovery of a significant courtyard villa at Upton (Challands and Middleton *pers. comm.*). Artis illustrates two mosaic floors at the Cotterstock site, although it is unclear if he actually dug at the villa. The overall plan of the main ranges of buildings has now been recovered by combining air photography and geophysical surveys with a minuscule amount of excavation (Upex 2001) and although the plan is spectacular in terms of size, a developmental chronology can only be inferred by comparison with sites such as that at Weldon (Smith *et al.* 1988). Thus, the dating and other details regarding Cotterstock still need to be resolved (Figs 4.3, 4.6) but the establishment appears to be set around four courtyards. One at the south-west is perhaps a garden area, next, a main courtyard surrounded by building ranges which must

A View of the Remains of a Roman Villa in Sutton Field, opposite Water Newton.

Figure 4.2. The villa at Ailsworth shown under excavation by Edmund Artis in the 1820s.

have formed extensive accommodation arrangements. This main courtyard may well have had a formal garden – again to be expected – and the modern surveys certainly suggest a formal gateway into the walled area, not dissimilar to that which existed at North Leigh, Oxfordshire (Wilson 2004). An adjoining courtyard to the east, with fewer buildings around its perimeter may well have been part agricultural or perhaps linked with the accommodation of workers on the estate. One rectangular set of rooms on the north side could well have accommodated an estate bailiff whilst the next courtyard to the east contains a less distinct set of rooms and/or buildings and may be exclusively agricultural. Antiquarian reports of 'digging' suggest that to the north, a spring produced a ready supply of water and reports of wooden pipes must be associated with expected bath(s) arrangements.

More recent discoveries, for example at Botolph's Bridge on the outskirts of modern Peterborough, give a tantalising glimpse of a site which will probably never be fully understood (Atkins and Spoerry 2015) although it clearly shows high-status arrangements by the array of finds which it has produced. During 2011, Oxford Archaeology East under the direction of Alex Pickstone excavated part of a large courtyard

Figure 4.3. The villa at Cotterstock showing three of the four courtyards.

villa at Walton within Greater Peterborough. The area had been preserved by its use as allotments and, staggeringly, nothing was ever reported to suggest a major villa in the area until part of the site was taken over for housing development. Excavation showed that the later villa fitted within an earlier Iron Age enclosure and has yielded elaborate wall-plaster, polychrome mosaics, hypocausts and a bath house – all of which reflected the wealth of the owners. The villa plan appears to be that of a fairly standard Nene valley courtyard villa, and so the detail which will be generated by the analysis of the site using modern scientific techniques will add enormously to our understanding of the chronological development and working of such sites (Pickstone 2012 and *pers. comm.*). It is the first major villa within the Nene valley to have been explored since the time of Edmund Artis in the 1820s.

Another site which was outlined by Artis, although he never produced any form of detailed plan, is that at Bedford Purlieus. Artis clearly marked this site down as a major villa, and the range of finds made in Artis's

day of statues, burials and pottery seemed to support this claim. Chief among these finds were statues of two charioteers and other fragments of sculpture which probably come from a grand funerary monument which must have implications for the site (Huskinson 1994, 35). The site is presently covered by dense woodland and little has been possible in terms of recovering a plan. However, recent small-scale excavation including a *Time Team* investigation (Simmons 2005; 2008; Wessex Archaeology 2010) linked with ground and LiDAR surveys have produced evidence which, when added to those shown by Artis on his 1828 plan, shows extensive groupings of buildings (Fig. 4.4).

Artis clearly related the 'villa' he saw at Bedford Purlieus with iron working – he recorded it as covering a large area, although again his lack of supporting explanatory text is annoying! He illustrated a large building range, with its open side appearing to face to the east and this is probably the same range encountered by the recent *Time Team* work, shown on Fig. 4.4 as 'M1'. This

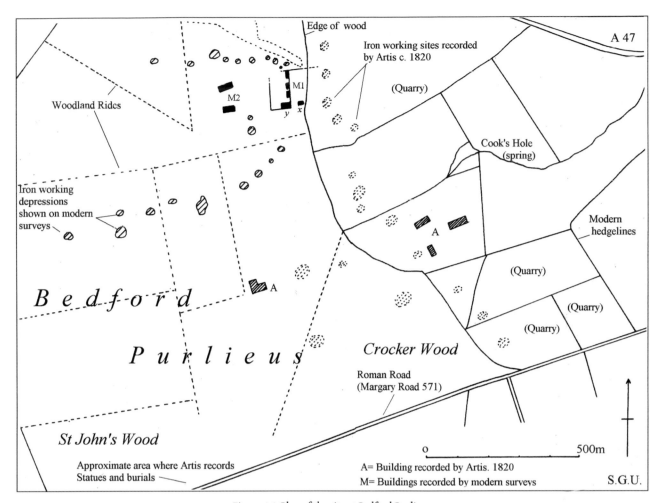

Figure 4.4. Plan of the site at Bedford Purlieus.

courtyard appears to extend from the present woodland into an area which was quarried during the 1970s and 1980s. Artis also showed other, isolated, structures to the south of this range and these can be plotted in the area to the south of Cook's Hole, named after a spring which feeds a small stream (A on Fig. 4.4). This area also has been quarried with only minor records having been made of any findings and little is known of these three buildings or of a fourth building (which must still exist within the woodland) located to the west. Although little was ever recorded when most of them were quarried away, the iron-workings in the area formed the basis of a paper which indicated extensive areas of roasting floors and smelting activities (Dakin 1968) and to some extent matched the illustrations which Artis published of how he thought the iron-working of the area was conducted (Artis 1828, plate X). The recent LiDAR survey also showed two newly discovered buildings (M2 on Fig. 4.4) to the west of the three-sided range shown by Artis and this, linked with small-scale targeted excavation, has allowed for the first time a modern plan to be assembled of the site (Fig. 4.4).

The overall interpretation of the site still remains difficult due in part to the dense tree and undergrowth cover within the woodland of Bedford Purlieus and of course to the lack of information about destroyed buildings within the area of quarrying to the east of the woodland. However, the scattered arrangement of buildings and the detail of Artis' range of rooms (which now, with the details from the modern surveys, appear to be separate structures arranged around a courtyard wall), requires the site's interpretation as a 'standard' courtyard villa to be questioned.

The recent part-excavation of building 'x' (see Fig. 4.4) indicated a substantial hypocausted bath house with box-tiles set into the walls, painted wall-plaster and a vaulted tufa ceiling. By contrast, building 'y' (see Fig. 4.4, 4.5), although it had walls of substantial herringbone masonry, lacked any form of luxurious finish or fittings, and seemed to be merely a functional and very basic range of rooms. In addition, during the excavations not a single coin or small find of metalwork (brooches/pins, etc.) were recovered and there was little pottery on the site, as if the disposal of rubbish was well controlled.

Figure 4.5. View of building 'y' at Bedford Purlieus under excavation in 2010.

Detail and information about this site remain tantalisingly limited but it does not have the plan, layout or finds which point conclusively to it being a conventional villa. Other possibilities as to its function do arise and these are closely linked with the extensive Roman metalworking sites which existed both around the immediate area of Bedford Purlieus and the area toward the modern villages of Laxton, Wakerley, Southwick and Fineshade, all sited to the west of Oundle (see Fig. 4.1). Surveys and excavations here have revealed that iron-working was conducted on a massive scale during the second to fourth centuries (Jackson and Ambrose, 1978; Jackson and Tylecote, 1988, Johnston 1987). How much control the army or the Roman state had over local iron-working is unclear. Sites may have been worked by landowners under some form of franchise from the authorities, or there could have been some more direct involvement by officials to control iron production and marketing. If officialdom were involved in supervising and controlling production then a 'central depot' may well have been required where manual workers and controlling officials required accommodation and it may be here that the site

at Bedford Purlieus fitted in, providing two contrasting sets of buildings, one luxurious and the other very basic. Such speculation linked to the rather 'open' plan of the site, with buildings dispersed amongst contemporary iron-working sites and quarry pits where the ore was being won, may all begin to suggest something which is either not a villa centre at all or some form of specialist villa whose operation and functioning we do not yet fully understand.

The lack of recent excavation limits our knowledge of many villa sites. For example, our understanding of the plan of the Mill Hill villa at Castor (see Fig. 4.9) is almost entirely based on the plans produced by Artis in 1828 (Artis 1828, plates 16-22), while the plan of the Apethorpe villa was almost entirely produced in the 1850s (RCHM(E) 1975, 8-9). The plots of Cotterstock and Upton, based on the recent aerial photography and geophysical surveys mentioned above, do provide accurate plans of the main ranges of buildings, despite the fact that no excavation has been possible at Upton and only the 'cleaning' of a nineteenth-century enclosure boundary ditch, which

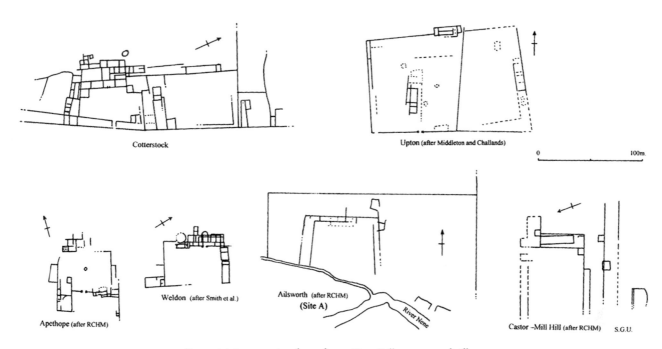

Figure 4.6. Comparative plans of some Nene Valley courtyard villas.

cut through walls at Cotterstock has been possible. However, plans of some of the courtyard villas, shown in Fig. 4.6, give some impression of the general similarity of these villas. The site at Ailsworth (site 1, Fig. 4.6), only known from air photographic evidence, appears to show a south-facing courtyard which opened onto the frontage of the River Nene. A similar river frontage arrangement must have existed at the adjoining villa at Ailsworth (Ailsworth 2) which is shown by Artis under excavation (Fig. 4.2). This seems to have been of a winged corridor design, with one wing immediately in front of the figure to the left of Artis' view and which is linked, by a subdivided corridor, to a small 'winged' room shown on the right of the illustration.

Although such comparative plans do give indications of scale and overall layout they raise more questions than answers with respect to how such establishments functioned. What was the use, for example, of the ranges of rooms which seem to line the edge of the Upton villa courtyard, and is the apparent subdivision of the main courtyard into two, linked to aspects of social division within the household, or to economic and agricultural divisions on the villa estate?

Some of the villa sites within the Lower Nene Valley open up enormous possibilities for future research and excavation. One such site sits just above the floodplain of the Nene at Fotheringhay and appears to have both Bronze Age and Iron Age antecedents in the form of ring ditches and field systems (Fig. 4.7). The main villa range, consisting of rectangular buildings, set in no

apparent courtyard or recognisable arrangement, is linked to what has been described before as a 'village street' which may have formed the accommodation for estate workers, supervised by a bailiff who lived in a building overlooking the village (RCHM(E) 1975, 8-10; Branigan 1987, fig. 34). It all sounds a plausible story of a working community farming the land – but it has never been tested by any large-scale excavation especially investigations dealing with the 'village' itself, although pottery distributions clearly suggest a link between the component elements of the whole establishment (Upex 2008, 142-3).

Other, more diverse complexes are also known, and here partial excavation has started to unravel the sequence. At Lynch Farm to the west of Peterborough a complex of crop-marks (Fig. 4.8 and 4.9) reveals an underlying Iron Age occupation of some magnitude and importance with a triple and quadruple ditch system annexing a large meander of the River Nene in which extensive settlement took place. This may be the centre of a sub-tribal group of the Catuvellauni and the nearby finds of high-status metalwork might support this claim (Upex 2008, 22-33; 2017; Peterborough Museum Collections). After a period of Roman first-century military occupation of the site, a series of buildings was constructed in a rather dispersed manner, and with no apparent focus or centre. Two structures which have been excavated (Fig. 4.8, site 2) are of the aisled-building type and another twelve buildings may well be of a similar form, although these are known only from parch marks on air photographs. The overall understanding of the site in the Roman period is masked

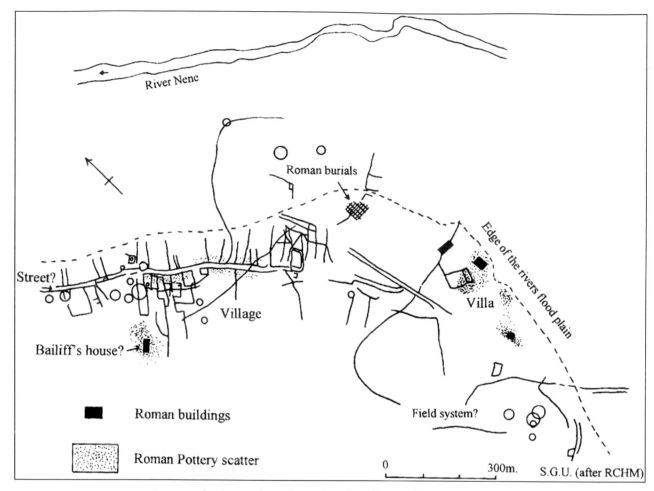

Figure 4.7. The site at Fotheringhay with a villa and its possible associated village.

and complicated by the mass of crop marks which exist over the whole area, but the arrangement may be similar to that which existed at Haddon (see Fig. 4.9), where excavation has revealed another plan of rather dispersed aisled buildings without any central focus. A similar site may have existed at Barnwell (French 1994; Hinman 2003; Upex 2015).

The distribution of villas in the Lower Nene Valley

Such arrangements of dispersed buildings may be geographically orientated towards the Fen Edge, compared to the more formal arrangements which exist to the west of the Nene where villas with courtyards seem to predominate. However, more research is required before a more definite statement can be made linking geographical distributions to villa forms. What can be said with some confidence is that the distribution of villas within the whole area of the lower Nene appears to be divided into three main groupings (Fig. 4.9). First, there are those villas which surround the Roman town of *Durobrivae*. Here there are six sites which are worthy of comment, all showing a substantial investment in a

developed and complex layout which is backed up by the recovery of surface finds in field-walking, consisting of painted plaster, hypocausting, *tesserae* and imported pottery, including samian pottery and *amphorae*. These sites are packed so close together that it is difficult to know what arrangements they had regarding any estate lands, and it has been suggested that they represent a wealthy elite who were linked to pottery production, metalworking or other industries which were operating within the suburbs of *Durobrivae* (see Upex 2008, 116-154). One site which may have been exceptional to this grouping is that underneath the modern village of Castor (Fig. 4.9, suburban villa no. 3), further discussed below.

A second grouping (shown in Fig. 4.9) consists of those villas where the buildings themselves appear to have either fronted the River Nene directly or were close to the river – sites at Fotheringhay, Sacrewell, Cotterstock and Yarwell fall into this category. A basic plot with putative estate boundaries developed by applying 'breaking-point' theory, suggests that their estates may have been small in size (when compared to villas on the higher ground with no Nene frontage) and would have

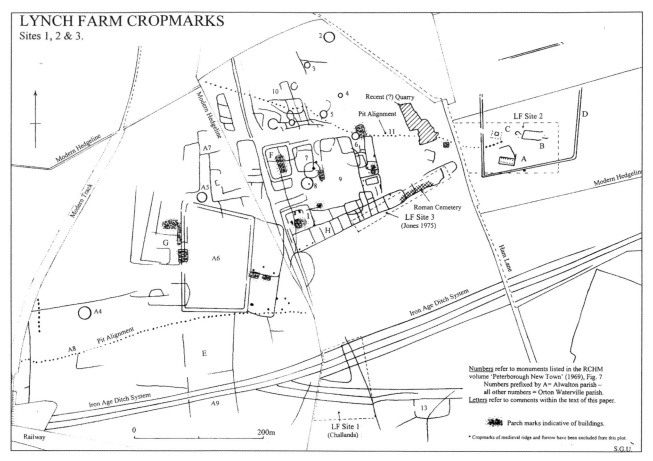

Figure 4.8. The complex site at Lynch Farm showing dispersed Roman buildings.

utilised a broad cross-section of topographical and soil variations. Meadow clearly would have followed the line of the Nene and its floodplain, fertile, well drained arable land would have been available on the gravel soils of the river terraces and inferior quality plough-land, grazing and woodland would have dominated the upper slopes of the valley on clayland villas within this grouping also appear to be fairly regularly spaced along the western bank of the Nene (Fig. 4.9).

The third grouping lies at some distance from the Nene frontage and is located on the higher interfluves of the valley system where poor soils, often clay, are located. Sites within this category include the villas at Apethorpe and Helpston, and the enigmatic site at Bedford Purlieus. The application of a 'breaking point' theory to these sites suggests that their estates areas could have been much more extensive than those which had river frontages. A more extensive land area on inferior soils could be expected as the fertility and productivity of such estate lands would be reduced when compared to the more fertile soils on the lower slopes of the river valley. It may also be true that parts of these larger estates had different farming regimes when compared to those

on lower slopes, including perhaps more grazing and woodland.

Almost nothing is known about how any of the villa estates functioned, and future excavation needs urgently to look into both palaeo-faunal and palaeo-botanical evidence in order to address this gap in our knowledge. At Barnwell, 5 km to the south of Oundle (see Fig. 4.1), recent analysis of the animal bone evidence suggests that cattle breeding was important and the large size of animals raises the question as to whether imported bloodstock was improving local breeds or whether selective breeding was taking place (Upex, B. 2015).

The organisation of the social and economic workings of villas is also poorly understood, although there is some evidence which points to the way that some estates may have operated. At the two adjoining sites of Yarwell and Fotheringhay, which both front onto the Nene, the plotting of secondary farmsteads discovered by fieldwork surveys could indicate two separate estate practices (Fig. 4.10). At Fotheringhay the villa has the possible workers' village nearby, already described above. If this did provide labour, both for the house and

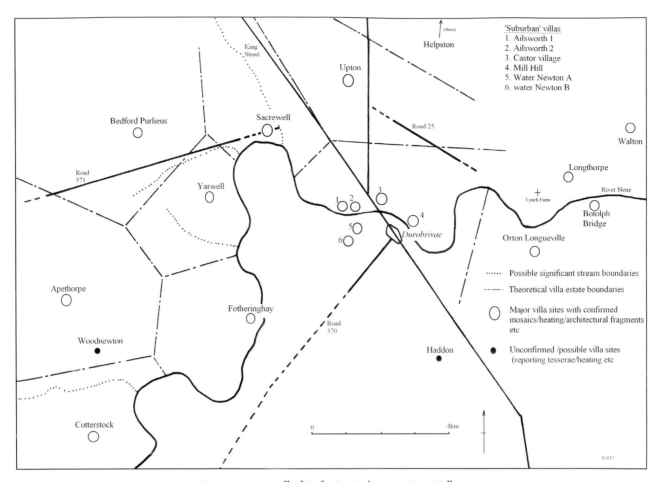

Figure 4.9. Major villa distribution in the Lower Nene Valley.

the estate, then the estate lands were probably farmed directly and perhaps under the control of a bailiff. The potential area of the estate land has already been shown in Figs 4.9 and 4.10 and when this area is scrutinised for smaller farmsteads there are only three. This provides a contrast to the potential estate area and the distribution of secondary farmsteads within the Yarwell villa's possible estate area where there are seven farmsteads. It may be that here the villa lands were farmed by a series of tenanted farms from which rent was paid in cash or in some form of produce such as cattle, wool or corn.

One last point regarding the distribution of major villa sites (those sites with mosaics, heating systems, baths etc) within the area relates to how they are completely absent on land in a broad area to the south the River Nene and the Roman town of *Durobrivae*. The plot of the major villa sites shown in Fig. 4.11 indicates that they are regularly spaced down the west bank of the Nene and between the Nene and the River Welland. The concentration of villas around *Durobrivae* also shows how they cluster on the suburban edge of the towns. However, between modern Peterborough and Huntingdon and in the area to the west of the Fen Edge between these two

centres there is a total absence of anything but small farmsteads, even though the quality of the soils and the slope of the ground is identical to those of the Nene's west bank. This anomaly, discovered as the result of intensive field-walking programmes within the area, has already been partly explored in print and is the topic of a further discussion which is in preparation (Upex 2008: Upex, in preparation). Why this area is devoid of major villa sites remains a problem, but it may be something to do with the way that the fenland was managed under probable state control.

Several writers have proposed that large areas of the fenland were taken into state management as an imperial estate and controlled from an official centre at Stonea (see Fig. 4.1). There may also have been sub-centres at such places as Godmanchester (Cambridgeshire), Sleaford (Lincolnshire), and Castor (Potter 1981; 1983; 1989; Potter and Potter 1982; Potter and Johns 1992; Jackson and Potter 1996; Fincham 2002; 2004; Upex 2008). Such an imperial estate may have been the accumulation of land confiscations in the aftermath of the revolt of Boudicca (AD 60) if not before (Upex 2008, 176–210) and it may have been expanded and formalised during

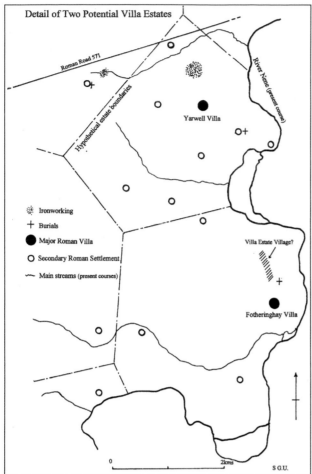

Figure 4.10. Possible villa estates at Yarwell and Fotheringhay.

the aftermath of Boudicca's revolt as extending to tribes other than the Iceni and including some of the sub-tribal groups who occupied the land to the west of the fenland and were within a 'Catuvellaunian confederacy'. Tacitus refers to the Iceni being joined in the revolt by 'neighbouring tribes' (Tacitus, *Annals* 14.30) and it is just possible that some of the northern Catuvellauni formed part of this group and suffered Roman retribution and land confiscations after AD 60 (see Frere 1967, 77 who suggests that areas of Corieltauvi territory could have been included in Tacitus's comment as well).

Another option is to see estates changing hands in the period when loans made by Seneca (presumable set against land) were later called in by Nero on Seneca's death in AD 65, and were surrendered as land areas rather than cash repayments. If such loans were taken out by landowners within the area in question, then failure to repay and the subsequent annexing of land by Nero into an existing and adjoining state-controlled area would seem to have been feasible and perhaps occurred with little basis for complaint by the Catuvellaunian elite (see Upex 2008).

Hadrian's reign when an impressive tower structure and new town were constructed at Stonea (Potter 1983, 28-30; Jackson and Potter 1996). Along with such developments there appears to have developed a fenland farming landscape devoid of large villas and consisting entirely of small native farmsteads and settlements. This landscape of small farmsteads is mirrored within the area between Peterborough and Huntingdon on the upland area where there is a similar lack of large villas. It is tempting to conclude therefore that the fenland Imperial estate continued out of the fen basin and up onto the higher ground in this particular region. Again, the question of why such an upland area, set within the northern territory of the Catuvellauni, should be taken into state control is odd, but there are possibilities. One is to view the confiscation of land in

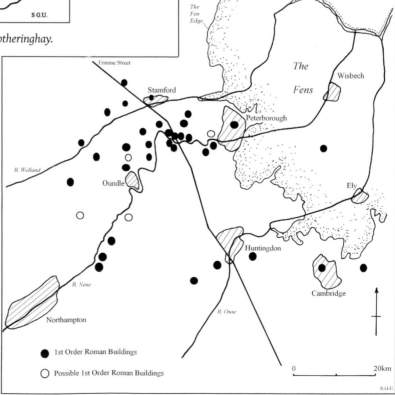

Figure 4.11. Major Roman buildings within the Fenland basin and the Lower Nene Valley.

51

Land confiscations may also have taken place under Septimius Severus in the aftermath of the revolt of Clodius Albinus in the 190s, although indications are that there was little support for the revolt in Britain (Salway 1981, 224-5). However, such a date for possible confiscations and for land being drawn into state control and incorporated into the pre-existing fenland estate is rather late and may have already allowed for villas to have developed in size and status and thus be detectable within the archaeological landscape. In fact, the area is devoid of any evidence that would point to such developments and so such estate reorganisations at this period would seem unlikely.

The *Praetorium* at Castor

Of all of the known major Roman buildings within the Lower Nene Valley, that under the modern village of Castor (Fig. 4.12) stands out as being exceptional and although it has in the past often been classed as a villa (Percival 1981, 13-15; Rivet 1968, 114, fig. 8; Salway 1981, 720), recent work has questioned the actual function of the structure. The site lies 1.5 km north of the Roman town of *Durobrivae* and early antiquaries such as William Camden in 1612 and William Stukeley in the 1720s were so

confused over the mass of walls, mosaics and other finds from Castor that they debated which of the two sites was actually that of the Roman town (Camden 1612; Stukeley 1885, 78-9). Much of what we know today comes from the work of Edmund Artis who recorded buildings around the church either through his own excavations or during schemes to excavate and lower road surfaces which led up the slope on which the medieval church is built. Artis illustrated his findings in a book which consists of engraved plates of views and plans of the archaeological features he saw and recorded around the village (Artis 1828). His general plan of the Roman features (Fig. 4.13) shows the massive scale of the building works which extend behind and on either side of the present church at the top of a naturally formed river terrace and extended down onto the lower part of the site and beyond the line of the former A47 road (Fig. 4.12 for this extent). In area the building ranges cover 290 x 130 m – or some 3.77 hectares (about 9.4 acres). Artis found that Roman rooms were arranged to the north, east and west of the church, and he numbered these on his plan A-D, F and H (see Fig. 4.13). His more detailed plans indicate specific room arrangements and the positions of mosaic floors and hypocausts. He also shows buildings to the south of the church, on the lower part of the site, where

Figure 4.12. View of Castor village from the east. The palatial Roman building extended from the right of the churchyard to beyond the road on the left of the picture. The 'North Range' extended beyond the church to east and west across the top of the sloping ground.

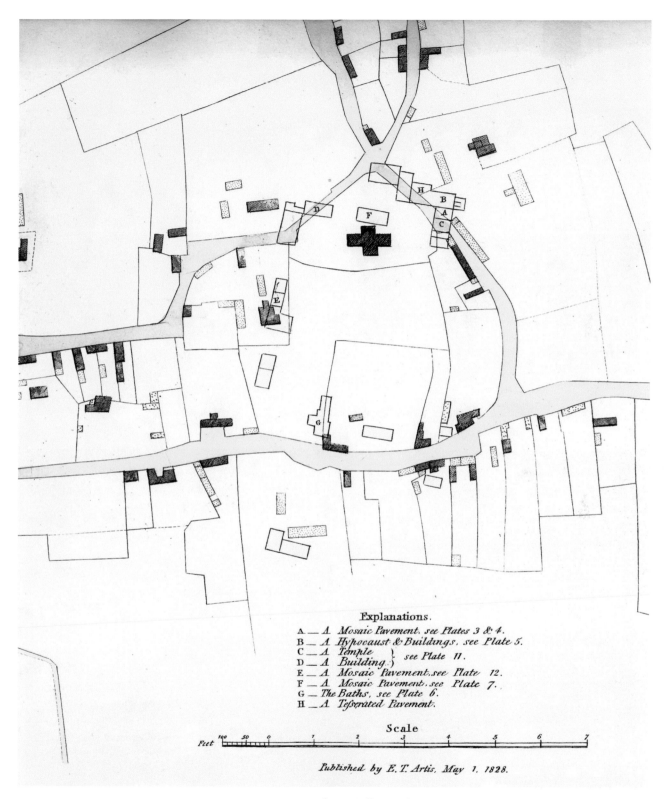

Explanations.

A — A Mosaic Pavement, see Plates 3 & 4.
B — A Hypocaust & Buildings, see Plate 5.
C — A Temple ⎫
D — A Building ⎭ see Plate 11.
E — A Mosaic Pavement, see Plate 12.
F — A Mosaic Pavement, see Plate 7.
G — The Baths, see Plate 6.
H — A Tesserated Pavement.

Scale

Feet 100 50 0   1   2   3   4   5   6   7

Published by E. T. Artis, May 1. 1828.

Figure 4.13. Artis' map of Castor village made in 1828.

he partly excavated a bath house (Fig. 4.13, G; see also Fig. 4.14), and a series of apparently isolated buildings, some of which contained mosaic floors (Fig. 4.13, Room E). His book of 1828 contained only plates, so there are numerous gaps in our full understanding about what he found, and also what he thought about the site. He was clearly impressed by the survival of various features and makes a comment in 1821 that he had seen '...walls of

53

Figure 4.14. Artis' excavations of the bath house below Castor church.

Figure 4.15. Roman walls protruding out of nineteenth-century garden walls at Stocks Hill, Castor.

Figure 4.16. Part of the massive wall foundations between Rooms 2 and 3 (see Fig. 4.18) of the 'North Range' at Castor. (Photo courtesy of G. B. Dannell and J. P. Wild)

More recent work at Castor was undertaken by Charles Green in 1956-7 who excavated in the area to the south of the church when it was designated for an extension to the graveyard (Green *et al.* 1987). Here Green found the remains of another bath house (Fig. 4.19) and later evidence for Saxon occupation over the site. However, it was during the 1970s and 1980s that renewed interest in the site really took place and attempts were made to first check the accuracy of Artis' plans and to explore other rooms which could be added to a composite plan of the whole site. To this end work to the north-west of the church took place under the direction of J. P. Wild and G. B. Dannell to test if the range of rooms shown by Artis to the north-east could be mirrored on the west side- and thus form a unified range of rooms on the upper part of the site (Dallas *et al.* 1972). Excavations were entirely within gardens in the village, which limited the scope of the archaeology, but work did reveal previously unplanned rooms on this side of what became known as the 'north range' (Fig. 4.18). Some rooms in this area (11 and 13) clearly had undergone earlier and probably antiquarian excavation and their original mosaic floors had been lifted (Upex 2008, colour plate 23). This may have been the work of Artis, although he never recorded working in this area of the site. However, the removal of a mosaic was something he had already done in another room of the 'Praetorium' (The Cedars, Room 'E', see Fig. 4.19) and this floor was given to William Fitzwilliam, 4th Earl Fitzwilliam (1748-1833), and relaid within the dairy at Milton Hall, just to the east of Castor (Upex 2008, Fig. 34). The excavations in the gardens of Elmlea (Fig. 4.19) during the 1970s also revealed massive wall foundations up to 2.00 m wide which indicated that the height of the structure could well have been of several storeys (Fig. 4.16). Added to this, the outside walls appeared to have been lime-washed and the vast amount of fired-clay roof-tiles suggests that the roof was tiled. The overall impression of the building, especially the ranges of rooms which were at the top of the slope and arranged in the area to the north of the medieval church, would have been spectacular and dominated the landscape and been visible from a considerable distance.

which are beautifully painted and from 10-11 feet high' (Artis 1821). He was so overwhelmed by the scale of the buildings, which he thought belonged to one unified structure, that he termed the site the 'Praetorium' and never appears to have referred to it as a villa.

Today all that can be seen of the site are sections of walls protruding beyond the lines of modern garden walls. For example, Fig. 4.15 shows part of the herringbone wall foundation at the junction between rooms A and B which Artis showed in his general plan of the site (Fig. 4.13) – this is part of the walling revealed when the gradient of the adjoining road was lowered in the 1820s.

Figure 4.17. Excavations at 'Castor Barns' (see Fig. 4.19). The extent of the building at Castor can be judged by the fact that the' North Range' extended beyond the church in the distance.

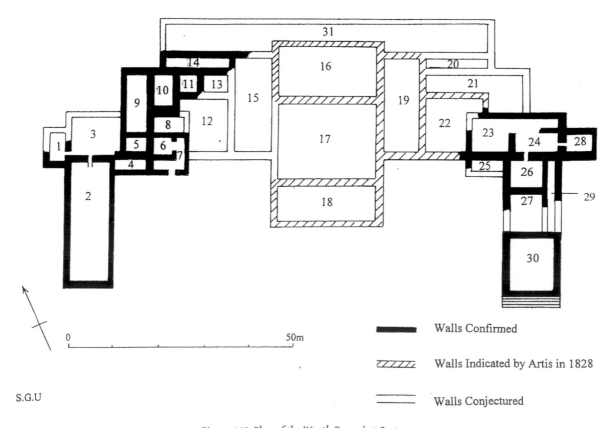

Figure 4.18. Plan of the 'North Range' at Castor.

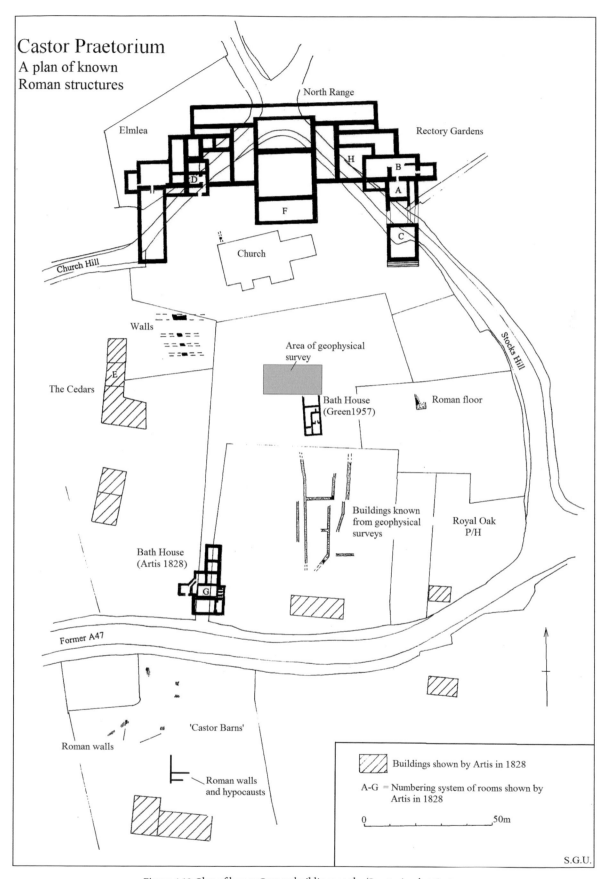

Figure 4.19. Plan of known Roman buildings at the 'Praetorium' at Castor.

A gazetteer of recent discoveries, including various watching briefs and evaluations sponsored by developers has added to the overall detail of the site (see for example Wessex Archaeology 2011). Recent work to the south of the former line of the A47 at Castor Barns has shown that Artis' two-roomed, L-shaped structure had additional rooms (some with hypocausts) immediately to its north. This area, which is shown within Fig. 4.17 and 4.19, emphasises the considerable extent over which the whole site is set out (for example, the so-called 'north range' of the Roman structure is behind the church tower).

Part of the problem of dealing with the plan provided by Artis is that it would appear to contain so many gaps in the arrangement of rooms that it is unclear whether the original Roman design was in fact that of isolated buildings, or that Artis simply did not excavate and record within the intervening areas. This point was partly answered by the recent excavations in the areas to the west, north and east of the present church where 'new' additions were added to the 1828 plan. Artis's 1828 plan also shows other problems such as the apparent misalignment of a room immediately north of the church marked on his plan as 'F' (see Fig. 4.13). This room seems to be not only detached from other rooms but also slightly out of line with the rooms shown to the north. To have expected Artis in 1828 to provide a complete and accurate plan of this whole site would be unfair, but by using the detail from Artis's plans and adding recent and additional information taken from all of the excavations which have taken place, it is possible to arrive at a 'best fit' plan of the north range of the Castor structure (Fig. 4.18). Here the rooms on the western side of the range have been substantially augmented by recent archaeological work so that a complex arrangement of some large and some small rooms appeared to exist in this area. Even here the larger rooms may have been further sub-divided, for example we know of Room 2 almost exclusively from Artis's work, and subdivisions might be expected here. The eastern wing of the north range, of which we know less than the western wing, has been drawn partly to mirror or balance the situation to the west. Artis thought that Room 30 was a temple and he showed it with steps leading up to what he assumed to have been a classical frontage. Later still Lewis (1966) also saw this structure as a temple but decided that it was probably a free-standing structure and not directly connected to the rooms to the rear (Rooms 26 and 27). The problem of the temple site was resolved during 2010 when *Time Team* dug into various parts of the site, including the south wall of Room 2 and found a similar 'stepped' foundation to that shown by Artis and re-excavated by Charles Green in 1957 (Artis 1828; Green *et al.* 1987). This stepped foundation was simply a series of offsets within the structure of the wall to add stability to the foundation and act as a form of revetment to the building which was set out along the top of the slope.

Thus the best scenario is to view the eastern wing of the north range as some form of grand entrance hall with the rooms behind functioning as reception rooms or even office accommodation. If this were the case then room 29 would have acted as a corridor leading to the rear of the range and, considering the slope of the ground to the south, may have incorporated steps up to the rear rooms.

This leaves the central rooms of the north range which are only known from the work of Artis and may of course have been further subdivided. Room 18, which is known to have had a mosaic floor (see Upex 2011, 77-81) has, for the purposes of this reconstructed plan, been shifted slightly to the north and east of where it is shown by Artis, so that it lines up with Rooms 16 and 17. Thus the conjectured arrangement is that of a tripartite series of rooms which lead up the slope of the ground from Room 18, through 17 and then to 16. This very formal layout, which is unusual for structures in Britain, may have parallels at grand buildings like Fishbourne, Great Witcombe (Walters and Rider, this volume) and Woodchester, which have entrance halls, followed by central areas – laid out as gardens in the case of Fishbourne – followed by audience rooms (Cunliffe 1971, figs. 23, 32, 38 and 42; Clarke 1982, fig. 1). How the rooms operated at Castor is at present impossible to determine but if the arrangement shown in Fig. 4.18 is close to the original design then it raises further problems of both how the roofing was organised and the access of light into the rooms. Both of these problems could have been partly overcome if room 17 was designed as an open space and formed a peristyle.

All the rooms across the north range shown in the conjectured plan also appear to reflect the problem the builders had with the sloping ground. From the back of Room 31 to the front of Room 18 the estimated difference in height is in the order of 5 m and the builders may have had to employ some of the walls running parallel with the contour as retaining walls – which may account, in part, for the extra width of walls between Rooms 4 and 5 and Rooms 8 and 10. Internally there will have had to be a whole series of steps to gain access to adjoining rooms. Artis shows one such arrangement between Rooms 24 and 26 in the eastern wing but it may also be that the L-shaped arrangement of Rooms 12 and 22 are designed for steps to lead up from the main areas of these rooms into upper suites of rooms.

If the rooms on the north range of the *Praetorium* are difficult to interpret with our present knowledge, then the buildings on the lower part of the site to the south of the church create even more of a problem in understanding- again largely due to their apparent disjointed and unconnected nature (see Fig. 4.19). It is possible to see an arrangement set around courtyards but until gaps between the known buildings are tested for other rooms which could link or unify the overall plan of this part of the site, any speculation regarding the overall layout is pure conjecture.

Figure 4.19 shows the plan of the whole of the site, with the conjectured north range (taken from Fig. 4.18) set to the north of the present church, and the collections of known Roman rooms and buildings forming the south range set at the bottom of the slope, to the south of the church. This 'simple' arrangement of a north and south range also conforms with the present understanding of the dating of the various elements of the site. All of the excavations which have taken place on the lower, southern part of the site have recently been re-appraised and appear to show that the area was occupied in the second and early part of the third centuries but then the buildings seem to have been either demolished or abandoned after this period (Upex 2011, 81-87). Green, for example, comments that the dating of the bath house he found in 1956-7 (see Fig. 4.19) 'reflected considerable activity on and around the site in the early years of the second century' but that the structure had probably been '....demolished before the Praetorium was built' (Green *et al.* 1987, 125). Similarly, the work to the south-west of the church conducted by Lucas (1998, 16), the work on the partly re-excavated baths found by Artis (Upex, 2011, 85-87) and the work to the south of the former A47 road in the area known as Castor Barns all found early- to mid-second-century material, but little evidence to suggest that occupation carried on into the latter part of the third century or beyond.

By contrast, the recent dating for the building(s) which form the north range appears to be later and suggest an initial building date of around AD 240. The finds from the site indicate that the buildings of the north range remained in use until the very end of the Roman period with occupation continuing into the early Saxon period (Dallas 1973; Upex 2011, 97-99). In some places this post-Roman occupation included post-holes cut into and through Roman mosaic floors, suggesting that people were living within the upstanding walls of the ruined Roman buildings. If the date of the construction of the north range is accurate and it was being constructed around AD 240 and with walls up to 2 m wide with, one might suppose, massive timbers to roof the structure, it

is just possible that some parts of the building could have been still standing well into the sixth and even seventh centuries. It is worth remembering that Artis saw walls standing to a height of 10-11 feet in 1828!

However, there was clear evidence that in of some parts of both the north and south ranges walls were being robbed out in the post-Roman period. In the north range, modern excavation has shown where stone robbers had systematically taken the quoin stones from walls and left the less desirable rubble of the herringbone walling. In some excavation trenches the ghost outlines of massive stones were found (Fig. 4.20) and the best indications are that such robbing took place in the early and middle Saxon periods. Indeed, close inspection of the medieval church at Castor reveals that several walls incorporate massive stones with typically Roman tooling. One particularly impressive area is that on the south-west corner of the church where large stones with Roman tooling have been used to form the quoins (Fig. 4.21). In other parts of the church fabric, robbed column sections have been stacked across the wall, and the re-use of Roman roofing tiles and bricks is common.

Such robbing and the use of stone taken from the Roman walls to construct the early walls of churches is well known (Woods 1970). However, at Castor the robbing may be linked with the whole site being taken over by St Cyneburgh (Kyneburgha) who founded a nunnery there in the seventh century (Green *et al.* 1987, 144-45; Dallas 1973, 17; Morris 2006, 175). The archaeological evidence for such a nunnery on the site is very poorly defined and there are no wooden or stone structures known which could be associated with the setting up of an early Christian establishment. However, the survival of seventh/eighth-century sculptural fragments and high-class metalwork and bone objects (Kendrick 1938, Pl. lxx, 2 and 169-70; Cramp 1976; 1977, 210-11; see also CAMUS Project, chap 6, 73) along with pottery suggests high-status occupation which may link Cyneburgh to the site.

The establishment of an early Christian settlement at the site may not be just coincidental. Early Christian activity during the Roman period within the area of Castor and *Durobrivae* is indicated by several finds which have either Chi-Rho markings on them or symbols which can be interpreted as early Christian. Chief amongst these finds is the treasure which comes from within the Roman town which has been described as the earliest liturgical plate from the early Church from anywhere in the Roman Empire (Painter 1999; Hartley *et al.* 2006, 210-222). Other finds include a complete lead tank impressed with a Chi-Rho from Ashton near Oundle which may have been for baptismal purposes (Guy 1977;

Figure 4.20. Photograph of excavations at the 'North Range' of the Praetorium at Castor showing the robbed positions of massive quoin stones. (Photo courtesy of G. B. Dannell and J. P. Wild)

1981; see also Thomas 1981, 113-121, for a review of early Christianity within the area of *Durobrivae*). Such finds pose the question of whether Christianity continued being the form of worship for some elements of the local population in the post Roman period and, if so, whether it continued through into the seventh century when it again became dominant – or at least emerged as a recognisable element within the archaeological and historical record.

Conclusion

So, what can we conclude about the function(s) of the *Praetorium* at Castor? There are several possibilities worthy of consideration (Mackreth 1984). The plan as it is shown in Fig. 4.19 is clearly complex and has many omissions which make the task of interpretation both difficult and requiring extreme caution. As a villa it certainly appears to be exceptional in its size and layout, and the nature of its original fittings with wall-plaster, mosaic floors, heating systems and imported finds elevate it to palatial proportions (Upex 2011). The differential dating between the lower and the upper parts of the site suggests radical re-arrangements during the early third century on a fairly massive scale which

appear to be linked with a shift of the site from the lower (south range) to the upper (north range) part of the site- and such upheaval would be curious on a villa site. This is not to say that local pottery or metalwork magnates were incapable of having the *Praetorium* built. However, the layout of rooms, as far as we understand them, especially within the north range is unlike the arrangements one would expect for conventional villas in Britain. Comparison has already been made with Fishbourne and Woodchester regarding the three central rooms which it would be easy to view as forming an entrance hall, peristyle and audience chamber.

Other options which have been considered include its construction and use by a guild or college – both of which are known on the Continent and in Britain (Frere 1967, 260; Wacher 1978, 172). The question here would be whether a local guild could afford the sheer scale and opulence of the building works.

As the residence for a high-ranking official, the site and buildings would seem very suitable but the problem comes with suggesting an official who would have needed to live at Castor. The idea of a provincial governor residing here would perhaps be limited by geography

Figure 4.21. Massive quoin stones built into the early medieval fabric of Castor church.

It is possible that the position of Castor just off Ermine Street, which formed the major arterial route to the north out of London, could have provided luxurious accommodation for a series of imperial progresses. For example, Hadrian came to the province in AD 122 and clearly spent time dealing with his new frontier arrangements and probably saw the area and the fenland for himself (Potter 1996, 678); Septimius Severus arrived in 208 with a large retinue, which included his wife Julia Domna and sons Caracalla and Geta, and went north to oversee the military reoccupation of the frontier. Imperial headquarters were set up at York, but Castor could have provided a convenient break whilst travelling from London (Frere 1967, 171). Later still, Emperor Constantius, who was succeeded on his death in York in 306 by his son Constantine the Great, would have also fairly certainly travelled along Ermine Street on the way north (Hartley *et al.* 2006, 15).

Precise dating of the Castor site would be significant here if any link were to be made between the site and an imperial visit. Dating the structures at Castor has always been problematic for several reasons. The site has been occupied from the Roman period to the present; it has been robbed from the Saxon to the Victorian period, and it has been dug over by various antiquarian excavations since the seventeenth century. Thus, most of the archaeological deposits have been disturbed, and even gaining access to the archaeological areas themselves is fraught as the entire site is under the present village and parish church at Castor. However, what dating we do have suggests occupation of the southern range from the mid second to early third century, which appears then to be followed by either stagnation or demolition on this part of the site and a switch to the northern range, which appears to have begun in the period c. 240 (Upex 2011, 92-97). None of these dates match directly with known imperial visits – or indeed visits of high-ranking officials – but this is not to say that the Castor site could not have been constructed for use by a whole range of senior officials who were either visiting Britain or at least travelling to the north on matters of state business.

(see Jones and Mattingley 1990, maps 5:4 and 5:7) whilst the post of a junior procurator, although perhaps linked with controls over local iron-working areas or fenland salt production may have been way below the status provided by the Castor accommodation. The site would seem too far south to have been the residence of a military official – one might assume that Lincoln or more probably York would be better placed to deal with frontier problems; whilst a link with an official belonging to the Saxon Shore fortifications would seem too far from the south coast (Mackreth 1984, 24). Apart from their proximity, it is also difficult to see any direct relationship between the Castor site and *Durobrivae*. The growing status of the town and its physical expansion seem hardy likely to have warranted such a major structure which could have dealt with aspects of local and regional government, especially one built just outside of the walled area.

One last option in an attempt to put Castor into a functional framework and even an historical context is to explore the links between the area of *Durobrivae* and that of Stonea to the south of the present town of March (see Fig. 4.1). Various writers make a case for imperial intervention and reorganisation within the fenland under Hadrian. The fenland may have become a state-controlled area which could initially have been formed shortly after the conquest of AD 43 and certainly in the aftermath of the revolt of Boudicca in AD 60 (Potter 1983, 28-32; 1996, 677-692; Potter and Johns 1992, 95; Malim 1992; 2005, 97-132; Upex 2008, 176-210). The laying out of a new, planned town and the construction of a tower-like structure of fairly massive proportions at Stonea have been seen as forming the centre of this imperial estate and acted as an organisational and tax/revenue centre for the control of fenland produce such as corn, meat, fish, salt and salted products. Potter makes the point that the site at Stonea was laid out between AD 130-150 and that, due to various reasons such as flooding and perhaps the fact that it was too isolated, remote and lacked links with the Roman road system, the tower was demolished in AD 220 (implying that state control was either removed or diminished) and the town then fell into decline (Potter 1996, 689).

The dates for the construction of Stonea (AD 130-150) match fairly closely the initial phase of work at Castor which is currently dated to the early second century. Equally intriguing is the date suggested for the demolition of the Stonea tower (AD 220) which is close to the date (AD 240) suggested for the second phase of work beginning at Castor with the construction of the north range. These dates could allow a line of argument which sees the *Praetorium* at Castor forming, in its first phase, a sub-centre for fenland administration which was under the central control of the major centre at Stonea. Other sub-centres have been suggested at Godmanchester, Grandford, Chatteris and West Deeping (Potter and Potter 1982; Jackson and Potter 1996; Evans 2003). The indications of a military presence suggested by Potter at Stonea (Potter 1996, 685-87) are lacking at Castor, although the slight evidence from the bath house excavated by Artis, which appears to have been laid out using precise Roman measurements, may hint at a military presence (Upex 2011, 85-87). The demolition at Stonea in c. AD 220 might then have seen the switching of the entire central fenland administration to Castor with the construction of the north range c. AD 240. The area around *Durobrivae* with its good road communications north-south and river access along the Nene, coupled with its growing political status and its flourishing industrial suburbs based on pottery production, local iron exploitation and rich agricultural land, may simply have been the ideal area from which to transfer a centre of state land management from its original and perhaps failing or isolated fenland centre. Certainly, if this is an accurate reading of the situation both at Stonea and Castor, then the impetus which such a switching of state control would have made, both in the personnel involved and the generated revenues and wealth which would have been channelled through the *Durobrivae* area, would go some way to explain why the area of the Lower Nene Valley and *Durobrivae* as a 'small' town expanded so rapidly in the post-Hadrianic period. There may be other links within the archaeological landscape which future work needs also to explore with regard to potential fenland administration from the area around *Durobrivae*. Might this help explain, for example, the cluster of villas (accommodating senior fenland administrators or elite local families who were concerned with fenland control) which developed just beyond the suburban fringe of *Durobrivae* and which have been outlined above?

Acknowledgements

Thanks are recorded to Rob Atkins for allowing me to view his work on the site at Botolph's Bridge prior to its full publication and to Adrian Challands and Paul Middleton for allowing me to quote details from their site at Upton. Alexandra Pickstone and the staff at Oxford Archaeology East have been particularly helpful regarding the site of the newly discovered villa at Itter Crescent, Walton. Figures 4.16 and 4.20 were kindly provided by G. B. Dannell and J. P. Wild. This paper has been considerably improved by several people, including Martin Henig, Grahame Soffe, Kate Adcock and Sylvia Upex who have kindly read through earlier drafts; any remaining mistakes are of course entirely my own.

References

Artis, E. T. 1821 In *Drakard's Stamford News*, 7 December 1821.

Artis, E. T. 1828 *The Durobrivae of Antoninus identified and illustrated in a series of plates, exhibiting the excavated remains of that Roman station, in the vicinity of Castor, Northamptonshire ...* Published by the author, London.

Atkins, R. and Spoerry, P. 2015 *A Late Saxon Village and Medieval Manor at Botolph's Bridge, Orton Longueville, Peterborough.* East Anglian Archaeology 153, Cambridge.

Branigan, K. 1985 *The Catuvellauni.* Alan Sutton, Gloucester.

Camden, W. 1789 *Britannia.* trans. R. Gough. London.

CAMUS Project 2004 *The Five Parishes, their people and places: a history of the villages of Castor, Ailsworth, Marholm with Milton, Upton and Sutton.* CAMUS, Castor, Peterborough.

Clarke, G. 1982 The Roman villa at Woodchester. *Britannia* 13, 197-228.

Cramp, R. 1976 Monastic sites. In D. M. Wilson (ed.), *The Archaeology of Anglo-Saxon England,* 201-52. Methuen, London.

Cramp, R. 1977 Schools of Mercian sculpture. In A. Dornier (ed.), *Mercian Studies,* 191-233. Leicester University Press, Leicester.

Cunliffe, B. 1971 *Excavations at Fishbourne, Vol I. The Site.* Reports of the Research Committee of the Society of Antiquaries of London 27, Leeds.

Dallas, C. 1973 The Nunnery of St Kyneburgha at Castor. *Durobrivae: A Review of Nene Valley Archaeology* 1, 16-17.

Dallas, C., Dannell, G. and Wild, J. 1972 Archaeology in Northamptonshire, 1971: Roman: Castor. *Bulletin of the Northamptonshire Federation of Archaeological Societies* 7, 13-19.

Evans, C. 2003 Britons and Romans at Chatteris: investigations at Langwood Farm, Cambridgeshire. *Britannia* 34. 175-264.

Frere, S. S. 1967 *Britannia. A history of Roman Britain,* Routledge and Kegan Paul, London.

Fincham, G. 2002: *Landscapes of Imperialism: Roman and native interaction in the East Anglian Fenland.* British Archaeological Reports (BAR) British Series 338, Oxford.

Fincham, G. 2004: *Durobrivae: A Roman town between Fen and Upland.* Tempus, Stroud.

French, C. A. I. (ed.) 1994 *The Archaeology along the A605 Elton-Haddon By-pass, Cambridgeshire.* Fenland Archaeological Trust & Cambridgeshire County Council, Cambridge.

Green, C., Green, I., Dallas, C. and Wild, J. P. 1986-7 Excavations at Castor, Cambridgeshire in 1957-8 and 1973. *Northamptonshire Archaeology* 21, 109-48.

Guy, C. J. 1977 The lead tank from Ashton. *Durobrivae: A Review of Nene Valley Archaeology* 5, 10-11.

Guy, C. J. 1981 Roman circular lead tanks in Britain. *Britannia* 12, 271-6.

Hartley, E., Hawkes, J., Henig. M. and Mee, F. 2006 *Constantine the Great: York's Roman Emperor.* Lund Humphries & York Museum Trust, York.

Hinman, M. 2003 *A late Iron Age farmstead and Romano-British site at Haddon, Peterborough,* British Archaeological Reports (BAR) British Series 358. Oxford.

Huskinson, J. 1994 *Roman Sculpture from Eastern England.* Corpus Signorum Imperii Romani (CSIR) Great Britain, Vol 1.8, British Academy, Oxford.

Jackson, D. A. and Ambrose, T. M. 1978 Excavations at Wakerley, Northants 1972-75. *Britannia* 9, 115-288.

Jackson, D. A. and Tylecote, R. F. 1988 Two new Romano-British iron-working sites in Northamptonshire: a new type of furnace? *Britannia* 19, 275-98.

Jackson R. P. J. and Potter, T. W. 1996 *Excavations at Stonea, Cambridgeshire 1980-85.* British Museum Press, London.

Johnson, A. G. 1987 *Fineshade Abbey.* Unpublished report for Northamptonshire Archaeological Unit, Northampton.

Jones, B. and Mattingly, D. 1990 *An Atlas of Roman Britain.* Blackwell, Oxford.

Kendrick, T. D. 1938 *Anglo-Saxon Art to AD 900.* Methuen, London.

Lewis, M. 1966 *The Temples of Roman Britain.* Cambridge University Press, Cambridge.

Lucas, G. 1998 *From Roman villa to Saxo-Norman village: An archaeological evaluation at The Cedars, Castor.* Cambridgeshire County Council Archaeological Report 260, Cambridge.

Mackreth, D. F. 1979 Durobrivae. *Durobrivae: A Review of Nene Valley Archaeology* 7, 19-21.

Mackreth, D. F. 1984 Castor. *Durobrivae: A Review of Nene Valley Archaeology* 9, 22-5.

Mackreth, D. F. 1996 *Orton Hall Farm: A Roman and early Anglo-Saxon Farmstead.* East Anglian Archaeology 76, Manchester.

Malim, T. 1992 *Stonea Camp: An Iron Age fort in the Fens.* Cambridgeshire County Council Archaeological Report 71, Cambridge.

Malim, T. 2005 *Stonea and the Roman Fens.* Tempus, Stroud.

Morris, A. M. 2006 *Forging Links with the Past: The Twelfth-Century Reconstruction of Anglo-Saxon Peterborough.* Unpublished PhD Thesis, University of Leicester.

Percival, J. 1981 *The Roman Villa: An historical introduction.* (2nd ed.) Book Club Associates, London.

Pickstone, A. 2012 Peterborough's lost Roman villa. *Current Archaeology* 23.5 (269), 28-33.

Potter, T. W. 1981 The Roman occupation of the central fenland. *Britannia* 12, 79-133.

Potter, T. W. and Potter C. F. 1982 *A Romano-British village at Grandford, March, Cambridgeshire.* British Museum Occasional Paper 35, London.

Potter T. W. 1983 *Roman Britain.* British Museum Press, London.

Potter, T. W. 1989 The Roman Fenland. In M. Todd (ed.), *Research on Roman Britain, 1960-89,* 147-173. Britannia Monograph 11, London.

Potter, T. W. 1996 Discussion and conclusions. In Jackson and Potter 1996, 671-694.

Potter, T. W. and Johns, C. 1992 *Roman Britain.* British Museum Press, London.

RCHM(E) = Royal Commission on Historical Monuments (England) 1975 *An Inventory of Archaeological sites in North-East Northamptonshire.* Her Majesty's Stationery Office (HMSO), London.

Rivet, A. L. F. 1969 (ed.) *The Roman Villa in Britain.* Routledge & Kegan Paul, London.

Salway, P. 1981 *Roman Britain.* Oxford University Press, Oxford.

Simmons, C. 2005 *Archaeological Recording at Sites S1, S2, and X. Bedford Purlieus National Nature Reserve, Thornhaugh, Peterborough*. Northamptonshire Archaeology Report 05/068, Northampton.

Simmons, C. 2008 *Archaeological Earthwork and Geophysical Surveys and Evaluation at Sites S1, S2 and S3, Bedford Purlieus National Nature Reserve, Thornhaugh, Peterborough*. Northamptonshire Archaeology Report 08/68, Northampton.

Smith, D. J., Hird, L. and Dix, B. 1988 The Roman villa at Great Weldon, Northamptonshire. *Northamptonshire Archaeology* 22, 23-67.

Stukeley, W. 1885 *Letters and Extracts from Diaries*. Surtees Society 80, Vol III.

Tacitus *Annals*. Edited by J. Fisher 1907, Oxford Classical Texts, Oxford.

Thomas, C. 1981 *Christianity in Roman Britain to AD 500*. Batsford, London.

Upex, B. R. 2015 The Animal Bones. In S. Upex 2015, 132.

Upex, S. G. 1993 *Excavations at a Roman and Saxon site at Haddon, Cambridgeshire, 1991-1993*. Privately printed, Peterborough Regional College.

Upex, S. G. 2001 The Roman villa at Cotterstock, Northamptonshire. *Britannia* 32, 57-91.

Upex, S. G. 2008 *The Romans in the East of England. Settlement and landscape in the Lower Nene valley*. Tempus, Stroud.

Upex, S. G. 2011 The *Praetorium* of Edmund Artis: a summary of Excavations and Surveys of the Palatial Roman Structure at Castor, Cambridgeshire 1828-2008. *Britannia* 42, 23-112.

Upex, S. G. 2015 A Roman farmstead at North Lodge, Barnwell: excavations 1973-1988. *Northamptonshire Archaeology* 38, 107-138.

Upex, S. G. 2017 *Iron Age and Roman settlement: Rescue excavations at Lynch Farm 2, Orton Longueville, Peterborough*. East Anglian Archaeology 163, Peterborough.

VCH = *Victoria History of the Counties of England: Northamptonshire 1*, 1902. Archibald Constable, Westminster.

Wacher, J. S. 1978 *Roman Britain*. Book Club Associates, London.

Wessex Archaeology 2010 *Bedford Purlieus Wood, Thornhaugh, near Peterborough, Cambridgeshire: Archaeological Evaluation and Assessment of Results*. Wessex Archaeology Report 71512, Salisbury.

Wessex Archaeology 2011 *Castor, Peterborough, Cambridgeshire: Archaeological Evaluation and Assessment of Results*. Wessex Archaeology Report 74155, Salisbury.

Wild, J. P. 1974 Roman settlement in the lower Nene valley. *Archaeological Journal* 131, 140-170.

Wild, J. P. 1978 Villas in the lower Nene valley. In M. Todd (ed.), *Studies in the Romano-British villa*, 59-69. Leicester University Press, Leicester.

Wilson, D. R. 2004 The North Leigh Roman Villa: its plan reconsidered. *Britannia* 35, 77-113.

Woods, P. J. 1970 Excavations at Brixworth, Northants 1965-1970: the Romano-British villa. *Journal of the Northampton Museum and Art Gallery* 8, *passim*.

5

Piddington, Northamptonshire: wealthy private farm or imperial property?

Roy and Diana Friendship-Taylor

Background

Piddington Roman villa (NGR SP 796 540) is situated within gently undulating countryside on an east facing slope, 6 miles (9.65 km) south-east of the Roman town of Duston, which lies on the western edge of Northampton. The site was discovered by workmen digging for limestone in 1781, when a complete mosaic was unearthed. Modern trial excavation began in 1959, and excavation has been conducted part-time by the Upper Nene Archaeological Society since 1979 (see Selkirk 2014).

A Late Iron Age settlement was established around the middle of the first century BC. After the Roman invasion in AD 43, there was a military presence, followed by wooden rectangular-roomed buildings in the later first century, and then a sequence of rectangular stone-built structures, culminating in a simple cottage type villa. From the second century this became an increasingly large winged-corridor-type villa with a courtyard. It also had two bath houses. At the end of the third century, it was abandoned and much of it was deliberately dismantled, with squatter-type occupation from the beginning to the end of the fourth century. The various phases are shown in Fig. 5.1.

There is a long history of almost unbroken human occupation in the vicinity of the Piddington Roman villa, from the Mesolithic to the Bronze Age periods, attested by some 1500 flint tools and a Bronze Age flint-knapping floor. Only the Early and Middle Iron Age periods are not represented, although there are sites of these periods less than 1 km to the south.

Late Iron Age and Roman activity was concentrated on the east- and west-facing slopes of a shallow valley, on well-drained boulder clay, with underlying oolitic limestone, close to the surface in places, together with deposits of fissile limestone and tufa; all three limestones were exploited during the Roman period. The soil is well-drained and provides good agricultural land. A spring-line occurs at the bottom of the valley (noted during the Victorian period for the perceived health-giving properties of the water). Other sources of water included a probable pond at the top of the western valley slope (piped to the villa site in the Roman period) and water accessed for the villa by at least one large well (8.5 m deep), from the second century. The site also lies just under 2 km from the Wootton Brook, a small tributary of the River Nene.

Late Iron Age occupation

The first detectable buildings are of Late Iron Age date from c. 50 BC. They comprise at least four D-shaped structures, with dark, organic-rich earthen floors, possibly used for storage or as animal shelters (Fig. 5.2). In about AD 25, occupation intensified, with the building of at least six substantial round houses and a small rectangular structure with plastered walls and cornbrash floor (similar to an example at Skeleton Green, Hertfordshire; Partridge 1981). A further circular structure has been interpreted as a shrine, since it contained structured deposits, including an imported glass flagon (c. AD 25; Denise Allen, *pers. comm.*).

Imported metalwork was associated with this phase. They included brooches, amongst them a Tiberian *Nertomarus* type stamped by the maker ROMI, from the Mosel region of Germany (Fig. 5.3; Mackreth 2011, plate 21, 6532). A fragment of a copper-alloy Etruscan 'spice strainer', dated to the late first century BC and associated with a round house of c. AD 25 (Fig. 5.4; Friendship-Taylor 2009; Michel Feugère, *pers. comm.*), is only the second example from Britain, the other being from the late Iron Age port at Hengistbury Head (Dorset). Among other imports represented were significant quantities of pre-conquest *terra nigra* and *terra rubra* pottery, mainly from northern Gaul, together with butt beakers and barrel-shaped beakers, all being mainly pre-conquest in date.

Other pottery types may date to the Late Iron Age occupation, or may be associated with the subsequent military phase (see below). Among these are lead-glazed flagons, early *amphorae,* including Dressel 1b (for wine in the early/mid first century AD from the Naples region) and early Dressel 20 (for olive oil from south-west Spain), arriving at Piddington around the conquest period. Egg-shell wares (white and black) are found in contexts just pre-or post-conquest.

Figure 5.1. General plan of the villa, showing all features and the main phases discussed in the text. (Drawing: Nich Hogben)

To view an online version of this plan please visit http://doi.org/10.32028/9781803273808-Figure5.1 or scan the QR code below.

Piddington phases

| 0 | 5 | 10 | 20 | 30 | 40 | 50m |

Key

- Phase 1 - early (military)
- Phase 1 - middle
- Phase 1 - late
- Phase 2
- Phase 4 - early
- Phase 4 - late
- Phase 5
- Phase 6

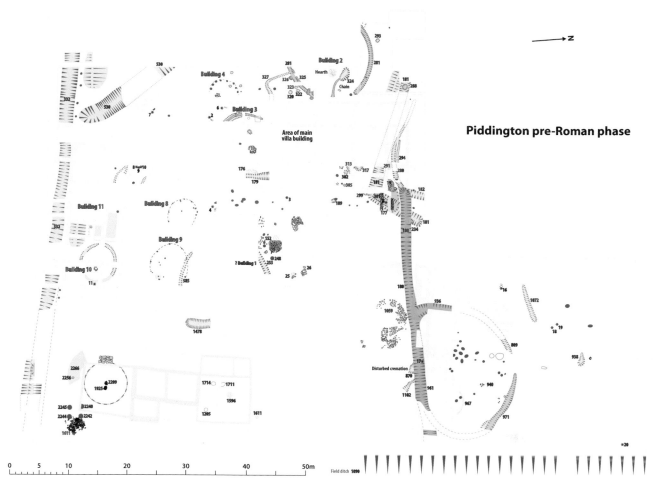

Piddington pre-Roman phase

Figure 5.2. The pre-villa phase, c. 50 BC – AD 44, showing four D-shaped structures, six round houses, circular structures (with the outline of the later villa). (Drawing: Nich Hogben)

Figure 5.3. Copper alloy Nertomarus brooch from the Mosel region of Germany, found in a round-house drip gully.

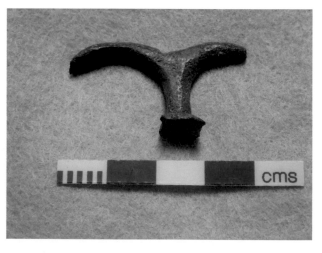

Figure 5.4. Fragment of an Etruscan spice strainer.

Piddington has also produced some of the earliest samian pottery in Britain (Tiberian form Dragendorff 29 bowls; G. Dannell, *pers. comm.*), in use in the Late Iron Age or military phase.

Channel-rimmed jars (also known as 'lid-seated jars') are well represented in pre-conquest contexts at Piddington and continue, with some modifications, into the second century. Detailed pottery research (Friendship-Taylor 1999) highlighted the geographical distribution of these jars in a definable area south of the upper reaches of the River Nene, including parts of south Northamptonshire, north Buckinghamshire, and north Bedfordshire. It is conceivable that this distribution defined the territory of a possible sub-tribe of the Catuvellauni, perhaps with its centre at Piddington.

Thus, it can be demonstrated that, on the eve of the Roman conquest, the late Iron Age settlement at Piddington was already a 'high-status' site, with the means, contacts and influence to acquire fine quality goods and foodstuffs from around the Roman Empire.

Roman military phase

The presence of a Roman fort in the field adjacent to the Iron Age settlement (and the main part of the later Roman villa complex) has been identified through aerial photography, undertaken by RCHM(E) and, more recently, by the authors during a series of helicopter flights, together with geophysical survey, field-walking and limited excavation.

Available evidence suggests that the Roman army arrived in this area in AD 44-45, perhaps as part of a strategy of establishing a temporary frontier at the River Nene. Professor Sheppard Frere (*pers. comm.*) was of the opinion that the legion was XIV, *en route* from Colchester to Wroxeter, via Piddington, followed by an early fort at The Lunt, Baginton. To the north-east, part of Legio IX is attested at Longthorpe (Frere and St. Joseph 1974) and Legio II was stationed at Alchester near Bicester, Oxfordshire, a similar distance to the south-west, where dendrochronological evidence indicated the establishment of a fort in AD 44-5 (Sauer 2005). The placement of Legio XIV at Piddington would account for a 'gap' in the known itinerary of Legio XIV.

Why was it decided to build a fort at this site? If Piddington lay at the centre of a sub-tribe within the Catuvellaunian territory (see above), it might be argued that the army would have been entering friendly territory, the local Britons welcoming the military presence as a buffer against any hostile neighbours, such as the Corieltauvi,

whose territory probably extended to the north bank of the River Nene (Friendship-Taylor 1999).

As described above, the site is also well-drained, provides good quality land and easy access to water. Although the fort was built on the side of a shallow valley, there would have been a good view across the gently undulating countryside, in most directions.

However, the native settlement would have been severely disrupted by its new neighbours, since a probable 'works depot' associated with the fort appears to have encroached over much of its area. If the Roman army were to keep the native population 'on side', it has to be supposed that steps were taken to re-house and appease them. Some of the best evidence for this works depot comes from underneath the first phase of villa-like buildings (the 'proto-villa', see below), and takes the form of two early latrine pits, located at right-angles to each other (Fig. 5.5, latrines 1 and 2). Finds included several pieces of a Claudian set of bone hinges for a copper-clad wooden box (Friendship-Taylor and Greep 2017).

A significant amount of evidence for military activity extended beyond the fort itself, which is clearly defined on its western side, for at least part of its length. A section was made through a modern field ditch, which proved that it is almost on the line of the outermost of three Claudian fort ditches. Until the fort itself is excavated, the existing evidence suggests that the main military presence lasted for about five to six years, with, perhaps, a small contingent remaining after the legion had moved on. Various dates have been suggested for the arrival of Legio XIV at Wroxeter, from AD 55 onwards, which would be compatible with the interpretation given to the timescale at Piddington.

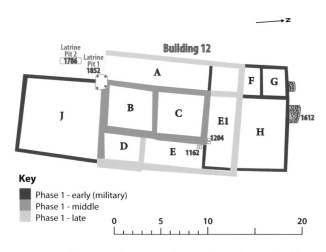

Figure 5.5. Phase 1; early rectangular wooden and stone buildings, forming the 'proto-villa'. For its position in relation to the later villa, of the second century onwards, see Fig. 5.1. (Drawing: Nich Hogben)

Romanisation

Certainly, by about AD 65, civilian life had returned to Piddington, with the construction of two rectangular timber buildings, with horizontal timbers laid directly on the ground and roofed with thatch or shingles, over the former military works depot (Fig. 5.5). A further building was added some five to ten years later.

In c. AD 75, a major 'tidying-up' was undertaken, with some site clearance, followed by the erection of a third building in the works depot area, but with much more substantial trench-cut footings, mostly filled with gravel and limestone cobbles; the fill of one trench comprised demolition debris from a bath house, possibly belonging to the fort. The resulting three buildings were eventually linked, creating a basic, but unmistakably Roman, seven-roomed villa, which has been termed the 'proto-villa' (Figs 5.4 and 5.5). It may be significant and symbolic that the largest, almost square, room virtually enclosed the site of the largest round house, which could be interpreted as a sentimental attachment to a native Briton's heritage, or a symbolic expression of Rome's domination of Britain, or simply coincidence. Finds associated with this phase include a small quantity of samian ware and brooches.

Who would now have been living at the site – might they have been some of the original, previously displaced, inhabitants or their descendants, or an imperial official?

Do we have a 'local boy made good', or a Roman citizen in the ascendancy? Available evidence does not provide an answer at this stage of our knowledge.

Towards the end of the first century AD, the building of what was to become a large and opulent stone villa was begun, on the upper valley slope to the west (Fig. 5.6). Both its position and, in due course, its ostentation, were designed to make a statement in the landscape. The late first-century main stone villa began, c. AD 90/100, as a modest, yet substantially founded 'cottage' house, comprising a simple range of five rooms, on a north-south alignment, with compacted cornbrash floors and two linked cellars. The first corridor may have been included in the original building phase, or added soon after. A separate east-west range of four rooms was added to form a south range, at an obtuse angle to the main wing, reflecting the angle of one of the, by then, partly-silted works depot Claudian ditches, later to be built over by a rear corridor at its south side.

Over the next century, the villa became progressively more elaborate; the cornbrash floors were replaced; the main corridor was now floored with small bricks, in an *opus spicatum* pattern; tessellated floors and mosaics were added. Decorative schemes adorned walls and ceilings (Wells 2011). An enclosing wall was constructed to define the area of the villa and some of its associated buildings and features. The foundations of the front (east-facing) wall are up to 0.5 m deep, presumably to support a wall

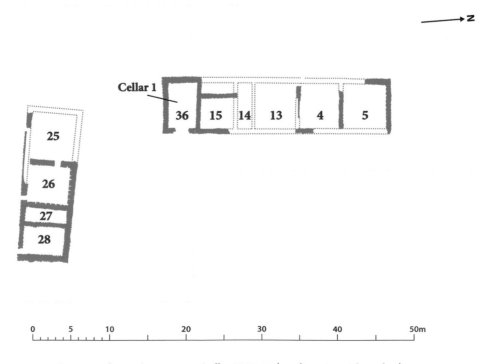

Figure 5.6. Phase 2; 'cottage- type' villa, AD 90-100/150. (Drawing Nich Hogben)

about 2.0-2.5 m high, whereas the foundations of the other three sides were laid directly on the subsoil, evidently supporting much less impressive walls.

The main corridor roof was covered with decorative grey/blue (deliberately overfired) *imbrices* and cream-coloured *tegulae*, whereas the main clerestory roof tiles were red, some given a red slip prior to firing, to enhance the colour. The front corridor comprised a low wall, externally plastered and painted red, supporting columns, constructed of limestone drums, roughly shaped, plastered and painted in red, purple/brown and white, in a charmingly naive attempt to copy classical columns, supporting a lean-to roof (Bidwell 1996, 27). The locally sourced fossiliferous limestone is impossible to turn smoothly, hence the plastering.

During the Hadrianic period, another stone building (Building 16) was established in the adjacent field, partly over the central of the three Claudian fort ditches, on its western side (Fig. 5.7). The building measured 41

m (north-south) x 17.5 m (east-west). It consisted of three linear rooms, later surrounded by a corridor or ambulatory in the later second century, in all a total of 13 rooms. The base of a staircase indicates that the building had two storeys and the collapse of the south-facing gable end of the earlier Hadrianic phase of the building, found lying outer face down to the south of the building in the fourth century enabled its height, of 10.2 m, to be calculated. The two rooms at the southern end of this building, at least, appear to have been well appointed, with wall-paintings depicting green leaves on a black background, flowers and stripes in a wide variety of colours (Fig. 5.8). Much of any potential evidence for the original use of the building would have been destroyed by a late second-century fire and its intensive reuse as an industrial building from the late third century and well into the fourth. Its position beside the main roadway from the east, as it enters the villa precincts, might suggest a multi-purpose role, designed to monitor arrivals and departures, receive incoming goods, act as a tack room (stabling has been tentatively identified

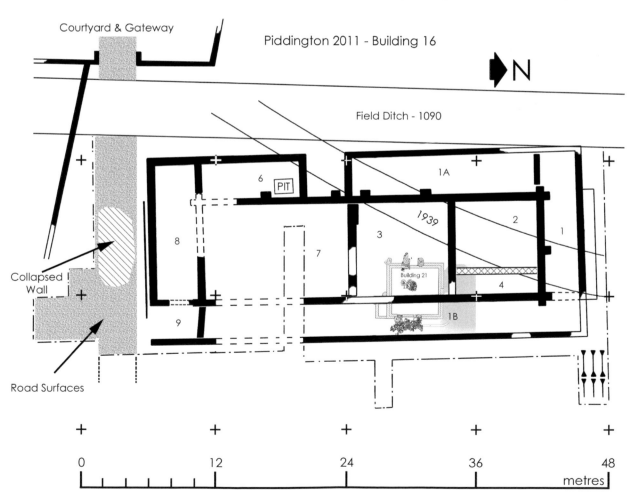

Figure 5.7. Building 16, which partly overlay the western fort defences. For its position in relation to the rest of the complex, see Fig. 5.1.

the other side of the road) and even to provide accommodation for a bailiff.

The villa continued to be developed throughout the later second century. An integral bath house was built in the corner between the main and the south wings. A second, detached, bath house was now added, north-east of the main building complex. The 'courtyard' arrangements became more formalised (Fig. 5.9), with a major series of large post-holes now defining the central 'garden' area from a 3 m-wide gravel walkway in front of the villa. Paired post-holes also ran from the south-east corner of the courtyard, continuing the gravel path down to a postern gate in the east boundary wall and beyond.

At least five parallel rows of post-holes, 2 m apart, packed with small fragments of limestone and tile (Figs. 5.9) are interpreted as supports for fruit trees/ bushes (no pollen evidence survived in the alkaline soil). Posts in the larger post-holes may have supported espalier apple or other fruit trees, as conjectured in interpreting the evidence for a garden at the Roman palace at Fishbourne (Cunliffe 1971, 124-6; 1998, chapter 7) and described by Pliny the Younger (*Ep.* 5.6), who planted them against a trellis in the gardens of his Tuscan villa.

A large, stone-lined well, over 2 m in diameter and 8.5 m deep, served the bath-house and other water requirements. An adjacent stone base would have supported a tank to which water was pumped (Fig. 5.10), to provide water to an irrigation system, carried into the courtyard garden through plank-lined channels between the rows of post-holes. The garden at Fishbourne Palace also had an irrigation system (Cunliffe 1998).

Associated with this period are a number of sub-floor tiles and *tegulae*, stamped TCV or TIB CL [SE]VERI, the interpretation of which may be crucial to our understanding of the site (Fig. 5.11; Tomlin and Hassall 2002, 367, nos 21-23; see also Tomlin 2016, 404-5, nos 19-20) The impressions of the letters have been created by superior quality metal dies, the 'SE' having been added to the 'VERI', in a slightly different style. The late Professor Sheppard Frere (*pers. comm.*) was strongly of the opinion that the names related to various villa owners, two in the second century, rather than being manufacturers' stamps (*contra* Tomlin and Hassall 2002,

Figure 5.8. Fragment of painted wall-plaster with a floral design, from Building 16.

367, n37). Tiberius Claudius brings to mind Tiberius Claudius Togidubnus, *Rex* of the Regni, for whom it has been suggested that the early phase at Fishbourne Palace was built, sometime after the conquest, in gratitude for his loyalty to Rome. Do we, therefore, have at Piddington the ruler of an Iron Age tribe, given the *tria nomina* for his co-operation at the time of the Roman conquest, with his successors still in residence in the mid to late second century?

Three other names are known from the site: Candida scratched her name on a poppy-head beaker (c. AD 60-150; Tomlin 2016, 405-6, no. 21), upside down, so that it would be legible when stored with others on a shelf; Saturninus, too, scratched his name on a tile (Tomlin and Hassall 2002, 367, no. 19), and Vatinia on a mica-coated dish (second/fourth century; *RIB* II, 2503.40); there are also a number of fourth-century initials scratched on (mostly) Black Burnished ware (BB1) dishes (Tomlin and Hassall 2002, 368, nos 24-26). A number of *styli* present on the site and a gladiator clasp-knife (see below) reinforce the fact that some of the villa's inhabitants were literate.

Setback, recovery, expansion and wealth

At the end of the second century, this expansion and evident opulence received a setback. A serious fire devastated most of the south wing of the main villa and the separate building (16) on the approach to the

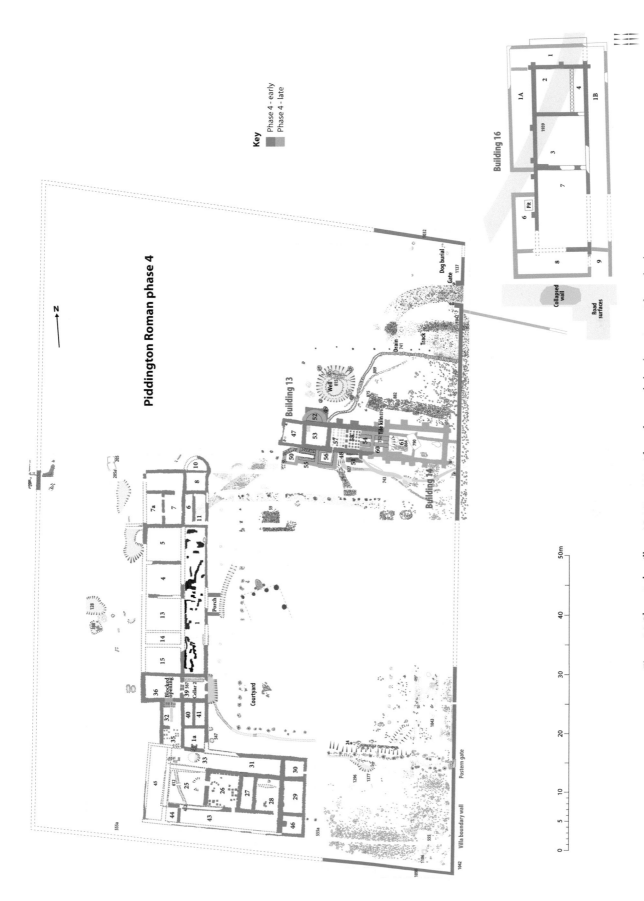

Figure 5.9. Phase 4; the villa, c. AD 160–c. 190, with garden post-holes. (Drawing: Nich Hogben)

Figure 5.10. Stone base for a timber water tank, for the garden's irrigation system, adjacent to the well.

Figure 5.11. Tiles stamped TIB.CL. [SE]VERI, the 'SE' being a later addition to the metal stamp.

corner, adding its own water supply from a source to the south-west, via a pipeline constructed of lengths of hollowed-out tree trunks, joined with iron collars, leading to a large water storage pond to the west of the bath house.

Mosaics and wall-paintings adorned many of the rooms at this time. A broad palette of pigments included expensive and rare colours, such as cinnabar (mercuric sulphide) from Anatolia, costing nearly nine times as much as the best quality red ochre. Its maintenance required time, using treatments with hot wax, to prevent it turning black when exposed to bright light (Mackenna and Ling 1991). Blue frit, also known as 'Egyptian blue', made of silica, copper and calcium compounds and a flux, was also used (Fig. 5.14). Eleven blue frit pellets were found at Piddington, twelve at Fishbourne. Susan Clegg (2014) analysed blue frit pellets from four sites: Fishbourne, *Verulamium*, Turners Hall Farm (Hertfordshire) and Piddington. She concluded that the examples from the last three were similar in composition and may have employed the same master craftsmen, while the material from Fishbourne was of a different composition. Nevertheless, its presence at these and a small number of other sites is one of the hallmarks of their high status.

Later in the third century, the detached bath house and the front boundary wall were demolished. The courtyard was then extended 20 m eastwards, over the fort's western defences (Fig. 5.12). A gatehouse in the new east wall (identified through geophysics) gave access to what have been tentatively identified as stables, now enclosed within the villa precincts, from where the villa would be approached on foot along the gravel path, through the postern gate, the tree-lined path continuing in a direct line to the porch along the villa frontage. This extension may reflect an increase in the number of inhabitants, and/or visitors to the villa, with the need to provide safe stabling or a compound for horses. Building 16, however, remained outside the confines of the new arrangements, accessible to all-comers, which suggests that the alteration was not made for defensive reasons, other than to prevent horses from escaping or being rustled.

villa. The distance between these buildings suggests a deliberate act of arson, rather than an accident.

After the fire, resources were available to carry out a programme of rebuilding in most of the damaged buildings and even to extend the main building by the addition of a north wing, creating a classic villa of winged-corridor type (Figs 5.12 and 5.13). It appears to have been a large open hall, without internal divisions, of unknown purpose. The opportunity was also taken to rebuild the integral bath house at the south-west

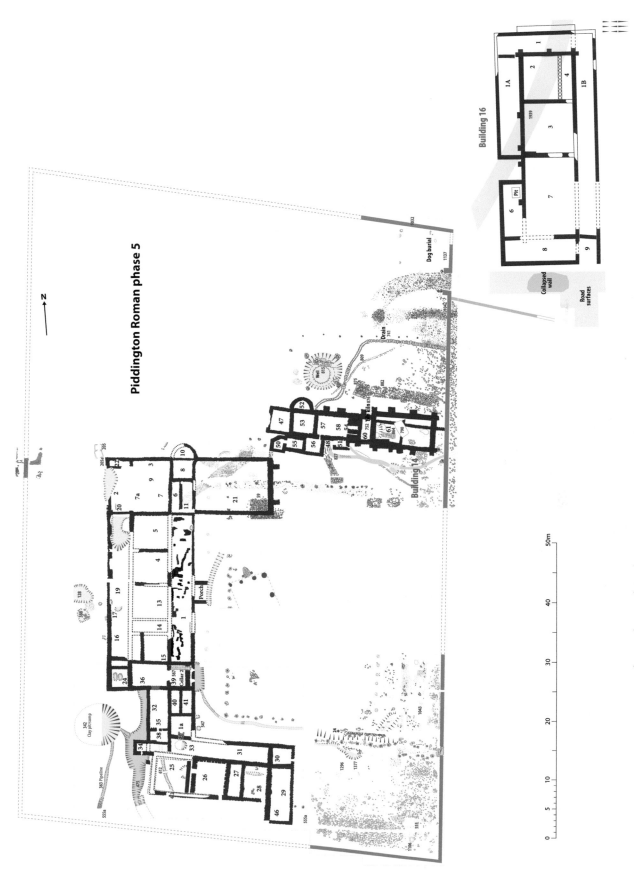

Figure 5.12. Phase 5; the post-fire enlargement, c. AD 190 – now a true villa of 'winged-corridor' type. (Drawing: Nich Hogben)

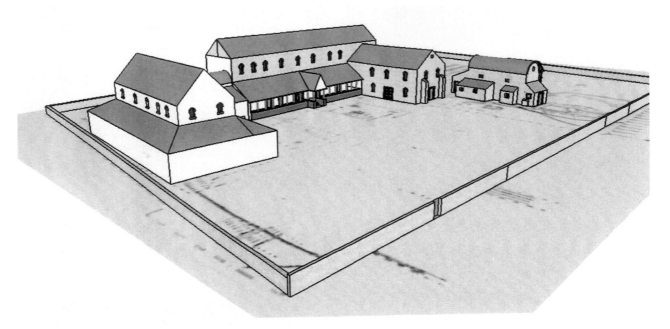

Figure 5.13. Computer-generated model of the third-century villa of 'winged corridor' type. (Roy Friendship-Taylor and Chris Lydamore)

Figure 5.14. Painted wall-plaster depicting a human face, against a blue frit background.

Piddington's central position, close to Watling Street (from around AD 60), would have made it a convenient place for an official *mansio*, however else the nature of the villa can be interpreted. Could this have been the original purpose of Building 16, which, throughout its life, was not included within either villa boundary wall arrangements, but remained accessible to 'outsiders'?

To this late period of development belong some of the most significant small finds. These include a large collection of geometrically-cut marbles (Fig. 5.15), mostly sourced from around the eastern Mediterranean, the shapes suggestive of a floral design (petals, leaves and stems), within a border, plus a piece of Egyptian porphyry (from the imperial quarries at *Mons Porphyrites*, Egypt). These pieces probably came from an item of furniture, perhaps a very generous diplomatic gift, datable to the third century by the inclusion of a small triangular piece of white marble from the Greek coast, known to have only been mined in the third century. Marbles were also brought from Portland, Dorset and Alwalton, near Peterborough, for wall decoration or cladding; a piece of polished grey conglomerate, from Sussex, with carved polished 'linen-fold' moulding, may have been used in a bath house. Three large fragments of flat 'Roman Stone', two cut into squares, one triangular, arrived

Figure 5.16. Gladiator (secutor) clasp-knife, third century (replica, as it would have appeared when new).

from a quarry producing ultra-fine limestone just outside Rome (David Peacock, *pers. comm.*).

The exquisitely detailed third-century gladiator clasp-knife (penknife), of copper alloy, with an iron blade, inset with two small circular silver settings, surrounded by copper-alloy rings, is of a quality unparalleled elsewhere in Britain (Fig. 5.16). It might have been kept on a writing desk where it would have served to sharpen quill pens; its presence fits in well with the other manifestations of wealth and luxury at this villa (Friendship-Taylor and Jackson 2001). Also dated to this period is a charming copper-alloy panther's head key handle, with vestiges of the iron key (Fig. 5.17).

The end of the Roman villa

However, life at Piddington was to change forever at the end of the third century. There is dateable evidence for a major refurbishment of the villa and its associated structures being contemporary with the Carausius/Allectus episode (AD 287-296). The inhabitants appear to have been displaced unceremoniously, leaving parts of the villa at various stages of reconstruction. There was presumably no anticipation of this event, otherwise such an ambitious project would not have been considered. Did the occupants make some unwise political allegiances which caught up with them at the restoration of Maximianus/Constantius, or could the change of use be coincidental in this respect? If the former, it suggests that the villa's occupants were sufficiently prominent for their political affiliations to have attracted 'official' notice.

The site may have been left unoccupied for a time, before being resettled by family groups, who modified the buildings into

Figure 5.15. A selection of the forty pieces of marble from around the eastern Mediterranean and a fragment of Egyptian porphyry, possibly from a table-top, made in the third century.

Figure 5.17. A third/fourth-century copper alloy key handle, in the form of a panther's head.

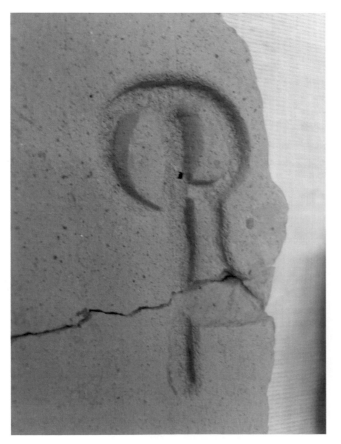

small units. They created a large communal room, with a massive hearth and bread oven, which was to be the hub of the settlement for much of the fourth century; a corn-drier was constructed, containing charred peas and wheat. Many of the trappings of fine living were still evident, but no respect was afforded the former villa buildings (which, in any case, had been left in a partially built state) and the inhabitants evidently lived in squalor among their food remains and other detritus.

The villa estate appears to have been turned over, much more obviously than in earlier phases, to a massive agricultural operation. It is suggested that, as is known in other parts of Britain, crops were intensively grown to support the beleaguered troops defending Rome's frontiers. To support this interpretation, a number of tiles of this period have a ligatured stamp: PRO[C], suggesting that the estate was now under procuratorial (imperial) control (Fig. 5.18) Alongside the agricultural operation, there is evidence for iron-working on a large scale, from smelting to finished ironwork. One of the centres of this operation was Building 16.

Figure 5.18. Roof tile, with ligatured stamp: PROC.

A wide variety of foodstuffs and other imported materials were still accessible and affordable to the occupants. This way of life continued until close to the end of the fourth century, or even into the fifth. The latest coin evidence comes from the early fifth century.

The final usage of the site was the burial of a number of Anglo-Saxons (at least four). One, found and 'lost' in 1781, is described as a warrior burial, with sword and other accoutrements (Parkins 1826). Evidence suggests a brief occupancy on or near the ruins of the villa at the end of the fourth/early fifth century. The 'sag' of the by-now filled-in well provided a convenient location for a small grubenhaus. Four of the burials were placed in the ruins of the third-century north wing of the main villa building.

Conclusions

Based on the evidence of the high status of the Late Iron Age settlement at Piddington and the possibility that its tribal chief had co-operated with the invasion forces, for which he had received Roman citizenship, there is a case for suggesting that his descendants were here in the later second century, based on the family's adaptation of the tria nomina, while retaining the 'Tiberius Claudius' elements. Indeed, he and his descendants may have continued to occupy the site, fulfilling an official regional rôle. Alternatively, it is possible that the Iron Age inhabitants were displaced and an imperial official was installed at the site, following the departure of the military.

The stone villa, begun in the later first century AD, was built in the prescribed Roman manner, right down to the wall and floor foundations, suggesting the involvement of military expertise. Throughout the second and third centuries, no expense was spared on the construction, amenities and decoration of the main villa, which underwent regular refurbishment. It would seem unlikely that this expense would have been within the means of an indigenous farming family, or perhaps even a significant local magistrate. Do the extensive trade contacts, which not only brought in a variety of foodstuffs from around the Empire, but carefully selected materials to enhance the villa, some notably present only at prominent sites elsewhere in Britain, suggest that this was the home of an individual/family with much wider influence? The marbles (about forty elements), from around the eastern Mediterranean and the Egyptian imperial porphyry, suggest a possible diplomatic gift. The gladiator clasp-knife, probably of Continental origin, may have been a souvenir from watching gladiatorial combats abroad.

The fact that the villa's exceptional wealth was sustained for approximately 200 years suggests that this does not just represent the good fortune or sustained position in society of one or more families. Rather, it points towards maintenance by the state of an official residence. Piddington villa has much in common with Fishbourne palace, albeit on a smaller scale: the early pottery assemblages and Roman military presence; the early villa-like buildings ('proto-villa'); early metalwork; the later first-century building phases; the exotic wall-painting pigments; the collections of marble and some of the garden arrangements; their demise at the end of the third century. Not least, too, there are the 'Tiberius Claudius' names (without the evidence for a Celtic cognomen in the case of Piddington). Was Piddington villa a farm, or an imperial property? It could have been either or both of these, but perhaps the evidence suggests that, in addition, the villa was the domain of a high-ranking regional or provincial official.

References

Ancient sources

Pliny, Ep. = Pliny the Younger, Letters, and Panegyricus. With an English translation by Betty Radice. Loeb Classical Library, Harvard University Press, Cambridge, Mass.; Heinemann, London, 1969.

Modern sources

Bidwell, P. 1996 The exterior decoration of Roman buildings in Britain. In P. Johnson and I. Haynes (eds), Architecture in Roman Britain, 19-29. Council for British Archaeology (CBA) Research Report 94, York.

Clegg, S. 2014 Blue Shade Hues. A study of blue pigments used by Romano-British wall-painters. University of Sussex DPhil thesis.

Cunliffe, B. W. 1971 Excavations at Fishbourne 1961-1969. Volume I: the site. Reports of the Research Committee of the Society of Antiquaries of London 26, Leeds.

Cunliffe, B. W. 1998 Fishbourne Roman Palace. Tempus, Stroud (revised ed.).

Frere, S. S. and St. Joseph, J. K. 1974 The Roman fortress at Longthorpe. Britannia 5, 1-129.

Friendship-Taylor, R. M. 1999 Late La Tène Pottery of the Nene and Welland Valleys, Northamptonshire: with particular reference to channel-rim jars. British Archaeological Reports (BAR) British Series 280, Oxford.

Friendship-Taylor, R. M. 2009 Mystery object – identified! Lucerna 37, 13-14.

Friendship-Taylor, R. M. and Friendship-Taylor, D. E. 1989-2015 Iron Age and Roman Piddington. Interim Reports. Upper Nene Archaeological Society, Hackleton.

Friendship-Taylor, R. M. and Greep, S. 2017 A Claudian pit group of bone hinges and box fittings from a 'military' latrine pit beneath the proto-villa at Piddington Roman villa. *Northamptonshire Archaeology* 39, 215-200.

Friendship-Taylor, R. M. and Jackson, R, 2001 A new Roman gladiator find from Piddington, Northants. *Antiquity* 75, 27-8.

Mackenna, S. A. and Ling, R. 1991'Wall paintings from the Winchester Palace Site, Southwark', *Britannia* 22, 159-171.

Mackreth, D. F. 2011 *Brooches in Late Iron Age and Roman Britain.* Oxbow, Oxford.

Parkins, Revd. S. 1826 Description in a letter dated 11 February 1826, to the Northamptonshire historian, George Baker, describing the recollections of 'an old labourer', who had discovered a mosaic and the burial, *c.* 1791..

Partridge, C. 1981 *Skeleton Green. A late Iron Age and Romano-British site.* Britannia Monograph 2, London.

Sauer, E. 2005 Alchester. In search of Vespasian. *Current Archaeology* 196, 168-176.

Selkirk, A. 2014 Piddington uncovered: beyond the Roman villa. *Current Archaeology* 297, p nos.

Tomlin, R. S. O. 2016 Roman Britain in 2015, III. Inscriptions. *Britannia* 47, 389-415.

Tomlin, R. S. O. and Hassall, M. W. C. 2002 Roman Britain in 2001, II. Inscriptions. *Britannia* 33, 355-71.

Wells, M. 2011 *Iron Age & Roman Piddington. The Painted Wallplaster: an art historical viewpoint.* Upper Nene Archaeological Society Vol. 1, Fascicule 8, Hackleton.

6

Whitley Grange villa, Shropshire: a hunting lodge and its landscape

Roger White

The excavation of a long-suspected villa site in the Rea Valley, 15 km west of the Roman town of *Viroconium Cornoviorum* (Wroxeter) in Shropshire located the remains of a small complex built around a courtyard. Only the southern and western sides of the courtyard had rooms attached to them, these being partly screened by a portico. On the north side was a small bath house with an indoor *natatio* and hypocausted rooms and on the west side was a large square room paved with a mosaic and flanking rooms of the same width but half the depth. Remains of a corridor leading to the furthest corner of the largest room hinted at access from a detached service wing. The complex was all of one build, dated to the last quarter of the fourth century by its mosaic. The last phase demonstrated dereliction of the baths suite but reoccupation of the remaining rooms by ephemeral buildings. It is argued both on the form of the building and its location within the landscape that the primary function of the complex was as a hunting lodge, an identification that fits closely with the known popular pastimes of the wealthy elites in the later Roman Empire.

Context of the study

The excavation of the Roman villa complex at Whitley Grange, Shropshire between 1995 and 1997 occurred as part of the larger Wroxeter Hinterland Project. The aim of this Leverhulme-funded research was to assess the degree and scale of landscape change brought about in the Roman period by the creation of an urban centre within a previously non-urban landscape, i.e. to assess the degree to which the successful implant of a Roman town on a non-urban native landscape brought about a Romanisation of that landscape, or whether it left that landscape and its inhabitants largely untouched economically and socially (Gaffney and White 2007, 22-33). The only secure means of answering this research question was to trace how far the Roman economic system, measured by its cultural material remains, could be located and mapped in the countryside around the Roman city. A study area of 1600 km² with Wroxeter at its core and its edges set at the nearest neighbouring substantial settlements about 30 km from the Roman city was sampled through systematic surface collection to provide the systematic database essential to providing a means to quantify the evidence of the penetration of Roman cultural material into the landscape. Crucially, the known lack in Shropshire of a Late Pre-Roman Iron Age phase, as defined by Martin Millett (1990, 9-39), meant that Roman material culture would stand out all the more clearly in such a survey.

The survey also provided a means of identifying new sites but also had a secondary aim of dating known sites and previous discoveries in the landscape. The study area is renowned for its high density of enclosure sites, identified from the late 1940s onwards by the systematic aerial photography of J. K. St Joseph, Arnold Baker and latterly Chris Musson but which had been little investigated by excavation (Whimster 1989; Gaffney and White 2007, 41-7). Another of the key aims of the Wroxeter Hinterland Project, therefore, was to carry out limited excavation of enclosure sites and also a suspected villa site. These excavations would hopefully provide some means of dating a number of sites but also, more critically, provide some measure of the adoption of Roman material culture and social practices (such as the adoption of Roman building materials and methods) in the native countryside. A secondary aim was to deliver archaeological training opportunities for students and the local community who provided the 400-strong volunteer force that did the hard work of systematic surface collection throughout the autumn, winter, and spring months (*ibid.* 62-3).

Identification of a villa site to excavate was not easy as few were known or suspected in Wroxeter's hinterland, but a promising site was identified at Whitley Grange in the Rea Brook valley, south west of Shrewsbury and west of Wroxeter. Intriguingly, two other villas were known to exist in the same valley but further to its west: Lea Cross which had been partially excavated in the late eighteenth century and from which a mosaic had been recorded (Cosh and Neal 2010, 309-10), and Cruckton which had been destroyed during the construction of a housing estate in the late 1940s and early 1950s with only minor observations being recorded (Houghton 1958). Aerial photography had identified a scatter of enclosure sites thought to be of Iron Age or Roman date in the same valley, and the Roman Road from Wroxeter due west to Forden Gaer and Caersws and beyond also ran along the same valley, but on the other bank from the villa. Lastly, the Roman roadside settlement at Meole Brace, identified and excavated in the early 1990s in advance of retail development on the edge of Shrewsbury (Hughes 1994), indicated a major point of Romanisation in the immediate vicinity of the possible villa at Whitley Grange (Fig. 6.1). The excavation at Meole Brace was the latest of a series of other smaller scale and earlier excavations that had been carried out in the area around Shrewsbury during the 1950s and '60s as the town expanded, these largely being conducted by Ernie Jenks, a locally based avocational archaeologist (Barker *et al.* 1991; Evans *et al.* 1999). Jenks had carried out a surface survey at Whitley Grange in 1976, along with Geoffrey Toms, which observed a scatter of Roman tile, stone blocks and roof slates over an area of 20 square metres and investigated an adjacent set of earthworks to the east, but no excavation was undertaken (Toms 1985). Taken together the archaeology of the Rea Valley offered, and still offers, a rich opportunity for understanding a potentially fully Romanised landscape of 'villas' and native enclosures which made the excavation at Whitely Grange potentially an opportunity of great value and significance for dating and characterising the nature of settlement in the valley (White 2007, 133). Surprisingly, the excavation provided the first opportunity for a large-scale research excavation of any villa in Shropshire, with huge potential for training and publicity opportunities for the project overall.

Fieldwork at Whitley Grange

As a first stage, surface survey was carried out on the available arable fields at Whitely Grange for Roman material and to attempt to pinpoint the possible location of the villa. This proved to be very effective at demonstrating the Roman date of the site, which was important as the existing Historic Environment Record had indicated that the site had been thought to be a medieval chapel. A geophysical survey was then carried out over the area producing the highest density of material this successfully locating areas of high resistance suggesting the remains of a Roman structure (Gaffney and White 2007, 95-7). The ensuing excavation uncovered the remains of a bath house. During this and the next two seasons of excavation nearly the full extent of the villa was uncovered.

The plan of the complex revealed over the three seasons comprised what appeared to be a single phase of construction with later evidence for reuse of some elements and robbing of others (Fig. 6.2). The complex was orientated north-east to south-west, with the bath suite at the northern end of the site and rooms on the longer western side. The south and east sides comprised a simple wall foundation with a gap in each signifying entrance points into an internal courtyard about 25 x 35 m in area. The centre of this courtyard was not excavated so it is not known if there was a central feature. An internal portico wall footing was located extending around the courtyard

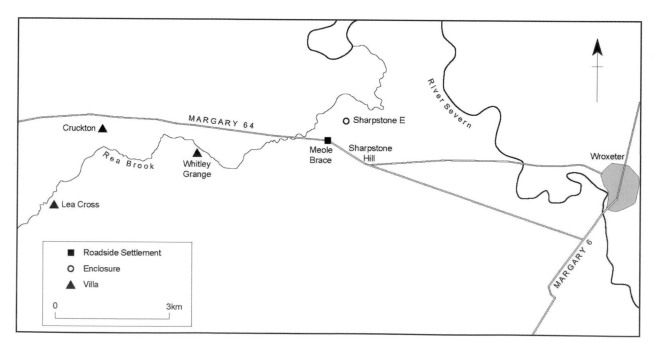

Figure 6.1. The landscape context of Whitley Grange and the Rea Brook Valley. (Drawing by Nigel Dodds)

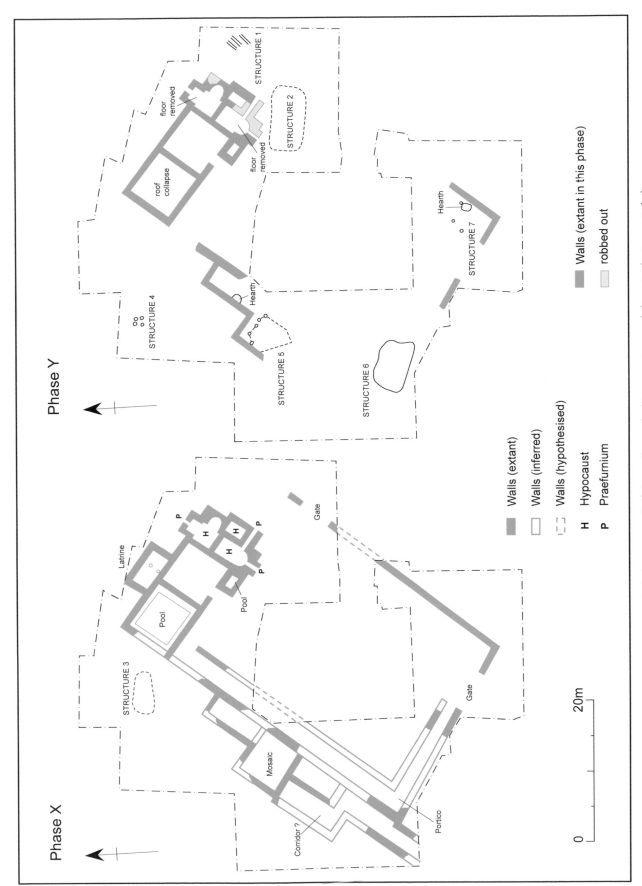

Figure 6.2. Phase plans of Whitley Grange villa (after Gaffney and White 2007, Figure4.24). (Drawing by Bryony Rider)

from the southern entrance to the northern end of the west range. Two column bases indicated perhaps a low wall (*pluteus*) surmounted by turned sandstone dwarf columns. Behind the western range and mirroring its outline was a corridor which began at the south-west corner of the main room in the western range. This corridor extended south out of the area of excavation and it is surmised that it led to a detached service area (Gaffney and White 2007, 101; fig. 4.24).

The principal components of the villa were the baths suite and western range (Gaffney and White 2007, 101-27). The baths suite was a simple rectangular structure 22 x 8 m divided into three equally sized parts (Fig. 6.3).

Figure 6.3. High level view of the excavated baths suite looking east towards Meole Brace roadside settlement. The natatio *is in the foreground. The wooded valley of the Rea Brook lies just beyond the villa.*

A centrally placed doorway in the south wall led from the courtyard into the central room which seems to have had a simple mortar floor. It was presumably a combination of *apodyterium* and *frigidarium*. A doorway in the north wall of the same room almost opposite but slightly to the west of the entrance led into a simple latrine with an internal division and a drain at the western end: this was flushed by the overflow from the neighbouring room, the western room of the bath house. This was an exceptionally well-preserved room comprising an intact *opus signinum* floor that did not reach any of the walls, stopping 0.5 m short. This gap was filled by a bench, largely ploughed away except on the south side where enough survived to show that it had been a tile-backed *opus signinum* construction with a quarter-roll fillet of *opus signinum* sealing the junction between floor and bench (Gaffney and White 2007, fig. 4.37). This room must presumably have been an indoor pool or *natatio* filled with water from the natural spring that still exists on the site. When excavated, its collapsed roof still survived (*ibid.* fig. 4.38). The remains comprised lozenge-shaped stone slates cut from micaceous flagstone visually identical to those found at Wroxeter. Interspersed among these were *tegulae* and *imbrices* denoting a mixed roofing of slates and tiles for polychrome effect (the same colour combination was noted in the mosaic borders). The heated rooms of the suite lay at the eastern end. Although the site of the doorway was not clear in the surviving masonry, it was presumably in the south-east corner of the central room, adjacent to a shallow tile-floored room 1.95 x 1.05 m internally that projected beyond the line of the wall. A small drain in the corner suggested this was foot bath (*ibid.* fig. 4.28). The baths proper comprised three rooms, two with apses. The first room, presumably a *tepidarium*, was 2.75 m square internally with an apse to the south, this being directly heated by a *praefurnium*. From there bathers could turn right into a small rectangular room 3.65 x 1.7 m in size, also heated directly by a *praefurnium* on the east side and which had an integral bench on the north side. The lack of any water or apse suggests this was a *sudatorium*. To the north of these rooms was a 2.85 m square *caldarium* with an apse to the east and a rectangular alcove (*alveus*) to the north, directly over the *praefurnium*. Externally, there was no hint of the apses, their curvature being buried within the wall thickness, but both the southern apse and the northern *alveus* attached to the *caldarium* symmetrically projected outside of the line of the walls (*ibid.* fig. 4.27).

The western range comprised three rooms placed centrally behind the 38 m long courtyard wall. A portico wall lay in front of this at a distance of 1 m so the rooms behind would have been invisible other than the upper walls and pyramidal roof of the main room which will have projected above the wall. The upper walls will have probably been provided with windows to allow light into the main room and, like the bath suite, it is likely that the roof will have been polychrome. The central room was 5.9 m square internally and seemed to have a broad doorway since the tessellated border extended over the wall line (Gaffney and White 2007, 119). Flanking rooms to the north and south were the same width as the main room, but only half its depth. They appear to have been entered from the main room rather than the portico, but their function was not at all clear. They were too narrow to have any obvious function measuring only 6.9 x 2.6 m internally. The original floor in the northern room was of pebbles set in lime mortar over beaten earth (*ibid.* 118). At the southern end of the range, a wall connected with the south-west corner of the main room and ran parallel with the wall of the flanking room for 11 m before turning at right angles to match the end of the flanking room creating a 4m wide corridor opening into the main western room at its south western corner (*ibid.* fig. 4.46). The wall of this corridor continued to run south out of the excavated area, joined by an eastern wall that formed a right angle with the south-eastern end of the south wall of the courtyard. The corridor seemed to be floored with pebbles while the flanking rooms apparently had a simple pebble in mortar floor (not all surfaces were fully excavated so the original floor finishes in the rooms were not always clear (*ibid.* 118)). The main room was provided with a polychrome mosaic of four colours: white, red, dark blue and greyish-green, laid on a thin skim of mortar with only a beaten earth surface beneath (i.e. there was no foundation, only a mortar skim to hold the *tesserae* in place). The design has been described in detail by David Neal and Stephen Cosh but was a four-by-four square design with a roundel at the centre containing a portrait head of Medusa (Cosh and Neal 2010, 310-3 ; Witts, this volume, fig 3.1). The coarser border was also tessellated but only using the greyish-green of the roof slates and red of the tiles to create outward facing stepped triangles and bands, perhaps echoing the appearance of the villa's roof. A deeper plain tile tessellated border lay against the west wall perhaps indicating the position for furniture or space for the attendants to move into the room from the corridor. The date of the mosaic, which was primary to the villa and which thus dates the whole

complex, is thought to be the third quarter of the fourth century (*ibid.*).

In sum, the villa complex comprised a courtyard, entered from the east but with a secondary entrance from the south which presumably led to the service buildings. On entering the courtyard, the visitors were facing onto the west range which had a central, square room and wide doorway with a mosaic floor fronted by a portico formed of a dwarf-wall with short columns. If the flanking rooms were not accessible from the portico they would have been invisible until entering the main room. Their plain decoration suggests that they may simply have been places where one changed for dinner in the main room. The only other visible doorway would have been on the north side which led into the middle room of the bath suite. The service corridor behind the main west suite would have been invisible and, while it was clear that further structures existed to the south of the excavated complex, it is highly unlikely that they represented anything other than a service wing. This was partly because immediately to the south of the villa the ground began to rise forming the valley side of the Rea Brook so there was inadequate space for a larger building.

It is not impossible that residential quarters existed away from the main bath house and the reception rooms; detached elements of villa buildings are certainly known elsewhere in the Roman West (Esmonde Cleary 2013b, 240-1). However, surface survey of the rest of field in which the villa was located, as well as in an adjacent field to the south and small-scale excavations on earthworks to the east failed to locate evidence for any other structures. The earthworks are thought to represent the remains of tile making facilities and an associated clay pit since there was clear evidence in the villa buildings that the tiles used during the construction had been made locally since some were over- or under-fired (Gaffney and White 2007, 101, 235). It must be concluded therefore that the complex was uncovered in its entirety with the exception of the putative service buildings.

While not germane to the interpretation of the original use of the villa, it is worth noting that there was a phase of reuse following the demise of the complex signalled by the collapse of the roof of the baths suite. A remanent magnetic date for the last firing of the northern *praefurnium* produced a date of AD 420-520 at 95% confidence or 450-500 at 65% confidence (Gaffney and White 2007, 141). The dating of this hearth is perhaps not very reliable in the light of the rejection of the dating of a similar features at Wroxeter (Lane 2014) but there was clear evidence that there was a reuse of the room even while ruinous. The disuse of the baths prompted the robbing of its fabric down to floor level, presumably to remove the large floor tiles but also the corners of the bath building where the largest of the ashlar blocks were located (Gaffney and White 2007, 127-9). There is no evidence that this robbing definitely occurred at the same time that small ephemeral structures were constructed next to the bath house, within the ruins of the main room in the western range, and at the two corners on the south side of the courtyard where the partially collapsed walls allowed a self-supporting structure to be erected, but neither can the possibility be excluded (*ibid.* 129-38). A hearth was found in the building at the south-east corner and another hearth was located in the ruins of the northern flanking room in the western range. Pottery of late fourth-century date, including rivetted black-burnished ware and a handful of later Roman artefacts including a glass bead and black jewellery, suggested occupation into the fifth century in line with similar cultural material assemblages characterised by Hilary Cool (Cool 2000; Gaffney and White 2007, 184; 189). I have been at pains to discuss this latest phase since the majority of the cultural material found on the site was directly associated with this phase and not with the use of the villa complex. The few areas associated with food preparation, for instance, were in the phase Y buildings constructed on the ruins of the

courtyard wall while there was correspondingly very little material that could be associated with the primary phase of the villa's use (Evans 2007, 157-9).

Whitley Grange villa in its landscape and social context

From the outset, it was clear that the results of the excavations at Whitley Grange were unusual and did not fit the expected pattern of a villa complex comprising a set of agricultural buildings and dwellings reflecting the existence of an agricultural estate, whether mixed, arable, or pastoral. Neither was it obviously a place of rural retreat for the elite on the model of many of the large late Roman villas of the south and south-west of Britain where large, elaborate status-orientated architecturally grand structures vie with each other for attention (Esmonde Cleary 2013a, 145-54). These too have their agricultural function, but they are very clearly orientated towards elite display. Whitley Grange too has its elements of display and grandeur, evidenced by a fine mosaic but also by a substantial bath house and elaborate decoration in the fashionable late Roman polychrome style (Gaffney and White 2007, 235-6; Fig 6.4). Yet these elements are all that it has. There is no hint

Figure 6.4. Aerial photograph of the excavation in 1996 showing the mosaic-floored room (foreground) and baths suite beyond. (Photo courtesy of RAF Shawbury)

of an agricultural base to the complex. It is possible that, detached from the building complex itself, there was a small settlement that produced an agricultural surplus from the land around the villa, but if so, its footprint was light and did not comprise structures made in Roman materials of stone or tile since there was no hint in the wider landscape of such evidence.

One other possibility that cannot be excluded, if only because we have inadequate evidence, is that Whitley Grange was an outlying complex of one of the other villas in the Rea Valley: at Cruckton or Lea Cross. Unfortunately, the evidence base is so poor that we cannot characterise these settlements, or for that matter date them adequately. The villa at Lea Cross was certainly prestigious enough to be equipped with a hypocaust and mosaic floor, but the plan recovered by Geoffrey Toms in the 1970s is clearly only partial (Cosh and Neal 2010, 309, fig. 318). Even less can be said of the remains at Cruckton since emergency recording was not able to recover even a basic outline of the remains (Houghton 1958, 26-7). The association of these two villas with Whitley Grange, and especially Cruckton since it is only a mile away, remains only a possibility but, since there is no evidence for any link it is assumed that there is none. Indeed, one cannot rule out the possibility that they too had the same function as suggested for Whitley Grange and that they too were specialist buildings connected not with each other but with town houses in Wroxeter. In order to understand the function of the villa complex we must therefore fall back on analysis of its layout as a first principle.

The first point to make is to establish the wider landscape context of the villa complex (Fig. 6.1). The buildings lie on the narrow flood plain of the Rea Brook valley, a small tributary of the Severn that rises between the northern end of the pre-Cambrian formations of the Long Mynd and Pontesford Hills and, on the northern side of the valley, the Long Mountain. The northern end of Long Mynd includes the Hope Valley and Stiperstones, both locations for the Roman lead industry in what became Shropshire with evidence for mining in the form of lead pigs dated to the Hadrianic period (White 2000; RIB 2404.28-30). The Roman road from Wroxeter headed due west from that city, across the saddle of Sharpstone Hill where it reused the line and surfacing of an Iron Age predecessor (Malim and Hayes 2010) to Meole Brace roadside settlement on the western flanks of Sharpstone Hill. Thence it crossed the Rea Brook to continue westwards on its northern bank through to Westbury, passing first Whitley Grange, then Cruckton and lastly Lea Cross. From Westbury the road followed the Rea Brook valley until it passed into the Camlad

valley and on to Forden Gaer rather than on the crest of Long Mountain as was suggested by Margary (Evans et al. 2010, 321). The three known villas lie in slightly different relationships to both the road and the Rea Brook. Whitley Grange lies 1 km to its south and on the south bank of the Rea Brook, but the road here runs along the northern crest of the steep-sided valley so in consequence it will not have been possible to cross it to get to the villa. Travellers on the road may have been able to see the villa, however, even if they could not reach it. At Cruckton, the villa lay almost equidistant between the Rea Brook and the road, no more than 400 m from either and so visible from the road. At Lea Cross the villa was situated like that at Whitley Grange: on the south bank of the Rea Brook but 2.5 km from the road and so unlikely to be seen from it. The spacing of these settlements is also worth noting: Wroxeter was 7 km from Meole Brace roadside settlement. The distance between Meole Brace and Whitley Grange was 3.2 km. That between Whitley Grange and Cruckton 2.4 km and that between Cruckton and Lea Cross 2 km (all distances as the crow flies: if there were no direct path between Cruckton and Lea Cross and travellers would instead have had to go up to the Wroxeter-Forden road, along it and then down to Lea Cross so that the actual distance travelled would have been more like 4.2 km). Thus, none of these villas was too far from Wroxeter: Whitley Grange was around 10 km from the city, Cruckton 12.4 km and Lea Cross probably around 15 km taking into account the distance from the Wroxeter-Forden road. In other words, all of these villas could easily be reached by horse within a couple of hours. Even on foot they could have been a simple day return trip from Wroxeter. The model here is more like the Russian *dacha* where the town's elite might travel out for the day or two to relax, returning to their town house after their brief stay.

The second point to consider is the wider landscape of the Wroxeter hinterland and Whitley's relationship to it. One element of the research into Wroxeter's hinterland that it was not possible to publish in the final report was a study carried out by a postgraduate student, Tony Maguire, that attempted to reconstruct the Roman landscape in which the town was located. The failure to publish was occasioned by Tony's sudden and unexpected death towards the end of his studies with us so that although he completed the work, we were not in a position to fully corroborate the research and to publish it, although it is still intended to do so as the results were very promising. To reconstruct the landscape, Tony plotted the enclosures within the study area, most of which had been identified by aerial photography, against the distribution of -*leah* (modern -ley) place names (Fig. 6.5). As is well-known, some -*leah*

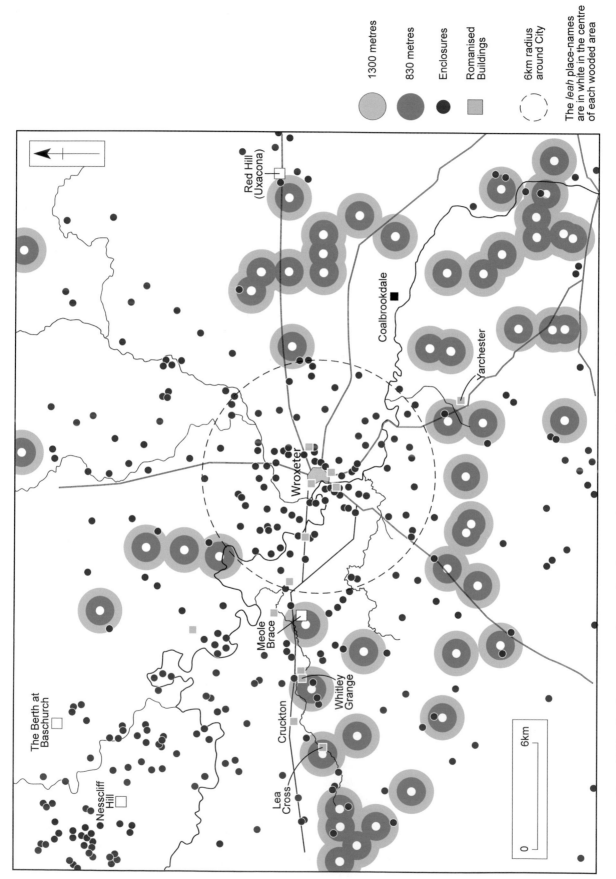

Figure 6.5. Map showing occurrence of cropmark enclosures in the Wroxeter Hinterland Survey study area with the occurrence of Anglo-Saxon –leah place names.
(Drawing by Nigel Dodds, after Tony Maguire)

place names are an indicator in the post-Roman period of secondary settlements created by clearings in existing woodland (Gelling 1992, 14-16), although Della Hooke informs me that -*leah* place names can also be taken to mean settlements in open-canopy woodland (D. Hooke, *pers. comm.*). Tony imported and displayed these names within the project GIS. He then created 830 m and 1300 m buffers around the place names to recreate the woodland that the -*leah* place names implied existed there. The resulting map demonstrates an almost mutually exclusive plot with extensive tracts of woodland along Wenlock Edge, Hoar Edge and the northern end of Long Mynd as well as a notable wooded area on the site of modern-day Telford and another on the sandstone hills of Clive and Grinshill north of Shrewsbury. Within a 6 km area around Wroxeter itself there are no -*leah* place names, as is also the case in the upper reaches of the Rivers Severn and Perry and the Roden and Tern, respectively north-west and north-east of Wroxeter. Where the -*leah* place names and enclosures do coincide is limited to two main areas. The first is an extensive tract of woodland extending north of Bridgnorth in the south east corner of the study area. The second is in the Rea Brook valley, where both Whitley Grange and Lea Cross are examples of -*leah* place names interspersed with enclosures.

Taken at face value, these results appear to suggest that enclosures largely avoided areas that were wooded in the post-Roman period. This implies that these woodlands existed too in the Roman period and that settlements did not tend to be located in these wooded areas, presumably because there was insufficient population pressure to occasion settlement in open-canopy or freshly cleared woodland areas, this pressure only arising in the post-Roman period. It seems highly unlikely, however, that there was no woodland for a 6 km radius around Wroxeter given the necessity of timber for fuel and construction at the very least so presumably those areas with dense enclosure settlement relied on managed woodlands of relatively small area. It may have been these areas that account for what slight evidence there is woodland regeneration in the post-Roman period, which is otherwise stable agriculturally (Rippon, Smart and Pears 2015, 254).

For the landscape of the Rea Valley, however, we appear to have a situation where there was extensive woodland, enough for areas later to be cleared for settlement, but also Roman settlement both in the form of villas and enclosures. While it is impossible to be certain, we may be seeing evidence here for a wooded landscape, more like a medieval park than farmland. If this were the case then, like a medieval park, the landscape may have

been actively managed to encourage game and thus provide the basis for hunting. This conclusion, alongside the unusual form of the villa, lies at the heart of the interpretation of Whitley Grange (and perhaps Lea Cross too) as a hunting lodge rather than a residence.

The architecture of the villa itself argues in favour of this interpretation since it provides only a very basic provision for the needs of visitors: a place to bathe and to perhaps eat a meal cooked in the adjacent service buildings and served up in the main room in the west range, while meeting these needs through conspicuous display. The inaccessibility of the villa from the Wroxeter–Forden road, whilst being entirely visible to any passer-by on that road, and the potentially semi-wooded landscape suggests perfect conditions for hunting. One can easily envision a hunting party setting out from Wroxeter to carry on a day's hunting in the park-like landscape west of the town, probably much as the friends of the late Roman historian Ammianus Marcellinus did: 'they embarked upon hunting expeditions – or rather parades, the strenuous part of labour being done by attendants' (Amm. Marc. XXVIII, 4.18; quoted in Matthews 1975, 2-3). Mosaics depicted these activities, notably that from Lillebonne (Seine-Maritime) which shows a stag-hunt with attendants, dogs, and bowmen such as might have been enacted in the landscape around Whitley Grange (Henig 1983, col. pl. 13). The resulting trophies could even be displayed in the villa, as appears to be the case with the villa at La Olmeda, Palencia (Spain) where the frontal skull bone and full antler set of a number of stags were apparently displayed in a corridor (A. C. King, *pers. comm.*). Once the hunt had been successfully concluded, the party could retire to Whitley Grange to bathe, relax and change into formal dining wear afterwards to eat the results of their day's action, prepared and served to them by the host's servants (Fig. 6.6). The social significance of this activity in the context of late Roman society should not be under-estimated. As Simon Esmonde Cleary has written;

> 'the entertaining of valued guests to a formal meal was another established way for a host to exhibit his regard for his guests while at the same time displaying his wealth and taste to impress them and to enmesh them in the bonds of reciprocal interaction' (2013b, 223-4).

While the thesis is difficult to prove conclusively, not least because the acidity of the soil denied any evidence from faunal remains and the conspicuous display of glass, plate, and servants, among other things, are intangible in the archaeological record, although well represented in the surviving art of the period (Dunbabin 2003). This interpretation fits very closely with the

Figure 6.6. A late Roman hunting party arrives at Whitley Grange villa.
(Reconstruction by Alan Duncan, Courtesy of Shropshire Museums Service)

interests and activities of the late Roman aristocracy: the *otium* or leisure that contrasted with the *negotium* of political and work-related activity (Brown 2012, 189-194; Matthews 1975, 1-31). Given the abundance of pictorial evidence of hunting from mosaics, wall-paintings and numerous silver vessels surviving from the late Roman world, the importance of hunting was paramount as a social activity (Esmonde Cleary 2013a, 104-121). It was an opportunity for social elites to compete with each other in hunting skills and bravery, as well as to relax after the hurly burly of the hunt in a baths suite (Esmonde Cleary 2013b, 242). Depictions of aristocratic feasting under awnings in the countryside alongside images of the hunt are a leitmotif of Late Roman art (Dunbabin 2003, 141-150). Whitley Grange thus provides the essentials for any successful day of 'competitive entertaining' to use Simon Esmonde Cleary's memorable phrase (Esmonde Cleary 2013a, 104): a landscape potentially full of game, including fish from the adjacent Rea Brook (which still has plentiful brown trout today), a small but well-appointed baths suite, and a place to dine elaborately with one's friends, waited upon by staff who have prepared the meal, and served it presumably on high-status silverware or pottery brought to the site for the purpose, presumably from Wroxeter. Whitley Grange thus offers an interesting model for landscape use within a late Roman context. It is evidently a sophisticated architectural complex firmly embedded in elite social practices seen with much greater grandeur elsewhere in the western empire (Esmonde Cleary 2013b, 215-228). Equally it is a relatively modest building providing these social functions in a pared down form so that it can only have functioned as a dependent settlement on a town rather than a fully developed elite villa building, such as those found in abundant numbers around Late Roman centres of power, like Cirencester, in which farming played a more significant role in the establishment's purpose (White 2007, 123-5, table 6.1; Esmonde Cleary 2013a, 126-32).

Acknowledgements

I would like to acknowledge here the help and advice received from Tony King, Martin Henig and Della Hooke who have all made valuable suggestions in relation to the final version of this paper. I hope I have interpreted their comments correctly, but if not then it is my fault, not theirs.

References

Barker, P. A., Haldon, R. and Jenks, W. E. 1991 Excavations on Sharpstones Hill near Shrewsbury, 1965-71. *Transactions of the Shropshire Archaeological and Historical Society* 67, 15-57.

Brown, P. 2012 *Through the Eye of a Needle. Wealth, the Fall of Rome, and the Making of Christianity in the West, 350-550 AD.* Princeton University Press, Princeton.

Burnham, B. C. and Davies, J. L. (eds) 2010 *Roman Frontiers in Wales and the Marches.* Royal Commission on the Ancient and Historic Monuments of Wales, Aberystwyth.

Cool, H. E. M. 2000 The parts left over: material culture into the fifth century. In Wilmott and Wilson, 2000, 47-65.

Cosh, S. R. and Neal, D. S. 2010 *Roman Mosaics of Britain. Volume IV Western Britain.* Illuminata Publishers and Society of Antiquaries, London.

Dunbabin, K. M. 2003 *The Roman Banquet: Images of Conviviality.* Cambridge University Press, Cambridge.

Esmonde Cleary, S. 2013a *Chedworth. Life in a Roman Villa.* History Press, Stroud.

Esmonde Cleary, S. 2013b *The Roman West, AD 200-500. An Archaeological Study.* Cambridge University Press, Cambridge.

Evans, E. M., Hopewell, D., Murphy, K., Silvester, R. J. and Toller, H. 2010 Gazetteer of roads. In Burnham and Davies 2010, 315-32.

Evans, C. J., Jenks, W. E. and White, R. H. 1999 Romano-British kilns at Meole Brace (Pulley), Shropshire. *Shropshire History and Archaeology* 74, 1-27.

Evans, C. J. 2007 The Roman pottery from Wroxeter's hinterland. In Gaffney and White 2007, 146-68.

Gaffney, V. L. and White, R. H. with Goodchild, H. 2007 *Wroxeter, the Cornovii, and the Urban Process. Final Report on the Wroxeter Hinterland Project 1994-1997. Volume 1. Researching the Hinterland.* Journal of Roman Archaeology Supplementary Series 68. Portsmouth, RI.

Gelling, M. 1992 *West Midlands in the Early Middle Ages.* Leicester University Press, Leicester.

Henig, M. 1983 *A Handbook of Roman Art. A Survey of the Visual Arts of the Roman World.* Phaidon, London.

Hughes, G. 1994 A Romano-British roadside settlement at Meole Brace. *Shropshire History and Archaeology* 69, 31-55.

Houghton, A. W. J. 1958 A Note on Excavations at the Roman Villa at Lea Cross During 1956-7 *Transactions of the Shropshire Archaeological and Historical Society* 56.1, 26-7

Lane, A. 2014 Wroxeter and the end of Roman Britain. *Antiquity* 88, 501-515.

Leonard, J., Preshous, D., Roberts, M., Smyth, J. and Train, C. (eds.) 2000 *The Gale of Life. Two Thousand Years in South-West Shropshire.* South-West Shropshire Historical and Archaeological Society / Logaston Press.

Malim, T. and Hayes, L. 2010 An engineered Iron Age road, associated Roman use (Margary Route 64) and Bronze Age activity recorded at Sharpstone Hill,

2009. *Shropshire History and Archaeology* 85 (issued 2011), 7-80.

Matthews, J. F. 1975 *Western Aristocracies and the Imperial Court A.D. 364-425.* Oxford University Press, Oxford.

Millett, M. 1990 *The Romanization of Britain. An Essay in Archaeological Interpretation.* Cambridge University Press, Cambridge.

Rippon, S., Smart, C. and Pears, B. 2015 *The Fields of Britannia. Continuity and Change in Late Roman and Early Medieval Landscape.* Oxford University Press, Oxford.

Toms, G. 1985 Whitley Chapel and Weir Meadow: a Romano-British site near Shrewsbury. *Transactions of the Shropshire Archaeological and Historical Society* 64, 13-16.

Whimster, R. 1989 *The Emerging Past. Air Photography and the Buried Landscape.* RCHM(E), London.

White, R. H. 2000 The Roman lead workings at Linley. In Leonard *et al.* 2000, 31-41.

White, R. H. 2007 *Britannia Prima. Britain's Last Roman Province.* Tempus, Stroud.

Wilmott, T. and Wilson, P. (eds.) 2000 *The Late Roman Transition in the North. Papers from the Roman Archaeology Conference, Durham 1999.* British Archaeological Reports (BAR) British Series 299, Oxford.

7

Moor Park, Hertfordshire:
two evaluations of an excavation of the 1950s

Victoria Leitch and Martin Biddle

Moor Park: Roman Villa or Sanctuary?

Victoria Leitch

Excavations at Moor Park Roman building, situated on a steep slope overlooking the Colne Valley near Rickmansworth in Hertfordshire (NGR TQ 080935), were carried out in 1955–6 after the Ministry of Public Building and Works scheduled the site as an Ancient Monument. The Merchant Taylors School Archaeological Society was subsequently given permission to excavate, assisted by the Rickmansworth Historical Society and local residents. A short note outlining the work carried out was originally published by Alan Millard (1956). However, this was never intended to be anything other than a preliminary report and thus contained no plans or images of the finds, and nor did it attempt to identify or contextualise the remains within the region or the period. Later, Martin Henig (1986) published a

description of the site's most important find, an Early Christian signet ring, of late fourth or early fifth-century date.

This paper serves as an interim report, awaiting the full publication of the 1950s excavations and its finds, to draw attention to this site and open up questions about its extent and use, with particular reference to the evidence for ritualistic behaviour on the site at different periods.

Moor Park is about 15 km south-west of *Verulamium*, just south of the River Colne (Fig. 7.1). There is evidence of occupation dating to Palaeolithic, Mesolithic, later prehistoric and Roman times in the nearby area, perhaps due to its favourable position on the south-eastern edge of the Chiltern Heights (Derricourt 1972, 2). About 1 km east of Moor Park villa are the Roman buildings at Sandy

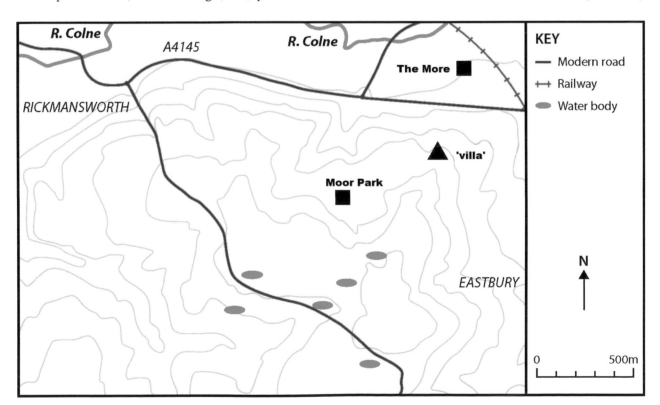

Figure 7.1. Moor Park: location sketch map, showing the 'villa' site, The More, and positions of possible water sources. (Drawing: Nich Hogben)

Lodge (which could conceivably have been on the Moor Park villa estate). Two stone buildings were excavated there in 1962 by the late Roger Jacobi, the earlier and more elaborate was over 6.1 m (20 feet) wide and 12.2 m (40 feet) long, with mainly fourth-century material on the site (Cotton, Mills and Clegg 1986, 66). There was an important find there of a second-century red jasper gem showing Victory in a *quadriga* (Henig 2007, no. 292). Another second-century masonry building at Hampermill, Watford, about 1 km east of Sandy Lodge, was discovered in 1930 (Derricourt 1972). It was less sophisticated than Moor Park and thought to be a native settlement with little evidence of Roman influence. Niblett (1995, 86-7) points out that peasant settlements (such as Hampermill) were often found about 1.5 km from the main villa, and so we can perhaps imagine that these three sites were somehow connected.

Looking further out, Moor Park is on the southernmost edge of a cluster of other Hertfordshire/Chilterns villas. They all lie close to roads or rivers. Many, for example Gadebridge Park and Park Street, date from the first century and saw improvements in the second, but became run-down in the mid to late third century (Branigan 1973, 63-77), which fits with the chronology of Moor Park. The reasons for this were political and economic instability. A revitalisation of the villas seems to have occurred around the beginning of the fourth century, with rebuilding, refurbishment, and in some cases, the addition of swimming pools. The area then suffered again in the mid to late fourth century (e. g. the Park Street villa was burnt and abandoned c. AD 361: O'Neil 1945, 29-30). However, the continued use of the forum at *Verulamium* in the fifth century might suggest trading and social links with the villas remained (Branigan 1973, 136). Hertfordshire villa sites have produced coins as late as AD 370-405, although in what form the villas were then occupied is more difficult to say.

Moor Park Excavations (Fig. 7.2)

The area of the 1950s excavation is shown in Fig. 7.2, probably the corner of a larger building, but the full extent of the construction is not known. The early building dates from c. AD 130 and after about a hundred years of disuse from around the end of the second century there was some alteration in the early fourth century, with at least another hundred years of occupation.

Room I (Figs 7.3, 7.4)

The so-called deep room was the only one to be fully excavated: the site notebook states that this room was deeper than the rest of the building. Its first occupation

phase dates from c. AD 120 to 230. From 120-150 it had an entrance in the north wall, three niches in the south wall and the east wall was cut to form a bench or shelf. From 150-200 the east wall was reduced to form a bench or shelf. Then from 200-230 there is a fire pit, suggesting a kitchen or bread-oven. This information suggests that it may have been a storeroom, which in fact was a practice taken from the Iron Age, where there was a preference for subsurface storage (Trow *et al.* 2009, 61). However, in the north-west corner of this sunken room there was a complete poppy-head beaker with a handful of bird bones underneath it, which was 'perhaps buried in a scooped out pit, upright' (site notes) and may be taken as a votive deposit. Further evidence that may support this view is that there were another six pots, more or less whole, found in other rooms at Moor Park. The floor was covered in a gravel layer that contained pottery of the late second century. From c. 230-300 the room does not seem to have been occupied. The room was then filled with rubble and in a second phase from c. 300 a hypocaust system was installed, which was deserted in AD 400 or later. The coins associated with this phase date to the late fourth century.

To look at the details, the doorway in the north wall (Fig. 7.2) and the west wall have fine white plaster painted with a red dado 61 cm (2 feet) high. The south wall has niches, just under 61 cm (2 feet) wide and 46 cm (18 inches) apart with a red painted band 7.5 cm (3 inch) around the edge of each; these were then blocked by the third century construction of a wall. The simple decoration of the walls is in line with other Romano-British villas, where elaborate decoration is rare (Perring 1989, 284). Similar niches have been found in *Verulamium*, such as Houses xxii, I, and xviii, I, suggested to be of domestic use, and in the cellars at Gorhambury (Neal *et al.* 1990, 47) and Shakenoak (Brodribb *et al.* 2005, 87). They are thought to be for *lararia* or sacred images (as evidenced at Lullingstone: Meates, 1963, 13), or perhaps for lamps (as suggested for the five niches at Chalk: Johnston 1972, 115-6).

The question of use is difficult to answer definitively, but we see a number of cellars from Roman Britain in the early second century (they were mainly built between AD 70 and AD 155: Perring 1989, 279), and it has been suggested that these might have been modelled on contemporary Gallic examples, which were generally thought to be for storage, particularly wine (Trow *et al.* 2009, 60-2). In the hinterland of *Verulamium*, such sunken rooms are known at Gorhambury villa (Neal *et al.* 1990, 45-8), evidently of some pretension, and at Gadebridge Park, thought to be for stabling (Neal 1974, 19-21). Another well-known cellar is recorded at the Ditches villa, Gloucestershire

MOOR PARK VILLA

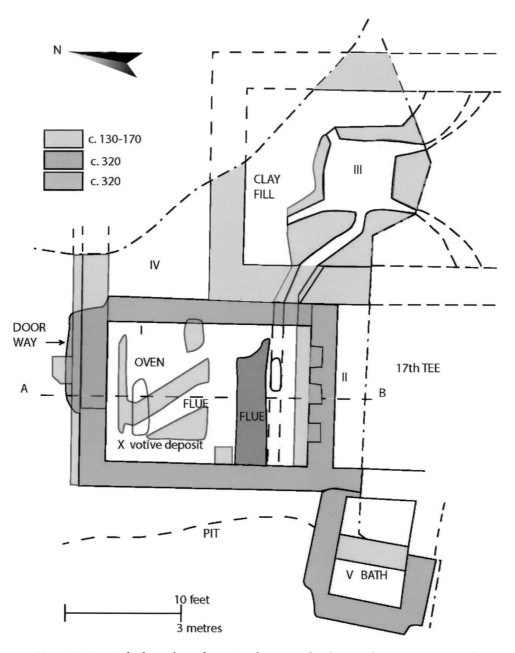

Figure 7.2. Moor Park: plan, redrawn from a site plan prepared in the 1950s. (Drawing: Nich Hogben)

(Trow *et al.* 2009, 26-9, 60). At Chalk, Kent, the excavators, looking at parallels in Germany, suggest the cellar was for storage, particularly wine (Johnston 1972, 121-2). The case of the cellar at Lullingstone villa, Kent, is interesting in that it began as a storage facility but by c. AD 180 had been refurbished as a *nymphaeum*, and sunken pots as votive deposits have been found there from several different phases of occupation, when the

house followed first Pagan and then Christian rituals (see Henig and Soffe, this volume; Meates 1963, 15-19). At *Verulamium*, 'a carinated beaker in fine grey ware of second-century type containing a worn *as* of Vespasian' (dated c. AD 140-150) was buried in the floor of *aedicula* A, thought to be a *lararium*, within the building in Insula xiv (Frere 1972, 57 and Plate XVIII). The presence of niches at Moor Park may point to a ritual role, emphasised by

Figure 7.3. Moor Park: Room 1, the 'deep room', looking south. Scale on ranging rod in feet.

Figure 7.4. Moor Park: Room 1, showing the three niches in the south wall. Scale rod in feet.

the possible votive deposit, the painted dado rail, and the later association with Christianity through the signet ring, suggesting, perhaps, that this was a 'reception' room rather than simply for storage. However, perhaps we need to be more flexible in our approach to its use. Such rooms may have had multiple uses, both functional and ritual: 'is it possible that cellars served as both cult rooms and stores; these functions can be complementary since fertility cults were directly concerned with the harvesting of agricultural produce?' (Perring 1989, 290).

An additional consideration, highlighted by Perring (1989, 285), is water supply – five of the known Roman cellars were set over natural springs and many others had water supply channels, with some evidence for ritual activity. Indeed, recent survey work in the area, which will be incorporated into the final report, also points to the importance of the site in terms of water supply – a gravity-fed water system from Moor Park Mansion, located up the hill from Moor Park villa, seems to have come from this hill to the villa, which probably received water from springs and/or ponds higher up the valley (Fig. 7.1).

Rooms II, III, IV and V (Fig. 7.2)

Room II was only partially excavated and had a thin mortar floor and associated second-century pottery. Room III is significant for having an inserted hypocaust with flues and the impression of two *pilae* in the clay floor. The north-west flue led into the main flue in Room I. This Room III hypocaust seems to be associated with fourth-century pottery and may have been used for a different purpose in the second-century occupation period. The bath in Room IV was destroyed by the construction of a sand-pit associated with the modern golf course. Room V overlays a second-century pit and has fourth-century pottery. It may have been a small tank or bath as it is lined with waterproof plaster. The Roman road running north-north-east to south-south-west on the western side of the building dates to the late first century.

The finds

Important finds from the site include some window glass, the signet ring and many late Roman coins. The ceramic finds (so far only briefly assessed) should also shed light on the connectivity of the site, with some interesting roller stamped flue-box tiles, probably of the second century, regional pottery including examples from Stow, Oxford, Nene Valley, *Verulamium*, and local coarse wares and black-burnished wares – both original and local imitations. Imports include Belgic pots, some unusual samian ware forms, dating mainly from the second to third centuries, and southern Spanish *amphorae* of Dressel 20 form, perhaps for fish-sauce or wine.

Discussion

Moor Park 'villa', partially excavated and with at least two discernible phases of occupation, raises more questions than it answers about the use of the rooms investigated and how the villa fitted into the political, religious, commercial and agricultural landscape. From the use of the cellar with its three niches to its possible religious significance, the presence, as suggested by the finger-ring, of late Roman Christianity, and the seeming lack of Anglo-Saxon culture in an area, this villa adds new evidence to our knowledge of country life in Antiquity. However, it also perfectly highlights the challenges of categorising villa types, which in Roman Britain were never as grand or uniform as those on the Continent, with their mix of native traditions, Roman influences, local conditions and available materials, and the need to widen our definition of their uses and reuses over time. From traditional villa to water-related cult centre, or shrine in the case of Moor Park, we should perhaps consider both interpretations as valid as the building evolved over time and space.

Moor Park 'villa', the Manor of the More, and Moor Park: the question of water supply
Martin Biddle

When I worked briefly on Alan Millard's excavation of the Roman building on Moor Park Golf Course in September 1956, while on embarkation leave from the army, I remember being struck by the sunken Room I with three niches in its south wall (Fig. 7.2, Room I, blue phase, *c.* 320). I thought then that it looked like a possible pool. Whether this is the case or not, I do not recall knowing that the smaller square room (Fig. 7.2, Room V) attached to the west wall of Room I, but structurally subsequent, was thought to be a bath. Both possibilities raise the question of the source of water supplied to this site lying at a height of just over 80 m aOD, above sea level, and some 30 m above the River Colne in the valley immediately to the north.

The same question arises in relation to the medieval Manor of the More, later a palace of Cardinal Wolsey and Henry VIII, which lies on the valley floor at a height of about 50 m aOD, 450 m (half a mile) to the north of the Roman site and 30 m below it. Excavations at The More by Alan Millard, Lawrence Barfield and myself for the Merchant Taylors' School Archaeological Society in 1952-5 showed that water was brought into the building from the fifteenth century onwards by a wooden pipe, and later distributed to all parts of the building by lead pipes (Biddle *et al.* 1959, 154, 156, 196, figs 5 (Section LM) and 6). Although the former had long rotted (leaving a circular void) and the latter had been removed when The More was demolished in the later sixteenth century (Falvey 2008, 98-99), it was clear that the water must have come from some higher source and not from the adjacent River Colne, and that in the sixteenth century it had been brought to the house in a lead pipe or pipes laid in a brick-built conduit passing through the principal gatehouse.

Fresh excavation at The More in 2012 by Wessex Archaeology for the BBC *Time Team* showed that the brick conduit survived intact some 55 m. south-south-east of the gatehouse running due south in a slightly uphill direction (Wessex Archaeology 2013, paras 1.5.13; 4.3.17, 19 and 36; p. 38; Figs 1 and 11). The surface of the intact vault of the conduit is shown on the Wessex Archaeology plan at approximately 97 m aOD. Since this level must be about 50m aOD, as the OS maps show, this must be a systematic error which affects all the levels given in that report.)

The problem of water supply is even more striking in relation to Moor Park itself, the great house built and rebuilt in the seventeenth and eighteenth centuries near the top of the hill at a height of about 87 m aOD, a little above the Roman 'villa' and high above the medieval manor house. The first house on this site was built about 1617 by Lucy Harrington, Countess of Bedford, who in the following decade surrounded the house with the elaborate gardens which have become famous from the description written by Sir William Temple, the statesman and essayist, who stayed there on his honeymoon in 1655. Thirty years later in an essay, *Upon the Gardens of Epicurus*, he described the gardens at Moor Park as 'the perfectest figure of a garden I ever saw, either at home or abroad' (Strong 1979, 141-6, with diagram on p. 145; see also Thacker 1994, 112-13 and Williamson *et al.* 2000, 11-12, 26-9). Roy Strong, judging Temple's description 'the most detailed evocation we have of a Jacobean garden' has drawn a diagram of 'a very large parterre', probably on the east side of the house which included two fountains and lower down a grotto with 'figures of shell rock-work, fountains, and waterworks'. 'On the other side of the house', Temple noted another garden 'all of that sort, very wild, shady, and adorned with rock-work and fountains'.

The gardens of Moor Park were reworked at least twice over the next century and a half. The house was rebuilt by Hugh May in 1673 and again as the present house for Benjamin Styles in 1720. The gardens redesigned for Styles in the 1720's, probably by Charles Bridgeman,

included to the north-east 'a large Octagonal peice of water' and a canal perhaps eight hundred feet long, with a second angular basin to the south-east (Bridgeman's design, now Oxford, Bodleian Library, Gough MS, MSGD a4, f. 58, is reproduced in Williamson *et al.* 2000, fig. 16). In the 1754-9 'Capability' Brown reworked the gardens again at great expense and 'undulated the horizon', but there seems to be little evidence at present of exactly what he did (Williamson *et al.* 2000, 42-4).

From 1617 or so the gardens of Moor Park required a constant flow of water sufficient to keep ponds full and fountains flowing, and presumably to service the house at all levels. There seems to be no contemporary evidence for the source of this water but Sally Jeffery, in establishing accurately for the first time the site of the Bedford house and its gardens, 'evidently well supplied with water features', has suggested that there must have been a 'hydraulic system that raised water from the river below and no doubt supplied a cistern at high level from which the fountains and waterworks were supplied by gravity' (Jeffery 2014, 163-4; substantial elements of the Bedford house, confirming its precise position and alignment, have now been shown to survive in the present house: Drury and Wrightson 2016). She also wondered whether 'the Bedfords [had] the means to build elaborate new gardens with costly hydraulics at Moor Park' (Jeffery 2014, 164). There is however evidence which suggests that the source lay not in a hydraulic system but in the ready availability of water in natural ponds higher up the hill above the house (see Fig. 7.1).

This source is a perched water-table at and above the 100 m contour, about 400 m south of and at least 13 m (43 feet) above the Moor Park mansion, and much higher above both the Moor Park Roman 'villa' and the medieval and Tudor Manor of the More. The existence of this supply can be seen today in a line of ponds tending in a north-north-east to south-south-west direction along and to either side of the road known as Batchworth Heath Hill, on Batchworth Heath itself, and inside Moor Park, to either side of Home Farm, and in the still filled circular pond known as the 'Old Pleasure Ground' lying due south-east of Moor Park house. These ponds, including several now disappeared, are seen most clearly, because coloured blue, on the OS 6-inch maps Hertfordshire Sheets XLIII.12 and XLIII.16 (revised 1896, 2nd edn. 1898).

In geological terms, these ponds appear to be surface water bodies occurring 'where the Pebble Gravels, glaciofluvial or river terrace gravels overlie less permeable strata, such as London Clay or till' (Catt 2010, 276), which here themselves overlie the Chalk.

It would seem that this ability to obtain a piped gravity-fed supply of good water from one or more these sources was used for The Manor of the More, following its great rebuilding in the mid fifteenth century, and may have been utilised, whether in a pipe or an open channel, as early as the Roman period to supply the 'villa' on the north-east slope of the hill down to the River Colne. The evident lavishness of the water supply together with the strong hints of ritual activity in the section of building excavated might well support the theory that the Roman site either was, or was closely associated with, a sanctuary at a spring.

References

Biddle, M., Barfield, L. and Millard, A. 1959 The excavation of the Manor of the More, Rickmansworth, Hertfordshire. *Archaeological Journal* 116, 136-199.

Branigan, K. 1973 *Town and Country: Verulamium and the Roman Chilterns*. Guildford.

Brodribb, A. C. C., Hands, A. R. and Walker, D. R. 2005 *The Roman Villa at Shakenoak Farm, Oxfordshire, Excavations 1960-1976*. British Archaeological Reports (BAR) British Series 395, Oxford.

Catt, J. (ed.) 2010 *Hertfordshire Geology and Landscape*. Hertfordshire Natural History Society.

Cotton, J., Mills, J. and Clegg, G. 1986. *Archaeology in West Middlesex: London Borough of Hillingdon from the Earliest Hunters to the Late Medieval Period*. London Borough of Hillingdon.

Derricourt, R. M. 1972 *The Romano-British Settlement at Hampermill, Watford*. Privately printed.

Drury, P. and Wrightson, D. 2016 Moor Park in the Seventeenth Century. *Antiquaries Journal* 96, 241-90.

Falvey, H. 2008 The More Revisited. *The Ricardian* 18, 92-99.

Frere, S. 1972 *Verulamium Excavations I*. Reports of the Research Committee of the Society of Antiquaries of London 28, Oxford.

Henig, M. 1986 An Early Christian signet ring from the Roman villa at Moor Park. *Hertfordshire Archaeology* 9, 184–5.

Henig, M. 2007 *A Corpus of Roman Engraved Gemstones from British Sites*. British Archaeological Reports (BAR) British Series 8, Oxford (3rd edition).

Jeffery, S. 2014 The Formal Gardens at Moor Park in the Seventeenth and Early Eighteenth Centuries. *Garden History* 42, 157-77.

Johnston, D. E. 1972 A Roman building at Chalk near Gravesend. *Britannia* 3, 112-48.

Meates, G. W. 1963 *The Roman Villa at Lullingstone, Volume 1 – the site*. Kent Archaeological Society, Maidstone.

Millard, A. R. 1956 Moor Park golf course, Rickmansworth, Herts. Interim report on the excavation of a Roman building. *Journal of the Ruislip and District Natural History Society* 6, 1-5.

Neal, D. S. 1974 *The Excavation of the Roman Villa in Gadebridge Park Hemel Hempstead 1963-8*. Reports of the Research Committee of the Society of Antiquaries of London 31, London.

Neal, D. S. 1977 Northchurch, Boxmoor and Hemel Hempstead Station: The excavation of three Roman buildings in Bulbourne Valley. *Hertfordshire Archaeology* 4, 1-137.

Neal, D. S., Wardle, A. and Hunn, J. 1990 *Excavation of the Iron Age, Roman and Medieval settlement at Gorhambury, St. Albans*. English Heritage Archaeological Report 14, Swindon.

Niblett, R. 1995 *Roman Hertfordshire*. The Dovecote Press, Wimborne Minster.

O'Neil, H. E. 1945 The Roman Villa at Park Street, near St Albans, Hertfordshire. *Archaeological Journal* 102, 21-110.

Perring, D. 1989 Cellars and cults in Roman Britain. *Archaeological Journal* 146, 279-301.

Strong, R. 1979 *The Renaissance Garden in England*. Thames and Hudson, London.

Thacker, C. 1994 *The Genius of Gardening: The History of Gardens in Britain and Ireland*. Weidenfeld and Nicolson, London.

Trow, S., James, S. and Moore, T. 2009 *Becoming Roman, being Gallic, staying British: research and excavations at Ditches 'Hillfort' and villa 1984-2006*. Oxbow Books, Oxford.

Wessex Archaeology 2013 *The Manor of the More, Northwood, Hertfordshire: Archaeological Evaluation and Assessment of Results*. Wessex Archaeology unpublished report, Salisbury.

Williamson, T. and Members of the Hertfordshire Gardens Trust 2000 *The Parks and Gardens of West Hertfordshire*. Hertfordshire Gardens Trust, Letchworth.

8

Great Witcombe, Gloucestershire: a reinterpretation of the site as a temple rather than a villa

Bryn Walters and David Rider

In the late 1960s, the first author of this paper was privileged to have taken part in the final excavations at Great Witcombe, directed by the late Ernest Greenfield. He has maintained a prolonged interest in the site ever since, which has led to the reinterpretation given below.

The Romano-British building at Great Witcombe (NGR SO 8995 1425) is one of the most enigmatic examples of Roman rural architecture to have been revealed in Britain. Ever since its discovery and excavation by Samuel Lysons in the early nineteenth century this building has been assumed to be the ornate *domus* of a wealthy landowner. However, there are problems with this interpretation, such as the absence of obvious living rooms, which will be discussed in detail in this paper. The alternative function of the buildings is for ritual purposes, focused on a central shrine with baths adjacent, in which water played a significant role.

The site occupies a fine location on the side of a south-east-facing slope of the Cotswold escarpment, approximately five miles south-east of Gloucester and one mile south-west of the village of Great Witcombe. The building sits on a steep hillside of Lias clay, just below a high scarp of the Inferior Oolite. In the passage beds between the clay and the limestone, the lithology changes to Cotswold Sands. Here is a spring-line offering fresh water before it descends a 30-degree slope to join with the Horsbere Brook. The abundance of water in this perched position is a major cause of slope instability, but at the same time appears to have been important for the function and interpretation of the building and its appurtenances.

Excavation History

The building at Great Witcombe was originally discovered by workmen extracting a tree stump on the estate of Sir William Hicks in 1818. Samuel Lysons was promptly invited to expose these remains; this he pursued with vigour, starting at the lower south corner of the site. Some walls were found to be more than two metres in height and still covered, in places, by painted plaster. A complete stone doorway capped by its lintel

(now lost) was seen when the tree stump was being removed. These features proved to be part of the lower suite of an extensive range of baths, terraced into the hillside. Attached to the north-east side was a curious 'shrine-like' room and an ascending stepped passageway (see Fig. 8.5, Rooms 1 and 2).

After his death, Lysons' preliminary account of these excavations was published in *Archaeologia* (Lysons 1821). This report contained important structural details of features that can no longer be seen on the site. Other details were recorded in watercolour illustrations now in the library of the Society of Antiquaries of London. When Sir William Hicks took over Lysons' excavations at Great Witcombe and revealed further features, he employed Thomas Lloyd-Baker to amend the site plan (Fig. 8.1).

In Elsie Clifford's report of 1954 are further references to features that have a major bearing on the interpretation of the building. Yet more information is contained in the site archive left by the last excavator, Ernest Greenfield, housed in the English Heritage store at Temple Cloud, Bristol (Wilson 1970, 294-5). These include letters between other antiquaries relating to various discoveries.

In this present text we use the original 'room' numbers as first applied by Lysons and then extended by later excavators. Where some of these 'rooms' were clearly corridors, thoroughfares and other compartments, we have sought clarity by applying other descriptive prefixes, where appropriate. All numbers, however, are those conventionally used throughout the exploration of the site.

Decorative stonework from Great Witcombe

In the archive store at Temple Cloud are significant architectural components from the site. These include fragments of marble and fine mouldings from architraves and entablatures. A lower half of a small, hollowed column (Fig. 8.2) and a rectangular stone panel with a central circular hole for a pipe offer evidence of a fountain. This, perhaps, was installed in an axial position with the 'well' at the foot of the portico (Fig. 8.5, 32).

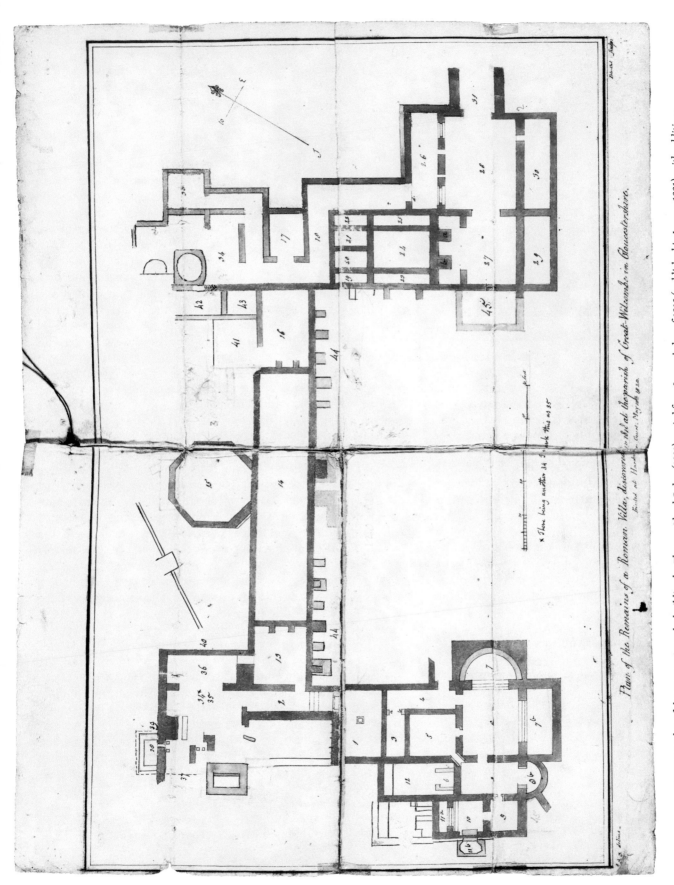

Figure 8.1. Plan of the Great Witcombe building by Thomas Lloyd-Baker (1820) copied from Lysons' plan of 1818 (published in Lysons 1821), with additions. (Copyright Lloyd-Baker Collection D3549/23/3/9. Reproduced by kind permission of Gloucestershire Archives)

Figure 8.2. The stepped base of the cantharus *fountain*

185). When, the drawings, reports and antiquarian letters are re-examined, we find architectural details that point to a very different interpretation of the nature and purpose of the Great Witcombe site.

Theoretical and artistic reconstructions

Over the past five decades several architectural reconstructions have been advanced at Great Witcombe. In 1977, David Neal speculated that there may have been upper storeys in the east and west wings of this building. He also suggested that the great frontal gallery had been covered by a pentice roof, pitched from a high rear wall (Neal 1977; McWhirr 1981). Given the relatively modest proportions of the wall foundation, we consider this unlikely.

Not cited by Leach (1998) are remains of up to three large open 'S' fretwork stone panels. Listed simply as 'balustrade' (Bevan in Leach 1998, 97), these decorative pieces are best described as a variation of the *acroteria* used to decorate pediments and roofs of sacred buildings. The best-preserved example tapers towards its top, while its base bears a V-shaped channel of the type otherwise found on stone roof finials (RCHM(E) 1976, pl. 28; Beeson, this volume).

A final item of note is a simple relief carving of a fish. This appears on an irregular oolite block that has been considered a possible *falsum* (Wright and Hassall 1973, 335). It is further discussed in this volume by Anthony Beeson.

Architectural Problems

Past restoration and physical reconstruction

Over many years, consolidation and reconstruction have been implemented at Great Witcombe. In some cases total rebuilding has been carried out. In other instances, important features recorded by Lysons, Lloyd-Baker, and Greenfield have been concealed or removed. All of these interventions now present an inaccurate rendering of the appearance of the building as first excavated. This problem has been identified in a survey and study by the Cotswold Archaeological Trust (Holbrook 2003,

Since 1977, further interpretations and reconstructions have followed. These include those of Graham Webster (1983), Guy de la Bédoyère (1991, 159-160), Bryn Walters (1993; 2000), J. T. Smith (1997) and a summary of Ernest Greenfield's excavations by Peter Leach (1998). Finally, an extensive survey of the site and its surrounding area has been made by The Cotswold Archaeological Trust (Holbrook 2003). In most of these studies, authors have empathised with Neal's objective in seeking a way to make the building work as a villa. Yet when we take the known ground plan as a working model, it is extremely difficult to see how this arrangement of modest rooms, passageways and baths could ever function as a comfortable country residence. The absence of obvious living rooms is particularly striking.

Reviewing an anomalous ground-plan

The building at Great Witcombe surrounds three sides of an elevated terraced courtyard. The central building, the north range, faces downhill where the upper terrace gives way to a poorly defined lower terrace. It is here that the disposition of further buildings and the configuration of a putative 'lower court' are poorly understood (Holbrook 2003, 196, fig. 9).

In his study on the social structure of Roman villas, published in 1997, J. T. Smith questioned the disposition of the rooms at Great Witcombe, commenting that 'the

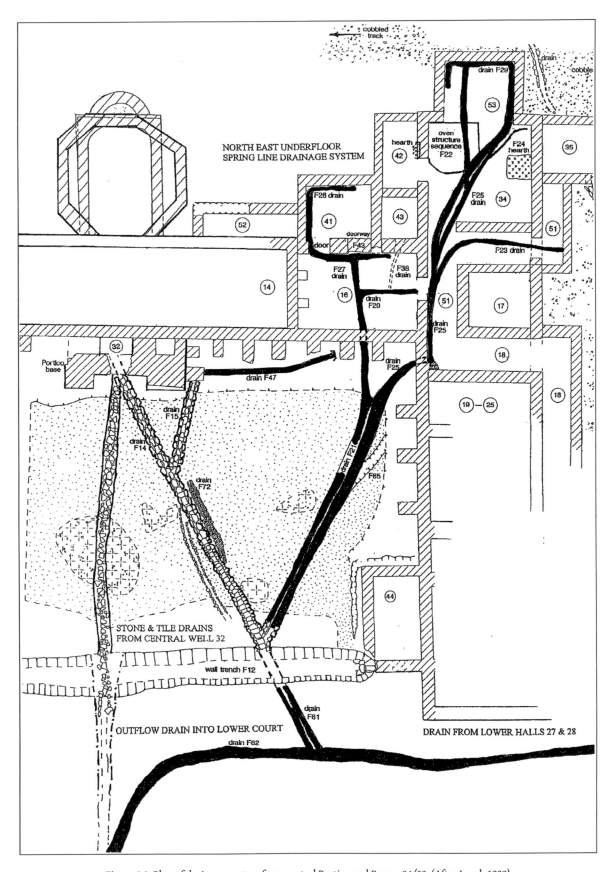

Figure 8.3. Plan of drainage system from central Portico and Rooms 34/53. (After Leach 1998)

way the rooms were used has never been worked out' ... 'Later, customary separation of function took place, the west wing incorporating the baths and the east wing some service function ...on the opposite side of the portico was a quite elaborate shrine' (Room 15).

Given the steep inclination of the hillside, it seems highly unlikely that a Romano-British landowner, even one with unlimited resources, would persist in contriving a home on such steep, waterlogged and unstable ground. Yet in the initial phase of construction the builders at this site were intent on cutting building platforms deep into the unstable clay of the hillside. Their early walls immediately demanded heavy supportive buttresses and required similar additions in the later phase. Just a little higher up-slope, the crest of the hillside offered a far better and safer position for the building, but this was ignored.

Determination to build at this location is certainly an important issue. In the case of a conventional Romano-British villa, two criteria would commonly guide its siting. A south-easterly axis would gain maximum daylight while a regular supply of water would serve the essential need of both residents and animals. At Great Witcombe both of these requirements are fulfilled, yet when significant architectural factors are taken into account, it is very difficult to accept that here was simply a functioning villa farmhouse showing somewhat unusual pretension. If it was not built as a home for a Romano-British landowner, then who designed this building and for what purpose?

Distinctive structural elements of this building include its impressive elevated central gallery, its elaborate projecting portico and its axially positioned tower or shrine. The west range is distinguished by two extensive suites of baths, one separated from the other by an enigmatic central 'shrine'. A further distinction is an absence of hypocausts from any other part of the building. Another peculiarity is the presence of two large latrines. Finally, the composition and design of the rooms in

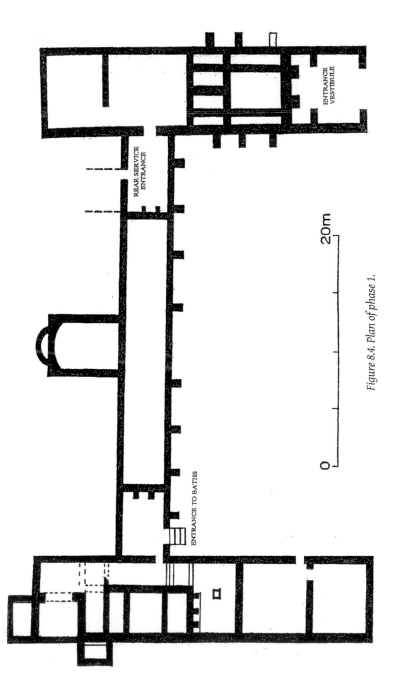

Figure 8.4. Plan of phase 1.

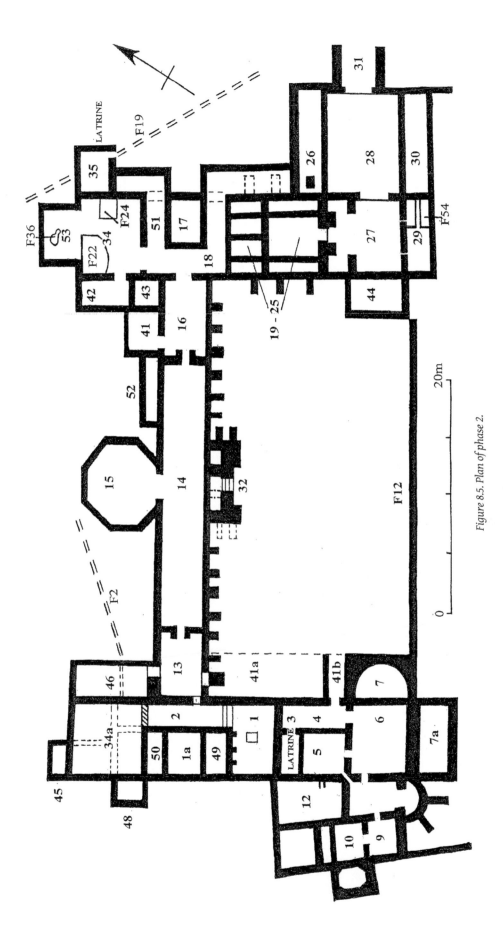

Figure 8.5. Plan of phase 2.

the east wing bear little resemblance to residential apartments.

In its first stone-built phase, the regular 'H'-shaped plan of this building is not remotely comparable with that of a conventional Romano-British villa. The layout of the building is rigidly formal, appearing more suited to public or ritual purposes (Fig. 8.4). Even after later enlargement, there are no hypocausts or mosaics as one might expect to see in the residential parts of a wealthy Roman house. The only exception is the bath suite, a facility that is so extensive that it appears better suited to a large social gathering. The central and east ranges of the building contain only cold-floored halls, small service rooms and passages. It is the interpretation that these apartments form a conventional Roman villa that now demands re-examination.

An abundance and over-abundance of water

Earlier writers have emphasised that the geology and hillside topography at Great Witcombe have presented this building with certain instability. When reporting on her 1938-39 excavations, Elsie Clifford pointed out that, 'The abundance of water must have added to the difficulties of the architect called upon to design so large a house on a sloping clay site' (Clifford 1954, 5). Much later, when reviewing the nature of this building, David Neal comments that 'from the start it must have presented very difficult structural problems...because the house was to be constructed on unstable subsoil prone to earth slip' (Neal 1977, 28).

The late Graham Webster, when discussing this site with the present writer, considered that the ground plan could not possibly function as a Roman country house. Similarly, in conversation, Ernest Greenfield also held doubts concerning the building's accepted interpretation as a villa. Despite these misgivings, it seems that, in published texts, there has been little enthusiasm for tabling alternative interpretations.

As at Chedworth, a spring-fed watercourse serves the site which at Great Witcombe passes beneath the central axis of building. Managing unpredictable spates of out-flowing ground water beneath a substantial man-made structure is an ambitious architectural undertaking. In this case it is surely tied to the essential siting and purpose of this building. At the centre of the lower terrace a further spring rose directly on the same central axis. It was towards this that all the drainage from the upper court was directed (Fig. 8.3, Rooms 14, 15, 34 and 53). It is at this point that we see that in both its primary and secondary phases of development, the whole building at Great Witcombe is better suited to the role of a water sanctuary.

Evidence for a lower court on the hill-slope

In this paper, discussion is focused on the visible apartments on the upper terrace, yet down-slope it is evident that a further array of structures has yet to be exposed. Surface indications of buildings were recognised here by the early excavators and, later, by Ernest Greenfield. In 1999-2000, these observations were confirmed when the land was contoured by Mark Corney and a Stratascan geophysical survey was conducted for English Heritage. A valuable overview of the surrounding archaeological features has been assembled by Neil Holbrook (2003, 187, fig. 4; 196, fig. 9). With its wet and unstable environment, it is difficult to see how this steep hill-slope could ever be chosen as a practical site for either a comfortable residence or a working farm.

Peripheral features

West of the exposed buildings, hillside ridges connect with a wide terrace. These appear to be ramps suited to the transportation of stone building materials to the site. Further west, another man-made terrace can be traced in the head of a deep combe in the High Brotheridge escarpment. Here, a waterlogged hollow, the springhead of the stream flowing south of the site, locally known as 'Tile Well', appears to be the source of the local Romano-British freestone. Some large quarried blocks still remain.

It has been proposed that in Antiquity the Celtic name of this minor river may have provided the name for nearby Roman town of *Glevum*. It is in the direction of Gloucester that this stream flows (Yeates 2009, 191-194). Today this stream forms the Horsbere Brook. This skirts the northern edge of the city before joining the upper reach of the Severn at Longford.

The terraced ridge descending the combe also leads towards a spring and a putative temple (see below; Holbrook 2003, fig. 9, site 14). This site is situated some 80 m west of the Roman buildings.

Reinterpreting the Main Building

Dating and building phases

The dating sequence for the construction of the main building is still subject to debate. Based on current assessments, it is possible that the first stone-built structure could have been completed early in the third century, perhaps in the period AD 200-230 (Fig.

8.4). Sporadic modifications may have followed before a second building phase saw major additions and remodelling in the first quarter of the fourth century, AD 300-330 (Fig. 8.5). In this discussion, particular construction dates are of lesser concern, our purpose being a reappraisal of the intended function of this building and its structural appearance during the first seven decades of the fourth century.

To aid the interpretation, we have divided the components of this building into three parts. This begins with the west range, first exposed by Lysons. The central range is next described and, lastly, the east range. The room and area numbers are those refined by Greenfield and maintained by Leach (1998, 4, fig. 4). These writers recognised five periods of activity on the site. In this present discussion our pertinent phases are just three: phase 1 – first stone building (Greenfield period 2) (Fig. 8.3); phase 2 – second extended stone building (Greenfield period 3). (Fig. 8.4); phase 3 – degradation stage (Greenfield and Leach's post-villa period 4).

The west range

In Room 1 in the west range (Fig. 8.6), Lysons exposed a central square *piscina*. This was surrounded by sandstone paving slabs. Three buttress-like projections against the north wall and a plinth-like feature adjacent to the entrance were also recorded. It was also noted that a pair of pivot-hinged doors had once surmounted a stone threshold of the doorway.

For Lysons, Room 1 appeared to have been 'appropriated to sacred uses'. He also noted that 'it did not appear to have communicated with any other'. This statement is misleading because access could be gained via a corridor (Room 2), to all parts of the building (Fig. 8.6, route R6) Although decay and collapse at the north end of this corridor has led to past misinterpretation, Lysons' plan clearly shows this interconnection. Where a low cross-wall survives at this north end, this appears to be no more than a threshold for steps to the upper baths (Rooms 13, 34a, 45, 46, 48, 49 and 50). A door in the east wall of the corridor (Room 2) connected with the front gallery of the central range by way of Room 13. From here access could be gained to the rest of the building and the courtyard via routes R1, R2 and R5. On-site, this route is no longer visible since Lysons' door into Room 13 has been obliterated by restoration masonry (Fig. 8.7).

A logical interpretation of the corridor (2) is a passageway ascending the hill-slope in two level stages, separated by steps. That steps in this passageway once served level sections is suggested by the horizontal composition of the painted wall panels seen by Lysons. Where extensive damage and disturbance is evident in this part of the building, it seems that much of this might be due to late Roman flooding after drainage arrangements beneath this building failed. This may have been exacerbated by conduit F2. This fed in water from the principal spring behind Room 15 (Fig. 8.6).

The lower baths in the west range (Rooms 3 to 12)

The lower bath suite was the first group of rooms exposed by Lysons. Most were very well preserved, although the two cold plunge pools (7 and 7a) had been damaged by down-slope ground movement (Fig. 8.8). The remaining rooms in this suite are well described and illustrated elsewhere (Clifford 1954, 18-22, fig. 2; Leach 1998, 5-11, fig. 5).

With no direct access from Rooms 1 and 2A, an enduring question has been how these baths were entered from within the main building? Lysons shows a door in the southeast corner of the corridor (Room 4), offering entry from the upper courtyard via a passage (41b) (Fig. 8.6, R4). Now a grassy hollow, this route is still discernible on the north side of the cold plunge (7). In his 1977 reconstruction, David Neal correctly places his entrance at this point, but suggests that these baths were intended for farm workers, who might approach across the courtyard alongside a wall from farm buildings in the opposite east range. Given that this is a lavish suite of baths, containing at least three mosaic floors (Cosh and Neal 2010, nos. 433.1-433.3), use by farm workers seems extremely unlikely.

Elsie Clifford sought a covered route to this entrance when excavating in the upper courtyard close to the west range frontage (Fig. 8.6, area 41a). Here she proposed that some form of tessellated passage or open veranda had led down-slope from Room 13 and alongside the front gallery of the central range. Although badly damaged, some tesserae offered some support for this conclusion.

Unlike the level area observed at Chedworth, the upper court at Great Witcombe appears to have retained a sloping elevation. Consequently, Clifford's external passage (41a) may have been stepped in the same manner as the passage (2) inside the building. The east range also had its own stepped arrangements. At the north end of the passage (41a), stonework with the appearance of a buttress footing is suspiciously larger than its counterparts. Lysons shows this to be an enlarged feature. Leach correctly considered this to be the base of a series of steps leading up to Room 13 (Fig. 8.6, R5; Fig. 8.7).

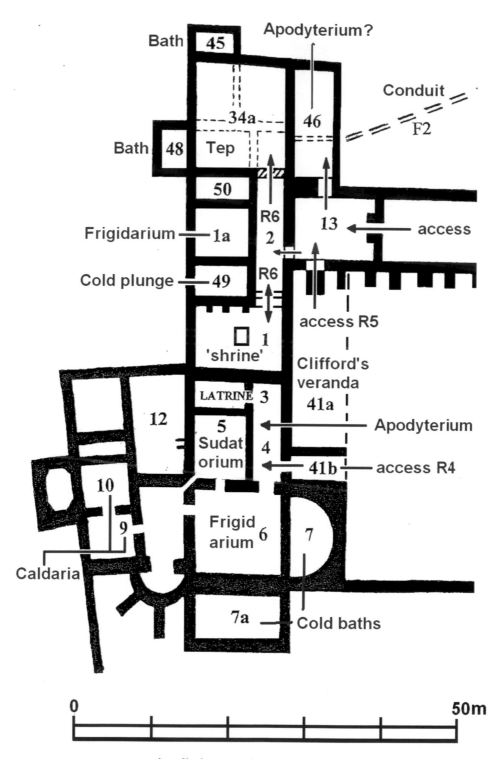

Figure 8.6. Plan of bath suites and access routes in the west range.

If Clifford's passage (41a) was truly the route to the west wing baths then Lysons' short wall on the northern side of his Room 41b must have been a structural retention from phase 1. If retained at a low level this could provide a threshold for the first step on to the ascending route to Room 13. The small space created at Room 41b might

then become an open antechamber into the lower baths. The internal corridor (4) might then be interpreted as the *apodyterium* (Fig. 8.6).

According to Clifford, Room 4 originally had a mosaic, or at least a fine red tessellated floor. Its south end gave direct access into *frigidarium* Room 6 (Fig. 8.6). In its north-west corner a further door led to latrine Room 3. Here, Lysons depicted two small square stones, perhaps intended to receive pivot hinges. Clifford and Greenfield's *apodyterium*, Room 5, with its own direct furnace, would have been too hot for a disrobing and dressing room. It is more likely to have been the *sudatorium*, rather than Room 10, as published in earlier reports. Rooms 9 and 10 appear to be *caldaria* of differing temperatures (Fig. 8.6).

Along the southern boundary of the upper court, Greenfield found a robbed-out foundation trench (Fig. 8.6, F12). In his reconstruction drawing, in 1998, Leach shows this as a full standing courtyard wall, although its height is completely unknown. At Chedworth, however, a similar single cross wall screened the upper court from the lower terrace. Eventually it was converted into an enclosed corridor.

While Greenfield's lost wall (F12), may have resembled the early arrangement at Chedworth, there is also an alternative. This would see no more than a low retaining wall, countering down-slope earth-movement without disrupting the view from below. One might also suspect

that originally, as at Chedworth, a flight of steps may have connected the upper and lower courtyards.

The upper baths in the west range (Rooms 1a, 13, 34a, 45, 46, 48, 49, 50)

During the first building phase at Great Witcombe, the upper baths in the west range (Fig. 8.9) were entered from the north-west corner of the courtyard by way of external steps leading up into corridor Room 13 (Figs 8.4 and 8.7). An internal route was also possible where the broad gallery gave access to Room 13 by way of some descending buttressed steps in the central range. These steps had undergone several modifications and had probably been constructed in the first building phase. Their use would have continued in building phase 2, when the baths were refurbished and combined with the lower baths via Clifford's external passage (41a). Past damage and decay in this part of the site has always made interpretation and dating of rooms difficult in the west range. In our study we offer a new reconstruction that gives particular attention to Rooms 34a and 46. We also offer a more logical interpretation of Room 13.

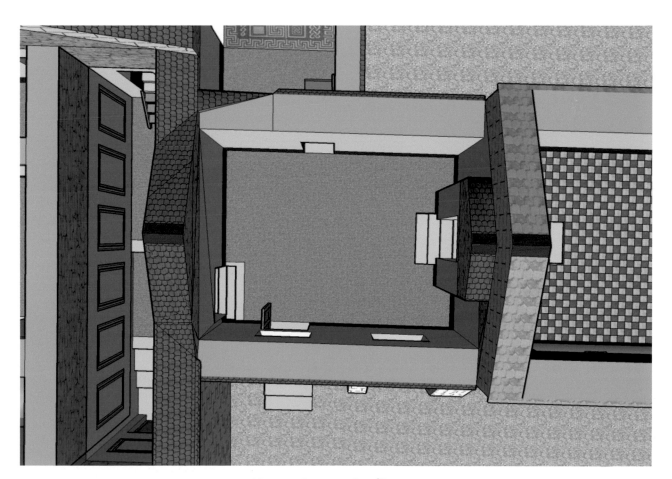

Figure 8.7. Reconstruction of Room 13.

In his 1977 paper, David Neal considered Room 13 to be a low cellar of no great significance, apart from supporting a higher floor accessing rooms above the baths from the level of the central gallery (14). On the evidence of the plans produced by Lysons and Lloyd-Baker, it is evident that Room 13 functioned as an essential antechamber connecting both sets of baths to the rest of the building (Fig. 8.7).

We have already suggested that during building phase 1, Room 13 would have been entered from steps in the corner of the courtyard. This route (R5) was maintained during building phase 2 when four doorways were in use in this room. On the nineteenth-century plans, just two of these doorways are shown. One in the west wall connected with the corridor (Room 2) (R6). In the north wall, a second doorway led up to Room 46 (Figs 8.1, 8.5, 8.6, 8.9, 8.10). Neither the door from courtyard (R5) nor the door to the broad gallery (Room 14) had been recognised at that time. They have since suffered from over-zealous restoration.

Leach assigned the upper baths to phase 2. This may have been partly based on a late third-century coin found beneath the lower floor surface of the tepid bath (Room 48). The coin could easily have been lost during a refurbishment of the bath in the late third/fourth century. This simple arrangement of baths originated from phase 1, and was interpreted as such by Greenfield in 1970 (Wilson 1970, 294-5).

In phase 2, access into the upper baths was possible from two doorways in antechamber Room 13. One gave access from the corridor (Room 2) (R6) and the other gave entry into Room 46 (Fig. 8.10). Lysons distinctly shows the second door centrally located in an exceptionally thick rear wall to Room 13. Today this is obscured by modern restoration, but its position is still betrayed by a faint irregularity in the stonework. It seems that this extra thick wall, shown on Lysons' plan, was intended to buttress higher ground where Room 13 had been cut back into the hill-slope during phase 1. The doorway

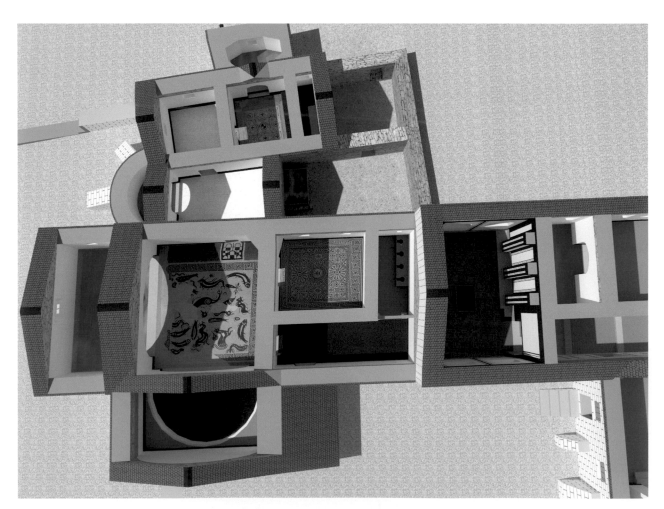

Figure 8.8. Reconstruction of lower baths.

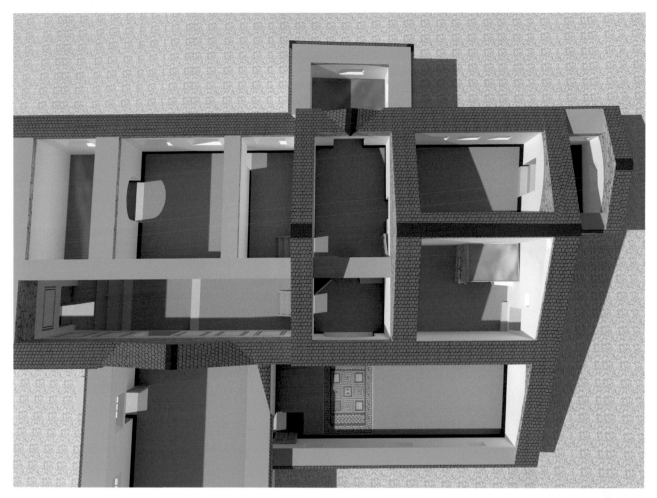

Figure 8.9. Reconstruction of upper baths.

Figure 8.10. Reconstruction of Room 46 arch into ante-chamber of upper baths.

would have been installed when Room 46 was added as an extension in the later third or fourth century.

After re-excavating Room 46, Elsie Clifford considered this to be an *apodyterium*. Here she recorded a 'concrete' floor, presumably *opus-signinum*. At its south end there was 'a mosaic strip 5 feet 6 inches in width' (Clifford 1954, 22). It seems, that this mosaic had been virtually destroyed in Antiquity because no mention of it is made by Lysons. (The mosaic depicted in our illustration (Fig. 8.9) is only a representation, based on a floor in Room 2 of the Colerne villa in Wiltshire). Lysons and Mrs Clifford both perceived a wooden division across Room 46, but Greenfield's excavation has since shown this to be part of his stone channel F2. This conveyed spring-water from behind Room 15 (Fig. 8.6).

In the upper baths, only a few fragments of surviving partition walls were recorded by Lysons and Lloyd-Baker. Greenfield identified signs of intense firing in the northeast corner of Room 34a. This appears to be the site of the *praefurnium* serving the *caldarium*. Here, the antiquaries plotted a large section of masonry adjacent to the north wall. This appears to be half of the supporting cheeks for a water tank above the furnace.

In the northern bath (Room 45), Lloyd-Baker recorded a hypocaust channel entering through the rear wall. This has since been filled with modern masonry. Until quite recently, the junctions of two small dividing walls could be traced in the exterior walls of Room 34a. Since these were recorded by Greenfield, the one against the north wall has disappeared. By connecting these points with fragments depicted by Lysons and Lloyd-Baker, it is possible to reconstruct a layout of rooms making up the lesser bath suite of the west range (Fig. 8.9). In this, the *tepidarium* in Room 48 acquires similar proportions to Rooms 1a, 49 and 50.

Despite the effects of earlier diggings and damage at Great Witcombe, successive excavations by Elsie Clifford and Ernest Greenfield recovered sufficient evidence to show that the west range was essentially dedicated to bath facilities and that, by the close of building period 2, these had been modified and expanded into two self-sufficient suites. In the lower baths we see substantial westward expansion and a generous provision of mosaic floors. In the northern suite we see modest external additions that appear to supplement an earlier range of unheated facilities comprising Rooms 1, 49 and 50 (Fig. 8.9).

While the provision of bath facilities at Great Witcombe is less generous than at Chedworth, the size and the twofold division certainly exceed the normal requirements of a conventional villa. Moreover, Chedworth's larger baths are well suited to substantial accommodation wings it was able to provide for its visitors. In some respects, it might be argued that while serving, perhaps, similar clientele, Great Witcombe was better suited to day visitors.

The octagonal tower and 'broad gallery' in the central range (Rooms 14 and 15)

During the early third century, a rectangular chamber occupied the prime axial position behind the grand gallery in the central range (Fig. 8.5). The rear wall of this chamber was curved to form an incipient apse. The centre of this wall gave way to an inner and smaller apsidal recess that appears to have been an internal water feature or *nymphaeum*.

During building phase 2, the first axial chamber was demolished to make way for a larger octagonal chamber or tower (15). Past interpretations have considered this chamber to be a *triclinium* where diners in this octagonal room might gain a view of the countryside (Holbrook 2003, 183). Given the narrowness of the door and the visual obstructions presented by the grand gallery and the *portico*, this has been an impractical suggestion. Yet when a full reconstruction is depicted (Fig. 8.11), it is evident that Room 15 was not intended to provide a vista of the landscape but was designed to become a vista itself. When viewed from the lower terrace, or indeed from the other side of the valley where Roman Ermine Street descends Birdlip Hill, Great Witcombe's tower was clearly the focal feature at this unusual perched site (Figs 8.11, 8.21, 8.22).

With water issuing from behind the rear wall of Room 15 there should be no doubt that this building was designed as a water shrine. This was implied by Smith in 1997. In two small drawings preserved in the library of the Society of Antiquaries, Lysons has recorded a small surviving section of an *opus sectile* floor that he had seen in Room 15 (Fig. 8.12). Here just sufficient survives to make a reasonable reconstruction of its original appearance (Fig. 8.13). When examining the same floor, Lloyd-Baker observed that 'the centre is imperfect but seems to have been finished off into a smaller octagon with triangular stones'.

We have already noted that in the Bristol archive store there are stone components suited to the construction of a water feature. When Lloyd-Baker adds that 'there is a drain beneath the floor leading to the well' we find further evidence that the management of water in this room was of prime importance. Part of this arrangement

Figure 8.11. Reconstruction of central gallery and octagon, an exterior perspective.

Figure 8.12. Reconstruction of internal view from the rear of octagon (Room 15).

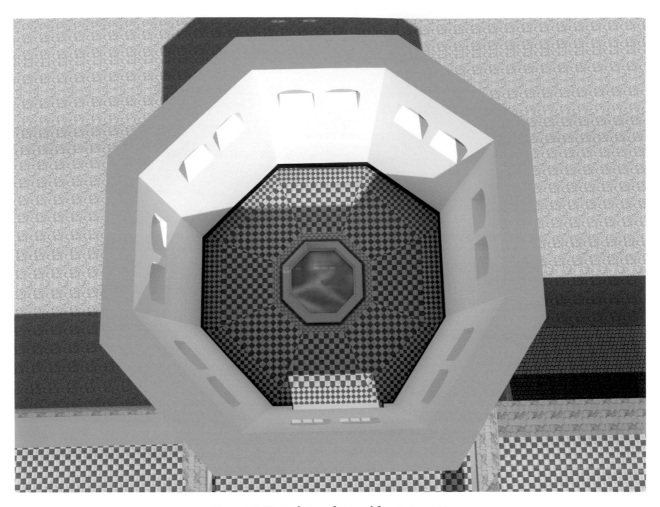

Figure 8.13. Vertical view of restored floor in Room 15.

appears to be an irregular rock-filled gully or 'French drain' contrived beneath Room 15. When Greenfield later examined this room, he found no trace of the floor, but he was able to record that the floor of the broad gallery (14) had most probably been at the same level and that both may have been finished with the same *opus sectile* surface. When excavating at the site with Greenfield, the author found a number of these tiles strewn across the courtyard. Here they seem to derive from past episodes of down-slope soil movement and winter flushes of groundwater.

The front gallery of the central range has been named both the 'grand gallery' and the 'broad gallery'. The width of its floor is approximately 4 m, a dimension that exceeds a conventional villa *porticus*. To maintain a level surface with tower Room 15, the floor of this gallery would have been elevated some 3 m above the upper courtyard. This would place this walkway substantially higher than the floors in the flanking chambers (13 and 16) necessitating descending well steps.

It seems that the walls at either end of the gallery may have extended upwards to provide gable ends for a ridged roof, rather than a pentice roof suggested by Neal. It would also be well within the capabilities of the builders to span a *porticus* 13 feet (4 m) wide with trusses. This could permit the gallery roof to sit on a lower and far lighter rear wall while projecting its roofline well above those of chambers 13 and 16. For the central section of the frontal gallery, our reconstruction proposes this differentiated roofline with stone-built gables supporting a pair of open fret *acroteria* as finials at each end (Fig. 8.11).

The portico and the stepped well in the central range (32)

During building phase 2, a massive portico was constructed over the central face of the broad gallery. Close to small steps fronting this structure the early excavators observed a sunken walled cavity, first perceived to be a well (32). This may have been in use during building phase 1 before being incorporated into the portico in phase 2.

There are several early references to this feature, which considered its role as a garden feature or a *nymphaeum*. When Lysons first uncovered the base of the portico it was already badly damaged and distorted by ground movement. His account refers to a 'cistern' being filled in with rubble. On-site, today, this is shown as a small tank. This interpretation is inaccurate, as the feature is composed of one of the original first period buttresses on its east side and a broader sidewall on the west. These two projections, then being linked by an outer cross wall, give the appearance of a hollow box-like chamber. In Lysons' day this seems to have been deliberately packed with rubble to create a large square pier in support of the portico. A similar construction seems likely on the other side of the well, but here the stonework has been extensively removed. Construction details are shown on Greenfield's plan (Wilson 1970, 294), and as bold black features in Holbrook (2003, fig. 9).

Figure 8.14. Reconstruction view of well 32, showing steps and pool.

At the centre of these two stone-built piers was a narrow portal with a short flight of steps, descending to a small semi-subterranean pool. This had been fed by Lloyd-Baker's drain, passing beneath the floors of Rooms 14 and 15 (Fig. 8.14). In the archive at Bristol is a smoothly finished stone panel with a central hole, which could have originated from the rear wall here. This water feature cannot be merely ornamental. Partly hidden from view, it was secluded yet accessible to those approaching the focal point of the site. Here was a further source of water, supplemental to the enshrined supply inside the towering octagonal chamber above.

It seems that the portico was structurally unsound soon after its construction. Frequent strengthening is evident, including further stone facing in support of the front elevation. Two broad buttresses were also added to the south-west and north-east corners, and yet two more were installed on the east side The foundation of the gallery wall still shows distortion caused by great lateral pressure exerted by the weight of this structure on an unstable and waterlogged slope. The later doubling of the number of buttresses reveals the persistence of this problem during building phase 2.

The constant strengthening of the portico emphasises its importance during the life of the building. Given the amount of water that could have risen at this focal point during periods of excessive rainfall, it is hardly surprising that its footings needed successive attention and reinforcement. The number of stone drains identified by Greenfield and the author emanating from here, emphasises the nature of this problem (Fig. 8.3).

During Greenfield's excavation, a pair of short captive pseudo-columns was found face down on the courtyard surface. These seem attributable to a fallen section of pilasters from the façade of the portico. A conserved example is illustrated in Fig. 8.15. Other items recovered from this area, and reported by Lysons, include fragments of Carrara marble embellishments. These suggest that the portico had an elaborate and prestigious finish. Here we might expect to see this structure pedimented and capped by a ridge roof connected to the crest of the gallery Room 14. Such a roof might then continue to connect with the forward face of the octagonal tower, creating a continuous cross ridge following the central axis.

Amongst the debris on the surface of the courtyard, Greenfield found fragments of white painted wall rendering bearing red relieving lines. Where this type of Roman external rendering is known elsewhere, its painted surface has been used to imitate regular courses

Figure 8.15. Attached dwarf column from front portico.

comprising the portico (13), the gallery (14) and the octagonal tower (15), had all been roofed with white oolitic limestone. This material could highlight this part of the building against a background of darker roofs elsewhere. This same roofing technique was employed at Littlecote Park in Wiltshire, where the roof of the mid fourth century triconchal cult building was highlighted in a similar manner. Here is another structure where the site plan and architectural embellishments distinguish it from buildings of everyday domestic use. Where *tegula* and *imbrex* tiles have been recovered at Great Witcombe, their conventional role as roofing material is less certain. Where observed *in situ* it is clear that many were used as construction material in hypocausts and the capping and flooring of drains.

For such an imposing structure, a stepped entrance on the central axis would have been expected. In France, the *naos/porticus* at Corseul offers comparison (see below; Fig. 8.23). In the case of the Witcombe building this was not possible due to the unstable and excessively wet nature of the ground at this point and which would have hindered maintenance of the drainage system, as well as obscuring the sunken well 32.

Taking an objective view of this evidence, what is actually revealed? Was this central section of the building an overtly ornate, but very cold dining and recreation area in a rich Roman farmhouse, or was this an impressive rural shrine set on an elevated podium? With white rendered walls from its foundation to its eaves, what impact did this building make on the surrounding landscape?

It seems that the entire central section of the upper building at Great Witcombe was created as an integral whole, its imposing portico presenting each visitor with a powerful reminder of classical architectural achievement. It seems that further emphasis was then added by the application of white rendering to the column-fronted gallery. Behind this façade, lofty windows in the high turret admitted light into the central octagonal chamber throughout the day. Here the light fell on a floor of *opus sectile* and a central octagonal pool or fountain. Beneath this tiled floor, excess water was guided down-slope to a secondary water source in the inner courtyard.

Antechambers and service rooms in the central range (Rooms 13 and 16, 41, 42, 43, 52)

Set either end of the broad gallery (14), Rooms 13 and 16 are both considerably lower than the gallery floor. With an estimated difference in height of some two metres, it has been suggested that here were once stairways

of ashlar blocks as revealed on one of the river-front buttresses at Weir Gardens near Hereford (Walker 1998, 6). Samples of this painted rendering remain in store at Temple Cloud, Bristol.

Evidence gathered from the courtyard during the Greenfield excavation indicates that roofs at Great Witcombe were covered with stone slabs. The majority of these were of old red sandstone, probably from the Forest of Dean. In front of the central range, however, quantities of cream/white oolitic roof-slabs and some Lias limestone examples were noted. Considering the elegance of other architectural embellishments, it is suggested here that the roofs of the central range, leading to upper storeys (Neal 1977, 34). We concur that both of these rooms housed important stairways but we are unconvinced that they ever served an upper storey.

On the original plans prepared by Lysons and Lloyd-Baker, two centrally placed internal projections are shown against the division walls separating Rooms 13 and 16 from the broad gallery (Fig. 8.1). Now rebuilt, they can still be seen. In the past, these projections have been interpreted as buttresses designed to support the massive raised foundation of the gallery (Neal 1977, 34; Leach 1998, 20), yet their size and orientation suggests that they would be virtually ineffectual for this purpose.

A more practical function for these features seems to be footings for steps leading up to the gallery floor. With doors in all other three walls of Room 13 it is evident that this was an active thoroughfare offering access to all parts of the building (Fig. 8.7). In Room 16, similar stairs would suit the door arrangements and a descent into the east range.

It seems that it was during Great Witcombe's first building phase that Room 16 was served by an exit door placed centrally in its northern wall (Fig. 8.5, F43). The chamber's eastern door then gave access to and from the central and eastern ranges (routes R3 and R7-9). During building phase 2, Rooms 41, 42, 43 and 52 were next constructed in the northern angle between these two ranges. This seems to have entailed the abandonment and blocking of door F43 and the construction of a new doorway into Room 41 (Figs 8.1 and 8.5). The eastern doorway in Room 16 still provided an essential connection between the two ranges. Where Room 52 has been added on the north side of the broad gallery, its narrow dimensions have suggested a further corridor (Neal 1977, 36: Leach 1998, 24).

The nature of the east range

When excavated, the rooms of the east range were mostly found to contain rubble, damaged floor surfaces and drains that had been left open and exposed by earlier excavations. During building phase 1 there can be little doubt that this part of the building was a well-built architectural match for its counterpart in the west range (Fig. 8.5). At that time, four distinct plan units can be seen in the east range. Here, the two southern units comprised an entrance vestibule (27) and a large compartment underpinned by close-set foundation walls (chamber/cavities 19-25). To the north, and prior to subsequent sub-division, two capacious rooms occupied the full width of the range (17/18/51 and 34).

The purpose of the underpinned section (19-25) was once thought to be a granary (RCHM(E) 1976, 73; Branigan 1977, 73; Morris 1979, 37, 189) but there are no signs of vents. Being filled with clay, the interstices between the walls are also unhelpful. The possibility of a high and heavy structure seems opposed by the instability of the hill-slope. The function of this part of the wing is resolved below.

The upper section of the east range (Rooms 17, 18, 34, 35, 41, 42, 51, 53)

During building phase 2, Room 34 was extended when an extension (53) was added to the north end of the east range (Fig. 8.16). We suggest that this enlarged and damaged room originally served as a *triclinium*. From beneath the floor of this dining room, two major drainage channels offered exit for rising and seeping groundwater during inclement times (Fig. 8.3).

Where water posed problems in this sub-floor, we suggest that conventional options for mortar and mosaic was discarded in favour of flagstones laid on a clay and fine rubble bedding. Although no stone flags survived *in situ* in Room 34/53, evidence of disturbed paving survived beneath the later hearths, in this room (Fig. 8.5, F22 and F24). Close to the latter, a further surviving patch has been previously considered to be 'possibly a remnant of floor foundation'. (Leach 1998, 24). Small rubble compacted in clay is a common bedding for flagged floors. As mortar under-bedding was not recorded in any of these rooms, flagged flooring seems more likely here during building phase 2.

If we are correct then Room 34/53 would have been better appointed in phase 2, as a principal room of the whole building. Its size was only exceeded by the grand aisled entrance hall (28). This would certainly suit communal or ritual dining requirements (Fig. 8.16). Unlike the multi-sided Room 15, its bi-partite plan is reminiscent of other apparent *triclinia* such as those at Kings Weston (room 4), Lopen (room 2) or the south range at Newton St Loe (Cosh and Neal 2005, 45, 248, 272). The substantial hearth F24, almost central to the east wall, might date to modification during or after building phase 2; this offering heat to what would have been a very cold chamber.

When first revealed in the nineteenth century, the large multi-phase hearth F22, set at the intersection of 34/53 was covered with collapsed stone *voussoirs*. These seem to have fallen from an arch formerly spanning the aperture between the larger and smaller bays of the room. This would be a typical architectural arrangement

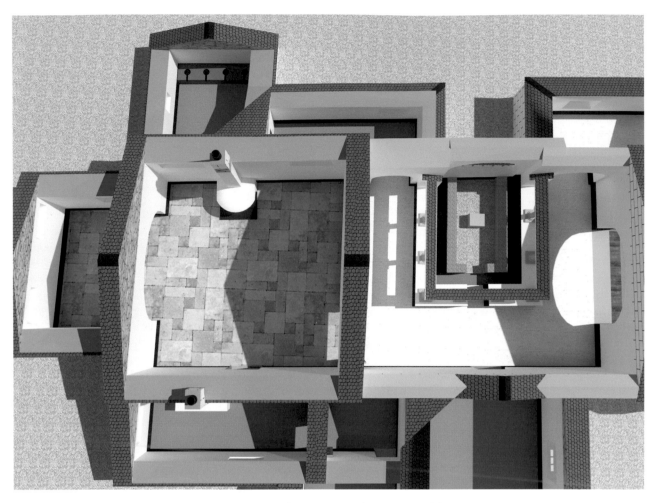

Figure 8.16. Reconstruction of interiors in north-east corner of the east range.

for a *triclinium*. Where there had been a door connecting Room 34 with Room 42, here, we suggest, was access to a side chamber appropriately equipped with a hearth or oven (Figs 8.1 and 8.5). Conceivably therefore, Room 42 had been the kitchen-pantry for the ritual dining room (34/53), with Rooms 41 and 43 providing ancillary kitchen storage and preparation space.

On the north-east side of Room 34, a square room (35) was identified by Greenfield as a large latrine. From here, a conduit-drain (Fig. 8.5, F19) led down-slope for at least 20 metres. Within its silt, toilet implements were recovered. A multiple latrine of this kind would be an unusual luxury in a British villa, but not in a public building catering for many people.

In order to create the *triclinium*, a new U-shaped corridor (51 and 18) partitioned the phase 1 room in such a way as to form Room 17 (Figs 8.5 and 8.16). This was now a small square space surround on three sides. The purpose for this has always been unclear, unless consideration is

given to the proposal put forward by David Neal (1977, 35). In this, he removes or lowers a section of the outer east wall, to create an open space and perhaps provide a view from his conjectured upper floor above Room 16. This modification would make the corridor (51/18) an open veranda or *atrium*.

Lloyd-Baker recorded an area of white tessellated floor in Room 18 and Greenfield recovered scattered *tesserae* in this area. In a number of respects Neal's proposal is very attractive, because it would only require a small removal of roof south of the *triclinium* to achieve a veranda. Moreover, this section of the building may already have been an open space in the phase 1 structure.

While we doubt the suggestion that a vista might have been gained from above room 16, we concur with the concept of an open veranda around a small garden court or *atrium*. We also recognise the advantage of admitting greater natural light into the building and contriving an open-air approach to both the dining area and the broad gallery. Where a door at the north corner of the veranda gave access to the latrine (35), this could offer welcome natural ventilation between this facility and the dining area. In the south corner a descending passage (18) led to the large, arcaded hall (28) on the lowest level.

The underpinned structure in the lower portion of the east range (walled cavities 19-26)

Narrow chambers, Rooms 19-25, have consistently posed difficult questions of reconstruction at this site (Figs 8.1, 8.4, 8.5). They are clearly not individual rooms but foundation supports for underpinning an internal structure of some kind. Lysons referred to them as being 'subterraneous, the spaces between them being filled with clay'. It is also rather modest in size; the sidewalls are far too narrow for a granary being 0.60 m and 0.80 m in thickness respectively, and why build it on such steep sloping ground? What is extremely significant is that this single structure is the only one not built on a levelled terrace cut into the hillside, but has been constructed intentionally - against the slope of the hill.

Attached to the extra-broad south wall of this underpinned structure, and contained with Room 27, are the remains of two large buttresses. In his reconstruction David Neal uses these to brace support for double storied living quarters. These he extends to a height of some 6-7 m. There being no cut terrace at this point, to support such a structure, we consider this to be an unlikely enterprise on such particularly unstable ground. This general problem is well demonstrated by distortion of the walls formerly visible, and now rebuilt, on either side of room 30. Similarly, on the opposite side of the courtyard, the plunge baths (7 and 7a) showed further ground movement. Greater instability is also evident below the façade of the broad gallery (14) where it seems that terminal collapse eventually occurred.

Upon excavation, the large buttresses in Room 27 and their attached wall, showed no sign of subsidence or collapse. This suggests that the underpinned structure had proved successful. We suggest that this was because this building had been relatively light in weight. Lysons states in his narrative, that the buttresses were of 'excellent masonry'. What did this mean? Were the stones of unusual dimension? Perhaps, like the columns along the broad gallery, these were of finer finish because they were internal and would be seen at close quarters.

We suggest that these internal foundations served as underpinning for a broad flight of steps, their low height being suited to the nature and slope of the hill. During building phase 1, these could have approached from the original entrance vestibule (27) where they might then be ascended to reach the upper part of the range. With suitable embellishment during building phase 2, these same steps might later serve the open veranda or *atrium* (Figs 8.5, 8.17, 8.18)

The external buttresses set against the east and west walls of this large stairway may have provided essential support against outward thrust from the roof above the stairs. This, we suggest, may have received little support from the internal cross-walls and timber piers within the body of the building. During building phase 2, construction of the descending corridor (18) necessitated the removal of two external buttresses on the east side of this structure. To compensate, it appears that the north wall of aisled Room 26 was specifically thickened to act as a brace against the outward thrust of the roof on this side.

The main entrance in the lower section of the east range (Rooms 25-31)

During building phase 1, the main entrance to the east range, and possibly to the whole building, was directed through the portals of a broad and imposing entrance in the south wall of Room 27 (Fig. 8.4). When found by Greenfield, this first entrance had been blocked up.

In our building phase 2, the principal entrance through the east range, was remodelled on a grand scale. With the original south entrance now blocked up, a new broad arched entrance is made through the east external wall of Room 27. This gave access to a finely finished arcaded hall, flanked by side aisles (Fig. 8.5, Rooms 26, 28 and 30; Fig. 8.18). This large reception space might be compared with the 'great fore-hall' of the 'guest house' at Lydney temple site. Here, Wheeler recognised a 'building devoted to public hospitality' (Wheeler and Wheeler 1932, 44-49).

Inside the aisled reception hall, there is evidence of a fine architectural finish. The base plinths for the arch piers had been chamfer-moulded, perhaps with the purpose of matching them with springers and arches of similar style. Amongst the rubble in this hall, Lloyd-Baker found fragments of a cornice and possibly a capital. In a drawing now held by the Society of Antiquaries, Lysons shows square columns with finely finished stone shafts. At a later date, these were incorporated into stone block walling, with portals fitted into the former west and east arches on the north side of the central aisle giving access to the now closed Room 26. The fine quality of this modification suggests this was undertaken before the site entered its degradation episode in our phase 3.

Figure 8.17. Reconstruction view from vestibule Room 27 to the main staircase.

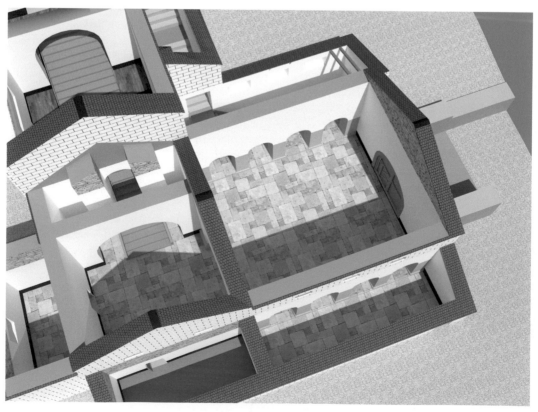

Figure 8.18. Reconstruction of interior of phase 2 aisled entrance hall.

Other modifications to the new main entrance may also be attributed to building phase 2. The addition of Room 44 on the west side of Room 27 extends the phase 2 reception suite into the courtyard (Fig. 8.5). Where the symmetry of this development matches the proportions of the baths on the opposite side of the courtyard, here we suspect the hand of a thoughtful architect. This arrangement might be compared with symmetry seen at Chedworth. With the addition of Room 29 we see similarly careful planning. Here the roofline of the aisle (30) seems to have been extended to complete the symmetry of the southern face of the east range.

Inside the arcade hall, on west end of the aisle (Room 26), Lysons records a heavy broken stone slab set some '7 feet' below his doorway at the mouth of the corridor (18). This, we suggest, may have been a base support for the turn of a right-angled timber stair giving access to the corridor (Fig. 8.19). Here, it seems, was a service route, by-passing the main staircase. Having attained height at this point, it seems that the rest of this corridor route was probably lined with gently stepped levels, similar to the corridor (2) in the west range.

Other Roman Buildings at Great Witcombe

A separate conventional villa

Sometime around 1820, Sir William Hicks uncovered a long rectangular building at the base of the hillside close to Horsbere Brook. This is sited some 90 m south-east of the main complex. Since this building has been relocated by Neil Holbrook's field survey, its outline has been interpreted as an apparent villa (Fig. 8.20, no. 8), perhaps with a projecting *triclinium* (Holbrook 2003, 197). The presence of this building and its putative identity reinforces our argument that the principal building at Great Witcombe was designed and used for a very different purpose.

A possible temple

A particularly interesting feature in the Holbrook field survey is site 14 (Fig. 8.20). This is sited some 80 m south-west of the main building where it occupies an up-slope position on the steepening hillside. At this spot, a large rectangular mound has produced Romano-

Figure 8.19. Angled timber stair and doorway in Room 26.

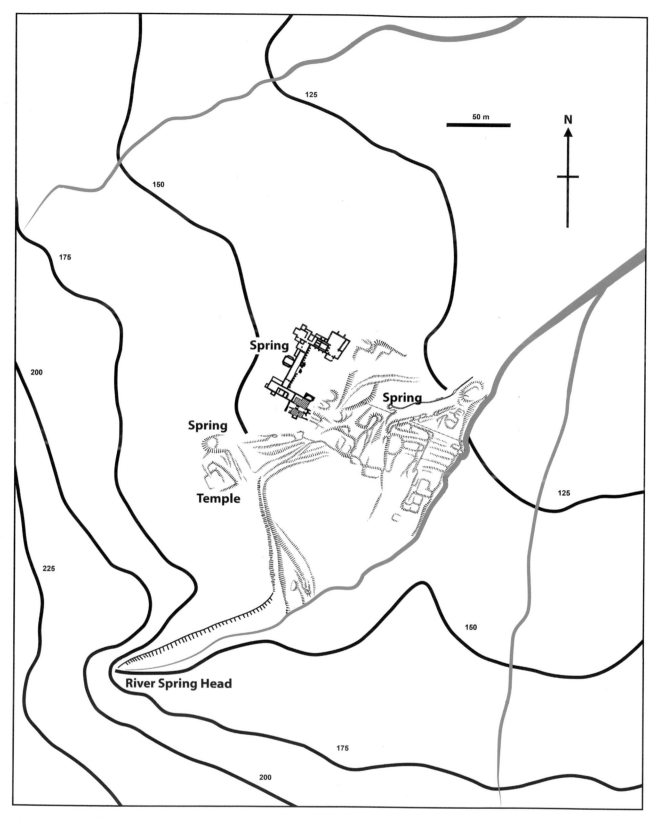

Figure 8.20. Roman buildings in the vicinity of the main complex at Great Witcombe. Main contour lines are shown except where they coincide with the survey detail. (After Holbrook 2003, Figure 9)

British building debris including large stone blocks and *tesserae*. For many years it has been suspected that here is the site of a substantial temple, perhaps akin to the 'Capitol' building at Chedworth (Holbrook 2003, 197). Traces of an adjacent wall, conforming to the alignment of this building, offer possible evidence of a *temenos*. The presence of this building adds further persuasion to the argument that, like Chedworth, the entire building complex at Great Witcombe was essentially built to serve spiritual needs linked to health-giving and curative properties attributed to a particular rising of groundwater.

Discussion

By the middle of the third century a simple hillside water shrine had been established. Constructed adjacent to a prolific spring-head it must have gained popularity and considerable patronage, as by the early fourth century it had been totally transformed with an elevated and towered octagonal hall, with an accessible well-head beneath its monumental central portico (Figs 8.21 and 8.22). The building was gleaming white with marble cladding, and roofed in pale oolitic stone slabs with rendered white painted walls. Its west range consisting of an extensive complex of baths, separated by a partially subterranean cult-like chamber. In the east range an impressive entrance was constructed with a broad stairway to elevate celebrants to the upper level, where a ritual dining room stood at the rear of an open garden *atrium*. Two substantial sets of latrines where provided, a facility normally reserved for public buildings. Overlooking the site to the west, was an almost certain temple beside the spring which supplied the building. Even further up the wooded west slope, the main spring-head for the river flowed from a marshy quarry from whence the stone for its walls had possibly been cut. South-east of the main building lower courts or gardens descended in terraces, flanked by other buildings probably incorporating accommodation

Figure 8.21. Reconstruction of the central octagon and portico of Great Witcombe in phase 2.

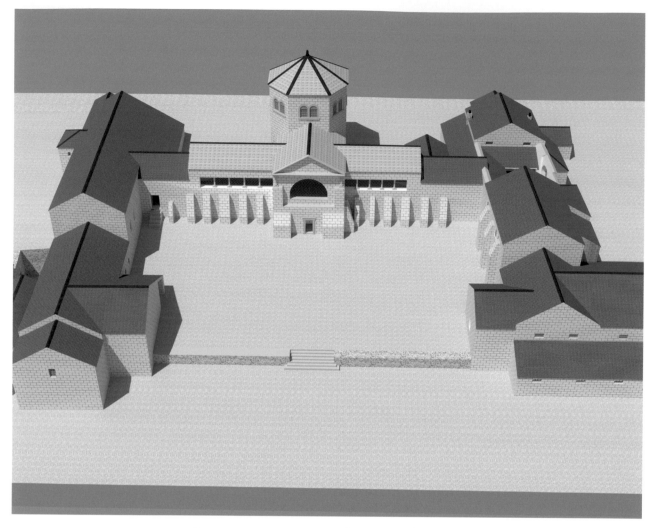

Figure 8.22. Reconstruction view of Great Witcombe, phase 2.

facilities for resident magi and far travelled pilgrims; with servant's quarters and workshops adjacent to the river.

By the time Theodosius outlawed pagan practices after AD 390, the site had already been abandoned to poorer farming families who debased the building by stripping out its finer fittings and used the decaying remains as humble dwellings and industrial facilities. The only positive agricultural implement to have been recovered from the site in over 200 years is a large iron coulter found by Samuel Lysons and presented to the British Museum by Sir William Hicks. By itself the coulter is insufficient evidence to argue for a farming villa; it may have been a ritual offering, or a surviving artefact from the later degraded farming community. By the early fifth century, the site was rapidly falling into decay, without regular maintenance its stone lined conduits silted

up and the springs, which were the original catalyst for its construction, sought alternative courses and undermined the human construction above, resulting in its collapse for future generations to untangle.

There is a striking similarity in the layout of Great Witcombe building with the temple complex at Haut-Becherel, Corseul (*Fanum Martis*) in Brittany (Fig. 8.23; Horne and King 1980, 399-400; Fauduet 1993; Bromwich 2014, 61-3; the writer is very grateful to Anthony Beeson for drawing my attention to this site). Though the Corseul structure is much larger, the octagonal *cella*, sited axially on a higher terrace to the rear of a broad *porticus*, with a projecting *naos/porticus*, provides a remarkable parallel to the upper court at Great Witcombe and both structures were elevated on cut terraces on the slopes of hills in order to be seen at a great distance. The plan of the building is complemented further by the right-

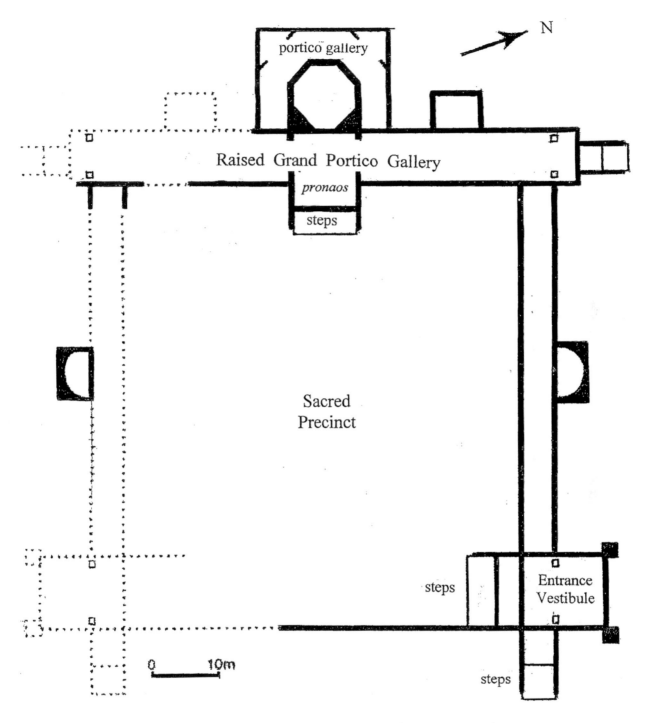

Figure 8.23. Plan of Fanum Martis at Corseul, France. (After Bromwich 2014)

angled entrance vestibule in the lower southeast corner of the courtyard, again as at Great Witcombe. There are also other structural similarities in the location and size of opposing chambers in the side wings. The Corseul building is an undisputed temple, possibly also linked with a nearby spring. The similarity in plan and topographical location of the Great Witcombe building argues convincingly that it too had a religious function. Acknowledgement is long overdue in recognising this site as one of the most spectacular and significant fourth-century rural shrines yet discovered from Roman Britain.

Acknowledgements

The writers would like to acknowledge the assistance and advice provided by the editorial team, especially Kate Adcock for constructive discussions, also Stephen Yeates and Harold Wingham for their invaluable assistance and information regarding the landscape features on the High Brotheridge escarpment.

References

Bédoyère, G. de la 1991 *The Buildings of Roman Britain,* Batsford, London.

Branigan, K. 1977 *The Roman Villa in South-West England.* Moonraker Press, Bradford on Avon.

Bromwich, J. 2014 *The Roman Remains of Brittany, Normandy and the Loire valley. A Guide Book.* Lucina Books, Peterborough.

Clifford, E. M. 1954 The Roman villa, Witcombe, Gloucestershire. *Transactions of the Bristol & Gloucestershire Archaeological Society* 73, 5-69.

Cosh, S. R. and Neal, D. S. 2005 *Roman Mosaics of Britain. Volume II South-West Britain.* Illuminata Publishers, London.

Cosh, S. R. and Neal, D. S. 2010 *Roman Mosaics of Britain. Volume IV Western Britain.* Illuminata Publishers, London.

Fauduet, I. 1993 *Atlas des Sanctuaires Romano-celtiques de Gaule, Les fanums.* Editions Errance, Paris.

Holbrook, N. 2003 Great Witcombe Roman villa, Gloucestershire: field surveys of its fabric and environs, 1999-2000. *Transactions of the Bristol & Gloucestershire Archaeological Society* 121, 179-200.

Horne, P. D. and King, A. C. 1980 Romano-Celtic temples in continental Europe. In W. Rodwell (ed.), *Temples, Churches and Religion in Roman Britain,* 369-555. British Archaeological Reports (BAR) British Series 77 (ii), Oxford.

Leach, P. 1998 *Great Witcombe Roman Villa, Gloucestershire, a report on excavations by Ernest Greenfield 1960-73.* British Archaeological Reports (BAR) British Series 266, Oxford.

Lysons, S. 1821 An account of the remains of a Roman villa discovered in the parish of Great Witcombe in the County of Gloucester. *Archaeologia* 19, 178-84.

McWhirr, A. 1981 *Roman Gloucestershire.* Alan Sutton, Gloucester.

Morris, P. 1979 *Agricultural Buildings in Roman Britain.* British Archaeological Reports (BAR) British Series 70, Oxford.

Neal, D. S. 1977 Witcombe Roman villa: a reconstruction. In M. R. Apted, R. Gilyard-Beer and A. Saunders (eds), *Ancient Monuments and their Interpretation,* 27-40. Phillimore, London.

RCHM(E) = Royal Commission on Historical Monuments, England 1976 *Ancient and Historical Monuments in the County of Gloucester, Volume One, Iron Age and Romano-British Monuments in the Cotswolds.* Her Majesty's Stationery Office (HMSO), London.

Smith, J. T. 1997 *Roman Villas. A Study in Social Structure.* Routledge, London.

Walker, G. 1998 The Weir Gardens, Swainshill, Hereford. *ARA The Bulletin of the Association for Roman Archaeology* 5, 5-6.

Walters, B. 1993 Great Witcombe. *Roman Research News* 7, 4.

Walters, B. 2000 Chedworth: Roman villa or sanctuary? *ARA The Bulletin of the Association for Roman Archaeology* 9, 10-13.

Webster, G. 1983 The function of the Chedworth Roman villa. *Transactions of the Bristol & Gloucestershire Archaeological Society* 101, 5-20.

Wheeler, R. E. M. and Wheeler, T. V. 1932 *Report on the Excavation of the Prehistoric, Roman and Post-Roman Site in Lydney Park, Gloucestershire.* Reports of the Research Committee of the Society of Antiquaries of London 9, Oxford.

Wilson, D. R. 1970 Roman Britain in 1969, I. Sites explored. *Britannia* 1, 268-305.

Wright, R. P. and Hassall, M. W. C. 1973. Roman Britain in 1972, II. Inscriptions. *Britannia* 4, 324-37.

Yeates, S. J. 2009 *A Dreaming for the Witches: A Re-creation of the Dobunni Primal Myth.* Oxbow Books, Oxford.

9

Chedworth, Gloucestershire: a question of interpretation

Bryn Walters and David Rider

Introduction

Over the past three decades, the most controversial re-interpretation of a Romano-British villa has been that put forward for Chedworth in Gloucestershire. It is one of the most popular and better-known Roman sites accessible to visitors in Britain, in the care of the National Trust since 1924. As a monument promoted for generations as a wealthy residential villa, it is understandable that the Trust would view an alternative interpretation with a certain amount of apprehension; consequently, the function put forward by the late Graham Webster and first published in 1983, literally fell on stony ground. Nevertheless, those who knew Webster and acknowledged his ability at recognising anomalies on a Roman site, respected his opinions and retained an open mind about his suggestions; allowing time and fresh evidence to prove or disprove a particular theory.

There is an unusual concentration of sites classified as villas in the immediate area of Chedworth, there being three within one and a half miles (2.4 km); Withington to the north-west, Compton Abdale to the north-east and Listercombe to the south-east. The first author's study of villa sites on the north Wiltshire downs surrounding Marlborough produced an average distance of between two and a half to three miles (4-5 km) between agriculturally designated villas (Walters 2001) and this pattern of distribution can be detected elsewhere in southern Britain. The close proximity of these villas around Chedworth implies that a smaller land holding was shared by all four sites. Unless, that is, the one at the centre, Chedworth, was not reliant on an agricultural economy.

The first author of this paper is well known for being an advocate of Webster's concept that the Chedworth building, and the satellite structures in its immediate hinterland, formed a sanctuary associated with healing (Webster 1983; Walters 2000), and would argue further that this had been the intention from its foundation in the second century. Investigations on the site over the past thirty years have done nothing to counteract this argument, and in point of fact, despite conflicting opinions, field work in recent years has added even further evidence to substantiate the proposal.

The existence of sanctuaries associated with thermal healing in Gaul and Germany is well documented (see Grenier 1960; Horne and King 1980; Budei 2016), some being vast and complex, with baths, hostels, temples and other infrastructure, such as Villards d'Héria (Nouvel 2011), Fontaines-Salées (Lacroix 1956; 1963), Alésia (De Cazenove *et al.* 2012) or Genainville (Mitard 1993). Examples in Germany include Heckenmünster (Binsfield 1969) and the smaller sanctuary dedicated to Apollo and Sirona at Hochscheid (Weisgerber 1975; see Wightman 1970). These sites exemplify the popularity for such facilities across Gaul and Germany; if such sanctuaries existed in continental Europe then why not in Britannia?

In relation to health and healing in general, four major schools of thought concerning health and medical matters were developed in the Hellenistic world and were imported into Rome, among which the 'Pneumatists' placed greater emphasis on the *pneuma*, or 'spirit', as the controlling factor (Cruse 2004, 48-50). Those who followed this doctrine believed in specific attention being given to the environment, the design and function of structural surroundings, water supply and bathing particularly. 'Methodism', championed by Asclepiades of Bithynia in the later years of the Republic was probably the more dominant ideal, being more attractive to the Roman psyche by regulating the consumption of food and wine, massage, gentle exercise and again bathing (Summerton 2007, 7). Such settings and pursuits may have been extensively displayed at Chedworth and Great Witcombe (see Walters and Rider, this volume).

Communal healing facilities, in the manner of present-day hospitals, did not form part of Roman life, the closest comparison being a *valetudinarium* in military bases (Jackson 1988, 134-7); individuals initially seeking consultations from a doctor or physician at the practitioner's urban residence. This does not rule out however that healing or recovery centres existed in more pleasant and peaceful rural environments, in line with the doctrine of the 'Pneumatists' cited above, well away from the hustle and bustle of city life. In Britain, the Lydney temple complex in Gloucestershire, founded for the cult of Mars Nodens, has long been acknowledged as such a healing sanctuary. It is unlikely that it existed in isolation, and similar institutions must have been established at many other places in the Romano-British landscape, but some examples have been misinterpreted as elaborate villas.

When Graham Webster produced his paper on the revision of a number of villa reports and interpretations in the classic volume *The Roman Villa in Britain*, he expressed the need to reassess the chronology originally proposed for a number of villas, pointing out that in certain cases historical, sociological and architectural aspects were lamentably defective (Webster 1969, 217), and in several cases this argument is just as relevant today. It is now recognised that the extensive expansion of the Chedworth building took place over a much shorter period of time around the turn of the third and fourth centuries, as opposed to Ian Richmond's assessment of gradual development over a longer period. Using evidence acquired since Richmond excavated at the site between 1958 to 1965, it is time to undertake a more analytical approach, to stand back from what has been a traditional interpretation of the remains at Chedworth for over 150 years, based on the outdated understanding and opinions of nineteenth and early twentieth-century investigators, unable to comprehend interpretative evidence; even though it was available at that time but not recognised or fully understood. As with any field of scientific research, consecutive specialists proposing a reassessment of evidence is normal procedure, and re-interpretation of archaeological sites is not exempt from this rule.

Considerable damage to the Roman remains at Chedworth in the seventeenth and nineteenth centuries, as the result of changes in land-use, stone-robbing and building, has undoubtedly destroyed large areas of previously stratified archaeological contexts. As a consequence, evidence for dating specific changes and identifying function is often unsatisfactory, and over the passage of time, earlier interpretations have not been sufficiently challenged or reassessed by succeeding scholarship.

With the exception of Webster in 1983, it is noticeable that there has not been a concerted attempt to reassess or challenge the conclusions advanced by Richmond since his paper on Chedworth was published in 1960. Subsequent articles and particularly the periodic guide-books to the site have simply maintained Richmond's suggestions as definitive for over 55 years, with little attempt at identifying alternative functions and disposition of the principal rooms, or the periods that subsequent changes were made to them. On many villas, after the main period of prosperity, usually the first seven decades of the fourth century, there came

a period of decline, usually post-370, when parts of buildings become adapted to the requirements of lower status occupants. Further degrading often subsequently took place in the early part of the fifth century with what used to be referred to as 'squatter' occupation. This decline certainly occurred at Chedworth, but has not been adequately identified owing to archaeological stratigraphy being disrupted or removed before the early twentieth century. Investigations and attempts to restore as much of the walling as possible in the nineteenth century, in order to smarten up the remains for visitors, has masked or removed important structural details; making phasing and functional interpretation problematic for later more highly skilled excavators. There are walls and other features shown on earlier published plans, along with areas of nineteenth-century consolidation, which do not belong to the extensive early fourth-century building. Similar problems have been identified on the site at Great Witcombe nine miles (12 km) to the west. This is a serious issue which has to be recognised, as such errors and structural remodelling lead to misinterpretation.

After the original exposure of the dual-courtyard building by James Farrer (Farrer 1865), acting on behalf of the owner, Lord Eldon, and its subsequent consolidation for public display, very little investigative work took place. In the early 1920's Welbore St. Clair Baddeley strove to preserve the site, raising sufficient funds for its purchase and transfer to the National Trust. Simultaneously, he published a romanticised article on rural life in Roman Britain for the *Illustrated London News*, basing it at Chedworth as a promotional feature (Baddeley 1924). Baddeley's interpretation was more imaginative than scholarly, incorporating the mistaken interpretation of G. E. Fox for example, in seeing the north baths as a *fullonica* for degreasing wool in fulling tanks and dyeing cloth (Fox 1905, 212-13), despite the evidence of mosaic floors and other sophisticated architectural embellishments. Beds of Fullers Earth used in such processing, which may have stimulated Fox's suggestion, overlie the oolite 100 feet (30 m) above the site. Many of the sentiments expressed in Baddeley's text survived in the collective conscientious of visitors and later students for many years, enduring to a certain degree ever since with the interpretation of the site as a wealthy villa, which is unfortunately now inextricably bonded into the archaeological literature. Shortly after the National Trust took over ownership of the site, Baddeley conducted his excavation of the temple originally identified by Farrer, approximately 800 yards (730 m) south-east of the villa's main entrance (Baddeley 1930).

With the exception of Lewis' comments (Lewis 1966) and Webster's 1983 reference to this monumental building, it has been virtually ignored, despite its significance in understanding the development of the overall site. Its proportions and structural details place it among the most impressive rural temples from Roman Britain and it would have dominated the approach to the Chedworth 'villa', implying that it must have held a prominent role in the function of the whole complex (see Fig. 9.1 for position, and reconstruction drawing, Fig. 9.13). Baddeley's account of this 'Upper Valley Temple', set into the hillside above a bend in the River Coln, contains a number of minor misconceptions and his text is difficult to unravel in places, but details can be elucidated to create a reasonable architectural impression of the building at the peak of its prosperity (see also Beeson, this volume). Baddeley recovered early samian pottery along with scattered coins including what he suspected to be a

small hoard ranging from Trajan, Hadrian and Marcus Aurelius, through to Julia Mamaea and Maximinus Thrax. If the coins had been offerings and concealed, this could indicate, along with the samian ware, that the probable origin of the temple dates from the mid-second century, the same period suggested for the structures forming the first phase of the adjacent 'villa' (Richmond 1960; Goodburn 1979/89), which would strongly suggest a complimentary reason for constructing those buildings also. The last coin in the hoard, of AD 235-8, implies the temple was still active in the mid third century, less than three decades from the 'villa's' huge expansion. What has to be questioned is why was such an imposing temple built so far from an urban community? Was it simply to grace the approach to a relatively small and insignificant second-century rural residence? A more detailed account of this site is given below (see The Satellite Buildings, 'The Upper Valley Temple').

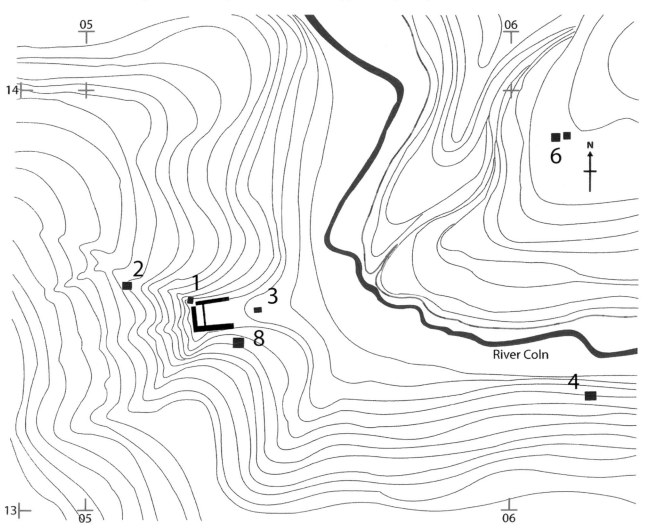

Figure 9.1. Chedworth valley, showing landform contours and the River Coln, and the location of satellite sites.
Key: 1, the nymphaeum; 2, 'The Capitol'; 3, 'The Lower Valley Temple'; 4, 'The Upper Valley Temple'; 6, Yanworth 1; 8, Chedworth Woods Enclosure. For other satellite sites, see text. The scale is provided by the National Grid kilometre tick marks at top and bottom.
(Drawing: Nich Hogben)

Farrer also identified the hillside building, which he called 'The Capitol' above the Chedworth baths in 1864 (Fig. 9.12), 'partially clearing several small rooms'. Baddeley proposed that it had been 'laid out as an octagon with eight internal cisterns around a *columbarium*', adding that it had been the chief water supply to the villa. It has been suggested to have been a mausoleum in the 2012 guide to the villa, as well as more recent publications (Esmonde Cleary 2013; 2014). This important building is also discussed in more detail below (see The Satellite Buildings, 'The Capitol').

In 1954, Eve Harris identified the latrine at the rear of the south wing (Rutter 1957), which was not fully excavated until the Trust appointed Ian Richmond to undertake a series of small excavations from 1958 until his death in 1965. More detailed work re-commenced under Roger Goodburn from 1977 until the start of the 1990's and with Philip Bethell, the property manager of the site, between 1994 and 2006. More recent excavations in 2009-10, in advance of constructing new public facilities over the west wing, revealed structural details that could explain certain features incorporated within the building (see

plan, Fig. 9.2). In the foundations of the west wing, courses of stone blocks at the base of the thicker rear wall in room 7 curved downwards, not as subsidence, as layers of stone blocks immediately above were perfectly horizontal; the lower stones being intentionally fitted into an earlier surface depression. It is likely that the central ancient spring channel descending the west slope referred to above, originally flowed where the centre of the west wing was to be built; consequently, broader corrective wall footings became essential.

Such additional bracing of Roman foundations is relatively common where builders encountered faults and hollows in the ground, but above the corrective foundation, the upper courses are normally reduced to the same dimension as the rest of the building. The additional thickening of the upper east and west walls to Room 7 implies that it was intended to build to a greater height at this point, even as early as the second century, despite the risk of structural weakness created by the possible conduit; the likelihood for which is resumed below when assessing the entrance into the upper court. Also, in 2010, immediately adjacent to the suggested

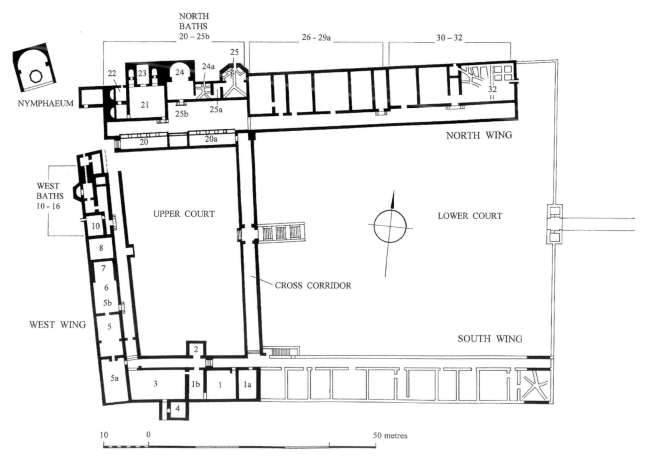

Figure 9.2. Plan of main site, c. AD 300-360, showing the suggested disposition of rooms and structural features.
(D. Rider, L. J. Thompson)

central water course, the excavations revealed the tilted foundation of the wall that made up the intervening corridor (Room 7), which no doubt had subsided owing to an unstable location. Depicted on earlier published plans of the fourth-century building, this wall must belong to a phase associated with the later fourth-century rooms, published as 5b, 6 and 7, which in the early fourth century was a single much larger bi-partite chamber around 36 feet in length (11 m), which it had been since the original phase in the second century (see below 'The West Wing').

In 1998-99 GSB Prospection Ltd conducted geophysical surveys in the upper half of the field east of the lower courtyard (Falfield), the intention being to locate the much sort after range of buildings associated with a 'home farm' establishment. Results were not forthcoming, no significant agricultural structures in a lower third court were located, a case perhaps for arguing that 'absence of evidence' implies 'evidence of absence'. It would appear that the well-known Roman courtyard complex had not therefore relied on a home-based farming economy for its upkeep during the period of its extensive early fourth-century redevelopment, and almost certainly, even from its earliest foundation. A further Sheffield University survey was undertaken in 2001 locating major features, the data for which has subsequently been lost.

What the 1998-99 survey did identify, was the known lower courtyard had been enclosed with a wall extending east of the main building, with a possible gate house aligned on the inner entrance between the upper and lower courts (Salway 2008). Remarkably, this is precisely what the artist Forrestier depicted in his Gothic illustration for Baddeley's article in the *Illustrated London News* in 1924. That a Roman building existed, approximately 150 m east of the recently identified entrance has been known for some time, and is included in the 1976 RCHM(E) Gloucestershire inventory as Chedworth building 3. Apparently, it was not incorporated into the 1998-99 survey, but had been indicated as a large circular feature on the 2001 Sheffield survey. A more recent programme of geophysics undertaken in 2012 by the National Trust on the south side of the Falfield, has identified at this location, what has been interpreted as the broad foundation of a large circular building with a smaller square structure on its west side (Papworth 2012). The 2012 survey has produced a palimpsest of further significant features and data, not necessarily contemporaneous, but nonetheless having a bearing on the interpretation of the complex. What should be expected outside the lower walled court are facilities accommodating visitor's mode of transport; a

shelter for horses and wheeled vehicles. The 2012 survey has identified what is interpreted as a large embanked enclosure parallel to the approach road on its south side and just in front of the main entrance. This might be interpreted as a paddock for visitors' horses, along with a small adjacent building which could have provided accommodation for grooms.

The lower entrance had been approached by a trackway flanked by ditches, leading up the slope from the river, and onwards through the lower court along a cobbled path, undoubtedly aligned on a flight of steps leading into the upper court, via a four-way semi-monumental arch set into an elevated corridor. Dominating the west wing, a towered projection rose as an architectural focal point (Salway 2008), Indeed, a tower is a real probability here, as suggested by the thicker east and west walls of Room 7 (Fig. 9.3).

A feature that remains enigmatic is the deviation of the axial alignment into the building upon reaching the higher courtyard. Why was the upper entrance off-set by approximately three metres to the north, and not aligned more formally on the entrance into the west wing as might be expected? In his essay on social structure, J. T. Smith identified this off-set entrance in his discussion on Chedworth, pointing out that it had been deliberately planned that way in order to emphasise the position and importance of the 'shrine' on entering the upper court. Inferring that when passing through the cross corridor, a clear visual perspective towards the *nymphaeum* would be gained through the gap, intentionally left between the two bath suites of the west and north wings. Smith recognised the *nymphaeum* as a focal point, signifying the importance of the source of the water flowing into the building (Smith 1978). A far better view of the *nymphaeum* would have been gained however, if the entrance had been maintained on the central axis, or even more so if off-set 3 m in the opposite direction to the south, this strongly suggests an alternative reason for the entrance being positioned where it is. If the curved foundation of Room 7 was intended to brace the wall set into a former stream bed, such a channel would have combined with the other two springs continuing down the slope, creating an even deeper and broader depression where an axial central entrance should be. Consequently, the builders would have foreseen a potential structural weakness for any steps set axially from the lower court. This could be the reason why the entrance is set off-centre. Placing the steps three metres south of the central axis might have put them over an even deeper depression. Therefore, the present location a little to the north on more solid ground, just above the hollow, was seen as the better

Figure 9.3. Computer-generated reconstructed view towards entrance tetrapylon *from lower court steps ('The High Place').*

option. Consequently, Smith's observation was only partially correct, as undoubtedly the upper court was designed to incorporate a view towards the *nymphaeum,* semi-mysterious and elevated on higher ground behind the two bath suites (Fig. 9.5). From the upper court a view of both water shrines, *nymphaeum* and 'Capitol' was undoubtedly achieved, emphasizing the significance of the source of the water and strengthening the interpretation of the sites function, even from as early as the second century.

Had there been no special status for the *nymphaeum* it could easily have been screened by the two bath suites being conjoined to form a double *thermae,* as at Great Witcombe, and fronted with a complete quadrangular *porticus* around the court. In addition to the two water shrines, and the 'Valley Temples', the other lesser buildings surrounding the 'villa' should be brought into the equation when considering the real purpose of the

complex as a whole. These are discussed below under 'The Satellite Buildings'.

This paper was complete and with the publishers when the Britannia monograph on Chedworth was published in the summer of 2022 (Esmonde Cleary, Wood and Durham 2022). It was thus too late for its conclusions to be discussed here or fully incorporated. In important respects, however, the authors have come to rather different conclusions from the available evidence discussed in this paper.

A functional reinterpretation

Of paramount importance in formulating a logical interpretation for the Chedworth complex is an appreciation of its topographical location. The principal dual-courtyard building had been constructed, from its beginning in the second century, on artificial terraces cut back into the limestone slopes at the head of a small narrow valley aligned 8 degrees north of due east. Luxury villas are predominantly aligned south-east or south. There must have been a significant reason, for selecting and modifying the landscape, at considerable physical and financial expense, in order to accommodate this building at this particular location. Immediately behind the 'villa' to the west, the valley rises with a steep slope creating a natural trapezoid vale formed by three distinct ancient water-worn combes, which converge to the point later adapted for the construction of the villa's west wing (Figs 9.1, 9.2, 9.15). In all probability, these three spring-lines were still moderately active at the commencement of the Roman era and were the catalyst for selecting the site for its intended function. Adopting the unconventional axis to the east-north-east may also have been intentional, as it is aligned on sunrises during the months of mid-summer. In the ancient world, water rising from the depths of the earth, combined with the light and warmth of the sun, were recognised as essential elements for the creation of life and the sustainment of health.

The following is a reappraisal of the extensive expansion and architectural appearance of the building in the first half of the fourth century, with an emphasis on its intended purpose. Contra to what has been maintained in earlier publications, fresh interpretations can be put forward for significant areas of the building for this period, and also the function of some of the rooms described in the sequence of guides to the site, as well as the inventory published by the RCHM(E) (1976, 24-8). On the plan of the dual-courtyard building (Fig. 9.2), many of the excepted 'residential' rooms are large for a 'house', while outwardly the overall composition is very simple, lacking the external architectural aggrandizement which is seen on wealthy fourth-century residential villas elsewhere in south-western Britannia, there is only one large polygonal apse (Room 25) and one internal apsidal bi-partite room (24), both in the north baths. Externally there are no elaborate late Roman exotic rooms, such as those found at Keynsham near Bath, Dewlish and Frampton in Dorset, or Littlecote, Wiltshire (see Walters 1996), the whole building appears utilitarian, resembling the plan of a large *mansio*. If it were not for the elevated *tetrapylon* leading to the upper court, the tower above Room 7 and the pillared frontage of the north baths, outwardly the complex is unexceptional. By contrast, the interiors incorporated an air of formal elegance, expressing a more public function. The disposition of the rooms in the west and north wings were similarly conceived, each containing a range of baths, large function rooms, a kitchen and large bi-partite feasting room at one end. Both buildings having the same

facilities suggests a division in activity, and not separate residential wings for an extended family, which for too long has been an established interpretation. If we are looking at a sanctuary associated with gods of healing, such rooms set aside for activities external to formal events are to be expected. These would have included a reception area which might have incorporated a daytime refectory, and there would have been other chambers at which pilgrims could attend religious seminars or meditations supervised by a resident *magus* or itinerant priests; or consultations with a physician, a *medicus*, or local apothecary practised in the use of herbal remedies as part of the anticipated cures. There are rooms in the north wing which would have been suitable for such purposes.

The upper court

It is paramount to understand the marked division and design of the upper court, in order to appreciate the function of the complex as a whole. Initially there must have been a huge financial commitment to create this semi-secluded terrace by building up the underlying rock and subsoil to remove the natural slopes of the ground. Excavations in 1979 demonstrated that an earlier single-walled division for an upper court had much later been substantially rebuilt to incorporate an enclosed corridor linking the south and north wings (Grew 1980, 384). This incorporated massive stone blocks, undoubtedly the retaining foundations essential to support the weight and pressure created by the huge amount of infill levelling the surface. In the spring of 2000, excavations confirmed that there had been no formal garden, the open area initially being grassed over had later been covered with stone slabs and gravel, suggesting the grass had been difficult to maintain; no doubt caused by the tread of many people creating a muddy surface.

When assessing the design of the upper court, it is obvious that there was never a vista down the valley to the east. Contrary to references expounding the setting of Chedworth as having fine landscape views down the valley (Richmond 1960; Esmonde Cleary 2014), from the west wing and any point within the upper court, the view down the Coln valley would have been totally obscured by the walls and roof of the cross-corridor. Upon arrival and closure of the almost certain paired entrance doors, then stepping into the court through the arched entrance, a visitor would have been confronted by a partially columned courtyard, strikingly similar to a medieval monastic cloister. The upper terrace was designed to be secluded and dominated by a singular view to the north-west, focused on the water-shrines, *nymphaeum* and 'Capitol' (Fig. 9.5). Certainly, in the first

Figure 9.4. Reconstruction view looking north over upper court from above Room 2.

half of the fourth century, the design of the building implies that it could not have been the private residence of a wealthy landowner. Dominating the entire north end of the upper court lay the elaborate larger baths, designed for the main intention of the site in general.

By adhering to Richmond's initial interpretations, the most recent publications on the villa seriously misinterpret the north baths, and reduces them to less than half-size. The east section containing Rooms 24, 25 and 25b is suggested to have been the main reception rooms, compensating for there being no axial *aula* on entering the west wing as on other 'residential' villas (Esmonde Cleary 2012; 2013; 2014). Considering the capital investment expended on this large building, if a wealthy owner had intended to create an impressive residence incorporating a suite of formal reception rooms, why were the original second-century rooms in the west wing retained and not dismantled, as happened to other parts of the second-century buildings in the north and south wings? The conclusion has to be that the established function of Rooms 5 and 5b-7 had been

too important for them to be replaced, so they were extended and made more elaborate instead; in much the same manner as that adopted for the axial room at Great Witcombe. The visitors' reception area to the building is discussed below.

The main entrance

The upper cross corridor

At the beginning of the fourth century, entry must have been gained by a substantial flight of steps, now buried beneath the site museum. On ascending from the lower courtyard, the façade of the cross-corridor and its arched entrance would have been visually impressive, but also rather intimidating, being silhouetted against the sky as 'the high place'; obscuring from view what lay beyond (Fig. 9.3). Its east wall would have been a solid construction fitted with small windows, screening the interior passage from the cold easterly winds and rain, and possibly matched the façade of the south wing. The steps gave access into a towered, four-way arched

Figure 9.5. Summer view from the upper court showing the 'Capitol' dominating the site. (L. J. Thompson)

entrance chamber, resembling a small *tetrapylon,* from which a formal reception area should be expected. If visitors turned to the right along the corridor, they would approach the north baths. Pass straight on and one entered into the tranquil upper court, dominated by the central tower above Room 7, the two water shrines on the slopes above and the impressive columned front of the north baths (Figs 9.4-9.6). However, turn to the left, and our visitor would have stepped down into the south wing containing the reception and accommodation facilities. A recent discussion on the covered 'galleries' around the upper court suggests there may have been no exit passage at the two ends (Esmonde Cleary 2013). This is not true, as there had originally been open passage into both the south and north wings. The cross corridor no longer gave access into the south wing as it has been blocked off at an unknown period, possibly the end of the fourth century when the site was divided up among lower-status family groups.

Finely tooled corner stones project beyond the butt-end of the blocking at the end of the inner west wall, indicating that it had originally been open (Fig. 9.7). The windowed east wall of the cross-corridor did not extend as far south as its opposite counterpart, and the blocking wall is butted against a squared end with a shallow east facing respond, suggesting that there had been yet a further entrance at this point connecting with the still buried south wing. The blocking wall itself turned at a right angle towards Room 1a, sealing off the south wing and separating its south-west corner from the rest of the building in the last decades of its existence.

Another doorway exists in the stonework at the north end of the west wall, accessing the north baths, seen today as a step leading into a grassed depression in the north-east corner of the upper court (Fig. 9.8). Excavations in 2016 identified a further doorway directly opposite, leading to the exterior of the building, this had been blocked at a later date by a massive buttress (see below). Consequently, it was possible to perambulate all around the covered portico-'galleries' of the upper court. The west wall facing into the upper court, and protected from the easterly winds, may have contained stone-built piers and dwarf columns similar to the opposite west wing and south portico each side of Room 2, giving the upper court its cloister-like appearance.

Figure 9.6. Reconstruction view of west tower and nymphaeum *from the upper court.*

Figure 9.7. Blocking at south end of cross-corridor, showing cut corner stones of west wall.

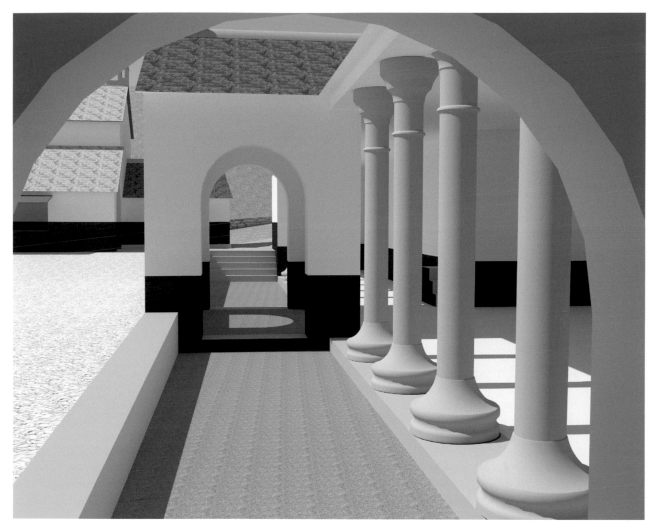

Figure 9.8. Entrance into Room 20a from north end of cross-corridor.

The south wing

The accommodation range

The south wing originally connected with the upper cross corridor and formed the administration unit for the building. In the first phase, of the second to third centuries, Rooms 1,1a, and 1b, forming the smaller south wing was elevated on a terrace cut into the south slope at the head of the combe, and as with the rest of the buildings at that time was single storied, whereas, the still buried eastern extension, later constructed on the much lower level, would have been double storied and intended to be the principal accommodation range. Excavations in 1983 identified that an earlier building had existed on the alignment of the lower south wing but had been dismantled to make way for the later, more elaborate structure (Goodburn 1984). Further excavations in 1997 identified substantial outer and inner walls for the east end of the south corridor which

had been fitted with a hypocaust. It was suggested by the excavators that the building may have been double storied, which improved the structural symmetry of the complex (Cleary *et al.* 1998a; 1998b). Sheltered by the steep hill behind it, for a large part of the year the south wing would not have benefited from the warmth of the sun, which accounts for the hypocaust channels identified in its front corridor, consequently it was not fronted with an open portico, but would have been completely enclosed, most probably with a similar gallery on the first floor. This would have resulted in a very different building with a solid façade pierced by rows of windows at two levels (Fig. 9.9). To relieve the starkness of its appearance the façade of the building could have been embellished with pseudo arcading or attached pilaster strips in stucco.

The floor level of the earlier south-west rooms (1, 1a, 1b) would have projected eastward with further rooms to form the upper storey, creating first floor *cubicula* for visiting

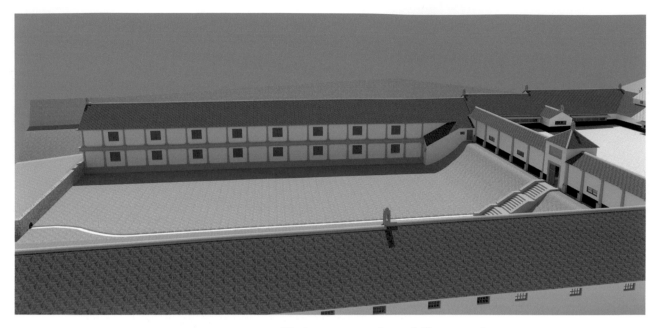

Figure 9.9. Reconstruction view of the lower court: south wing (left) to tetrapylon *steps.*

patrons. This suite of rooms being elevated sufficiently to benefit from sunlight along its south wall in the summer months, with splayed windows located below the roof line for illumination. It is also likely that the steep hillside behind this building would have been clear of trees, in order to maximise as much sunlight and warmth on the rear of the building for further months of the year. The explanation for the cross-corridor above the lower court, providing covered access directly from the accommodation area to the north baths and function rooms in the sunnier north wing, is that visitors were being lodged here.

The whole of the enlarged south wing from Room 3 eastwards could have fulfilled the same purpose as the *mansio*-like 'guest house' at the Lydney temple west of the Severn estuary. When excavating the Lydney building, Mortimer and Tessa Wheeler collectively identified ten ground floor guest rooms in the north and west wings and suggested that there had been an upper floor level. If matched with those below, along with an additional four in the upper east wing, this would make a further fourteen, totalling 24 guest rooms for paying clientele (Wheeler and Wheeler 1932). In time it may prove possible to match this with ten to twelve rooms on the ground floor of the south range at Chedworth also, of which at least one at the east end had been fitted with a hypocaust and mosaic. If repeated on the floor above, another twelve could be added, making up to 24 guest rooms in the south wing, an identical estimate to the number provided at Lydney.

Constructed with an upper storey, the building would have required a flight of stairs, approximately where the steep bank is on site today, leading down from the upper cross-corridor and reception area giving access to the heated lower corridor and its adjacent chambers. As the principal accommodation area, the building would have needed to retain as much internal warmth as possible generated by its hypocausts, but if an internal stair had been constructed without doors at the top and bottom, the heat generated to warm the lower floor would have been lost by up-draught through any open stair well, whereas an enclosed external stair, with doors at the top and bottom would have aided the retention of warmth on the lower ground floor (Fig. 9.9). There may be evidence for such a facility on site today represented by the already mentioned east facing respond at the south end of the cross-corridor, reminiscent of one side of a doorway. As a parallel, the foundation for an external stairway has been identified on the façade of the villa house at Littlecote in Wiltshire (Phillips, Thompson and Walters 2005), as well as on a side building of a villa near Chiseldon, also in Wiltshire (Walters forthcoming). The roof would have spanned the whole building, closely matching the height of the range of rooms on the north side of the lower court, being more-or-less at the same level as all the other single storied buildings. In this way, it provided a better architectural composition.

The south-west corner

In the light of what has been proposed above, a more logical reinterpretation for the group of rooms forming the south end of the upper court, incorporating Rooms 1 to 3 can be advanced. Today, visitors enter the site by crossing this area of the south wing, with no clear

138

understanding of what must have been a very significant part of the building. Consolidated outlines for robbed-out walls, along with right-angled tarmac paths, sloping and varied levels of deep grassed embankments and hollows, surrounded by differing levels of conserved walls, make this area of the building totally incomprehensible to visitors; and yet, this section of the building fulfilled a most important function. Today, a wall separates Rooms 1b and 3 from the adjacent higher corridor linked with Room 2 on its north side, the wall being a relatively modern reconstruction above its surviving part-robbed foundation to create a safety barrier for visitors passing the deep grassy hollow. This area contains evidence for several periods of change, which can be broken down for convenience into three main stages: the second/third-century rooms (1, 1a, 1b), the extended fourth-century building, and finally a lesser quality structure of the late fourth-fifth century, when the building was sub-divided between small family groups engaged in minor agricultural activities.

Reception and utility area

Rooms 1, 1a, 1b, 2, 3, 4, 5a

In their *Notes on the Roman Villa at Chedworth* published in 1873, Buckman and Hall intuitively identified the south end of the upper court as an administration area, stating; 'The few buildings on the south side seem to have served the purpose of offices, or servants' apartments' (Fig. 9.10). On entering the south corridor, visitors would step down before turning right to ascend up to Room 2. A considerable number of the coins found on the site originated from Room 2, which emphasises the point that pecuniary exchanges had taken place here. A short walk along the raised corridor and the doorway into Room 3 is encountered, the second largest room in the whole building. On published plans and on site today is marked the position of an oven; inconveniently blocking the entrance. Obviously, the oven is not an early fourth-century feature, belonging to either the later period when the complex was in decline and subdivided, or is much earlier, built in the open before Room 3 was constructed. On the evidence of this awkwardly located oven, along with Richmond's suggestion in 1960, this very large room has been identified as the principal kitchen, and is illustrated as such in the 2012 guide-book, despite the lack of evidence for a cooking range or other facilities for the preparation of food.

Today half the room falls away as a steep grassed embankment, but originally it must have been timber-floored above the hollow. Fires for ovens, and cooking ranges, along with heated oils, would make a hollow wooden floor extremely dangerous for a Roman kitchen! Room 3 is far more likely to have been the formal reception room, similar to the 'fore-hall' in the 'guest house' at Lydney and also the arcaded Rooms 27 and 28 at Great Witcombe. A door central to its south wall 'conveniently' gave access to the latrine (4), via a closed corridor. The latrine is at a much lower level than the proposed timber floor of Room 3, and must have been accessed via descending steps, now lost. Based on early fourth-century pottery in its sewer outlet and following an observation by Richmond, Goodburn suggested the latrine was dismantled in the early fourth century. This pottery might well have been residual having been discarded at the rear of the building, to fall into the sewer during later demolition. As a public building, a modest form of communal chamber would be required, other than the formal ritual dining rooms (5 and 32). In such a room morning repast could be taken and small midday meals served, all of which could have been prepared in the adjacent room 5a, long interpreted as being used solely as the furnace and wood store for heating Room 5. Compared with the fuel stores for the west and north baths, Room 5a is excessively large, and though considered as 'unlikely' by Richmond, (who favoured the improbable Room 3 as a kitchen), having a terraced solid floor Room 5a is far more appropriate, and safer, to contain kitchen facilities as well (though, like Room 3, no evidence for such has yet been recorded here). For example, in order to fire the hypocausts for the villa house and baths at Littlecote, access to the internal *praefurnium* was gained through its kitchen. The hypocaust in Room 5 may have been infrequently used, and consequently did not require an exorbitant amount of fuel storage. Occasional firing of the adjacent hypocaust is unlikely to have disrupted the principal use of Room 5a as a kitchen, ideally located for servicing both Room 3, as a form of refectory, and Room 5 the Bacchic ritual feasting hall.

Additionally, Room 1b could have been adapted and given an upper floor level during its rebuild corresponding with the adjacent higher corridor on its north side, along with the floor levels in 2 and 3. Integrated with Room 2, upper 1b, directly and proportionally opposite, would have become part of the public reception rooms, the 'porter's lodge' as at Lydney. No door into upper Room 1b is shown today, the present wall being a nineteenth-century safety barrier. The lower level of Room 1b, having a concrete floor, could have been a low ceiling storage chamber alongside Room 1, which may have been timber floored as a utility room along with Room 1a, also with a concrete floor. Such rooms would have been essential, even in a residential villa, for storing dry foods, wine and oil *amphorae*, ancillary furnishings

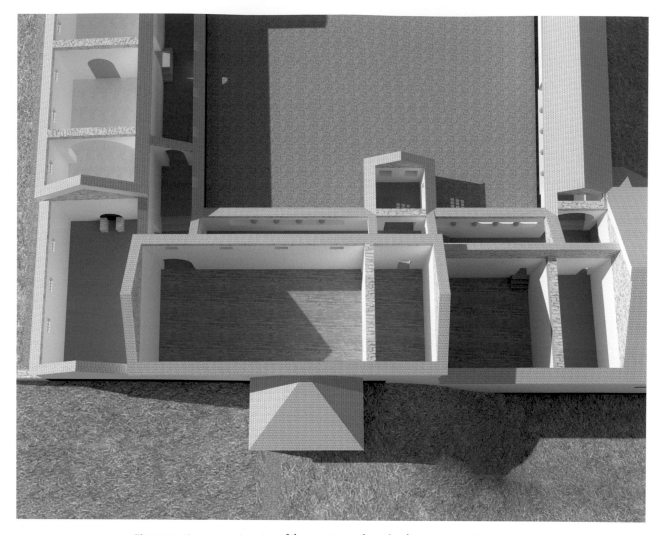

Figure 9.10. Reconstruction view of the interiors in the utility/reception area: Rooms 1-5a.

and other household equipment, not to mention minor accommodation for resident servants. Relegated to rooms of insignificance today, for the first half of the fourth century, this corner of the building can be re-interpreted as the administration, reception and utility area for visiting patrons, this being the function for the upper level of Room 1b conjoined with Room 2, where clientele's monies changed hands upon arrival, along with a refectory and latrine in Rooms 3 and 4, the main food preparation area and principle kitchen in Room 5a and storage/utility rooms in Rooms 1, 1a and lower 1b.

The west wing

What would normally be the principal residential wing of a wealthy villa, with axial reception rooms incorporating a fine entrance overlooking the landscape to the south, at Chedworth consists of two large formal chambers (Rooms 5 and 5b-7) aligned along the length of the building with no external view, a suite of baths

(10-16), and a room of undefined purpose (8). Having a standard front *porticus* width of 8 feet (2.45 m), with its floor 3 feet (0.92 m) lower than the internal rooms, would have allowed Rooms 5 and 5b-7 to easily accommodate clerestory openings above the *porticus* roof line. Additionally, if the entrance porch projecting into the upper court had a small, ridged roof spliced into the timbers of the *porticus*, even more head room would have been created for entering the building at this point, allowing the *porticus* roof to be constructed at an even lower level on its outer retaining wall piers and dwarf columns; permitting the internal ceilings to be dropped to an even lower level. Nonetheless, the rooms would still have been lofty, perhaps in the region of 10-11 feet (3.35 m). Room 5, and possibly part of Rooms 5b-7 had been fitted with a hypocaust, so heating, when required, was not a problem, and both being large function rooms, the high ceilings would have made them more impressive. This would make windows within the *porticus* unnecessary, allowing the number of columns along the façade to be reduced between stone and tile piers. This design being repeated on three sides of the upper court and the east section of the north wing. Fully open columned porticoes were probably not as common as many restoration artists have depicted over the years owing to the unreliable British climate, even in Roman times. Where they did exist, they were most probably along the lines described above and fitted with shutters hinged from a heavy timber lintel across the dwarf columns, which could be lowered during inclement weather, also providing protection for any mosaic decorated passages.

The thicker east and west walls of Room 7, undoubtedly supporting a tower, conceivably also buttressed a vaulted ceiling below its roof, its super-structure probably being constructed in timber to reduce the weight. Located at the centre of the building, externally it would have highlighted the significant chamber below. If the tower was fitted with deep clerestories on its south side, late sunlight would have illuminated the end north wall of Room 7, which may have been decorated in a manner relative to the intended function of the room which would impress upon entry. Such a fresco would also have been visible through the intervening central door connecting with Room 5. Remains of a *pelta* mosaic survives in the present Room 5b, truncated by the construction of a wall for the later Room 6. It is the surviving part of an end panel to an even more extensive and elaborate floor, obliterated when this large central room was subdivided by the later Room 6 and its adjacent passages. If this interpretation is correct, Room 5b-7 would have been truly spectacular. This large room, approximately 36 feet (11 m) in length, intentionally retained from the earliest period, was afforded an eminent location and in all probability was the most significant room in the whole building (Fig. 9.11). Sited centrally it might reflect a similar function to that of the octagonal towered hall at Great Witcombe.

At the south end of Room 5b-7 is the bi-partite Room 5, floored with the extremely fine 'Bacchic' mosaic (Fig. 9.12), long accepted as the *triclinium* of the 'villa', it should more appropriately be interpreted as a ritual feasting hall, its centrally located door ceremonially interconnecting to the principal hall (5b-7). The floors in Room 5 and the later Room 6 have been attributed to the same period around the mid-fourth century (Cosh and Neal 2010), based on comparable details recognised in rooms 4, 5, 6 and 10 at Woodchester, and a specific tessellated swastika-meander cornering technique being used on both Chedworth mosaics 5 and 6. There is no reason not to suppose, as with other border designs, that such a corner meander was used by successive

generations of mosaicists. The much finer mosaic of Room 5 and the destroyed floor with the *pelta* pattern in Room 5b-7 are better attributed to the elaborations around the beginning of the fourth century, and the lesser quality mosaic in Room 6 and its adjacent passages might belong to a period after the site had ceased to be used as a sanctuary in the late fourth century, perhaps as a result of the discouragement of pagan worship at this time, with the mosaic craftsmen simply copying the earlier cornering technique in the adjacent room.

Unquestionably however, there are striking differences in the craftsmanship of the mosaics in Rooms 5 and 5b which suggests more than one school of mosaicists had been working at Chedworth during the extensive early fourth-century rebuild. This is also reflected in the quality and style seen in the *porticus*, and, if contemporary with these elaborations, the west baths too.

The original smaller Room 5 appears to have been a heated room, its hypocaust connecting through to Room 5b-7. It was later extended to the south with a larger hypocaust by removing its end wall. The *pelta* panel mosaic in Room 5b and the lower mosaic in the west *porticus*, being of much the same artistic quality, were possibly laid during the earliest phase of expansion, with the much finer floor in Room 5 being laid a short while later by more skilled craftsmen following the extension of Room 5. The two fine acanthus-scroll panels at the south end of Room 5 are unquestionably paralleled with the same scheme in room 12 at Woodchester, which Cosh and Neal tentatively place in the first half of the fourth century. The acanthus panels at both sites strongly suggest the hand of the same craftsman. The dating phases proposed for Woodchester are woefully inadequate and too much reliance has been placed on stylistic elements within the mosaics. Considering the extent of the additions to the Chedworth building around AD 300, and the probable need to reach an early completion date, it is not inconceivable that flooring contracts were issued to different firms. The variation in style reflecting different standards of competence rather than commissions spread over many years. Cosh and Neal do, indeed, concur that different craftsmen probably worked concurrently on the extensive number of mosaics being laid at Woodchester (Cosh and Neal 2010, 213); might this also have been the case at Chedworth?

In the early second century, the floors in these rooms were much lower, being raised later, perhaps in the third century when Rooms 5 and 5b-7 were fitted with a hypocaust. The roof may also have been raised at that

Figure 9.11. Reconstruction view of the interiors of west wing Rooms 5-5a, 6, 7.

time, coinciding with the construction of the east-facing corridor/*porticus*. Subsequently the two geometric mosaics referred to above were added. It was probably in the early fourth century that Room 5 was extended with a larger hypocaust and magnificent mosaic. How access was gained into these sumptuous chambers remains unresolved; the present two sets of cumbersome pyramid steps leading into Room 5a and the adjacent baths were constructed on top of the *porticus* mosaic, and consequently they must belong to the later post-sanctuary period, when Room 5b-7 was subdivided with Room 6. Initially, dual opposing slab-built steps must have been built against the inner wall, similar to the surviving example in the north baths and mostly confined within the plain outer border of the *porticus* mosaic, without disrupting the visual flow of the central tessellated panels. The baths at the north end of the building (10-16) consist of traditional *thermae* of damp heat. As at Great Witcombe, they are separated from the larger baths for reasons not entirely clear today, possibly indicating a division of functions between the west and north wings.

The north wing

East of the north baths, Rooms 26 to 29a have been attributed to the earlier second century, and 30 to 32 to the later fourth, sometime up to c. AD 380. Structural evidence suggests that Rooms 30-32 had been attached after the construction of the *portico*/gallery fronting Rooms 26 to 29a, which was added at the beginning of the fourth century. A construction date leading up to AD 380 is extremely late to build an elaborate suite of rooms associated with formal dining. Fragments of a fine mosaic was found in the heating channels of Room 32, the largest heated room in the whole building. The construction evidence for this extension needs to be seriously reassessed, as logistically this extensive dining complex should be much earlier, being added immediately following construction of the front *porticus* at the beginning of the fourth century, and probably simultaneously with the construction of Rooms 24 to 25b; not up to eighty years later. The coin series for the site appears to terminate with issues of Gratian, AD 378-83, suggesting this imposing suite of rooms must

Figure 9.12. Room 5 Bacchic mosaic. (Painting by L.J. Thompson)

date well before 380. Richard Reece identified just over 360 coins from the site, 'far exceeding that of other published Cotswold villas'; adding further, 'Chedworth lacks issues after AD 383 which reached *Corinium* in large numbers, it would seem likely that the villa had either ceased to function, or to use coins by AD 386' (Reece 1960). The 2012 souvenir guide to the site suggests that this second, and considerably larger, dining room, may have been a summer *triclinium*. If so, why construct such a large, expensive and complex hypocaust with two firing points? Also, in the later fourth century on many sites, hypocausts were being closed down, blocked up, reduced in size; or not constructed at all.

The single-storied north wing caught sunlight for most of the day and most probably was graced with an open *porticus* during fine weather (Figs 9.13, 9.14). The front of the building has been badly robbed of its stone, probably for burning to produce lime (a large lime kiln of seventeenth-century date having been found behind the north wing) (Goodburn 1979, 22; Bethell 2006, 5). Raised hypocausts implies that some of the internal rooms were elevated above the level of the *porticus* floor, and as with the west wing and north baths, access was

gained by steps (Goodburn 1979). The east end of the *porticus* is almost 10 feet in width (3.05 m), which would make its roof line higher. Its entrance was at the west end where it connects with the large colonnaded hall of the north baths (25b), allowing ample head room to be gained through a probable arched opening set at this point. Excavations in 2016 revealed a foundation for an arch respond here abutting the stone slab threshold. More significant was the extensively worn-down state of the *tesserae* borders at the east end of the Room 25b mosaic where it abutted the stone threshold. The edges of the *tesserae* had been rounded into their interstices, suggesting that large numbers of feet, probably in hobnail shoes, had passed through here. Had this building been a private residence with only servants and family perambulating the passages in soft soled footwear, the mosaic border would not have worn down to such an extent. Like the west wing, this broad arched opening to the north *porticus,* would allow the roof to be constructed at a low level on its front wall to permit the installation of clerestory openings. Having a southerly aspect, a considerable amount of daylight could have shone into this range of large rooms, which may have accommodated less formal activities, but more

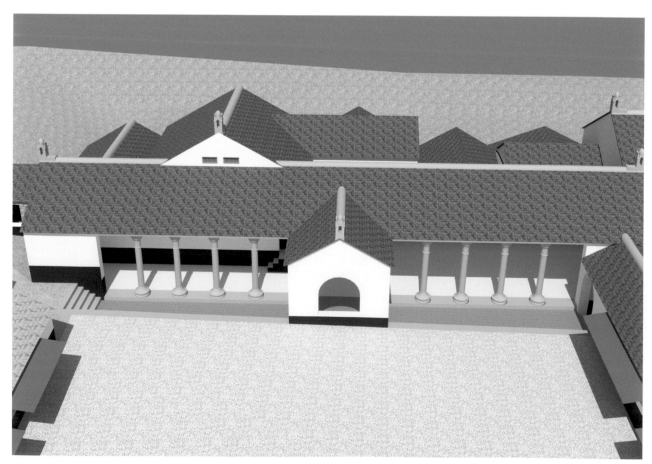

Figure 9.13. Reconstruction view of north baths façade and roof-scape.

Figure 9.14. Reconstruction view to the south-west from exercise 'veranda' Room 25b in the north baths.

specifically, could have housed the resident officiating *magus* or *magi*. In which case it may be significant that the only landscape vista down the valley, which could have been gained from any part of the entire building, was in fact from the *porticus* of the north wing, by looking south-east, across the outer courtyard wall towards the bend of the river and; the 'Lower and Upper Valley Temples' (see below).

The north baths

The north baths are amongst the most important buildings in the whole complex, fed by the waters descending from two sacred buildings, the 'Capitol' and the *nymphaeum*; both being the reason for the bath's construction and continuing development from the second century onwards. Elaborate bath suites formed some of the principal buildings in a healing sanctuary, as bathing in what had been deemed waters from a sacred spring, were not solely intended to cleanse the physical body but also to provide relaxation and uplift of an individual's spirit as one of the remedies for a variety of debilitating conditions; and for our period, contrary to published sources, the north baths had been equipped with the expected facilities of a standard traditional suite of baths for that time.

The north baths incorporate the most complicated sequence of changes on the whole site, consequently this discussion will concentrate on the most likely arrangement belonging to the first half of the fourth century. Taking into account the size of these baths, designed for a considerable number of people, it is not surprising they underwent frequent remodelling. Goodburn followed on from Richmond's work here, and with the loss of vital structural and stratigraphic evidence by post-medieval stone robbing and nineteenth-century exploration and consolidation, he had a thankless task trying to make sense of the maze of interlocking foundations and alterations; for without total excavation, incorporating demolition of parts of the building, an understanding of the development of these baths, is nigh impossible; as expressed in the 1979/89 guides to the site. Though incorporating Richmond's interpretations, these guides have been the most analytical and comprehensive attempt to describe the baths to have been published (up to the time of writing). The most recent site guide also maintains earlier descriptions, and deletes Rooms 24, 24a, 25, 25a-b, at the east end suggesting they might be the main reception rooms for the whole building; repeating Richmond's earlier misconception. It is clearly evident elsewhere on the site that structural changes and lower status downgrading were implemented in the later fourth century, including the subdivision of Room 5b-7, the construction of the pyramid steps in the west *porticus,* the blocking off of the cross corridor into the south wing, possibly the clumsily positioned oven in the doorway to room 3, closure of the latrine, and the massive buttress inserted into a doorway at the north end of the cross corridor. Most recently in 2017, excavation of the elaborate Room 28 in the north wing identified, above the damaged mosaic floor, a dense layer of ash associated with a central tile-built hearth suggestive of low-status industrial use (Papworth forthcoming). Equally so, late changes and downgrading would have been made in the north baths, which need to be reassessed and attributed more carefully.

The question of laconica

There has been a consistent opinion that *laconica* played a significant role in the north baths during the early fourth century (Richmond 1960), being based on changes made to the damp heat baths (Room 22) (Goodburn's Phase 4). A shallower hypocaust had been introduced (10 inches deep (26 cm)), possibly fired with charcoal from the Phase 3 stoke-hole in the north wall. By raising the basement floors and doing away with the heated water baths to form a unified floor surface, a *laconicum* is suggested as having being created. The mosaics in Room 22 had been extensively damaged, and the former *tepidarium* was coarsely patched with *opus signinum* around a large fallen stone block, 'left *in situ*'; the collapsed stone block implies that the building was in an advanced state of decay. Such degraded modifications and repairs would be quite unacceptable among the fine interiors of the first half of the fourth century, it is suggested therefore, that these changes and coarse repairs to Room 22 should also be relegated to the inferior alterations of the later fourth or early fifth century. Richmond realised that Room 22 had undergone 'a long and complicated history', and whilst making a reasonable assessment of the 'late' changes to this room, his final phasing and

function in particular was misplaced. Reducing the depth of the underfloor heating chambers in Room 22 almost certainly had nothing whatsoever to do with dry-heat bathing, being introduced much later, probably in order to create a drying floor for lower status agricultural activity. This would also account for the destruction of the two mosaics which had graced the earlier damp-heat baths in order to reduce the heating chambers beneath. Late agrarian activity is evidenced by a large millstone found in Room 26, charred grain in late midden deposits over the upper court and a pit containing charred grain cut into the corridor of the south wing.

It is highly unlikely that there was ever any *laconicum* at Chedworth in the fourth-century, which was very much an early type of intense hot dry baths, predominantly of the first and second centuries, favoured by the military especially and requiring extra-large furnaces, not reduced ones. In the later third and fourth centuries this form of dry bathing had completely fallen from use in domestic buildings. What did continue was the alternative lesser dry-heat rooms, *sudatoria,* and it is far more likely to be that system which was incorporated at Chedworth (and Great Witcombe also). We propose that Goodburn's Period 3 damp-heat Room 22 continued into his Period 4, though still with the stoke room (19), which formally heated the *caldarium* of Period 2, being dismantled. This functional identification is also proposed for these rooms by Cosh and Neal (2010, 65-66). This small *caldarium* and *tepidarium* could have functioned quite adequately with the stoke hole inserted in the north wall with the hot water tank encased above it. An almost identical arrangement existed in the small north baths at Littlecote (Phillips, Thompson and Walters 2005). Richmond's 'shallow hypocaust' belonging to a lower-status floor for drying beans or grain at the end of the fourth century.

Interpreting the north baths

The reinterpretation presented here logically describes the disposition of rooms in the north baths, to serve a sanctuary in the early fourth century, and consequently does not entirely correspond with Goodburn's, Richmond's, or other recent interpretative texts (Esmonde Cleary 2012; 2013; 2014). For this period, the baths can be divided into five areas, incorporating an almost monumental façade fronting an open relaxation or exercise hall, a modest damp-heat suite, a very elaborate *frigidarium,* a large *apodyterium,* and a suite of dry-heat rooms, *sudatoria.* The mosaic-floored open-sided room is referred to as a 'wide veranda' by Goodburn who, as with the other open porticoes, never designated it an identification number in his guides to the site. It was confusingly numbered in 1976 by the RCHM(E) as Room 25a, which is the room number Goodburn attributed to the small intervening chamber between Rooms 24a and 25. (This error with Room 25a was unfortunately incorporated into Cosh and Neal's volume in 2010). The 2012 site guide logically designated Goodburn's veranda as Room 25b, the number adopted here.

The north baths had a special status, and to emphasise this, it was architecturally embellished in a manner superior to any other part of the building. On site today are the base sections of two large columns, which originally formed part of a colonnade fronting the baths above a sunken passageway (20), set alongside the revetment supporting the upper court at its north end. This has been consolidated for visitors and leads up the adjacent flight of steps, and clearly implies an association with the *nymphaeum,* and also access to the lesser baths in the west wing (feature 20 has been omitted from the 2012 site guide). In the north-east corner of the upper court a stepped doorway ascends from the entrance cross-corridor (Fig. 9.8), into what is now an elongated grass depression parallel to a continuation of the colonnade wall, the grass rising as a low embankment on its south side to the level of the upper court. This grassy hollow complements the pathway (20) fronting the colonnade to the west, separated from it today by the outline of the earlier cold bath; undoubtedly this hollow could represent another sunken passage (20a), which has never been exposed, but provided entry to the north baths from the accommodation area in the south wing.

The north baths frontage

Situated midway along the baths frontage is the cold plunge belonging to the earlier baths. The retaining wall of the upper court abuts the south-west corner of the former cold bath, likewise the opposite grassy embankment stops at its south-east corner. This clearly suggests that the walls of the early cold bath were retained in the fourth-century elaboration, as both sunken passages (20 and 20a) terminate against it, implying it had been adapted to suit the changes, perhaps as an ornamental entrance, kiosk or shrine between two rows of columns, or even retained as a cold pool as part of the open hall Room 25b. This structure is only slightly broader than Room 2, immediately opposite on the other side of the upper court, providing an element of architectural symmetry. Similar opposing square rooms occur in the enclosed courts at Lydney and Great Witcombe.

The structure of the cold bath, retained as a projecting feature, would have braced any outward thrust pressure

along the top of the colonnade from a ridged roof covering the broader section of the mosaic hall (25b) below. That a roof had originally spanned this hall is suggested by its fine geometric mosaic, proffering the floor an element of protection from the inclement British weather. In 2014 excavations over Room 25b exposed areas of previously unrecorded mosaic, the finer decorated central panels were extensively worn and damaged, possibly caused in part to environmental exposure in the very late period, but more likely by the neglect of lower status occupants at that time. The better-preserved outer borders, laid with larger and more deeply set *tesserae*, were consequently more resilient to weathering. Excavations in 2016 revealed the purpose of the massive blocking-up of the outer doorway at the north end of the cross corridor. This outer portal must have created a structural weakness for the arch at the corner of Room 25b caused by the outward thrust of its roof. Consequently, a massive buttress was inserted into the abandoned doorway to resist this pressure. Additional buttressing was gained by the inner wall and roof at the north end of the cross-corridor.

In a similar manner, the interior of the western section of the colonnade was also roofed, being half the width of the main hall, a pent roof would have been set against the outer wall of the *tepidarium* (22) and *frigidarium* (21). Blending with the ridge of the main roof it provided perfect symmetry to the roof line when viewed from the upper court. This lesser roof would also have been braced by the wall at its west end beside the passage (20) steps.

The two surviving column bases have a lower shaft diameter of 13 inches (0.33 m). The formula for calculating the original height of a column shaft is to multiply the lower diameter by eight, this would make the two Chedworth column shafts 8 feet 8 inches (2.65 m). Add on the combined dimensions of the moulded base, capital and header stone and a full column height in the region of 11 to 12 feet (3.35-3.65 m) is obtained. When spaced proportionally either side of the kiosk a truly impressive pillared frontage of eight tall columns emerges (Figs 9.13 and 9.14). Clearly these are not the baths of a Romano-British farmer.

Disposition of the early fourth-century north baths

Passing through the colonnade from the sunken passages (20/20a), one would have entered the open floored hall (25b), intended as a shaded place for relaxation on warm days or an area for exercise, resembling a genteel gymnasium. Facing south it benefited from the summer sun, the transit of which would have cast the passage of shadows from the columns across its mosaic floor through the day, creating a truly atmospheric and relaxing ambience in the chamber, admirably suited to the doctrine of the ancient 'Pneumatists' and 'Methodism' of Asclepiades cited above (Fig. 9.14).

Directly opposite the suggested kiosk or entrance, is the bi-partite apsidal Room 24, initially labelled as a *laconicum*. Goodburn (1979, 20) indicated that due to the size of the room its heating system would have made, 'a somewhat cool and ineffective *laconicum*'. Most recently it has been classified as a reception room. For our early fourth-century period, Room 24 is more likely to have been a mildly heated *apodyterium*, appropriately located between the damp and dry heat bath suites, unusually large to serve a private residence, but not a more public facility. It would need to have been entered by paired steps from the mosaic hall (25b), (identical to the restored pair at the corner of Room 21 today), now lost along with its attached wall to stone robbing.

Internal doorways would have led into the *frigidarium* (21) on its west side and the dry heat rooms through the east wall; thresholds for which are also now lost. Inserted around the end of the third century between the earlier small baths and the west wall of Room 26 of the second-century north wing, Rooms 24a, 25 and 25a formed the dry heat bath system, not the reception rooms to a villa. This suite incorporated a dry *tepidarium* in Room 24a (converted from an earlier stoke room), the flues for which may still have connected with the proposed *apodyterium* (24). The blocked opening, shown on earlier published plans, between Rooms 24a and 25b, must have been sealed at this time. The small intersecting ante-chamber (25a), led to a probable *sudatorium* in Room 25. The purpose of Room 25a has vexed others in the past, but its purpose was probably intended to curtail loss of heat from Room 25, bathers closing the doors as they moved from room to room, maintaining the temperature in the *sudatorium*. Room 24a would have functioned as a cooling-off chamber on leaving the *sudatorium*. Devoid of a tepid plunge it was sufficiently large to hold a *labrum*, where bathers, on leaving the *sudatorium* could splash-wash perspiration from their bodies before crossing the *apodyterium* (24) into the *frigidarium* (21).

Goodburn (1979, 22) points out that the hypocaust in Room 24a appears not to have been used. Being a fairly small chamber acting as a *tepidarium* without a bath, it would not require any intensive heat, though this would also make the *apodyterium* (24) much cooler. Goodburn suggested that Room 24a was even later changed back into a stoke room, presumably serving a remodelled Room 24 when much later, the baths were reduced and

downgraded. The *praefurnium* forming part of the area in Room 19 was probably dismantled earlier, on the construction of Goodburn's Phase 3, when the furnace for the damp-heat baths (22) was introduced through the north wall.

A small doorway in the corner of the *tepidarium* connected with the large *frigidarium* (21), previously published as the *apodyterium* for a *laconicum*. *Apodyteria* are the entry rooms to baths used for undressing and are not equipped with elaborate cold plunge baths. This impressive cold room, with columns partitioning the immersion baths, was also partly lined with marble and resembles the plan of *frigidaria* seen in public bath suites elsewhere, probably being modelled on the same principle, as it was intended to serve many people at a time. Though much larger, a similar arrangement for a *frigidarium* is paralleled in the legionary baths in the fortress at Caerleon (Zienkiewicz 1986, 31-3). The dual steps at the corner of Room 21 provided a convenient direct access from the *frigidarium* into the open exercise hall (25b). The north baths would have been the principal *thermae* for ritual bathing in the sacred waters of the sanctuary. The water, flowing down from the 'Capitol' passed through the *nymphaeum* and was piped into the *frigidarium*, replenishing the three immersion pools with fresh 'sacred' water. An interesting comparison of this large multi-pooled *frigidarium* can be made with that of nearby Great Witcombe, the *frigidarium* of the larger baths on that site was also equipped with two large plunge pools, capable of accommodating a sizeable group of people at a time.

Discussion of the Main Building

Impressive though the complex may have appeared at a distance when approaching from the east (Fig. 9.15), the primary criticism in accepting Chedworth as a wealthy rural residence, is its claustrophobic and certainly cold location for a large part of the year. The axis of the building, aligned 8 degrees north of due east, is compacted into a narrow steep sided combe at the head of a broad valley exposed to the cold winds funnelled into it from north-eastern Europe. This contrasts austerely with the more traditional south or south-easterly aspect of the greater majority of residential villas in this country, which are generally laid out in more open landscapes, frequently just below raised ground affording a screen from the north and north westerly winds, being aligned to gain the maximum amount of sunlight and warmth; frequently benefiting from a fine view of the landscape to the south. Chedworth had no vista from rooms around its upper court, the view being blocked by the upper cross-corridor and no view was available from within the lower

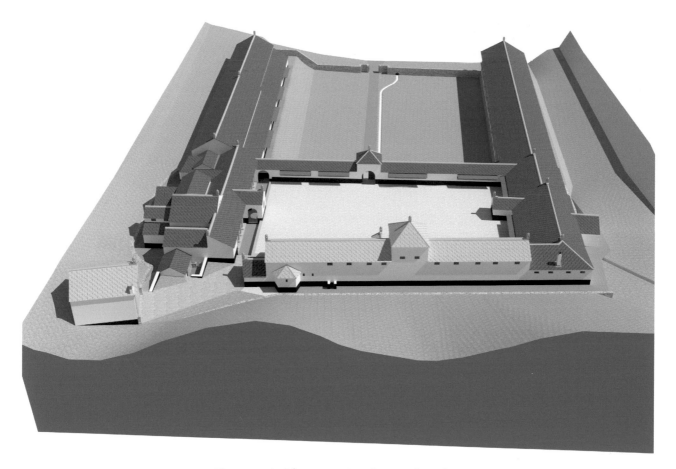

Figure 9.15. Aerial reconstruction of courtyard complex.

court, also screened by the recently identified enclosure wall. The only vistas were from the north *porticus* towards the 'Valley Temples' and from the upper court upwards to the water shrines, 'Capitol' and *nymphaeum* (Fig. 9.5). The overall plan of the building is rigidly formal, resembling a state-controlled lodge or *mansio* with an inordinate emphasis on communal bathing and dining. In the nineteenth century a large number of mosaic floors were revealed, though predominantly geometric in design, and evidence suggested that even more had formally existed; to date eighteen mosaics are suspected as having graced the building; this does not have to imply a series of wealthy owners. Around the mid fourth century the remodelling of the healing temple and 'guest house' at Lydney included at least 23 similar mosaics (Cosh and Neal 2010).

The topographical location for this building must have been dictated by some other natural phenomenon, necessary for the intended function of the complex, and summer sunrises is a possible answer, which would have been caught by the towered clerestories above Room 7 and the 'Capitol', bringing the first light of day into the two most significant sacred chambers on the

site. The 'Capitol' was the source of the sacred waters into the *nymphaeum* and baths, the principal reason for the location of the complex. A similar intention can be proposed for the octagonal chamber at Great Witcombe. Along with summer sunrises, the triple spring-lines on the upper hillside behind the west wing provided the perfect combination of natural phenomena to establish a healing retreat. The north combe supplying the baths and the larger combe to the south very likely providing a perpetual flow of water to flush the latrine behind the south wing, which would account for its location at that point. Furthermore, nothing has been discovered at the site to convincingly argue for an agrarian economy to support such a structure for the greater part of its existence. There are no storage buildings, malting furnaces, barn-like structures or surrounding field systems. The iron tools which have been preserved, including sheaths for small wooden spades, a small plough shoe, a mattock for breaking small areas of ground, could be interpreted as items for maintaining kitchen gardens, which may have existed on suspected narrow field terraces behind the west and north wings, or they may have originated from a very late small-holding. The iron shears in the site museum are rather small for shearing sheep and more likely had been used for pruning shrubs or hedges.

Archaeology is essentially concerned with interpretation and as with any academic debate, all proposals and theses should be put forward and openly aired along with all available evidence. In 2005-6 the National Trust initiated a renewed policy to bring together all known records and material recovered from the site since its discovery in 1864, incorporating a Data Service and a new Publication Policy, gaining the services of Peter Salway as Specialist Adviser on Roman Britain, who published a resumé in *Britannia* (Salway 2008). Current assessment now suggests that the exposed double courtyard complex was extended more-or-less in unison late in the Roman period, around the beginning of the fourth century and did not develop piecemeal over a longer period, as proposed by Richmond. This implies a massive construction programme, transforming what had been a series of small detached structures into a much larger unified complex, made up of a suite of reception rooms with a latrine, a large towered axial 'ritual' chamber, two elegant dining rooms, substantial and ornate bath suites, and a double storied accommodation wing.

Interpretations over the years have incorporated the long-standing antiquarian view that Chedworth was a well-appointed residence of a wealthy landowner, while Fox and Baddeley saw the north wing as industrial, John Smith believed that the complex could fall within his 'unit-system' in which a villa was divided up into multiple tenancies (Smith 1978), and, as stated at the beginning of this paper, Graham Webster fired the initial salvo in favour of a sanctuary (Webster 1983). More recently, Salway has proposed that the building was an investment property, an 'asset' in a real estate portfolio (Salway 2009); and in the past decade the site has been interpreted as a rich man's occasional hunting lodge (Esmonde Cleary 2012; 2013). At least there is an element of agreement, that the site does not fall into the excepted category for a standard Romano-British villa. The 'investment' proposal is not without merit and Salway is justified in putting the idea forward, as a possibility for some of land ownerships in late Roman Britain. However, from the environmental viewpoint, it is unlikely that an absentee property speculator would consider acquiring or building such an inhospitable property as seen at Chedworth. Investors would surely select a more comfortable property for their money, an estate on a more profitable landscape, with a residence laid out on a sunnier alignment with a vista to the south or south east, an infinitely more desirable prospect for an investment portfolio, along the lines of nearby villas such as Turkdean or Withington.

The theory proposed for such absentee owners was based partially on suggestions that there was little sign of the hypocausts identified being extensively fired (Bethell 2007; see also Salway 2009, 49). This does not form a cogent argument against the theory for a healing sanctuary, as there could be any number of reasons why the hypocausts might appear to have been under-used. This problem has been identified on other sites, not least on the writer's (BW) excavations at Littlecote Park, where the circular channelled hypocaust in the central room of the main house, appeared to have never been used. Moreover, the *sudatorium* of the house baths at Littlecote showed little sign of intensive heat; yet the central room in the house and its bath suite had undoubtedly been inhabited and continually used from the second to fourth centuries when the internal *praefurnium,* set adjacent to the cooking range in the house kitchen, saw extensive firing. Evidence suggests that virtually the whole building now displayed at Chedworth is a late construction, resulting in insufficient time for some hypocausts to show prolonged exposure to heat before the building was abandoned as a public amenity. A further explanation might be that accumulated ash could have been regularly cleared away so as not to inhibit up-draught. It is also not unknown for a hypocaust to have been inefficiently designed, failing to create a good up-draught to produce substantial heat, which may well have been the case for the central room at Littlecote. Possibly a *praefurnium* may have been structurally refurbished by replacing heat damaged tiles and masonry shortly before abandonment.

For a sanctuary at Chedworth, considering its north-easterly alignment, with the cold damp penetrating winds, patronage of the site may have fallen sharply during the inclement colder months of the year, if not closed down altogether during the winter, negating any need for extensive heating, and equally so during the periods of high summer. Finally, and more especially, it is being recognised on other sites, that the hypocaust system was falling out of favour from the mid fourth century, being too expensive to maintain and internal fireplaces were being introduced instead, fine examples being at Great Witcombe, the Newport, Combley and Carisbrooke villas on the Isle of Wight, and at the Bignor and Sparsholt villas (Johnston 1978). Therefore, suggested paucity of hypocaust activity is in itself insufficient evidence to argue for a wealthy absentee patron.

Smith's suggestion that the property was multi-tenanted continued the idea that it was housing separate families of a farming community. Smith's unit-system is very plausible on several other sites in this country, and fits in well with the division of properties between a fourth generation claimant and a sitting occupier in Celtic law, as outlined by C. E. Stevens (Stevens 1947), an example being the North Leigh villa in Oxfordshire, which undoubtedly accommodated three distinctly separate families (Walters 2009). However, the overall evidence suggests that this is certainly not the case at Chedworth. Only at the end of the fourth century was it surely so, long after the original proprietors who had embellished the building, vacated it to lower status farming communities, in exactly the same manner as occurred at Great Witcombe.

The recently proposed suggestion that the site was a hunting lodge has been based on a small number of bones from game animals, including specimens recovered from the late midden deposits above the upper court, some arrow heads and parts of several stone statuettes of Diana (Esmonde Cleary 2012; 2013). The midden deposit in the upper court suggests that it dates from the degraded period at the end of the fourth to early fifth century. The lower-status occupants now having free range of the countryside to take wild animals at will, there no longer being high status masters on the adjacent villa estates to control illicit hunting. Excavation of the undoubted hunting lodge in Littlecote Park, albeit late seventeenth-eighteenth century, produced faunal middens containing thousands of bones from game animals, not just a few. The fragmented statuettes recovered from Chedworth could indeed represent the hunting deities suggested, including a relief depicting Apollo Cunomaglos and statuettes of Diana (Henig 1993, nos 21-2, 110; 2022, 254, 256-8) but there is evidence for other deities here as well, including Bacchus on the major figural mosaic, and presumably a water-deity in the *nymphaeum*.

A religious healing sanctuary need not have been associated with a single Roman deity; there may have been others assimilated with local nature deities and this diversity can be recognised among the sculptures found at Chedworth. Healing sanctuaries incorporated special facilities expected at such establishments, including a number of separate shrines or temples in the surrounding landscape where offerings and pleas for improved health might be made to favoured deities, and such structures unquestionably existed in the immediate surrounding area (Fig. 9.1). Bathing in 'sacred waters' in elaborate *thermae* was conventional and this facility was most certainly provided. Activities included communal ritual feasting, to celebrate the favoured god, who would have been linked, in syncretic fashion, to a local deity; at least two dining rooms are recognisable at present in the plan of the building, one of them being Room 5 in the

west wing, with its mosaic implying an association with the rituals of Bacchus (Fig. 9.12) and the much larger Room 32 at the east end of the north wing, intuitively proposed as having been a single chamber with a raised dais (Goodburn 1979).

The hypocaust at its east end probably being higher than that of the adjacent larger floor, provided an elevated dining area, similar to communal dining in a medieval hall and perhaps was intended for the resident *magi* accompanied by higher-status guests. As a second dining room, it has been suggested that Room 32 may have been a summer *triclinium* (Esmonde Cleary 2012; 2013), an unnecessary classification for the inclement province of Britannia.

In fact, despite consistent references to their identification by archaeologists, even the standard *triclinium* is extremely rare in Britain, as has been argued convincingly by Patricia Witts (2000). Ritual feasting did not require pilgrims to recline on curved *stibadium* or classic *triclinium* couches, such furnishing would limit the number of diners; in a classically styled *triclinium* only nine persons could be accommodated. It is far more likely that in a ritual feasting room, diners sat at tables on benches or chairs around the sides or down the centre of the room, as Goodburn correctly suggested for Room 5 and in a medieval fashion for Room 32. There are images of such a scene on a mosaic from Carthage dated to the mid fourth century, now in the Bardo museum, which shows diners seated in groups of three at tables ranged around the sides of a large room with servants distributing food (Dunbabin 1978, 124, pl. XI). On the surviving area of the mosaic, at least twenty are attending the banquet, and there may have been more, the number equating with the ratio of possible guest rooms proposed above for the south range at Chedworth.

The satellite buildings

When assessing the function of the Chedworth complex, it is essential to give serious consideration to the number of minor buildings, the small un-investigated sites, and landscape features in the immediate vicinity (Figs 9.1 and 9.16). Collectively there are at least six to seven possible lesser buildings within a radius of approximately 900-1000 m of the courtyard 'villa', the better known being the 'Upper Valley Temple', the 'Capitol' overlooking the baths and the *nymphaeum* below it. In her survey of temples from Roman Britain, Ann Woodward identified that some 21 per cent were located on hill tops or adjacent to springs (Woodward 1992, 19-20). The outlying structures at Chedworth must be

Figure 9.16. Suggested winter view of the Chedworth complex looking south-east from above the 'Capitol' showing satellite buildings.
(L. J. Thompson)

associated with the central complex as it is most unusual that a large villa should be surrounded by at least three undoubted shrines, with the likelihood of there being several others, instead of extensive field systems and livestock enclosures; in this respect, for a villa in Britain, at the present time Chedworth is probably unique. In 2011, in an area of recent tree clearance at the east end of the high ridge above the south wing, the writer (BW) identified on an aerial image, a substantial single ditched trapezoid enclosure, directly above and south of the buried main entrance into the 'villas' lower court. The earthwork may have been pre-Roman but could have been re-used much later. A geophysical survey of part of its interior in June 2012 located linear trenches and post pits for a possible timber-built structure. If the enclosure had contained a tall timber building it would have dominated the entrance into the 'villa' and be visible from all points of the adjacent valley. This site is listed as 8 on the distribution plan (Fig. 9.1). With the exception of this recently located enclosure, The Royal Commission Inventory of 1976 itemises the other sites below.

(1) The nymphaeum (RCHM(E) 1976, 26, plan, no. 17)

This ornate structure channelled the known water supply into the site, and as pointed out above, its size and embellishment implies something far more significant than a reservoir for a house; the structure appearing to have been highly ornamented. An uninscribed altar, 2 feet in height (0.61 m) was found buried beneath the late floor in 1865. Set back to the rear of the main buildings, the *nymphaeum* is mis-located and too large to be an ornamental garden water feature, it is more akin to a discretely located shrine, from which the spring would have flowed for the benefit of the pilgrims patronising the site and bathing in its waters, similar to the aquatic supply at Bath, Lydney and Great Witcombe, and many other water sanctuaries in Gaul and Germania. The angular shaped flagstones with the incised Chi-Rho monograms, accepted as originating from the floor of the *nymphaeum*, point to an act to Christianise a pagan structure (see Cosh, this volume). There may well have been a short-lived Christian phase at Chedworth, which converted the *nymphaeum* to a detached open baptistery, as implied by the Chi-Rho monograms – for which the flowing water would be suitable (Henig 2004, 14-17). The *nymphaeum* has to be associated with the other sacred satellite buildings in the vicinity and seen for what it is, one of a series of shrines set into the surrounding landscape.

(2) 'The Capitol' (RCHM(E), 1976, 28, building 2)

Sited in a prominent location approximately 170 yards (162.5 m) above the baths (Fig. 9.16), the building was identified by James Farrer in 1864 who devoted 'only a few hours labour to this place, which was discovered the day before I left the county,..several small rooms were partially cleared...and fragments of pillars, justify the inference that a building of some importance has also existed in this part of the wood.' (Farrer 1865). This probable tower-like building was suggested by Canon H. M. Scarth to have been a temple, circular in form sitting on a hillside terrace above the two bath suites (Scarth 1869). Baddeley refers to it being laid out as an octagonal wheel design (as at Weycock in Berkshire or Pagans Hill, Somerset), but here consisting of eight internal 'cisterns' centred on a *columbarium* and having been the chief water supply to the 'villa'. This suggests an octagonal central pool beneath a high clerestory tower (similar to Great Witcombe), only here surrounded by side chambers at ground level, not dissimilar to the octagonal 'baptistery' style baths at Holcombe in Devon and more especially the octagonal temple of Apollo Cunomaglos at Nettleton Scrubb on the Fosse Way in Wiltshire, suggested elsewhere, as having served as another healing sanctuary (Burnham and Wacher 1990, 190-1). The relief depicting Apollo Cunomaglos at Chedworth might be significant in this respect, as Pagans Hill, Somerset was also of this form and George Boon suggested that a sculpted hound belonged to this deity (Boon 1989; see also Haeussler 2019). Probably elaborated in the early fourth century with a polygonal exterior, this building perhaps had a circular second-century predecessor, the same as the early phase at Nettleton Scrubb (Wedlake 1982).

Fine architectural details were recovered from the site including column fragments, a shell-headed niche and glass *tesserae*; the building clearly having been an elaborate hillside spring-line temple. In more recent years a small copper alloy bust possibly of the god Saturn is reported as having been found in the area of this lost building; probably originating from a vessel or piece of ritual furnishing (Henig and Goodburn 1982). In the 2012 guide to the villa, it is described as a mausoleum (Esmonde Cleary 2012), which is highly unlikely considering its proximity and association with a main source of water.

This important building is recorded as being destroyed during the construction of the Cirencester to Cheltenham railway between 1889 and 1892 (Esmonde Cleary 2013). However, during visits to the site by the writers, surface features and scattered cut stones west of the redundant railway track indicated that a substantial part of the building may have survived destruction. In June 2013, with the co-operation of the landowners, the writers engaged in a radar scan of the area. This resulted in the identification of a small room and a limited excavation of its north and east walls revealed at least four to five courses of stone blocks, along with a further wall at a different alignment passing beneath an adjacent tree, and evidence for other parts of the structure near-by. Clearly a substantial part of the 'Capitol' still survives (Walters 2013). The building had been constructed beside the northern water-cut combe, descending towards the north-west corner of the main building and may have been intended to symbolise the primary source of the spring head, supplying the *nymphaeum* and the baths below. It is also considered, however, that the exposed small room, 3.2 m square was an additional external chamber attached to one of the facets of Baddeley's octagonal wheel design. If repeated on all sides of the central tower it would have made for a more stable and impressive construction (Fig. 9.16). These side rooms are suggestive of a sequence of sleeping chambers in an *abaton*, commonly found at healing sanctuaries across the Empire, and more locally at Lydney. N.B. Recent re-examination of the plans drawn up in 2013 (see above) suggests that the structure might in fact be of pentagonal form.

(3) 'The Lower Valley Temple' (RCHM(E) 1976, 28, building 3)

Approximately 135 yards (150 m) east of the still buried 'villa' gate house, and towards the end of the lower field, lies a low knoll described in the 1976 Inventory as an artificially raised area 40 feet (13 m) across, and 50 feet (17 m) north of the modern public approach road; which produced Romano-British building debris after ploughing. This suggests a structure smaller than the detached agricultural buildings frequently found on villa estates, but is close in size to that of the 'Upper Valley Temple' 600 yards (550 m) to the south-east. It was casually suggested by Webster in 1983 to be the possible 'gate house' for the 'villa'.

The geophysical survey conducted by the National Trust in 2012 has clearly identified a large circular building some 20 m in diameter, with a smaller square building on its west side (Papworth 2012). Sited south of, and roughly half-way along the approach road leading up into the 'villa' entrance, the circular building is too large to be a mausoleum and is most probably yet another substantial shrine. Though slightly smaller, this newly identified building may be comparable to the second-century temple *cella* dedicated to 'Vesunna' at Périgueux in the Dordogne; it is, however, larger than the first-century example on Hayling Island (King and Soffe 2013).

The 2012 survey recorded part of an inner circle of foundation pits, as opposed to an interior circular foundation recognised on other similar structures, these pits conceivably supported a sequence of arches as the base for a towered *cella*. Its broad outer wall suggests an enclosed rotunda as opposed to a more traditional open ambulatory. This would have created a large open circular hall within the building rather than an enclosed *cella*. Roofing timbers above the outer rotunda, set into the superstructure of the *cella*, would have provided additional stability for a tall edifice above the lower arcade, not unlike late Roman baptisteries. A wide gap is indicated in the outer wall on its east side, the traditional location for the main entrance in such buildings.

Located so prominently on the axial approach into the complex presupposes a shrine of considerable significance. It is possible that the fragment of a curved *acroterium* in the site museum, may have originated from the upper part of this newly identified shrine, though Beeson has put forward an alternative location (Beeson, this volume). This substantial building may have been approached, via the raised terrace descending from the north-east, from the structures at the edge of Yanworth Wood (see below, Yanworth 1) and it would have been clearly visible from the north wing in a vista of sacred structures incorporating the 'Upper Valley Temple' beyond.

(4) 'The Upper Valley Temple' (RCHM(E) 1976, 28, building 4).

Almost 46 feet square externally (14 m), this building is one of the larger rural temples recorded from Roman Britain, but has unfortunately been seriously damaged by extensive quarrying, the site being known as 'Old Quarry' as early as 1820. On the evidence of Hadrianic coinage and sherds of second-century samian ware, a foundation in the Antonine period appears very probable. Partially exposed by Farrer in 1864 and again by St Clair Baddeley in 1925-6, it lies approximately 700 yards (640 m) south-east of the main courtyard building and has not been afforded the discussion and structural examination it undoubtedly deserves.

Baddeley published an article on his investigations at this site, also illustrated by Forestier, in *The Illustrated London News* in 1928, and his formal report two years

later (Baddeley 1930). Forestier made a reasonable attempt with his depiction of the temple, but he must have been given limited information by Baddeley, with the consequence that there are a number of inaccuracies: notably the height of the building, his reconstruction is too low and out of proportion, appearing somewhat squat, as the columns along the front are too short, probably having based them on the dimensions of the single complete drum measured by Baddeley (discussed below). Forestier also appears to have been unaware that the walls of the temple very likely narrowed at least twice from the very broad foundation courses, the thickest on any rural temple in Britain and he omitted to incorporate the smaller columns seen on site into the side walls to create an open ambulatory (discussed below). The *cella* wall was also depicted crossing the full width of the interior creating a narthex, this also being most unlikely. The accompanying drawing (Fig. 9.17) is a reinterpretation by the first author (BW) and L. Thompson (see also Beeson, this volume).

An elderly quarryman related to Baddeley that he and his brother had carried off over 300 loads of stone from the building around 1871-72 for the construction of, and repairs to, cottages and gateways in the village of Yanworth on the opposite side of the valley, where they can be seen in walls to this day (Fig. 9.18). The lower walls of the temple, partly surviving in the nineteenth century some four courses high, were built of massive finely finished stone blocks averaging 4 feet in length (1.22 m), quite exceptional for a temple in Britain and referred to by Farrer as being 'cyclopean' in scale, with many others scattered around awaiting transit off the site. The building had been constructed on a broad terrace cut back into the slope of the hill above the valley floor. On the evidence of various sizes of column fragments, its frontage must originally have supported a columned portico with an ambulatory surrounding the *cella*, remains of which was seen by Farrer and others, but which had been destroyed by Baddeley's day. On the evidence of the surviving *in situ* stones in its south-west corner, the lower walling could have stood 4 feet high (1.20 m), the lower course, 5 feet in breadth (1.50 m) protruded slightly as a chamfered off-set. At the south-west corner, the stones extended westwards, forming what was mistakenly interpreted as part of an attached structure, possibly a priest's house, owing to a scatter of inaccurately described 'hypocaust' tiles. These were more likely to have been discarded *pilae* bricks used in the interior walls of the temple (several of the tiles are recorded as being impressed with animal paw and hoof prints). This stone-built extension, recorded as 7 feet 6 inches (2.30 m) in breadth, should be identified as a corner buttress and was suggested as such by Lewis

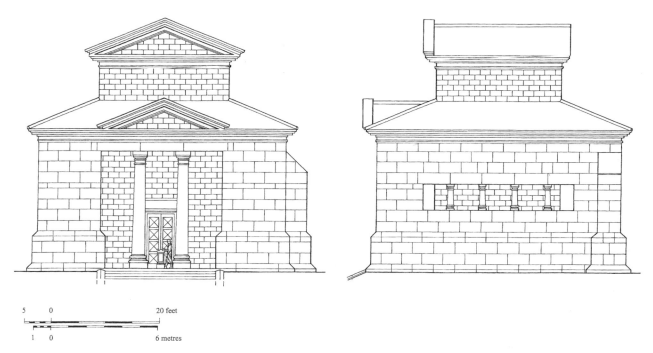

5   0   20 feet

1   0   6 metres

Figure 9.17. Reconstruction of the 'Upper Valley Temple'. (B. Walters and L. J. Thompson)

(1966, 18). The chamfered stones at the base of the temple supported two further courses, the third level at the south-west corner also being chamfered on its upper face, suggesting the walls narrowed again from that level, but could have continued above it to an unknown height, creating a screen wall 4 feet (1.20 m) in thickness and easily 8 feet in height (3 m) to carry the ambulatory columns above the floor inside. This is not improbable considering the scale of the building and thickness of its foundations. A smaller column base and capital probably originating from the ambulatory exists, along with other large cut stone blocks, at the entrance to a cottage in Yanworth (Fig. 9.18, A & B). Another column is preserved at the adjacent 'villa'.

Among the architectural details identified by Baddeley was a column drum 18 inches (0.50 m) in diameter and 2 feet 7 inches (0.80 m) in height, along with other similar broken drums. That the columns had been built in sections indicates they had been very large. If Baddeley's complete drum originated from the base, when applying the formula of multiplying the diameter of a column shaft by eight it would have been around 12 feet (3.65 m) high (the approximate height depicted by Forestier). However, the elderly quarryman reported to Baddeley that he had found an even larger column drum; if this had a diameter in the range of 24 inches (0.61 m) and originated from the base, this would suggest a shaft of 16 feet (4.88 m). The complete columns, incorporating the moulded base, capital and header stone, each approximately around

12 inches deep (0.30 m), would create columns in the region of at least 19 feet in height (5.80 m), suggesting that they must have graced the front of the temple. Considering the scale of the foundations and breadth of the building this estimate is quite acceptable and of better proportion to that depicted by Forestier. Other pieces of architecture recovered included what Baddeley describes as a fragment of architrave; Lewis (1966, 41) identified it as being the only fragment of stone entablature recovered from a rural temple in Britain (at the time he was writing).

Also recovered was a moulded capital, fragments of smaller columns, stone *voussoirs,* along with smaller well finished stone blocks, both probably surviving from the *cella*. Blocks of calcareous tufa, undoubtedly used as vaulting within the building, hexagonal sandstone roofing slabs and many terracotta tiles, no doubt from string courses in the *cella* walls. The interior of the building had been badly disturbed by routing out the more easily carried blocks from the *cella* and its foundations. Baddeley relates that the *cella* had been completely obliterated before his investigations, but in 1867 was 'clearly traceable' by Mr J. W. Grover. Fragments of scattered *opus signinum*, and what Baddeley referrers to as 'several *opus signinum* bricks' 12 x 7 inches (0.30 x 0.18 m) may have come from the original floor surface. Farrer found fragments of mosaic discarded near the south-west buttress, possibly originating from a panel within the *cella*. Whether the temple was a Romano-Celtic form, with a lantern peaked pyramid

Figure 9.18A & B. Column base and capital in Yanworth village. (L. J. Thompson)

roof (Lewis's (1966) Romano-Celtic type 1A) (Fig. 9.17), or on the evidence of the massive proportions of its front columns and fragment of entablature, a classical pedimented structure, is open to speculation. Baddeley cut trenches into the slope forward of the north front wall overlooking the river valley, and located, under collapsed building debris, broad terracing 4 and 8 feet (1.23 and 2.45 m) respectively front to rear and 2 and 3 feet in height (0.61 and 0.92 m), which he correctly interpreted as foundation platforms for the construction of a flight of stone steps, long since robbed out. The full breadth of these terraces was not identified but they extended 12 feet (3.96 m) north of the temple wall. Baddeley suggested they may have continued for 100 feet (over 30 m). A curious pit, lined with compacted rough stones, was located on the central axis just inside the entrance, in the fill of which were found two stones, both 'pierced' by 'two small clean-cut holes' and stained green with copper oxide suggesting they had originally been attached to something made of copper-alloy. This pit may have been dug for a ritual foundation deposit or, far more likely, a firm stone-packed base to support either a statue of the incumbent deity, standing impressively at the head of the approach steps, or a large altar visible from the valley below.

It has been suggested that the building may have been a mausoleum, on account of some human bone found by Farrer in his excavation, and of a single fragment of human jaw-bone recovered by Baddeley from the fill of the pit. This interpretation has been proposed for the building in recent publications on Chedworth (Esmonde Cleary 2012; 2013). The building, however, is excessively large for such a purpose in Roman Britain and some way from a public road; the normal location for such a structure. The bone fragments are much more likely to have been residual from an earlier burial, disturbed during the construction of the building. The consensus remains that it had once been an impressive temple, though not necessarily dedicated to Silvanus, as proposed by Esmonde Cleary in 2014. The figurine from the site, recorded by Baddeley (1930, 261; Webster 1983, 20, no.22) is not of Silvanus (Henig, *pers. comm.*).

Dominating the view from the valley to the north-west, as well as being inter-visible from the north *porticus* of the 'villa' and all the satellite sites in the area, such a lavish religious building, so far from an urban conurbation and located so close to the approach into the 'villa' testifies that it was a very significant part of the whole Chedworth complex, and unquestionably a major reason for its existence, including the foundation of the 'villa' in the second century.

(5) Workers' settlement (RCHM(E) 1976, 28, building 5)

Identified by James Farrer in 1865, 250 yards (229 m) due south of the 'Upper Valley Temple' (4) on a natural hillside platform, a number of walls associated with Roman pottery and evidence of metalworking covering a considerable area. Webster suggested that this may have been the settlement for the workers servicing the sanctuary along with small smithies producing metal votives (Webster 1991, 111). Such industrial areas are quite common near temple sites, housing the personnel and workshops for maintaining the main buildings as well as manufacturing metal votives.

(6) Yanworth 1 (RCHM(E) 1976, 135)

Recorded in the Royal Commission inventory as being located on almost level ground at the south-west corner of Yanworth Wood, 900 yds (825 m) north-east of the 'villa' entrance is a feature, most certainly a building platform approx. 25 ft by17 ft (7.60 m x 5.20 m) with building stones, including a further large rectangular block 65 yds (59.50 m) to the north-east. Roman building material, fourth-century pottery and coins were scattered over the area between two presumed buildings. It has been considered as a possible small settlement, but its position on the north side of the valley, sited directly opposite the 'Upper Valley Temple' and consisting of only two small stone-built structures, is suggestive of a pair of further shrines. It is undoubtedly connected, by a raised trackway 10 ft wide (3 m), to the recently identified large circular structure, the 'Lower Valley Temple' (3).

(7) Cassey Compton (RCHM(E) 1976, 37, Compton Abdale)

Situated on a curve of the River Coln south of the hamlet of Cassey Compton, and 1300 yards (1200 m) north of the 'villa', this site is something of an enigma (Fig. 9.19), and is included here with some reservation there being very few detailed discoveries from the site, it being simply referred to as 'undated earthworks' in the RCHM(E) 1976 volume. Although Richmond originally considered this site to be Roman, it was mostly excluded from the RCHM(E) Inventory, which suggests a medieval origin. The lower part of the site consists principally of a square mound surrounded on three sides by an embankment and an elongated axial hollow falling towards the river on the west side, the whole enclosed by a loop in the river. On its east side a dry conduit bisects the site, above which extends a steep slope cut with a series of terraces which may very well be medieval. The lower ground plan and close proximity to the river and flood plain looks most unlike a medieval habitation site,

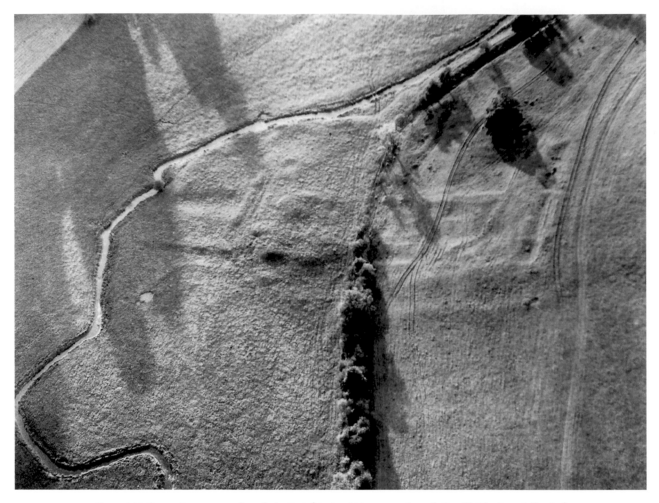

Figure 9.19. Cassey Compton earthworks in 1962. (National Monument Record, Harold Wingham Collection)

and seems too small for a mill. Romano-British sherds have been recovered from the fields close by, and a few pieces of Roman pottery, a cut stone block and a single *tessera* were recovered on the surface of the earthworks many years ago. The site has never been investigated, but the evidence may be suggestive of a Roman origin, later adapted in the medieval period. The possibility of a spring line shrine should not be dismissed for the time being, as the site would certainly have been inter-visible from the 'Upper Valley Temple' and the small buildings at the edge of Yanworth Wood.

(8) Chedworth Woods Enclosure (Walters 2013)

This trapezoidal earthwork (Figs 9.20 and 9.21), having undoubted rounded corners at its west end, suggests it might be Roman, but it also resembles similar late prehistoric enclosures. Banked only at the wider west end, it is open to the east where a narrow hollow way ascends the hill roughly on its central axis, cutting the bank off-centre on its west side, considered here to be a much later track. Being open-ended it cannot

have been intended to hold livestock, and is unlikely to have formed part of a chain of defensive works. In the Roman period, from this elevated and probably tree-less location, the other satellite buildings would all have been inter-visible, especially the 'Valley Temples' below. A geophysical survey over the south-west corner of its interior identified possible linear trenches and post-pits, suggesting a timber-built structure, but no datable material was identified from the ground surface (Sabin and Donaldson 2012; Walters 2013).

Conclusions

The reinterpretation for the Chedworth building, outlined above, along with the points arguing a reassessment of function, have to be weighed in conjunction with the unusual quantity of religious and cult-like artefacts which have been recovered, far more than has been identified from any other 'residential villa', or from many a conventional temple in Britain; whereas in the counter-balance, there are no obvious agricultural contexts until the very final period. Structurally what

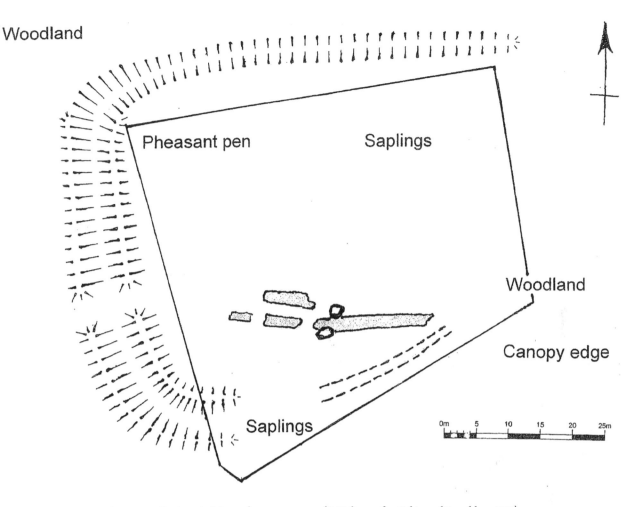

Figure 9.20. Site 8: resistivity and contour survey. (B. Walters, after Sabin and Donaldson 2012)

has to be recognised are the extensive ranges of baths, the ornate almost ceremonial conjoined rooms in the west wing, spacious dining rooms, and probable double-storied accommodation block in the south range; all of which implies a more public usage for the buildings. This point is emphasised further by the erosion on stone surfaces caused by the tread of large numbers of feet during a relatively short passage of time. This extreme abrasion is indicated by the wear of the border *tesserae* at the entry into the south corridor from Room 25b, but most dramatically on the threshold between the *frigidarium* and *tepidarium* in the west baths where the stone has been totally worn through at its centre. Even allowing for heavy duty shoes to protect the feet from the heat of the *caldarium* floor, the wear is too excessive for a family villa.

The sculptured pieces gathered from all the buildings in the complex form an unusual assemblage for a 'villa'. These include several pieces from statuettes of Diana mentioned above, the non-inscribed altar from beneath the floor of the *nymphaeum*, and a number of small 'votive'

altars with incised figures of a male warrior, presumably a local equivalent to Mars, and a bronze thumb possibly hacked from a Sabazius cult hand (Webster 1983/1991). In 1998, a pewter libation bowl was recovered from the north wing, an unusual item to find in a wealthy country house, but quite acceptable in a religious one, especially if the resident *magi* had resided there. Among the coin assemblage, many specimens appear to have been deliberately debased as though to ritually 'kill them' as votive offerings to the spirit world. Several items betray signs of iconoclasm, which may also have been the fate of the central panel of the Bacchic mosaic in Room 5; and not solely the result of its eventual collapse into the hypocaust. The survival intact of the small altars implies they had been buried or concealed as 'votives', thereby escaping iconoclast destruction.

Finally, the deeply incised Chi-Rho emblems on the suggested 'coping' slabs from the *nymphaeum*, unquestionably symbolises a later Christian 'cleansing of the waters', and thereby, a de-paganising of the site in its entirety. How long the sanctuary lasted into the

Figure 9.21. Aerial view of site 8 earthworks above the 'villa' in 2010. (Copyright Get Mapping plc)

fourth century eludes us, even though a large number of the coins recorded cover the period AD 364 to 378 they appear to end by 383. Theodosius' edict for the closure of temples and household shrines in the early 390's would appear too late for the cessation of its activities, as later degraded structural changes to the building had almost certainly begun before then. Perhaps the popularity for such healing activities had waned by the later 370's making the facility unprofitable, resulting in the building being sub-divided among lower-status families engaged in agricultural activities; as recognised at Great Witcombe around the same time.

The similarity of architectural style and facilities at Chedworth and Great Witcombe is striking. Both were built on artificially terraced hillsides, adjacent to a perpetual supply of water with an elevated court surrounded by a range of formal public rooms dominated by a central tower. Feasting rooms, latrines, lesser and greater bath suites fed from a *nymphaeum,* along with adjacent hillside temples; all implying a like mind in

their conception. Nine miles apart (15 km), set in the Gloucestershire limestone hills, could both have been commissioned and designed by the same school of *magi*?

Appendix: Clerestory lights or windows?

Artistic reconstructions of Roman villas in Britain invariably incorporate clerestory lights below the upper roof line to illuminate interiors. In a great many cases, if the ground floor was maintained throughout a building at the same level as the entrance passage, this is a serious misconception. Too often artists (and archaeologists) fail to calculate the internal ceiling height required to accommodate clerestory windows above a *porticus* roof, which can only work where floor levels in the internal rooms are much higher than the side passageways, or in 'basilica' style buildings with a roof-high central nave. A building, with an average portico 8 feet wide (2.45 m) and ground floors all at the same level, would require an internal ceiling of at least 15 feet (4.57 m) due to the dimensions of structural details above the summit of the portico roof, the pitch of which would be at a minimum 25 degrees, and where it joins into the main structural wall, the line of its upper tile level could easily reach 10 to 11 feet (3.35 m) above its floor. If a portico is wider its upper roof line will be correspondingly higher and the ceiling height inside the building proportionally higher again. A portico 10 feet wide (3.05 m) would require the internal ceilings to be at least 17 feet (5.20 m) high. Such high ceilings are not a sustainable proposition for houses in the cold northern climate of Britannia. Any heating provided would be substantially lost and wasted in the upper void of a room. The majority of single-storied residential buildings in Britain would have lower ceilings in the region of around 10 feet in height (3.05 m), illuminated by windows set into the main inner structural walls, within a fully columned or arcaded open porticus, or by high splayed windows set into the rear walls, where there was no outer corridor. The main roof of such buildings would have spanned its full width, including the front portico/corridor, reducing the overall height and accumulated weight of the building. Chedworth, however, presents an unusual and most interesting structural challenge.

References

Baddeley, W. St Clair 1924 The country life of the Romans in England. *The Illustrated London News*, July 12, 1924, 68-75.

Baddeley, W. St Clair 1928 The shrine of an unknown Roman-British god. *The Illustrated London News*, December 1, 1928, 1043-44.

Baddeley, W. St Clair 1930 The Romano-British temple, Chedworth. *Transactions of the Bristol & Gloucestershire Archaeological Society* 52, 255-64.

Bethell, P. 2006 *Chedworth Roman Villa*. National Trust Guide, London.

Bethell, P. 2007 *Chedworth Roman Villa Archaeological Assessment. Summary of recent archaeological interventions 1977-2006.* Unpublished Atkins Heritage Report.

Binsfeld, W. 1969 Das Quellheiligtum Wallenborn bei Heckenmünster. *Trierer Zeitschrift* 32, 239-68.

Boon, G. C. 1989 A Roman sculpture rehabilitated: the Pagans Hill dog. *Britannia* 20, 201-17.

Buckman, J. and Hall, R. W. 1873 *Notes on the Roman Villa at Chedworth, Gloucestershire; with a catalogue descriptive of the articles deposited in the Museum attached to it; with a plan.* C. H. Savory, Cirencester.

Budei, J. 2016 *Gallorömischer Heiligtümer. Neue Studien zur Lage und den räumlichen Bezügen.* Verlag Franz Philipp Rutzen, Mainz and Ruhpolding.

Burnham, B. and Wacher, J. 1990 *The Small Towns of Roman Britain.* Batsford, London.

Cleary, R., Goode, J. and Bethell, P. 1998a Chedworth, Chedworth Roman Villa, in Archaeological Review 1997. *Transactions of the Bristol & Gloucestershire Archaeological Society* 116, 196-9.

Cleary, R., Goode, J., Bethell, P. and Cosh, S. 1998b Archaeological investigations at Chedworth Roman Villa. *Glevensis* 31.

Cosh, S. R. and Neal, D. S. 2010 *Roman Mosaics of Britain, Vol. IV, Western Britain.* Society of Antiquaries of London, London.

Cruse, A. 2004 *Roman Medicine.* Stroud, Tempus.

De Cazenove, O. *et al.* 2012 Le lieu de culte du dieu Apollon Moritasgus à Alésia. Phases chronologiques, parcours de l'eau, distribution des offrandes. In De Cazenove, O. and Méniel, P. (ed.), *Etudier les Lieux de Culte en Galle romaine*, 95-121. Editions Monique Mergoil, Montagnac.

Dunbabin, K. A. 1978 *The Mosaics of Roman North Africa.* Oxford Monographs on Classical Archaeology, Oxford.

Esmonde Cleary, S. 2012 *Chedworth Roman Villa, Gloucestershire.* National Trust site guide, Warrington.

Esmonde Cleary, S. 2013 *Chedworth: Life in a Roman Villa.* The History Press, Stroud.

Esmonde Cleary, S. 2014 Imperial country life. *Country Life* September 24, 2014, 114-17.

Esmonde Cleary, S., Wood, J. and Durham, E. 2022 *Chedworth Roman Villa. Excavations and re-imaginings from the nineteenth to the twenty-first centuries.* Britannia Monograph 35, London.

Farrer, J. 1865 Notice of recent excavations in Chedworth Wood, on the estate of the Earl of Eldon, in the County of Gloucestershire. *Proceedings of the Society of Antiquaries of Scotland* 6.2, 278-83.

Fox, G. E. 1905 Notes on some probable traces of Roman fulling in Britain. *Archaeologia* 59, 207-32.

Goodburn, R. 1979 *The Roman Villa Chedworth.* National Trust site guide, London.

Grenier, A. 1960 *Manuel d'Archéologie gallo-romaine, IV, Les Monuments des Eaux.* Picard, Paris.

Grew, F. 1980 Roman Britain in 1979. I, sites explored. *Britannia* 11, 346-402.

Haeussler, R. 2019 *Apollo Cunomaglos*, Lord of the Wolves. *Bandue. Revista de la Sociedad Española de Ciencias de las Religiones* 11, 65-82.

Henig, M. 1993 *Roman Sculpture from the Cotswold Region.* Corpus Signorum Imperii Romani (CSIR) Great Britain 1.7, British Academy, Oxford.

Henig, M. 2004 The arts of Rome in Carlisle and the civitas of the Carvetii and their influence. In McCarthy, M., and Weston, D. (ed.), *Carlisle and Cumbria. Roman and Medieval Architecture, Art and Archaeology. British Archaeological Association Conference Transactions* 27, 11-28.

Henig, M. 2022 The sculptured stone. In Esmonde Cleary *et al.* 2022, 254-63.

Henig, M. and Goodburn, R. 1982 A Roman bronze bust, possibly from Chedworth. *Transactions of the Bristol & Gloucestershire Archaeological Society* 100, 251-53.

Horne, P. and King, A. C. 1980 Romano-Celtic temples in continental Europe: a gazetteer of those with known plans. In W. Rodwell (ed.), *Temples, Churches and Religion: Recent Research in Roman Britain,* 369-555. British Archaeological Reports (BAR) British Series 77, Oxford.

Jackson, R. 1988 *Doctors and Diseases in the Roman Empire.* British Museum Press, London.

Johnston, D. E. 1978 Villas of Hampshire and the Isle of Wight. In Todd, M. (ed.), *Studies in the Romano-British Villa,* 71-92. Leicester University Press, Leicester.

King, A. and Soffe. G. 2013 *A Sacred Island. Iron Age, Roman and Saxon Temples and Ritual on Hayling Island.* Hayling Island Excavation Project, Winchester.

Lacroix, B. 1956 Un sanctuaire de source du IVe siècle aux Fontaines-Salées (Yonne). *Revue Archéologique de l'Est et du Centre-Est* 7, 245-64.

Lacroix, B. 1963 Un sanctuaire de l'eau de plan circulaire aux Fontaines-Salées. *Revue Archéologique de l'Est et du Centre-Est* 14, 81-114.

Lewis, M. J. T. 1966 *Temples in Roman Britain.* Cambridge University Press, Cambridge.

Mitard, P.-H. 1993 *Le Sanctuaire Gallo-Romain des Vaux-de-la-Celle à Genainville (Val-d'Oise).* Centre de recherches archéologiques du Vexin français, Guiry-en-Vexin.

Nouvel, P. 2011 Les sanctuaires de Villards-d'Héria (Jura). Apport des travaux anciens et récents. In Guichard, V. (ed.), *Aspects de la Romanisation dans l'Est de la Gaule, Vol. 2,* 619-27. Collection Bibracte 21, Bibracte/Glux-en-Glenne.

Papworth, M. 2012 *Report on a Geophysical Survey of the south part of the field immediately east of Chedworth Roman Villa. 17 July 2012.* National Trust.

Phillips, B., Thompson, L. and Walters, B. 2005 *Littlecote Roman Villa. An Illustrated Guide.* 2nd edition, Association for Roman Archaeology.

Reece, R. 1960 Coins from the Roman Villa at Chedworth. *Transactions of the Bristol & Gloucestershire Archaeological Society* 78, 162-5.

Richmond, I. A. 1960 The Roman Villa at Chedworth, 1958-59. *Transactions of the Bristol & Gloucestershire Archaeological Society* 78, 5–23.

RCHM(E) = Royal Commission on Historical Monuments (England) 1976 *Iron Age & Romano-British Monuments in the Gloucestershire Cotswolds.* Her Majesty's Stationery Office (HMSO), London.

Rutter, E. 1957 Chedworth Roman Villa: an exploratory trench. *Transactions of the Bristol & Gloucestershire Archaeological Society* 76, 160-4.

Sabin, D. and Donaldson, K. 2012 *Earthworks south-east of Chedworth Roman Villa Gloucestershire.* Archaeological Surveys Ltd., for The Association for Roman Archaeology.

Salway, P. 2008 A publication policy for Chedworth. *Britannia* 39, 253-6.

Salway, P. 2009 When is a villa not a villa? *Current Archaeology* 232, 48-49.

Scarth, H. M. 1869 On the Roman villa at Chedworth, Gloucestershire, discovered in 1864. *Proceedings of the British Archaeological Association* 25, 215-27.

Smith, J. T. 1978 Villas as a key to social structure. In Todd, M. (ed.), *Studies in the Romano-British Villa,* 149-85. Leicester University Press, Leicester.

Stevens, C. E. 1947 A possible conflict of laws in Roman Britain. *Journal of Roman Studies* 37, 132-4.

Summerton, N. 2007 *Medicine and Health Care in Roman Britain.* Shire Archaeology 87, Princes Risborough.

Walters, B. 1996 Exotic structures in 4th-century Britain. In Johnson. P., and Haynes. I, (ed.), *Architecture in Roman Britain,* 152-62. Council for British Archaeology (CBA) Research Report 94, York.

Walters, B. 2000 Chedworth: Roman villa or sanctuary? A re-interpretation of a well-known site. *ARA Bulletin of the Association for Roman Archaeology* 9, 10–13.

Walters, B. 2001 A perspective on the social order of Roman villas in Wiltshire. In Ellis, P. (ed.), *Roman Wiltshire and After. Papers in honour of Ken Annable,* 127-46. Wiltshire Archaeological and Natural History Society, Devizes.

Walters, B. 2009 Roman villas in Britain: farms, temples, or tax-depots. *Current Archaeology* 230, 30-35.

Walters, B. 2013 The Chedworth Roman Villa Environs Project. *Association for Roman Archaeology News* 30, 16-19.

Webster, G. 1969 The future of villa studies. In Rivet, A. L. F. (ed.), *The Roman Villa in Britain,* 217-49. Routledge & Kegan Paul, London.

Webster, G. 1983 The function of the Chedworth Roman 'villa'. *Transactions of the Bristol & Gloucestershire Archaeological Society* 101, 5-20; also in Webster 1991, 95-111.

Webster, G. 1991 *Archaeologist at Large.* Batsford, London.

Wedlake, W. J. 1982 *The Excavations of the Shrine of Apollo at Nettleton, Wiltshire, 1956-1971.* Reports of the Research Committee of the Society of Antiquaries of London 40, London.

Weisgerber, G. 1975 *Das Pilgerheiligtum des Apollo und der Sirona von Hochscheid im Hunsrück.* Habelt, Bonn.

Wheeler, R. E. M. and Wheeler, T. V. 1932 *Excavation of the Prehistoric, Roman, and Post-Roman Site in Lydney Park, Gloucestershire.* Reports of the Research Committee of the Society of Antiquaries of London 9, Oxford.

Wightman, E. M. 1970 *Roman Trier and the Treveri.* Rupert Hart-Davis, London.

Witts, P. 2000 Mosaics and room function: the evidence from some fourth-century Romano-British villas. *Britannia* 31, 291-324.

Woodward, A. 1992 *Shrines and Sacrifice.* B. T. Batsford, London.

Zienkiewicz, J. D. 1986 *The Legionary Fortress Baths at Caerleon, vol.1 The Buildings.* CADW, Cardiff.

10

Acroterial decoration and *cantharus* fountains

Exotic architectural stonework from Great Witcombe and Chedworth

Anthony Beeson†

This paper discusses several distinctive pieces of Romano-British decorative and architectural stonework that were discovered at the Gloucestershire sites of Great Witcombe and Chedworth in the nineteenth century. They comprise a series of pierced panels ornamented with confronted S-shapes and part of an ornamental *cantharus* fountain. It traces the history of their discovery and the origins of their design, comparing them with other examples from Britain and the Roman Empire. It also explores their significance in connection with the claims that these sites have a religious status and suggests their original architectural settings within the complexes.

Several Roman sites in rural Gloucestershire and the Cotswolds have produced a wealth of decorative and architectural stone fragments, some of which are highly unusual survivals, whilst others are at present unique in Britain. The abundance of high-quality freestone in the district permitted the Roman builders and sculptors free rein to produce some of the finest architectural stonework to be found in Britannia, and in a quantity to ensure that, even after centuries of despoliation, a sufficiency remains to show the quality and sum of what had originally existed.

The great importance of Chedworth, until recently, was the fact that perhaps all of the stonework excavated on the site was still there and available for inspection and interpretation. At one time this was also the case at Great Witcombe, but new policies in the 1980s saw that collection banished to a store miles from the site, where it perhaps gained more security but could no longer be readily evaluated or inspire the casual visitor. Alas, this has now largely occurred at Chedworth as well with many interesting pieces now housed in a National Trust store at Sherborne in Gloucestershire. Part of this paper has had a very long gestation and sprang from a visit made to Great Witcombe as a 21-year-old in 1969 when I first discovered, and was excited by, the most complete of the pierced panels kept with other stonework in rooms 5 and 6 of the bath building there. Over the years I have sought out other examples in order to elucidate their original purpose.

In February 1818, labourers working on the estate of Sir William Hicks at Great Witcombe, Gloucestershire, uncovered a six-foot long stone that proved to be the lintel of a doorway leading to a finely decorated cult room containing a small, square, central pool continuously fed by piped spring water (Fig. 10.1). Many bones and skulls of bullocks, goats and stags were discovered in this room and the approach passage together with what Samuel Lysons, the great Gloucestershire antiquary, identified as an iron sacrificial axe. Lysons came at Hicks's request and excavated here, but he was to die in 1819 before he could properly publish his work. However, his paper posthumously published in *Archaeologia*, together with the many drawings and watercolours he produced during the excavation for an unrealised publication (now in the Society of Antiquaries collection at Burlington House, London) still remain to elucidate the site. Of the cult room he wrote,

'Several circumstances tend to prove that the first room discovered (No. 1 on his plan) had been appropriated to sacred uses; indeed it would be difficult to imagine, for what other purpose it could have been designed. The decorations of the walls sufficiently indicate that it could not have been designated for any mean use; the stone just within the doorway, separated from the pavement by a border of brick tiles, seems to have been the base of an altar, and the recesses above mentioned were probably designed for the reception of statues, as well as to strengthen the wall built against high ground. The *piscina* or cistern was a common appendage of the Roman temple or other sacred edifice. The bones and horns found in this place, were no doubt of those victims. This building seems to have been that kind of chapel or place of worship which sometimes formed a part of the Roman dwelling house; and was denominated *Sacrarium*. On the outside of this building, in the court No. 12, was found the figure of a lyre cut in stone, 2 feet 3½ inches (70 cm) high, and part of another, which seem to have been placed on this building. (Lysons 1821, 180)

Figure 10.1. The cult chamber, Room 1, at Great Witcombe as first uncovered and recorded in watercolour by Samuel Lysons in 1818. The painting is a marvellous, yet previously unpublished, record of the room's decorative plaster. To the right of the small but deep central pool may be seen the large S-panel. (D. Rider)

Another Gloucestershire villa, founded between AD 60-150 at Wortley, near Wotton-under-Edge, has provided a parallel cult cellar with glazed splayed windows, painted plaster and two smaller niches. Beneath its *opus signinum* floor the room was criss-crossed by two channels believed to have fed, through rising water, a central lead font or basin, placed above their juncture (Wilson *et al.* 2014, 12-17, 22-26, 39-42, figs. 12-20). Interestingly, the square cult room at Great Witcombe with its central pool also recalls the crypt beneath the *cella* of the Temple of Serapis (known as the *Ginnasio*) at Syracuse in Sicily, which was built in the style of an Iseion. The crypt, reached by a staircase, also possessed a niche for a statue in its west wall.

Acroterial decoration

It is, however, the decorative figures of lyres that concern us here. Although quite roughly carved and finished they were striking and attractive ornaments and designed 'in a high style of art, and bid fair to vie with some of the boasted remains of Italy herself' (Clarke 1850-8; Figs 10.2

and 10.3). One survives only as a fragment but the finest one that Lysons illustrates clearly shows the decorative quality that they must have had when new (RCHM(E) 1976, pl. 28). The design is simple but effective. Two antithetic S-shapes stand back-to-back separated by a central, slightly tapering, and gently waisted, upright, which protrudes between the upper curves of the Ss to form a focus. Although now roughly flat-topped this upright may originally have been finished with a rounded or triangular top. Incised decoration appears on only one face of the piece suggesting that it was only to be viewed from that side. Two chiselled horizontal lines, representing a tying band, ornament the upper part of the design where the necks of the Ss meet the central upright. A single horizontal line, representing another tying band, appears at the foot just above the lower volutes. Above this on the front of the central upright, is a long, open-topped, rectangular panel. Its upper limits curve outwards below the necks of the Ss. All volutes are roughly inscribed with spirals and rather resemble jam sponge rolls in appearance. The sweep of the lower parts of the Ss are suggested to the eye at the volutes

Figure 10.2. Lysons' watercolour drawing of the large pierced panel from Great Witcombe as first found but with additions by the author to show all of the decoration on the piece. (D. Rider and A. Beeson)

Figure 10.3. The S-panel as exhibited at Great Witcombe in 1966. By this date the upper section of the panel had been further damaged and wired together.

and corners by the simple use of chip carved triangles (Fig. 10.4). Originally the decorative lines would most likely have been picked out in red on the white stone in the manner of contemporary carved inscriptions to make the decoration more obvious to the viewer. Surviving stonework from Great Witcombe (Fig. 10.5) shows that at least some parts of the façade of the complex were rendered white and also painted with false masonry joints in red as also survives *in situ* on the south-eastern façade of the north-western revetment of the riverside water shrine or villa at New Weir, Swainshill, near Kenchester in Herefordshire (Walker 1998). This was a common form of exterior decoration both in the Roman and the medieval world but evidence for it is rarely encountered in Britannia, which makes it all the more strange that these important pieces have never been published. At Great Witcombe, the lyre shape created by the Ss and central upright is contained by two outer and undecorated supports, only one of which has survived. When Lysons found the panel, the surviving section was in one piece, but its fragility was illustrated by the fact that by the late 1960s when I first encountered it on site and became interested in it, the upper part had been broken into three pieces, and was both cemented and wired into place (RCHM(E) 1976, pl. 28). Now in store, the mortar has been removed and only two pieces appear to have survived. These no longer join and are not kept together (Figs 10.6 and 10.7). All that survived of a second panel was the banded portion of the upper central section which is also illustrated in plate 28 of the RCHM(E) volume. It could not be located in the English Heritage store whilst researching for this paper. Neither the drawing of the large panel done by Lysons nor that published by Blagg (2002, 76) is wholly accurate, but the former has been amended in the attached plate here to include all of its decoration (see Fig. 10.2).

That Lysons firmly believed that they had been placed high on the building is evidenced by the existence of two pencil sketches or 'doodles' that exist on his excavation drawings in the Society of Antiquaries' collection in Burlington House, London (Figs 10.6 and 10.7). There he positioned them as roof finials sitting at either end of the roof ridge, with their narrow sides facing out from the gables and to be seen full-on from the

Figure 10.4. Detail of the chip and incised decoration on the large panel.

Figure 10.5. A previously unpublished fragment of whitened stone from Great Witcombe, presumably from the façade of the building. Painted with false joints in imitation of red-mortared ashlar masonry it is a rare clue to as to external decoration of at least part of the structure.

side view of the roof. This particular sketch restores the roof over room 1 itself as clad in stone hexagonal tiles, which was presumably what Lysons discovered in its ruins. Unless the result of a re-roofing programme or a polychromatic roof, this contradicts the idea that the early building was roofed in terracotta tiles, although Lysons' watercolour of the room after excavation shows neatly stacked terracotta and stone tiles (Leach 1998,131; see Fig. 10.1). In another drawing Lysons placed one double S as a central pediment ornament within a gable. On both sketches, obviously only remembering the lyre

Figure 10.6. The large panel as it survives.

Figure 10.7. The detached neck of the larger panel showing the symbolic rope binding and the top of the central upright.

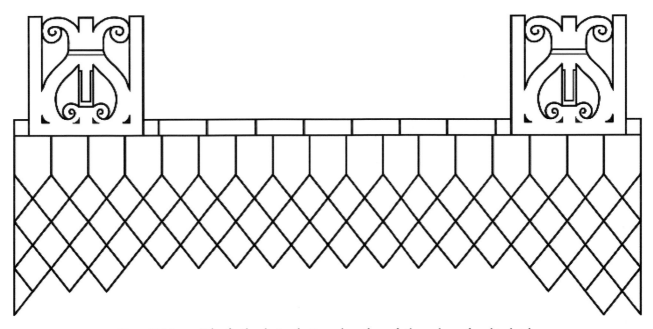

Figure 10.8. Lysons' idea for the placing the S-panels on the roof ridge, redrawn from his sketch.

Figure 10.9. Lysons' alternative placing of the panels as a tympanum or gable decoration redrawn from his sketch to include the outer supports. When deprived of its uprights the similarity of the Great Witcombe S-motif to the acroterion *at Assos (Figure 10.11) is striking.*

shape, he forgot to include the outer uprights. As the originals are so faint, they have been redrawn for the purpose of this publication together with their uprights (Figs 10.8 and 10.9). The prospect that they might have been balustrade panels such as one might find along an open-sided corridor or balcony as has been suggested in more recent times does not seem to have occurred to him (Clarke 1850, 10, pl. 1, fig,1). As this paper will show, they may only be termed as 'balustrading' in so far as that term is used architecturally to describe the false balustrading applied as decoration or screening to roof-lines in Renaissance and later classical architecture.

Certainly, their shattered condition suggests that they had indeed fallen from a great height, rather than been smashed for reuse as building materials at some later period. The very nature of their fretted decoration would have made them of limited use as salvaged blocks for rebuilding and even less if broken up, although burning for lime may have been their intended fate. As the ruins were subjected to heavy stone-robbing over the centuries, it is perhaps remarkable that so much good quality architectural stonework still remained on the site to be found. It also illustrates just how much there must have been originally.

The S-shape motif

Although the antithetic or confronted S-motif (sometimes referred to as a double-volute scroll) does broadly resemble a lyre, with the central strengthening upright acting as the strings, this is only because in this instance the device is seen as a single element and not part of a series. The motif is an ancient one but here is highly stylised. To my knowledge the origin of the cresting design has not previously been traced in a British publication, but it originally derives from the *anthemion* or honeysuckle, with its S-shaped petals. In classical design it was probably first used by the Ionian Greeks, who themselves had borrowed it from earlier eastern civilisations. The curling petals of the central palmate often sprang from a base composed of confronted S-shapes, that, when used in a frieze, would form a running scroll. As time passed the S-shapes were enlarged so that when used as a single motif they often became the dominant feature of the design. In architecture this was particularly pertinent in the case of antefixes and acroterial decoration. The temple of Aphaia (c. 500 BC) on the island of *Aegina* had a spectacular pierced acroterion ornament flanked by pairs of *korai* or maiden statues at the apex of each pediment at either end of the building (Kowalczyk 1927, pl. 46 1; Marquand 1909, 239; Fig. 10.10), whilst the Doric temple of Athena at *Assos* (c. 530 BC) in Turkey had fine but solid examples above the central pediments. One is displayed on the restored façade of the temple in the archaeological museum, Istanbul. Notable here are the naturalistic tying bands of

Figure 10.10. A restoration of the spectacular acroterion *ornament from the Temple of Aphaia on the island of* Aegina, *c. 500 BC. The lower section with its central palmate between the scrolls is the ancestor of the Great Witcombe design. (1920s postcard)*

rope linking the Ss as in the stylised examples at Great Witcombe (Fig. 10.11). Not generally found on Roman examples, these traditional bands therefore link the Gloucestershire design back to the sixth century BC and earlier. Even before these surviving temple acroteria, and around 550 BC and for about thirty years beyond, it became the fashion in Attica to use the confronted S as the capital for grave *stelae*. These were then topped by statues of the Sphinx or Medusa. A superb pierced example that consists only of S-shapes and bears a close ancestral relationship to the Great Witcombe design is in the Museum of Fine Arts, Boston. The double-volutes are outlined with incised lines painted in black and red (Boardman 1985, pl. 228).

By Etruscan times the confronted S-design had become part of a standard decorative repertory and was used for the cresting of sacred buildings. It appears to have sometimes taken the place of individual antefixes and to have been placed as a frieze both along the sides of the edifice above the *sima* or gutter at roof edge level, and also climbed up the slopes of the pediments to join the central acroterion ornament. These were often *anthemion* palmettes. In other words, the original design for the *anthemion* had been split in two with the lower part (the base of the S) forming the cresting and the upper (the palmette) the *acroterion* (Fig. 10.12). As time passed these elements also would change (Hamlin 1916. 128-130, Figs. 156, 157).

Figure 10.11. The acroterion *decoration of the Temple of Athena at Assos as displayed in Istanbul archaeological museum. The decoration is dominated by the antithetic Ss whilst the cords tying the necks and bases of the volutes indicated at Great Witcombe are present here.*

Delicate examples of cresting survive in terracotta. The British Museum has on display a particularly fine Roman example in painted terracotta composed of interlaced double-volutes. This Italian piece dates from the first century BC (GR.1892 1-21.49; Terracotta D712; Fig. 10.13). Also in Italy, and from the same era and the following century, both of the villa complexes attributed to Pompey the Great at Albano and the maritime villa of Tiberius at Sperlonga have yielded examples of terracotta cresting that, with the addition of a palmette above the central upright, bear great resemblance to the design at Great Witcombe. The former example is displayed in the Museo Civico at Albano whilst the latter is in the site museum at Sperlonga. A first-century AD example, also in terracotta but featuring Victories crowned with palmettes between confronted Ss is illustrated by Kowalczyk (Kowalczyk 1927, 110). Allied to these is the fascinating brick and marble temple-tomb façade from Grottarossa on the Via Flaminia and now partially reconstructed in the Antiquarium Malborghetto, in Rome. Here an Antonine building copied the techniques of Etruscan and early Roman builders in a historical pastiche of terracotta and marble (Fig. 10.14). The S-cresting here was in marble and given tapering leaf-topped uprights

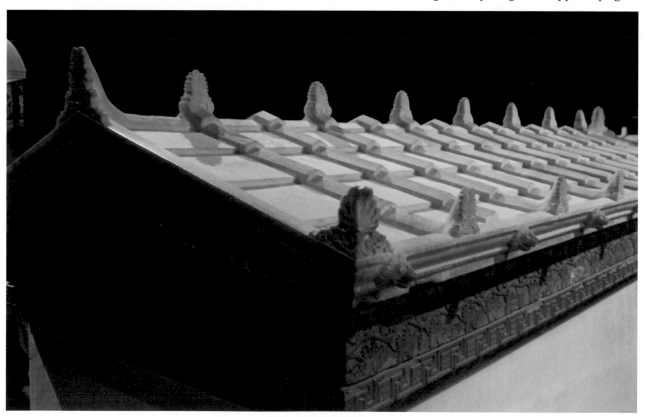

Figure 10.12. Royal sarcophagus from Sidon.

Figure 10.13. A first-century BC Roman painted terracotta cresting of interlaced double-volutes in the British Museum.

Figure 10.14. Detail of the marble S-cresting from Grottarossa. (Andrew Foster)

either side of each pair of Ss. These uprights and all later ones, however far-seemingly removed, have their origin in the blending of two aspects of the traditional design. Firstly, there is the broad central sword-like leaf of the *anthemion* palmette, and below it, and rising from between the Ss of the base a triangular topped stem or handle if the palmette itself is interpreted as a fan. No doubt when used in pierced cresting as at Grottarossa, uprights also provided additional strength to the panels, which in theory rather than execution, have strong connections with those from Great Witcombe (Messineo 1991, 130-134, figs 154-7; Thomas 2007, fig. 155 a, b). An intermediary stage in the development may be seen on a first-century AD bronze Sabazius relief from Rome, in the National Museum, Copenhagen, where a pediment of a shrine is topped by alternate single and double leafed palmettes (Godwin,1981, 160, fig. 130). A sestertius of AD 64-68 shows the *sima* of the rectangular temple of Janus in the Roman Forum crested with *anthemia* alternating with uprights that mask the roof completely (Cassanelli 2002, 208-209, fig. 208 (6)). To illustrate how the traditional *anthemion* palmette itself gradually became debased to resemble several pairs of S shapes either side of a broad blade-like upright, one only needs to regard those carved on blocks recovered in Istanbul from the excavated church of Saint Polyeuktos of AD 525 and now displayed adjacent to the ruins in the archaeological area known as Saraçhane Park. Although the fronds curl in the opposite direction to those at Great Witcombe there is again a band around the S petals tying them to the upright.

According to Blagg (2002, 75-6) the S-shape is used outside of Britain not only as a cresting ornament but also as a screen decoration. However, the examples that he gives do not accord with the latter interpretation and all are surely to be interpreted as roof decorations. Over many years of research into the use of this S-pattern in architecture I have not discovered one sure example of it having been used as a screen or balustrade. Even when pierced, stone screens and balustrades commonly conform to a small corpus of traditional designs and generally are made in imitation of wooden examples (see Beeson 2019a, figs 14, 21, 22, 31). The confronted and antithetic S however, always appears in connection with the roofs of buildings apart from on a *lararium* from Quinta de Marim, Portugal, where they are stacked to form pilasters (Beeson 2019a, fig. 7). Even when used decoratively on a tombstone or inscription, as on the fragment from Cadder in Lanarkshire, they are placed near the top of it as a running decoration. A bizarre example of this survives in a religious relief sculpted in a conflated Roman and Celtic art style from Trier now in the Rheinisches Landesmuseum. Two bands

of decoration appear in the upper half of the stone. In the lower field a man stands by a container from which curls a huge vine, whilst above them runs a running decoration of Ss and blade like uprights (Pobé 1961, 71, pl. 197). On buildings, Blagg writes only of its use as a cresting for raking pediments but a fragment of a relief showing the Temple of Apollo from Vienne now in the Musée Lapidaire de Vienne clearly shows it in use as a continual decoration also along the sides of the temple above the building's *sima* (Formigé 1949, fig. 27). It might be termed an antefix frieze although some solid panels may also have acted as an addition to the guttering for roofs (Fig. 10.15). Its origin in this position may be illustrated by the *anthemion* antefixes with their S-shaped bases that decorated the same position on Greek religious structures. Excellent examples in miniature survive on the roofed sarcophagi from the royal necropolis of Sidon, now in Istanbul Archaeology Museum (see Fig. 10.12). It might be suspected that buildings using it as a raking pediment decoration also had their eaves ornamented in the same way.

Examples of S-friezes survive at sites and in collections principally throughout the northern provinces of the Roman Empire, to where it must have spread and evolved from Italy. In France an example may be cited from *Andemantunnum* (Langres) and preserved in the Musée Lapidaire, together with acroterial ornaments from the same structure (Espérandieu 1907-1981, IV, 266). Also at Saint Laurent-sur-Othain, a single S from a rare pierced antefix frieze abuts what appears to be an acroterion base carved on one face with a pipe-playing satyr and on another with a dancing Bacchante (Espérandieu 1907-1981, XIV. 40, cat. 8449, pl. xliv 8449,1; Fig. 10.16). In the Musée Alésia, Alise-Ste-Reine, is a reconstructed pediment to a chapel of Venus that spectacularly preserves two thirds of the S and upright cresting together with its acroterial ornaments (Fauduet 1993, 77). A second- to third-century AD pipe-clay shrine to Venus, discovered in a grave at Quai Arloing, Lyon and now in the Musée Gallo-Romain de Lyon-Fourvière, displays either a circular pediment or (more likely) an open apsidal courtyard surrounded by a wall crowned with a continuous S-cresting (Fig. 10.17).

Rescue excavations in 2014 at the site of the second century religious precinct at Pont-Sainte-Maxence (Oise) in Northern France reported 'S-balustrade' fragments amongst the architectural elements found around the temple *cella* in the centre of a vast precinct. These were around 50 cm in height. The building faced a huge rectangular pool with an apsidal southern side (Brunet-Gaston and Gaston 2016, fig. 122). Likewise, at Windisch (*Vindonissa*) in Switzerland part of a classical

Figure 10.15. A rare portrayal of an S sima cresting on the temple of Apollo at Vienne as recorded on a relief in the Musée Lapidaire, Vienne.

Figure 10.16. The end element of an S-cresting frieze from St Laurent-sur-Othain. The terminal block may have been the corner element of a pediment and is decorated on two faces with a satyr and a bacchante. (From an early French postcard)

Figure 10.17. Pipe-clay shrine to Venus, from Quai Arloing, Lyon, in the Musée Gallo-Romain de Lyon-Fourvière. The S-cresting should be seen as standing upright on top of an apsidal wall surrounding an open shrine with a central statue standing within a niche.

temple pediment from a shrine outside of the fort has been reconstructed at the museum with its elaborate S cresting running up the raking side (Gessner-Siegfried 1912, 13-14, Westwand, cat. 5-6; Simonett 1947, 98-9).

A similarly elaborate decoration embellished a mausoleum in a walled enclosure at Wavre, Belgium (Drack 1988, fig. 255). In the internal courtyard of the Musée d'Art et Histoire, Geneva are two sections from a continuous S-frieze. There the base of each block has been angled so that it could be set on a similarly shaped base for stability, presumably once more on a raking pediment. Here the upper edge of the 'plate' behind the Ss has been shaped to echo their curve (Figs 10.18 and 10.19). *Carnuntum* in Austria has yielded several stones from the pediment of a temple from the Heliopolitanum sanctuary in the Mühläckern suburb of the town (see below). These include the apex stone together with a palmate *acroterion* decoration. Of great interest is the fact that the Ss are not in antithetic pairs as is usual, but march in file, one behind the other down the sloping sides of the pediment, each separated by a blade-like leaf (Ertel 1991, fig. 28). From Cologne, and in the Römisch-Germanische Museum, the gable of a *lararium* is ornamented with a continuous fluid S-cresting motif more akin to those of Etruscan buildings (Borger 1977, 89, fig. 26). The rear of the famous third-century Mithras relief from Dieburg, and now in the Dieburg Kriesmuseum, has the group of Phaeton-Mithras and Sol backed by the temple of the Sun, the pediment of which is crowned by S-cresting (MacKendrick 1970, 180, fig. 6.19). The use of the S-motif as a decorative feature on the pediments of gravestones is particularly common in Germany. The Steinhalle of the Landesmuseum, Mainz preserves several examples. The finest is that of Gnaeus Petronius Asellio, dating from the first century AD, and aping in appearance a temple tomb (Selzer 1988, 148, cat. 70) whilst that of Gaius Atilius Scruttarius (Selzer 1988, 136, cat. 47) is also decorated with the S-and-uprights frieze. A slight variant to these designs with elongated Ss occurs on the gravestone of Gnaeus Musius (Selzer 1988, 73, col. pl. 49). An early third-century AD gravestone from Salzburg in Austria has the image of the

Figure 10.18. A block from a frieze as preserved at the Musée d'Art et Histoire, Geneva.

Figure 10.19. Blocks from a continuous frieze as preserved at the Musée d'Art et Histoire, Geneva. The base of each block has been angled to sit on a similarly shaped base.

deceased man in a niche below a band carved with a dolphin. Above this is a single large confronted Ss motif that appears to have been originally flanked by uprights (Heger 1974, 211, cat. 92, fig. 92) in the manner of that from Great Witcombe. This gravestone refers of course to the S-topped grave *stelae* of the sixth century BC (Fig. 10.20).

In Britain the spectacular bearded second- or third-century Medusa pediment from a probable mausoleum in Chester is this country's finest illustration of the motif in use architecturally (Toynbee 1962, 158-9, cat. 84. pl. 91; Henig 2004, 33 no.104, pl. 29; Fig. 10.21). It is also, incidentally, one of the best in the entire Empire. What are missing from it are the eave and gable *acroterial* decorations, which lines on the *acroterion* corner bases suggest were the traditional *anthemion* in design and

carved on separate blocks. A fragment of what may be another tombstone or *lararium* survives at Corbridge with the finely carved motif being only 3 cm in height (Blagg 2002, 234, pl. lxviii) and again at Cadder, Lanarkshire, in the top left-hand corner of a slab (Keppie 1984, 46, cat. 126, pl. 32.) The S-cresting in a degenerate and misunderstood form can also be found on the recently discovered gravestone of Insus from Lancaster. Here the Ss are placed on their sides between the uprights (Bull 2007, 20).

Apart from tombstones, Britain has the remains of full-sized S-motif roof cresting. Corbridge has produced a cache of examples from the classical temples on the site (Forster and Knowles 1909, 351; fig. 14.29). Like the more accomplished examples from *Vindonissa* and Geneva these are carved on solid panels of stone (Fig. 10.22).

Figure 10.20. *The S-motif with supporters used as an acroterion decoration above a gravestone. Drawing of a relief built into the wall of a building in Nonnbergasse, Salzburg.*

Figure 10.21. *The bearded Medusa pediment from a mausoleum at Chester preserves Britain's finest illustration of the S-cresting used on a raking pediment.*

Figure 10.22. *Cresting block from a temple at Corbridge.*

Figure 10.23. *Angle block from a temple* tympanum *from Corbridge.*

Probably the background of such blocks may well have been painted blue or red to give a 'transparency' to them with the motifs then picked out in white. One surviving Corbridge panel has a blank and angled area at its left end that was intentional rather than a later fracture. This suggests that the piece was fitted into the lower left-hand corner of the *tympanum* of the pediment as part of the latter's decoration, a novel if not unique form of decoration at this period (Fig. 10.23). Use of the raking pediment decoration on the lower register of the *tympanum* is extremely rare in architecture but may be found as far back as on the sixth-century BC terracotta pediment of the Gelan treasury at *Olympia* (Yalouris

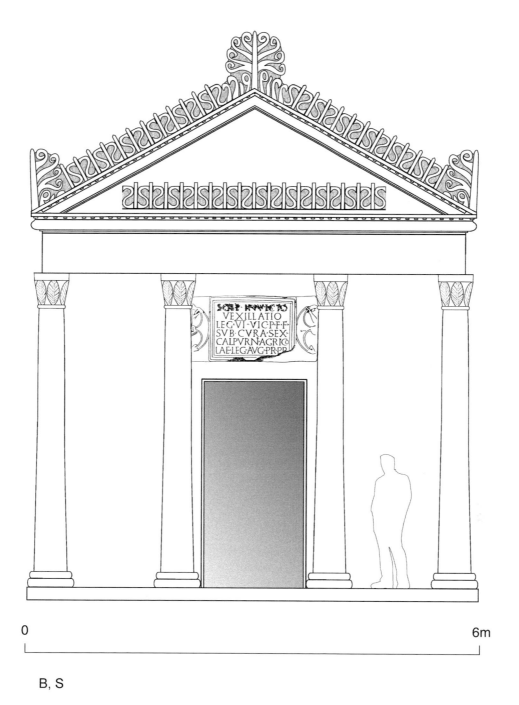

VEXILLATIO
LEG·VI·VICP·F·F·
SVB·CVRA·SEX·
CALP·VRN·AGRI©
LAE·LEG·AVG·PR·PR

0   6m

B, S

Figure 10.24. Reconstruction of the façade of one of the temples at Corbridge. (N. Hodgson)

1987, 87, pl. 86b). Was this example at Corbridge, like the Grottarossa pediment, another Antonine pastiche of ancient architectural decoration? The Corbridge Ss have strong serifs and the best preserved have well defined and round-topped uprights that protrude well above the tops of their S-shapes. S-panels in a different scale from the site suggest that more than one of the temples was decorated in this way. After years of the blocks being dismissed as probable screen panels, a recent survey of Corbridge's architectural stonework, jointly conducted between Tyne and Wear Museums and English Heritage, and allied to the author's own research, has finally officially recognised them as the *sima* and pedimental decoration that they undoubtedly are through an exciting new survey that illustrates the benefits of a thorough study of a site's Romano-British architectural stonework (Hodgson 2009, 97-101, figs 22-3; Hodgson 2010a; 2010b; Fig. 10.24).

At the enigmatic site at Well in Yorkshire, the excavations conducted by R. and D. Gilyard-Beer between 1938 and 1947 uncovered an isolated and finely built ashlar structure. It was described as a plunge bath and was built on an extravagantly massive scale with finely worked blocks up to 4 feet 6 inches (1.37 m) long. Measuring 39 feet 10 inches by 15 feet (12.14 x 4.57 m), it was almost as large as the Lucas or eastern bath at Bath. The most interesting aspect of this site is that this massive pool and the nearby hot baths were built on a public scale, and were certainly out of proportion to the modest dwelling house traced there. Gilyard-Beer suggested that it had been built as a place of ceremony and was probably a water shrine and healing centre connected with the worship of the goddess Brigantia under her guise of a water deity, Dea Nympha Brigantia. He suggested that the house was for the priest and other personnel attendant on the baths and shrine. No temple building was ever found but the pool itself may indeed have been the sacred focus of the complex rather than being a secular plunge or swimming pool. Interestingly the tradition that the spring had sacred and healing properties hung on into the Middle Ages at Well. For our purposes the most exciting object found in the infilling of the Well pool was a cresting slab decorated with antithetic Ss. This was of Magnesian Limestone and measured 1 foot 8½ inches by 11½ inches (52.1 x 29.2 cm). It was boldly carved on one side with the traditional design of S-shaped figures divided by uprights. Like the Corbridge examples, all of the figures stand proud of the background and are chamfered to catch light and shadow (Fig. 10.25). The excavator recognised its architectural significance and compared it with the examples from Corbridge and the Chester tombstone. This block was no doubt one of a series cresting the walls or pediments and denoting the purpose of the pool or

an adjacent structure (Gilyard-Beer 1951, 34, 69, pl. X b). Excavations on the site of the possible temple *temenos* of the Antonine era in Insula VI at Cirencester (building VI, 1) uncovered three fragments of architectural stonework in a late rubble deposit. Two curved pieces and one 'vertical shaft' were suspected by Thomas Blagg as having come from 'an S-screen' (Holbrook 1998, 139). These are now in the Corinium Museum Resource Centre at Northleach, but proved impossible for the author to access for study, as they are stored out of reach of any available ladders within the building.

What is noticeable about all the examples seen is that they seem to have ornamented edifices and structures that in some way were sacred, whether these were temples, shrines, temple tombs, or gravestones. The confronted or antithetic S was not a motif of general decoration, rather, it appears to have come to be used in a less obvious but similar fashion to the so-called 'Horns of Consecration' which ornamented the roofs of sacred structures in the earlier Minoan and Mycenaean cultures and denoted their sanctity to the onlooker, or to the Cross for Christian buildings today. A seemingly unique adaptation appears on a third-century AD monolithic garden *lararium* from the villa at Quinta de Marim, Portugal, where pilasters formed of double-Ss, placed one above the other, form pilasters topped with lotus flowers flanking the statue niche (Beeson 2019a, fig. 7). The sacred carriage or *pilentum* discovered at Città Giuliani near Pompeii in 2021 is ornamented with a panel of confronted Ss denoting its sanctity (Beeson 2021, 24, fig. 2).

Acroterial decoration at Great Witcombe

At Great Witcombe, Walters has postulated that the site was more likely to have been a religious establishment devoted to a water deity than a villa (Walters and Rider, this volume; Walters 2000, 12). This of course echoes but greatly expands upon Lysons' opinion of the Room 1 as a cult chamber. A terracotta pinecone found in area 41 immediately outside of the cult chamber gives additional support to the room's identified purpose (Smith 1939, 194, pl. xliv; Clifford 1954, 68-69, pl. XI). Elsewhere on the site from area 67, what is surely part of a terracotta crested serpent, but identified as part of a roof finial, is worth a mention here (Leach 1998, 101, 102, fig. 31,1). Can it be simply a coincidence that what was possibly the most sacred room in the complex has yielded up the remains of two of these S-panels? I believe that is not the case and also that they were originally displayed high on the outside of the building denoting that this part of the complex at least was sacred. It might also be suggested that more would have decorated the roof of the *cella*-like (and probably tower-like) central octagonal

Figure 10.25. Cresting block from the site at Well in Yorkshire.
(Andrew Foster)

Room 15 of the north terrace, especially if (as seems likely) it was fronted by a roof structure stretching across the great colonnaded terrace gallery to form a classical and pedimented façade on its southern side. What has not previously been noticed by those studying Great Witcombe is the remarkable and striking similarity that the basic design of the complex bears with the *Fanum Martis* temple in the Sanctuaire de Haut-Bécherel at Corseul in north-west France. There, again on the western side of a sloping courtyard, a polygonal *cella* (that at Witcombe replaced a rectangular one) is fronted by a raised terraced colonnade that becomes part of the temple's pronaos. Only sections of the Corseul precinct have been excavated but, apart from the similarities of the *cella* and its congregational corridor, as at Witcombe, there is also an entrance hall on the corner of the eastern wing. There may even be a connection with water as, interestingly, the Corseul temple faces in the direction of the sacred spring at Saint-Uriac, approximately 400 m eastwards (Provost 2010, col. pl. 1, 133, 190, fig. 160). Fragments of limestone arcading found by Greenfield suggest that the dwarf columns of the Great Witcombe gallery once supported arches which would have given the façade a far more classical appearance than has hitherto been suggested (Leach 1998, 97, 98, fig. 29, 19). This would especially have been the case had the columns been founded on square pedestals. The unusual aspect of the Great Witcombe S-panels when compared to other existing examples is their great size. They are fretted from slabs of stone which were approximately over 71 cm (2 feet 4 inches) square when complete. The piercing does, of course, cut down their weight considerable and they are reasonably easy for two men to handle. As only parts of two sure panels have turned up so far, and another enigmatic fragment that may have been a third, one has to consider the prospect that there never were many (Fig. 10.26). The fact that the Ss are bordered with uprights for strength might suggest that the pieces stood alone and were not part of a repeating decoration. This being said, it must be admitted that as we have only one side of the design then we could be looking at the end element of a continuous run and that the opposite and lost side adjoining the left-hand S would not have had an unattached upright but either abutted an antithetic S or an upright attached to the next stone. The exceptional size of the piece would seemingly rule it out from being a continuous *sima* cresting, and yet an additional find from nearby Chedworth (and referred to below) must make that a real possibility (Fig. 10.27). When seen as such the decorative appeal of the design is only too evident, as is illustrated by the survival of a large-scale bronze cresting from Écija, Spain, mentioned below. The *lacunae* of the fretted stones give an appearance of a reversed series of sacred ivy or lotus leaf shapes. The author's personal opinion is that it seems more likely

Figure 10.26. An unpublished enigmatic fragment from Great Witcombe that may be part of a third S-panel or an element of a continuous run.

that at Great Witcombe they were indeed single elements that decorated the roof eaves or gable. A series of three or four isolated pieces regularly spaced along the length of the eaves in the manner of temple antefixes might be an alternative possibility to a continuous run, although a use as acroterion ornaments above the gables seems perhaps more likely (Fig. 10.28). However, stylised versions of large confronted Ss spaced along a palace building's eaves do appear on a mosaic of Theseus and the Minotaur from the villa of Torre de Palma, Monforte, Portugal, and now in the National Archaeological Museum in Lisbon (Inv. No. 999.149.1; Fig. 10.29). A remarkable nineteenth-century revival of the motif, using large individual confronted Ss to decorate the gutter-line of a house, survives at Rua de Gil Pais in the Portuguese town of Torres Novas and clearly illustrates their decorative potential in architecture (Fig. 10.30).

Given the theory that Great Witcombe functioned as a sanctuary wherein water played an important part, it is perhaps worth alluding to the possibly superficial similarity that the stone panels have with the head of Neptune's trident on the Hellenistic mosaic from the House of the Trident on Delos. There, confronted Ss (albeit reversed to those at Great Witcombe) are interspersed between the three tangs of the weapon (Bruneau 1974, 31, fig. 33).

Some idea of how the Great Witcombe ornaments may have been used is given by a pipe-clay shrine found in Gutter Lane, London and now on display in the Museum of London. Here the apex of the pediment is ornamented by a large *acroterion* ornament consisting of antithetic Ss.

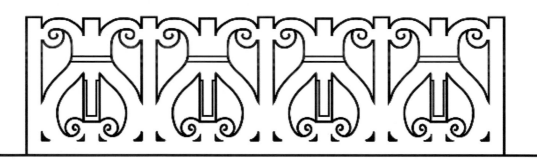

Figure 10.27. The Great Witcombe S-panels used as sima *or eave decoration; Above, single panels as spaced decoration and* below *as a running cresting.*

Figure 10.28. The Great Witcombe S-panels used as acroterial decoration.

Figure 10.29. Knossos palace crowned with a row of stylised double S's from a mosaic of Theseus and the Minotaur from Torre de Palma, Portugal. The ornament at the rear left has the author's interpretation of the design superimposed.

Figure 10. 30. Ceramic double S's decorating the gutter-line of a nineteenth-century house at Rua de Gil Pais in Torres Novas, Portugal.

179

Bands link the heads of the S-shapes as at Great Witcombe and a swelling protrudes up and beyond these to form the apex of the design (Fig. 10.31). One is reminded of the terracotta acroteria on the Etruscan temple from Alatri as reconstructed at the Villa Giulia in Rome (Reich 1979, 46) and (at a distance) of the giant volutes that appeared on Etruscan and early Roman temple pediments such as on the sixth-century BC Temple of Mater Matuta in the Forum Boarium, Rome (Bertoletti 1999, fig. 42; Stamper 2005, 40-44, fig. 28). At the Musée Alésia, Alise-Sainte-Reine, there is a miniature shrine found at Mount-Auxois that preserves its acroterial ornaments. The plain raking slopes of the pediment are dominated by an ornament of confronted Ss at the apex (Fauduet 1993, 11).

Graphic reconstructions of Romano-British buildings often forget that pediments of important structures were commonly provided with acroterial decorations in the Graeco-Roman world. That Roman Gloucestershire was not unfamiliar with such impressive antefix or *acroterion* ornaments is evidenced by the spectacular 0.69 m high example found in Gloucester north-east of the cathedral before 1860 (Toynbee 1962, 165-6, cat. 96, pl. 103; Henig 1993, 58, no. 173, pl. 42; Beeson 2019b, 35. figs 7, 8). Here a female head is backed and framed by an *anthemion* palmette of S-shaped petals. The tall central leaf of the palmette rises behind the head as a dominant feature echoing at a distance the uprights found on S-friezes. This female head, backed and crowned by a palmette bears comparison with the wild-haired Medusas on stone antefixes from Agos, France and now in the Musée de Comminges (Espérandieu 1955, XIV, 13, cat. 81114-81116, pl. xvii) and more anciently in the archaic terracotta female antefixes of the temples of the Greek cities of southern Italy (Marquand 1909, 163-4, fig. 191). Also from Gloucestershire, a small moulded half-leaf terracotta *acroterion* ornament from the corner of a gable was discovered in a tile kiln during an excavation conducted by the television programme *Time Team* at the site of a Roman villa at Coberley in 2007 (Fig. 10.32). Excavations at a spectacular sited walled complex in South Gloucestershire in 2018 by Archaeoscan uncovered a unique British example of a recurvant horned *acroterion* similar to those depicted on some Mediterranean mosaics (Beeson 2019b, 34-35, figs 1-10; Fig. 10.33).

Elsewhere in the province, acroterial ornaments are a rare survival and are generally connected with funerary architecture, such as the tragic mask from Towcester now in the British Museum (Brailsford 1964, 55; Huskinson 1994, 32, no. 67, pl. 24). What is often forgotten, however, is that some buildings were adorned with bronze roof ornaments rather than stone. Survivals throughout the Roman world show that cornices, doors, altars, statue bases and reliefs were just some of the few architectural items commonly sheathed, ornamented or cast in bronze. The value of the metal as scrap sealed the fate of most such decorations but rare examples survive. Avenches in Switzerland has yielded half of a gilt bronze *anthemion acroterion* decoration from a temple in the Granges-des-Dîmes sanctuary (Bögli 1989. 17, 20, fig. 18; Drack 1988, 234, pl. 216) and two heavy bronze acanthus leaves probably from a pediment at a villa site at Gorge de Loup, Lyon, are now displayed in the British Museum. Nor should the large gilded bronze dolphins from a substantial relief frieze in Vienne be forgotten (Boucher 1964, 3-15). It is unlikely that quality buildings

Figure 10.31. A pediment from a pipe-clay shrine found in Gutter Lane, London and crowned with an antithetic S acroterion ornament suggests how those from Great Witcombe may have been used.

Figure 10.32. A moulded terracotta corner acroterion decoration from the early tile kiln found at Coberley villa, Gloucestershire, during the Time Team excavation. (Time Team)

Figure 10.33. An interpretative reconstruction of a recurvant horned acroterion from a site in South Gloucestershire.

in Britannia would have been substantially different in appearance from those found elsewhere in the Northern Provinces, so such bronze architectural embellishments may have been reasonably common on edifices of note. Indeed, tantalising fragments do survive from Britannia and no doubt more remain unrecognised in collections. The richly leafed bronze cornice with silver foil highlights from Silchester and the famous goose head *cheniscus* from a relief on the Great Monument at Richborough, now in the British Museum (Coombe *et al.* 2015, 74, no. 132 pl. 77) are just two examples: likewise the remarkable bronze bracket in the shape of a finger complete with nail, that was found in St Michael's School Yard, *Verulamium* (insula XIX) by A. D. Saunders and J. Lunn in 1955 (accession number 1988.256; Coombe *et al.* 2015, 119-20, no. 221 pl. 82) which was probably used to secure the great Purbeck marble dedicatory inscription from town's basilica (Boon 1974, 120, figs 34ff: Cunliffe 1968, 101-102, pl. LVIII). A wonderful survival of gilt-bronze cresting in Écija Museum, Spain, illustrates what was possible in metal ornamentation, and consists of two joined elements of a run of elaborate double Ss from a pediment or roof (Fig. 10.34; Museo de Écija, EPE 04/s.n. 2005). Gilded on one side, it decorated a first-century

Figure 10.34. A fragment from a large-scale run of gilded bronze S-cresting from a major temple at Écija, Spain. It was probably once fixed within the tympanum *of the pediment, as on the Corbridge shrine. (Copyright Museo de Écija).*

181

temple in the forum of *Colonia Augusta Astigi* (Écija, Seville) and had fallen into an adjacent rectangular stepped pool at the rear of the building during the latter's demolition or destruction. The proximity of the stepped pool and water is of note. The cresting's uprights have lily-flower terminals while nail holes in the upper volutes suggest that it was fixed to a backing, probably within a *tympanum* as at Corbridge, or onto an entablature. Lead was poured around the base as another fixing agent. Apart from being an exceptional survival of bronze architectural ornamentation, the cresting is of particular importance in that the motifs are even larger than those from Great Witcombe. The fragment, currently not fully restored, measures 1.33 m in length by 0.90 m in height and 5-8 mm in thickness. Each of the two surviving S panels measures 0.66 m in length by 0.90 m in height. Its excavator, the archaeologist Sergio García-Dils de la Vega, believed the cresting to be a balustrade, but this is questioned by Écija Museum's Director, Antonio Fernandez Ugaide, who also believes that it decorated the roof of the building (Ugaide, *pers. comm.*, October 2021; García-Dils and Gutiérrez 2014, 1635-38, figs 1-3; García-Dils 2015, 226-230, figs 141-2).

If, as here suggested, the Great Witcombe ornaments were used as acroterial decoration, then they would have sat upon rectangular *acroterion* blocks at the apex of a gable or proper pediment (see Fig. 10.28). The base of the surviving panel has been provided with a shallow V-shaped channel some 10 cm in width to act as the *female* socket to a corresponding lost *male* feature on the *acroterion* block (Fig. 10.35). This was no doubt done to provide some stability for the piece as it was not mortared into place but simply placed there. This channel led Lysons to assume that they might have sat upon the ridge pole of the building, but this was surely not the case as they are decorated to be seen from one side only and also their weight would put an enormous strain on the roof structure and the footing would hardly have been a stable one for such a position. An inverted V-shape is also cut into the base of the South Gloucestershire horned *acroterion* and also the Gloucester female head (Beeson 2019b, 34-35, figs 1-10).

Spaced and isolated *anthemion* ridge pole decorations to enliven a long roof were certainly employed in antiquity as are depicted on the Sidon sarcophagi and existed as spaced ridge tiles on the roof of the Temple of Aphaia, *Aegina*, but generally these were smaller and, by the time of Witcombe building, were more likely to resemble the finial example from Chedworth mentioned below (Marquand 1909, 123, fig. 155; Henig 1993, 75, cat. 237, pl. 57, 237; see Fig. 10.12).

Figure 10.35. The V-shaped setting channel on the underside of the Great Witcombe panel.

A series of S-panels from the second century AD, 'temple A' at the Jupiter Heliopolitanus sanctuary in the *vicus* at *Carnuntum* in Austria, and another fretted example from Frankfurt am Main have been identified as cresting for a ridge pole, but these are only 20 cm in height as opposed to over 71 cm for the Witcombe example (Ertel 1991, pl. 33, fig. 28-29; Meier-Arendt 1983, 33, Cat. 7). Although certainly a possibility, a continuous ridge pole cresting would be unusual, so notwithstanding their small size and given the evidence of the Vienne relief, one must still question whether these *Carnuntum* and Frankfurt examples were not actually decorations of the *sima* rather than from the roof ridge. Likewise, a long run of small-scale *sima* S-cresting is built into the exterior wall of the chevet of Nôtre Dame Cathedral, Le Puy-en-Velay, France (Fig. 10.36).

Proof that the Great Witcombe shallow footing channel was soon deemed to be insufficient protection against possible disaster may be evidenced by the fact that at some period at least three holes were cut into the stonework at the bottom and rear of the central upright and lower curled ends in order to insert metal ties or stanchions to prevent the panel from shifting or falling

Figure 10.36. Edwardian photograph showing panels of Roman S-cresting from the sima of a shrine or mausoleum reused in the exterior wall of the chevet of Nôtre Dame Cathedral, at Le Puy-en-Velay, France. (Beeson Collection)

forward from its base in a gale on this hillside spot. In doing so it seems that the right-hand roll volute of the base was cut back from the rear to half the width of the rest of the Ss (Fig. 10.37). One sees the same sort of stanchions in place nowadays as a safety precaution on free-standing Victorian ornamental pediments and roof ornaments that are exposed to the elements. Most likely it was the salvaging of this metal that was the ultimate cause of the ornament's destruction as several V-shaped hammer marks appear on the stone in this area. These metal stay-irons are also indirect evidence against Lysons' vision of the pieces having sat upon the ridgepole or as ornaments within the *tympanum* or triangle of a gable. In the former instance there would have been nothing substantial to have anchored them to and in the latter the sheltered position would not have required it nor really provided much scope to anchor it because of the presumably close proximity of the wall behind. When viewed from the side it also is evident that the panel tapers in width from the top to the base as another attempt both to lighten its weight and to provide stability (Fig. 10.38). It is noticeable that care has only been taken to decorate one face of the panel showing that it was only intended to be viewed from that side. This is further evidence against it having been a balustrade. The metal ties would have been placed on the side from whence the human force necessary to move them would have arisen,

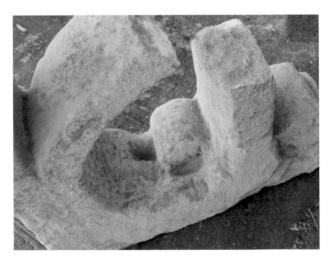

Figure 10.37. Holes for fixing metal ties to the rear of the Great Witcombe S-panel.

but this is the undecorated side. It seems unlikely that one would present this undecorated side most closely to the viewer. It should be noted that most, if not all of the smaller examples from pediments are only decorated on one side.

The architectural stonework from Great Witcombe is simple but generally elegant in execution and design and of the best British materials. Fragments of imported

Figure 10.38. Tapered side profile of the large panel showing the V-shaped setting channel.

Figure 10.39. A previously unpublished relief from Great Witcombe, featuring a fish on a raised band, suggests that a narrow frieze of fishes similar to those found on some Romano-British mosaic floors was a feature of part of the building.

marble and floors in the gallery and octagonal chamber of *opus sectile* hint at further lost grandeur and much expenditure. No decorative sculptural pieces survive in the store beyond the unpublished right-hand section of a rectangular block, carved in relief with a fish on a raised horizontal band that may originally have been part of a frieze of fishes. Below the band and under the fish's tail are chiselled what appears to be the letters IXI (or IXV) but may equally be the commencement of a somewhat crude decorative border of lozenge decoration in the form of IXIXIXI (Fig. 10.39). Although no sure evidence of pediments survives amongst the cornices and mouldings it may be merely the fact that the vital angle blocks are missing. However, the lack of proper pediments is no reason to discount acroterial decoration. Proof that otherwise undecorated roofs could sometimes bear such large decorated blocks on their gables may be seen on the buildings illustrated on the mosaic of Pasiphae and Daedalus from the house of Poseidon, *Zeugma*, and now in Gazientep museum (Önal 2009, 17-21; Fig. 10.40). That the ornaments held a prominent position at Great Witcombe is suggested by graffiti of what are described as 'lyres'

that are scoured on two stones from the site (RCHM(E) 1976, 61). In addition to ornaments at their apex, gables and pediments were commonly provided with acroterial decoration at their corner angles known as *acroteria angularia*, and it may be there that these or additional ornaments were set (see Fig. 10.28). It is probable that room 1 was the southern climax of the western wing in the complex's earliest days although the direction of its roof structure is problematic. Did it have a single gable or pediment at its southern end or a pair east and west or on all three sides? Certainly, it was built at a higher level than Room 3 and the rooms of the southern baths and it is most likely that even at a later date its gable(s) and roof with its ornaments would have still dominated all later additions to the south (Neal 1977, fig. 3).

Acroterial decoration at Chedworth

Great Witcombe is not the only Roman complex in the Cotswolds to yield remains of confronted S decoration. At Chedworth two examples have been found. Arguably the most interesting is the least well preserved and consists of two confronted Ss, joined together by a horizontal link or stretcher, but with no uprights (Goodburn, 1983, pl. 12; Fig. 10.41). The link, presumably, is a symbolic reference to the traditional rope bindings. The length of the piece on its base is approximately 69 cm (2 feet 3 inches), just slightly smaller than that from Great Witcombe. The outer curve of one of the S-shapes preserves part of a second stretcher, which with the absence of uprights, suggests that this was not an isolated free-standing decoration as is postulated at Great Witcombe, but was once part of a continuous decorative S-cresting on a building.

Figure 10.40. Buildings with plain gables decorated with large acroterial ornaments from the Pasiphae and Daedalus mosaic from Zeugma, Turkey.

Figure 10.41. The Chedworth S-panel. The curved base suggests that it once ornamented the walls of the nymphaeum. *The links that joined the S's remain in the centre and on the right-hand side.*

The original effect that such a linked cresting would have had when complete may be seen in the attached reconstruction of a short length of it and also as depicted on the raking sides of an eighth-century AD relief of a pediment or *tympanum* from Istria (Kowalczyk 1927, pl. 158; Fig. 10.42). This illustrates that links occurred both at the top and bottom of the Ss (Fig. 10.43). An earlier variant occurs on the mausoleum at Wavre where the stretchers form continuous rods through the top and bottom volutes of the Ss (Drack 1988, fig. 255). What is of great significance with the Chedworth piece, but has previously been ignored, is that the gently curved base rail to which the Ss are joined indicates that it once decorated an apsidal or circular structure (see Fig. 10.41). The diameter formed by the stone's curve would nicely fit above the apse of the sacred *nymphaeum* building in the north-west corner of the site (Fig. 10.44). Indeed, an experiment by the author with a paper template taken from the piece proved that it exactly matches the curve of the *nymphaeum* apse. One is reminded of the bold *anthemion* and lotus *acroteria* crowning the circular Temple of Vesta as it appears on a sestertius of AD 22 (Cassanelli 2002, 208-209, fig. 208 (4)). The effect must have been very similar on the apsidal structure (Fig. 10.45). The absence of more examples from the site may be a result of the kiln that was established on the north bank near the *nymphaeum* in the seventeenth century in order to burn the available stonework for lime. Perhaps the cresting ended at the front of the apse with *acroterion* pedestal bases similar to those from Saint Laurent sur Othain where the S-cresting also shows no evidence of uprights either (see Fig. 10.16). The S of the latter example retains

Figure 10.42. The Chedworth S-cresting restored after the pediment relief from Istria and the cornice decoration at Wavre.

*Figure 10.43. An eighth-century AD pediment relief from Istria shows the same kind of linked S-decoration that existed at Chedworth.
(From a postcard c. 1920)*

Figure 10.44. The Chedworth nymphaeum. The cresting would have ornamented the top of the curving back wall regardless of whether or not this structure was originally roofed in antiquity.

Figure 10.45. The solid S-panel that may have formed part of the Chedworth nymphaeum's tympanum or acted as the central element of the running S-cresting.

a top rail but comparison with other survivals makes it unlikely that the Chedworth cresting had one. Either way it would have looked (and physically been) a delicate ornamental finish to the building it decorated. The fact that the cresting is well finished on both sides suggests that it was expected to be viewed by the public from both inside and outside the nymphaeum and also that it would not have been obscured by any roofing over the apse. The flat underside of the piece bears a very neatly cut hole and adjoining longitudinal slot for a now robbed metal pi-clamp to secure it to another panel (Fig. 10.46).

Also from Chedworth, and discovered in the western baths, is a large rectangular slab decorated in relief with antithetic Ss either side of a pillar (Goodburn 1983. Pl. 13; Henig 1993, 74, cat. 236, pl. 57, cat. 236). An off-centre notch cut in the upper edge perhaps to hold a water pipe suggests a secondary use at a later date and possibly at the same time as border slabs from the nymphaeum were also reused in the baths. This decorative relief may have once formed the central panel of the nymphaeum pediment's tympanum (if such actually existed), allied to the design postulated at Corbridge. Alternatively, if the shrine was originally open to the sky and lacked a proper roof, half dome, or pedimented front, and had the walls merely capped with a cresting, then the solid panel may have formed the central element above the apse for the run of Ss girdling the wall top either side of it. The blind relief panel is decoratively in keeping with the postulated S-cresting of the same structure, with the horizontal stretchers linking the top and bottom loops of the Ss, indicating that it was designed to match the pierced fragment on the curved base from the site. Where it differs from any other S-design is in the treatment of the Ss themselves. These are incredibly fluid in conception, with the lower volutes almost tucked behind and flowing onwards, and with their entire bodies heavily fluted. Were they perhaps designed to symbolically represent the flowing waters of the spring? The Chedworth panel's central pillar is surmounted by a V-shaped crown of what appears to be four lanceolate leaves. This may

Figure 10.46. Underside of the curved Chedworth cresting panel showing the neatly cut fixing slot for a robbed metal pi-clamp to fix it to an adjoining panel.

be a schematic capital, a reference to the traditional palmette design or even an allusion to spouting water. Published restorations of the architectural elevation of Chedworth's *nymphaeum* have not been convincing and the current attempts are probably the least so of all (Bethell 2008, 1, 20; Goodburn 1979, pl. 3; Forestier 1924, 74-75). With the omission of the columns *believed* to have formed part of its decoration, the restoration painted by the historical illustrator Amédée Forestier is, with some reservations, possibly closest to the original appearance of the structure if roofed in antiquity. Certainly, it accords with the suggested half-domed restoration given by John Ward in 1911 who also records that the interior was 'painted a bright red' (Ward 1911, 249-50). However, the author's personal opinion is that the *nymphaeum* broadly resembled the structure as it survives today: open to the sky but with higher walls surmounted by a simple entablature and crowned by the cresting, the details of which could be seen and appreciated both by those approaching it from the complex or from the hillside above (Fig. 10.47). Indirect support for this idea comes from the pipe-clay shrine to Venus now in the Musée Gallo-Romain de Lyon-Fourvière, Lyon (see Fig.

10.17). The goddess is depicted as standing in a niche beneath what seems to be a horseshoe-shaped pediment surmounted by a running cresting and fronted by side columns. I believe that, rather than imagining that a new form of structurally unsound circular pediment is intended on this piece, it actually portrays a statue standing in a niche but set back within an open apsidal enclosure with the walls topped by an S-cresting and their façades each fronted by a column. The piece should be viewed as attempting to show depth and perspective. We should view it as an attempt to give an illusion of depth such as one encounters on some of the tomb façades at Petra that depict all forecourt walls, courts and gateways, before the main building as one façade and as showing on one plane several elements of the building's architecture. It is possible that the two fragmentary statues, one with a fern support, discovered behind Room 5a may originally have stood on the attached pedestals flanking the entrance to the *nymphaeum*.

Another interesting feature preserved at Chedworth is an elaborate roof finial seemingly designed to ride somewhere along the ridge of a roof as an eye-catcher and

Figure 10.47. An interpretative reconstruction of the Chedworth nymphaeum *with the curved S-cresting based on the terracotta shrine from Quai Arloing, Lyon (Figure 10.17). Fragmentary statues found to the rear of Room 5a may have stood on the front pedestals.*

not at its end (Goodburn, 1983, pl. 12; Henig 1993, 75, cat. 237, pl. 57, 237). This finial had decoration on three storeys but has lost most of its upper element. The decoration appears to be leaf-shaped when viewed from the angles but forms antithetic Ss when seen from the front or sides.

What is noticeable about the examples of S-panels from Great Witcombe and Chedworth is that although the inspiration for the motif originates from the same tradition, their execution and design is quite different at each site and it is difficult to believe that they were the work of the same craftsmen. Dating is of course very difficult, but with the obvious revival of interest in the Antonine period in earlier decorative forms as evidenced by the Grottarossa cresting, one might suggest some time in the late second or third century AD which would accord well with the most recently suggested founding date for Great Witcombe of about AD 200 (although Clifford suggested a century earlier) and with the majority of other datable examples in the northern provinces. Chedworth's examples may be later than this, if the somewhat late construction date of around AD 300 for the *nymphaeum* is to be believed, but an earlier, second-century construction is probably far more likely. The latest use of the S-motif

yet discovered by the author in Roman Britain is to be found on the sides of a decorated lead coffin (grave 295), occupied by a two-year old in an expensive gypsum burial at the Butt Road cemetery in Colchester. Dated by the excavators to around AD 320-45, the lead inner coffin has a lid ornamented with circles, stylised woollen fillets (as used to adorn sacrificial animals, and depicted as hanging from the wrists of Artemis of Ephesus) and shells, symbolic of Venus and rebirth. Whether or not the long side panels of nine S-mouldings can be seen as symbolic of water and the Styx or simply used as a decorative but sacred ornamentation is unclear (Crummy 1993, 123-125, 161, fig. 2.69).

In 1928, St Clair Baddeley suggested that the impressive temple in Chedworth Wood standing above the River Coln in a headwater valley of the Thames had been the second-century focus of a religious centre that had existed in the area since earliest times. Amédée Forestier produced a reconstruction of the building under his direction (Baddeley 1928, 1014, 1015, 1044; Forestier 1928, 1015; Fig. 10.48). A second-century temple would of course be the ideal candidate for S-cresting, but none was reported from the site. Graham Webster postulated

Figure 10.48. A reconstruction by Forestier, under the direction of the excavator, of the impressive Antonine temple found in Chedworth Wood. A temple of this period would have been an ideal candidate for S-cresting.

189

that Chedworth was not a normal villa but a religious complex and recent suggestions have linked the obscure local goddess Cuda with the site (Walters and Rider, this volume; Webster 1983, 5-20; Bethel 2008, 21; Yeates 2004, 2-8; Yeates 2006). Bryn Walters has agreed with Webster and further argued the same for Great Witcombe whilst the same was suggested by Gilyard-Beer for the site at Well (Walters 2000, 10-13; Walters 2009, 30-35; Gilyard-Beer 1951, 42-43). All three sites had indirect evidence for water cults and all have provided examples of S-cresting. Of course, it does not mean that because a religious shrine exists in an establishment that the entire complex should be interpreted as devoted to religion, but it does I believe show that the motif itself only appears on sacred structures (Salway 2008, 253-256; Salway 2009, 48-49). The obvious similarity of Great Witcombe's design with the *Fanum Martis* temple in the Sanctuaire de Haut-Bécherel at Corseul (see above) adds further weight to the argument especially given the proximity of the latter complex to the sacred spring at Saint-Uriac (Bromwich 2014, 62; Floquet 2001).

Cantharus fountains at Great Witcombe and elsewhere

Apart from the S-panels, Great Witcombe has also produced evidence of something else that is a unique survival from Roman Britain, but until now has not been recognised as part of the *cantharus* fountain that it surely is (Fig. 10.49). One of the most frequently encountered images in the art of the Roman Empire is the *cantharus*, or sacred wine goblet associated with the Bacchus. Although the shape and form varies, it is generally a two-handled stemmed and footed vessel. Allied and often identical in appearance with the *cantharus* is the *crater*

Figure 10.49. The stepped base of the cantharus *fountain from Great Witcombe (D. Rider)*

or wine-mixing urn (Önal 2009, 96-97) which enjoyed the same symbolism. Present-day studies of Roman art in Britain generally conflate the two under the term *cantharus*. In Roman Britain, as elsewhere, it is an almost ubiquitous motif in mosaic design. As a symbol of the wine god it not only referred to the pleasures of the cup and the ecstasy achieved through it, but also to the deeper mysteries of the deity. Bacchus was associated with water turning to wine and his cult also gave the hope of rebirth. Indeed the Christians adopted the *cantharus* into their own sacred imagery syncretising it with the cup of Christ. The sacred importance of water at Witcombe perhaps adds a deeper meaning to this perhaps than that of merely a decorative piece.

Possibly because of their connection with water, *canthari* were commonly designed as fountains to ornament buildings and gardens throughout the Empire. They also appear as such on many a mosaic. Sometimes these mosaic fountains stand in symbolic mosaic pools in the centre of pavements or dominate apses. Often the pools are inhabited by lotus flowers and buds or flanked by dolphins (both symbols of rebirth). Although attributes of both Venus, the goddess of renewal, and also of Neptune, dolphins likewise alluded to the episode of Bacchus changing the Tyrrhenian pirates into such creatures. Occasionally the entire floor alludes to water in a more obscure way such as on the famous Oceanus mosaic from Building 8, Insula IV, *Verulamium* (Neal 2009, 326, fig. 299). There the central bust of the sea god is surrounded by a swastika meander border holding panels of lotus flowers and four *cantharus* fountains, two of which feature central feed pipes protruding above the rim. Also from Building 3, Insula XXVIII, *Verulamium*, comes a depiction of a *cantharus* fountain with dolphins' tails entwined with its handles (Neal 2009, 350-1, fig. 327-8). Two jets of water shoot from the centre of the vessel into the mosaic's symbolic pool. A similar but fragmentary example survived in Building 10, Insula IV in the same town (Neal 2009, 333, fig. 306a and b). As a fountain the *cantharus* was easily adopted into early Christian art as representing the Fountain of Life.

Only about 14 cm (5.05 inches) of the lower part of the socle or stem of the *cantharus* survives from Great Witcombe, hitherto unrecognised in the collection of small finds from the site (Fig. 10.50). The surviving piece consists of the stepped turned base of the socle with a diameter of about 15 cm (6 inches). Such a base occurs on a simple bronze *cantharus* urn from Pompeii and now in the Naples Museum (inv. 37098) (Ward-Perkins 1976, 135, cat. 137). The fragment appears to be of limestone although a fine sandstone is often used at the site for architectural details. The surface appears to have been lime-washed in antiquity

Figure 10.50. The cantharus *fountain base from Great Witcombe, showing the central hole to accommodate a feedpipe. (D. Rider)*

unless this is a natural lime deposit gained whilst it was in use. When perfect the piece would have stood about a metre (3 feet 3 inches) in height (Fig. 10.51). The evidence that it was a fountain survives in the 2.50 cm (1 inch) hole drilled through the centre of the socle to accommodate a lead feed pipe. Mosaics such as the gladiator mosaic from Augst clearly depict how these fountains functioned

Figure 10.51. An interpretative reconstruction of the Great Witcombe cantharus *fountain with a low feedpipe. (D. Rider and A. Beeson)*

(Berger 1971, pl. 6). The lead pipe would generally be attached to an ornamental bronze pipe that would rise above the water level in the bowl of the fountain and provide a focus to the display with sound and movement (Bowe 2004, 11, fig. 7). The length of the pipe no doubt depended on the pressure of the water supplying the fountain, whether this was from a water tower or spring at a higher level, but some obviously protruded more than a foot above the water level as may be seen on the mosaic of deer drinking from a fountain, from Carthage and now in the British Museum (inv. no. MLA 1858, 4-2.90; Hinks 1933, 48; Fig. 10.52). Sometimes the pipe was fitted with a pierced rose to provide a spray as on the parrots and fountain mosaic in the Musée Gallo-Romain de Lyon. Occasionally this rose would continue the Bacchic theme of the *cantharus* and take the form of a *thyrsus* topped with a pine cone, as in the superb example believed to be from Pompeii and now in the British Museum (Walters 1899, 2579; Fig. 10.53) or the shorter one from Avenches (Bögli 1989, 67, 69, fig. 79). A mosaic from the House of the Masks in Sousse, Tunisia, features plain *canthari* in its spandrels holding *thyrsoi* topped by a single ivy leaf. Bacchic ivy rather than water sprays from the vessels on this floor (Foucher 1965, 16, fig. 21). *Cantharus* and bowl fountains generally only had an inlet pipe which kept the water level high in the bowl (Jashemski 1979, 332, fig. 530). The outlet generally was in the basin in which they stood. *Cantharus* fountains might have decorative, scalloped or beaded rims to direct water overspill or a plain edge to allow a hopefully even overflow all around. The possible lime deposit on the surviving piece might suggest that the latter was the case here. Some designs saw the bowls pierced and fitted with bronze panther or lion spouts, as is suspected at Darenth, Kent (Beeson 2019a, 79, figs 43, 79).

The relatively narrow diameter of the Great Witcombe socle foot suggests that it held an upright and deep *cantharus*-shaped top rather than a wider bowl-style fountain (Mattusch 2009, 66 –67, 203, figs 14 and 15, 91; Bowe 2004, 32, fig. 30) although it must be admitted that a great many designs were in use at least in gardens in the Roman world (Farrar 1998, 87-89; Jashemski 1979, figs 470, 471, 475, 480; Mattusch 2009, 171, fig. 64). Comparison with the rest of the stonework from the site would suggest that it was probably of simple but elegant design, lathe turned and without decoration (Önal 2009, 96-97; see Farrar 1998, fig. 87; Beeson 2019a, figs 43, 58, 79, 80). Handles, if any, could have been attached afterwards, as at Bad Kreuznach and might have been of stone or bronze (see Fig. 10.51).

To have a fountain in the house or garden was a huge status symbol in the Roman world. In a town it illustrated that one had the wealth and influence to be allowed to tap into the public water supply. Where

Figure 10.52. Deer drinking from a cantharus fountain provided with a tall feedpipe on a mosaic from Carthage and now in the British Museum.

this was impossible or too expensive, a water tower discretely hidden and perhaps filled by hand or pump could provide a sufficient head of water for long enough to impress and amuse one's guests when the fountains were turned on. In country houses local springs could be tapped and occasionally would provide a good head of water for a fountain. That at Woodchester in Gloucestershire near to the site of the great Roman villa, still powers an impressive fountain in the manor garden whilst at Fishbourne a water tower fed the garden's fountains (Cunliffe 1971, I, 129-132, figs 37-38, pls 38a and b). Fragments from fountain statuary are not uncommon from sites throughout Britannia and range from the huge and spectacular fish-shaped spout found near Tockenham in Wiltshire (Henig 1997, 35-36, fig. 5; Beeson 2019a, 38-39, figure) to the wealth of stonework fragments at Chedworth and North Leigh villa that include pieces from ornamental fountains and basins (Beeson 2019a, 42-43, figure). However, to my knowledge, no *cantharus* fountain has yet been identified. The gardens at Fishbourne Roman Palace had the remains

of several simple bowl-shaped fountain basins but none surviving were from a *cantharus* (Cunliffe 1971, II, 37-41 figs 21-23, pl. II b).

In the villa at Bad Kreuznach in Germany a *cantharus* fountain has been restored from remains found to the centre of a walled hexagonal pool set in the middle of the Oceanus mosaic and provides a wonderful illustration of the effect this must have had. The position of fountains and pools within houses can often be surmised by the damage caused to floors and mosaics when the lead pipes conducting the water beneath them were ripped out. Evidence of such destruction in important rooms can be found at Woodchester, possibly Chedworth and at Great Witcombe itself in the central octagonal chamber (15) of the northern wing. On the great floor of the *aula* at Woodchester water nymphs with flowing jugs occupied the spandrels of the great Orpheus pavement and there is a tradition that mosaic fish were part of the lost central panel in a pool. At Chedworth, notwithstanding the hypocaust, it is possible that the Bacchus and

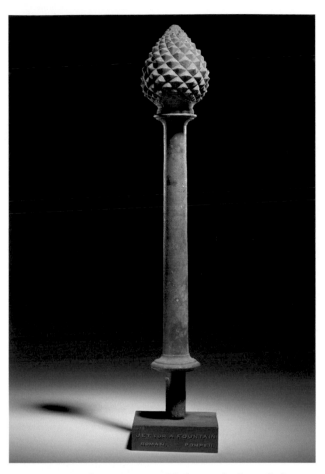

Figure 10.53. A rare bronze ornamental feedpipe in the shape of a thyrsus. Reputed to be from Pompeii and now in the British Museum. The pine cone is pierced and forms the rose. (Trustees of the British Museum)

seasons mosaic of Room 5 may have surrounded a raised and walled octagonal pool similar to that at Bad Kreuznach and would have been admirably suited to a central *cantharus* fountain. The summer reception room at Bignor with its hexagonal sunken pool surrounded by mosaic panels featuring Bacchante dancers is again the ideal place to imagine a Bacchic *cantharus* fountain. The original location of the *cantharus* fountain at Great Witcombe must of course remain a matter of speculation. With such abundant water at the site, it is unlikely that it was the only such decorative water feature in the complex either within or outside in the gardens. As there is no documentation to state when it was found one suspects it was an early find made by Lysons or Hicks suggesting that it came from the immediate area of the building itself. There are two main locations where it would have been displayed to the greatest effect. The prime one is within the postulated octagonal pool of room 15, where there would have been a sufficient hydraulic head of water to allow a gentle flow from the feed pipe into the bowl of the *cantharus* (Fig. 10.54). The second choice might be in Room 32, the *nymphaeum* incorporated into the lower part of the central portico below and south of Room 15. Lysons had suggested that part of this supporting structure incorporated a water tower, and three drains ran southward from it, indicating the presence of considerable amounts of water (Leach 1998, 42, fig. 10). A fountain set within a central niche in this structure would have enjoyed a good head of water and have been a public display of the benefits of the site. If the entire Witcombe complex *was* a sacred one then this

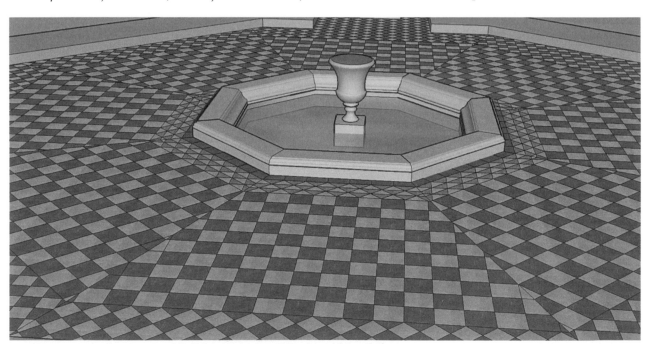

Figure 10.54. A suggested reconstruction of the Great Witcombe cantharus fountain as it might have appeared in situ in the octagonal pool of Room 15. (D. Rider and A. Beeson).

nymphaeum may even have served as an approachable public dipping place, much as existed at the overflow from the great reservoir at Bath.

The exciting survival of this unpublished *cantharus* fountain fragment amongst the items in the English Heritage store illustrates only too well the problems faced by researchers into decorative art and architecture in Roman Britain, especially when dealing with items excavated in past decades and now re-buried from public and academic consciousness in that most tiresome of institutions, the museum store. One wonders how many more such fragments lie undetected in stores away from public view? It also highlights the importance of sites like Chedworth and North Leigh where most stonework found on the site has been on display and easily available for study. Sadly, recent developments at Chedworth connected with the revamping of the site, have seen important items of stonework that were previously on view, once again sent off to a store and the link broken. Britain unfortunately lacks the *lapidaria* or stone museums often housed in redundant churches that are found on the Continent, where such items are displayed for all to see.

Conclusion

The Roman buildings at Great Witcombe and those at Chedworth have produced a remarkable collection of rare architectural and decorative stone fragments, the study of which is still in its infancy. The pierced S-panels follow in a long tradition of the use of this motif for the ornamentation of the roofs of sacred structures throughout the Graeco-Roman world, a fact that suggests their original positioning in both of these Gloucestershire sites where worship connected with water has been attested. To judge by other examples throughout the northern Empire they are likely to date from some time in the third century following a revival of interest in earlier decorative forms in Antonine times. These Gloucestershire examples are unique for their great size and suggest that they may have been used architecturally in a slightly different and evolved way from those surviving elsewhere. For a site such as Great Witcombe, where water was obviously of great significance, the *cantharus* fountain fragment is further proof of the importance of that element to the inhabitants. It is an iconographical link between the sacred nature of the decorative S-panels and the holiness of the water. It stands as a unique three-dimensional survival of a decorative piece that must have been quite commonly encountered in the province both in art and reality but has previously not been discovered.

References

Baddeley, W. St Clair 1928 The shrine of an unknown Roman-British god. *The Illustrated London News*. 1 December 1928, 1014-1015, 1044.

Beeson, A. 2019a *Roman Gardens*. Amberley, Stroud.

Beeson, A. 2019b A new acroterion from South Gloucestershire. *Association for Roman Archaeology News* 42, 34-35.

Beeson, A. 2021 The four-wheeled processional carriage from the Città Giuliana excavation. *Association for Roman Archaeology News* 45, 24-26.

Berger, L. and Joos, M. 1971 Das Augster Gladiatorenmosaik. *Romerhaus und Museum Augst Jahresbericht 1969-1970*.

Bertoletti, M., Cima, M. and Talamo, E. 2004 *Sculptures of Ancient Rome. The collections of the Capitoline Museums at the Montemartini Power Plant*. Electa, Milan.

Bethel, P. 2008 *Chedworth Roman Villa, Gloucestershire*. National Trust Guidebook, London.

Blagg, T. F. C. 2002 *Roman Architectural Ornament in Britain*. British Archaeological Reports (BAR) British Series 329, Oxford.

Boardman, J. 1978 *Greek Sculpture, the Archaic Period*. Thames and Hudson, London.

Bögli, H. 1989 *Aventicum. The Roman City and the Museum*. Société Suisse de Préhistoire et d'Archaéologie, Basel.

Boon, G. C. 1974 *Silchester: the Roman Town of Calleva*. David and Charles, Newton Abbot.

Borger, H. 1977 *Das Römisch-Germanische Museum, Köln*. Georg Callwey, Munich.

Boucher, S. 1964 Les grands dauphins de bronze doré du Musée de Vienne (Isère). *Gallia* 22.1, 3-15.

Bowe, P. 2004 *Gardens of the Roman World*. Getty Museum, Los Angeles.

Brailsford, J. W. 1964 *Guide to the Antiquities of Roman Britain*. British Museum, London.

Bruneau, P. 1974 *Mosaics on Delos*. Diffusion de Boccard, Paris.

Brunet-Gaston, V. and Gaston, C. 2016 Le sanctuaire de Pont-Sainte-Maxence 'Le Champs Lahyre' (Oise). In A. Bazin, and J.-P. Blazy (eds), *À la Romaine! Résidence Privée, Construction Publique en Gaule du Nord*, 119-25. Archéa, Roissy.

Bromwich, J. 2014 *The Roman Remains of Brittany, Normandy and the Loire Valley. A Guide Book*. Lucina Books, Peterborough.

Bull, S. 2007 *Triumphant Rider. The Lancaster Roman Cavalry Tombstone*. Palatine Books, Lancaster.

Cassanelli, R. and Massimiliano, D. 2002 *Ruins of Ancient Rome: The Drawings of French Architects who Won the Prix de Rome 1786-1924*. Getty Museum, Los Angeles.

Clarke, J. 1850 *The Architectural History of Gloucester, from the Earliest Period to the close of the Eighteenth Century*. T. R. Davies, Gloucester.

Clifford, E. M. 1954 The Roman Villa, Witcombe, Gloucestershire. *Transactions of the Bristol & Gloucestershire Archaeological Society* 73, 5-69.

Coombe, P., Grew, F., Hayward, F. and Henig, M. 2015 *Roman Sculptures from London and the South-East.* Corpus Signorum Imperii Romani (CSIR). Great Britain, Vol. 1, Fascicule 10. British Academy, Oxford.

Crummy, N., Crosan, C. and Crummy, P. 1993 *Excavations of Roman and later Cemeteries, Churches and Monastic Sites in Colchester, 1971-88.* Colchester Archaeological Report 9, Colchester.

Cunliffe, B. W. 1968 *Fifth Report on the Excavations of the Roman Fort at Richborough, Kent.* Reports of the Research Committee of the Society of Antiquaries of London 23, London.

Cunliffe, B. W. 1971 *Excavations at Fishbourne, 1961-1969.* 2 vols. Reports of the Research Committee of the Society of Antiquaries of London 26, London.

Drack, W. 1988 *Die Römer in der Schweiz.* Raggi-Verlag, Stuttgart.

Espérandieu, É. 1907-1981 *Recueil Générale des Bas-Reliefs, Statues et Bustes de la Gaule Romaine.* 14 vols. Imprimerie Nationale, Paris.

Farrar, L. 1998 *Ancient Roman Gardens.* Sutton, Stroud.

Fauduet, I. 1993 *Les Temples de Tradition Celtique en Gaule Romaine.* Errance, Paris.

Floquet, C. 2001 *Le Temple de Mars, Corseul.* Gourin.

Forestier, A. 1924 Found thanks to a whining ferret! The fourth century Roman villa at Chedworth. *Illustrated London News* 12 July 1924, 74-75.

Forestier, A. 1928 Did the Romans worship Father Thames here? A reconstruction. *Illustrated London News* 1 December 1928, 1015.

Formigé, J. 1949 *Le Théâtre Romain de Vienne.* Audin, Vienne.

Forster, R. H. and Knowles, W. H. 1909 Corstopitum: Report on the excavations in 1908. *Archaeologia Aeliana*, series 3. 5, 305-424.

Foucher, L. 1965 *La Maison des Masques à Sousse. Fouilles 1962-1963.* Imprimerie du Secrétariat d'Etat aux Affaires Culturelles, Tunis.

García-Dils de la Vega, S. 2015. *Colonia Augusta Astigi. La evolución urbana de Écija desde la Protohistoria hasta la Antigüedad tardía.* Universidad de Sevilla, Seville.

García-Dils de la Vega, S. and Rodríguez Gutiérrez, O. 2014 El recinto de culto imperial de colonia Augusta Firma Astigi (Écija, Sevilla). Evidencia de un cerramiento metálico en el templo principal. In J. M. Á Martínez, T. N. Basarrate and I. Rodà de Llanza (ed.), *Actas del XVIII Congreso Internacional de Arqueología Clásica: Centro y periferia en el Mundo Clásico,* II, 1635-38. Museo Nacional de Arte Romana, Mérida.

Gessner-Siegfried, A. 1912 *Katalog des Kantonalen Antiquariums in Aarau.* H. R. Sauerländer, Aarau.

Gilyard-Beer, R. 1951 *The Romano-British Baths at Well.* Yorkshire Roman Antiquities Committee Research Report 1, Leeds.

Godwin, J. 1981 *Mystery Religions in the Ancient World.* Thames and Hudson, London.

Goodburn, R. 1983 *The Roman Villa Chedworth.* National Trust, London.

Hamlin, A. D. F. 1916 *A History of Ornament.* The Century Company, New York.

Heger, N. 1974 *Salzburg in Römischer Zeit.* Salzburger Museum Carolino Augusteum, Salzburg.

Henig, M. 1993 *Roman Sculpture from the Cotswold Region with Devon and Cornwall.* Corpus Signorum Imperii Romani (CSIR). Great Britain, Vol. 1, Fascicule 7. British Academy, Oxford.

Henig, M. 1997 The sculpture. In Harding, P. and Lewis, C., Archaeological investigations at Tockenham,1994. *Wiltshire Archaeological and Natural History Magazine* 90, 35-36.

Henig, M. 2004 *Roman Sculpture form the North-West Midlands.* Corpus Signorum Imperii Romani (CSIR). Great Britain, Vol. 1, Fascicule 9. British Academy, Oxford.

Hinks, R. P. 1933 *Catalogue of the Greek, Etruscan and Roman Paintings and Mosaics in the British Museum: Mosaics.* British, Museum, London.

Hodgson, N. 2009 *Hadrian's Wall 1999-2009. A Summary of Excavation and Research.* Titus Wilson & Son, Kendal.

Hodgson, N. 2010a The reconstruction of legionary temples at Corbridge. *ARA The Bulletin of the Association for Roman Archaeology* 20, 16-20.

Hodgson, N. 2010b Roman architectural fragments at Corbridge; a survey and study. *Arbeia Journal* 9, 1-42.

Holbrook, N. 1998 *Cirencester. The Roman Town Defences, Public Buildings and Shops.* Cirencester Excavations V. Cirencester.

Holbrook, N. 2003 Great Witcombe Roman Villa, Gloucestershire: field surveys of its fabric and environs, 1999-2003. *Transactions of the Bristol & Gloucestershire Archaeological Society* 121, 179-200.

Huskinson, J. 1994 *Roman Sculpture from Eastern England.* Corpus Signorum Imperii Romani (CSIR). Great Britain, Vol. 1, Fascicule 8. British Academy, Oxford.

Jashemski, W. F. 1979 *The Gardens of Pompeii, Herculaneum and the Villas destroyed by Vesuvius.* Caratzas Brothers, New York.

Keppie, L. J. F. and Arnold, B. J. 1984 *Scotland.* Corpus Signorum Imperii Romani (CSIR). Great Britain, Vol. 1, Fascicule 4. British Academy, Oxford.

Kowalczyk, G. and Köster, A. 1927 *Decorative Sculpture.* E. Benn, London.

Leach, P. 1998 *Great Witcombe Roman Villa, Gloucestershire. A Report on excavations by Ernest Greenfield, 1960-1973.* British Archaeological Reports (BAR) British Series 266, Oxford.

Lloyd-Baker, O. (undated) *Notes on Witcombe Villa. Manuscript from notes taken by Mrs Clifford from Col. Lloyd-Baker after Miss Olive Lloyd-Baker of Hardwicke Court.* Copy in Bristol Reference Library.

Lysons, S. 1821 Account of the remains of a Roman villa discovered in the Parish of Great Witcombe, in the County of Gloucester. *Archaeologia* 19, 178-183.

MacKendrick, P. 1970 *Romans on the Rhine.* Funk & Wagnalls, New York.

Marquand, A. 1909 *Greek Architecture.* Macmillan, New York.

Mattusch, C. C. 2009 *Pompeii and the Roman Villa.* Thames & Hudson, London.

Messineo, G. 1991 *La Via Flaminia da Porta del Popolo a Malborghetto.* Quasar, Rome.

Neal, D. S. 1977 Witcombe Roman Villa: a reconstruction. In M. R. Apted *et al.* (ed.), *Ancient Monuments and their Interpretation,* 27-40. Phillimore, London.

Neal, D. and Cosh, S. 2009 *Roman Mosaics of Britain. Vol III, Part 2, South-East Britain..* Illuminata Publishers, London.

Önal, M. 2009 *Zeugma Mosaics, a Corpus.* Istanbul.

Pobé, M. 1961 *The Art of Roman Gaul.* Galley Press, London.

Provost, A., Mutarelli, V. and Maligorne, Y. 2010 *Corseul. Le Monument Romain du Haut-Bécherel. Sanctuaire public des Coriosolites.* Presses Universitaires de Rennes, Rennes.

Reich, J. 1979 *Italy before the Romans.* Elsevier-Phaidon, Oxford.

RCHM(E) = Royal Commission on Historical Monuments, England 1976 *Ancient and Historical Monuments in the County of Gloucester. Volume One Iron Age and Romano-British Monuments in the Gloucestershire Cotswolds.* Her Majesty's Stationery Office (HMSO), London.

Salway, P. 2008 A Publication Policy for Chedworth. *Britannia* 29, 253-256.

Salway, P. 2009 When is a 'villa' not a villa? *Current Archaeology* 232, 48-49.

Selzer, W. 1988 *Römische Steindenkmaler. Mainz in Römischer Zeit.* Philipp von Zabern, Mainz.

Simonett, C. 1947 *Führer durch das Vindonissa-Museum in Brugg.* Speer Verlag, Zürich.

Smith, R. A. 1939 Roman fir-cone of terra-cotta. *Antiquaries Journal* 19, 194, pl xliv.

Stamper, J. W. 2005 *The Architecture of Roman Temples; The Republic to the Middle Empire.* Cambridge University Press, Cambridge.

Thomas, E. 2007 *Monumentality and the Roman Empire.* Oxford University Press, Oxford.

Toynbee, J. M. C. 1962 *Art in Roman Britain.* Phaidon Press, London.

Walker, G. 1998 The Weir Gardens, Swainshill, Hereford. *ARA The Bulletin of the Association for Roman Archaeology* 5, 5-6.

Walters, B. 2000 Chedworth: Roman villa or sanctuary? *ARA The Bulletin of the Association for Roman Archaeology* 9, 10-13.

Walters, B. 2009 Roman villas in Britain; Farms, temples or tax-depots? *Current Archaeology* 230, 30-35.

Walters, H. B. 1899 *Catalogue of the Bronzes in the British Museum. Greek, Roman and Etruscan.* British Museum, London.

Ward, J. 1911 *Romano-British Buildings and Earthworks.* Methuen & Co, London

Ward-Perkins, J. 1976 *Pompeii AD 79.* Imperial Tobacco Ltd, London.

Webster, G. 1983 The Function of the Chedworth Roman villa. *Transactions of the Bristol & Gloucestershire Archaeological Society* 101, 5-20.

Wilson, D., Bagnall, A. and Taylor, B. 2016 *Report on the Excavation of a Romano-British Site in Wortley, South Gloucestershire.* British Archaeological Reports (BAR) British Series 591, Oxford.

Yalouris, A. and Yalouris, N. 1987 *Olympia; the Museum and Sanctuary.* Ekdotike Athenon, Athens.

Yeates, S. 2004 The Cotswolds, the Codeswellan and the goddess Cvda. *Glevensis* 37, 2-8.

Yeates, S. 2006 *Religion, Community and Territory: Defining religion in the Severn Valley and adjacent hills from the Iron Age to the early medieval period.* British Archaeological Reports (BAR) British Series 411, Oxford.

11

The stones with Chi-Rho inscriptions at Chedworth

Stephen R. Cosh

On 9 July 1864, less than a month into the formal 'excavation' of Chedworth Roman villa, Revd Samuel Lysons, the nephew of his more famous namesake, visited the site. Recognising an entrance, he wondered whether, as in other cultures, there might be an inscription on what he termed the 'foundation stone'. He had one of the workmen 'turn it over' and was delighted to see, carved into it, a Chi-Rho, the Christian monogram comprising the first two letters of Christ in Greek. This suggested to him that the Roman owner was a Christian (Lysons 1865, 76-79; 1867, 236-37).

The presence of the Chi-Rho featured prominently in most of the early accounts of the villa. We now know of three Chi-Rhos inscribed on three separate slabs which all have a distinctive angular shape (Fig. 11.1). There has been much hypothesising about the significance of the Christian symbols and the stones themselves. It has long been recognised that they were originally the coping stones on the rim of the octagonal pool in what has become known as the *nymphaeum*, and the slabs were removed in antiquity to be re-used elsewhere.

So where did Lysons discover his 'foundation stone(s)'? In more recent times the Chi-Rho inscriptions are sometimes said to have been found incised or scratched on the rim of the pool, but this is shorthand or a misunderstanding. Most modern scholars describe them as having been built into the steps leading to the western bath-suite from the northern end of the *porticus* (for example, Richmond 1959, 22; Goodburn 1972, 24; RCHM(E) 1976, 26; Thomas 1981, 220). An examination of the nineteenth-century evidence is necessary to ascertain whether this is indeed correct.

The most worthwhile approach is to examine the descriptions of the find-spot in rough chronological order of publication. The earliest account by the first site excavator, James Farrer, writing at the time of the excavation, gives only a vague reference that the Chi-Rho was found 'in another part of the ruins' after describing (today's) Room 5 (Farrer 1866, 279). This implies that it was some way from Room 5, the grand dining room at the southern end. In 1865 Samuel Lysons stated that he discovered 'beneath the foundation-stones ... the Christian monogram twice repeated' and a little

later: '[beneath] the foundation-stone of the principal entrance of the villa' (Lysons 1865, 76; Lysons 1867, 236). The stones were turned over on Lysons' direction, and at least one was moved to the site museum which was built very shortly afterwards. It is unlikely that subsequent writers saw the stones *in situ*. In 1867 John Grover, expanded the description of the find-spot to: 'under part of the foundation of the steps leading into the corridor' assuming that this was the 'principal entrance' to which Lysons alluded (Grover 1867, 224). By his own admission he had not visited the site at that time and was relying on Lysons' published pieces (Grover 1868, 132). Revd Harry Scarth further expanded on the above in 1869, interpreting 'foundation' as the 'lowest step': 'under the steps leading from the long corridor into the *villa urbana...* under the lowest step'; and then added: '... there is a flight of steps leading into [the western baths] out of the corridor. Under these was found the Christian monogram' (Scarth 1869, 217-18).

It very much looks as though successive writers have elaborated on earlier accounts, almost like a Chinese whisper, and perhaps ended up with a false premise regarding the location under the flight of steps, which has since been interpreted as built into them. Of course, we do not know whether these gentlemen had other information. Scarth may well have attended the meeting of the Archaeological Institute in Warwick on 2 August 1864 at which Lysons read a 'memoir' on Chedworth and the Christian monograms (*Archaeological Journal* 21, 1864, 391), which was apparently never published, but it probably differed little from the one he read at a Cotteswold Naturalists' Field Club meeting which was (Lysons 1867). When Scarth led the tour of Chedworth villa during an excursion of the British Archaeological Association on 15 August 1868, Grover was present, but, although there was plenty of discussion reported about the nature of the octagonal pool, the stones with the Chi-Rhos were not mentioned in the congress proceedings (*Journal of the British Archaeological Association* 25, 1869, 400-405). The location under the steps to the baths as stated by Scarth seems inherently unlikely: the workman could hardly 'turn over' the lowest step of a flight.

Following a visit to Chedworth villa subsequent to his first article, Grover, after mentioning what he had previously

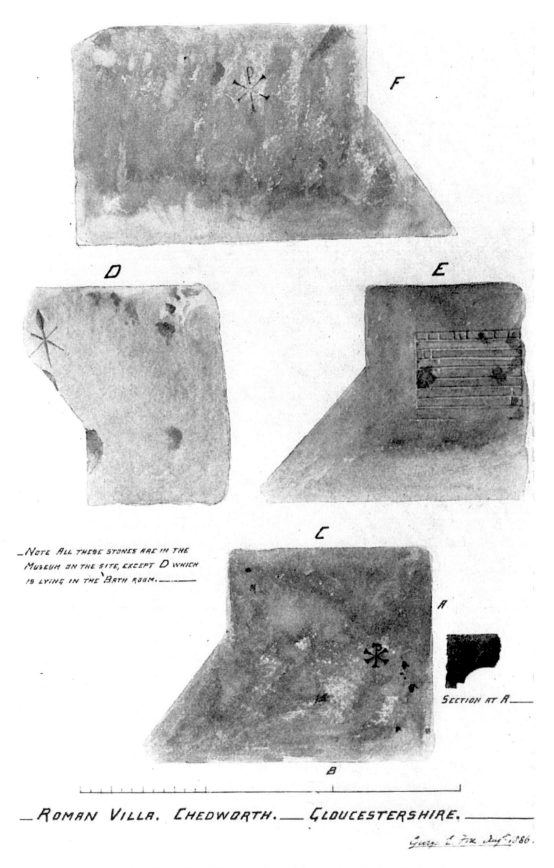

Figure 11.1. George Fox's 1886 watercolour of the angular slabs from Chedworth.
(Courtesy of the Society of Antiquaries of London)

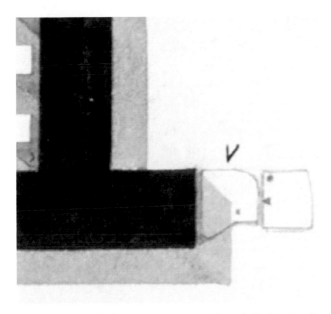

Figure 11.2. Detail of George Fox's 1886 plan of Chedworth villa. (Courtesy of the Society of Antiquaries of London)

said about Lysons' find, states: 'The *chi rho* also occurs on a door-step' (Grover 1868, 132). This sounds more like Lysons' account, and conceivably could be something that he had heard referring to the original discovery rather than another one. However, in August 1886 George Fox made a watercolour of four inscribed slabs (Fig. 11.1), three of which include the Chi-Rho monogram, so Grover's statement should perhaps be taken at its face value. It is interesting in this context that on the plan of the Chedworth villa made by George Fox in 1886 and now in the library of the Society of Antiquaries of London, he shows the doorstep to, or threshold of, Room 26a in the northern range. It comprises two stone slabs: one has the distinctive angular shape and the same width as the other slabs believed to have come from the rim of the octagonal pool, and the other almost square piece has the same width as the angular slab (though turned 90 degrees) (Fig. 11.2). It is almost certainly not the doorstep referred to by Grover, as that slab was being displayed in the site museum when Fox made his drawing of it. The fact that two doorsteps or thresholds were formed by these angular stones, makes it more likely that the original two discovered by Lysons were used in the same way, as his term 'principal entrance' suggests. It would seem almost certain that all three were part of the same building phase and their installation must have closely followed the levelling of the pool and at least the partial demolition of the *nymphaeum*.

It should be noted that Lysons found two Chi-Rhos under the 'foundation-stone(s)' and published line-drawings of them, one elaborate and the other somewhat simpler, side by side (Fig. 11.3a; Lysons 1865, 76). This was the

basis for Grover's earlier illustration, engraved by J Jobbins, which shows them as separate but these are among other images of Chi-Rhos from elsewhere (Fig. 11.3b; Grover 1867, pl 10). In Grover's later version there is a continuous background of stone but this must be fanciful as only single Chi-Rhos appear on the existing slabs (Fig. 11.3c; Grover 1868, pl 12). By the time George Fox saw and drew them in August 1886 (Fig. 11.1) the slab with the more elaborate Chi-Rho was in the site Museum while the one with the more sketchy example was, according to the note on his drawing, 'lying in the bath room'. It would seem that Fox's slab D is inscribed with the simpler of the Chi-Rhos found by Lysons, but the other is either on slab C or F. C is the more likely as the rho has a prominent serif at the top.

From Lysons' description, the 'foundation stone(s)' appear to be a single entity, formed of at least two parts bearing the Chi-Rhos, and, logically, the 'principal entrance' might well be that in the centre of the western *porticus*. It is difficult to see how two of the irregular-shaped stones were arranged, assuming that the two Chi-Rhos were on the same sides in relation to one another as Lysons implies, especially if they were slabs D and C. When the perhaps less likely pair of slabs (F and D) are placed together, they form a near perfect rectangle about 1.22 m by 0.5 m, which might well have been taken to be a single slab broken across the middle (Fig. 11.4); the Chi-Rhos would be in the same relative position as on Lysons' drawing. The length of the two stones as put together is less than the width of this central doorway (the opening is about 1.8 m). However, the arrangement would fit exactly when placed beside the southernmost stone of the step which has the same width. The Chi-Rho slabs were taken away for display, and it is quite possible that the two misshapen ones at the entrance as it appears today are their Victorian replacements (Fig. 11.4). Although the northernmost is unlikely to be a primary feature, the central one does show considerable wear, and therefore appears to be original. Alternatively, Lysons' stones may have been laid over this excessively worn step. It should be noted that the only one of these angular slabs illustrated *in situ* has the point facing outwards rather than being interlocked with a similarly-shaped stone.

If these first slabs were indeed part of the door-step at the central entrance to the western *porticus*, then it was very unlikely to have been an original feature. The mosaic flooring the *porticus* at this point was very susceptible to wear, and there is evidence that the much-damaged 'threshold' panel was laid to replace the centre of an earlier mosaic in the mid-fourth century presumably because its predecessor was damaged. Assuming that the

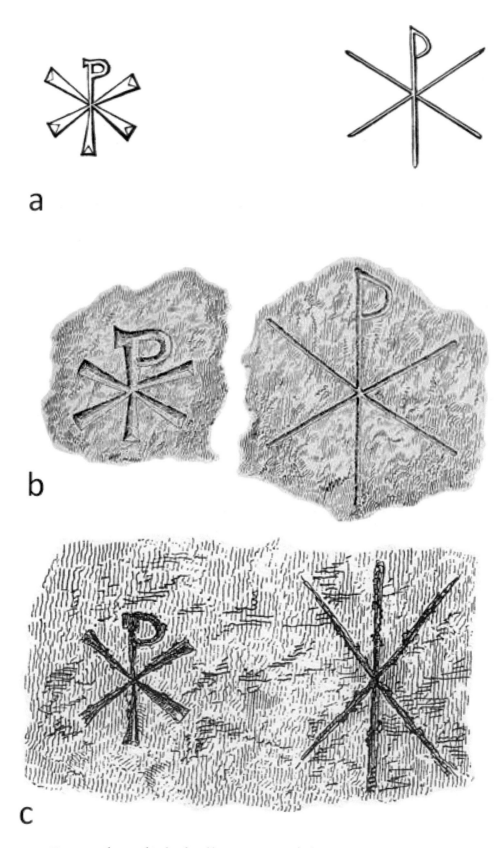

Figure 11.3. The two Chi-Rhos found by Lysons in 1864: a) after Lysons 1865, drawing on p 76; b) after Grover 1867, pl 10; c) after Grover 1868, pl 12.

slabs were not part of the mid-fourth century flight of steps leading to the western baths, it is quite conceivable that the original step at 'the principal entrance' was replaced or covered towards the end of the century if not later.

A less likely alternative is that Lysons' 'principal entrance' was at the centre of the cross-corridor, close to where the site museum/hunting lodge was built; it certainly had grand architectural pretensions. Graham Webster, without explanation or referencing, stated that the stones bearing Chi-Rhos were 'built into steps of the east wing' (Webster 1983, 13); this is probably a mistake and 'west wing' was meant, following other scholars since Scarth. Nevertheless, this location is a possibility, especially as two stones used for the step at the north end of this corridor are right-angled trapezia with the appropriate angle to have been part of the masonry which formed the rim of the pool below the coping stones. However, the cross-corridor may not have been revealed as early as 9 July 1864.

The threshold of Room 26a represents the only certain provenance for one of the re-used angular slabs. The exact find-spots of other similarly-shaped pieces no longer *in situ*, six in all, are unrecorded. Charles Thomas stated that one with a Chi-Rho was found 'in the north bath-suite' but this is a mistake: one has merely been displayed there, and still is (Thomas 1981, 220). It is known that the octagonal pool itself 'when first discovered was filled with rubbish and broken stones' as well as 'a large pillar' (Farrer 1870, 251). Although it

is impossible to say for certain if this debris included any parts of the rim, this is quite likely. It is not easy to envisage how the oddly-shaped pieces formed the coping of the pool's rim before it was levelled – they are not the expected trapezoidal shape as is sometimes erroneously stated (RCHM(E) 1976, 26). Figure 11.5 shows the most likely configuration, so that the pieces form the internal angles with rectangular and triangular slabs between them. The three known Chi-Rhos could all have been drawn by somebody sitting on the rim of the pool when the stones were still in place, albeit very awkwardly and randomly, just prior to demolition or at any point in the pool's history during the fourth century. On Fig. 11.4 showing the conjectural juxtaposition to create the 'step', the Chi-Rhos are in the same orientation, more or less level and the same distance from each end. This suggests that they were carved after their removal and just before their secondary use, but this may be coincidence. However, when the two other inscribed pieces illustrated by Fox are put together in the same way to form the putative second door-step alluded to by Grover, the Chi-Rho would also have this same orientation; at 1.10 m in length, almost the equivalent of four Roman feet, there are various possible doorways of the correct width. A protective element at an entrance would be wholly appropriate and there are many examples of a 'pagan' equivalent, but, as at least two were on the underside (assuming that they were not turned over in antiquity or, indeed, by Farrer's workmen prior to Lysons' intervention), this seems to defeat such a purpose; the notion that 'pagan' stones were 'Christianised' before re-use cannot be

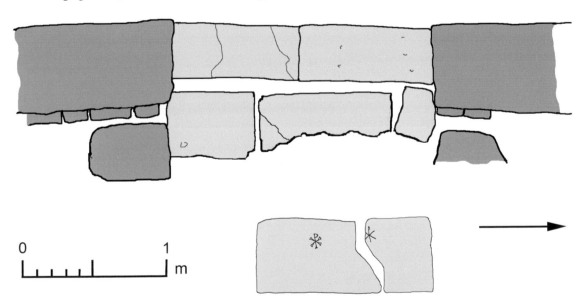

0   1   m

Figure 11.4. Two slabs put together to form a rectangle and shown at the same scale as the plan of the central entrance to the western porticus. (Drawing: S. R. Cosh)

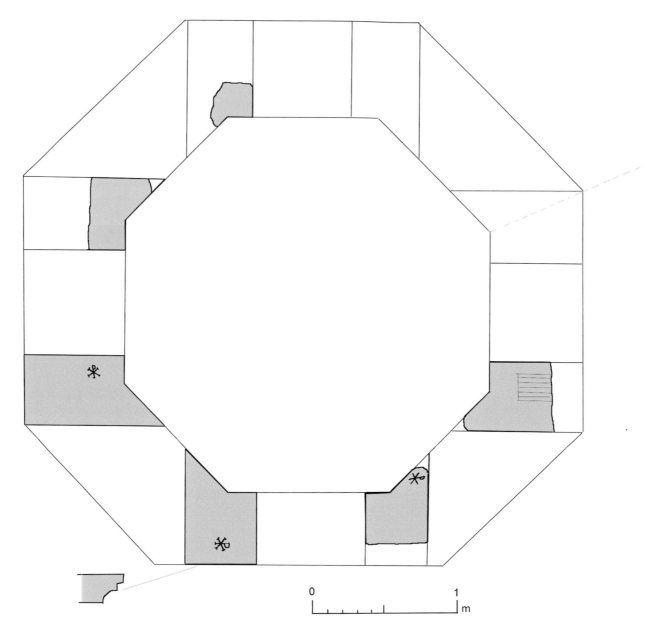

Figure 11.5. Probable configuration of the coping stones on the rim of the octagonal pool. (Drawing: S. R. Cosh)

ruled out (Webster 1983, 11) and the Chi-Rhos may have been hidden from sight to avoid having to walk upon the name of Christ. For Charles Thomas 'possibly the proprietor's family once Christianised their shrine, and successors eschewed the new religion' (Thomas 1981, 220). If, for whatever reason, the inscriptions were made when the coping stones were in their original position on the pool's rim, the less-weathered or uninscribed side of the stone may have been preferred as the surface of the new step and the Chi-Rhos ended up underneath to be discovered by Samuel Lysons 1500 years later. We should be thankful for his vigilance, for as he himself stated: '...the probability is that had I not been present, and searching for these evidences, the stones would

have been thrown away with the rest of the rubbish and lost' (Lysons 1867, 237).

But something that Lysons did not notice, and, as far as the author is aware, nobody else has to this day, is that the better of his Chi-Rhos is accompanied by the Greek letters *alpha* and *omega*. The latter, as 'ω', is just visible to the right of the Chi-Rho on photographs taken with raking light (Fig. 11.6); the *alpha* on the opposite side from the *omega* is less apparent because of a chip in the stone, but the faint marks can be seen as an *alpha* in the form of an 'A' (Fig. 11.7). The first and last letters of the Greek alphabet often occur in this form either side of a Chi-Rho reflecting the words in the New Testament:

Figure 11.6. Photograph of the Chi-Rho with alpha *and* omega *encircled. (Photo: S. R. Cosh)*

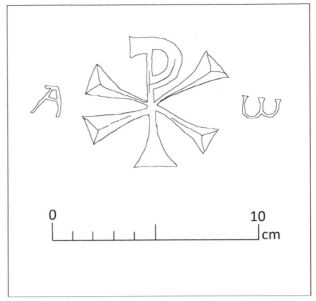

Figure 11.7 Interpretative drawing of Fig. 11.6. (Drawing: S. R. Cosh)

'I am the Alpha and the Omega' (Revelations 1.8 and 21.6) and there are several Romano-British examples in various contexts (Thomas 1981, 88-90, fig 6), including the famous reconstruction of the wall-painting from the supposed house church at Lullingstone villa, Kent. The arrangement of an *alpha* and *omega* flanking a Chi-Rho was also featured on coins of Magnentius (AD 350-353), its earliest datable use, and could have provided a model for the Chedworth example; it at least suggests that the Chi-Rhos were inscribed after AD 350.

Acknowledgement

Thanks are due to Dr Martin Papworth, the National Trust archaeologist, for sharing a photograph of the threshold of the main entrance.

References

Farrer, J. 1866 Notice of recent excavations in Chedworth Wood, on the estate of the Earl of Eldon, in the County of Gloucester. *Proceedings of the Society of Antiquaries of Scotland* 6, 278-83.

Farrer, J. 1870 Letter to Rev. Prebendary Scarth. *Journal of the British Archaeological Association* 26, 251-52.

Goodburn, R. 1972 *The Roman Villa: Chedworth*. National Trust, London.

Grover, J. W. 1867 Pre-Augustine Christianity in Britain as indicated by the discovery of Christian symbols. *Journal of the British Archaeological Association* 23, 221-30.

Grover, J. W. 1868 On a Roman Villa at Chedworth. *Journal of the British Archaeological Association* 24, 129-35.

Lysons, S. 1865 *Our British Ancestors: who and what were they? : an inquiry serving to elucidate the traditional history of the early Britons, by means of recent excavations, etymology, remnants of religious worship, inscriptions, craniology, and fragmentary collateral history.* John Henry & James Parker, Oxford.

Lysons, S. 1867 Notes on the Roman Villa at Chedworth. *Proceedings of the Cotteswold Naturalists' Field Club* 4, 233-39.

RCHM(E) 1976 = Royal Commission on Historical Monuments (England), *Ancient and Historical Monuments in the County of Gloucester*, vol 1, *Iron Age and Romano-British Monuments in the Gloucestershire Cotswolds.* HMSO, London.

Richmond, I. A. 1959 The Roman Villa at Chedworth, 1958-59. *Transactions of the Bristol and Gloucestershire Archaeological Society* 78, 5-23.

Scarth, H. M. 1869 On a Roman Villa at Chedworth, Gloucestershire, discovered in 1864. *Journal of the British Archaeological Association* 25, 215-27.

Thomas, C. 1981 *Christianity in Roman Britain to AD 500.* B. T. Batsford, London.

Webster, G. 1983 The Function of Chedworth Roman "villa". *Transactions of the Bristol and Gloucestershire Archaeological Society* 101, 5-20.

12

The St Laurence School villa, Bradford on Avon, Wiltshire

A Late Roman estate centre and early post-Roman church

Mark Corney

*To the memory of my father, Clifford Corney, 1928-2015,
who did so much to encourage my pursuit of archaeology.*

Location and Archaeological Context

The St Laurence School villa complex (Fig. 12.1) covers an area of approximately 2 ha (5 acres); it is located on the north-western edge of the historic Wiltshire market town of Bradford on Avon and sits on an Oolitic limestone plateau at a height of 102m OD (ST 817615). The location commands extensive views to the south, with a vista across the western end of the Vale of Pewsey and the northern escarpment of Salisbury Plain. To the east, the western scarp of the Marlborough Downs is visible some 18 km distant. The location is well-drained and permanent springs rise some 500 m to the north of the villa. The Anglo-Saxon and later centre of Bradford on Avon is located at the bottom of a steep-sided valley, beside a ford across the River Avon, approximately 1 km to the south-east of the villa site.

On a promontory overlooking the River Avon, 500 m to the south-east of the villa, is the site of an early first millennium BC hillfort, Budbury. Largely destroyed without record by housing development in the decades following World War II, one small area was excavated by G. Wainwright in 1969 (Wainwright 1970). This established the site as a bivallate enclosure of approximately 2.8 ha (7 acres). Wainwright's investigations suggest a construction date during the eighth century BC and abandonment by the fourth century BC. A small assemblage of fourth-century AD Roman coins and ceramics may hint at Late Roman, or even early post-Roman reoccupation. Unpublished salvage recording to the east of Budbury in the late 1970's and early 1980's recorded an extensive scatter of mid to late Iron Age material as well as Romano-British material associated with a series of ditches and pits (Wilts HER; A. Powell, *pers. comm.*).

Before the discovery of the villa complex, the evidence for Roman occupation in Bradford was relatively slight but significant. Besides the material from the vicinity of Budbury hillfort, five stone coffins of later Roman date are known. Four come from the plateau, within 500 m of the villa site. The same area has also produced occasional stray finds of Roman pottery coins and building materials. A further stone coffin was found at the foot of the hill below Budbury hillfort, near Barton Orchard, before 1907. The presence of stone coffins indicated that there ought to be a Roman settlement of some substance in the area. The first significant hint of a major building complex came in 1976 when part of a bath house was discovered during building operations and excavated under difficult circumstances by the late Alison Borthwick and Roy Canham. The bath house was located at one corner of the St Laurence School playing field, adjacent to a modern housing estate. It was a well-built structure and displayed the standard Roman bathing arrangement of hot (*caldarium*), warm (*tepidarium*) and cold (*frigidarium*) rooms. The building was dated to the later third century AD, continued in use into the early fifth century AD and included a complex network of very well-built stone-lined drains. The cold plunge bath incorporated a number of re-used fine architectural fragments suggestive of an earlier stone building of some pretensions and large quantities of high-quality painted wall-plaster. This structure is now known to have formed part of the west wing of the main villa complex (Fig. 12.2, Building 4). Late first and second-century material was also recovered in some quantity although no structures of this date were revealed. The 1976 excavation remains unpublished (Roy Canham, *pers. comm.*).

Beyond the immediate environs of Bradford on Avon, the Wiltshire SMR records a considerable number of find spots of later prehistoric and Roman material as well as a large number of cropmark sites ranging from field systems and tracks to enclosures, many of the latter displaying morphological characteristics typical of the later prehistoric and Romano-British period. Other Romano-

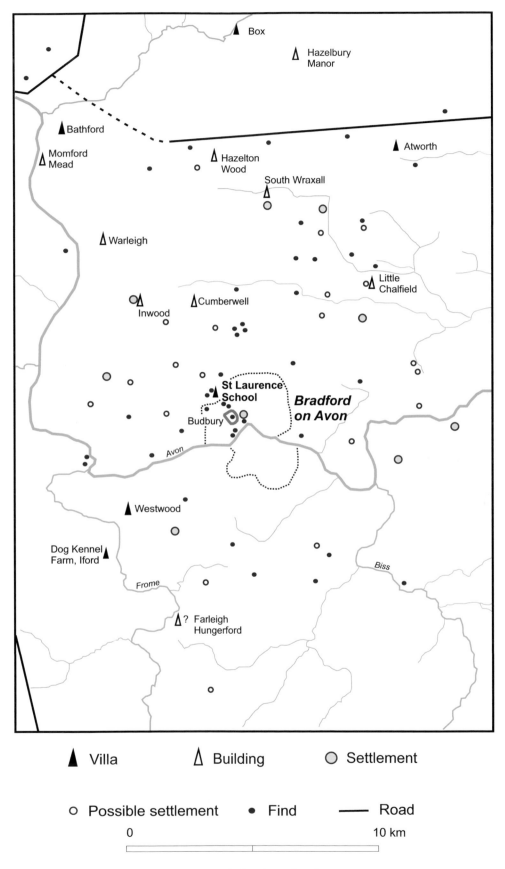

Figure 12.1. Site location and environs.

205

British structures or villas are known at Box, some 7 km to the north (Brakspear 1904; Corney 2012; Hurst 1987), Atworth, 5 km to the north-east (Mellor and Goodchild, 1942; Erskine 2008), Westwood, 2 km to the south-west (Wilts SMR), Iford, 5 km to the south-west (Page 1906), Farleigh Hungerford, 6 km to the south (Wilts SMR) and Bathford, 6 km to the north west (Scarth 1864).

The known Roman road system is represented by the main London to Bath route, Margary 53, running from east to west approximately 5 km north of the villa site. Other, minor routes are suspected but await confirmation through fieldwork. The nearest large urban settlement is at Bath, *Aquae Sulis*, 8.5 km to the north-west of Bradford on Avon. This major healing sanctuary will also have provided a wide range of administrative and market services to be expected of a major 'small town' (Burnham and Wacher 1991; Cunliffe 1995). At Westbury, 10.5 km to the south-east, a large but poorly understood industrial complex is probably another local market centre (Corney 2001). The nearest *civitas* capital is at Cirencester, *Corinium Dobunnorum*, some 43 km to the north-east and it is within the administrative territory of this centre that the villa was most probably located.

Figure 12.2. Site plan based on excavation, geophysical survey and air photography.

The discovery and plan of the villa complex (Figs 12.2 and 12.3)

The staff and pupils at St Laurence School had long been aware of strange marks appearing on the school playing field during long hot spells in the summer. It was widely believed that these marks showed the outline of a buried building although no report was made. It was only in the summer of 1999 that the parchmarks were planned by a Bradford on Avon architect, Martin Valentin, who passed the information on to the then Wiltshire County archaeologist, Roy Canham. An aerial photographic sortie was arranged through English Heritage and the resulting photographs, coupled with Valentin's plan, revealed the plan of a south-facing winged corridor building 38 m (118 ft) by 18 m (56 ft) with at least fifteen rooms (Fig. 12.2, no. 1). Following the confirmation of a villa building, students from the University of Bristol undertook a geophysical survey of the school playing field under the direction of Richard Tabor and the author (Fig. 12.3). This added further detail to data derived from the air and ground survey and revealed the existence of a second house of identical size and plan. This was on the same alignment as the first building discovered and set 30 m (100 ft) to the west of it (Fig. 12.2, no. 2).

The overall plan revealed by the non-invasive methods is without close parallel in Roman Britain. Although paired villa structures are widely known (Smith 1978; 1997) they are usually linked by a corridor, arranged around a court or, as in the case of Halstock in Dorset, connected by a probable tower over an entrance passage between the two houses (Lucas 1993). In most examples of this type of villa plan, the two 'houses' are rarely on an identical alignment or dimensions and Smith (*ibid.*) has suggested this may reflect the differing status of the respective occupants. In the case of St Laurence villa an alternative interpretation is offered.

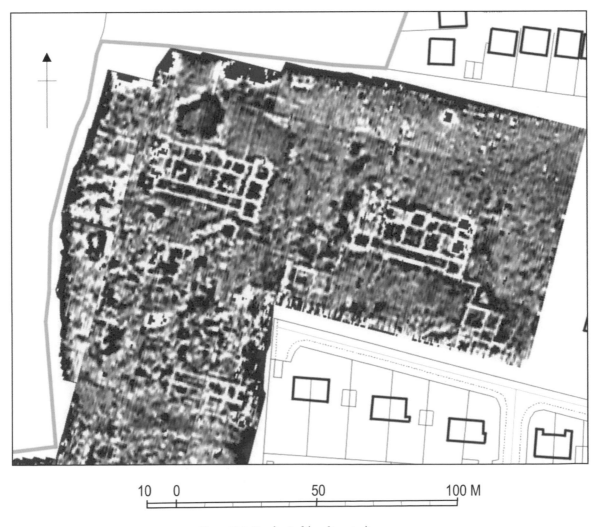

10 0   50   100 M

Figure 12.3. Geophysical (gradiometry) survey.

The eastern house (Building 1) has two ranges projecting to the south (Buildings 4 and 5). The western arm (Building 4) housed the bath-suite first excavated in 1976. The full extent of the ranges is unknown as they extend under a modern housing estate; although evidence (mainly in the form of Pennant sandstone roof tiles and other building debris) derived from a garden survey of adjacent houses suggests that they may be up to 70 m (over 230 ft) in length. The western house (Building 2) does not have attendant ranges, although the geophysical survey has recorded other buildings immediately to the south, comprising two small square structures, measuring 6 x 6 m, and a small, three-roomed building with a corridor along its south side (Fig. 12.2, no. 6). The latter is on a slightly different alignment to Buildings 1 and 2 and may be part of an earlier complex of buildings associated with the earliest phase of the bath-suite excavated in 1976.

The excavated evidence

No evidence for pre-Roman occupation was recovered although where the bedrock was revealed under Building 2 it was seen to be deeply scored by ploughing pre-dating the construction of the building (Fig. 12.4). Later prehistoric features, including Budbury hillfort

(Wainwright 1970), field systems and settlements are known within a short distance of the villa site (Canham 2014; Hawke 2005; Last *et al.* 2016). All the structures excavated between 2002 and 2004 are of later Roman date, probably constructed towards the end of the third century.

Building 1

Building 1 (Fig. 12.5) measures 38 m (118 ft) by 18 m (56 ft) and has at least fifteen rooms on the ground floor, based on the evidence of the magnetometer survey, air photography and parchmarks recorded on the ground in the summer of 2003. In 2002 and 2003, a north-south trench, measuring 20 x 8 m was excavated through the centre of the building. This produced evidence for two phases of construction and subsequent modifications. The walls, all of local limestone, were laid directly onto the underlying bedrock. External walls averaged 1 m in width and internal walls 0.8 m.

Upon removal of the turf and the base of a truncated post-Medieval ploughsoil, an extensive and dense spread of rubble, including finely dressed limestone blocks, derived from the collapse of the villa was exposed, recorded and removed. This sealed further debris, largely

Figure 12.4. Pre-villa plough-marks under Room 1, Building 2.

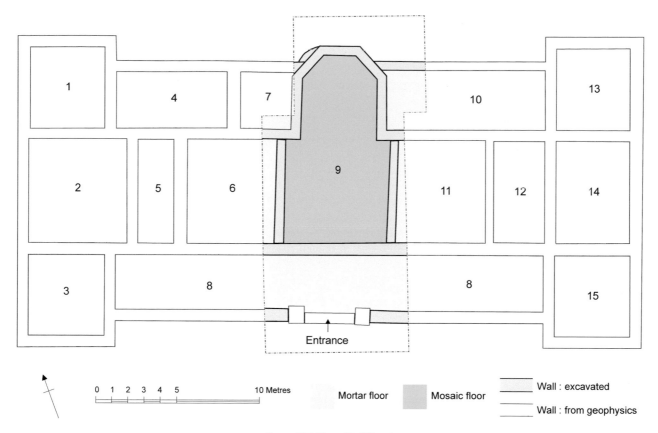

Figure 12.5. Plan of Building 1.

comprising large quantities of Pennant sandstone roof tiles, suggesting that the building gradually decayed and collapsed. No evidence of organised or large-scale robbing was recorded.

At the southern end of the excavated area was part of the *porticus* (Room 8) fronting the house with a monumental entrance. The entrance is constructed from two limestone blocks forming a threshold 3.2 m wide (10 ft). At each end was a squared limestone block measuring approximately 1 x 1 m and on each of these were the faint stains indicating pillar bases 0.8 m in diameter (Fig. 12.6). A threshold of this width would have required a double-leafed door. Pronounced wear on the eastern side of the threshold supports this and suggests that this half of the entrance was the main side of entry, although slighter wear on the west demonstrated that both doors were opened on occasion. The degree of wear on the east side suggests a prolonged period of use. Abutting the entrance, the outer walls of the *porticus* (and all of the other excavated walls of the building) were constructed of limestone rubble, with finely dressed facing stones all set in a hard yellow mortar. The *porticus* was 3.5 m (11 ft) wide with a floor of hard, pale yellow mortar that was much worn with rough repairs using limestone chips mixed with fragments of Pennant sandstone roof tiles. From the surface of the *porticus* floor came much painted wall-plaster, mainly of a deep red and cream colour and fragments of window glass. This suggests that the *porticus* was fully enclosed and did not take the form of an open fronted colonnaded gallery.

The north wall of the *porticus* retained evidence for a mortar threshold of similar width to the main entrance. This gave access to a bi-partite room (Room 9) 6.25 m (19.5 ft) square with a rectangular chamber, measuring 4.4 m (13.8 ft) by 5.3 m (16.6 ft) leading into a semi-hexagonal apse. This apse had replaced an earlier rounded one, part of the foundation of which was exposed on the north-west corner. This was clearly of a different build, with a hard pale cream mortar and was constructed from a finer grained limestone than its successor. Further evidence of rebuilding was noted in the wall dividing Rooms 9 and 6.

The building appears to have been kept free of rubbish and dating evidence for the Period 1 structure was scant, but the small assemblage of pottery and coins suggests construction during the period c. AD 250-300 and the Period 2 rebuild to the middle of the fourth century AD and is associated with the laying of a fine mosaic floor in Room 9. The reason for the rebuilding is unknown, but the Period 2 walls incorporate limestone blocks with evidence of burning. The faces of the walls of Room 9 all

Figure 12.6. Threshold to Building 1. View from the south.

Figure 12.7. Building 1, Room 9, mosaic floor, as excavated.

retain traces of painted wall-plaster and quarter-round plaster moulding. The *in situ* plaster is all of a deep red colour, although other fragments from the collapse of the structure indicate an ornate upper scheme with panels including mock marble designs employing shades of green, purple and yellow. Other fragments depict foliage and possible architectural motifs.

The floor of Room 9 features a well-executed polychrome mosaic (Fig. 12.7). Dated on stylistic grounds to c. AD 350-360 by David Neal, it is best preserved in the northern half of the room where it features a central rosette and knot motif with the four corners filled with stylised foliage; a *cantharus* flanked by a pair of dolphins facing away from the *cantharus*, occupied the apse (Cosh and Neal 2005; Witts, this volume). The southern half of the mosaic has suffered considerable damage in a late Roman or early post-Roman phase (see below), but had included four 'cushion' motifs and a central panel of unknown design, now lost. The style of the floor has affinities with the South Western Group A, the central rosette being closely paralleled on a floor from nearby Bath (Cunliffe 1969, pl. 82 b) and the cushion motifs on a floor from the villa at Brislington on the eastern outskirts of Bristol (Cosh and Neal 2005, 328-330).

Of greatest interest was the discovery and partial excavation of a circular stone platform carefully sited in the centre of the southern part of the bipartite chamber, Room 9 (Figs 12.8 and 12.9, 425). The south-western half was fully excavated and the north-eastern half was cleaned and planned but otherwise left undisturbed. The platform was 5.6 m in diameter and edged with dressed limestone blocks. On the north-west side two courses survived *in situ*. Within the platform kerb a single layer of undressed limestone blocks had been carefully placed in a packed soil matrix which produced four fourth-century coins, the latest a

House of Theodosius issue dating to c. AD 388-402. No evidence of a floor surface survived but the presence of two courses of kerbing indicates that this must have been at least 0.3 m high. In the centre of the platform was a circular hollow 2.1 m in diameter and 0.3 m deep which had removed the central panel of the underlying mosaic and exposing the underlying mortar base (Fig. 12.9, 429). In the south-east quadrant of 429 a pit, 437, 1m in diameter and of unknown depth, had been cut through the mosaic floor and had an upper fill of small loose limestone fragments. (Fig. 12.9, 437). This is interpreted as a soakaway associated with 429.

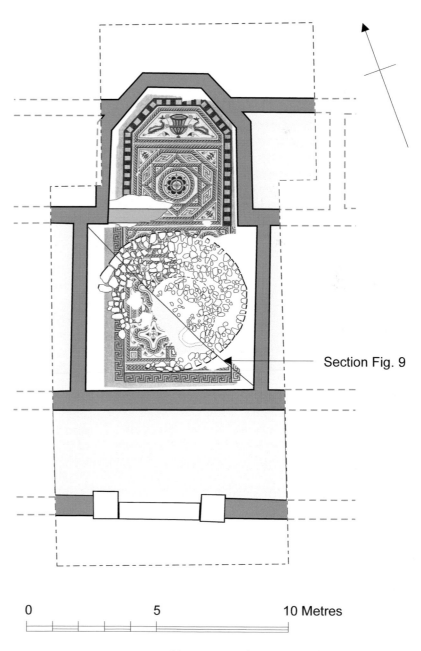

Section Fig. 9

0   5   10 Metres

Figure 12.8. Building 1. Room 9 plan as excavated.

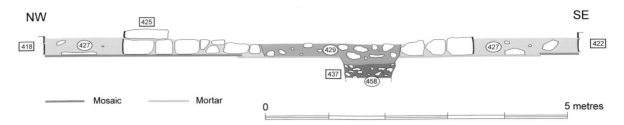

NW   SE

Figure 12.9. Building 1. Room 9 section through platform.

The platform was sealed by a thick deposit of Pennant sandstone roof tiles mixed with limestone rubble, dressed blocks and fragments of wall-plaster demonstrating that the structure had stood within the building whilst it was still roofed. The interpretation and significance of the stone platform is discussed below.

The survival of Building 1 as a villa house beyond the fifth century is difficult to determine. The coin list for the building runs from c. AD 270 to 402, the latest being two *Salus Reipublicae* issues of the House of Theodosius, including the example from the circular platform. The small ceramic assemblage comprises common later fourth century coarse wares such as South-East Dorset Black-Burnished ware (BB1), local types and Oxford Colour-Coated wares including forms dating to the second half of the century. Four conjoining sherds in BB1 are from a type 18 bowl; a form recognised as continuing in production into the early fifth century (Gerrard 2010), was recovered from the mortar floor of the *porticus*, Room 8.

Building 2

Building 2 is 30 m west of Building 1, is on the same alignment and has identical dimensions. It has at least seventeen rooms based on the evidence of the magnetometer survey, air photography and parch-marks recorded in the summer of 2003. The walls were of similar dimensions to Building 1 and laid directly onto the underlying bedrock. In the debris from the building were many finely dressed limestone blocks, Pennant sandstone roof-tiles and part of a Bath-stone roof finial in the form of a *quadrifrons*.

The west end of the building, comprising three rooms (Fig. 12.10, 1, 2 and 3), was fully excavated and an additional trench examined part of the central suite including an apsidal-ended room (Fig. 12.10, 5, 8 and 9). The building produced no evidence for interior décor. No *tesserae* or pieces of painted wall-plaster were recovered, and it appears to have been unadorned.

In Rooms 1 and 2 the floors were composed of compact, rammed limestone laid directly onto the underlying

bedrock; the latter scored with plough-marks, presumably made by an iron-tipped ard and pre-dating construction of the building. In Room 2 the limestone cobbles were covered by discrete burnt deposits which in turn were sealed by extensive spreads of Pennant sandstone roof tiles, many still intact. A door 1.2 m wide in the west wall of Room 2 opened onto an external cobbled surface. Against the south wall of Room 2 was a remarkably small stokehole feeding a hypocaust in Room 3. The hypocaust chamber had been excavated into the bedrock to a depth of 1.4 m and large limestone *pilae* arranged in an unusual and irregular fashion supported a crude floor of large Forest Marble slabs, many of which had collapsed into the void below (Fig. 12.11). None of the slabs retained any traces of mortar on their upper surfaces and it appears that they were intended to function as the floor of the room. Against the north wall of Room 3 was an irregular pit containing eighteenth-century pottery and clay-pipe fragments. This had removed at least five stone *pilae*, the impressions of which were clearly visible in the mortar skim which formed the floor of the hypocaust chamber. The pit is the only evidence for an otherwise undocumented discovery of part of the villa prior to recent investigations.

Following abandonment of Room 3 the flags either collapsed or were deliberately demolished and the voids used to deposit domestic rubbish. The pottery was of later fourth century date and similar in character to that recovered from Building 1. The latest coin is an issue of the House of Valentinian, 364-378. The deposit also included a large assemblage of animal bone dominated by sheep and cattle, many with evidence for butchery.

In the central range Rooms 5, 6, 7 and 9 were partially examined. This produced evidence for two phases on construction. The first phase included Rooms 5 and 9 where the walls were set in a hard pale cream mortar identical to that observed in the first phase apse in Building 1. If a symmetrical plan is assumed, then the unexcavated room to the east of Room 9 should also belong to this build and may originally been of a simple tripartite building subsequently enlarged to produce a ground plan identical to Building 1 with Room 6 becoming the *porticus*. The floors in 5, 6 and 9 comprised compact, rammed limestone laid directly onto the underlying bedrock and of identical character to those recorded in Rooms 2 and 3. In the apsidal room on the north side of the building, Room 8, no floor survived but large quantities of nails recovered here may suggest that timber planking was used. As in Rooms 1 and 2, the bedrock in Room 8 was also deeply scored by plough marks pre-dating the construction of the building (Fig. 12.12).

The central room, 9, was found to contain a well-built, stone-lined flue, which exhibited clear traces of intensive heat. The lower fill also contained a thick deposit of charcoal. The northern end and western side of the structure was bonded into the walls of the room showing it to be an original feature of the first phase structure and retained in use after the enlargement of the building. The plan of this flue suggests that it is part of an agricultural kiln, probably consisting of two flues and covered with large stone slabs and used to parch grain or as a malting floor. The upper fill of the flue contained the capital of a small limestone column and a large quantity of Pennant sandstone roof tiles, many still intact and still retaining the nails used to affix them to the roof timbers (Fig. 12.13).

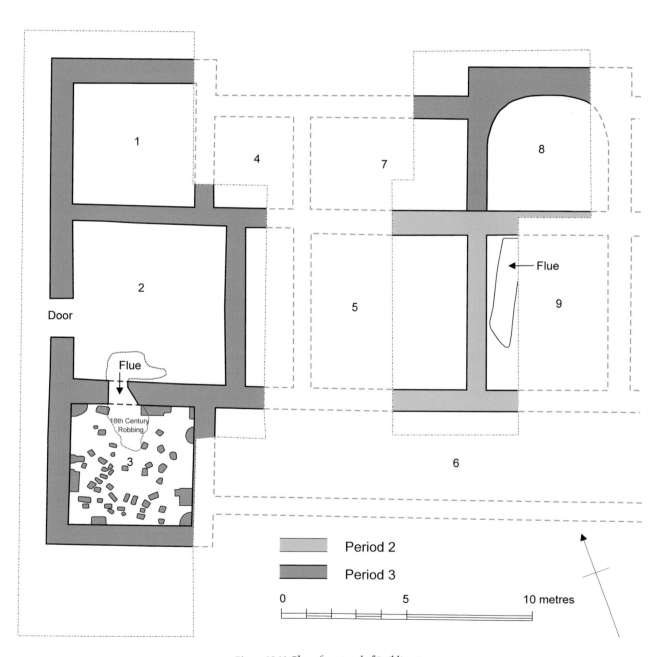

Figure 12.10. Plan of west end of Building 2.

Figure 12.11. View of Room 3, Building 2 under excavation. View from the north.

Figure 12.12. View of Room 8, Building 2 showing pre-villa plough-marks. View from the east.

Figure 12.13. View of Room 9, Building 2, showing collapsed roof tiles in the flue. View from the east.

The remains of three neonate human burials were found within Building 2. All were found within the northern range of the building, placed against the inner face of the north wall in Rooms 1, 7 and 8.

The function of Building 2

Despite the very formal plan of Building 2 and the quality of the construction which undoubtedly presented a grand exterior, the interior was of a very different character. The hypocaust in Room 3 has many unusual features; there are no vertical flues in the walls for *tubuli* and the large slabs over the *pilae* bear no trace of a mortar surface and there were large gaps between the slabs. The stokehole is remarkably small and it is difficult to reconcile these features with a conventional heated domestic room. An alternative interpretation is that the room was designed to function as a smokehouse for the curing of meat and other produce. To the author's knowledge such a room is without parallel in other Romano-British villas. Possible smokehouses, as free-standing structures, have been identified elsewhere in Britain such as at Castleshaw fort, Greater Manchester (Bidwell and Hodgson 2009, 73) and a recently excavated example at Pineham in Northamptonshire (Chapman *et al.* 2014).

The placing of a large double-flue kiln or oven in the central room, 9, as part of the original construction, is also unusual, this location usually reserved as the principal reception area in a standard Romano-British villa house.

Building 2 performed a number of functions central to the economic base of the villa estate. It was designed as a utilitarian working building behind a grand façade mirroring that of the main house, Building 1, some 30 m to the east. The agri-industrial interpretation would also explain why Building 2 lacks the additional ranges housing a bath-suite, kitchen and other ancillary rooms present on the south of Building 1. Some domestic occupation is also indicated by the presence of bone pins and a stone gaming die. Other part of the building may have housed estate workers.

Building 4, bath-suite

The west range of the main villa, Building 4, was first investigated in 1976. In 2004 part of the suite was re-examined. This was largely confined to the removal of the 1976 backfill and the detailed recording of the structural remains. This identified three phases of construction (Fig. 12.14). The eastern side of the suite

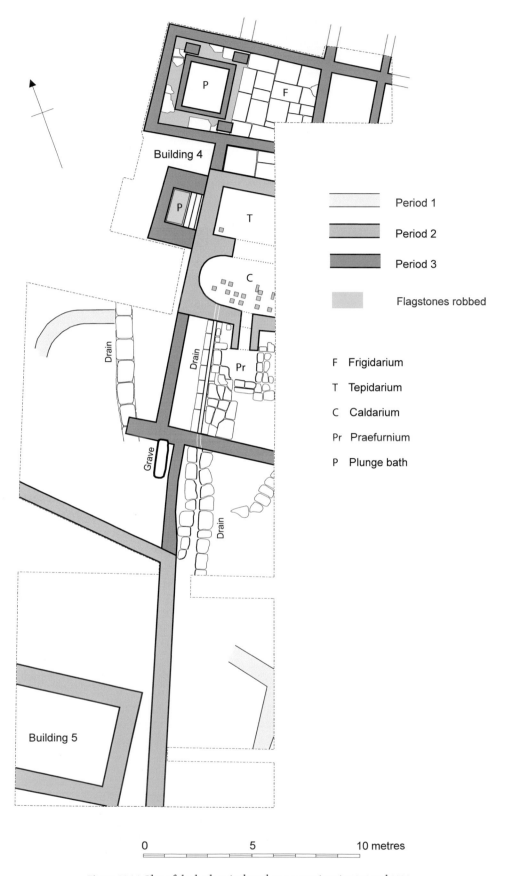

Figure 12.14. Plan of the bath-suite based on excavations in 1976 and 2004.

is now inaccessible under garages and houses of the adjacent housing estate. This estate was built during the 1960's and although there are no records of discoveries during construction there is no doubt that further substantial buildings associated with the villa complex must have been encountered and destroyed.

The *frigidarium* was floored with carefully smoothed and cut Pennant sandstone flags. At the west end was a plunge bath measuring 3 x 3 m, with three large stone bases at the corners, a fourth having probably been robbed. The bases were fashioned from re-used moulded stones, probably from a cornice, derived from an earlier building. To the south was a narrow room leading into the *tepidarium* with a small rectangular bath on the west entered by two steps. The *caldarium* lay to the south with the *praefurnium* beyond. Examination of the remains showed that the *tepidarium* and *caldarium* belong to an earlier phase with the *tepidarium* bath and *frigidarium* range being later additions. A further room was added to the south of the *praefurnium*. A wall at least 15 m in length was revealed running south from the *praefurnium* and had a compact cobbled surface to the east, perhaps forming part of a service yard. Parchmarks and geophysical survey show that the bath-suite lay at the southern end of a range of many rooms extending southwards from the south-west corner of Building 1. A corresponding east range, Building 3, is known from geophysical survey but its full extent is now lost under the adjacent housing estate. A complex series of well-constructed stone drains ran south from the bath-suite with another to the west of the *praefurnium*. Some of the covering stones appear to have been salvaged and re-used from another structure. Dating evidence is sparse but based on comparisons of mortar and building materials the *frigidarium*, *tepidarium* bath and room to the south of the *praefurnium* are identical to the mid-fourth century phase of Building 1. The earlier phase of the bath-suite comprising the tepidarium and *caldarium* may be contemporaneous with the first phase of Building 1 dated to c. 250-300. This may have begun as a detached suite.

To the south and west of the baths, short and fragmentary lengths of unmortared pitched limestone footings were observed and ascribed to the earliest phase of construction, possibly pre-dating the main villa complex. The westernmost wall is curved and is cut by one of the drains.

To the south of the bath-suite the north-east corner of Building 5 was examined. This had a rough cobbled floor which produced a dispersed hoard of 21 later third-century 'barbarous' radiates copying issues of the Gallic Empire. All were in a very fresh condition and two still had casting flash attached, possibly indicating manufacture on site.

Burials

Apart from the infant burials recorded from Building 2, two inhumation burials were excavated, one being 50 m to the south-west of Building 2, where part of an inhumation cemetery was located. The excavated burial was aligned north-west to south-east, and was a prone and decapitated burial with head placed at the feet (Fig. 12.15). Apart from hobnails at the feet of the skeleton no grave goods were present. Decapitated and prone burials are a predominantly Late Roman practice and although relatively uncommon are not regarded as necessarily deviant (Philpott 1991, 71-89; Tucker 2015). The outlines of two further graves on the same alignment were recorded but not excavated.

Burial 2 was an isolated inhumation located immediately to the south-west of the bath-suite *praefurnium* (Fig. 12.16). It was aligned north-east – south-west with the head at the northern end. The northern end had been cut into the wall the southern boundary of the *praefurnium* with the head resting against large limestone block. The lower legs were tightly packed between two large upright stones. The partial lining and pillow-stone is a

Figure 12.15. Burial 1. View from the south.

Figure 12.16. Burial 2. View from the west.

characteristic of late and post-Roman burials in western Britain (Philpott 1991, 63) with numerous examples from the large cemeteries at Cannington (Rahtz *et al.* 2000, 104-5) and Henley Wood (Watts and Leach 1996, 57), both in Somerset, although here the graves are aligned east-west. At the time of writing radiocarbon determinations from both inhumations are awaited.

Discussion

The investigations at the St Laurence villa have revealed a large villa complex and estate centre. Although later first and second century material and reused architectural fragments are present, the main complex is only constructed after the middle of the third century with major additions in the mid-fourth century, including the enlargement of the bathing-suite and the provision of a fine mosaic floor in Building 1. The focus of earlier activity remains unknown and may now be lost under the adjacent housing estate.

The plan of the complex is highly symmetrical with the two main structures, Buildings 1 and 2, being of identical plan and on a common alignment. Building 2 has been identified as a large agri-industrial unit with an external appearance identical that of the main villa house, Building 1. Building 2 has produced evidence for a smokehouse and a large double-flue drier or malting kiln as being part of the original construction thus indicating the building was designed from the outset as an integral part of the villa's ability to process produce from the estate. Whilst the ground plan of both buildings falls within a well-known design of Romano-British villa houses, the configuration of Buildings 1 and 2 shows a

clear intention from the outset to use the architecture of the complex to convey a very grand façade to those approaching the site from the south. It could even be said that the owner or owners had a strong sense of an architectural landscape in commissioning such a design. The elevated and commanding position of the villa complex, overlooking the Avon Valley, would have presented a very impressive sight visible for a considerable distance to the south and east.

The late to early post-Roman circular structure placed within Room 9 of Building 1 is a remarkable and important discovery. Such features rarely survive post-Roman disturbance or ploughing and, given the relatively ephemeral nature of the construction, would not necessarily have been recognised in earlier antiquarian investigations of other villa sites in the south-west.

The interpretation of the structure requires careful consideration. The position, symmetrically placed in the centre of the principal public room of the Roman house, is undoubtedly deliberate and can be demonstrated stratigraphically to have been constructed while the house was still standing and roofed. The dating evidence points to the very late fourth or early fifth century. It will have been a dominant feature to anyone entering the house through the grand double-door main entrance and was clearly of considerable importance. In form the structure is a platform with a centrally placed feature cut through the underlying mid-fourth century AD mosaic. The structure is identified as a Christian baptistery, an interpretation endorsed by Henig (2015, 25) and Bowes (2008, 176-7). The apse beyond the room, with the mosaic depiction of a *cantharus* flanked by dolphins would remain accessible and could quite conceivably have become a church (Henig *ibid*.). Within the centre of the circular platform would have stood the font, made either of brick or lead. Baptismal fonts of brick or lead are known from later Roman Britain and some 29 lead examples are now known from Britain and many are decorated with various Christian motifs, including the Chi-Rho monogram (see Booth *et al.* 2011 for a recent overview). Brick or masonry fonts are rarer but where known have strong parallels with continental examples. The best known is the particularly fine brick font, associated with a timber church, which still survives within the late Roman fort at Richborough in Kent (Brown 1971). Further examples in eastern England include Icklingham in Suffolk (West and Plouviez, 1976) or Ivy Chimneys in Essex (Turner 1999). A possible western British example comes from West Hill, Uley, Gloucestershire, where a fifth-century church and baptistery have been proposed as succeeding a temple dedicated to Mercury (Woodward and Leach 1993; Petts 2003, 70-71).

Although at St Laurence the font is now absent, the platform, central circular setting and the adjacent soakaway pit strongly supports the interpretation as a baptistery. The nature of the baptismal font at St Laurence will remain unknown but Booth *et al.* (2011, 271) note that the majority of the lead fonts occur on rural settlements rather than villas and Henig has observed; 'In an island where an increasingly large percentage of the population was Christian, portable fonts such as these may have given way to larger and far more permanent structures such as that recently discovered at Bradford on Avon. We should look for others.' (Henig 2015, 28). The rarity of portable lead fonts from villa sites and western Britain would strongly suggest that the St Laurence example will have been of brick, perhaps similar to the example from Richborough.

The reconstruction a baptismal scene based on the lead font from Walesby in Lincolnshire published by Thomas (1981, 221-225, fig. 41) is the depiction of a rite that would have been familiar to those witnessing and undergoing baptism at St Laurence. In the scene Thomas, following Toynbee (1964, 354), accepts the scene as being set within a building, probably a baptistery in Britain. Thomas further states; 'The scene is good presumptive evidence for the existence of a baptistery....in late Roman Britain' (Thomas 1981, 224).

Although other Romano-British churches and baptisteries are known (Henig 2015), the St Laurence site gives clear evidence for the conversion of a villa into a place of public Christian devotion. This contrasts for example with the private Christian house church at Lullingstone in Kent which occupies a peripheral position within the villa and no baptistery has been recognised (although the main central mosaic has cryptic allusions to Christian beliefs; Henig 2015, 24). At two other villas in western Britain, Lufton in Somerset and Holcombe in east Devon, large octagonal buildings have been claimed as baptisteries (Todd 2005) although this interpretation is challenged by Henig (2006).

The conversion of villas and estate centres into churches and baptisteries is paralleled in fifth-century Gaul where members of aristocratic families become bishops and maintain both secular and spiritual power (Bowes 2008; Van Dam 1985; Collis, this volume). The best-known Gallic literary source is provided by the letters of Sidonius Apollinaris, aristocrat, landowner and Bishop of Clermont writing in the later fifth century. A letter to from Sidonius to his friend Elaphius, living in Rodez, is especially illuminating where he says to Elaphius, 'Your letter tells us that the baptistery so long in the builder's hands is now ready for consecration.' (Sidonius Apollinaris, *Letters* 4.15).

We do not have such documentary sources for Britain although St Patrick's opening statement in his *Confessio* tells us that his father was a deacon and his grandfather a priest (*Confessio* 1) and that he was captured at his '*uillula*', a description which Dark (1993) has argued may refer to a villa or an estate.

The archaeological evidence from the St Laurence villa shows that the site undergoes a transformation in the early fifth century. It remains an estate centre for an unknown period and also becomes a Christian centre to serve the rural community dependent upon the villa and the landowning family who, like in Gaul, may also include a bishop. How long this continues is uncertain but the provision of a substantial stone baptistery and the pattern of wear on the villa threshold would suggest use over a number of years. A transformation of the estate on the Gallic model described is a strong possibility and this may have had a major influence on the emergence of Bradford on Avon as an important Middle Anglo-Saxon centre.

Postscript: beyond the fifth century

Evidence for late Roman Christianity in western Britain is well-documented (see Petts, 2003). This ranges from mosaics, Hinton St Mary and Frampton in Dorset being the best known, to cemeteries such as Poundbury outside of Dorchester. Probable Christian structures or cemeteries succeeding pagan temples and continuing into the post-Roman period are known at Lamyatt Beacon (Leech 1986), Brean Down

(ApSimon 1965), Henley Wood (Watts and Leach 1996), Cannington (Rahtz *et al.* 2000) all in Somerset, and Uley, Gloucestershire (Woodward and Leach 1993) to name but a few. The evidence of the cemeteries in particular shows British Christian communities continuing into the post-Roman period. The provision of a large baptistery at Bradford on Avon must have played an important role in the establishment of these emerging communities in west Wiltshire.

West Wiltshire is an area where evidence for an Early Anglo-Saxon presence is sparse. In a recent review of the Early Anglo-Saxon period in Wiltshire, Eagles notes the paucity of fifth to seventh-century material in the region (Eagles 2001, Map 11.1), he further notes the survival of a number of British and related place-names across the county (*ibid.*, Map 11.2). In a further article Eagles argues for the survival of a British Christian community in west Wiltshire, where Brittonic is still widely spoken and that the meeting between St Augustine and British Church leaders in 602 or 603 may have taken place in the area, possibly near Kemble, on the Fosse Way some 30 km north-east of Bradford on Avon (Eagles 2003). It is probable that this British Christian community will have had its origins in the Late Roman Period.

Finally, it is worth briefly discussing the assimilation of the Bradford on Avon region into the Anglo-Saxon Kingdom of Wessex. Under Ine, king from *c.* 688 to 726, Wessex expands westwards and in 705 Bradford on Avon is one of a number of estates granted to St Aldhelm in Wiltshire, Somerset and Dorset on his appointment to the newly-created see of Sherborne. Aldhelm was related to the royal house of Wessex and had a long and distinguished clerical career having taken orders under an Irish monk, Maildubh, at Malmesbury and subsequently became Abbot there (Lapidge 2007). Aldhelm was acknowledged by Bede as a great Anglo-Saxon scholar and man of letters, fluent in Latin as well as English. He is known to have visited British communities in Dumnonia, which apart from Devon and Cornwall probably included parts of Somerset and western Dorset at this date and he is known to have corresponded with British and Anglo-Saxon rulers (Smith 2013). Could Aldhelm's links with the native British Christian communities in western Britain have influenced Ine in his choice as Bishop of Sherborne? Was the estate granted at Bradford on Avon given in recognition of Aldhelm's contact with western British Christian communities and reflect the survival of such a community here?

King Ine appears to have been aware of the established Christian tradition in the western part of his newly expanded kingdom with him sponsoring 'new' foundations at Glastonbury and Wells. Both locations have produced evidence of Late Roman and early post-Roman activity. At Wells excavations between 1978 and 1993 established that the Saxon church overlay a Late Romano-British tomb, argued by Rodwell to be a *martyrium* (Rodwell 2001, 53-54). It is worth recalling here that Yorke (1995, 190) has noted the prevalence of 'British' names in the king lists of the early House of Wessex, including Cædwalla, Ine's predecessor.

Although Aldhelm's centre at Bradford on Avon is thought to lie away from the villa site in the Avon valley, possibly in the vicinity of the Late Anglo-Saxon church of St Laurence (Haslam 1976; Hinton 2009), we may speculate whether the lands granted to him were in part a fossilisation of the villa estate where the Christian community of the area was born.

At Bradford on Avon we have for the first time in fifth-century Britain archaeological evidence for the conversion of a villa into a Christian centre including a baptistery. As such the results of the excavation have placed the site as one of the most important and exciting discoveries in recent years and is of international significance. It may also give an insight and the rationale for the creation of an important Anglo-Saxon centre at Bradford on Avon by St Aldhelm in 705.

Acknowledgements

The excavations at St Laurence School, Bradford on Avon were supported by a number of institutions and the generosity of the people of Bradford on Avon. Thanks are extended to the staff and Governors of St Laurence School for permission to excavate and provision of many support facilities; to BBC *Points West*, BBC2, public donations, Bradford on Avon Preservation Trust, Bradford on Avon Lions and Ex Libris Press. All three seasons, 2002-4, were supported by the University of Bristol as part of their Certificate in Archaeology programme. The 2002 season was a joint venture between the Universities of Bristol and Cardiff with Peter Guest acting as Co-Director. It is a particular pleasure to acknowledge the generous grant aid made by Bradford on Avon Town Council and The Association for Roman Archaeology. A special thanks is extended to Sophie Hawke who greatly assisted in liaising with St Laurence School.

References

Ancient Sources

Patrick, *Confessio* = Hood, A. B. E. (ed. and trans.) 1978 *St Patrick: his writings and Muirchu's Life.* Phillimore, Chichester.

Sidonius Apollinaris = Anderson, W. B. 1936 (ed. and trans.) *Poems and Letters of Sidonius Apollinaris.* Loeb Classical Library 296, Harvard University Press, Cambridge, Mass.

Modern Sources

ApSimon, A. 1965 The Roman temple on Brean Down, Somerset. *Proceedings of the University of Bristol Spelaeological Society* 10.3, 195-258.

Bidwell, P. and Hodgson, N. 2009 *The Roman Army in Northern England.* Arbeia Society, South Shields.

Booth, P., Cameron, E. and Crerar, B. 2011 A Roman lead 'tank' from Wigginton, North Oxfordshire. *Oxoniensia* 76, 266-72.

Bowes, K. 2008 *Private Worship, Public Values, and Religious Change in Late Antiquity.* Cambridge University Press, Cambridge.

Brakspear, H. 1904 The Roman villa at Box. *Wiltshire Archaeological Magazine* 33, 236-269.

Brown, P. D. C. 1971 The church at Richborough, Kent. *Britannia* 2, 225-31.

Burnham, B. and Wacher, J. 1990 *The 'Small Towns' of Roman Britain.* Batsford, London.

Canham, R. 2014 *A Land Through Time: a Lidar survey of part of the Bradford Hundred.* Ex Libris Press, Bradford-on-Avon.

Chapman, E., Hunter, F., Booth, P., Pearce, J., Worrell, S. and Tomlin, R. S. O. 2014 Roman Britain in 2013. *Britannia* 45, 307-95.

Corney, M. 2001 The Romano-British nucleated settlements of Wiltshire. In P. Ellis (ed.), *Roman Wiltshire and After. Papers in Honour of Ken Annable,* 5-38. Wiltshire Archaeological and Natural History Society, Devizes.

Corney, M. 2012 *The Roman Villa at Box.* Hobnob Press, Salisbury.

Cosh, S. and Neal, D. 2005 *Roman Mosaics of Britain. Volume II South-West Britain.* Illuminata Publishers & Society of Antiquaries, London.

Cunliffe, B. W. 1969 *Roman Bath.* Reports of the Research Committee of the Society of Antiquaries of London 24, London.

Cunliffe, B. W. 1995 *Roman Bath.* Batsford, London.

Dark, K. R. 1993 St Patrick's Uillula and the fifth-century occupation of Romano-British villas. In D. Dumville (ed.), *Saint Patrick AD 493-1993,* 19-24. Boydell, Woodbridge.

Eagles, B. N. 2000 Anglo-Saxon presence and culture in Wiltshire, *c* 450-*c* 675. In P. Ellis (ed.) 2000, *Roman Wiltshire and After: Papers in Honour of Ken Annable,* 199-233. Wiltshire Archaeological and Natural History Society, Devizes.

Eagles, B. N. 2003 Augustine's oak. *Medieval Archaeology* 47, 175-178.

Erskine, J. and Ellis, P. 2008 Excavations at Atworth Roman villa, Wiltshire 1970-1975. *Wiltshire Archaeological Magazine* 101, 51-129.

Gerrard, J. 2010 Finding the fifth century: A late fourth- and early fifth-century pottery fabric from South-East Dorset. *Britannia* 41, 293–312.

Guy, C. J. 1981 Roman circular lead tanks in Britain. *Britannia* 12, 271-277.

Haslam, J. 1976 *Wiltshire Towns: the archaeological potential.* Wiltshire Archaeological and Natural History Society, Devizes.

Hawke, S. 2005 *Survey of Earthwork Features at Upper Bearfield, Bradford on Avon.* Unpublished report.

Henig, M. 2006 Neither baths nor baptisteries. *Oxford Journal of Archaeology* 25, 105-7.

Henig, M. 2015 The origins of Christian Britain: From mystery cult to Christian mystery. In P. Barnwell (ed.), *Places of Worship in Britain and Ireland, 300-950,* 15-32. Rewley House Studies in the Historic Environment 4, Oxford.

Hinton, D. A. 2009 Recent work at the Chapel of St Laurence, Bradford on Avon. *Archaeological Journal* 166, 103-209.

Hurst, H. 1987 Excavations at Box Roman villa, 1967-8. *Wiltshire Archaeological Magazine* 81, 19-51.

Lapidge, M. 2007 The career of Aldhelm. *Anglo-Saxon England,* 36, 15-69.

Last, J., Carpenter, E. and Evans, S. 2016 *West Wiltshire: National Archaeological Identification Survey. Lowland Pilot Project Report.* Historic England Research Report Series 38, Swindon.

Leech, R. H. 1986 The excavation of a Romano-Celtic temple and later cemetery on Lamyatt Beacon, Somerset. *Britannia* 17, 259-328.

Lucas, R. N. 1993 *The Romano-British Villa at Halstock, Dorset. Excavations 1967-1985.* Dorset Natural History and Archaeological Society Monograph 13, Dorchester.

Mellor, A. and Goodchild, R. 1942 The Roman villa at Atworth, Wilts. *Wiltshire Archaeological Magazine* 49, 46-95.

Page, W. 1906 Romano-British Somerset. *VCH Somerset,* Volume 1.

Petts, D. 2003 *Christianity in Roman Britain.* Tempus, Stroud.

Philpott, R. 1991 *Burial Practices in Roman Britain: A survey of grave treatment and furnishing A.D. 43–410.* British Archaeological Reports (BAR) British Series 219, Oxford.

Rahtz, P., Hirst, S. and Wright, S. 2000 *Cannington Cemetery.* English Heritage Monograph 17, London.

Rodwell, W. 2001 *Wells Cathedral. Excavation and Structural Studies 1978-93.* English Heritage, London.

Scarth, H. M. 1864 *Aquae Solis, or notices of Roman Bath.* London.

Smith, J. M. H. 2013 Writing in Britain and Ireland, c. 400 - c. 800. In C. A. Lees (ed.), *The Cambridge History of Early Medieval English Literature,* 19-49. Cambridge University Press, Cambridge.

Smith, J. T. 1978 Villas as a key to social structure. In M. Todd (ed.), 1978, *Studies in the Romano-British Villa,* 149-185. Leicester University Press, Leicester.

Smith, J. T. 1997 *Roman Villas: A Study in Social Structure.* Routledge, Abingdon.

Thomas, C. 1981 *Christianity in Roman Britain to AD 500.* University of California Press, Berkeley.

Todd, M. 2005 Baths or baptisteries? Holcombe, Lufton and their analogues. *Oxford Journal of Archaeology* 24, 307–11.

Toynbee, J. M. C. 1964 *Art in Britain under the Romans.* Clarendon Press, Oxford.

Tucker, K. 2015 *An Archaeological Study of Human Decapitation Burials.* Pen & Sword Books, Barnsley.

Turner, R. 1999 *Excavations of an Iron Age Settlement and a Roman Religious Complex at Ivy Chimneys, Witham, 1978 – 83.* East Anglian Archaeology 88, Chelmsford.

Van Dam, R. 1985 *Leadership and Community in Late Antique Gaul.* University of California, Berkeley.

Wainwright, G. J. 1970 An Iron Age promontory fort at Budbury, Bradford On Avon, Wiltshire. *Wiltshire Archaeological Magazine* 65, 108-166.

Watts, L. and Leach, P. 1996 *Henley Wood: Temples and Cemetery Excavations 1962-1969.* Council for British Archaeology (CBA) Research Report 99, York.

West, S. E. and Plouviez, J. 1976 The Roman Site at Icklingham. *East Anglian Archaeology* 3, 63–125.

Woodward, A. and Leach, P. 1993 *The Uley Shrines: Excavation of a ritual complex on West Hill, Uley, Gloucestershire 1977-9.* English Heritage Archaeological Report 17, London.

Yorke, B. 1995 *Wessex in the Early Middle Ages.* Leicester University Press, London.

13

Dinnington and Yarford: two villas in south and west Somerset

Anthony C. King

With a contribution by Christina Grande

This paper is concerned with two villas in southern and western Somerset. Both were excavated by the University of Winchester, in conjunction with Somerset County Council; the first to be dug, Dinnington (NGR ST 404135) was excavated initially in 2002 for a *Time Team* Channel 4 programme (Gallagher 2005), later continued as part of *Time Team's Big Roman Dig* in 2005 (Somerset County Council *et al.* 2005). These latter excavations were undertaken with the University of Winchester, and subsequent excavations on the site continued until 2007. The second villa to be considered here, Yarford (NGR ST 202303), was excavated 2003-5 as part of the Southern Quantocks Archaeological Survey (SQAS), which had been initiated in 2000 by the university as a research project to examine later prehistoric and Roman settlement in a previously under-investigated area.

The interest of these two sites lies primarily in their position on the western margins of the villa zone (King 2004). However, they are very different in size and, by inference, status; Dinnington is a villa of considerable size, and can be related to the well-known group of villas clustered around Ilchester. By contrast, Yarford is a relatively modest villa, but situated very much on its own with no close neighbours of villa type. The aim of this paper is to describe both villas and to discuss their nature and cultural connections, particularly in the late Roman period. Both sites also have significant post-Roman phases, in the case of Dinnington demonstrably running into the late fifth or early sixth century. The implications of the occupation of these sites at such a late date are also explored.

Dinnington

The location of Dinnington is an interesting one (Fig. 13.1), since it lies to the south of the rich wetlands of the Somerset levels, and also to the north of higher ground running along the Somerset-Dorset border. This is also the position of Ilchester, and approximately fifty villas or analogous structures, many of which are close to either the main Roman road in the region, the Fosse Way, running north-east to south-west through the town of Ilchester, or the lesser Roman road running from the north-west, i.e. from the Somerset Levels, to Ilchester, and then towards Dorchester.

Ilchester and the Fosse Way, together with all the villas, were positioned to take advantage of this communications corridor, and also to exploit the fertile agricultural land in the region. The town itself probably owes a great deal in terms of its positioning to the nearby hillfort of Ham Hill (RCHM(E) 1997), one of the largest and most significant Late Iron Age sites in this part of south-west Britain.

Dinnington itself lies very close to the Fosse Way, about 15 km to the south-west of Ilchester. It is in the small valley of the Lopen Brook, and immediately on the other side of the brook is another small villa at Crimbleford Knap, Seavington St Mary (Fig. 13.1, no. 36; Graham and Mills 1995). Several hundred metres downstream is another, apparently courtyard-style villa, at Priory Mead, Hinton St George, that has been explored by geophysics and trial excavation (Fig. 13.1, no. 37; Graham 2003), and at c. 1.5 km downstream is a further large villa at Lopen village (Fig. 13.1, no. 38; Bellamy and Graham 2004).

Although close to the Fosse Way, the villa is not in fact easily visible from the road, especially for travellers coming up the Fosse Way from the south-west, since a low hill obscures the view. However, there appears to have been a roadway running off the Fosse Way at the point where it crosses the Lopen Brook. This roadway was located in the geophysical survey and links to the east wing of the villa, where the main entrance was positioned.

As well as being close to the Roman road, the villa was adjacent to a stream, the Lopen Brook. The valley of this stream has remains of at least four villas along the 3 km length that it shares with the Fosse Way, and it seems that the coincidence of these two topographic features with good agricultural land and the proximity of the Roman town of Ilchester ensured that villa development was particularly dense in the vicinity of Dinnington and Lopen.

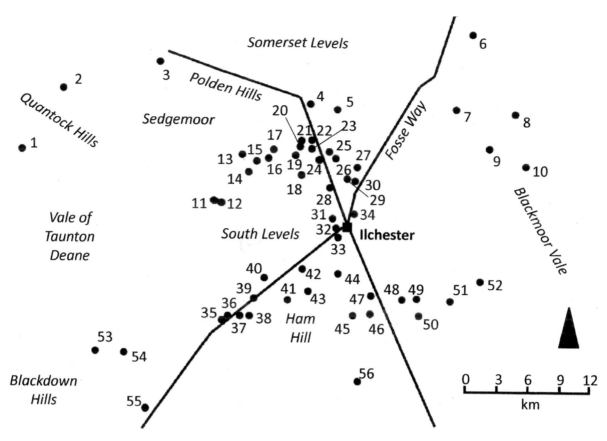

Figure 13.1. Map showing Yarford (no. 1), Dinnington (no. 35) and other Roman villas in the Ilchester region (data from Taylor 2006, with additions). Key: 1, Yarford; 2, Spaxton; 3, Bawdrip; 4, Street; 5, Butleigh; 6, Chesterblade; 7, Ditcheat; 8, Redlynch; 9, Bratton Seymour; 10, Wincanton; 11, Hambridge; 12, Drayton; 13, High Ham; 14, Wearne; 15, Low Ham; 16, Pitney 2; 17, Pitney 1; 18, Melbury; 19, Bancombe Hill; 20, Bradley Hill; 21, Lugshorn; 22, Littleton 2; 23, Littleton 1; 24, Somerton; 25, Hurcot; 26, Windmill Hill Wood; 27, Chessalls Lane; 28, Catsgore; 29, Kingsdon; 30, Lytes Cary; 31, Pill Bridge Lane; 32, Ilchester Mead; 33, Sock Dennis Farm; 34, Costello Hill; 35, Dinnington; 36, Crimbleford Knap; 37, Priory Mead; 38, Lopen; 39, Watergore; 40, Pikes Moor; 41, Blackbarrow; 42, Stanchester; 43, Ham Hill 1 & 2; 44, Lufton; 45, West Coker; 46, East Coker; 47, Westland; 48, Bradford Abbas 2; 49, Bradford Abbas 1; 50, Thornford; 51, Lenthay; 52, Castleton; 53, Whitestaunton; 54, Wadeford; 55, South Chard; 56, Halstock.

Layout of the villa, and site phasing

Evidence of Iron Age and early Roman land use was suggested by a curving ditch on the eastern side of the villa complex, and linear features within its courtyard area. No coherent traces of occupation or structures were found, however, and it therefore seems likely that the villa developed on a largely unoccupied site. Dating for the earliest building work relies on a few pieces of late first and second-century fine wares in the overall pottery assemblage, and suggests limited activity prior to the main construction phases in the third and fourth centuries.

Geophysical survey in 2002 and 2005 (Fig. 13.2; GSB Prospection 2002), combined with a vertical air photograph taken by the Ordnance Survey in 1973, demonstrated that the villa was laid out on three sides of a courtyard. The east and west wings were c. 70 m in length, connected by a much longer north wing, c. 120

m long. However, the site sequence shows that the villa may not have been one complete three-range building until the final stage in its development, but initially was a series of aligned buildings around a courtyard. The fourth side of the courtyard was not built up, and seems to have been defined by boundary ditches for an east-west droveway passing alongside the villa. Another double-ditched droveway or road ran from the centre of the east wing at right angles to it in an easterly direction, eventually reaching the Fosse Way c. 500 m away. The local topography indicates that this would have been the only point at which the villa was visible from the Fosse Way, and therefore this double-ditched feature may have formed the main entrance to the villa buildings.

Preliminary landscape investigation noted the rectilinear nature of the field boundaries around the villa. The fact that the principal axis of these matches that of the Roman villa may indicate that many of these

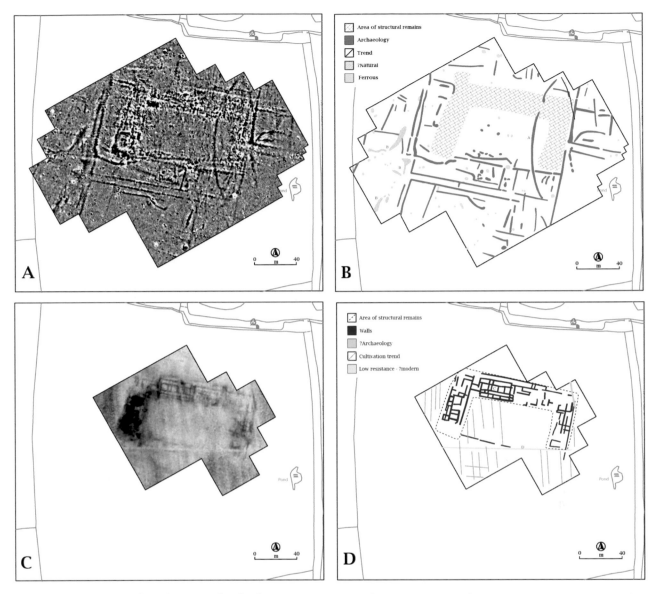

Figure 13.2. Dinnington: geophysical survey, undertaken by GSB Prospection. A: gradiometer survey, B: gradiometer survey summary interpretation, C: resistivity survey, D: resistivity survey summary interpretation. (Survey plot courtesy of John Gater of SUMO Geophysics)

boundaries replicate the pattern of a field system that was in existence in the Roman period. It is possible that elements of this pattern may in fact be earlier, as the nearby Fosse Way, a major early Roman road, can be seen to cut through it.

The earliest phase probably dated to the late first/second century and was indicated by a linear stony feature (possibly foundations for a timber-framed building), and a hearth/kiln in the north range of the later villa. These were later truncated by masonry walls of more than one phase. No complete room or feature was evaluated in this area, but the evidence suggests expansion from slight masonry structures to more substantial ones in the later Roman period.

The north wing was excavated in its western sector (Fig. 13.3), and yielded a sequence indicating that individual rectangular buildings were initially erected, one of which links spatially and perhaps physically with the north end of the west wing. These were replaced by a large, probably aisled or porticoed building, with massive foundations, that ran along most of the length of this wing (Fig. 13.3, A). It would have been the dominant building within the villa as a whole, as it was considerably larger and longer than both the west and east wings. There was little evidence of the standard of its interior decoration, because the excavated levels were largely of foundations and robber trenches rather than substantive walling. *Tesserae* and some fragments of coloured wall plaster indicate some embellishment of

225

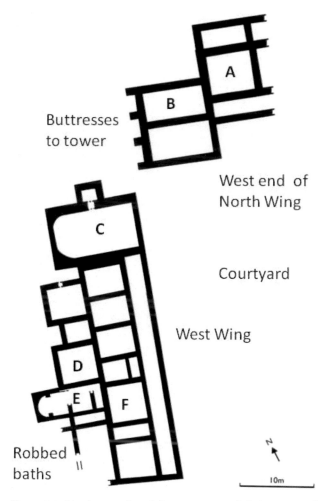

Buttresses
to tower

West end of
North Wing

Courtyard

West Wing

Robbed
baths

10m

Figure 13.3. Dinnington: plan of the west wing and the western end of the north wing. The letters indicate features referred to in the text.

stratigraphy and state of preservation. It was probably first laid out as a porticoed range in the late third/early fourth century. It had high levels of visual display and contained at least three rooms with mosaics and decorative polychrome walls initially, together with a bath range at its southern end. Stylistically, the best-preserved mosaic is probably of early/mid fourth-century date (Fig. 13.3, F; Fig. 13.4), and consisted of eight rectangular panels arranged in an octagon around a destroyed central motif (Cosh and Neal 2005a, 207, no. 196.4; 2010, 402, no. 196.4). The surviving peripheral panel contained a dolphin. The base of the next panel possibly contained a bust, and in the corners, triangular panels contained vases and leafy tendrils. The walls of this room were decorated with two successive layers of red painted plaster, and fallen plaster from the upper part of the walls and ceiling indicated a polychrome scheme of decoration, probably in panelled areas of different colours (Spiller 2007).

The rooms of the west range were connected together by a corridor or portico on the eastern, courtyard, side. The courtyard wall had four surviving courses of oolitic limestone blocks, implying a dwarf wall and colonnade or a solid corridor wall. Elsewhere in the west wing, a Ham stone lathe-turned column capital was found in an overlying demolition level, which may have come from a portico colonnade or entrance feature. The floor of the portico was a tessellated chequerboard design in grey and red *tesserae* (Cosh and Neal 2005a, 205, no. 196.1; 2010, 399, no. 196.1), thus giving an indication that the portico had this style of flooring over some considerable part of its length. Only a small section of courtyard was excavated. It was not paved, but a possible Ham stone flag and mortar feature may have formed an eaves drip gutter to the portico.

The insertion of a large hypocausted hall (Fig. 13.3, C), with extensive figurative mosaic, into the north-west corner of the villa, was a subsequent improvement, to be dated probably to the middle of the fourth century (Fig. 13.5). It cut across the portico, and served to fill the north-west corner formed by the west and north wings. It was probably a prestigious winter dining room and reception area, positioned to be visually dominant in the north-west corner of the villa courtyard. Its hypocaust was a composite of pillars of stone in the central area, with channels under most of the flooring area. Large stone slabs must have formed the basis of the suspended floor, but these were systematically removed by the time of the destruction of the room. The floor itself was a high-quality polychrome mosaic, of geometric guilloche patterns framing a series of pictures (Figs 13.8 and 13.9; Cosh and Neal 2005a, 205-6, no. 196.2; 2005b; 2010, 399-

the wing, but their quality in comparison with the west wing suggests that the north range of the villa was not the main living or reception zone.

Little excavation was carried out in the east wing, and no complete room was revealed. However, an oven/furnace feature was identified, combined with a wide range of domestic and high-status pottery, of predominantly third/fourth century date. A notable fragment of mosaic was recovered; only c. 5 cm across, it was made up of tiny *tesserae*, c. 2-3 mm in size, in a variety of colours. This must have been part of the *emblema* of a fine-quality mosaic, unfortunately broken up into pieces too small to identify in terms of decorative scheme. The mosaic fragment was from an upper level associated with the demolition/collapse of the east wing, and therefore its original provenance within the villa is uncertain.

The west wing was more extensively excavated and formed a major focus of the project because of its good

Figure 13.4. Dinnington: mosaic with marine theme, in room F in Fig. 13.3, showing the corner design and the central section of one of the sides.

Figure 13.5. Dinnington: the apsidal hall, room C, from the west.

401, no. 196.2). The whole floor had been shattered and scattered in antiquity, possibly the casualty of robbers seeking to remove the flagstones of the suspended floor, or even a deliberate destruction of the mosaic for other, perhaps ideological or political motives. The date of this destruction is not ascertainable with accuracy, due to the paucity of artefacts from the homogeneous fill in the hypocaust that contained the mosaic fragments. Some pottery and coins of late fourth-century date indicate that destruction possibly happened before the end of the Roman period, or perhaps early in the fifth century. There are no traces of the serious fire that damaged the southern part of the west wing (see below), and it is conceivable that the hall had already been destroyed before the fire episode. Alternatively, its massive construction made it more resistant to the fire, and its south wall acted as a fire-break. If this was the case, the relative sequence of the fire and the mosaic's destruction in the hall cannot be pinned down.

Returning to the north wing, a construction episode probably contemporary with the development of the apsidal hall was the addition of a tower-like structure to the south-west corner of the large range of the north wing (Fig. 13.3, B). This new room overlay the demolished remains of earlier rectangular rooms (see above), and had four large supporting buttresses, giving the impression of a two (or more) storied square projecting tower that formed a visual stop to the length of the north wing, and made it a version, albeit on a massive scale, of the typical portico-and-tower (or winged corridor) arrangement of many villas. The purpose of the tower is unknown; it may have been functional, perhaps a granary or similar (see Ferdière 2019), but equally its close proximity to the apsidal hall may suggest a more prestigious architectural elaboration of the north-west corner of the villa as a whole.

Following construction of the apsidal hall (room C), subsequent development of the west wing took place behind the main range. Three rooms were added to the west side of the original range of rooms, creating a façade facing to the west. One, at least, of these rooms had a hypocaust and probably a mosaic as well, but all trace of it had been removed when the hypocaust was converted into a probable corn-drier by the driving of a series of holes through the suspended concrete floor (Fig. 13.3, D).

This conversion from a relatively high-status use into more utilitarian character is seen within the original west wing rooms as well. Three of the smaller rooms, including the one with the marine mosaic (Fig. 13.3, F), appear to have been used for grain storage. The mosaic had been damaged across the majority of the decorative zone, especially in a wide band running from the north-west across the centre of the panels (see Cosh 2005 for discussion of damage to mosaics in the Late Roman period). In places this damage penetrated below the cement base into the underlying make-up. The damage was not random, but was formed of indentations c. 10 cm across in the mosaic. These had removed or shifted the *tesserae*, and overall formed a pattern of lines across the floor, orthogonal to the walls and floor design. Their purpose is uncertain, but an interpretation as the base of wooden partitions for grain storage is suggested, on the evidence of the burnt grain found overlying the mosaic. Where the *tesserae* had been removed a thin earthen floor was found (and was also located in the other

rooms as well), which probably represented activity contemporary to the grain storage within the now downgraded room, and is probably to be associated with a crude new layer of red painted plaster on the walls. The date of this activity is uncertain, but appears to lie in the later part of the fourth century, or conceivably early in the fifth century. Pottery and coins from overlying layers run to the end of the fourth century, and there is a radiocarbon date of 410-570 cal. AD (2σ calibration of 1573±25 BP, Wk16584) from a sample taken from the charred cereal grains overlying the floors.

The evidence for grain storage was preserved in a layer, 2-5 cm thick, of charred grain and other burnt material spread over the damaged floors (Fig. 13.6). Preliminary results indicate that wheat was the primary grain to be stored, while barley was also present. The charred grain therefore seems to represent sacks or bins of cereals that had been destroyed in a significant fire that affected much of the west wing and its portico.

Figure 13.6. Dinnington: view from the north of excavations in the west wing; in the foreground a layer of burnt grain in room F, with square gridded sampling scheme visible.

Over the burnt grain layer was another burnt layer, c. 5 cm thick, of somewhat different complexion, in that it contained shattered roof slate fragments, probably from destruction of the ceiling and roof during the fire. A possible cause for the fire is identifiable in the portico. Mortar had been laid across its tessellated pavement, to form a rough floor and the basis for blacksmithing activity, seen in the clear traces of burning and remains of furnace foundations, together with pieces of slag and hammer scale.

The stratigraphic sequence in this part of the villa continued in the form of a thick overlying layer of rubble derived from the collapse or destruction of the walls. On the west side of the destroyed buildings, however, in the area of a ruined set of baths (Fig. 13.3, E), there was less evidence of rubble and destruction, as it had been cleared away. Instead, a thick dark layer, up to a metre in depth in places, built up, analogous to the dark-earth deposits found largely on late and post-Roman urban sites (Macphail *et al.* 2003). There were quantities of animal bones in this deposit, dominated by cattle, but a surprising aspect was the equally high percentage of horse bones (c. 30%), many of which showed signs of skinning and butchery, and included a complete skeleton (Fig. 13.7). It seems that the ruins of the villa were used as an animal-processing area, probably for hides and meat, and also as a rubbish dump (Rodbourne 2008; Firmin 2014, 52, Table 4; see Cross 2011 for ritual aspects of horse burials – probably not the case here; see Poole 2013 for discussion of hippophagy in post-Roman Britain).

Adjacent to the horse burial, about 8 m to the west of the west wing, were the badly preserved remains of an adult human skeleton, probably female and relatively elderly. It was carefully laid out, with head to the north, and can be regarded as a 'small-scale transitional burial' in the definition of Dodd (2021, 68). It is possible that an area to the west of the villa was used for casual, but tidy burials of both animals and humans, during this late period of occupation.

The north wing at this time had a large spread of dark fill and rubble, overlying the ruined and robbed remains of the tower at the south-west corner of the north wing (Fig. 13.3, B). The date of this activity is unknown, but post-dates the fire and burnt grain episode in the west wing, implying a probable date in the fifth or even the sixth century.

Figure 13.7. Dinnington: horse skeleton from very late or post-Roman phase. It was found immediately to the west of the west wing, close to an area within the ruined baths that showed evidence for processing of horse and cattle bones, probably for hides and meat. The skeleton was of a male pony (similar to Exmoor ponies), aged about 4 years, and had cut marks indicating skinning, and partial disarticulation in order to fit into the pit. Why the animal was buried entire is not known.

Mythology at Dinnington villa

Christina Grande

The excavations at Dinnington have revealed glimpses of an opulent residence that was embellished with high-status interior decoration and artefacts. Amongst the building rubble dumped, late in the site sequence, in the demolished south-western tower of the north wing, was found a fragment of sculpted local limestone. Although fragmentary, it clearly has interlocking hands and arms around a muscled torso (Fig. 13.8, A). This would make it potentially part of a group depicting Hercules wrestling with Antaeus. In complete versions of this mythological episode, the heroic superman wrestles with the Libyan giant, lifting him forcibly from the earth, his mother Gaia, thereby conquering Antaeus by removing him from the source of his strength (as in the sculpture from Catania, Sicily; Fig. 13.8, B, or the mosaic from Avenches, Switzerland; Rebetez 1997, 71-4). This image had been a favoured subject for artists of the Greek world who relished the action-packed theme to demonstrate Hercules' triumph over impossible odds, a mirror for human struggle and triumph over adversity.

Roman patrons in Italy and throughout the Romanised world demonstrated their knowledge of fashionable Greek culture by decorating their homes and gardens with copies and adaptations of celebrated pieces of Greek art as well as new versions of long familiar stories from Greek mythology. The Latin version of Hercules and Antaeus was clearly familiar to Roman culture, and

was used by the first-century AD poet Lucan in his epic *Pharsalia* (4.581ff; see Saylor 1982), Ovid (*Met.* 9.183), Statius (*Theb.* 6.894ff) and others. If the Dinnington fragment was indeed part of a Hercules and Antaeus group, this is a very exciting find, given the scarcity of mythological sculpture from Roman Britain, prompting questions about why the image was selected and what part it may have served within the villa's visual or conceptual scheme. The image of Hercules and Antaeus is very rare in Roman Britain, and almost all examples are late Roman. The Dinnington fragment is the only known sculptural depiction in Britain, but it is known in other media, for instance the mosaic at Bramdean, Hampshire (early fourth century; Witts 2005a; 2005b, 54-5; Smith 1977, 144; Neal and Cosh 2009, 167-9, no. 308.2), the pepper pot from the Hoxne Treasure (fourth century; Johns 2010, 85-8, no. 34), a circular relief from a silver vessel in the Capheaton Treasure (second/third century; *ibid.*; Henig 1984, 117-18), a glass intaglio from Richborough (first century; Henig 2007, no. 437) and another probable example in glass from Silchester (third century; *ibid.* no. 521). It is therefore an important piece, both for its contribution to the cultural life of the villa and for the use of Greek mythological iconography by a sculptor in Roman Britain.

The large but shattered mosaic in the apsidal hall (see above) is the other element of the villa having mythological scenes. Although the mosaic fragments are mostly very small, showing perhaps an eye or section of hair, a few fragments are capable of very tentative

Figure 13.8.A Dinnington: Hercules and Antaeus sculpture, found in a rubble layer over corner tower (Fig. 13.3, B); height of stone: 14 cm.

Figure 13.8.B Marble table support depicting Hercules and Antaeus, found off the coast of Catania, Sicily. Greek/Hellenistic, 200-100 BC. Museo Civico 'Castello Ursino', Catania, inv. no. 56.

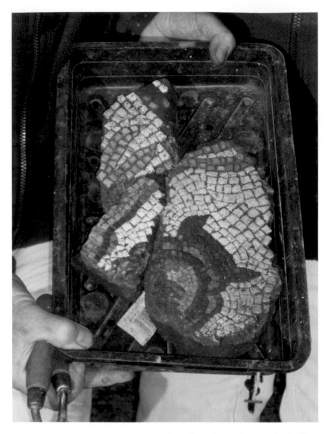

Figure 13.9. Dinnington: mosaic of Daphne, from the apsidal hall, room C, photographed at the time of excavation.

to the Roman world via Ovid's *Metamorphoses* (1.452ff). Another fragment looks to be the head and wing of a Cupid. A further fragment seems to portray a helmeted head, perhaps Minerva or an armed hero (Fig. 13.10). If it is possible to identify something of the relationship between these scattered mythological scenes, as a result of further reconstruction, it would certainly contribute to our understanding of this large villa and perhaps even the philosophical or religious interests of the owners.

The Ilchester area is rich in villa mosaics depicting mythological scenes, most notably the famous depiction of Dido and Aeneas from Low Ham (Cosh and Neal 2005a, 253-7, no. 207.1), based on Virgil's *Aeneid*. Ovid's *Metamorphoses*, too, was clearly read and exploited for visual depictions at four or more other villas in the region (Cosh and Neal 2005b, 25; Croft 2009). Classical learning and *paideia* were thriving, at least for a high-status sector of the population (see Scott 2000, 126-7), and display of this was keenly pursued by villa owners in the region.

Dinnington in Late Roman Britain

Dinnington is a large villa, comparable in size to some of the best-known Romano-British villas, such as Chedworth or Brading, but a little smaller than the biggest (Woodchester, North Leigh, Bignor, etc.). The current state of knowledge suggests it is arranged around three sides of a courtyard, with a possible gateway and wall on the fourth (southern) side. The west wing has high-quality interior decoration, and probably represents the main focus in terms of social display. However, the north wing has a lower level of interior decoration, but was the longest wing of the villa, and thus has positional significance. It is possible that this was the original part of the villa, the central role of which was reduced by development of the west and east wings, so that the focus moved to the west wing. This shift is seen at other villas, notably Bignor (Frere 1982; Aldsworth and Rudling 1995, fig. 3; Rudling and Russell 2015).

identification. For example, two sections that belong together seem to be the head and fingers of Daphne as she turns into a laurel tree at the moment she is captured by Apollo (Fig. 13.9). This story was familiar

The east wing is the least understood part of the villa, currently, and it seems to have been more utilitarian in character. It is often the case that one of the wings in larger villas had agricultural and small-scale manufacturing installations such as driers and furnaces (e.g. North Leigh, Brading; see Branigan 1988, 47-9; Wilson 2004). The entrance droveway, running from the Fosse Way, does, however, lead up to the middle sector of the east wing, and there may have been an entrance into

Figure 13.10. Dinnington: mosaic with possible helmeted headdress, from the apsidal hall, room C. Greatest dimension across diagonal of the photo: 22 cm.

the villa's courtyard at this point. It seems unlikely that this was the major entry point into the villa, which was possibly on the south side, through the wall and possible gateway there. Visually, however, the east wing formed the façade of the villa for visitors coming from the north via the droveway from the Roman road, and therefore we would expect embellishment of this façade above the utilitarian level of the usage that it concealed within the wing itself.

All large villas had one or more bath buildings, sometimes one in each wing, as at North Leigh. Baths can be highly elaborate architecturally, especially in late Roman West Country villas, such as Lufton or Holcombe (Walters 1996). The west-wing baths at Dinnington are relatively simple by comparison.

All these features of the villa pale into insignificance upon consideration of the large apsidal hall. Reconstruction of its appearance would assume an eastern entrance facing onto the courtyard, probably with low-pitched roof and a gable forming a pediment. The room cuts across the earlier portico, and there does not appear to be a new portico positioned further into the courtyard, so a side entrance at the south-east corner, entered from the truncated portico, can also be envisaged. In volume, we would expect the hall to have approximately the same height as its width, thus giving an internal height to the top of the walls of c. 7.5 m, and a possible overall height to the gable of c. 10 m or more. At its western end, externally the room was rectangular, whilst internally it was apsidal. In terms of the roofline, this makes for simplicity in reconstruction, but internally the apse implies a probable vault, and therefore either an arch to complete the vault where it meets the main body of the hall, or a continuous barrel vault running the length of the room, with an east-west main axis. There is no evidence for projections in the apse area, consonant with pilasters, or springing for an arch, so it is possible that the barrel vault roof reconstruction should be preferred. Its size, and insertion into the pre-existing plan, invites immediate comparison with the apsidal room 26 at Box (Corney 2012, fig. 27; Hurst 1987), which is slightly larger, at 6.8 m diameter for the apse, and 12.5 m length, but similar in date and also likely to have been a winter dining or reception room. At Dewlish, an apse was added to a large reception room, probably a summer dining room, resulting in a roughly similar sized arrangement overall (Ellis 1995, 172; Putnam 2007, 99-100). Box, Dewlish and Dinnington are amongst the largest such rooms known from villas in Britain (Ellis 1995, 177; see also Cosh 2001).

In regional terms, Dinnington is within the group of villas clustering around Ilchester, ancient *Lindinis* or *Lendiniae* (Fig. 13.1; Branigan 1976, fig 3). This town appears to have developed into a significant centre by the Late Roman period, probably as a *pagus* centre, or even as a *civitas* capital (Leach 2001, 55-6). Certainly, the rural settlement pattern demonstrates a concentration of villas, of various sizes, and mainly of third and fourth-century date (Leech 1982; Leech and Leach 1982, 76-80). There is an apparent growth in wealth, too, to judge from the number of villas with mosaics of this late period – or alternatively a growth in social competition and status display manifested in villa mosaics (see above). Dinnington is at the larger end of the range of villas in the region, comparable in surface area to Pitney I and Halstock (Branigan 1976; Lucas 1993).

More locally, there are several contemporary villas and other settlements in close proximity to Dinnington, notably Lopen (Bellamy and Graham 2004), the mosaic at which indicates an equivalent to Dinnington in terms of decoration and display (even if the surface area and layout of Lopen is at present not well understood). As well as the clustering effect round Ilchester, local geographical factors probably played a significant part. The major Roman road, the Fosse Way, ran only 250 m from the villa, and its presence must have had an effect on both the siting of the villa and its ability to transport surplus products to markets in Ilchester and beyond. Secondly, the villas at Lopen, Priory Mead, Crimbleford Knap and Dinnington are all in the fertile valley of the Lopen Brook that crosses the Fosse Way at this point. Was the valley particularly suited to villa development as a result?

The hey-day of Dinnington in terms of its wealth and visual display appears to have run through much of the fourth century. A major change occurs towards the end of the century, with two possibly linked events. The most dramatic, in many ways, was the deliberate destruction of the large mosaic in the apsidal hall. The dating of this event is somewhat uncertain, due to the open stratigraphy above the destruction debris, and therefore the easiest interpretation is to attribute the episode to robbing activity. This could have taken place in either the ultimate years of the Roman period or at some point afterwards, and was probably motivated by the desire to recover the large stone slabs forming the suspended floor, that must have underlain the mosaic. The mosaic itself was of no consequence to the robbers, and approximately 10-15% of it was thrown back into the hypocaust, and subsequently excavated. A more speculative alternative hypothesis is that the mosaic was destroyed for ideological or political reasons, which would place the event much more certainly within the late Roman period. For this to be the case, we must envisage the owner being on the wrong side in a dispute about local or national power (e.g. the suppression of the supporters of Magnentius; see Webster 1983, or a similar episode), or religion (possible Christian suppression of a pagan notable). However, it must be stressed that the likelihood of either scenario has to remain speculative.

We are on firmer ground when considering the change of use that is apparent in the west wing. Agricultural storage (grain bins), grain drying and light industry (metalworking) take over from the relatively smartly appointed living and reception rooms in this part of the villa, possibly at the same time as the apsidal hall mosaic is destroyed, and the tower (a granary?) is added to the south-west corner of the north wing. Activity seems to be well-organised and carefully zoned, so is certainly not the 'squatting activity' that used to be the prevalent interpretation of such late occupation of villa sites (see Dodd 2021, 69-70). The villa becomes more of a working farm, and clearly sees less emphasis on fine living and classical culture. There may have been a change in ownership, or in the location of the owner (i.e. no longer present on the site itself), and if any speculation about the deliberate destruction of the apsidal hall mosaic is correct, that event and the change of use may be linked.

Zonation of activity during this period did not prevent the catastrophic fire that destroyed the remaining structures in the west wing. Fire-risk activity, such as metalworking in furnaces, was close to the grain storage area, and may have been the cause of the disaster. Dating of this event may well run into the fifth century, if the radiocarbon date of AD 410-570 on burnt grain (see above) can be taken as a guide. (Corroborative radiocarbon dates are in process of analysis as this paper is being written.) The implication is that the farming activity at Dinnington outlasted the nominal end of Roman control, and continued for some time into the fifth, or even the sixth centuries. And this was not in fact the end of the story, since subsequent activity is well-attested, in the form of animal-based agriculture, with possible specialisation in the processing of horse carcasses, probably byres for cattle, and their butchery as well. This could easily run into the sixth century, and thus would be contemporary with nearby high-status centres such as South Cadbury (Leach 2001, 123-4; Alcock et al. 1995).

The final phases at Dinnington are clouded with chronological uncertainty, which will need further research to elucidate (see Leech 1982, 249-51; Gerrard 2004; 2011). At present, it is best to conclude discussion of this site by stressing the importance of the sequence for our understanding of the changes in use that villas underwent in their final decades (see Leech and Leach 1982, 80-1, for Somerset; Putnam 2007, 150-2, for Dorset). At Dinnington, it was a dramatic change from early/mid fourth-century opulence and engagement with classical culture, to working farm, to fire and ruin, culminating in post-Roman usage of the ruined structures for animals, and ultimately as a source of stone.

Yarford

Yarford forms one of the sites investigated as part of the Southern Quantock Archaeological Survey, which had the aim of studying and characterising a sample of new sites in the southern part of the Quantock Hills, by means of geophysical survey and excavation.

The sites had originally been discovered by aerial photography, particularly following a Somerset County Council commissioned survey. This resulted in the discovery of at least 100 enclosures and other signs of archaeological activity, which was a revelation for a zone little-studied archaeologically hitherto. As a consequence of this, the project was set up to continue archaeological study of these sites, to gain more detailed data through geophysical survey and, above all, to gain chronological data through excavation of a sample of sites (Fig. 13.11; Wilkinson and Thorpe 2000). The sample was chosen to reflect the varying topography of the Quantocks, in particular to test the hypothesis that the sites on high ground (e.g. Ivyton) had a poorer material culture than those in less exposed and more favourable positions lower down the slopes. A subsidiary aim was to undertake soil sampling to assess the threat to the sites as a result of recent agriculture (Wilkinson et al. 2006).

Yarford was the fourth site in the Project, after Stoneage Barton (2000), Toulton (2000) and Volis Hill (2001). The three earlier sites all proved to be of Iron Age and Roman date, with Bronze Age activity also detected at Volis Hill. Excavations at Yarford took place in 2003, showing that it, too, was of Iron Age and Roman date. However, an unexpected find in that year was that part of the site was occupied by a small Roman villa. This could not be fully excavated in 2003, so excavations continued in 2004-5, together with a fifth site, at Ivyton (on a Bronze Age and Iron Age site).

The site is located on the lower slopes of the Quantocks, facing south-west, towards the Vale of Taunton Deane and the Blackdown Hills beyond. The underlying geology is a shaly slate, relatively easy and free-draining. The soil is good quality agriculturally, and is currently farmed for a variety of crops, including cereals and legumes.

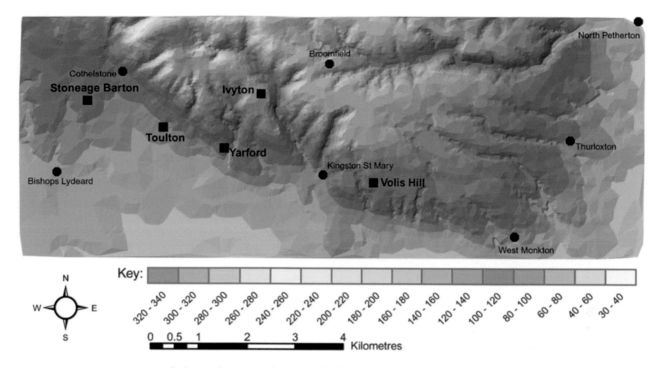

Figure 13.11. Yarford: map showing site location and other Southern Quantocks Archaeological Survey sites.

The site's position on the south-western slope of the Quantocks is very favourable. It is at about 90 m elevation, about a third of the way up the hillside. The slope, however, is moderate, enabling cultivation of surrounding fields without too much difficulty. This position in the Quantocks has traditionally been regarded as good, in that it avoids the water drainage problems of the valley, and also the exposure of the higher slopes. Water for the site was probably obtained from a small stream in a narrow valley just to the east of the site and c. 15 m below it. Springs also exist in the vicinity of the site.

In terms of the local archaeology, the nearest previously known site is the Iron Age and Roman settlement at Norton Fitzwarren (Burrow 1982, 94), c. 3 km south in the valley, along which a routeway to the coast may have existed. A small Roman fort is known at Wiveliscombe (Webster 1959), c. 12 km west, and the nearest Roman town is Ilchester (*Lindinis*), 30 km east-south-east (see Leach 2001, 52ff).

Geophysical survey was undertaken over an area of very clear crop-marks seen in the aerial survey (Fig. 13.12; Turner 2003). The most obvious feature was a D-shaped enclosure, of two concentric ditches, apparently overlying an earlier field-system. Three dark areas in the north-east corner of the enclosure could not be interpreted before excavation, but proved to be the rubble overlying the Roman villa.

The Late Iron Age enclosure

The D-shaped enclosure was suggestive of a late prehistoric settlement, as seen in many sites in south-west Britain. The excavations demonstrated that this was indeed the case (Fig. 13.13), but more unexpectedly established a late date for the enclosure. Analysis of the pottery from the ditches indicates a Late Iron Age date, and it is possible that the enclosure was set up in the first century BC or first century AD.

The inner ditch was a substantial feature, about 2.5 m across and 1.8 m deep (see below), and could have served a defensive purpose, especially when combined with a putative rampart internally and the outer ditch (which was slightly shallower and less wide). Terminals to the ditch were located on the east side, together with a stone-packed post-hole, which was almost certainly the southern part of a gate structure.

The site sequence

Excavation of the concentric ditches established not only a Late Iron Age date, but also the rapid infilling of the ditches after a relatively short lapse of time. There appears to have been a deliberate levelling of the enclosure, such that the ditches remained only as shallow features from the first century AD onwards.

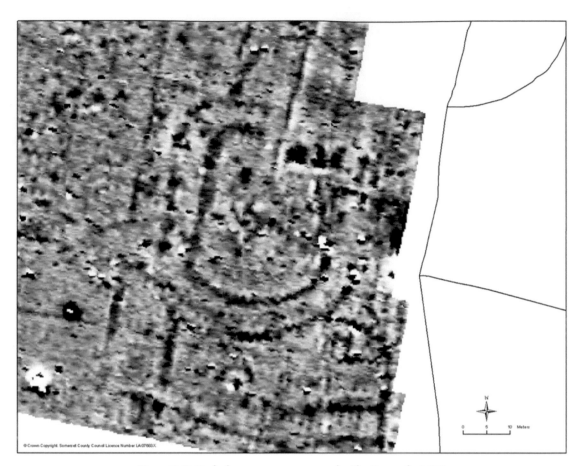

Figure 13.12. Yarford: magnetometer survey, by Alex Turner for SQAS.

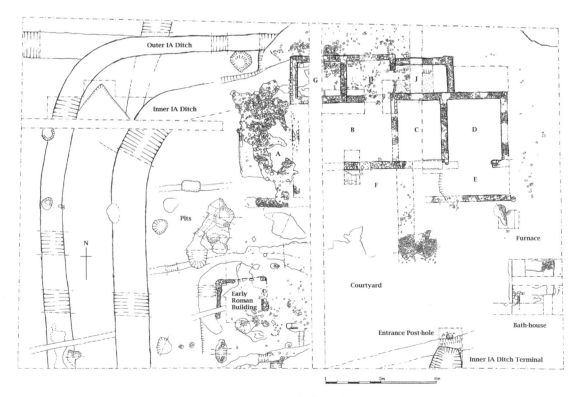

Figure 13.13. Yarford: site plan.

Sparse evidence for structures in the interior seems to reinforce the impression that the enclosure only had a brief active life. Some inter-cut pits and a possible foundation slot for a circular structure were found, however, which indicated a certain level of activity continuing into the Roman period.

The next sign of activity took the form of pottery deposition in the mid to late second century. A decorated samian ware bowl and a lidded coarse ware jar containing a penannular brooch were found on the western periphery of the excavated area, adjacent to the western sector of the outer ditch. The jar and brooch in particular are suggestive of some form of deliberate deposition, but not apparently a burial, as no overtly funerary traces were found.

It was probably at this time that the first phase of the villa site came into existence. Within the old enclosure, and respecting the old ditch lines, were found traces of dry-stone rectilinear buildings. Their form was very simple, and may indicate that the occupants were continuing effectively a traditional lifestyle, with the additional uptake of some of the indicators of 'Roman' culture, i.e. samian ware and rectilinear architecture. The site seems to have been a small farmstead at this time, similar to others that have been investigated in the Quantocks by the research project.

The villa

The next major phase, and a significant development for the site, was the construction of a villa. The date when this occurred has not been determined accurately. However, construction in the late third century is the most likely date.

The villa was of row type, with a portico, that is a row of domestic rooms (Fig. 13.13, A-D) linked by a portico or verandah (E-F). There is no sign of corner towers, which would indicate an example of the widespread 'winged-corridor' villa. To the rear of the main row were three further rooms, of which G and H were integral to the original construction, and J was an addition, almost certainly a kitchen. Room usage within the villa is uncertain, apart from the kitchen and the probable dining room in rooms D and E. However, room H had remains of a hypocaust, and was probably a heated living room of some sort.

The front portico (F) was carefully paved in cut flagstones, as quite commonly found in rooms in villas in the region (see Martin and Driscoll 2010), and may have been open to the elements on the south side, since a Ham stone lathe-turned dwarf column was found in the abandonment rubble of the villa. At the eastern end of the portico, the flagstones were replaced by a mosaic which formed the entrance to the most important room in the villa (D). This had a wide arched or lintelled opening from the portico, into the most important room in the villa, which had a mosaic and painted plaster decoration (see below).

Just to the south-east of the portico was a small bath-house with a plunge bath at its north end and hypocausted rooms further south, in all forming the east side of the courtyard in front of the villa. This had been badly robbed in ancient times, and its precise plan is poorly understood.

The mosaic

One of the major features of the villa was a polychrome mosaic in rooms D and E (Fig. 13.14; Cosh and Neal 2010, 406-8, no. 493.1; King 2005). It has an interesting design, made up of a central square containing a representation of a *cantharus* or wine-mixing vessel, surrounded by a thick band of *guilloche*, the rope motif found on many Romano-British mosaics. This is the centre of a rectangular grid of *guilloche*, arranged to form nine panels. The four corner panels have floral motifs in them, but the other panels are transparent, as it were, to allow an underlying circular design, also formed of *guilloche,* to show through.

The *cantharus* is arranged so that someone entering the room would look at it upside-down, but this was probably because the room was a dining room (*triclinium*). The diners would have been seated or lain on couches around the back and sides of the room, with the villa owner at the north-west corner. Thus, they would have the *cantharus*, a symbol of conviviality and feasting, in front of them as they ate.

The *cantharus* also dates the mosaic to the fourth century stylistically, and there is a similar one on a mosaic from Pound Lane, Caerwent, South Wales (Cosh and Neal 2010, 355, no. 483.24). The Yarford mosaic has an old design for the fourth century AD. When first partially uncovered in 2003, David Neal considered it to be a second-century design, on the basis of good parallels for the overall design from North Hill, Colchester, which are datable to the second century (Neal and Cosh 2009, 97-100, nos 291.15-16). However, once the whole mosaic had been uncovered, it was apparent that in fact it was a late Roman mosaic making use of an old design. It is not seen elsewhere in the West Country, and at present, it is not clear whether this is a one-off mosaic, or laid by one of the local workshops, such as the one based in Ilchester (see discussion of this mosaic in Witts, this volume).

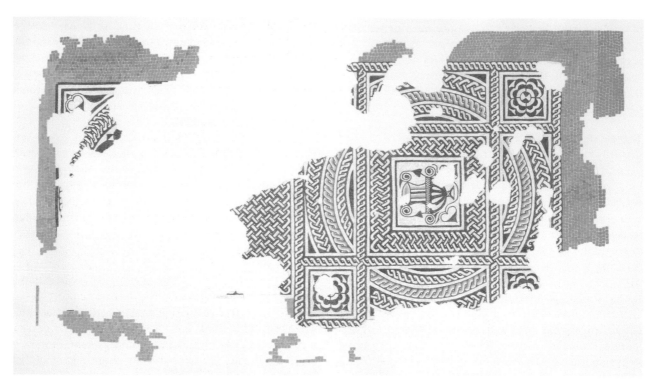

Figure 13.14. Yarford: the mosaic in rooms D and E. (Illustration by S. Cosh and D. Neal)

The Yarford villa and its owner

The excavations have shown that one room of the villa was highly decorated and would have looked very smart, since the walls were decorated with polychrome wall-paintings, as well as the floor having a mosaic. The room was open to the south, into the portico, and in fact the mosaic continued into this area, which acted as a sort of vestibule for the *triclinium*. The design in this area was badly damaged, but seems to have been a semicircle, probably with a floral motif within it, and a mat of *guilloche* under the opening between the two rooms. Almost certainly, the portico had a window or opportunity to see the view from the *triclinium*, as the prospect over the Vale of Taunton Deane would have been a feature of the villa.

One of the most intriguing aspects of the villa is its position well to the north-west of other known villas in the region (Fig. 13.1), the nearest being the small villa at Spaxton, c. 7 km north-north-east, on the other side of the Quantocks ridge (Fig. 13.1, no. 2; Somerset HER no. 10802; Cosh and Neal 2005a, 189–90). Yarford is, in fact, one of the most westerly villas in the entire south-west peninsula, although it should be realised that new research may uncover other examples, perhaps in the Vale of Taunton, or around Exeter. As it stands, however, Yarford is right on the boundary of the so-called 'villa-zone' that stretched across southern and eastern Britain

(King 2004). In a sense, the villa owner was isolated, a pioneer of Roman taste in a region otherwise dominated by settlements in the Iron Age tradition. This is remarkably similar to the location and cultural isolation of the Abermagwr villa, near Aberystwyth, the plan and size of which are also very analogous to Yarford (Davies and Driver 2018).

Who did the owner invite to dinner in his smart *triclinium*? Did other villa owners travel in their carriages the 20 miles or so (c. 32 km) over the Quantocks to visit him? Or was the mosaic and room there to impress the locals, who may well not have seen this level of decorative elaboration, at least not in the local area?

Yarford was probably within the ambit of the nearest Roman town, Ilchester, which was considered to be part of the territory of the Durotriges, the Roman *civitas* or administrative district centred on Dorchester and present-day Dorset. Ilchester is regarded as the northern capital of the Durotriges, particularly during the fourth century when Yarford was fully developed. To the south-west of Yarford, the *civitas* was the Dumnonii, centred on Exeter and Devon. It is possible that the Quantocks marked the north-western boundary of the Durotriges, and that the Brendon Hills and Exmoor were Dumnonian.

Building on this distinction, an interesting comparison can be made with the site at Maundown, near

Wiveliscombe (Context One Archaeology, *pers. comm.*). This was a small settlement of round-houses, dating back to the Late Iron Age, but continuing into the Roman period. Inside one of the round-houses was a third-century coin hoard in a pot, apparently deliberately buried under a slate forming part of the central hearth of the house. This clearly demonstrates a reasonable level of wealth at the site, but at the same time a cultural preference to preserve that wealth in cash, rather than invest it in Roman-style mosaics and wall-plaster. Maundown lies within the postulated territory/*civitas* of the Dumnonii, and may be a marker of the boundary of the 'villa zone' in much the same way as Yarford, with its Roman villa, within the territory of the Durotriges a few Roman miles to the east.

The end of the Yarford villa

The high point of the villa's existence was probably in the early to mid fourth century, in much the same way as Dinnington and many other villas in Roman Britain. This was when the main reception room was in use, and when the villa reached its largest ground-plan.

In the late fourth century, things started to change. Room D is redecorated with plainer, largely white wall-plaster, probably because the old scheme had started to decay, rather than purely for fashion reasons. The mosaic itself also started to erode, so that patches appeared in its surface (Fig. 13.15). Mosaicists were not employed to repair it, however, and the patches remained. They form a pattern, with four holes in the mosaic in a line from north-west to south-east across the middle of room D. Probably this is due to some activity or construction (in wood?) positioned over the mosaic. At about the same time, two small holes were punched through the mosaic and its concrete base, both on line with the centre of the room in a north-south direction. These probably represent post-holes to support the collapsing roof or ceiling of the room. Finally, large burnt areas are visible on the mosaic, and a thick burnt layer with small pieces of shale, burnt antler, building debris, pottery and coins of the late fourth century, accumulated over the floor. This seems to represent some sort of workshop activity rather than destruction, and may date to the late Roman period or even the immediate post-Roman period in the early fifth century. Other rooms in the villa, particularly room C, also have the same deposit in them.

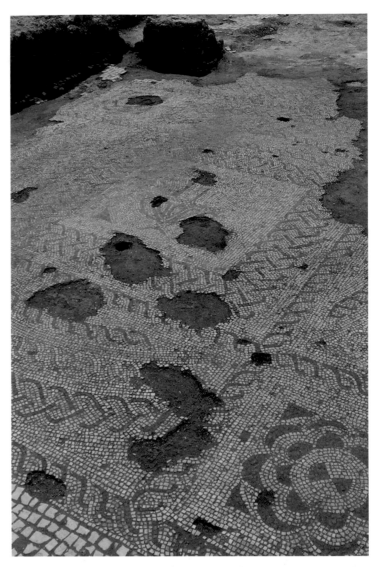

Figure 13.15. Yarford: the mosaic in rooms D and E, showing Late Roman damage to the mosaic.

Unlike one of the other enclosure sites in the SQAS research project, Stoneage Barton, where a cemetery of late sixth to seventh century date was excavated (Webster and Brunning 2004), there is no evidence of later post-Roman activity. The building was overlain by the rubble of its collapsed walls – undisturbed and unknown until rediscovery in the twenty-first century.

Acknowledgements

At Dinnington, grateful acknowledgment is due to the landowner Mike Holloway and his family, for their close interest in the excavation. *Time Team* (Wildfire Television) and Channel 4 undertook initial excavations in 2002, followed by the *Big Roman Dig*, which was broadcast live from the site in July 2005. The University of Winchester was the partner organisation at this event, and continued the project until 2007. Alan Graham provided vital assistance on site throughout, and was instrumental in initial recording of the findings from the exploratory trenches. John Gater of SUMO Geophysics undertook the geophysical survey of the Dinnington, and kindly supplied the plots that form Fig. 12.2. At Yarford, grateful thanks are due to the Tetton Estate for permission to excavate, and the enthusiastic interest and help of Peter and Jane House, the tenant farmers. Bob Croft, Somerset County Archaeologist, was instrumental in setting up both excavations, and in smoothing the way each season. Thanks are also due to Chris Webster, Somerset County Council, who ran a community excavation as part of the Quantocks project; Steve Minnitt, Somerset County Museum, who identified the coins, and David Neal and Steve Cosh, who expertly recorded the mosaics. Richard McConnell of Context One Archaeology kindly provided information and access to the Maundown site during its excavation. Pat Witts, Bryn Walters and Grahame Soffe also made useful and stimulating comments during visits to the sites. Finally, Nathalie Barrett has provided essential post-excavation assistance.

The excavations at Dinnington and Yarford have been generously funded by the University of Winchester, Wildfire Television, the Roman Research Trust and the Maltwood Fund of Somerset Archaeology Society. The archive and finds from both sites are destined for Somerset County Museum, Taunton.

References

Ancient Sources

Lucan, *Phars.* = Duff, J. D. (ed. and trans.) 1928 *The Civil War (Pharsalia)*. Loeb Classical Library, Harvard University Press, Cambridge, Mass.

Ovid, *Met.* = Miller, F. J. (ed. and trans.) and Goold, G. P. (rev.) 1916 *Metamorphoses*. Loeb Classical Library (2 volumes), Harvard University Press, Cambridge, Mass.

Statius, *Theb.* = Shackleton Bailey, D. R. (ed. and trans.) 2004 *Thebaid*. Loeb Classical Library (2 volumes), Harvard University Press, Cambridge, Mass.

Modern Sources

Alcock, L., Stevenson, S. J. and Musson, C. R. 1995 *Cadbury Castle, Somerset. The Early Medieval Archaeology*, University of Wales Press, Cardiff.

Aldsworth, F. and Rudling, D. 1995 Excavations at Bignor Roman villa, West Sussex 1985-90. *Sussex Archaeological Collections* 133, 103-88.

Bellamy, P. S., and Graham, A. H. 2004 *Mill House, Lopen, South Somerset. Archaeological Excavation, October-November 2001*. Terrain Archaeology Report 5092.1, unpublished report.

Branigan, K. 1976 *The Roman Villa in South-West England*. Moonraker Press, Bradford on Avon.

Branigan, K. 1988 Specialisation in villa economies. In Branigan, K. and Miles, D. (ed.), *The Economies of Romano-British Villas*, 42-50. Department of Archaeology and Prehistory, University of Sheffield, Sheffield.

Burrow, I. 1982 Hillforts and hilltops 1000 BC–1000 AD. In Aston, M. and Burrow, I. (ed.), *The Archaeology of Somerset*, 82-97. Somerset County Council, Taunton.

Corney, M. 2012 *The Roman Villa at Box. The story of the extensive Romano-British structures buried below the village of Box in Wiltshire*. Box Archaeological and Natural History Society, East Knoyle.

Cosh, S. R. 2001 Seasonal dining-rooms in Romano-British houses. *Britannia* 32, 219-42.

Cosh, S. R. 2005 What the Romans should never have done. The destruction of Romano-British mosaics in Late Antiquity. *Mosaic* 32, 5-11.

Cosh, S. R. and Neal, D. S. 2005a *Roman Mosaics of Britain, volume II, South-West Britain*. Illuminata Publishers and Society of Antiquaries of London, London.

Cosh, S. R. and Neal, D. S. 2005b Daphne at Dinnington. *Mosaic* 32, 23-5.

Cosh, S. R. and Neal, D. S. 2010 *Roman Mosaics of Britain, volume IV, Western Britain*. Society of Antiquaries of London, London.

Croft, B. 2009 *Roman Mosaics in Somerset*. Somerset County Council Heritage Service, Taunton.

Cross, P. J. 2011 Horse burial in first millennium AD Britain: issues of interpretation. *European Journal of Archaeology* 14, 190-209.

Davies, J. L. and Driver, T. G. 2018 The Romano-British villa at Abermagwr, Ceredigion: excavations 2010-15. *Archaeologia Cambrensis* 167, 143-219.

Dodd, J. 2021 Transitional burials in Late Antique villas in the north-western provinces: assessing distributions and characteristics. *European Journal of Archaeology* 24.1, 68-88.

Ellis, S. P. 1995 Classical reception rooms in Romano-British houses. *Britannia* 26, 163-78.

Ferdière, A. 2019 De nouvelles formes de stockage de céréales à l'époque romaine en Gaule: quel changements, avec quel(s) moteur(s) ? In Martin, S. (ed.), *Rural Granaries in Northern Gaul (6th century BCE – 4th century CE)*, 73-105. Brill, Leiden and Boston,.

Firmin, P. 2014 *Faunal Remains from Dinnington Roman Villa: west wing*. BA Dissertation, University of Winchester.

Frere, S. S. 1982 The Bignor villa. *Britannia* 13, 135-95.

Gallagher, B. 2005 *Dinnington Somerset: an interim report on the archaeological evaluation by Time Team 8-10 May 2002.* Time Team, unpublished report.

Gerrard, J. 2004 How late is late? Pottery and the fifth century in southwest Britain. In Collins, R. and Gerrard, J. (ed.), *Debating Late Antiquity in Britain AD 300-700*, 65-75. British Archaeological Reports (BAR) British Series 365, Oxford.

Gerrard, J. 2011 Crisis, whose crisis? The fifth century in south-western Britain. *Archaeological Review from Cambridge* 26.1, 65-78.

Graham, A. H. 2003 *A Romano-British building in Priory Mead, Hinton St George, Somerset.* Unpublished report.

Graham, A. H. and Mills, J. 1995 A Romano-British Building at Crimbleford Knap, Seavington St Mary. *Proceedings of the Somerset Archaeology and Natural History Society* 139, 119-34.

GSB Prospection 2002 *Survey results. 2002 / 47 Dinnington, Somerset.* Geophysical survey report for Time Team.

Henig, M. 1984 *Religion in Roman Britain.* Batsford, London.

Henig, M. 2007 *Corpus of Roman Engraved Gemstones from British Sites.* British Archaeological Reports (BAR) British Series 8, Oxford (3rd edition).

Hurst, H. 1987 Excavations at Box Roman villa, 1967-8. *Wiltshire Archaeological Magazine* 81, 19-51.

Johns, C. 2010 *The Hoxne Late Roman Treasure. Gold jewellery and silver plate.* British Museum, London.

King, A. C. 2004 Rural settlement in southern Britain: a regional survey. In M. Todd (ed.), *A Companion to Roman Britain*, 349-70. Blackwell Publishing, Oxford.

King, A. C. 2005 A mosaic in western Somerset: Yarford, Somerset, excavations 2003-5. *Mosaic* 32, 19-22.

Leach, P. 2001 *Roman Somerset.* The Dovecote Press, Wimborne.

Leech, R. H. 1982 The Roman interlude in the South-West: the dynamics of economic and social change in Romano-British south Somerset and North Dorset. In Miles, D. (ed.), *The Romano-British Countryside. Studies in rural settlement and economy*, 209-67. British Archaeological Reports (BAR) British Series 103, Oxford.

Leech, R. H. and Leach, P. 1982 Roman town and countryside 43-450 AD. In Aston, M. and Burrow, I. (ed.), *The Archaeology of Somerset*, 62-81. Somerset County Council, Taunton.

Lucas, R. N. 1993 *The Romano-British Villa at Halstock, Dorset. Excavations 1967-1985.* Dorset Natural History and Archaeological Society Monograph 13, Dorchester.

Macphail, R., Galinié, H. and Verhaeghe, F. 2003 A future for Dark Earth? *Antiquity* 77, 349-58.

Martin, P. and Driscoll, S. 2010 *Excavation of a Romano-British Site, Butcombe, Somerset. Season One, 2009.* Absolute Archaeology, Trowbridge.

Neal, D. S. and Cosh, S. R. 2009 *Roman Mosaics of Britain, volume III, South-East Britain.* Society of Antiquaries of London, London.

Poole, K. 2013 Horses for courses? Religious change and dietary shifts in Anglo-Saxon England. *Oxford Journal of Archaeology* 32, 319-333.

Putnam, B. 2007 *Roman Dorset.* Tempus, Stroud.

RCHM(E) = Royal Commission on Historical Monuments (England) 1997 *Ham Hill, Somerset. A new survey.* Unpublished report.

Rebetez, S. 1997 *Mosaïques. Guide-complément à l'exposition réalisée par le Musée romain d'Avenches 17 mai – 26 octobre 1997.* Musée romain d' Avenches, Avenches.

Rodbourne, B. 2008 *The Investigation [of] the Roman horse burial found during Excavations at a Roman Villa in Dinnington, Somerset 2007.* BA Dissertation, University of Winchester.

Rudling, D. and Russell, M. 2015 *Bignor Roman Villa.* History Press, Stroud.

Saylor, C. 1982 Curio and Antaeus: the African episode of Lucan *Pharsalia IV. Transactions of the American Philological Association* 112, 169-77.

Scott, C. 2000 *Art and Society in Fourth-Century Britain. Villa mosaics in context*, Oxford University School of Archaeology, Oxford.

Smith, D. J. 1977 Mythological figures and scenes in Romano-British mosaics, in Munby, J. and Henig, M. (ed.), *Roman Life and Art in Britain.* Oxford, British Archaeological Reports (BAR) British Series 41, 105-93.

Somerset County Council, University College Winchester and Channel 4's Time Team 2005 *Project design for an archaeological research project at Dinnington, Somerset (ST 404 135).* Unpublished report.

Spiller, J. 2007 *Painted Wall-Plaster from Yarford and Dinnington in Somerset, England.* BA dissertation, University of Winchester.

Taylor, S. C. 2006 *Roman Villas around Ilchester, Somerset.* BA dissertation, University of Winchester.

Turner, A. 2003 *Geophysical Survey Report. Yarford, Somerset.* Unpublished report, University of Winchester.

Walters, B. 1996 Exotic structures in 4th-century Britain. In Johnson, P. and Haynes, I. (ed.), *Architecture in Roman Britain*, 152-62. Council for British Archaeology (CBA) Research Report 94, York.

Webster, C. J. and Brunning, R. A. 2004 A 7th-century AD cemetery at Stoneage Barton Farm, Bishop's Lydeard, Somerset, and square-ditched burials in post-Roman Britain. *Archaeological Journal* 161, 54-81.

Webster, G. 1959 An excavation at Nunnington Park, near Wiveliscombe, Somerset. *Proceedings of the Somerset Archaeology and Natural History Society* 103, 81-91.

Webster, G. 1983 The possible effects on Britain of the fall of Magnentius. In Hartley, B. and Wacher, J. (ed.), *Rome and her Northern Provinces: papers presented to Sheppard Frere*, 240-54. Alan Sutton, Gloucester.

Wilkinson, K. N. and Thorpe, I. J. N. 2000 *The Southern Quantock Archaeological Survey. Project Design, draft*

2.0. Department of Archaeology, University of Winchester.

Wilkinson, K. N., Tyler, A., Davidson, D. and Grieve, I. 2006 Quantifying the threat to archaeological sites from the erosion of cultivated soil. *Antiquity* 80, 658-70.

Wilson, D. R. 2004 The North Leigh villa: its plan reviewed. *Britannia* 35, 77-113.

Witts, P. 2005a The lost mosaics of Bramdean: the Days of the Week and Hercules and Antaeus. In *Actes du IXe Colloque International pour l'étude de la mosaïque antique et médiévale*, vol. 1, 235-45. Collection de l'Ecole Française de Rome 352, Paris.

Witts, P. 2005b *Mosaics in Roman Britain. Stories in stone.* Tempus, Stroud.

14

The Ashtead Roman villa and tileworks

David Bird

The geology of the historic county of Surrey is very complex, like the other Wealden counties (i.e. Sussex and Kent). The soils that result are often poor or difficult to work; as Brandon and Short note (1990, 8), 'much of Surrey has never been a very promising environment for agriculture'. It should come as no surprise, therefore, that Surrey does not seem to be a land of many Roman villas and it was historically a very rural county with a comparatively low population (Bird 2004, 73-83; see Bird 2017).

Those villas that are known, whatever definition of the term is used, show an uneven distribution probably influenced by access to the better soils and a good water supply. For most, the siting seems to favour geological boundaries and it may be suggested that this indicates a mixed economy (for discussion see Bird 2004, 83-87 and for a wider area around London, Bird 1996, 220). In an uncertain world, the first aim must have been a degree of self-sufficiency, and being able to exploit different environments would have been important: if one option suffered as a result of the weather, etc, then another might fill the gap. Choice of site may also have been influenced by pre-existing Late Iron Age settlements, where there may therefore have been other factors affecting the Roman-period siting. Recent work has made a strong case for such continuity at the Chiddingfold, Ashtead Common and Abinger villas (Graham and Graham 2011, 188; Howe *et al.* 2014, 246-7; Bird 2014, 5), where the first-two named are not well placed for agricultural potential. Indeed, a case can be made that Chiddingfold, apparently Surrey's largest villa but in one of the least favourable settings, is more likely to have had later Roman-period use as a ritual centre, perhaps linked to an important spring in a relatively remote place (Bird 2002).

It is inevitably difficult to be certain about the main function or functions of most of the possible villas in the county. It would be of great interest to be able to demonstrate that some at least made use of land in long estates crossing several geological boundaries as was the case with the historic parishes, which seem to have been laid out to make possible the exploitation of many different kinds of environment (Bird 2004, 85). This can only be speculation at present, although work at the three sites mentioned above has been attempting to gain greater understanding of the land around the villas rather than examining only the central core of buildings.

As noted, the Ashtead Common site is located in a setting where conditions are not favourable for farming. This very spot was described by early twentieth-century soil scientists as 'the unmixed London Clay at its worst; undrained, sour, and cold, saturated all the winter and cracking wide during the drought, it has little economic value except for timber' (Hall and Russell 1911, 84-5). They did not, however, consider that the clay might have another use, for the manufacture of ceramic objects. That potential was recognised in the Roman period and now provides us with a very clear example of a villa closely associated with an industrial site. A nearby field system has been postulated as Roman in origin (Blair 1991, 29-30) but this does not seem very convincing; for example, a very regular layout is postulated but it does not relate to the equally regular approach road. There may of course have been a more extensive estate that included dependencies on the better soils to the south, such as a newly discovered site less than 3 km to the south-west (Priestley-Bell 2014, 208-210). There is in fact a possible villa near the parish church, also on the better soils; Lowther (1934, 83-4) was of the opinion that it replaced the Ashtead Common building in the third century. If so, it might be suggested that this happened when the tilery business came to an end, although it would be difficult to establish any of this with certainty.

The Ashtead project

The Ashtead Roman villa and tileworks project started in 2006, with the main fieldwork phase ending in September 2013. It is part of a wider programme of work undertaken by Surrey Archaeological Society's Roman Studies Group since it was founded in 2004. The project aims to reassess earlier work on the site and assist the Ashtead Common rangers in the management and interpretation of the scheduled monuments and other important archaeology in their care. Although it is in Surrey, the Common is one of the open spaces owned and managed by the City of London. It is a National Nature Reserve and Site of Special Scientific Interest particularly for its ancient oak pollards and related wildlife, which all had to be taken into account in planning archaeological work, for example in terms of time of year and location of trenches. The overall tree cover and other vegetation (see for instance Figs 14.6 and 14.8), a long walk to the site and the heavy clay subsoil also affected the work, which was only made possible by the wholehearted support of the rangers and their estate office – and, of course, that of the many volunteers who carried out the work in all weathers.

As fieldwork was only completed later in 2013 what follows can only be an interim statement, because detailed work on the finds is still in progress. There is in any case only room here for a brief summary of a very complex site. It lies not far to the west of Epsom (and, more pertinently, the Roman-period nucleated settlement at Ewell; Bird 2004, 60-2), near the crest of a low hill on the London Clay, and was first excavated in the period 1924-1929 by A. W. G. Lowther, with the crucial assistance of A. R. Cotton, who owned the site. Cotton was then the Clerk of Epsom Rural District Council and he used his experience to raise funds and other support for the excavation, as well as taking a full part in the dig himself (Fig. 14.5). A separate bath house was found first (with what, for a villa, is a very unusual circular *laconicum*) and then a villa

house whose plan has been described by J. T. Smith (1997, 112) as 'unique' in the north-west Empire (see Figs 14.4 and 14.7). A straight metalled road was recorded leading to the villa, probably as a branch from Stane Street, the London to Chichester road, which passed through Ewell. Considerable evidence for a tileworks was also noted, in the shape of a wide scatter of wasters and burnt material, but was unfortunately not mapped and only vaguely located in publications (Lowther 1929, 1; 1930, 132).

Lowther was in his early twenties when he started the dig, and he was clearly learning as he went along. He was then training as an architect but was also gaining some archaeological experience working as an unpaid assistant for the Guildhall Museum, salvaging information from development sites in London (Anon 1973, 405). After Ashtead he carried out several important excavations in Surrey and elsewhere on an amateur basis and was a key member of Surrey Archaeological Society for many years. He published the results of the Ashtead excavation with commendable speed but did so while the dig was in progress; there are three reports in sequence, and they are interpretation as much as report (Lowther 1927; 1929;

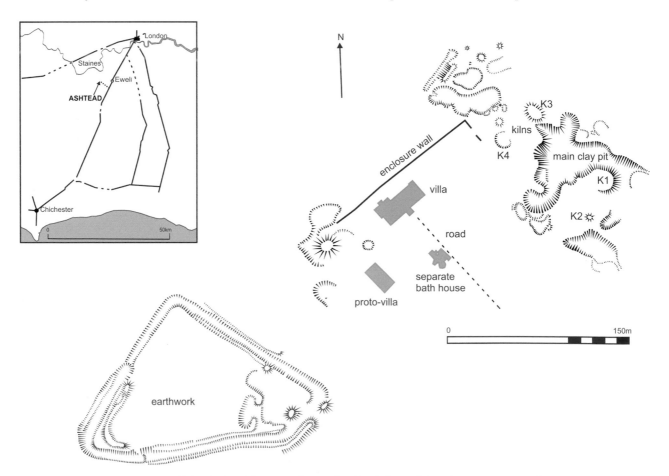

Figure 14.1. Overall sketch plan. (Illustration by David Bird and Alan Hall, based on Hampton 1977, fig 2, 30 and surveying by David and Audrey Graham)

1930). There is plenty of information about the finds but only occasional details of their location, let alone their stratigraphic context. Only a few site notes have survived and as some of those we have are literally on the back of an envelope it is probable that there were only ever a few actual records, apart from planning, made on site. Contemporary press reports, particularly those in *The Times*, are therefore of great value, as they were clearly written by someone who was well-versed in the archaeology of the site, probably Lowther himself. Together with surviving lecture notes they help to date the sequence of excavation and provide a *terminus ante quem* for when certain finds were discovered (and therefore to some extent where), and even provide information not in the site reports, such as the nature of the painted wall plaster from the separate bath house. The excavation was, however, probably better carried out and recorded than most at the time.

Lowther gave very little information about the tileworks but his discoveries led him to make more general studies of some of the finds, such as the roller-stamped tiles (now usually called 'relief-patterned': Fig. 14.2) and the so-called 'lamp chimneys' (Lowther 1948; 1976). He also provided a little more information about the site when reconsidering its dating thirty years or so later (Lowther 1959) but this must be treated with caution. In this paper he dates the excavation, specifically including the separate bath house, as between 1926 and 1928. His own earlier reports and the press records make it absolutely clear that the dig started in 1924 and there was a major season on the bath house in 1925. It seems that in 1959 he must have been writing – perhaps at speed under pressure of deadlines – from a somewhat faulty memory. This could explain other examples of inconsistency, such as where certain coins were found. Thus any apparently new information in the later paper must be treated with caution, which is unfortunate.

In the 1960s the late John Hampton (best known now for his work on aerial photography) undertook a detailed survey of the area around the villa, from an enigmatic triangular earthwork in the west to what must be unusually well recorded Roman-period clay pits in the east (a simplified plan was published; Hampton 1977 fig. 2, 30; see Fig. 14.1). Hampton also traced an enclosure

Figure 14.2. Relief patterns on box tiles recorded from Ashtead. (*After Betts* et al. *1994, passim*)

wall around part of the villa site and the locations of a number of possible kiln (K) sites. He excavated part of one of these (K3), finding a mass of burnt and unburnt clay, charcoal, broken tile and tile wasters and pottery. It was then considered to be a possible tile clamp site but is now thought more likely to have been a waster and rubbish heap.

It is the intention of the current project to revisit every aspect of the earlier fieldwork and all available information has been gathered together (John Hampton has kindly passed on his own finds and records, together with other relevant material). New fieldwork was planned to provide a date for the triangular earthwork, re-examine key aspects of the plan of Lowther's house and its development through time, and gain a better understanding of its immediate surroundings and of its associated tilery. Hampton's survey, carried out when the site was more open, has been crucial as an aid to navigating a site now covered in dense woodland. Not until very recently has the use of LiDAR data become an option; a brief review of what is available suggests that the survey was very accurate and missed little of consequence. In what follows cardinal points are given in accordance with 'site north' as marked on Fig. 14.1.

Earthwork to villa

At the start of the project the triangular earthwork was surveyed in detail by a team led by David McOmish of English Heritage. It had usually been considered as medieval (Lever 1978), but the report suggested that it had several phases and that it might be prehistoric in origin (McOmish and Newsome 2007, 11). This was later confirmed by a single section across the enclosure on the western side. Not only was it possible to show that there had been at least three phases, but the primary silt of the recut of the ditch in its second phase conveniently supplied large fragments of storage vessels that are to be dated to some point around the Roman

conquest. Geophysical survey and minimal excavation in the interior of the earthwork also hints at possible occupation at this time. Material from the third phase ditch suggests that the earthwork may still have been in use in the second century.

Roughly half-way between the earthwork and the house found by Lowther, another building was located by following up surface indications noted by John Hampton and the results of magnetometer survey carried out by Archaeology South-East (Tibble 2007, figs 5 and 6). Excavation was somewhat restricted by tree cover but it was possible to record a building with flint wall foundations. An original rectangular structure approximately 14.5 x 6 m internally, with traces of internal divisions, had been extended by additions along three sides. On the other side, that to the west (Fig. 14.3), there was an unusual structure on the line of the wall, marked by carefully made gaps either side of a 1.72 m stretch of wall which had a covering tile course (there was no sign of such a course anywhere else on this wall). The gaps were of different lengths, 470 mm and 610 mm, but it is difficult to interpret them as anything other than the setting for large squared posts either side of an imposing entrance. If this is correct it is curious that

Figure 14.3. Overhead photograph of part of the possible proto-villa, showing the north-west corner of the original building with traces of internal walls and the addition to the north (left). The tiled 'entrance' shows clearly; subsequent excavation showed that the foundations continued across the gap on each side at a lower level. (Photo: Alan Hall and David Graham)

it faces west while the additions that wrap round the building are on the other three sides (see further below).

A further line of post holes may indicate that there was eventually a portico along the eastern side. One wall of the earliest part of the building overlay a large shallow pit which contained early Roman pottery. This included some early imports, Gallo-Belgic types and native style grog-tempered jars etc, all suggesting pre-Flavian to early Flavian activity (Louise Rayner, *pers. comm.*). Other meaningful stratigraphy is limited and while the general area of the building has later first-century pottery there is also second-century material and a great deal of relief-patterned tile of more than one pattern as well as combed box tile. The tile, window glass and the overall quality of the pottery suggest that this was a building of some pretensions, starting as a proto-villa. The detailed sequence must await the completion of the finds reports but it is probable that the first building was constructed in the later first century. It is very tempting to see it as a natural progression from the earthwork, in a similar fashion to a site such as the Ditches villa (Trow *et al.* 2009, 45 and *passim*) but in this case sited outside; perhaps the elaborate entrance was intended to face back to the old site.

The two buildings found by Lowther were both re-examined, although little work was undertaken at the separate bath house partly because the area had been thoroughly dug over in the 1920s and partly because of nature conservation requirements (Fig. 14.4). This limited work confirmed the location and as a bonus supplied some relief-patterned tile

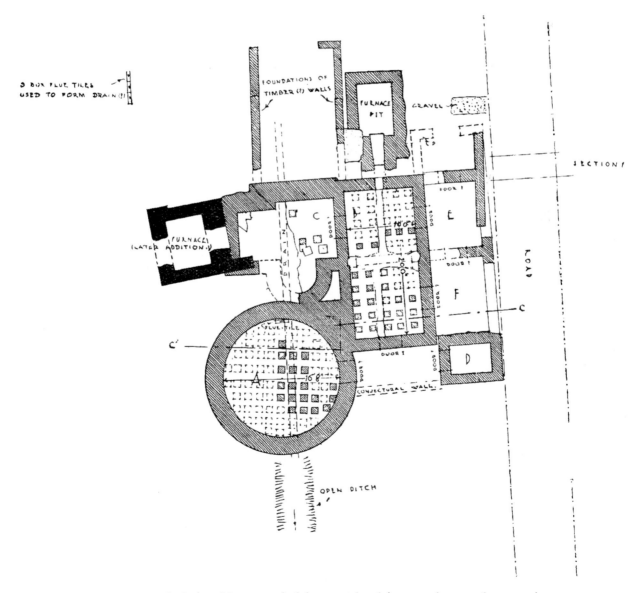

Figure 14.4. Lowther's plan of the separate bath-house at Ashtead. (From Lowther 1930, plan opp. 148)

Figure 14.5. Contemporary photo of Lowther (left) and Cotton standing behind room B of the separate bath house, with the circular laconicum *to the right.*

fragments (with occasional exceptions it is not possible to be sure of the original location of the tiles from Lowther's reports). It also confirmed the existence of the circular *laconicum*, a feature that seems to be very unusual on villa sites (Fig. 14.5): Perring mentions only Eccles (Kent) and Ashtead, with a suggested dating to the Neronian period and the early second century respectively (Perring 2002, 175; see Walthew 1975, 196). In each case this should be open to revision and they could well be more nearly contemporary.

The 'house' was tested in several places, subject to restrictions imposed by its scheduled status and the close proximity of veteran trees. Where possible trenches were sited to re-examine the oddities in the building's plan and to allow for deeper excavation where it was hoped that post-Roman robbing (or the 1920s excavations) would make it possible to go below the later floor levels with minimal disturbance to surviving archaeology. This led to the discovery of evidence for the existence of a number of periods, the earliest being the construction of

a chalk-floored building with beam slots (Fig. 14.6). The '3″ chalk deposit (pre-villa)' noted by Lowther on the final plan (1930, fig. opposite 148; reproduced here as Fig. 14.7) was part of this building and although little of its plan could be retrieved it is certain that the structure occupied a different footprint from the later stone-founded building, going beyond it to both south and east (its northern and western extents are not known). This discovery and that of the newly-found building to the west changes the way in which the layout of the whole site can be seen. It may indicate that there was an early house with a chalk-floored outbuilding to its left front and a separate bath house to the right, the whole complex facing east, replaced later on with Lowther's 'house' becoming the main building and the complex facing south. Current work on the finds suggests that there was pre-Flavian activity on all three sites.

The chalk-floored building must have been demolished before the later periods on the Lowther house site, which had flint foundations, probably for dwarf walls

Figure 14.6. View looking east across the eastern end of the Lowther house. The prominent wall in the centre of the trench is the outer wall of the tile-floored gutter; a few tiles can be seen still in situ. Nearer the camera a small portion of the inner wall of the gutter and then just a trace of the eastern outer wall of the villa can be seen. These features have partially removed the earlier chalk-floored structure which can be seen nearer the camera and at the far end of the trench continuing further east than the later building. (Photo: David Bird)

and a timber superstructure, although as the site was later robbed this cannot be regarded as certain. As excavation proceeded it became increasingly clear that the site had received very little backfilling in the 1920s, and that many of the walls recorded as standing by Lowther were in fact robber trenches. Nevertheless, where it was tested, his plan of the later building was shown to be accurate, and Smith's 'unique' plan was not the result of inadequate excavation. Anomalies such as the junctions of rooms 10-13, and of 4, 6 and 7, did exist as shown on Lowther's plans. Excavation in 2012 also confirmed his discovery of an underfloor parallel channel heating system in room 4, and the hypocaust in room 6 with more conventional *pilae*, but completely lined with box tiles starting from the sub-floor level (Fig. 14.8). This arrangement had been anticipated when the tiles were made

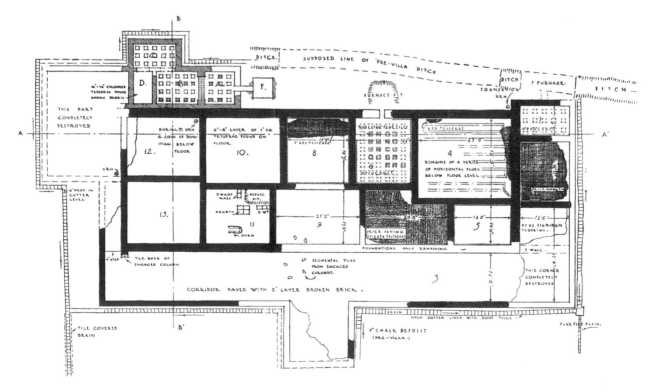

Figure 14.7. Lowther's plan of the Ashtead house. (From Lowther 1930, plan opp. 148)

Figure 14.8. Contemporary photo of work in progress in room 6 of Lowther's house in 1926, looking south-east, and more or less the same view in 2012. Note the parallel sub-floor channels in room 4 in the background; the herringbone brick floor of room 7 is to the right. (Modern photo: Stella Fagg)

as about half had openings cut into the front face pre-firing. The adjacent room 7 had a herringbone brick floor, something of a rarity in Britain (Perring 2002, 127); it was the second floor in this room (Lowther 1930, 136).

Because of the restrictions on excavation it was not possible to gather enough evidence to establish the full sequence of phases of the Lowther house overall and it remains difficult to understand its development. It is, however, clear that there was an earlier period with several phases. For example, it was possible to show that room 6 was earlier than rooms 4 and 7, and that room 11 appears to pre-date rooms 10, 12 and 13. There were probably intervening phases and finally a later period building in which the floor level of the whole structure was lifted by around 300mm, extended at the east and west ends and given the unusual tile-based drain or gutter round three sides. The raising of the level was achieved by the use of demolition material from the earlier building or large quantities of yellow clay, and probably took place towards the end of the second century. If so, the new building may not have been in use for many years before the site was abandoned, except for robbing activities, relatively early in the third century.

Continuing work on the finds may make it possible to establish a better understanding of the phasing of the Lowther house and how it relates to the proto-villa and the separate bath-house. The new evidence has however, probably inevitably, made it clear that Black's suggestions (1987, 110-114) for phasing can no longer stand. Fortunately, this is not the place for a detailed discussion of the phasing as it is only relevant in this paper to discussions of the inter-relationship between the villa and the tilery, which will be considered further below.

The tileworks

Considerable attention was paid to the area west of the Lowther house to gain a better understanding of the tilery. Hampton's enclosure wall was located and further tested but it did not prove possible to trace it much further either to west or south. It seems clear enough, however, that the wall was intended to enclose the villa complex and separate it from the tileworks. What survived of the wall was flint built with a bonding course of broken *tegulae*, flanges uppermost as in the walls of the villa gutter; it is probably to be dated relatively late in the sequence and may have replaced the ditch known to run across close to the north side of the Lowther house. This ditch was not traced further in the recent excavations but was shown to have two phases when sectioned near room 8 in 2008.

It was hoped that evidence would be found for workshops associated with the tileworks, but it did not prove possible to locate any certain buildings. It may be that they were mostly timber-built, perhaps set on ground beams as seems to be a common practice in the South-East (Bird 2000, 159). Spreads of pottery, flint and tile in a number of places indicated what might be termed 'activity areas' and these probably had associated structures. Hampton found two locations with tile and flint rubble and pottery that are sufficiently remote from the known buildings for it to be unlikely that they simply indicate rubbish disposal from them. A third was added by test-pitting in 2012, and a small trench attempting to pursue the line of the enclosure wall to the south found instead a layer of tile rubble which would have been dismissed as no more than that had it not been for the way the rubble ended neatly in straight lines with a right-angle corner. This could well have been a rough base for a workshop or drying shed. Goodchild found a large area with a layer of broken tile fragments at the Wykehurst Farm, Ewhurst, tilery, which he interpreted as a 'paved brickyard' used for drying tiles before firing and for a tessera-making workshop (Goodchild 1937, 79-80).

A double-flued tile kiln at Horton to the north of Ashtead Common (Goodchild 1937, 90-92) has been seen as part of the Ashtead industry but current research suggests that it is more likely to be medieval. The earlier archaeological work had not found any tile kilns as such on the Common itself and this was a major aim of the project. The original intention was merely to locate and test some kilns but in the event it became necessary to devote considerable attention to the kiln, or as it turned out kilns, first discovered in 2009 and further excavated over the next five years. The site was chosen to test an anomaly identified in magnetometer survey by Archaeology South East, just south of the waster and rubbish mound K3 excavated in part by John Hampton (Cole and Meaton 2008, figs 5 and 6). Excavation was particularly difficult when it was dry as the whole area consisted mostly of burnt and unburnt clay and masses of tile, all of it varying from rock hard to very soft. The proximity of a veteran tree also made it impossible to tackle the full area of the stokehole. Further complications were caused because it was only after the first two seasons that it became apparent that there were two kilns, one built on top of the other (for further information about the kilns, see Bird 2016).

The first kiln had been built into a large rectangular pit with sloping sides and a deeper trench along the middle for the central flue. The kiln itself was about 3.5 m long and 3.25 m wide internally and the flue extended eastwards beyond it towards the stokehole by about 1.6 m.

Figure 14.9. The tile kilns from the west showing the tegula structure at the end of the central flue and the stokehole retaining walls in the foreground. The full width of the front walls and part of the interior of the kiln can be seen further back. The prominent ledge visible in the central flue marks the point to which the first period flue was cut down. (Photo: Stella Fagg)

The whole structure was tile-built, with the walls made up from fragments laid flat with a straight side outwards and then a rubble infill. At the stokehole end of the flue there were flanking tile-built walls on either side, one at an angle (Fig. 14.9). The kiln probably had eight inclined side flues, each about 150 mm wide made by laying tiles across the area and 'growing' the flue walls out of them as they reached the appropriate height, with the aid of plastered clay. Evidence for repairs to the central flue suggests a considerable period of use, as does the build-up of its fill, with several separate charcoal levels over burnt clay and debris. The tile walls in some places were reduced almost to crumbling clay and had certainly been replaced in patches near the stokehole end.

Eventually the decision was taken to replace the kiln with another built on top of it. The first kiln was sliced off at a level about a third of the way up the side flues and the remains packed up with around 250 mm of clean yellow clay. The central flue arches were cut off close to the springing point (Fig. 14.9) and the flue was packed solid with burnt clay and tile rubbish to form a new floor level. New central flue walls were built up on the cut-down first-period walls, laid across the remnants of the earlier side flues and forming an outer edge for their yellow clay packing. This packing was covered with tiles to provide a base for a new set of side flues, also of the inclined type, and again probably eight in number. The side walls this time were free-standing with the sloping flues made of rubble and plastered clay (Fig. 14.10). The evidence for this part of the upper kiln structure was confined to the back of the kiln, as it had apparently been robbed out further to the east. At the back, elements of the central arch of one side flue wall survived in a collapsed state, and vitrification of the central flue tiles was specially marked. The first kiln's outer walls must have been built up further for the second period but not much survived. Where it did at the back (west side), it was apparently only roughly built. The oven floor level of the upper kiln must have been well above current ground level.

Figure 14.10. Overhead view of the back of the tile kilns with east at the top. The back wall of the kilns is about half way up the photo, with, to the west, the tiled approach to the kiln and to the east the collapsed flue arch marked by over-fired tiles. A second side flue wall shows near the top of the photo on the edge of the trench. (Photo: Stella Fagg)

Two features of the earlier kiln appear to be unusual survivals, one even perhaps unique. At the stokehole end of the central flue a set of *tegulae* had been placed on edge to continue the line of the walls and then turn across the flue, leaving a small gap which had been bridged by a tile (found broken and collapsed into the gap). Part of such a structure had previously been recorded at Hartfield (Rudling 1986, 198 and plate 15B) but the Ashtead example presumably survived more-or-less complete because of the way the kiln was sealed by its successor. At the south-west corner of the kiln, a carefully formed structure made from *imbrices* in line had been laid through and outside the back wall, probably just above oven floor level. Clearly both features are related to control of the air flow through the kiln. It seems that once the firing temperature was reached, the fire was pushed under the oven floor and the flue-end was blocked with *tegulae*, leaving a small gap to allow assessment of colour and make it possible to give more or less air. There must have been a temporary chimney above the back of the central flue too, hence the vitrification there, and the

imbrex structure (no doubt one on each side) would then be intended to supplement the system, with the aim of drawing the heat right through to the back corners of the kiln. The kiln did not survive sufficiently well to show if there had been similar vents along the sides, as has been recorded elsewhere (Charlier 2015).

The area outside the back of the kiln was also examined, providing clear evidence for a tiled approach that is to be associated with the first-period kiln (Fig. 14.10). It continued the line of the central flue exactly and was defined by side walls which sloped up to the west, presumably to the contemporary ground level. There can be little doubt that it was intended to assist loading and unloading of the kiln. There seem to be few recorded parallels but those at Eccles and Heiligenberg kiln 1 might be noted (McWhirr 1979, 157-8; Le Ny 1988, 77 and fig. 38, 98); Ashtead's seems to be the best survival. What seemed to be another tiled surface was found at a higher level close to the north-west corner of the kiln but it is possible that it was intended, at least in part, to support a post. A varying number of tiles laid flat were also found adjoining each of the other corners and not elsewhere, and while seen in isolation there was no reason to suppose that they were used as post pads, when taken together it is hard to find another explanation. It seems likely that they supported a cover structure of some kind, to afford protection from the weather. There is a well-recorded example of a cover building at Crookhorn, Hampshire (Soffe *et al.* 1989, 64-8 and fig. 14, 60), where it may be noted that there was more than one phase, which, together with uneven ground and varying lengths of posts, could be the explanation of the variability of the tile features at Ashtead.

The kilns were placed on the edge of the main clay pit, whose Roman date has been supported by radiocarbon dating in work carried out by Professor Martyn Waller of Kingston University to investigate the vegetational history of the area (Waller 2010, 741). The clay pits have not been tested by archaeological excavation, but a roughly circular depression near to and west of the kilns was sectioned in 2013 to test a theory that it might be a puddling pit. It turned out to be over 2.5 m deep, a pit with sloping sides and layers of curious mottled fills obviously related to kiln activity (and a great deal of tile but virtually no pottery). Micromorphological analysis has confirmed the presence of trampled horizons and furnace rakings and provided information about the local environment (Banerjea and Batchelor 2014). Whatever the purpose of the pit, it had been thought appropriate to mark it by the placement of a face pot in the lowest silt level, which contained many large fragments of tile wasters. The pot (Fig. 14.11) was probably placed complete, perhaps as either a thank offering or plea for a successful firing, and later shattered as the pit was filled. It is quite likely to date to the Antonine period, which is also suggested by pottery from the K3 mound (Joanna Bird, *pers. comm.*), and may imply that the first-period kiln was in use in the later second century. Both kilns were sampled for archaeomagnetic dating (by a team from Museum of London Archaeology), in the hope that the unburnt yellow clay filling in the first-period kiln would have shielded the earlier kiln from the later one's heat, but unfortunately they produced virtually identical dates, those for the last firing of the final period being within the range AD 205-225 at 95% confidence (Noel 2011).

Figure 14.11. The face pot; the lower piece probably belongs elsewhere but gives the correct impression. Height of pot is about 200 mm.

This evidence together with that for considerable use of the first kiln (and the effort involved in its construction) might suggest that it was in use for several years and was then replaced close to the end of the second century. Current evidence suggests that the final period of the Lowther house, when it was rebuilt at a higher level, could have started at about the same time. Might the raising of the levels at both house and kiln have been part of a site-wide attempt to deal with a particularly wet period around AD 200? The problems that could occur on this site are well illustrated by events in 1927, when the excavations were 'badly hampered by the excessive rain. For most of the three months available the ground was badly waterlogged and at times work was only made possible by cutting ditches and draining off the water' (Anon 1929, xix).

It is very likely that the known kilns represent a late phase of tile-making activity at Ashtead. There is still a great deal of detailed work to be done on the chronology of tile production on the site but it seems likely to start in the late first century and continue through to the early third century. The main clay pit alone covers a wide area indicating that there must have been a major industry in action over a considerable period of time and there seem to have been many other subsidiary pits. Based on the size of the main pit and information supplied by Redlands, Hampton calculated (1977, 34) that Ashtead could have supplied enough tile to roof fifty villas its own size, as well as producing other kinds of tiles. The concentrations of tile debris known near the eastern end of the main pit (Fig. 14.1, K1 and K2) are very likely to be waster dumps near earlier kilns. Analysis of tile samples collected from them in 2013 suggests that they differ slightly from later products which may support the suggestion that they represent earlier activity.

Analysis of pollen from the main pit (Waller 2010) suggests that peat accumulation began soon after the abandonment of the tileworks. Woodland cover (predominantly oak and hazel) began to increase and there is evidence suggestive of grazing for the rest of the Roman period which may indicate that the later use of the Common as wood pasture started at this time.

Discussion

London Clay covers a wide area around the City and this makes it difficult to trace the distribution of tiles from the Ashtead tilery as any tiles made from the clay will tend to be similar (see Betts 2017, 371). A programme of analysis has therefore been set up using inductively-coupled plasma spectrometry (ICP) to analyse the chemical features of tiles from different production centres and consumer sites and compare the results. The series of four tests so far carried out under the guidance of Ian Betts and Mike Hughes have demonstrated how difficult it is to draw conclusions even using this method, but it is hoped that in due course, together with analysis of the contexts of the many relief-patterned and combed flue tile fragments from the site, it will provide more precise dating for some of these products and offer an insight into their marketing. The wide variety of tile types at Ashtead will also be studied, including many found by Lowther and not fully published (which may account for errors in Brodribb's survey; e.g. 1987, 56, fig. 22.4 and 74, fig. 32.1).

The study of finds that is now in progress should also provide a better dated sequence for the structures and the development of the site. The intention is to re-examine all previous discoveries; as a result of seeing the site at first hand, it has become increasingly possible to 'read' clues in the reports and unpublished material.

There is an early reference to Roman pottery and silver coins having been 'met with' in an area not far to the east of the villa (Paget 1873, 3). The description of one coin strongly suggests a Republican type and the information could be taken to suggest a mid-first century AD hoard of *denarii* (I am grateful to Richard Reece for discussing the evidence). Such a find would not be out of place in view of the evidence now available for activity at about this time at the nearby earthwork. The early pottery from the sites of all three of the buildings reinforces the impression of higher status, as does a fragment of a Claudio-Neronian decorated samian bowl of form Hermet 4 (Joanna Bird, *pers. comm.*) from the recent excavations on the Lowther house site. This seems to be a particularly unusual find.

Other finds from the site demonstrate that the 'Roman' aspects continued. A gold Hercules club earring found by chance in 1936 is one of a handful of examples in Britain, with other gold examples known from Birdoswald and the Walbrook in London. Cool notes that those from Ashtead and Birdoswald 'have the blue or turquoise enamels that are typical of Classical enamelling on gold, and are otherwise known in Britain only on the bracelet from Rhayader', and suggests that these may have been the products of a second-century British workshop producing 'luxurious gold jewellery' (Cool 1986, 231 and *passim*). A bronze cockerel from a composite statuette of Mercury, a seal-box lid (Andrews, 2013, 437) and a samian inkwell (see Monteil 2008, 183) are all likely to be linked to economic activity. The many different kinds of tiles including those for attached columns and heating systems also reinforce the 'Roman' aspect. The best-known find from the site, the dog and stag patterned box tile (apparently the only one of its kind to feature animals), had a design that included well-made letters with serifs and stops (Fig. 14.2, die 6). The letters might be interpreted as (G[aius] I[ulius] S[...]) and (I[ulius] V[...] FE[cit]), perhaps the site owner and a skilled tile maker respectively.

Another unusual and very 'Roman' object is the decorated stone slab that may have been intended for an inscription (perhaps just painted) of which fragments were found by Lowther in the gutter round the later house (1929, 6 and pl. III; 1930, 136, fig. 11). Recent study suggests a date around the late first century and draws attention to the crossed *cornucopiae* and globe device which is in accord with the symbolic visual language of Empire. 'This does not mean that the plaque was official, though the owner may have been a veteran from the army, a civil servant or someone who merely wished to identify her/himself with the ruling power' (Coombe *et al.* 2013, 107-8 and pl. 74, no. 199).

The possibility that the owner was a military veteran accords well with other evidence from the site. Walthew (1975, 196; see Lowther 1959, 73) drew attention to a possible 'military' aspect in the shape of the circular *laconicum*. The straight metalled approach road might also suggest a 'military' aspect. The face pot (Fig. 14.11) is one of the late Gillian Braithwaite's type 13D, made in *Verulamium* or London and probably to be dated to the Hadrianic or Antonine periods (Braithwaite 2007, 261-4; fig J7, 272). She comments (2007, 255) that both face pots and *tazze* seem to have been 'closely associated with the army and the military community in the western provinces.' Ashtead can now be shown to have both (for a high quality *tazza* see, for instance, Lowther 1929, pl. Vb, opp. 8). As significant is the recent discovery in finds processing of a fragment of a carrot amphora (Isabel Ellis and Louise Rayner, *pers. comm.*), a class described as 'commonly associated with early military sites in Britain and Germany' (Peacock and Williams 1986, 109). A recent survey by Daniel Howells noted that the *only* villa to have produced such a find was Fishbourne (!) and reached the overall conclusion that that they occurred 'predominantly in elite military situations, particularly at legionary fortress sites' (Howells 2009, 77 and 79).

Attention is thus drawn to the lettering on the dog and stag tiles, which the ICP analysis has established were made on site. The form of the G, with a separate hook, seems to be unusual, but is paralleled on some Legio XX tile stamps. It is noticeable that they are almost the only Legio XX stamps where the letters have serifs (Frere and Tomlin 1992, 175-194; 2463.21 is apparently the only example that has serifs and a normal G). Warry (2006, 80-1 and pl. 5.8) comments on this group of stamps with 'unusual lettering' and 'curiously-shaped "G"s', noting that they can be linked to production by a civilian contractor, probably named Aulus Viducius, working at Tarbock near Liverpool (see Swan and Philpott 2000, 56). He suggests that manufacturing box tiles was a difficult task and that they were made for the military by specialist contractors (Warry 2006, 86). He also points out (2006, 81 and note 37) that 'two of the unstamped *tegulae* [at Tarbock] had a letter 'V' signature incised onto their upper surface, which is rare and RIB records only one other site [Castleshaw] that has produced 'V' graffiti', adding that 'there is also one tile from Ashtead with a 'V' signature in this [i.e. Warry's] survey'. Other marks on the Ashtead tiles may hint at a 'military' link, such as hobnail boot impressions (Warry 2006, 14; D6 in table). Viducius can be dated to AD 126 (Warry 2006, 64-5, where he makes a very good case), and where this can be identified the unusual tiles belong to Warry's *tegula* cutaway group dated AD 100-180 (Warry 2006, 63 and 81). It may therefore be significant that three of the eight coins known from Ashtead are Hadrianic and are associated with the separate bath-house.

A military establishment as such at Ashtead is unlikely, but it seems reasonable to propose that in the second century the owner was an ex-soldier, someone like Gaius Longinius Speratus, a veteran of Legio XXI Primigenia, who seems to have owned a private tileworks in southern Germany around the end of the second century (Brandl and Federhofer 2010, 69). Perhaps G.I.S was a veteran of Legio XX, making good use of contacts from his earlier career, or was someone with close links to that unit. Julii are represented in Legio XX, including one possibly of British origin (Birley 1979, 84-5). A fragmentary Julius tile stamp (in capitals with serifs) is known from Chester and Holt (Grimes 1930, 141 and fig. 59.16) and some of the tiles with unusual 'Gs' come from Holt, where tile production is dated from the late 80s to around 150 (Warry 2006, 59). Intriguingly there is an interesting object from Holt, supposedly the die for a *mortarium* stamp, bearing the name IVLI VICTORIS (Grimes 1930, 131 and fig. 57.8). It is apparently unused and has not been found on any *mortaria*, so was perhaps created for the sake of it (I am grateful to Kay Hartley for her comments on this object). The die has an edging of diagonal lines which also appear along one edge of the dog and stag tiles but on no other relief-patterned tile. Such edging is, however, common on *mortarium* stamps and this particular die uses plain letters.

We might also note Julius Vitalis, a craftsman of Legio XX buried at Bath probably in the later first century (*RIB* 156). Scott (2017, 303, 315) points out that the use of *faber*, without a qualifying adjective, might well mean someone associated with the building trades (although he does not suggest a skilled tile maker in this particular case). While tempting, however, it would clearly be straining credibility to suggest that Julius Vitalis or Julius Victor is Ashtead's I.V. The names would be common enough and even a link between die 6 and other relief-patterned dies probably containing I and V (dies 13 and 33) seems unlikely (*contra* Betts *et al.* 1994, 45) as the patterns have little in common. It is also interesting but probably no more than coincidence that the overall plan of the Holt complex (Grimes 1930, fig. 2) is matched by that at Ashtead at roughly the same scale, with the main clay pit at the eastern end, then to the west first the kilns, next a house and baths and then an enclosure (which at Holt housed barracks).

G.I.S might thus be dated to the 120s and a case can be made for this dating to relate also to the circular laconicum and the 'inscription'. The face pot and associated evidence point, however, to a later date while some of the other 'military' evidence including the laconicum could be pre 100. The tilery itself is likely to have been in production on a considerable scale, though not necessarily continuously, for 100 years or more, mostly across the second century. The large quarry (and other clay pits), likely longevity of the known (and dated) kilns, probable earlier kilns and likely dates of the relief-patterned products all point in this direction. The new discoveries, however, change the once simple picture of a villa and associated tileworks established together on a new site, perhaps starting around AD 100. It is now necessary to consider the prehistoric origins of the site and the strong argument for continuity from the Late Iron Age into the Roman period, with finds suggestive of high status occupation. How and when did it come about that an owner saw the site's potential as a tilery and how is it possible to fit a military veteran into the story, as well as allowing for more than one generation if the tilery continues for 100 years or so?

In view of the experimental nature of some aspects of construction at Ashtead, consideration should also be given to a possible link to the early developments in tile technology in Britain suggested by Lancaster (2012) with reference to sites in Sussex. Of particular interest is the villa at Angmering where Lancaster notes the similarities with Ashtead but assumes that the latter is later and second century (Lancaster 2012, 427, n. 29). Angmering has a room completely jacketed with box-tiles taken right down to sub-floor level, with openings in the front of the box-tiles made pre-firing and with them set into the floor ('set in place before the floor surface was added'), and with *pilae* made from one larger base tile with smaller ones in the stacks (Lancaster 2012, 427). In every case this is paralleled in Ashtead's room 6. It must be likely that these rooms are more or less contemporary. Angmering is well placed to have had reasonably close links with Ashtead; it is more or less due south of Pulborough, not far away from Stane Street.

Lancaster (2012, 424) suggests that the innovatory approach to baths construction is probably to be dated to around the later first century. She thinks that those involved are 'unlikely to have been military experts' but were possibly 'a mix of local Britons and Gallic immigrants' who were 'skilled and confident terracotta craftsmen' and 'confident heating engineers' (Lancaster 2012, 436). How this might relate to the idea of a military veteran being involved at Ashtead is difficult to explain. We might consider an early owner whose son(s) had joined up (possibly even abroad) and returned after completing service (this might even be the explanation for the probable Republican coins already noted: see above and, for example, Walton 2012, 62). But it seems as likely that a new owner, G. I. S, took over at the time of the construction of the Lowther house. *If* he was a Gaius Julius, he is most likely to be non-British in origin.

So perhaps this and other evidence would fit best with a legionary veteran taking over early in the second century, presumably by purchase, although of course that raises interesting questions about how he would know of the site and its potential. A romantic suggestion would see him married to a daughter of the original site owner, having met her while on service in London (a suggestion I owe to Nikki Cowlard). Even if so, it looks as though production continued across most of the second century so there must be more than one generation involved – a family firm, possibly with links elsewhere. The new broom towards the end of the second century could mark another new owner, but could just be a new generation or a forced response to site conditions.

Jones' discussion of the Roman 'family firm' (2006, 218-243) is of interest in this context. He notes that 'it was common for the elite paterfamilias to invest in mining, quarrying and manufacturing enterprises'; citing the activities of the elder Cato, which included, relevant to discussion below, buying estates 'rich in forest'. Varro similarly advocated the exploitation of resources including clay pits. Jones also points out that 'in the second century the particular commercial interest of emperors was in the production of lead pipes and bricks'. An example is tiles stamped as from the Tiber valley estate of Domitia Lucilla, who was the mother of Marcus Aurelius (Jones 2006, 218-220). There was clearly good money to be made out of making tiles. The high quality gold earring and other objects from Ashtead do not seem out of context in this world.

No doubt many villa owners in Britain would have sought to make sensible use of their available resources. There is some evidence in favour of specialisation in the area around London (Bird 1996, 223, 227; 2012). Ashtead's siting clearly favoured tile production, and probably also timber (Hall and Russell 1911, 85). The owner may also have had an interest in the production of chalk and/or lime from nearby pits of probable Roman date (Bird 2004, 77), perhaps all part of the provision of 'building supplies'. Another string to the owner's bow may have been the production of pottery; study of the finds from Hampton's excavation of K3 suggested the possibility of manufacture on site. Current work on the finds is confirming that there is local pottery production that is very likely to have been at the tileworks (Joanna Bird and Louise Rayner, *pers. comm.*).

It is probable that other tile kilns in the South-East were associated with villas as part of a wider production of 'building supplies'; some possible examples are noted here. The kiln at Reigate was probably part of an enterprise that also produced Reigate stone, as faulty blocks from a quarry were used in the kiln front wall (Howe *et al.* 2005, 280; Emma Corke, *pers. comm.*; for a slight hint at a possible villa site see Williams 2008). Proximity and an unusual pear-shaped tile suggests a link between the Wykehurst Farm tilery and the Rapsley villa, which may also have had nearby stone quarries (Hanworth 1968, 31-2; Goodchild 1937, 93-4). The tile kiln at Hartfield in Sussex may well have been associated with the building at nearby Garden Hill and with iron-working activity (Rudling 1986; Money 1977). The villa at Eccles, Kent, had a nearby tilery and pottery production (Detsicas 1983, 162, 167-9) and might well have been involved in ragstone quarrying. Crookhorn in Hampshire is probably another site with a villa and associated tileworks (Soffe *et al.* 1989). This tilery is likely to have been long-lasting: produce seems to have included *tegulae* stamped TIFR dated by Warry (2006, 156) to AD 100-180. As the known kiln has archaeomagnetic and pottery dating to the early fourth century this suggests production over a lengthy period.

The Ashtead Common site was clearly a major industrial establishment, but it has so many unusual features that it is difficult to see it as a simple example of a working villa. Many questions remain and the project is still very much a work in progress, but it should help to gain this most interesting site the attention it deserves.

Acknowledgements

Thanks are due first and foremost to all those who toiled on the site in all weathers and those who have put in many hours of hard work on the finds. The constant flow of suggestions and challenges to possible interpretations have contributed greatly to the growing understanding of the site. Margaret Broomfield, David Calow, Emma Corke, Nikki Cowlard, Isabel Ellis, Audrey Graham, David Graham, Alan Hall, and Gillian Lachelin all had key roles at various times. John Hampton's work in the 1960s laid the foundations for the project and he was consistently helpful. The Ashtead rangers were always welcoming; the project was only possible because of their assistance. Officers of Natural England and English Heritage (particularly Richard Massey and Ann Clark) were also very supportive. David Hartley and the Leatherhead and District Local History Society have provided important information as has Bill Archer, one of Arthur Cotton's grandsons. Richard Reece, Paul Tyers and Kristina Krawiec all provided help with specific queries. Joanna Bird, Louise Rayner, Ian Betts and Mike Hughes have made important contributions to the continuing work on the finds. Joanna has also provided welcome general assistance with this paper, as have the editors.

References

Andrews, C. 2013 Are Roman seal-boxes evidence for literacy? *Journal of Roman Archaeology* 26, 423-438.

Anon 1929 Report of Council for the year ending December 31st, 1927. *Surrey Archaeological Collections* 38.1, xvii-xxi.

Anon, 1973 Obituary of Anthony William George Lowther, esq., ARIBA. *Antiquaries Journal* 53.2, 405-6.

Banerjea, R. Y. and Batchelor, C. R. 2014 *Ashtead Common, UK: micromorphology analysis.* Unpublished report, project no. 187/14, Quaternary Scientific, School of Human and Environmental Sciences, University of Reading.

Betts, I. 2017 The supply of tile to Roman London. In D. Bird (ed), *Agriculture and Industry in south-eastern Roman Britain*, 368-83. Oxbow, Oxford.

Betts, I., Black, E. W. and Gower, J. 1994 A corpus of relief-patterned tiles in Roman Britain. *Journal of Roman Pottery Studies* 7, passim.

Bird, D. G. 1996 The London region in the Roman period. In Bird, J., Hassall, M. and Sheldon, H. (ed.), *Interpreting Roman London, papers in memory of Hugh Chapman*, 217-232. Oxbow Monograph 58, Oxford.

Bird, D. G. 2000 The environs of *Londinium*: roads, roadside settlements and the countryside. In Haynes, I. Sheldon, H. and Hannigan, L. (ed.), *London Under Ground. The archaeology of a city*, 151-174. Oxbow, Oxford.

Bird, D. G. 2002 Chiddingfold Roman villa: a suggested reinterpretation. *Surrey Archaeological Collections* 89, 245-8.

Bird, D. G. 2004 *Roman Surrey*. Tempus, Stroud.

Bird, D. G. 2012 Croydon, crocus and collyrium. *London Archaeologist* 13.4, 87-90.

Bird, D. G. 2015 Excavation at Cocks Farm, Abinger 2014. *Bulletin of the Surrey Archaeological Society* 450, 1-5.

Bird, D. G. 2016 Ashtead Common, Surrey (England): Roman tileworks. *Rei Cretariae Romanae Fautores Acta* 44, 317-324.

Bird, D. G. 2017 Rural settlement in Roman-period Surrey. In Bird, D. (ed.), *Agriculture and Industry in south-eastern Roman Britain*, 111-133. Oxbow, Oxford.

Birley, A. 1979 *The People of Roman Britain*. Batsford, London.

Black, E. W. 1987 *The Roman Villas of south-east England*. British Archaeological Reports (BAR) British Series 171, Oxford.

Blair, W. J. 1991 *Early Medieval Surrey. Landholding, church and settlement before 1300*. Alan Sutton Publishing, Stroud, and Surrey Archaeological Society.

Braithwaite, G. 2007 *Faces from the Past: a study of Roman face pots from Italy and the western provinces of the Roman Empire*. British Archaeological Reports (BAR) International Series 1651, Oxford.

Brandl, U. and Federhofer, E. 2010 *Ton und Technik. Römische Ziegel.* Schriften des Limesmuseums Aalen 61, Theiss Verlag, Stuttgart.

Brandon, P. and Short, B. 1990 *The South East from AD 1000.* Longman, Harlow and New York.

Charlier, F. 2015 Des fours de tuiliers romains avec évents latéraux bas. *Société Française d'Étude de la Céramique en Gaul, 31. Actes du Congrès de Nyon 14-17 Mai 2015.* Saint-Paul-Trois-Chateaux, France.

Cole, R. and Meaton, C. 2008 *A detailed topographical and geophysical survey of Ashtead Common, Surrey. Report Number: 2008025 Project No. 3235.* Unpublished report, Archaeology South-East, Portslade.

Cool, H. E. M. 1986 A Romano-British gold workshop of the second century. *Britannia* 17, 231-7

Coombe, P., Grew, F., Hayward, K. and Henig, M. 2013 *Roman Sculpture from London and the South-East.* Corpus Signorum Imperii Romani (CSIR), Great Britain vol. I, fascicule 10, British Academy. Oxford.

Detsicas, A. 1983 *The Cantiaci.* Alan Sutton. Gloucester.

Frere, S. S. and Tomlin, R. S. O. (ed.) 1992 *The Roman Inscriptions of Britain (RIB), 2, Instrumentum domesticum, fasc. 4.* Alan Sutton, Stroud.

Goodchild, R. G. 1937 The Roman brickworks at Wykehurst Farm in the parish of Cranleigh. With a note on a Roman tile-kiln at Horton, Epsom. *Surrey Archaeological Collections* 45, 74-96.

Graham, D. and Graham, A. 2010 Recent investigations on the site of the Roman buildings at White Beech, Chiddingfold. *Surrey Archaeological Collections* 96, 175-189.

Grimes, W. F. 1930 Holt Denbighshire: the works-depot of the twentieth legion at Castle Lyons. *Y Cymmrodor* 41, *passim.*

Hall, A. D. and Russell, E. J. 1911 *A Report on the Agriculture and Soils of Kent, Surrey and Sussex.* His Majesty's Stationery Office (HMSO). London.

Hampton, J. N. 1977 Roman Ashtead. In Jackson, A. A. (ed.), *Ashtead, a village transformed,* 26-34. Leatherhead.

Hanworth, R. 1968 The Roman villa at Rapsley, Ewhurst (parish of Cranleigh). *Surrey Archaeological Collections* 65, 1-70.

Howe, T., Jackson, G. and Maloney, C. 2005 Archaeology in Surrey 2004. *Surrey Archaeological Collections* 92, 235-289.

Howe, T., Jackson, G. and Maloney, C. 2014 Archaeology in Surrey 2011-12. *Surrey Archaeological Collections* 98, 275-295.

Howells, D. 2009 Consuming the exotic: carrot amphorae and dried fruit in early Roman Britain. *Journal of Roman Pottery Studies* 14, 71-81.

Jones, D. 2006 *The Bankers of Puteoli. Finance, trade and industry in the Roman world.* Tempus. Stroud.

Lancaster, L. C. 2012 A new vaulting technique for early baths in Sussex: the anatomy of a Romano-British invention. *Journal of Roman Archaeology* 25, 419-440.

Le Ny, F. 1988 *Les Fours de Tuiliers gallo-romains. Méthodologie; étude technologique, typologique et statistique; chronologie.* Documents d'Archéologie Française (DAF) 12, Paris.

Lever, R. A. 1978 The earthwork in Ashtead Woods and its suggested age. *Proceedings of the Leatherhead and District Local History Society* 4.2, 45.

Lowther, A. W. G. 1927 Excavations at Ashtead, Surrey. *Surrey Archaeological Collections* 37.2, 144-163.

Lowther, A. W. G. 1929 Excavations at Ashtead, Surrey. Second report (1927 and 1928). *Surrey Archaeological Collections* 38.1, 1-17.

Lowther, A. W. G. 1930 Excavations at Ashtead, Surrey. Third report (1929). *Surrey Archaeological Collections* 38.2, 132-148.

Lowther, A. W. G. 1933 Bronze-Iron Age and Roman finds at Ashtead. II Pottery from the Roman villa. *Surrey Archaeological Collections* 41, 97-8.

Lowther, A. W. G. 1934 The Roman site near the parish church of St Giles at Ashtead. *Surrey Archaeological Collections* 42, 77-84.

Lowther, A. W. G. 1948 [but undated] *A Study of the Patterns on Roman Flue-tiles and their Distribution.* Surrey Archaeological Society Research Paper 1, Guildford.

Lowther, A. W. G. 1959 The date of the Roman buildings and brickworks on Ashtead Common. *Proceedings of the Leatherhead and District Local History Society* 2.3, 73-5.

Lowther, A. W. G. 1976 Romano-British chimney pots and finials. *Antiquaries Journal* 56, 35-48 [prepared for the press by F. H. Thompson].

McOmish, D. and Newsome, S. 2007 *Ashtead Common, Leatherhead, Surrey. Survey and investigation of an earthwork enclosure.* English Heritage Research Department Report 37/2007.

McWhirr, A. 1979 Tile-kilns in Roman Britain. In McWhirr, A. (ed.), *Roman Brick and Tile.* British Archaeological Reports (BAR) International Series 68, 97-189, Oxford.

Money, J. H. 1977 The Iron Age hill-fort and Romano-British iron-working settlement at Garden Hill, Sussex: interim report on excavations, 1968 -76. *Britannia* 8, 339-350.

Monteil, G. 2008 The distribution and use of samian inkwells in Londinium. In Clark, J. *et al.* (ed.), *Londinium and Beyond. Essays on Roman London and its hinterland for Harvey Sheldon.* Council for British Archaeology (CBA) Research Report 156, 177-183, York.

Noel, M. 2011 *Ashtead Roman villa, Ashtead Common, Surrey. Archaeomagnetic analysis of a Roman tile kiln. Scientific dating report, 2011.* English Heritage Research Department Report 80/2011.

Paget, F. E. 1873 *Some Records of the Ashtead Estate (and of its Howard possessions: with notices of Elford, Castle Rising, Lebens and Charlton).* Privately printed, Lichfield.

Perring, D. 2002 *The Roman House in Britain*. Routledge, London.

Peacock, D. P. S. and Williams, D. F. 1986 *Amphorae and the Roman Economy. An introductory guide.* Longman, London.

RIB = Collingwood, R. G. and Wright, R. P. 1965 *The Roman Inscriptions of Britain. Volume 1, Inscriptions on stone.* Oxford University Press, Oxford.

Rudling, D. R. 1986 The excavation of a Roman tilery on Great Cansiron Farm, Hartfield, East Sussex. *Britannia* 17, 191-230.

Scott, I. 2017 Ironwork and its production. In Bird, D. (ed.), *Agriculture and Industry in south-eastern Roman Britain*, 301-329. Oxbow, Oxford.

Smith, J. T. 1997 *Roman Villas. A study in social structure.* Routledge, London.

Soffe, G., Nicholls, J. and Moore, G. 1989 The Roman tilery and aisled building at Crookhorn, Hants, excavations 1974-5. *Proceedings of the Hampshire Field Club & Archaeological Society* 45, 43-112.

Swan, V. G. and Philpott, R. A. 2000 Legio XX VV and tile production at Tarbock, Merseyside. *Britannia* 31, 55-67.

Tibble, M. 2007 *A detailed topographical and geophysical survey of Ashtead Roman villa and environs, Ashtead Common, Surrey. Project No. 2798.* Unpublished report, Archaeology South-East, Ditchling.

Trow, S., James, S. and Moore, T. 2009 *Becoming Roman, being Gallic, staying British. Research and excavations at Ditches 'hillfort' and villa 1984-2006.* Oxbow, Oxford.

Waller, M. 2010 Ashtead Common, the evolution of a cultural landscape: a spatially precise vegetation record for the last 2000 years from southeast England. *The Holocene* 20.5, 733-746.

Walthew, C. V. 1975 The town house and the villa house in Roman Britain. *Britannia* 6, 189-205.

Walton, P. 2012 *Rethinking Roman Britain: coinage and archaeology.* Collection Moneta 137, Wetteren, Belgium.

Warry, P. 2006 *Tegulae. Manufacture, typology and use in Roman Britain.* British Archaeological Reports (BAR) British Series 417, Oxford.

Williams, D. 2008 A Roman ditch at 80 Doods Road, Reigate. *Surrey Archaeological Collections* 94, 330-3.

15

Lullingstone Roman villa

Art and social status in the Kent countryside

Martin Henig and Grahame Soffe

With a contribution by Anthony King

The excavation of the Roman villa at Lullingstone was initiated by Ernest Greenfield with Edwyn Birchenough in 1949, but was later taken over by the administrator, Lieut-Col. Geoffrey Meates, steward of Lullingstone Castle until 1961; in its later stages the labour force consisted largely of schoolboys, not unusual for semi-amateur excavations at the time. However, a number of more professional archaeologists became involved, amongst them Brian Philp who worked on the temple-mausoleum and bath-suite, and Rosamond Hanworth whose passion for mosaics, perhaps fired by those of Lullingstone, would lead her to become the organising genius behind the Association for the Study and Preservation of Roman Mosaics (ASPROM) and the great mosaic Corpus (Soffe 2015-16, 49-51, fig. 2). The site was adopted by the Ministry of Public Building and Works, and what was regarded as the main house of the villa with its mosaics was enclosed for protection under a cover building.

Meates wrote a 'popular' account of the excavation of the villa (Meates 1955) and a fuller excavation report twenty-four years later (Meates 1979), when his memories and those of others must have faded. After considerable post-excavation work, for example on the wall-painting, the finds were appraised by various specialists in a volume submitted by the excavator for publication shortly before his death and published two years later (Meates 1987). Inevitably the excavation must be viewed as a product of its own time. Nowadays other questions might have been asked about the wider environment and associated and less glamorous structures (cf. Mackenzie 2019, chapter 2). Moreover, a modern approach to pottery dating affects the way we might appreciate the villa's history, removing as it does the third-century hiatus (see Appendix).

The Villa: Its nature as revealed by the excavations

The villa has become a showpiece, one of the few open to the public in south-eastern England, and is in the guardianship of English Heritage. It is widely regarded as a typical villa. In questioning this assumption, it needs to be reiterated that without the rich material yielded by the excavation and indeed the quality of subsequent research on the material evidence, we would be in no position to qualify the original conclusions and, indeed, in doing so the villa emerges as more significant and more unusual than it might have appeared to be twenty years ago. Nevertheless, what we write here does require some qualification. The lack of evidence for a substantial range of reception rooms and *cubicula*, does raise the question of whether the entire villa has been located or whether there might be other associated wings or detached buildings even on the other (east) side of the River Darent. A modern geophysical survey of the ground east of the main building would potentially produce important evidence. How did this villa fit into its landscape and how does it compare with other villas in the vicinity both in its middle empire phase and in Late Antiquity?

Its beginnings may, indeed, have been that of a fairly small, standard villa centred on a winged-corridor house of the late first century AD. The building as we have it (Fig. 15.1) was evidently enlarged in the second century but not significantly, although as we have suggested there may well have been other structures associated, not just for agricultural purposes (barns and granaries including, of course, the very large granary on the north side of the courtyard, which is prominent in the English Heritage reconstruction painting of the site, Fig. 15.2; Mackenzie 2019, fig. 2.2 and cover; Wilson 2009) but as extra domestic space, to allow for much more accommodation than seems possible on the villa as we now have it. One of the suggestions for further such provision is a putative south wing, running down to the River Darent from the south end of the villa building as currently housed under the modern cover building. A simple detached building, c. 5 m to the south of the baths of the main villa building was excavated by Meates, and appears in the report as the South Outbuilding (Meates 1979, 132-6, figs 34-5), but not on any of the reconstructions or the overall plans of the site in the final excavation report. The walling was only partially uncovered due to restrictions on the limit of the trenches, but it seems to have been a separate building, with footings for clay/wattle upper walling, and therefore a simple structure, not a further wing of the main villa itself. Meates dated this outbuilding to the late second into the mid-third century, but the list of coins and other finds suggests that occupation may have continued in some form into the fourth century. He also hypothesised that it ran as a rectangular building to the south (as indicated on the plan in Wilson 2009, 20; redrawn here as Fig. 15.1). However, it could have run in a south-easterly direction towards the River Darent,

and thus have formed part of a range that would enclose the south side of the open space between the main villa building and the river, with the granary forming the north side. An opportunity to check this alternative layout, and explore the area further, came about when groundworks were undertaken in the area to the south-east of the main villa building in 2007/08 (Sparey-Green and Hoskins 2009; Ward 2008). Roman rubble was present, but unfortunately no structural remains were located, and thus a full-length south wing equivalent to the granary on the north side of the complex (Fig. 15.2) continues to be a hypothesis rather than a proven entity.

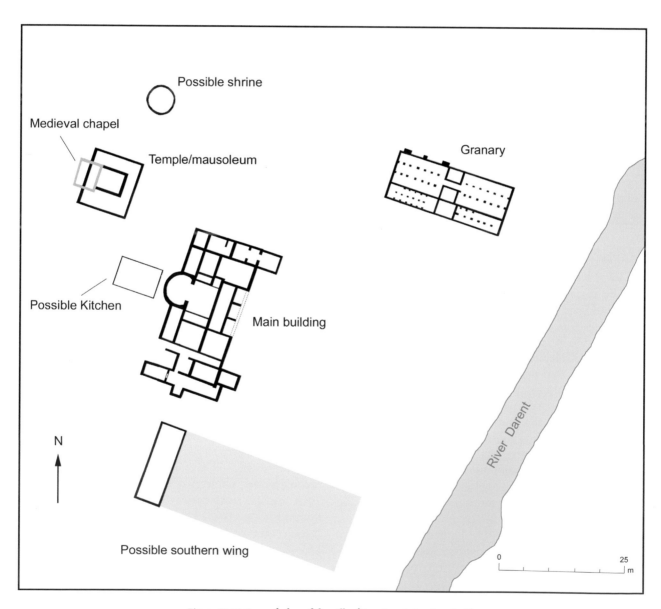

Figure 15.1A General plan of the villa. (Drawing: © Stephen Cosh)

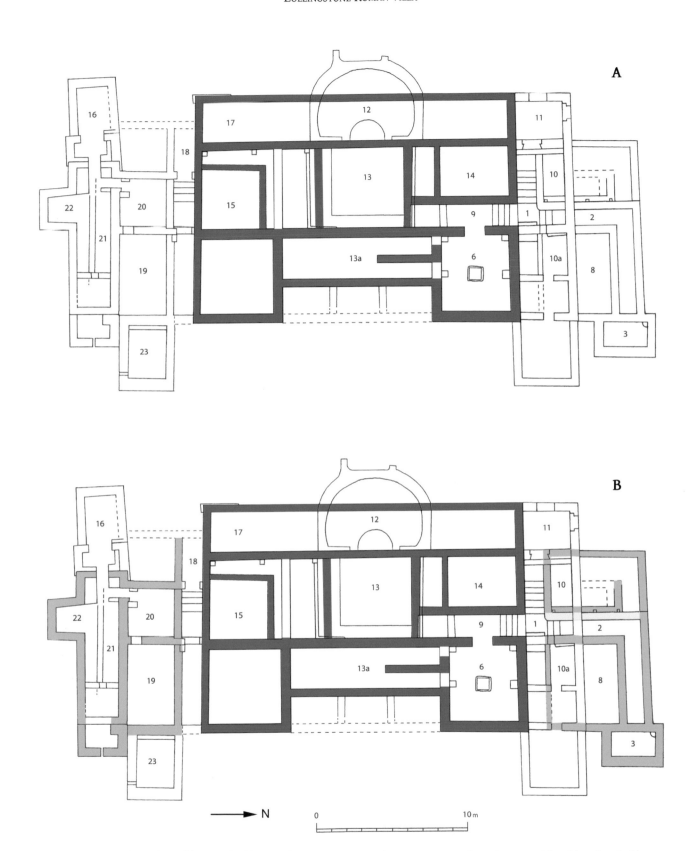

A

B

N

0   10 m

Figure 15.1B Phase plans of the main building. **A** *Phase 1, AD 80-150:* **B** *Phase 2, AD 150-275. (Drawing: © David Neal/Stephen Cosh)*

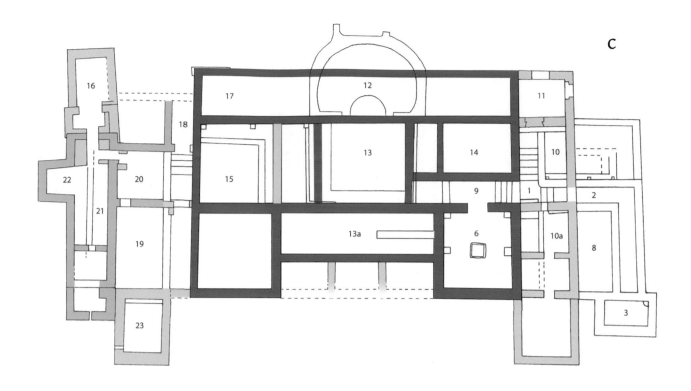

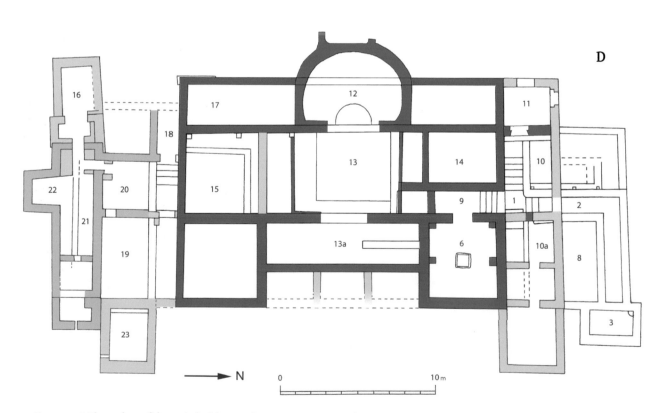

Figure 15.1B Phase plans of the main building. **C** *Phase 3, AD 275-350;* **D** *Phase 4, AD 350 and later. (Drawing: © David Neal/Stephen Cosh)*

Figure 15.2 Reconstruction of Lullingstone villa in its landscape setting in the late fourth century A.D. Apart from the main building with temple-mausoleum behind, a garden is shown running down to the River Darent, with the granary on the north side. The circular shrine, the possible detached kitchen and the south wing opposite the granary are not shown. (Painting: Peter Urmston, © Historic England Archive)

The structure now visible to the public would seem, for the most part, to have been given over to ceremonial functions, bathing, dining and religious. Indeed, the building, being sited very close to the River Darent, surely had a highly significant religious function from early in its life, alongside any presumed residential, use. West of the villa a circular structure was probably built as a shrine while the cellar of the main building itself, Meates's 'Deep Room', was furnished with a prominent niche within which three water-nymphs were painted. This is a richly coloured fresco executed in a classical style with considerable vigour and it is a work of the highest quality which can be dated to the last quarter of the second century (Davey and Ling 1981, 136-8, pls LIV and LV; Meates 1987, 9-11). As the building is situated alongside the River Darent it is tempting to see this as a functioning *nymphaeum* dedicated to the local nymphs. It is possible that there was a free-standing figure of Venus here, perhaps on a small scale within the niche, comparable to the bronze statuette of Venus found in the cellar of a house in *Verulamium* (Toynbee 1964, 83-4, Pl. XVIII, c, d). There were *nymphaea* at Chedworth, Gloucestershire (although this was not a standard villa, see Walters and Rider, this volume) and

at the North Wraxall villa, Wiltshire (Andrews *et al.* 2013). Other aspects of the contemporary painted décor associated with the cult room, including date-palms and trellis-work (Meates 1955, 99-101, fig 7a) remain distinctive amongst the paintings from Roman Britain and could be suggestive of foreign, even oriental, taste, although they are not obviously of a religious nature in themselves. Certainly the villa has every sign of being richly appointed in the second half of the second century; apart from the frescoes there is evidence that the *frigidarium* of the baths had a tessellated floor with a fine mosaic panel at its centre, subsequently destroyed (Neal and Cosh 2009), 386, mosaic 361.2). It is possible, of course, that the principal reception room of the main house had a mosaic floor subsequently replaced by the important and familiar fourth-century mosaics.

The villa as a possible refuge for governor Pertinax: the evidence of art

Two of the best-known finds from Lullingstone are the pair of marble busts carved in Greek marble (Fig. 15.3). One of them (bust 1) is complete and bears some resemblance to portraits of Antoninus Pius although,

Figure 15.3 Archive photo of the cellar (or deep room) with the busts re-positioned as found.
(Photo: Historic England Archive, © Kent Archaeological Society)

in detail, it does not appear to correspond with known portraits of that emperor (Coombe *et al.* 2015, 11-13, no. 21). The second portrait (bust 2) is of a younger man in the style of the later second century (*ibid.*, 13-14, no. 22) and appears to be identical to that of a portrait in the archaeological museum at Aquileia which has been identified by Richard de Kind (2005) as Publius Helvius Pertinax at about the time he was governor of Britain and before he – very briefly – became emperor. The only other probable portrait of a governor of Roman Britain is a marble head of a middle-aged man found near Hawkshaw Castle, Peebleshire in the late eighteenth century. The hairstyle is suggestive of an early Trajanic date, and Miles Russell and Harry Manley (2015, 162-167) have indeed suggested it represents Trajan, but the physiognomy with the pursed lips and downturned mouth are not those of the emperor, and it is far more likely that this too is a portrait of one of his most trusted deputies in Britain, most probably a governor, presumably a successor to P. Metilius Nepos, governor in AD 95.

That the Pertinax bust at Lullingstone was of special contemporary significance is suggested by the manner in which it was deliberately damaged in Antiquity. It has not only been decapitated, hacked from the upper torso, perhaps with an axe, but its shoulders have been carefully sawn off. The suggestion originally made at the time of discovery that the shoulders were trimmed in order to fit it into a putative niche is hardly tenable because symbolically the removal of the shoulders would have removed the arms, rendering the figure impotent, and thus insulted the very genius of the subject. The same treatment was accorded to a marble bust of Geta recovered from the Thames at London but now in the John Paul Getty villa at Malibu in California, which likewise had the shoulders sheered off (and in this case his ears cropped) suggestive, in this case of *damnatio memoriae* following his murder at the order of his brother Caracalla who assumed supreme power shortly after the death of Septimius Severus in AD 211 (Coombe *et al.* 2015, 14-15, no. 23). The desecration of Pertinax's image most likely took place somewhat earlier, in 186 at the end of his governorship in Britain (AD 185-186) when it is recorded that there was a revolt amongst some of the military in Britain. The suggestion is that Pertinax owned Lullingstone, perhaps as an occasional 'bolt-hole' from London and that the place was sacked by disgruntled soldiers. The undamaged bust would in its early Antonine style fit Pertinax's father P. Helvius Successus, and of course there would have been no reason for the assailants, almost half a century later, to harm that.

Important contributory evidence is provided by a beautiful cornelian ring-stone from a gold signet-ring (Fig. 15.4), very much finer in quality than the average intaglio from a provincial site (Henig 2007). The gem had been levered out of its setting leaving flecks of gold in a crack. Such a gold ring could at this time only be legitimately worn by a man of Equestrian or Senatorial status. The subject, Victory writing on a shield leaning against a trophy is distinctly military, and perhaps alludes to Pertinax's distinguished military service in Marcus Aurelius' wars (cf. SHA Pertinax II.7-9). Such intaglios may have been gifts, distributed to officers who had distinguished themselves. Dr Adrian Marsden (2011) has tentatively assigned three gems found respectively at Caistor St Edmund, Norfolk, Stainfield, Lincolnshire

Figure 15.4 Plaster impression of cornelian intaglio depicting Victoria signing a shield which is attached to a trophy. 23 mm by 19 mm. (Photo: © Martin Henig).

and Newstead, Roxburghshire, all of which figure Victory respectively crowning Fortuna, Hercules and a trophy to Severus' wars in Britain. However, he accepts the probably earlier date of the Lullingstone intaglio which was found outside the villa and was probably associated with second-century coins scattered in the looting of valuables in the events described. The bullion (gold and silver) was presumably removed by the mutineers while the base-metal coins and a possibly incriminating signet gem were discarded.

That there were widespread disturbances in Kent at this time is implied by the discovery of two murdered soldiers with their swords still in their scabbards unceremoniously dumped in a pit within the city walls of Canterbury (Goodburn 1978, 469-71, figs 19 and 20); the swords have now been re-dated by Brian Gilmour to the late second century (Gilmour 2009) and that is entirely consistent with the period when the Lullingstone villa would appear to have been ransacked. Furthermore, a marble head of Commodus, dating from about the time he became emperor in AD 180, which had clearly been hacked from a statue or bust, has been found at Richborough and recently entered the collection of Sandwich Museum (Hayward and Henig 2019). Although it could well have suffered mutilation subsequent to his damnatio memoriae following his assassination in 192, it might well have been desecrated by disaffected soldiers in 186, in the same incident that led to the damage to the Pertinax bust.

The building, as excavated and displayed at Lullingstone, was surely too modest to serve as a governor's main country house? Admittedly, like the two busts and the gem, the painting of the nymphs and other fragments of painting recovered from the Deep Room are of excellent quality, but even supposing that there have been major losses from the building, there is none of the luxury such as exotic marble veneers or mosaics we might have expected from the residence of an upper-class Roman.

There are two possible explanations. One of them is that we do not have the complete villa, but only part of it. Presumably the two busts were not originally placed on the steps of the cellar but were prominently displayed, probably in the atrium or the main public room. Was there another residential wing, separate from what could be regarded as a detached baths and dining-room suite? In that case there is a possible parallel at Littlecote, Wiltshire, where a detached building with baths and a triconch apse close to the River Kennet lies a short distance away from the main house of the villa (Walters 1996; Phillips 2022, 39-48). The mythological mosaics here certainly date to the second half of the fourth century (Cosh and Neal 2005, 350-356) but that is also true of the Lullingstone mosaics (see below).

Secondly, we happen to know that Pertinax, who came from freedman stock, had considerable commercial acumen and indeed, according to the *Historia Augusta*: 'he bought up many farms [in Liguria] as well as adding buildings to his father's shop which he retained in its original form' (*SHA* Pertinax III.4) presumably out of *pietas*, in sentimental regard for his father's memory. In other words, here was a man for whom maximising profits coupled with a simple life-style were more important than extravagant luxury. Lullingstone might thus have been just another commercial acquisition, perhaps along with other estates in the Darent valley (Black 1987, 222, fig. 25), exploiting water-resources, agricultural land, and woodland. In this regard it is worth remembering that there is now primary evidence for the sale of property in Kent some 60 years earlier, in a text transcribed on a wooden stylus tablet comprising part of the deed of sale of a wood called *Verlucionium* '*in civitate Cantiacorum*'. It was found dumped in the Walbrook, and the assumption must be that the transaction had taken place in London where Pertinax or his factors must surely have bought Lullingstone (Tomlin 1996). Thus, it is plausible that Pertinax, who knew that his sojourn in Britain would be short, even though of course he could not have anticipated its precipitate end, was happy with a very modest rural bolt hole from affairs of state. However, in either case, the fact that the busts were displayed presupposes that the villa house or at least its entrance hall (*atrium*) had a public function where clients, and those who wished to seek favour from the governor, as representative of the emperor, would have come to pay their respects. The very possession of the two marble busts of father and son was thus, inevitably, a flaunting of an aspirational family with influence and power.

Although, as stated, Lullingstone was just one of a number of villas in the Darent valley, at about sixteen miles (26 km) from London it would certainly have made a convenient rural retreat for the governor when he was not in the north on campaign, on circuit as a judge or required for miscellaneous reasons elsewhere in his province. As a weekend home, indeed, its relationship with regard to the provincial capital, *Londinium*, inevitably reminds us of the younger Pliny's Laurentine villa (Pliny, *Ep.* 17) which he tells us was seventeen miles from Rome 'so that having finished your business in the City, you can spend the night there after completing a full day's work'. Just as Pliny did he might have traveled in a vehicle and, indeed, Lullingstone has yielded an axle-cap from such a carriage embellished with a lion's mask for protection (Meates 1987, 71 and 74, fig. 30, no. 148); though this comes from a fourth-century pit it is very likely earlier. There is also – and of course this is not in the least an unusual find – at least one harness fitting from the site (Meates 1987, 74, fig. 30, no. 158). Pliny's villa was extravagantly furnished compared with the main house at Lullingstone, but in the first place Pertinax would have known that he would only use his Lullingstone retreat on a few occasions during a short and strenuous governorship after which, in all probability, he would never see it again, and secondly his tastes were very much simpler and more abstemious than Pliny's. Even so, as noted above, there were other buildings to north and south of the main house, rendering Lullingstone a rather larger villa than it is currently presented by English Heritage, though still without any real luxury in its appointment like that for instance of the late first-century villa at Fishbourne, the probable residence of the client king Tiberius Claudius Togidubnus. It would, nevertheless, have needed, apart from the granary, stabling for horses, a carriage house, and accommodation for the governor's retinue.

It is, however, highly significant that the busts were retained after the violent incident in which Pertinax's was decapitated, and this suggests either that later generations of owners were related to Pertinax in some way or else that they were clients of the family. They, at least, must have continued to respect the memory of the former governor and (briefly) emperor and of his father by re-erecting the two busts, albeit the former still in a damaged state, within the 'cellar room'. This room indeed had a continuing religious function well into Late Antiquity. Relevant to this is a renewed study of the pottery by Anthony King (see Appendix), which shows that there was, in fact, no hiatus between the late second century and the later third century as the excavators had believed.

Lullingstone villa in the early fourth century

In the early fourth century the niche containing paintings of the nymphs was filled in for some reason, possibly because the nymphs were venerated in some more suitable place and a temple-like building was built near the circular shrine though this served as a tomb, containing two coffined burials though one was subsequently removed. The surviving lead coffin is ornamented with pecten-shells indicative of the sea over which the dead pass over to the Isles of the Blessed. The woman was buried with two silver spoons which can be dated to the early fourth century (Meates 1987, 61-63, fig. 23, nos 54 and 55) and pottery vessels for dining and drinking, as well as a box inlaid with incised bone fittings of which seventeen were recovered, all geometric apart from a protective device, a vigorously rendered mask of Medusa, carefully placed at the head of the coffin; the Medusa is comparable in style to incised female heads from a casket excavated in a villa at Fordham, Essex which is likewise of fourth-century date. The Lullingstone box comes from a small group of fourth-century wooden boxes decorated with figural and geometric shapes, though perhaps only on one side (Stephen Greep, *pers. comm.*). It probably contained a set of glass counters from a game, also recovered. These grave goods suggest that this young lady of the house was, nominally at least, still a pagan. Such élite tombs are not unexpected in the vicinity of a villa and, indeed, the nearby Keston villa, Bromley, was associated with a cemetery containing a substantial circular tomb and a rectangular tomb. Several stone coffins and a sarcophagus embellished with a recessed ansate plaque on one side, prepared for an inscription, were recorded there (Philp *et al.* 1999, 45-60, cf. fig. 23).

In the house itself, pagan practices still persisted as is evidenced by the votive deposits interred in pits dug into the floor of the cellar room, most probably as dedications to the two busts set up here, presumably now regarded as the household gods or as *imagines* of the ancestors. Similar deposits of late Roman date are recorded from the building excavated at Moor Park, Hertfordshire (Leitch and Biddle, this volume).

Avitus and the mosaics: from pagan to Christian

Around AD 350 or so, the space which probably always served as a dining room was extended with an apsed area to take a curving bench or *stibadium* on the coarsely tessellated area surrounding a figured mosaic depicting Europa, the beautiful Phoenician princess being abducted by Jupiter who has taken the form of a bull (Fig. 15.5). Here, in this alcove, the villa owner (*dominus*) and his guests would have dined on formal occasions. In the contiguous rectangular room was another mosaic with a representation of the hero Bellerophon, mounted on the winged horse Pegasus, performing the task set for him by King Iobates of Lycia to kill the monstrous, fire-breathing, Chimaera (Neal and Cosh 2009, 379-85, mosaic 361.1; Mackenzie 2019, chapter 3). Few fourth-century mosaics are known in south-east Britain compared with the wealth of such floors, many of them figural, in the west, and most of these are in London. Of course, these mosaics were very much a feature of élite society, of the small landowning class which exercised social and political power over its dependents. The luxurious quality of these floors, their subject matter and setting all reflected the ideology of the local *dominus* (Scott 2000).

The bi-partite arrangement of two figured panels, one in the apsed area, which it is convenient to call the 'dining

room' (a function it surely served, as well perhaps as being the setting where the *dominus* received his clients) and the other in the contiguous rectangular area which has been described as the 'audience chamber' is replicated in other mosaic floored rooms for instance in the West Country, for example at Hinton St Mary (Cosh and Neal 2005, 156-60, mosaic 172.1) or on an even grander scale at Frampton (*ibid.* 134-7, mosaic 168.2), the second an enigmatic complex of buildings on the flood plain of the River Frome, which include amongst their subjects two images of Neptune leading to the suggestion that this was a sanctuary dedicated to water gods (Putnam 2007, 86-89) – one recalls the earlier nymphs shrine at Lullingstone. While the Lullingstone mosaics cannot be assigned to the same workshop, they are most plausibly to be attributed to the same south-western workshop tradition. Although Neal and Cosh reject this Durnovarian link, it nevertheless seems the probable source of direct influence for two reasons. First the very lithe quadruped animals and the very fleshy dolphins portrayed in the mosaic resemble similar creatures on mosaics from that region, and secondly, the innovative and adventurous use of myth at Lullingstone is characteristic of the south-western tradition; indeed the Bellerophon scene is indeed figured on both the Frampton and Hinton St Mary mosaics while the subject of Europa and the bull is also to be found on a mosaic at Keynsham though here the bull sits placidly and has not yet taken off over the sea (Cosh and Neal 2005, 239-44, mosaic 204.10). These connections hint, if no more, that the mosaicists who laid the Lullingstone mosaics came from one of the centres in the West Country.

The mosaic in the 'audience chamber' depicts Bellerophon and the Chimaera and is further detailed with four fleshy dolphins and two bi-valve shells thus indicating that Pegasus is flying over the sea. This scene is contained within a cushion-shaped guilloche border and surrounded by busts of the Seasons of which three, Spring, Autumn and Winter remain. These are, most probably, rather more than space-fillers, and are designed to emphasise the order of the Universe over which the gods preside, and which was kept in order on earth by the guidance of the landowning class through the careful management of their estates (Scott 2000, 147-54). The panel in the apse of the 'dining room' depicts Europa reclining on the back of the bull, almost naked and holding a mantle which billows out above her as though caught by the wind. She is preceded by one cupid and followed by a second who holds the bull's tail, virtually the same arrangement as shown on a later fourth-century mosaic depicting Europa and the bull from Djemila (*Cuicul*) in Algeria (Robertson 1988, 85 no. 164) although there both cupids hold flower baskets,

Figure 15.5 Mosaic of Europa and the Bull, the Four Seasons, and Bellerophon and the Chimaera. (Photo: © Historic England Archive)

the bull's head is turned and Europa's legs are reversed from the manner shown at Lullingstone and the whole scene is set in a crowded marine environment with dolphins, fishes and other marine fauna. The two images probably share the same iconographic source, although the simpler linearity of the Lullingstone mosaic with its more limited use of colour is much more effective and stylish as a work of art (compare Robertson 1988, 85 no. 162, Lullingstone, with no. 164, Djemila). At one level the theme of the mosaic is merely playful, celebrating the dominating power of sexual passion and this is emphasised by a two-line verse inscription on the chord of the apse (RIB II, no. 2448.6):

INVIDA SI TA[VRI] VIDISSET IVNO NATATVS
IVSTIVS AEOLIAS ISSET ADVSQVE DOMOS

If jealous Juno had seen the swimmings of the bull, she would more justly have gone to the halls of Aeolus.

Inscriptions are very rare on mosaics and in Britain only the Frampton mosaic, of which mention has been made above, provides a ready parallel and both poems are oblique references to what is shown and not, as on so many other mosaics in other provinces , merely identifying labels . The Lullingstone couplet alludes to an episode in the *Aeneid* (1.50) in which Juno visits Aeolus, ruler of the winds, asking him to brew up a storm in order to wreck Aeneas' ships. How much more readily would Juno have done so if she had seen her husband cavorting with the beautiful Europa. Anthony Barrett (1978, 311) points out that the elegiac couplet is essentially Ovidian and indeed the story of Europa and the Bull is to be found in Ovid's *Metamorphoses* (2.835-75). Stephen Cosh has further suggested that the couplet is reminiscent of an epigram by Martial (14.180) thus adding a further poetic influence to the text (Cosh 2016). The composer, doubtless the villa owner, was thus demonstrating his prowess in verse composition which he had no doubt learned at school under a *grammaticus* in the first stage of his higher education which consisted of grammar, syntax and composition, where both Virgil, Ovid and indeed Martial were standard texts (Newby 2007, 190-93). If he was brought up and educated in Britain this would be valuable evidence for a fairly high standard of Latinity amongst the élite of the province, which is supported by the popularity of mosaics depicting mythological scenes in fourth-century Britain, some of which, amongst them those from Low Ham, Somerset, Boxford, Berkshire and Ketton, Rutland which seem to be derived from illustrated manuscripts of literary works most probably in the possession of the patron (Henig 2019; Henig 2022a and b), and such a refined standard of literacy can, in any case, be confirmed albeit in a fully Christian context from the surviving writings of St Patrick and later of Gildas (Howlett 2007).

Of course, the subject of the images and the sentiment expressed in the couplet are suggestive of the ethical problem of misbehaving gods who can get away with rape, and mortals who live at the whim of divine jealousy and manipulation. The story of the Trojan fleet, refugees from the sack of Troy, seeking safety at Carthage with Queen Dido and its consequence is, of course, expressly the theme of one of the best Virgilian pavement to survive from anywhere in the empire, almost certainly derived from an early illustrated codex. It portrays Aeneas' arrival, his love affair with the queen, the royal hunt culminating in the embrace of the couple in a cave (here suggested by two flanking trees) where the struggle in Aeneas' breast between love and duty is conveyed by depicting him fully clad in armour while Dido is naked and vulnerable. The central panel shows Venus flanked by two cupids, one with a torch raised representing the triumph of duty in the case of Aeneas while the other holds a torch lowered symbolising Dido's despair and suicide, a victim of love. This mosaic was set on the floor of the *frigidarium* of the villa baths at Low Ham, Somerset and is now in Taunton Museum (Cosh and Neal 2005, 253-7, mosaic 207.1; Henig 2022a, 27-29). A contemporary fourth-century mosaic, recently uncovered in the *triclinium* of a Lusitanian villa, depicts an episode from the end of the *Aeneid* (12.926-50) where the victorious Aeneas with his Phrygians confronts the suppliant Turnus and his horrified, defeated Rutilians (Caetano and Mourão 2011). From the denouement of Virgil's poem we know that Aeneas was overcome in the end by personal hatred and, in consequence, he slays his adversary. But was this acceptable behaviour? Was not this, rather than a display of the Roman ideal expressed by the phrase *parcere subiectis et debellare superbos* (*Aeneid* 6.851), a case of raw emotion blinding the hero's judgment, preventing him from doing the right thing? What is shown on that mosaic is the moment before the sad climax, while there would still have been time for him to display noble compassion. A similar moral question arises in the case of the newly discovered Romano-British mosaic from Ketton, Rutland in the three scenes ultimately derived from the *Iliad*, showing the conflict between Achilles and Hector, the humiliating treatment of Hector's body and its subsequent ransom by Priam (Henig 2022a, 30-32). Newby (2007) points out that such sophisticated, mythological subject matter allowing for moral and philosophical debate at the dinner table such as is found in Britain as well as elsewhere in the late Roman West, contrasts strongly with the general boorishness of much of the North African mosaic repertoire with its emphasis on wild-beast fights and gladiatorial displays.

However, there is probably even more to be discerned beneath the surface in elucidating the iconography displayed by the Lullingstone mosaic with its elegant inscription, than immediately meets the eye, and this takes us somewhat beyond the average expected school exercise, or even what we might imagine to be the common run of educated, dinner-table philosophic discussion. As both David Howlett (2007) and the late Professor Charles Thomas (1998) have demonstrated, drawing in Howlett's case on fifth and sixth-century literary works and in Professor Thomas's on insular gravestones, there was a continuing tradition of cryptography at least in western Britain which must have started in Roman schoolrooms. The first word of the Lullingstone couplet, 'Invida', is itself amuletic as was noted by W. H. C. Frend (1955, 14-15) in an important paper on fourth-century religion in Britain where he noted that the word *invidia* ('envy') is employed as a charm against the Evil Eye on several North African mosaics; it is, indeed, equivalent to the apotropaic phallus sometimes figured for exactly the same reason on mosaics (e.g. Johns 1982, 64, fig. 46). However there is more: if one takes the final 'a' and proceeds to counts seven letters at a time and highlights the eighth, the name, *Avitus* is revealed which is very probably that of the villa owner himself (see Henig 1997; Thomas 1998, 47-53; Henig 2015b, 24). If this interpretation is accepted the Lullingstone mosaic is only the third presently known from Britain to record the name of a villa owner. The others are the near contemporary mosaic depicting the god Bacchus from the villa at Thruxton, Hampshire bearing the name of Quintus Natalius Natalinus and his clients (?) the Bodeni (Henig and Soffe 1993), and that on the recently discovered Boxford Mosaic, Berkshire dedicated to Caepio and his wife Fortunata (Beeson, Nichol and Appleton 2019, 55-56).

The name Avitus is not a surprise as it appears to have been quite popular in the Late Roman West and some of those bearing the name were certainly of high status: indeed, one Gaulish bearer of the name Eparchius Avitus was briefly emperor (AD 455-6) before being deposed (see Collis, this volume). One might wonder whether the nickname (*signum*) of the Lullingstone Avitus was not 'Taurus' because, apart from an 'I' in place of the required 'r', all the letters are there, and the bull which has rather a jolly smile on his face, thus might refer both to Jupiter and to the villa owner, Avitus, figured here mythologically as an earthly Jupiter, master of his estate and thus providing an image of his own élite power (see Scott 2000). Further, it can hardly fail to be noted that both lines begin with an 'I' and end with an 'S' and that was surely deliberate. The letters 'IS' may have been significant, as a protective charm or amulet employing the first and last letter

of the Holy Name, Jesus. Moreover, if one follows a somewhat similar procedure of counting letters in the second line as that which revealed the name Avitus in the first, though, this time, commencing with the first 'I' and counting sevens one reveals 'Iesu' although for completeness we need the fifth letter 's' which is obtained by counting five to the final 'S' which completes the word, 'Iesus'. The cryptography here is assuredly a little amateur, certainly not perfect although not bad for a non-professional after a good average education from a *grammaticus* which would have consisted of the major classics in Latin as read in the fourth century and games with letters and numbers; and together with the literary accomplishment of the couplet, provides a surprising tribute to the range and quality of Roman education in Roman Britain (see Thomas 1998).

In addition it may be observed that both Frampton and Hinton St Mary mosaics depict the Bellerophon theme with Chi-Rho emblems in adjoining panels, at Hinton St Mary set behind a bust, most probably of Christ. Two other mosaics of late Roman date depict the Bellerophon myth; one from Croughton, Northamptonshire (Neal and Cosh 2002, 234-236, mosaic 86.1) simply depicts Bellerophon, mounted on Pegasus, in the act of slaying the Chimaera as at Frampton, Hinton and Lullingstone, but a section of a mosaic floor excavated in 2017 in what must have been the main room in the villa at Boxford, West Berkshire also depicts this scene (Beeson 2017-18) though the complete excavation of the mosaic in 2019 revealed that this was but one of a number of subsidiary myths, the main subject being Pelops' wooing of Hippodamia, daughter of King Oenomaus and centres on the latter's death as a result of Pelops bribing his charioteer Myrtilus to loosen his master's linchpin so that the wheel of his chariot came off (Beeson, Nichol and Appleton 2019). It is likely that the sources for the myths on that floor derive from an illustrated copy of Hyginus' *Fabulae*, more properly *Genealogiae*, and if so the Bellerophon episode at Lullingstone also points to a popular, literary source, studied by members of the provincial élite at school. In any case the Bellerophon and Chimaera episode was clearly a remarkably popular theme in Roman Britain, where it acquired a Christian significance. A few decades before the date of these mosaics, Methodius, who was probably bishop of *Olympos* in Lycia as we have seen the homeland of the myth, identified (*Convivium* 8, 10 and 12) the fire-breathing Chimaera with the seven-headed dragon of the Apocalypse, thus revealing Bellerophon as a type of Christ (Henig 2012). The image thereby evokes a tough muscular Christianity of active 'Works' and is suggestive of the sort of faith the British heresiarch, Pelagius, acquired in his formative years before such commonplace ideas were challenged by St Augustine.

Another aspect of the iconography of these mosaics may be considered. The imagery of the Hinton St Mary pavement may have had direct reference to Psalm 22 in the multiple images of deer beset by hounds recalling verses 16 and 20, which beseech God for deliverance from the dogs encompassing the psalmist (Hartley *et al.* 2006, 92-93, fig. 38; 204-205, no. 190). Bulls, too, encircle him, compared in verse 12 to 'a ravening and roaring lion'. The latter could well be exemplified at Frampton, Hinton St Mary and Lullingstone, by the Chimaera. In addition, might Europa's bull on the Lullingstone mosaic, with its temptation of carnal desire exemplify the bovine enemy evoked by the psalmist, and thus at a deeper level assume a different and darker meaning from that suggested above as merely the owner's personal *signum*? Is it then, truly a 'bull of Bashan' carrying off the Christian soul, here figured in the guise of the hapless maiden, Europa? Verse 21 of the psalm proclaims: 'Save me from the mouth of the lion! From the horns of the wild oxen you have rescued me.' There could have been a subtle allusion to that verse, that prayer, in the juxtaposition of both parts of the Lullingstone mosaic, Bellerophon's Chimaera with the lion on one section of the floor, and Europa's bull and the bull of Bashan on the other. Therefore, just as at Hinton St Mary (and possibly even Frampton, despite its multiple myth scenes as well as the Chi-Rho and *cantharus*) we should not completely rule out the possible use of the mosaic chambers at Lullingstone for Christian worship before that was transferred, as we will see, to a more suitable setting. It might be noted that there are the remains of a *cantharus* in the border to the left of the Bellerophon scene at Lullingstone, while the panel below, between it and the Europa scene, includes ten equal-armed crosses and three swastikas. Although it would be pressing the point to claim that these necessarily have a Christian significance, it is legitimate to wonder whether they might have been interpreted here as Christian symbols.

Nevertheless, we should not dismiss the significance of the classical myths on the highly educated and subtle cultivated Late Roman mind. Like so many other mosaics from Roman Britain, the Ovidian/Virgilian *stibadium* room and its linked chamber reveal the importance of a sophisticated literary culture in the middle of the fourth century, in Britain as elsewhere. Peter Brown (2012, 185-207) sees the mythological mosaics of Britain, Spain and Aquitania as echoing the easy and relaxed world of Ausonius in which the rich or middling rich, both Christian (as here) or Pagan (as at Thruxton) could participate in enjoying complex works of art with highly esoteric and polyvalent interpretations.

It is also hard not to believe that Avitus was, or at least became, a Christian some time before an upper suite of rooms was converted into what was certainly a dedicated house church around AD 385 (Bowes 2008, 130-133; see back cover, this volume). Indeed, did he commission the mosaics to mark his conversion while at the same time reassuring visiting villa owners who came to dine with him that he had not abandoned classical *paideia*? Apart from the evidence of the mosaics there were found fragments of glass bowls with engraved scenes, similar to others which are certainly Christian in nature (H. E. M. Cool and J. Price in Meates 1987, 128-30, fig.54, nos 338 and 339). The addition of the church on an upper floor would have provided Lullingstone with the same sort of elite processional way as probably existed in a pagan context at Brading on the Isle of Wight, where the votary passed from the realm of death in the tomb through the heavenly realms to the sun (Henig 2013). At Lullingstone, a procession may have led from the point of departure for the enquirer with the Bellerophon mosaic, at one level, signifying the eternal battle between good and evil, through the Europa room, the point of true conversion, up the stairs to finally encounter the full mystery of the Christian faith, expounded in fresco rather than mosaic in the upper room. Something similar may be observed in the suite of mosaics at Frampton, where a succession of mythological panels culminate in an apse with a Chi-Rho and a chalice representing the Eucharistic feast as the goal of the pilgrimage (Cosh and Neal 2005, 130-140, mosaic no.168).

The house church and its frescoes

The frescoes in the upper rooms, perhaps painted a decade or more later than the mosaics (Davey and Ling 1981, 138-45, pls LVI-LIX; Meates 1987, 11-40; Bowes 2008, 131-132; Henig 2015b, 24), certainly define a house or villa church complete with a narthex for *catechumens* – at a slightly earlier stage before the upper rooms were frescoed to serve as a church perhaps the mass was celebrated below: the Bellerophon room could have served as a narthex and the Europa exedra as the church proper, though the overtly pagan imagery of the mosaics could never have been regarded as altogether satisfactory whatever its esoteric explanation. With regard to the painted house church, apart from the Chi-Rhos displayed both on the south wall and in the narthex the main theme reconstructed to date is along the western wall, where the décor included a line of *orantes*, men with both arms raised in the *orans* gesture, which, as the name implies, was the usual attitude of prayer employed by early Christians, as can also be seen for example in the case of the *Donna Velata* in the Catacomb of Priscilla in Rome, likewise of fourth-century date

(Charles-Murray 2007, 52-53, fig.40). The Lullingstone *orantes* are clad in richly coloured dalmatics, garments very similar to those worn today by deacons in churches, although it should be emphasised that by themselves these have no liturgical significance at Lullingstone; it is rather that clergy have continued to vest themselves in the manner of well-to-do, fourth-century gentlemen! The Lullingstone figures, indeed, probably represent the assembled worshipping community at Lullingstone or at least the male, élite part of it, who would have stood in front of the painting facing east at the mass. Whether these were simply regarded as members of Avitus' own extended family, a monastic group established by him in the manner of Paulinus of Nola (see below) or a more extensive community of Christians is uncertain (though the clothing, suggestive of people of high rank, argues against the Lullingstone congregation being socially very diverse). We may imagine that the priest would have employed a silver chalice and other vessels like those from Water Newton, Cambridgeshire (Painter 1999) presumably presented by the villa owner and his friends when celebrating the mass.

Just as the marble busts at an earlier stage in the villa's existence reflected the power of the rulers of the empire and their deputies, the Lullingstone *orantes* thus manifest the veneration of a higher power, the Court of Heaven. The transition was easily made. At the other end of the empire, at Luxor in Egypt, under the Tetrarchy and some seventy years before the Lullingstone paintings, the Pharaonic temple was converted into a military fort complete with a shrine to the imperial cult replete with paintings in which richly dressed dignitaries are gathered around the sacred images of the emperors (McFadden 2015, especially 104 and 119, figs 6.1 and 6.16) providing a sort of prototype for the Lullingstone Christian congregation. For them, of course, the focus for veneration was not the earthly emperor but the Trinity, symbolised by the Chi-Rho. Although the Chi-Rhos and the *orantes* are the most familiar elements of the frescoes here, it is evident in figural fragments from other walls that they did not stand alone, for in addition, the décor included panels which almost certainly figured Biblical scenes. Despite this being to date the finest, or at least the best-known, example of a house church in the Roman West with unique wall-paintings, 'important as evidence for the development of Christianity and of Christian painting in the fourth century' (Charles-Murray 2007, 63, note 20) it is regrettable that so much still remains so many years after its discovery to be pieced together and the whole scheme fully elucidated.

Even so, from details of what has been restored, it is possible to observe the same sophisticated taste apparent in the slightly earlier mosaics. For example, as Nicola Cronin (now Nicola Barham) in one of the most thoughtful reviews of the nature of Romano-British Christianity has pointed out that one of the *orantes* previously thought to have a curtain behind him seems to be shouldering a yoke, reminding us of Jesus' words in Matthew 11:30: 'For my yoke is easy and my burden is light' (Cronin 2006, 137-8). Cronin (*ibid.* 138-9) also singles out the Chi-Rho in its jeweled wreath, essentially a ring of flame, together with the flanking pair of doves and a stream of water below, as all being striking allusions to the Holy Spirit. The lively sophistication revealed here takes us into a world in which Christian theological speculation was as fully understood and appreciated as Classical myth had been (and as we have seen, indeed, still was in aristocratic circles).

Cronin writes of Romano-British Christians such as Avitus and his circle: 'they were distinctly Roman (in their use of classical *topoi*), distinctly British (in their artistic preferences and style) *and* distinctly Christian' (Cronin 2006, 139). If this should be obvious, it is too often forgotten. However, it is possible that Avitus later in life or his heir towards the end of the century took the path of Ausonius' pupil Paulinus of Nola who renounced his wealth and turned a villa into what was, in fact, a monastic community (Brown 2012, 108-23). Whether or not fashionable dining continued here in the same manner as previously, the emphasis was now certainly centred on the house church, as indeed was the case in the villa at Bradford on Avon, Wiltshire where the main reception room was adapted to serve as a church and baptistery (Bowes 2008, 176-8; Corney, this volume). One might legitimately ask whether there was a dedicated baptistery at Lullingstone, using water from the River Darent or was there rather a lead tank of a type widely disseminated in south-east England including one from Walesby, Lincolnshire, probably depicting a baptismal scene (Hartley *et al.* 2006, 208, no. 194) and another from Flawborough, Nottinghamshire depicting both the Christian Chi-Rho and a number of *orantes* (Hartley *et al.* 2006, 208-9, no. 195)? Despite Crerar's skepticism (Crerar 2012), we continue to believe that these bulky vessels were most probably brought from an ecclesiastical centre in a town, out into the countryside, perhaps at Easter time, for the purpose of baptising the peasantry. Lullingstone and Bradford on Avon, Wiltshire do not, of course, stand alone in Europe as villas supporting house churches and some of the continental examples of Christian complexes like that of Villa Fortunatus in north-east Spain (Bowes 2008, 133-5) were on a vastly more lavish scale. Ultimately such sites could become the location of monastic estates which continued to exercise secular as well as spiritual power and influence.

Lullingstone at the end of the Roman period and after

How long Lullingstone remained, in part at least, as a 'normal' residential villa or whether, as was sometimes the case, its latest existence was converted into a designated Christian religious site is not at present known. The excavators and the author of the present Lullingstone guidebook (Wilson 2009, 31 and 34) place its end in the fifth century but the basis for this is simply the general absence of coins which in any case are virtually non-existent as site finds later than the very beginning of the century. The temple-tomb was partly incorporated into a chapel on the site which, in the form in which it survived as a ruin into modern times, looks basically Romanesque though it might well have had earlier Anglo-Saxon origins? Indeed, did the mausoleum itself become a place of worship even during the period in which the house church remained in use? Was it, indeed, believed to be the resting place of especially holy people, 'the very special dead' as Peter Brown (1981, 69-85) describes them, if not of actual martyrs? (Henig 2008, 198-9). The sequence from villa and mausoleum to church is generally difficult to substantiate but may have been true in several instances where a later church overlies a villa as at Southwell, Nottinghamshire, and there is persuasive evidence that such may likewise have been the case at Thorney Island, on the site of Westminster Abbey, where there is evidence pointing to a villa and a mausoleum in the area of the later monastery (Henig 2015a). John Blair (2005, 70-71) cites two further cases in Kent of the re-use, under Frankish influence, one of a Roman mausoleum in the late sixth or early seventh century in east Kent at St Martin's, Canterbury, and the second at Stone-by-Faversham, although without positing continuity from the Roman period. The issue of continuity does, however, require sympathetic consideration, whether as true continuity in the form of regular worship or simply of folk memory by local Christians over a generation or so. To these should be added Eccles, near Maidstone, where a large villa has been excavated (Detsicas 1977; Stoodley and Cosh 2021), and where evidence for Christian continuity is suggested by the place name itself (Blair 2005, 24).

An unusual hanging-bowl, the Lullingstone bowl, was found in 1859 associated with a 'Saxon' burial north of the Lullingstone villa (Bruce-Mitford 2005, 175-9, no. 43). Like other such bowls it has enameled escutcheons though the imagery of the applied plaques which includes prominent double axes, deer, birds and fish is highly distinctive. The naturalistic stag has been compared with a similar animal on the Book of Durrow and has led to suggestions of a north British origin, although it may rather be of local Kentish manufacture, and quite a large proportion of known hanging bowls come from this part of the country. The Lullingstone bowl has been ascribed to the late seventh-eighth century, though it might be somewhat earlier. The earliest hanging-bowls have been dated back as early as the late fourth and early fifth centuries in late Roman times, and the type was very likely intended for hand-washing. In Christian context this would have included ritual ablutions by the priest before celebrating the Eucharist, and indeed the find spots of some such bowls, notably from a grave at St Paul-in-the-Bail, Lincoln, probably dating soon after the foundation of the church in 627 (Bruce-Mitford 2005, 191-9, no. 53), and from St Martin-in-the-Fields, London are certainly suggestive of their Christian use (Harris and Henig 2010, 31). The Lullingstone bowl provides another example, dating from the Conversion period in Kent. However, a glass bowl of late fifth-century date from a sixth-century cemetery in Darenth Park, Dartford, a few miles further north in the Darent Valley may provide further evidence for the continuance of Christian culture in the Lullingstone region (Webster, Harden and Hassall 1980). Moulded on the base is a prominent Chi-Rho, and around it an inscription which commemorates, in a phrase which echoes the language of Christ in John's Gospel (14:6), St Rufinus, probably the martyr St Rufinus of Soissons, killed with one Valerius in the Great Persecution. Incidentally, Kent may have had its own local martyr called Sixtus, whose cult continued through the fifth and sixth centuries only to be suppressed at the time of the Augustinian mission (Sharpe 2002, 123-125; Blair 2005, 24).

Throughout its history Lullingstone remained an unusual and distinctive villa, if it was ever truly a villa in the classical sense of the word. Although the excavated building is small its high status (albeit muted in terms of luxury) is evinced by the late second century through the presence of the marble portrait busts and the high quality cornelian intaglio from a gold signet ring which suggest a link to the Roman governor, Pertinax, though it is hard to see the building, at least as excavated, as large enough for an élite residence which would have needed to house a large staff, especially if the resident was a governor. And yet by the early fourth century there were very rich burials in a grand mausoleum, figured mosaics (the only ones of this period yet discovered in Kent), and subsequently a richly decorated house church. That there seems always to have been an important religious aspect in the arrangement of the building is indicated by the cellar ("deep room" as Meates styled it) with its paintings of the nymphs, and by the mosaics in the triclinium, depicting two Classical myths. The latter are perhaps already indicative of the owner's Christian leanings which would have become much more overt with the construction of the church.

Conclusion

In speaking and writing of another site, Chedworth, discussed elsewhere in this volume, the late Dr Graham Webster often posed a seemingly obtuse question: 'Where is the villa?' We saw what he meant by this; there were peculiar aspects at Chedworth which did not fit squarely with a 'normal' villa and these are explored in another contribution to this volume. Lullingstone is very different from Chedworth; it is much smaller to start with, but the same question can be posed.

Although grander, and more elaborate as well as multi-phased, the main house at Lullingstone has something in common with the triconch building at Littlecote, Wiltshire with its figural mosaics, there alluding to a pagan (Orphic/Dionysiac) cult (Cosh and Neal 2005, 350-55) which provided a dining hall and cult centre for votaries but no living accommodation. However, this building was set only a few metres away from the main, residential house. As with the position of Lullingstone, it too was situated beside a fast-flowing stream, there the River Kennet, and in that case almost certainly exclusively served the purposes of cult (Walters 1996; Phillips 2022, 39-48; Cosh and Neal 2005, 350-355). In other words, by analogy, most of the actual residential and ancillary agricultural buildings of Lullingstone (apart from the granary) are yet to be found and fully investigated. If the mosaics at Lullingstone were in use at the same time as the house church above to provide a processional way, comparison could also be made with the villa at Brading, likewise a winged-corridor house where a succession of mosaic-floored rooms in the west wing are suggestive of a processional way from the realm of death symbolised by tombs guarded by the Egyptian gods Anubis and Thoth through the realm of the heavens to the sun (see Henig 2013; Tomalin, this volume) and possibly also at Frampton where the sequence of mosaics may have begun with the realm of Neptune and ended with the Christian symbolism of Chi-Rho and chalice (Cosh and Neal 2005, 130-140, mosaic no. 168). In the case of Brading at least there were important additional buildings, an aisled hall providing a north range and other structures to the south (Cunliffe 2013), and it appears likely that at Frampton apart from the mosaic rooms uncovered by Lysons, there were other elements comprising the villa.

Secondly, as hinted above, the finding of a hanging bowl in the vicinity of the villa and the fact that a later church was constructed on the site in the Middle Ages may indicate its former sanctity was not forgotten and that it remained a place of Christian significance and continuity through the intervening centuries. So, the possibility of investigating whether there was a far longer sequence here needs to be undertaken with a depth and subtlety which was not available to Col. Meates and his excavation team.

Appendix: Lullingstone villa during the third century
Anthony C. King

Col. Meates suggested in his final report that the main house was abandoned c. AD 200 until c. 280, with some occupation continuing in an outbuilding AD 200-220 (Meates 1979, 20-24). This break in continuity was used as a basis for suggesting that ownership changed between the villa of the second century and that of the fourth. It appears, though, that in various parts of the villa there was activity during the third century.

In the central room of the range of rooms built onto the north side of the early winged-corridor house in the third phase, a wall was created to form its northern boundary which became the northern wall of the main building of the villa. This over-ran the demolished remains of the earlier (phase 2) extension. This room (Meates's room 10) and the other rooms extending from it to the east were part of a hypocaust system with a raised floor which may never have been used, and within the room up against its new wall a deposit accumulated that contained a *denarius* of Severus Alexander, two East Gaulish samian plain ware vessels and a samian beaker with incised decoration (Meates 1979, 50-1; Oswald 1952a; Pearce 1952). This deposit is listed in the present writer's discussion of potential third-century deposits with samian ware (King 2013, Gazetteer C33) and has an adjusted coin date of periods IXa-IXc (c. 222-60; King 2013, Appendix 6, no. C33; Table 3.I). The room at the eastern end of the hypocaust system also contained a *denarius* of Julia Maesa from its concrete floor and a very worn *sestertius* of Faustina I from the mortar of its east wall. No evidence of material later than the early/mid third century is given, despite the dating of the walling work by the excavator to the late third century reoccupation. This part of the villa (and the villa finds in general) in fact contains a surprisingly large number of early third-century coins and late Central Gaulish and East Gaulish samian ware (listed in Pearce 1952 and Oswald 1952a; cf. also Reece 1987, 49; Simpson 1987, 160-4; Meates 1979, 49-51, 69-70, fig 13a-b). This points to an active early third-century phase, probably due to the villa's inhabitants dumping rubbish and levelling material on its north side.

Elsewhere, the southern bath-suite contained samian ware that suggests construction in mid/late second century, with use and alterations subsequently. There is no clear evidence of abandonment, although a change of use in one of the rooms is indicated by a rubble floor with post-holes in it, with coins of Claudius II and Allectus (Meates 1979, 92-4). The well-known SVAVIS motto-beaker found in a small pit in the floor of the cellar (deep room) (Meates 1979, 35-7) probably dates to the late second or early third century (Pollard 1987, 172-3, 268, 292-3; cf. Symonds 1992, chapter 7). Its date of deposition is unknown and may be late third century or later, but the cellar in general appears to have been kept clean throughout the third century (or cleaned out thoroughly during the fourth century). No accumulation of abandonment debris was present in this room. The detached possible kitchen building contains samian ware of form 30 dated to the period AD 160-90 (not described in the 1979 report but probably Central Gaulish phase IV (as defined in King 2013, chapters 1 and 5; cf. also Heiligmann 1990, 156), to judge from the dating and the brief details given), Rhenish black-gloss ware, and Nene Valley colour-coated ware with barbotine decoration. All point to a late second- or early third-century date. The subsequent hill-wash layers which mark the abandonment of this outbuilding contain disturbed late second/early third-century pottery and coins of Tetricus I and Carausius (Meates 1979, 107-8). At the same time, another outbuilding, the granary, was first being occupied, since rubbish in and around its foundations contained pieces of samian ware, including samian *tesserae*, Rhenish and Nene Valley wares, and coins of Postumus, the Tetrici, Aurelian and Allectus (Meates 1979, 115-6). Lastly, the building at the west end of the south range appears to have been constructed in the late second century, but was demolished in the middle of the third, to judge from two pieces of samian ware of forms 33 and 18/31, and a coin of Valerian from the clay wall debris (Meates 1979, 134-5, fig 35). Subsequent debris has coins of Gallienus to the fourth century.

In sum, there was considerable activity at the villa during the third century, in the form of rubbish dumping, building construction, alteration and demolition. A phase of abandonment is not justified, and thus does not provide a basis of evidence for a change of ownership (for which archaeological evidence of this sort is inherently unsuited anyway). Abandonment in the early/mid third century, particularly of buildings such as villas and town-houses, is often inferred in excavation reports. If, however, the revised chronological scheme for samian ware in the late second and early third centuries, as given in King (2013, chapters 4-5) is applied, together with the evaluation of other fine wares by Pollard (1987), Symonds (1992) and others, many of these abandonment phases are not justified, or at least are much shorter. A consequence that follows from this is that economic and social interpretations of the period may need to be revised if more sites continue into the early third century than hitherto thought.

References

Ancient sources

Hyginus, *Fabulae* = Marshall, P. K. (ed.), *Hygini Fabulae*, Teubner edition, K. G. Saur, Munich, 1993 [revised edition 2002]

John = *The New Oxford Annotated Bible, New Revised Standard Version.* Oxford University Press, Oxford, third edition.

Martial = *Martial Epigrams.* Loeb Classical Library, Harvard University Press, Cambridge, Mass.; Heinemann, London, 1993.

Matthew = *The New Oxford Annotated Bible, New Revised Standard Version.* Oxford University Press, Oxford, third edn.

Methodius, *Convivium* = Migne, J.-P., *Patrologia Graeca* XVIII, col. 27-220 *Convivium Decem Virginum*, Imprimerie Catholique, Paris, 1857; English translation, Roberts, A. and Donaldson, J., *Ante-Nicene Christian Library: Translations of the Writings of the Fathers down to AD 325*, vol. XIV, T. & T. Clark, Edinburgh, 1869.

Ovid, *Metamorphoses* = *Publius Ovidius Naso.* Loeb Classical Library (6 volumes), Harvard University Press, Cambridge, Mass.; Heinemann, London, 2014.

Pliny, *Ep.* = *Pliny the Younger, Letters, and Panegyricus. With an English translation by Betty Radice.* Loeb Classical Library, Harvard University Press, Cambridge, Mass.; Heinemann, London, 1969.

Psalm 22 = *The New Oxford Annotated Bible, New Revised Standard Version.* Oxford University Press, Oxford, third edition.

SHA Pertinax = *Scriptores Historiae Augustae.* Loeb Classical Library, Harvard University Press, Cambridge, Mass.; Heinemann, London, 1967-68.

Virgil, *Aeneid* = *Virgil; with an English translation by H. Rushton Fairclough.* Loeb Classical library 63-64, Harvard University Press, Cambridge, Mass.; Heinemann, London, 1934-5. [Revised edition, 2001-2]

Modern sources

Andrews, P. *et multi alii* 2013 Two possible *nymphaea* at Truckle Hill, North Wraxall, Wiltshire. *Archaeological Journal* 170, 106-53.

Barrett, A. A. 1978 The literary classics in Roman Britain. *Britannia* 9, 307-13.

Beeson, A. 2017-18 The Boxford Bellerophon mosaic. *ARA Bulletin of the Association for Roman Archaeology* 24, 86-92

Beeson, A., Nichol, M. and Appleton, J. 2019 *The Boxford Mosaic. A unique survivor from the Roman age.* Countryside Books, Newbury.

Black, E. W. 1987 *The Roman Villas of South-East England.* British Archaeological Reports (BAR) British Series 171, Oxford.

Blair, J. 2005 *The Church in Anglo-Saxon Society.* Oxford University Press, Oxford.

Bowes, K. 2008 *Private Worship, Public Values, and Religious Change in Late Antiquity.* Cambridge University Press, Cambridge.

Brown, P. 1981 *The Cult of the Saints. Its rise and function in Latin Christianity.* University of Chicago Press, Chicago.

Brown, P. 2012 *Through the Eye of a Needle. Wealth, the fall of Rome and the making of Christianity in the West, 350-550 AD.* Princeton University Press, Princeton.

Bruce-Mitford, R. 2005 *A Corpus of Late Celtic Hanging-Bowls.* Oxford University Press, Oxford.

Caetano, M. T. and Mourão, C. 2011 A 'portrait' of Book XII of the *Aeneid*: the mosaic from the House of the Medusa (Alter do Chão, Portugal). In Şahin, M. (ed.), *11th International Colloquium on Ancient Mosaics. October 16th – 20th 2009, Bursa, Turkey,* 205-223. Zero books, Istanbul.

Charles-Murray, M. 2007 The emergence of Christian art. In Spier, J. (ed.), *Picturing the Bible. The earliest Christian art,* 50-63. Yale University Press for Kimbell Art Museum, Fort Worth.

Coombe, P., Grew, F., Hayward, K. and Henig, M. 2015 *Corpus Signorum Imperii Romani. Great Britain. I.10. London and south-east England.* British Academy, Oxford.

Cosh, S. R. 2016 The Lullingstone mosaic inscription – a parody of Martial? *Britannia* 47, 262-266.

Cosh, S. R. and Neal, D. S. 2005 *Roman Mosaics of Britain. II. South-West Britain.* Illuminata Publishers and Society of Antiquaries of London, London.

Crerar, B. 2012 Contextualising Romano-British Lead Tanks: a study in design, destruction and deposition. *Britannia* 43, 135-166.

Cronin, N. 2006 *Sumus novi dei*: approaches to a renewed understanding of the identity of the Romano-British Church. In M. Henig (ed.), *Roman Art, Religion and Society. New Studies from the Roman Art Seminar, Oxford 2005,* 127-140. British Archaeological Reports (BAR) International Series 1577, Oxford.

Cunliffe, B. 2013 (ed.) *The Roman Villa at Brading, Isle of Wight. The excavations of 2008-10,* 253-64. Oxford University School of Archaeology Monograph 77, Oxford.

Davey, N. and Ling, R. 1981 *Wall-Painting in Roman Britain.* Britannia Monograph 3, London.

De Kind, R. 2005 The Roman portraits from the villa of Lullingstone: Pertinax and his father P. Helvius Successus. In T. Ganschow and M. Steinhart (eds), *Otium. Festschrift für Volker Michael Strocka,* 47-53. Greiner, Remshalden.

Detsicas, A. P. 1977 Excavations at Eccles, 1976: final interim report. *Archaeologia Cantiana* 93, 55-9.

Frend, W. H. C. 1955 Religion in Roman Britain in the fourth century AD. *Journal of the British Archaeological Association* 3rd series, 18, 1-18.

Gilmour, B. 2009 Victims of crime? Ferrous technology and origins of two pattern-welded long swords from Durovernum Cantiacorum (Canterbury, Kent). In A. Giumlia-Mair *et al,* (eds), *Proceedings of the 2nd International Conference on Archaeometallurgy in Europe, Aquileia 17-21 June 2007.* 250-61. Associazione Italiana di Metallurgia, Milan.

Goodburn, R. 1978 Roman Britain in 1977. Sites explored. *Britannia* 9, 404-72.

Harris, A. and Henig, M. 2010 Hand-washing and foot-washing, sacred and secular, in Late Antiquity and the early Medieval period. In M. Henig and N. Ramsay (eds), *Intersections: The archaeology and history of Christianity in England, 400-1200. Papers in honour of Martin Biddle and Birthe Kjølbye-Biddle,* 25-38. Archaeopress, Oxford.

Hartley, E., Hawkes, J., Henig, M. and Mee, F. 2006 *Constantine the Great. York's Roman Emperor.* York Museums and Gallery Trust, York.

Hayward, K. and Henig, M. 2019 A marble portrait of Commodus from Richborough, Kent. *Association for Roman Archaeology News* 41, 13-14.

Heiligmann, J. 1990 *Der „Alb-Limes". Ein Beitrag zur römischen Besetzungsgeschichte Südwestdeutschlands.* Theiss Verlag, Stuttgart.

Henig, M. 1997 The Lullingstone mosaic: art, religion and letters in a fourth-century villa. *Mosaic* 24, 4-7.

Henig, M. 2007 The Victory-gem from Lullingstone Roman villa. *Journal of the British Archaeological Association* 160, 1-7.

Henig, M. 2008 'And did those feet in ancient times': Christian churches and pagan shrines in south-east Britain'. In D. Rudling (ed.), *Ritual Landscapes of Roman South-East Britain,* 191-206. Oxbow Books, Oxford.

Henig, M. 2012 From Romano-British hero to patron-saint of England: the transformations of Bellerophon and his Chimera. In E. Setiri (ed.), *Myth, Allegory, Emblem. The many lives of the Chimaera of Arezzo,* 137-50. Aracne, Rome.

Henig, M. 2013 The mosaic pavements: their meaning and social context. In Cunliffe 2013, 253-64.

Henig, M. 2015a 'A fine and private place': the sarcophagus of Valerius Amandinus and the origins of Westminster. In W. Rodwell and T. Tatton-Brown (eds), *Westminster: I. The Art, Architecture and Archaeology of the Royal Abbey,* 23-33. British Archaeological Association Conference Transactions 39.1, London.

Henig, M. 2015b The origins of Christian Britain: from mystery cult to Christian mystery. In P. S. Barnwell (ed.), *Places of Worship in Britain and Ireland 300-950*, 15-31. Shaun Tyas/Rewley House Studies in the Historic Environment 4, Donnington.

Henig, M. 2019 The Vergil mosaic from Low Ham Roman villa, Somerset. *Association for Roman Archaeology News* 42, 29-30.

Henig, M. 2022a High culture in Roman Britain. Epics of Troy and Carthage. *Antiqvvs* 4.2, 27-32.

Henig, M. 2022b High culture in Roman Britain, The Myths of Ovid and Hyginus. *Antiqvvs* 4.3, 13-18.

Henig, M. and Soffe, G. 1993 The Thruxton Roman villa and its mosaic pavement. *Journal of the British Archaeological Association* 146, 1-28.

Howlett, D. 2007 Continuities from Roman Britain. In L. Gilmour (ed.), *Pagans and Christians – from Antiquity to the Middle Ages. Papers in honour of Martin Henig presented on the occasion of his 65th birthday*, 175-188. British Archaeological Reports (BAR) International Series 1610, Oxford.

Johns, C. 1982 *Sex or Symbol. Erotic images of Greece and Rome.* British Museum Press, London,

Jones, M. and McFadden, S. 2015 (eds) *Art of Empire. The Roman Frescoes and Imperial Cult Chamber in Luxor Temple.* American Research Centre in Egypt/Yale University Press, Yale.

King, A. C. 2013 *Coins and Samian Ware. A study of the dating of coin-loss and the deposition of samian ware (terra sigillata), with a discussion of the decline of samian ware manufacture in the NW provinces of the Roman Empire, late 2nd to mid 3rd centuries AD.* British Archaeological Reports (BAR) International Series 2573, Oxford.

Mackenzie, C. K. 2019 *Culture and Society at Lullingstone Roman Villa.* Archaeopress, Oxford.

Marsden, A. 2011 An intaglio featuring Victory and Fortuna from Caistor St Edmund, Norfolk and a putative glyptic workshop connected to the Severan campaigns in Britain. *Oxford Journal of Archaeology* 30, 427-34.

McFadden, S. 2015 The Luxor Temple paintings in Context. Roman visual culture in Late Antiquity. In Jones and McFadden 2015, 104-133.

Meates, G. W. 1955 *Lullingstone Roman Villa.* William Heinimann Ltd, London.

Meates, G. W. 1979 (ed.) *The Roman Villa at Lullingstone, Kent. Vol.1 The Site.* Kent Archaeological Society Monograph 1, Maidstone.

Meates, G. W. 1987 (ed.) *The Roman Villa at Lullingstone, Kent. Vol.2. The Wall Paintings and Finds.* Kent Archaeological Society Monograph 3, Maidstone.

Meates, G. W., Greenfield, E. and Birchenough, E. 1952 The Lullingstone Roman villa, second interim report. *Archaeologia Cantiana* 65, 26-78.

Neal, D. S. and Cosh, S. R. 2002 *Roman Mosaics of Britain. I Northern Britain.* Illuminata Publishers and Society of Antiquaries of London, London.

Neal, D. S. and Cosh, S. R. 2009 *Roman Mosaics of Britain. III South-East Britain.* Illuminata Publishers and Society of Antiquaries of London, London.

Newby, R. L. 2007 Inscribed mosaics in the late Roman Empire: perspectives from east and west. In Z. Newby and R. L. Newby (eds), *Art and Inscriptions in the Ancient World,* 179-99. Cambridge University Press, Cambridge.

Oswald, F. 1952 Notes on the samian. In Meates *et al.* 1952, 41-9.

Painter, K. S. 1999 The Water Newton silver: votive or liturgical? *Journal of the British Archaeological Association* 152, 1-23.

Pearce, B. W. 1952 Detailed coin list. In Meates *et al.* 1952, 67-76.

Phillips, B. 2022 *Littlecote, Wiltshire: Archaeological excavations in the Park.* Hobnob Press, Gloucester.

Philp, B., Parfitt, K., Willson, J. and Williams, W. 1999 *The Roman Villa at Keston, Kent. Second Report (Excavations 1967 and 1978-1990).* Kent Archaeological Rescue Unit, Dover.

Pollard, R. J. 1987 The other Roman pottery. In Meates 1987, 164-302.

Putnam, B. 2007 *Roman Dorset.* Tempus Stroud.

Reece, R. 1987 Commentary [on the Roman coins]. In Meates 1987, 48-51.

RIB II = Frere, S. S. and Tomlin, R. S. O. 1992 (eds), *The Roman Inscriptions of Britain, Volume II, Fascicule 4.* Alan Sutton Publishing, Stroud.

Robertson, M. 1988 Europe 1. In *Lexicon Iconographicum Mythologiae Classicae, IV. Eros-Herakles,* 76-92. Artemis Verlag, Zürich and Munich.

Russell, M. and Manley, H. 2015 Trajan places: establishing identity and context for the Bosham and Hawkshaw heads. *Britannia* 46, 151-169.

Scott, S. 2000 *Art and Society in Fourth-Century Britain. Villa Mosaics in Context.* Oxford University School of Archaeology Monograph 53, Oxford.

Sharpe, R. 2002 Martyrs and local saints in Late Antique Britain. In A. T. Thacker and R. Sharpe (eds), *Local Saints and Local Churches in the Early Medieval West,* 75-154. Oxford University Press, Oxford.

Simpson, G. 1987 The decorated and plain samian pottery. In Meates 1987, 153-64.

Soffe, G. 2015-16 Rosamond Hanworth: an aristocratic English archaeologist at home and abroad. *ARA Bulletin of the Association for Roman Archaeology* 23, 48-61.

Sparey-Green, C. and Hoskins, R. 2009 *Lullingstone Roman Villa. Watching brief during improvement of visitor facilities.* Canterbury Archaeological Trust Ltd for English Heritage, Canterbury.

Stoodley, N. and Cosh, S. R. 2021 *The Romano-British Villa and Anglo-Saxon cemetery at Eccles, Kent: A summary of the excavations by Alex Detsicas with a consideration of the archaeological and linguistic context.* Oxford, Archaeopress.

Symonds, R. P. 1992 *Rhenish Wares. Fine dark-coloured pottery from Gaul and Germany.* Oxford University Committee for Archaeology Monograph 23, Oxford.

Thomas, C. 1998 *Christian Celts. Messages and Images.* History Press, Stroud.

Tomlin, R. S. O. 1996 A five-acre wood in Roman Kent. In J. Bird, M. Hassall and H. Sheldon (eds), *Interpreting Roman London. Papers in memory of Hugh Chapman,* 209-15. Oxbow Monograph 58, Oxford.

Toynbee, J. M. C. 1964 *Art in Britain under the Romans.* Clarendon Press, Oxford.

Walters, B. 1996 Exotic structures in 4th-century Britain. In Johnson, P. and Haynes, I. (ed.) *Architecture in Roman Britain,* 152-62. Council for British Archaeology (CBA) Research Report 94, York.

Ward, A. 2008 *An archaeological Watching Brief at Lullingstone Roman Villa, Lullingstone, Kent.* Canterbury Archaeological Trust Ltd for English Heritage, Canterbury.

Webster, L., Harden, D. and Hassall, M. 1980 The Darenth Park bowl. *Antiquaries Journal* 60, 338-340.

Wilson, P. 2009 *Lullingstone Roman Villa.* English Heritage Guidebook, London.

16

Clinging to Britannia's hemline: continuity and discontinuity in villa estates, boundaries and historic land use on the islands of *Vectis* and *Tanatis*

David Tomalin

Similarities in their geography and geology prompt a comparison between Britannia's two southern near-shore islands and the nature of their villa communities. On *Vectis* (Isle of Wight) at least 32 villa/Roman buildings are suspected within some nine ancient land units. These divisions, historically regarded as 'centons', were once associated with the mustering of the Isle of Wight's medieval militia. With some minor variations, these boundaries also defined 'tythings' for the annual task of tithe collection in both cash and grain. The author postulates Roman *annona* collection over a patchwork of minor ownerships blanketed by comparable apportionments of land. Analogies are drawn with Gaelo-Celtic land division of the 'ceathrú' and 'rundale' type as exemplified in the Aran Islands and in the configuration of ancient Irish townlands. Brading's mosaics may carry a secondary allusion to *annona* collection as well as the operation of a commercial fleet. Where, in Kent, *Tanatis* (Isle of Thanet), shows a similar intensity of villas, it lacks demonstrable evidence of integral prosperity focused around what economic geographers and others would term a 'central place' or 'local centre' (Von Thunen 1996; Hingley 1989, 111–120). Differing patterns of indigenous ownership, a shortage of shipbuilding timber and lack of maritime acumen are considered. Both islands offer geographic models for reconstructing other villa economies, not least by considering land boundaries that may override and transect personal ownerships.

The nature of the two islands

Hovering at the hemline

Recognised by Suetonius (8.4.1) and mapped by Ptolemy, the island of *Vectis* (Isle of Wight) has often been relegated to the position of an appendage in studies of Roman Britain (Ptolemy 2.3.14; see Rivet and Smith 1979, 487–89). The Solent seaway separates Wight from mainland Britannia where a crossing distance of at least 3–5 km must be anticipated. At the western end of this channel, a shorter crossing distance, from the tip of Hampshire's Hurst Spit, may be discounted on account of fast and treacherous currents and a fatiguing 2 km trek across a shifting train of unstable shingle (Fig. 16.1).

On *Vectis*, an area of 381 square kilometres exhibits villas and ancient land boundaries covering an array of differing lithologies. Sometimes likened to a slice of streaky bacon, the geology of this island offers an extensive northern tract of Tertiary clayland (zone 1), two ranges of chalk hills (zones 2 and 2a) and a broad Greensand vale (zone 3). The sandy soils of the latter are broken in two places by small clay inliers (sub-zones 3a and 3b). In West Wight, the northern claylands are interrupted by an unusual outcrop of Oligocene limestone (zone 4). Beneath a shallow mantle of pastoral and arable topsoil, lies a hard resistant natural 'pavement' of karst limestone bedrock, crazed with grikes and clints.

On the southernmost coast of the island, and set below an imposing inland cliff, we find an ancient linear rock chaos where massive rotational and compound landslides have created the Isle of Wight's 'Undercliff' (zone 5). Here, Nature's fertile hand has masked an apron of slumped and tilted Upper Greensand failure blocks. Here, large segments of the ancient inland cliff-line have slid towards the sea. These have reached an uneasy repose in a wooded coastal zone that is 9km long and no more than 0.5 km wide. Modern episodes of fissuring and ground movement are a reminder of continuing instability here, yet there are traces of determined Romano-British occupation intermixed with talus and rubble. On the northern, or Solent, margin of Wight, a long process of Holocene downwarping has produced a ria coastline where shallow drowned valleys offer the navigator sheltered creeks reaching towards the interior of the island (Fig. 16.1, sub-zones 1a).

As an insular afterthough, clinging to the hemine of Britannia, Vectis deems to claim a unique geographic distinction until we turn to the geomorphological anomaly of the Isle of Thanet.. At the south-eastern extremity of Britain, here is another chalk and sandstone landscape (Fig. 16.2). Here we see a scatter of Roman villas that is similarly proportional to the available land area (Fig. 16.3 & Appendix 1, A & B).

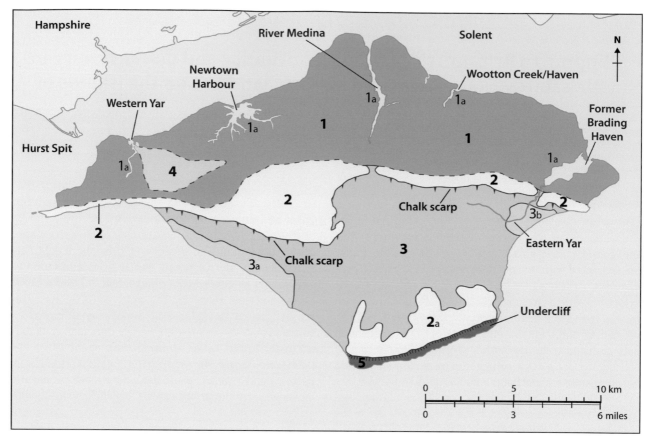

Figure 16.1. The natural zones of Wight. **1** Northern forested claylands, with inlet sub-zones 1a; **2** Central Chalk downland, with southern downland sub-zone 2a; **3** Greensand vale, with minor clay outliers sub-zones 3a and 3b; **4** Plateau of Bembridge Limestone; **5** Undercliff rock chaos and apron of coastal ground instability.

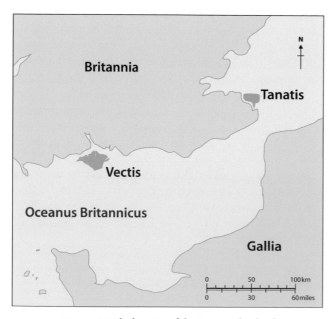

Figure 16.2. The location of the Roman islands of Vectis and Tanatis.

The Isle of Thanet's separation from Kent is now acknowledged by no more than its name. A 'saltwater moat', the Wantsum Channel, once presented a ferrying distance of approximately 1km, until natural siltation and drainage engineers intervened. Once a seaway open to Roman and medieval shipping, the Wantsum was extinguished at the close of the eighteenth century. Today, it is ploughed farmland (Figs. 16.3 and 16.4).

On this Romano-British island of *Tanatis* we find a land area of some 90 square km that was formerly severed from the Cantiacian mainland (Ptolemy 2.3.14; Rivet and Smith 1979, 468–69). Some 16 square km must now be added to Thanet for its reclamation of lands or 'innings' on the former floor of the Wantsum. In Figure 16.5 we see that the geology of this island comprises some 82% chalkland (zone 2) and some 10% Thanet Sand (zone 3). The latter is confined to a discrete area on the southern boundary with the Wantsum Channel between the village of 'Minster-in-Thanet' (Minster) and Pegwell Bay (Fig. 16.7).

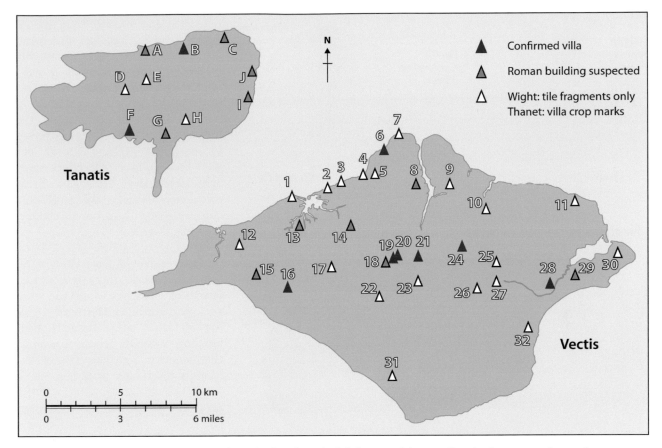

Figure 16.3. Vectis and Tanatis are near-shore islands with similar lithologies. Both have a villa to land ratio around 1:1,100 hectares (adjacent mainland coastlines are omitted).

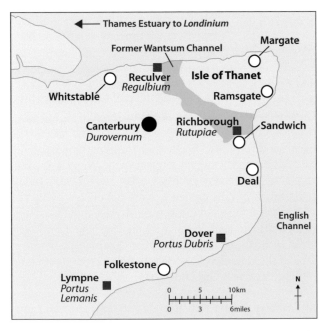

Figure 16.4. The ancient course of the Wantsum Channel and the former detachment of the Isle of Thanet from mainland Kent. The coastline of this channel is approximate. Squares denote Roman shore-forts. Open circles denote modern coastal towns.

With extensive chalklands covering both *Vectis* and *Tanatis*, we find excellent laboratory conditions in which to examine some of the opportunities, obstacles, preferences and prejudices that influenced villa development and land use in two detached portions of Rome's great economic holding in southern Britain (Fig. 16.6). In Appendix 2, Table D, Thanet's natural zones 2 and 3 show general parity with similar lithological zones in Wight.

Villas and settlement in the Vectensian landscape

Like so many regional studies in Roman Britain, the number of recognised villas in the land of *Vectis* has varied according to individual perceptions and criteria. In this text, confirmed villas and those perceived to be so, by aerial photography or by chance discovery of building materials, are all simply cited as 'villas'. This makes for easy expression, but the reader must weigh this caveat as well as the caution that the discovery and confirmation of more villas will alter current estimates of land/villas ratios.

Eleanor Scott's national corpus of 1993 listed thirteen villas on Wight (Scott 1993, 101–2). From personal knowledge I would currently discount entry IW10 for

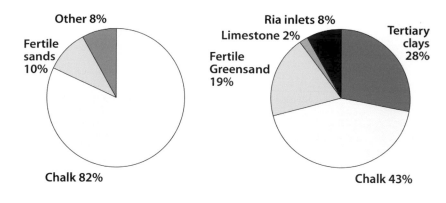

Natural zones of Thanet **Natural zones of Wight**

Figure 16.5. The geological base of the natural zones of Tanatis and Vectis.

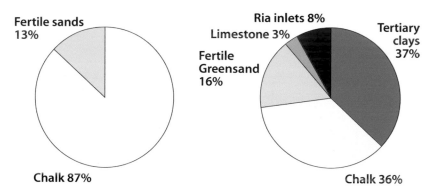

Villa locations on Thanet **Villa locations on Wight**

Figure 16.6. Pie diagram showing preferred villa locations on Thanet and Wight.

four thousand hectares (Appendix 2, Tables E and F). Chalkland settlement, it seems, had been thoroughly established throughout the cantons of the Atrebates and the Regni (Appendix 2, Table G). In the Dorset homeland of the Durotriges, the intensity of chalkland villas increases to one villa to around 825 km² per villa in a county that offers some 50% alternative lithologies. (This calculation excludes the geographic clustering of villas around Ilchester; see King, this volume, Fig. 13.1.)

On the Tertiary clays and sands of the Hampshire Basin there is a virtual dearth of villas, yet where the same geology reappears in northern Wight, the incidence of scattered Roman building materials reveals a reversal that amounts to some 37% of the Island's total land area (Fig. 16.6). Nevertheless, like the terrain of the Atrebates and Regni, the Vectensian chalklands are also particularly well attended by villas. Here their intensity increases to a mean of one villa to around 870 km².

When dealing with Roman buildings on the Vectensian chalk, a little latitude must be allowed. Two confirmed villas, at Brighstone (Rock) and Brading sit at the foot of the chalk scarp where they are abutted by chalky hill-wash. The foundations of the Rock villa at Brighstone actually straddle the Chalk/Greensand junction; Brading's foundations sit on the Greensand yet, like Rock, this building is essentially wedded to the south-facing scarp of Wight's median range of chalk downs (Figs 16.9 and 16.36). Today, persistence of this choice is well demonstrated by the siting of the farms of Compton, Mersley and 'Newbarn' (Shorwell). In each case we find that the farmhouse attends the interface between the sheep-cropped scarp-face of the downland and fertile Greensand ploughland of Wight's zone 3 (Fig. 16.8).

At Combley, a villa also attends the same median range of Wight chalkland, yet it is sited on Tertiary clays some 300 m north of the chalk outcrop (Fig. 16.3, no. 24). A certain geographic pragmatism seems evident here because this location also offers ready access to a reliable spring in a locality where water is less accessible

Newchurch, for this concerns no more than an isolated corn-drier. At Newport, entry IW11 should be combined with IW12 yet these adjustments are of little weight, for when all evidence for detected Roman building materials is brought together, the total number of sites is currently 32. This allows for several individual buildings in the Bowcombe valley being counted as a single assemblage at a site that generally conforms to Richard Hingley's definition of a 'local centre' (1989, 25–29). Although land allocations might seldom be equable, and other types of contemporary landholding may have rivalled or exceeded the estates of villas, it is interesting to see that on both islands the mean available land per villa is just a little over 1100 hectares.

Even in simple tabular form the incidence of Roman buildings in Wight's natural zones presents some notable surprises. A glance at the villas of Hampshire and Sussex shows a clear preference for chalk terrain where the mean available land per villa registers between three and

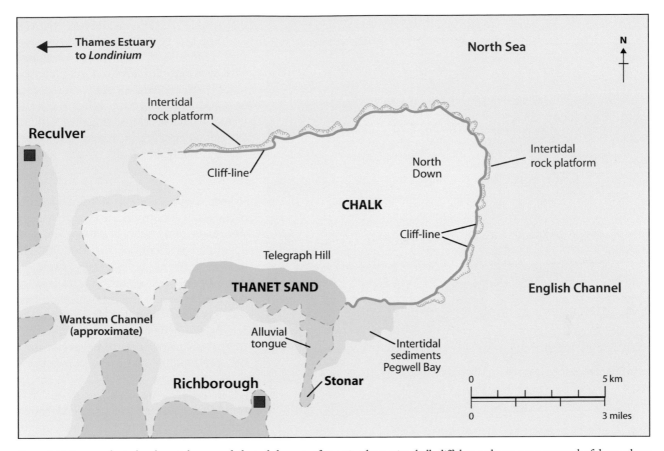

Figure 16.7. Some geological and coastal geomorphological elements of Tanatis. Obstructive chalk cliffs bar seaborne access to much of the northern and eastern coastline. The Thanet Sand offers high fertility. The precise configuration of the Stonar alluvial tongue in earlier times is uncertain.

on the chalkland slopes. In the Newport suburb of Shide, we find a further villa sited just 300 m north of the dip-slope of the chalk. A further geographic factor influencing the siting of this villa will have been the close proximity of the river Medina as well as its head of navigation that is just 900 m away (Figs 16.9 and 16.25, site 1).

West of Newport, in the parish of Carisbrooke, we find the chalk valley of Bowcombe where an array of poorly understood Roman buildings sits close to the course of the Lukely Brook (Figs 16.9 and 16.25, sites 4–6). It is indeed in West Wight rather than East Wight that most of our under-investigated Roman buildings have been found. There are no obvious

Figure 16.8. Compton Farm, Freshwater 2021. One of Wight's few villa-style farms still focused on downland sheep. Its scarp-foot location mirrors the villas of Brading and Rock. In the foreground, the fertile Greensand 'bench' can be ploughed after having been well manured by the sheep. The stone farmhouse is traditional, comfortable and clearly enlarged, a process of progressive improvement we see in so many Romano-British villas.

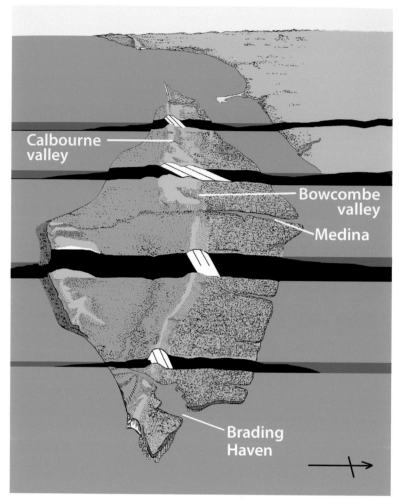

Figure 16.9. Vectis turned and sliced. A perspective view showing the Island's axial chalk downland. In the foreground, in East Wight, is a steep Chalk cuesta. West of the Medina River the gentle dipping Chalk provides broader downland and extensive sheep-grazing.

discernible attraction is the rich colluvial floor of the Bowcombe valley. Here we find agricultural prosperity combined with a geographic advantage of 'central place' (Figs 16.9 and 16.21). This includes east and west axial approaches along the Island's median chalk ridge as well as convenient northerly access and egress via the navigable head of the Medina estuary.

In East Wight, the steep anticlinal folding of the Chalk has produced an acute cuesta where no more than a narrow band of downland is available for exploitation. In West Wight, where the angle of dip relaxes, the upper dry valleys of Bowcombe and Calbourne once offered rich grazing terrain of unimproved grassland, unchanged by agriculture (Fig. 16.9). Here is a resource that was certainly well exploited at the time of Domesday.

It is in this same western arm of the Chalk zone that some of the principal round barrow cemeteries of the Island are to be found. These indicate that earlier populations of Islanders had already established a particular interest in the agricultural assets of this zone. Strung out along a relatively narrow Chalk outcrop, it seems that the distancing of the chalkland villas may have particularly suited the territorial management of flourishing numbers of sheep. Much later, in Tudor times, history tells of conflict and litigation when rustling and boundary disputes followed in the wake of the wandering flocks.

causal factors in fieldwork or sampling to account for this. It is noticeable, however, that the siting of many of Wight's villas seem attracted to positions where a convenient passage may be gained between the north-west coast and the larger tracts of the Island's chalk downland (Figs 16.9 and 16.15).

When we examine the incidence of Vectensian villas in relation to the size of each of the Island's natural zones, there can be no denying that an overriding preference lies with the Chalk. While this outcrop accounts for no more than 16% of the Island's surface, 36% of the detected Roman buildings lie on or at the margin of this zone. A simple explanation might claim that Wight's agricultural wealth lay at the scarp-foot and spring-line junction of the Chalk and the Greensand, yet there are certainly additional factors that have also nurtured Roman building in this environment. A

Villas, perceived villas and the topography of Thanet

On the island of *Tanatis* we find little opportunity to compare Romano-British settlement within contrasting geological zones because the greater part of this landscape is simply composed of Chalk (Figs 16.5, 16.6 and 16.7). Unlike Wight, the Chalk topography of Thanet is less prominent. East of the Wantsum Channel it steadily rises to a maximum of no more than 55 m at Telegraph Hill. Near the cliffs of North Foreland, the summit of Northdown approaches a similar height. This island is too small to accommodate a well-developed valley system but at Margate there are two converging north-draining combes at Dane and Shottendane (Fig. 16.10, combes 1 and 2). Further west another shallow

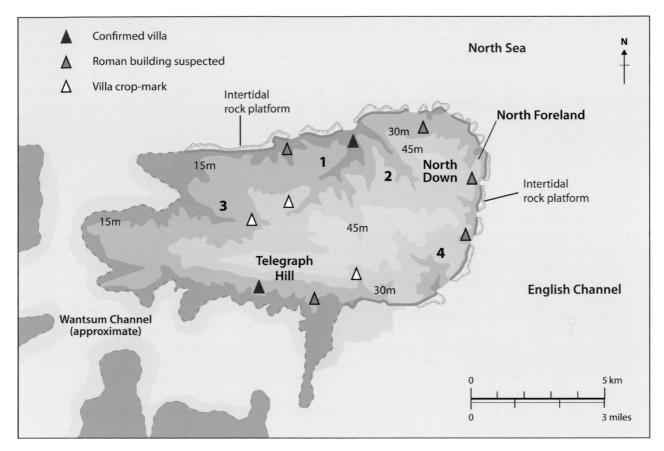

*Figure 16.10. Thanet's villas and its topographical relief, showing the locations of chalk combes: **1** Shottendane Valley; **2** Dane Valley; **3** Acol; **4** Ramsgate, St Lawrence.*

valley is occupied by the hamlet of Acol (Fig. 16.10, combe 3). For grazing animals, each of these valleys offers a water supply that can be otherwise elusive on most of the chalk upland.

The number of villas on Thanet is not easy to define. Writing in 1983, Alec Detsicas followed the Ordnance Survey in recognising only the Tivoli Park villa at Margate, a stone building with frescoes and hypocaust, inadequately recorded in 1924 (Haverfield *et al.* 1932, 121–122). In her gazetteer of Kent villas, Eleanor Scott (1993, 102–9) identified eight sites on Thanet; these were prefixed KE and listed by their parishes. In this present text, a total of ten sites have been assigned letters in Figure 16.3 and they are further listed in Appendix 1, Table B, where Scott's county and parish numbers are also given.

Three of these ten sites had been perceived only from aerial photography. A general appraisal by Gerald Moody (2008, 140, fig. 84) observed that a cob-built dwelling at Cottington Hill, Ebbsfleet, ill-befitted the status of a villa. Since evidence of stone buildings has since been noted near the neighbouring Ebbsfleet shore by Jay

(1990), this general location may be postulated as the site of a further potential 'villa' community (Fig. 16.3 site H; Jones 217, 190, fig. 1, sites J1 and J2).

The present distribution map differentiates between incidental traces of built remains and firmer evidence of a villa. In the latter category may be placed just two. These are Tivoli Park, Margate and the Abbey Farm villa at Minster (Figs 16.11 and 16.12, sites B and F). Greater caution may admit only the latter (Lacy and Mullen, 2019, 77, fig. 1) although this is not a course adopted in the study. A larger figure of nineteen 'probable villas' has also been recently plotted by Jones (2017, 190, fig 1), although his text alludes to only a dozen or so, of which only the Abbey Farm villa at Minster, is named (Appendix 1, Table C).

The siting of Thanet's villas and buildings deserves comment. It seems that the Tivoli Park, at Margate, may have gained a particular topographical advantage in its sheltered position. This villa sits near the floor of Shottendane Valley, the only sizeable dry chalk combe on the island. Seemingly, its occupants could utilise good arable colluvium and a water supply suited to human settlement and the pasturage of animals. In some respect this begs comparison with Wight's Bowcombe valley, where a similar agricultural advantage appears to have been seized.

As in the case of *Vectis*, the distribution of Bronze Age round barrows on Thanet offers a general guide to past foci of human activity. In the village and parish of Minster, the early winged corridor villa at Abbey Farm (Figs 16.3 and 16.7, site F) is sited on the island's localised outcrop of Thanet Sand. This lithology could certainly offer a good agricultural return because Minster secured a particularly impressive rating in its listing of Domesday plough-teams. Since the seventh century, the village has also hosted a successful monastic community. With the abbey and villa (site F) sharing the same locale, this site exudes well-established prosperity. An assemblage or 'super cemetery' of round barrows on the chalk ridge above the village offers further reassurance (Fig. 16.11, cemetery MM).

At Acol, a perceived Roman building attends the head of the lower Acol Valley where a trail of neighbouring round barrows can be found in the Minnis Bay–Brooksend area (Fig. 16.11, site D, cemetery MB). East of Acol, 'villa E',

at Woodchurch, is attended by a smaller cluster of Early Bronze Age barrows (Ac) near the village of Acol. Devoid of adjacent round barrows, it seems that the Tivoli Park villa (Fig. 16.3, site B) might owe less to earlier prehistoric agricultural activities and more to later landings and longshore interests ranged over the adjacent sandy shoreline of Margate Bay. A similar situation might be postulated for the Westgate villa (Fig. 16.3, site A). This overlooks the sands of the Channel coast.

Near the northern tip of the island, the villa site overlooking Palm Bay is set in close proximity to barrows assembled on the adjacent slope of Northdown (Fig. 16.3, villa site C, cemetery Nd). At Ramsgate, the perceived villa at site H shows no obvious proximity to local and earlier barrow building activities.

Of Thanet's ten villa sites considered in this study, sites C, D and E are nearer to the Island's principal barrow cemeteries. For sites A, B, C, I and J it appears that coastal positioning has been a major determinant. In Figure 16.11 we also see that villas at sites C, F, G and H might claim both traditional onshore and offshore interests by virtue of their positioning. There is no particular reason to believe that barrow cemeteries mark the

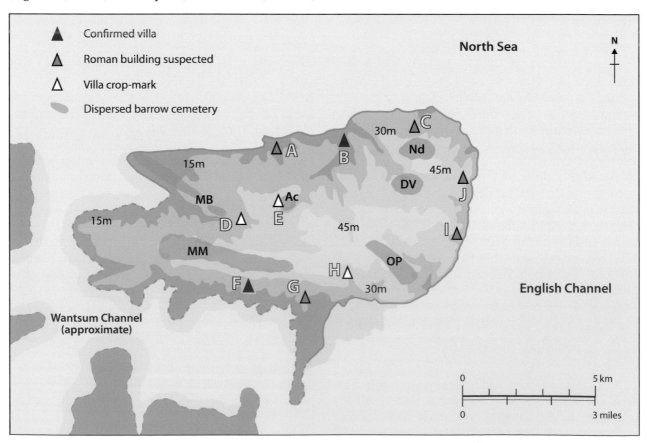

Figure 16.11. Thanet's villas and their relationship with earlier human activity represented by Bronze Age barrows. Perceived barrow concentrations are: Acol (Ac); Monkton/Manston (MM); Minnis Bay–Brooksend (MB); Northdown (Nd); Ozengell–Pegwell (OP), and Dane Valley (DV).

specific location of Bronze Age settlements, but it has been observed elsewhere that barrow groups commonly signify settlements in the neighbourhood. Often such settlements are positioned down-slope, where shelter and water can be found and barrows can be viewed in a hilltop silhouette (Tomalin 1991; Woodward 2002, 74).

Maritime Resources

Harbourage, anchorage and maritime opportunism on Tanatis

It would be all too easy to assume simple agricultural pragmatism to be the single governing factor in the siting of villas on our two islands. On *Tanatis*, where a total of ten villas can either be recognised or perceived, at least 50% might claim a maritime interest (Fig. 16.12). Set near the northern cliff-line, Margate sites A, B and C all claim convenient access to individual landing places. These are opportune spots on an unaccommodating coast that is largely barred by cliffs and fronted by a dangerous wave-cut platform. The term 'gate', as used in Margate, Ramsgate, Westgate and Kingsgate, refers to a gap in a high chalk cliff-line where rare access can be gained to a beach (Glover 1976, viii).

Gerald Moody adroitly reminds us that cliff-recession has progressively truncated Thanet's cliff gaps, sometimes leaving their floors in a steepened or semi-perched position with reduced access to the shore (Moody 2008, 31–33). These 'gates' appear to be a principal determinant for the settling of enterprising communities seeking particular maritime opportunities such as fishing, oystering and the facility to launch and land boats. This is well demonstrated on the Channel coast of Thanet at Dumpton Gap and Stone Gap, Ramsgate, where traces of Roman buildings occur where a break in the cliff-line leads to a small landing cove (Fig. 16.12, sites I and J; Moody 2008, 145).

Set in its chalk combe, Tivoli Park villa at Margate (Fig. 16.12, site B) overlooks a particularly accommodating landing place on Margate Sands. This shore is attended by an offshore anchorage now known as 'Margate Roads' (Figs 16.12 and 16.13; also, Tomalin 2006, 38). For mariners, this is clearly the best placed of all of the villas attending Thanet's 'cliff and gap' coastline.

On the southerly margins of *Tanatis* a shallow and sheltered coastline offers further convenient landing-

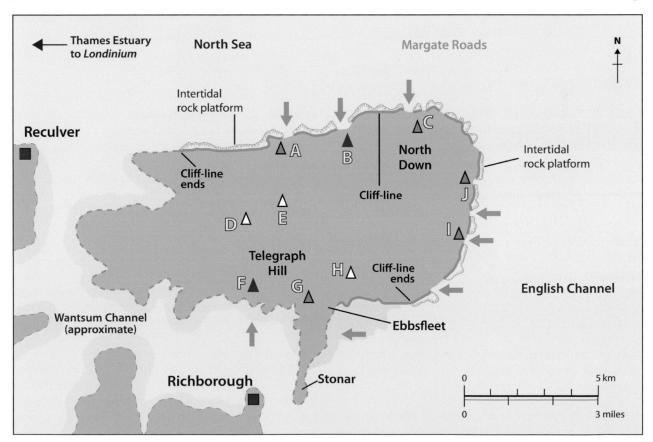

Figure 16.12. The villas of Tanatis and their coastal proximities. Coves with historically attested beaching points are arrowed. Most are served by gaps or 'gates' in an obstructive chalk cliff-line. On the seaward shore of the Stonar tongue the Early Saxon landing-point at Ebbesfleet/ Wippisfleet is also shown. Historically, Margate Roads has offered a substantial offshore anchorage.

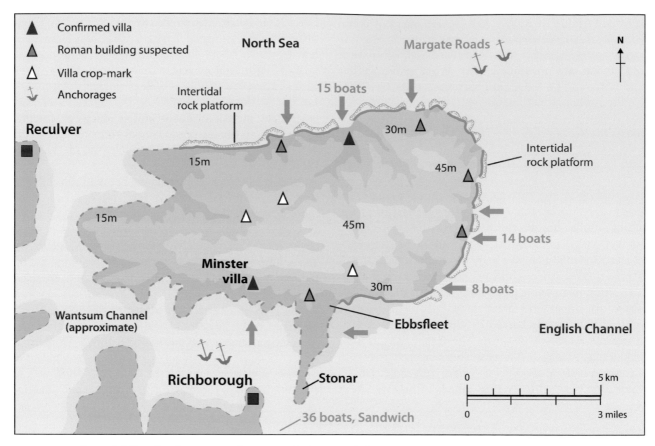

Figure 16.13. Villas and cliff-gap beaching points. Thanet's Elizabethan record of resident harboured boats on the more accommodating beaches is shown. The historic offshore anchorage of Margate Roads is also identified.

places. At Cottington Hill (Fig. 16.12, site H), traces of a Roman building lie close to a long-favoured beaching point at Ebbsfleet, where history alleges the landing of Hengist and Horsa as well as the later arrival of St Augustine. Recently, further evidence of Roman stonework has been noted closer to this shore (Jones 2017, 190, fig. 1).

Where the villa at Minster borders the southern coastline, maritime interests may have been more pragmatic (Fig. 16.12, site F). While this house occupies particularly high-grade agricultural land, it is also very well placed to control ferrying and the provisioning of craft in the Wantsum anchorage. Provisioning of the Richborough garrison should also be considered. If we accept a similar claim for villa site H, near Pegwell Bay, then some three-quarters of Tanatian villas show particular proximity to the sea.

Writing in the mid sixteenth century, William Camden records a very similar predilection on this island, where the inhabitants 'are extremely industrious, getting their living like amphibious animals, both by sea and land'. It seems that this is a clumsy but well-meant compliment,

for he goes on to enthuse that these islanders are at home 'in both elements, being both fishermen and ploughmen, farmers and sailors' (Camden 1581 and 1695, 201).

Another helpful witness of the sixteenth century is the Canterbury evangelist, schoolmaster and antiquary, John Twyne. Writing around 1530 he describes the changing state of the Wantsum Channel when, in living memory, 'not small boats but greater barks and merchant vessels often sailed backwards and forwards betwixt the isle and the mainland' (Brayley 1817, vol. 1, 4–5). Here, severed from Kent, is a truly insular community making every practical use of terrestrial and maritime assets that may have undergone little change since Romano-British times.

Prompted by Camden's reference to an 'amphibious' population of islanders, we should now consider just what the maritime interests of Romano-British Thanet may have been. Like the island of *Vectis*, the climate and soil conditions were particularly well suited to cereal production. Some later writers such as Walley Oulton (1820, 29) perceived virtual agrarian perfection on this island, especially in the parish and the villa environs of Minster (a.k.a. Minster-in-Thanet). Oulton went on to explain that 'the manner of agriculture here is different from that in any other part of the kingdom' and that 'common red wheat can be grown almost all over the island'. Elsewhere, we are told that the quality of the rich loamy soil between Monkton and Ramsgate is so good that 'there is seldom occasion to fallow it' (Brayley 1817, vol. 1, 9).

At the time of Domesday, the manor of Minster had an astonishing deployment of forty plough-teams. With a bountiful agricultural resource such as this, there could be only one hurdle on the track to prosperity. This would be the shipping of the island's produce to market. In the early nineteenth century this was achieved by Thanet hoys shipping out some '24,000 quarters' (some 300 metric tonnes) of corn *per annum* (Brayley 1817, vol. 1, 48).

Writing in 1981, Keith Muckelroy made the point that ancient sailing craft should and would seldom rest idle (Muckelroy 1981, 294). This observation introduces the possibility that Tanatian seafarers, in their need to overcome the moat of the Wantsum, might venture much further afield in their bids to make full economic use of their craft. It seems, from the distribution of villas on Thanet, that there was more happening on this island than the simple growing and home consumption of grain. In the configuration of the Wantsum Channel we find an immense natural harbour capable of accommodating grain transports alongside military craft. On its western shore, the establishment of the Claudian military base at Richborough hints at pre-Conquest maritime activities well established in the vicinity of the Wantsum's natural harbour. Early transactions include the acquisition of a variety of imported Gallic tableware, since recovered from various parts of Thanet (Moody 2008, 132–35).

The siting of some of Thanet's villas leaves little doubt that the cliff-and-gap coastline may have accommodated craft of another kind. An account from a Tudor maritime survey of 1565–66 (8 Eliz.) helps to sketch in the possibilities (Oppenheim 1926, 298). Given the rocky nature of this shoreline, it is not surprising to find that the number of boats accommodated in each of these bays seems proportional to the size the inlet (Fig. 16.13). Thus, on Margate's broad and accommodating beach we find fifteen boats, ranging from 1 to 16 tons, in regular use. At Ramsgate, where the beach is more constricted, there were fourteen boats ranging from 2 to 16 tons. Where the beach at Broadstairs is narrow and small, we find just eight boats, none of which are suitable for anything other than local fishing. Helpfully, the survey adds that the fourteen vessels at Ramsgate provided a livelihood for seventy seamen who were responsible for fishing and carrying grain to market (Oppenheim 1926, 298–99).

Villas, harbourage, anchorage and Vectensian maritime opportunism

Turning from *Tanatis* to *Vectis*, we find maritime factors that are broadly similar. In the first instance we can identify a significant offshore anchorage that, like the Wantsum haven, served a wider strategic function for military and civilian craft destined elsewhere. This appears to be the haven identified by Ptolemy as the *Magnus Portus* (Ptolemy 2.3.3; Rivet and Smith 1979, 408). Here was an area of sheltered Solent water where ships might weather out adverse conditions in the English Channel, or assemble in convoys for longer journeys along the Atlantic seaboard or into the *Oceanus Germanicus*.

In practice, this 'great port' may well have embraced an array of favoured anchorages in these waters (Fig. 16.14). Medieval and later history suggests a total of at least ten particular mooring locations in the Solent, where mariners could find 'good riding' and the security of anchoring in 'firm ground'. Where the sea floor has been archaeologically sampled, four of these offshore locations have produced Roman 'gash goods' where ships have discarded waste items while waiting at anchor (Tomalin 2006).

On the island of *Vectis*, the importance of the navigable ria inlets is explicit where Roman buildings attend Brading Haven and the Medina estuary. To these we can add further traces of coastal buildings close to the northern creeks of the Luck, Newtown Harbour and the Western Yar (Fig 16.15). These include the known villa at Gurnard (villa 6) and perceived buildings at Newtown, Saltmead, Thorness, Sticelett, Thorley and Shalfleet (Fig. 16.3 sites 2, 3, 4, 5, 12 and 13). In total we can recognise that 33% of Vectensian villas may claim overt maritime interests by virtue of their siting. Later, in this discussion, we shall see that this may well be an under-estimate, because historic analogy suggests that wealthy operators and investors in seafaring activities might find little reason to reside particularly close to the source of their maritime income. This is an argument that might similarly be advanced for a wealthy villa like Bignor, West Sussex, where the navigable Arun offers a valuable shipment route for Wealden and downland products and produce. This could include the region's *annona* shipments and generous supplies of iron and wool.

Elsewhere, on Britannia's coast, displays of opulent mosaics in the Lincolnshire villas of Horkstow, Roxby and Winterton may signify comparable maritime investment around the mouth of the Humber (Neal and Cosh 2002, mosaic sites 53, 58 and 68). Cargoes entering and leaving

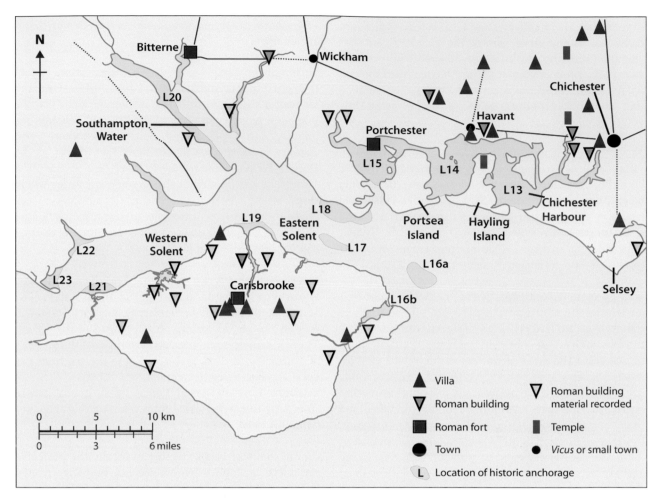

Figure 16.14. Villas, indeterminate Roman buildings and historic anchorages of the Solent region and the Magnus Portus. Seabed strews of Roman ceramics have been identified at locations L16a, L18, L19 and L21. Notation after Tomalin 2006.

Ptolemy's 'Safe Haven Bay' (2.3.4) at Scarborough might similarly account for a further flaunting of prosperity in the Yorkshire villas of Harpham and Rudston (Neal and Cosh 2002, mosaic sites 132 and 143).

When we come to consider a relationship between landing places and villas on *Tanatis* and *Vectis*, we find a convincing link in at least 36% of the collective villas on these two islands. On *Vectis*, the prime natural harbours in the Medina estuary and Brading Haven are both attended by coastal villas, while there is implicit evidence of further buildings near the seaward reaches of Newtown River and the Western Yar (Fig. 16.15). West of Cowes, a minor silted inlet at the mouth of the Luck stream at Gurnard has produced shoreline evidence of another villa, supported by an antiquarian record of a 'Roman wooden quay' (Kell 1866; Motkin 1990; Tomalin 2006, 66, villa 40).

With land-locked buildings adjacent to the axial Chalk spine of Wight, it appears that the villas at Combley and

Rock probably claimed their own respective landing places at Wootton Haven and perhaps Grange Chine (Fig. 16.15). Both of these locations have produced strews of artefacts at or near on the shoreline. While a third of Vectensian villas claim maritime interests by virtue of their siting, these are topped by a figure of at least 50% on *Tanatis* where villas attend recognised coves and 'gates'. The size of Thanet, however, means that most of its stone Roman buildings are inevitably close to the coast.

Prosperity, sophistication and obligation at the coastal villa of Brading

If we draw some select analogies from the Norman organisation of the Isle of Wight, perhaps we might envisage a villa like Brading to be simply one component of a large administrative parcel of land embracing an array of ownerships. This could include various 'freehold' and 'leasehold' arrangements held together by a common local mechanism for gathering rents and

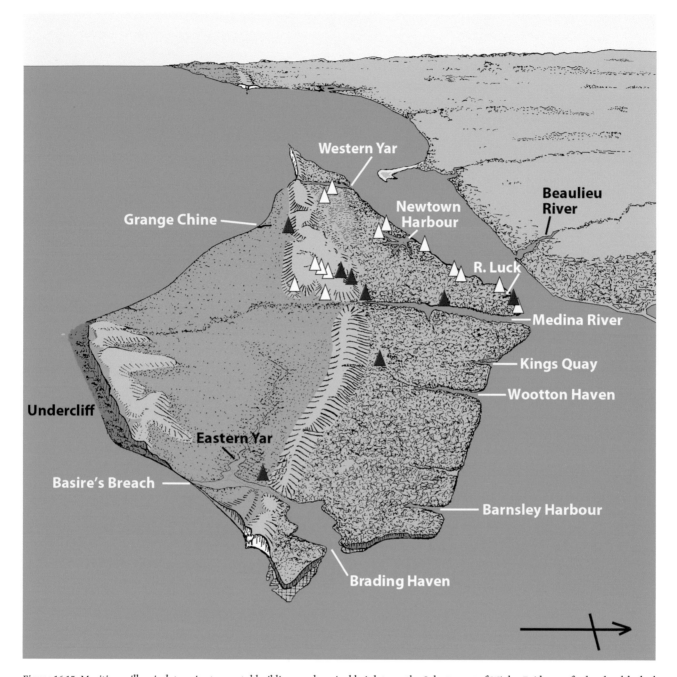

Figure 16.15. Maritime villas, indeterminate coastal buildings and navigable inlets on the Solent coast of Wight. Evidence of other land-locked buildings is omitted.

taxes. To this we might add some logistical obligations to meet certain naval needs.

Sited just 0.5 km from the former shore of a large natural haven, the villa at Brading was ideally positioned for organising both agricultural production and the export of produce. In the floor of room 12 we find iconography that drew its message from the highest levels of contemporary classical philosophy (Beeson 1997; Witts 2004; Wilson 2006; Neal and Cosh 2009, 262–80; Henig

2013). Here, it may be argued, an Aratean view of the Earth and the Cosmos is subtly conveyed for the benefit of a discriminating Romano-British dilettante (Wilson 2006; Tomalin forthcoming).

For local folk entering this principal room, the floor of the outer bay offers a more direct message. Here we see Medusa's central medallion surrounded by man's eternal toils of shepherding, ploughing/sowing, crop-tending and harvesting (Figs 16.16 and 16.17). These panels are multi-

Figure 16.16. The terrestrial themed floor in the outer bay of room 12 in Brading villa. In the projecting panels of the saltire, the four seasonal farming tasks are overseen by Medusa. Adapted from an engraving published by Thomas Morgan, 1886.

communicative, alluding also to rustic preoccupations with flocks, crops, vine and, perhaps (in Neal and Cosh 2009, mosaic no. 331.6e), the management of orchards and woodland. The latter may be symbolised by Daphne, who, Ovid reminds us, was transformed into a laurel tree (*Metamorphoses* 1.552). For those of classical outlook, human transformations might be found by inference in all four saltire panels (Fig. 16.18). Here, perhaps, the mosaicist has also reminded the credulous of the fate of the dilatory.

The iconography in this floor also reminds its viewers that all four of these seasonal activities may be summarily

confounded by the caprice of the weather (Winds). These uncertainties are ever present within the uncompromising timetable of the Seasons. Here, as at Bramdean, Hampshire, are powerful reminders of the unceasing challenges and responsibilities that the local farming community must meet as days pass and the year unfolds.

In the basal panel of the Brading floor, the depiction of Triton, Tritones and Nereids is an explicit reminder of the further challenges that members of this villa community must overcome, when venturing to sea (Figs 16.19 and 16.20). Elsewhere, it is argued that these two particular

Boreas

Eurus

Zephyrus

Notos

Figure 16.17. Seasonal farming tasks in the Medusa saltire in the outer bay of the room 12 mosaic at Brading villa.

*Figure 16.18. Allusions to human transformations in Ovid's Metamorphoses
are conveyed in the room 12 saltire at Brading.*

Figure 16.19. With his steersman oar, Brading's Triton assumes the role of navigator, master and captain. With his bowl of oysters, he offers the fruits of the sea. Yet in his nether regions perhaps we glimpse our villa owner's alter ego. His coiled tails intimate speed and efficiency, his spear-like penis a piratical ability to ravage. (This image has been graphically enhanced.)

Figure 16.20. In Brading's maritime panel, a muscular Triton, possibly Gaaeos, alludes to the power of the sea and, the bounty of its lurking fish. His crook symbolises his helpful disposition. His female companion is perhaps Leukothea, a deified guardian of seafarers. Here is potent imagery for an insular community focused on its maritime assets and the harvesting and shipment of its grain. (This image has been graphically enhanced.)

depictions of daughters of Nereus may represent Akte and Leukothea. In myth, these are, respectively, a guardian of the shore and a guardian of mariners (Tomalin forthcoming).

While room 8 at Brading is conventionally positioned to serve as a household dining room (*triclinium*), room 12 is well suited to be an audience chamber where, among other activities, tenants, bailiffs and defaulters on *annona* might be summoned. Set firmly at the head of the inner bay, we may envisage the chaired adjudicator. His agenda may ensure that quotas and responsibilities within his jurisdiction are fulfilled within the seasonal calendar that is articulated in the polychrome imagery set out at his feet. (See Neal and Cosh 2009, 273 for a general view of this floor and its border image, in which the sun is represented by a swastika.)

Elsewhere, the present writer argues that the weak and damp bedding of these mosaics and the provision of a remote and cramped bath house makes this principal residence at Brading best suited to the summer visits of an absentee *dominus*. The seasonal iconography of the mosaics in room 12 also befits an annual summer residency, perhaps terminating on or shortly after the specific date of 10 September (Tomalin forthcoming).

Villas, markets and exports in an insular setting

Set at the epicentre of the island of *Vectis*, the Bowcombe valley accommodates at least seven Roman stone buildings. Here is evidence that a geographer's 'central place' has long been present in the island of *Vectis*. Caution is needed here because when Christaller proposed such a theoretical entity, in 1933, he postulated a homogeneous or undifferentiated landscape in which a central trading hub might eventually emerge within a lattice of equidistant rural settlements. Economies in transport costs and the exercise of rational choice, he suggested, would pre-determine this centralised position.

Moving from the theoretical to the practical, Richard Hingley has advanced the term 'local centres' for settlements of *vicus* size scattered across the Romano-British landscape (Hingley 1989, 86–94). Since these simple civil trading communities can be either enclosed or unenclosed, they offer an appealing analogy with the perceived settlement on the valley floor at Bowcombe. As *vici* are frequently sited at convenient gathering points on Roman roads, their origins may differ from the generally unplanned evolution of the central place.

In Wight, however, Bowcombe and its medieval successor, Newport, fulfilled the role of a central place, while Hingley's alternative term of 'local centre' acknowledges

the influence of wider determining factors. When a fine Norman church was eventually constructed by the brethren of Lyre, the importance of the Bowcombe valley was confirmed. Yet shortly after this event, it was navigational opportunities and maritime interests that eventually secured a shift of the population to a waterfront position at Newport (Figs 16.21 and 16.22).

Defence of this Bowcombe community was first marked by a fortified stronghold or 'enclosure' on Carisbrooke's Castle Hill. Its eventual replacement by a Norman castle suggests that geographic conditions concerning the economic organisation of the Island may have seen little functional change between the Roman Conquest and the first invasion of tourists and entrepreneurs in the mid-nineteenth century.

If the Bowcombe/Carisbrooke community simply evolved and functioned as Wight's central place then, using Christaller's standard geographic model, we might predict one or more tiers of subordinate and contributory settlements set relatively equidistant across the rest of the Island. While we may perceive some evidence of this in Figure 16.21, plain Christallerian arguments such as these have been commonly criticised for their disregard for varied topography, unevenness of resources and the influence of pre-established populations (Preston 1983).

Within the confines of Wight, variable access to good quality farmland and limited access to ports has certainly skewed the interests and viabilities of smaller communities. Nevertheless, we must allow that a central place has indeed evolved and retained its singular function on this island while shifting its position by about 1.6km over the course of a millennium (Fig. 16.22).

An appealing alternative to the Christaller model is to view the emergence of Romano-British Bowcombe and its ensemble of Romano-British buildings as a product of 'central flow'. Such a process would promote this community's on-going vitality by engaging with a wide spectrum of the Empire's markets (Taylor 2007). In the previous model, Bowcombe's role could be largely re-distributive, as Newport is today, but in the second scenario it could gain increasing prosperity from the economic health and wealth of the Empire. Here is a mechanism by which the general economic status of Romano-British *Vectis* might be raised, while purpose and explanation might be added to account for its generous number of villas.

In Figure 16.23 the principal geographic and economic attributes of *Vectis* are set out in schematic form. Here we see a simple division between agricultural wealth in

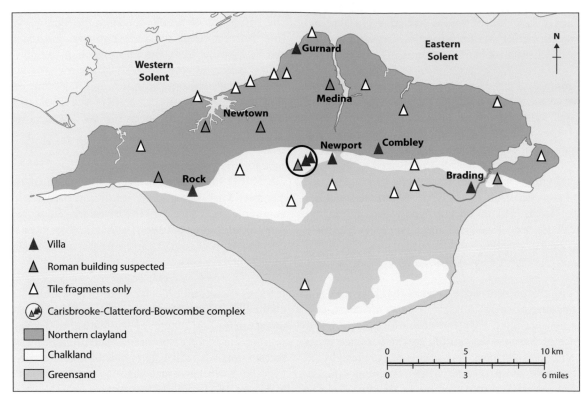

Figure 16.21. Bowcombe Valley, as the 'central place' of Vectis. Chalkland grazing and fertile Greensand are the Island's principal farming assets. Villas and unconfirmed Roman buildings are partly satellite to Bowcombe (circled) but, like Thanet, several are also drawn to maritime 'gateways' on the coast.

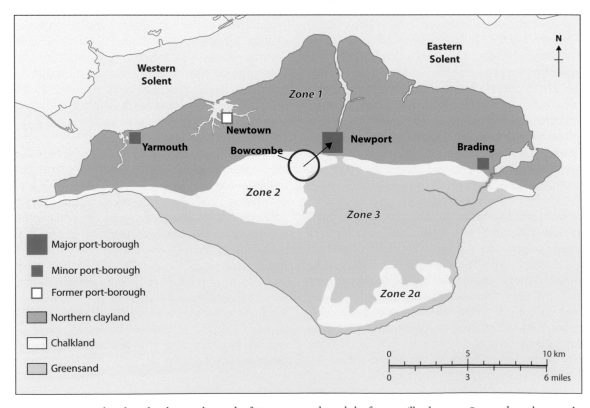

Figure 16.22. In medieval Wight, the port-borough of Newport supplanted the former villa cluster at Bowcombe to become the Island's new 'central place'. In zone 1, minor port-boroughs and an extinct example at Newtown failed to secure sufficient access to the prosperous chalklands of zone 2 and the fertile Greensand vale of zone 3.

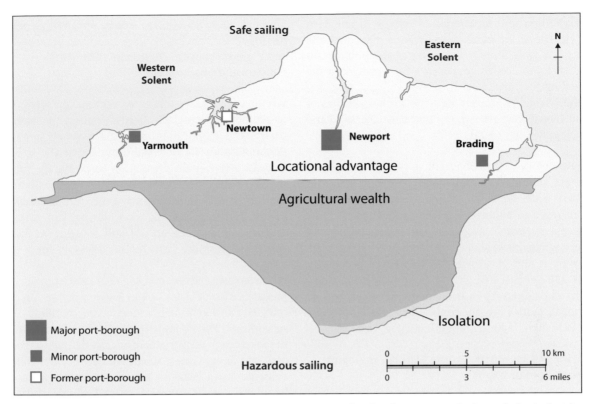

Figure 16.23. The principal economic zones promoting the development of medieval Newport as the 'central place' of Wight. Newtown is a failed port/borough, and Yarmouth and Brading are poorly developed coastal communities. Unlike Newport, all three are peripheral to the principal source of agricultural wealth. The Romano-British population would find similar constraints.

Figure 16.24. Brading villa regained its ancient coastal configuration under flood conditions in February 1994. Here, the villa still lies under the old pitched roofed cover building at the centre of the picture. In the foreground, Brading Down retains its ancient sheep-cropped grassland.

southern Wight and locational advantage in northern Wight. In the latter zone, a key role is played by the Solent's navigable creeks where vital shipping access can be sustained. With southern Wight providing the principal agricultural wealth, it is significant that it is only the navigable Medina and the former reaches of Brading Haven that offer ready maritime access to and from this zone (Fig. 16.24).

The southern coastline of Wight is generally beset by dangerous sailing conditions and poor opportunities to secure safe landings. Navigational impediments are confirmed in evidence from medieval times. Then we see the inevitable ascent of the town and port of Newport, while the weaker hinterlands serving the ports of Yarmouth and Newtown fail to deliver prosperity (Fig. 16.22). On the strength of later historic analogy, an isolated community in the Undercliff might find its maritime activities largely confined to small craft best suited to inshore fishing and pilotage (Fig. 16.23).

Insularity and insecurity: some historic analogies from post-Roman Wight

In a document dated 1352–53 we find that Wight's principal families are 'bound by their tenure' to defend the Island's central retreat at Carisbrooke Castle (Worsley 1781, 36). This is the fortress erected on the site of an earlier walled stronghold known as the 'Lower Enclosure'. In recent studies, a Late Saxon date has been advanced for this 'enclosure' (Young 2000), yet the nature of its building materials shows particular accord with local Romano-British quarrying practice. The presence of Roman tile and pottery within its interior cannot be denied (Tomalin, 2002).

In a further medieval document, we find a list of provisions allotted to the defenders of Carisbrooke Castle (Worsley 1781, 37). These include '10 tuns of wine; 100 quarters of wheat; 100 quarters of malt; 50 quarters of beans and peas; 100 quarters of oats; with salt, coals, wood and other munitions'. Perhaps these offer an outline of some more ancient military necessities once raised or funded within Wight's territorial land units and sent by responsible villa owners to a central military depot and assembly point at the Lower Enclosure.

In the past, analogies have been drawn between Carisbrooke's 'Lower Enclosure' and the forts of the Saxon Shore, but the case has always foundered on the enclosure's inferior size and the weak and heavily truncated nature of its atypical stone rampart (Rigold 1969, 134; Johnson 1976, 141–42; Cotterill 1993, 236; Young 2000, 16–19; Pearson 2002, 62; Philp 2005, 216–18;

Tomalin 2002, 55–60). For some, an analogy with the fortified civil enclosure at Gatcombe, Somerset, may carry greater appeal (Branigan 1975; Hingley 1989, 72; Smisson and Groves 2004).

Whatever defensive measures Vectensians were obliged to maintain during the fourth century, it seems that their basic vulnerabilities would ever be unchanged. Documentation in medieval times shows the size of the Island's active male population to be barely sufficient to deter or evict determined intruders. Given that reinforcements were urgently sent from Southampton, Devon, Stafford and London during the fourteenth century, we can see an old and integral weakness in Wight life (Worsley 1781, 76; Hockey 1982, 98).

When Saxons, Frisians and Bagaudae were pursuing their predations across the *Oceanus Britannicus*, we can be sure that Romano-British Islanders were certainly no less susceptible. The documented panics and precautions of the fourteenth century seem equally befitted to the third and fourth centuries, when we see no archaeological evidence for a resident Island garrison to protect the population. At the same time, we glimpse little more than a pastiche of true military architecture in the walled defences of the 'Lower Enclosure' at Carisbrooke.

In the valley below the Lower Enclosure, we find a tantalising scatter of poorly understood Roman buildings. These extend over a distance of some 2 km along the valley floor, where the Lukely Brook passes through water meadows and the remnants of abandoned ponds. These buildings begin with the Carisbrooke villa and can be traced upstream, via Clatterford villa, to a concentration of buildings in the vicinity of Bowcombe Farm (Figs 16.25 and 16.26). Despite weak archaeological investigation, here we detect a large and prosperous community that immediately challenges any geographic conjecture of a single consolidated villa estate.

Land division for fiscal and strategic purposes

Now that we can recognise a clear clustering of Romano-British villas in the Bowcombe valley, it appears that a number of prosperous Vectensians were assembled far too close to each other to maintain individually consolidated landholdings. The alternative might mean all manner of ownerships dispersed throughout the major land units of *Vectis*. This could allow each unit to encompass an entire patchwork of farmlands, forest, chalkland grazing, coppices, pastures, dwellings and appurtenances held under customary native law. While some of these properties might be held by an array of principal Vectensian landowners, we must recognise

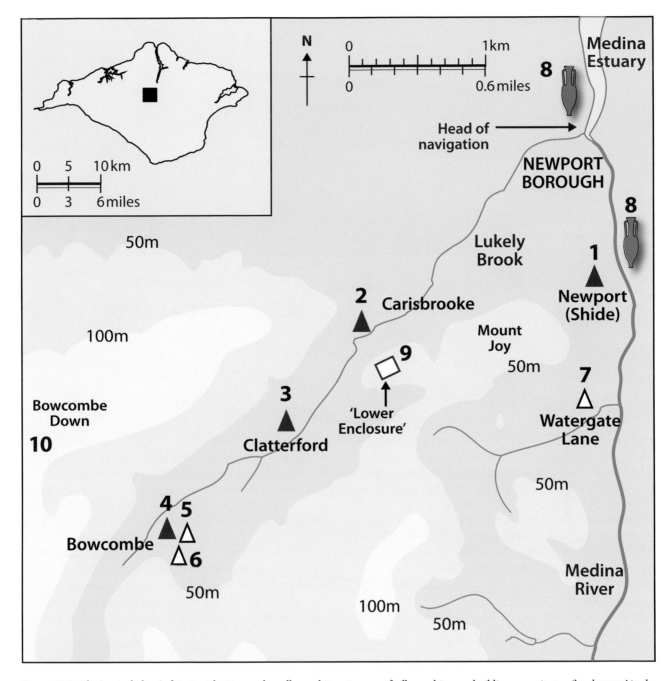

Figure 16.25. The 'central place' of Vectis. The Bowcombe valley and its entourage of villas and Roman buildings constitute a 'local centre' in the organisation of Roman Wight. The walled 'Lower Enclosure' at Carisbrooke endorses the importance of this location. Key: 1 Newport (Shide) villa; 2 Carisbrooke villa; 3 Clatterford villa; 4–6 Bowcombe Roman buildings; 7 Corn-drier and building materials; 8 Riverside occupation; 9 Roman fort; 10 Briquetage.

that others might be held by more distant owners at home on the British mainland and, perhaps, much further afield.

If we are prepared to see the nine or so linear divisions of *Vectis* fulfilling no more than a fiscal and administrative role, then it seems that the lower section of the Bowcombe valley may have accommodated

a substantial, and perhaps principal, tranche of the Island's social and economic elite. What we are denied is an adequate indication of that all-important balance between resident and non-resident ownership. For the purpose of insular security, however, much might have been gained by maintaining a wide spread of individual holdings where owners would be highly motivated to defend, to death, that which was theirs. This strategy

Figure 16.26. The Bowcombe Valley. The epicentre of Roman and Saxon Wight. Key: 1 Carisbrooke parish church with Roman coin hoards adjacent; 2 Carisbrooke villa; 3 Clatterford villa; 4 Carisbrooke Castle with 'Lower Enclosure'; 5 Lukely Brook; 6 Anglo-Saxon occupation and productive centre; 7 Newport villa (concealed below hillside).

we see in later times when, for the purpose of nurturing a strong fighting population, individual islanders were prohibited 'from holding farms, lands, or tithes exceeding the annual rent of ten marks' (Worsley 1781, 72; Statute 4 Henry 7, cap. 16).

Ancient land division on Thanet

A brief appraisal of historic land division on Thanet begins with the parishes of Broadstairs and Ramsgate (Fig. 16.27). Part of the boundary between these two parishes appears to follow an ancient stream. The upland extension of this line hints at old divisions, perhaps enclosing ancient grazing rights on former downland on Northdown and on hilltop ground in the Manston area (Fig. 16.11, locations Nd and MM).

Other parish boundaries of the island seem distinctly unhelpful. Those delineating the parishes of Minster, Monkton, Sarre, St Nicholas-at-Wade and Margate commonly display a serrated or tabular outline. These irregular configurations are typical of subsequent re-castings and modifications. Later, we shall see in this discussion that changes of this type can be surprisingly old.

The urban expansion of Margate has been responsible for further confusion, including the subjugation of the medieval manors of Birchington and Woodchurch (Appendix 3, Table H). It may, however, be no accident that, a little north-east of Telegraph Hill, three of the island's parishes converge, on high ground at Manston. Was this, perhaps, the spot where earlier land division was once brokered?

St Mildred's Lynch or 'Cursus Cerve'

Like Wight, it seems that the Isle of Thanet was once divided into principal east and west territories. Whereas the central division of Wight was drawn along the natural course of the river Medina, Thanet's historical division was once artificially imposed by an ancient baulk or bank known as St Mildred's Lynch. It seems that this boundary formerly separated Minster, or 'Thacket' Manor, from the manor and later parish of Monkton. In the year 670, Thacket Manor was in the possession of Ecgbhert (Egbert), King of Kent (664–73). Historically, it has been claimed that the boundary dates from this time (Lewis 1723, 52).

In his account dated 1723, John Lewis observed that 'the west part of the parish (Minster) is bounded by a Lynch

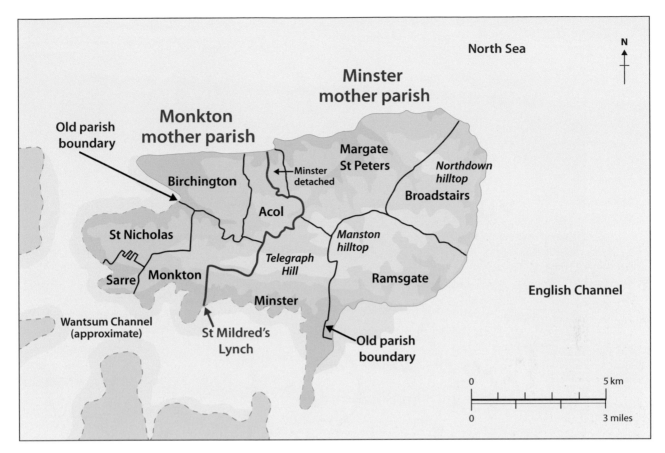

Figure 16.27. The bifurcation of Thanet into east and west zones dominated by the pre-Conquest and later possessions of St Augustine's Abbey at Canterbury (Monkton) and the See of Canterbury (Minster). These mother parishes were once divided by St Mildred's Lynch (the Cursus Cerve). Ancient daughter parishes are also shown. The coastline of the Wantsum Channel is approximate.

or Balk which goes right across the Island to West-gate and which is the bounds of the Mannor as well as the Parish, that way. This, the crafty Monks persuaded the silly people was the track where Domneva's deer ran thro', now it is generally called St Mildred's Lynch. The Lynch has formerly been much broader than it is now, many Farmers who occupy the land on to it, or near it, having, thro' a covetous humour, not only dug up the mold or top of it to lay on their sowing land, but in some places ploughed in upon it.'

It appears that the fourteenth-century Augustinian chronicler William Thorn was the source of the beguiling medieval tale concerning the hind. This fanciful story attributes the boundary to a monastic foundation in the year AD 670 (Hasted 1800; Britton 1808, vol. 5, 987). Then, it is claimed, Egbert (*Ecgbhert*), King of Kent, awarded the land to Abbess Domneva (*Domne Eafe*). History asserts that the flight of the released hind was used to ascertain Divine Will. The result, it was claimed, was a generous allocation of land to the nunnery that was later known as St Mildred's (Rollason 1982).

Around the years 1410–11, the boundary, allegedly defined by 'the course of the hind', was mapped by Thomas of Elmham. His *Mappa Thaneti insulae* was later copied and published by John Lewis in 1736 and by Charles Hardwick in 1858 (Rollason 1980, 7; Moody 2008, 37–38). On the map we see Thanet's twelve principal medieval settlements numerically halved by the course of the *Cursus Cerve* (Fig. 16.28). On this map we also find manors marked by an image of a church; the 'cursus' is helpfully labelled with a leaping hind. It seems that a beacon brazier perched on Telegraph Hill near Alland and another located near Birchington then served the needs of mariners (Figs 16.27 and 16.28).

Given that the story of the hind is so delightfully fanciful, we might ponder whether the '*cerf*' boundary could have marked some earlier distinction such as a Romano-British land division or the limit of ancient woodland. The name *Cursus Cerve* applied to this bank clearly associates it with deer, and this implies some appropriate cover of woodland. There remains the possibility that this land division was already in existence at the time of King Egbert when it was then used to define Church lands and

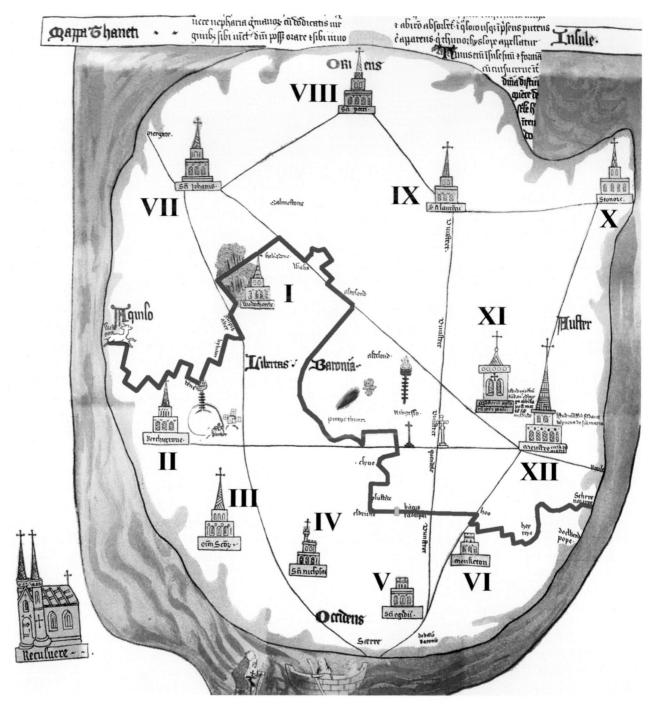

Figure 16.28. Mappa Thaneti *insulae, drawn by Thomas of Elmham (c. 1410–11). North is to the left, with Reculver church. The map shows a well-balanced distribution of settled communities with two groups of six churches divided by the boundary of the 'Cursus Cerve' (marked by the leaping hind at mid-left). The fine lines are roads. Map after Charles Harwick's printed version of 1858 with Roman numerals since added for ease of reference.*

Royal hunting rights. Thanet's lost deer now live on in the name Hartsdown, near Tivoli Park.

The historic woodland of the island is more elusive. In Domesday we find reference to no more than 5 acres of woodland, set in the manor of Monkton. These were deemed sufficient for a tax of ten pigs. On his map of c.1410, Thomas of Elmham inks in a tree or two that seem to convey the arboreal environs or origins of Woodchurch. Writing of Thanet in 1796, John Boys concludes that there is 'hardly any coppice-wood throughout the whole of it'.

304

Ancient land division on Wight

It takes no more than a glance at the map of parochial Wight to see that all parishes are set within a framework of larger transect territories or units (Fig. 16.29). At first glance, these units appear to be at least seven in number while, arguably, another might be perceived in the geomorphological detachment of the 'Isle of Bembridge'. It is little known, however, that an additional north–south boundary once bisected the mother parish of Arreton. Unadopted as a parish boundary, this now lurks as an anonymous Whippingham-Arreton hedge-line running from Palmers Brook to the crest of the Undercliff near Whitwell (Figs 16.29 and 16.30, WAHL).

The fact that this boundary has been so well concealed and largely overlooked hints at its considerable antiquity. This is supported by a suite of dates obtained by optically stimulated luminescence (OSL). These come from two adjacent cross-sections cut through this boundary at Standen Heath (Fig. 16.30, site D). Here a primary date of c. 100 ± 130 BC has been postulated for its construction. It then seems that the bank and ditch may have been repaired or modified, sometime between the eighth and the fourteenth centuries (Schwenninger 2012). Caution arises where anomalies in the field samples now make further corroborative dating desirable.

In the mother parish of Carisbrooke, the configuration of daughter parishes Atherfield, Kingston and Gatcombe hint at the presence of another vertical division that may have slipped from sight. This could bring the total number of territorial units to as many as ten (Figs 16.29 and 16.38, sub-units 4a and 4b). The comparative sizes of their allied mother parishes are given in Appendix 3, Table I. It seems that these ancient 'bacon-slicer' boundaries will continue to tantalise us until hard-won archaeological evidence is extracted from the surviving banks and ditches along their course. The outstanding question is: just how old might these territories be?

In East Wight a somewhat dubious record offered by a supposedly lost charter tells of 50 hides of land in Brading. It is claimed that this was gifted to St Wilfred by King Ine of Wessex in the year 704 (Page 1912, 158; Margham 2000, 119–20). This is the earliest of all of

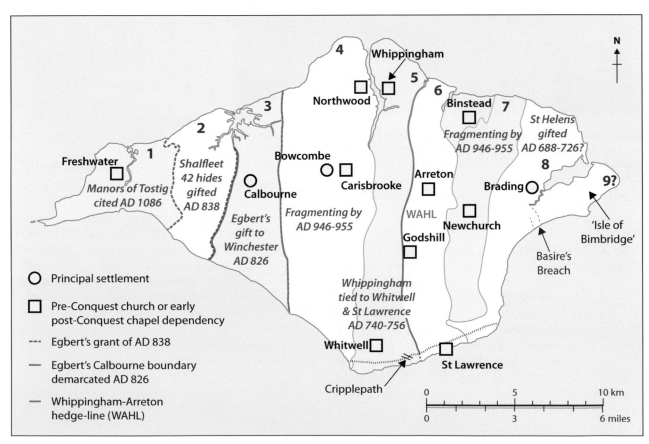

*Figure 16.29. A general reconstruction of Wight's pre-Norman land units, defined by the boundaries of the Island's mother parishes. The dates of their fragmentation into smaller units attest their antiquity. Mother parishes are: **1** Freshwater; **2** Shalfleet; **3** Calbourne; **4** Carisbrooke; **5** Whippingham once with Whitwell and St. Lawrence; **6** Arreton with Godshill; **7** Newchurch; **8** St Helens. The early status of 'Isle of Bimbridge' [Bembridge] (**9**) is uncertain. The Whippingham-Arreton hedge-line (WAHL) is also shown.*

Figure 16.30. The Whippingham-Arreton boundary follows Palmers Brook southwards from A to its rising at B. Here it changes to a hedged bank with ditch, passing over the Isle of Wight's median chalk spine and entering the Greensand vale to C and beyond. OSL dates obtained at D suggest a Late Iron Age or early Roman origin. E marks the site of Combley Roman villa. (Courtesy Google Earth Geoinformation Group, 2015)

the last two names equate with Whitwell and St Lawrence, then we find the first two places strung from north to south along land unit 5 (Fig. 16.38), where they appear to confirm its integrity in the eighth century (Kokeritz 1940, lviii). Whitwell lies close to the southern chalk outcrop of Wight, where Domesday later reveals particular agricultural prosperity. St Lawrence, however, in the Undercliff, is aligned with Unit 6 although it is virtually severed from this unit by an impassable cliff-line. A diagonal route via the 'Cripplepath' offers a singular link with Whitwell and unit 5 (Fig. 16.32).

In West Wight, charter references to early boundaries are more revealing. In a review of the mother parish of Carisbrooke, Jamie Sewell (2000) suggests that interest in the physical demarcation of major land boundaries may not have emerged until the Late Saxon period. It was then that rulers like King Edgar (AD 959–75) were enforcing the idea that churches that provided pastoral care for laity should be supported by specific payments of food rent (tithes). As this was to be drawn from each lay recipient in the church's care, here was a powerful reminder to all Islanders to think specifically in territorial terms.

Wight's named land transactions – if it can be trusted! After 1066, King William's reappraisal of his new English kingdom seems to have prompted a number of hurried forgeries, mostly concerning church lands. It must be allowed that Brading's lost charter as well as some other Isle of Wight land charters may have been fabricated at this time. John Margham reminds us that it is likely that Calbourne charter S274 was also forged by the monks of Winchester in the eleventh century (Margham 2006, 91). Given the underlying need for such subterfuge, the contemporary bounds and details cited in these documents were probably real enough.

In the area covered by the land units of Whippingham and Arreton, another eighth-century document was issued by King Cuthred sometime between AD 740 and 756. This links properties at Whippingham, *Muleburnan*, and *Banewadan*. If we accept the view of Kokeritz that

While this argument is both logical and attractive, it also acknowledges that there had been a 'time before' when each 'pre-parish' community had been bound to a territory that might be similarly cohesive yet, perhaps, less concerned with its precise physical boundary or line on the ground. Sewell considers that each of these earlier Saxon communities had still been obliged to pay tax by a *feorm* or food-rent that was overseen by a local collector or King's Reeve.

It seems possible that this concept of payment-in-produce differed little from the collection of the Romano-British *annona*. This being the case, we are bound to ask whether the north–south transect territories of the Island, be they marked or unmarked on the ground, approximate to ancient units for rent gathering and food payment that had long retained their usefulness. With the encouragement of the OSL date for the

Whippingham/Arreton hedge-line, here is an attractive proposition that we are bound to pursue.

A helpful clue lies in the fragmentation of Wight's major land units. Contrary to Jamie Sewell's suggestion of a Late Saxon genesis, it is evident that fragmentation of these units was already underway before the close of the tenth century. This is evident in the Bowcombe/Carisbrooke unit where, in the period AD 958–76, King Edgar gave Atherfield, in Unit 4, to the Bishop of Winchester and thence to the parish of Brighstone in Unit 3. It also appears that along the boundary between Unit 3 (Calbourne) and Unit 4 (Bowcombe/Carisbrooke), a segment of land at Watchingwell was given to the Wiltshire abbey of Wilton before the year 968 (Finberg 1964, 30, charter 15; Margham 2006, 88–91, charter S766). After some reductions and modifications, this estate eventually seems to be transfixed within the parish boundary of 'Shalfleet Detached' (Margham, ibid.; fig. 18; this text Figs 16.35 and 16.36).

A further Late Saxon alienation concerns land at Bowcombe. This was remotely held by a royal estate in Amesbury, Wiltshire (DB, Wilts, 1,3; DB, Hants, IoW, 1,3). In the past, persistence of a dispersed personal estate of Roman of sub-Roman date has been pondered (Jones 1961, 229–31; Applebaum 1983, 345–46; Myres 1989, 213).

Of all the fragmented accounts of Wight's Anglo-Saxon land boundaries, charter S724 is particularly pertinent to our current enquiry. In this document we find the delineated bounds of the complete territorial 'unit' we have now numbered 3 in Figures 16.29 and 16.38. According to the surviving copy of the charter, this land, described as 30 hides, was conveyed by King Egbert in the year AD 826 to the Bishop of Winchester (Page 1912, 218; Finberg 1964, 29; Margham 2006, 91–96).

It is generally agreed that there are sufficient identifiable points in the delineations in this document to identify this estate with the bounds that define the mother parish of Calbourne. This would be recognised before the alienation of its daughter parishes of Mottistone and Brighstone (Margham 2006, 91–98, fig. 30). These bounds are also reiterated in a second charter concerning Wilton Abbey (Margham 2006, 96–98, charter S1581). Here, we find a substantial coast-to-coast segment of West Wight where some 4,187 hectares of land have held their geographic integrity at least since the ninth century. In the centre of this ancient tract sits the villa of Rock (Fig. 16.35).

Land unit 3 (Figs 16.35 and 16.38) seems far too large to befit the estate of the modest Roman farm or villa we see at Rock. It might, however, befit a demarcated patchwork of various Romano-British occupancies and ownerships drawn together for the purpose of levying and collecting a tax such as the annona. In this, the villa of Rock might play a particular role.

Due to their abutment to each other, it certainly seems that Shalfleet and Calbourne land units (2 and 3) may have been renewals or re-allocations by Egbert of pre-existing blocs (Fig. 16.29, units 2 and 3). Because these particular gifts lie close to each other in both time and space, it has been suggested that these were once viewed as a unified bloc, recognised during or before the year AD 826 (Cahill 1980, 23). Together, they could produce a landholding of some 9,702 hectares. Arguably, this larger bloc could be part or all of the 300 hides, or 'one quarter of the Island' given by Caedwalla to Bishop Wilfred on the event of his enforced Christian conversion of Islanders in AD 686 (ASC; Bede, EH, Bk. IV, ch. XVI; Hockey 1982, 7).

Perhaps a remaining portion of the King's gift to Wilfred was either of the adjoining units of Bowcombe (4) or Freshwater (1); no information prior to Domesday survives for either. Had Caedwalla drawn up new boundaries in the seventh century or had he accepted what he found? Once more, we must allow that the critical documents may have been forged to reinforce privileges enjoyed by the Bishopric of Winchester in the eleventh century (Margham 2006, 91). Nevertheless, the dates claimed by these documents and the traditions to which they allude could push local cognisance of these territories further back in time.

Having pressed the use of our land units back to within 350 years of Roman departure, it now seems that Romano-British recognition of these ancient territories could be a beguiling possibility. Some might even say 'probable' when adding some of the highly persuasive evidence gleaned from villa/parish estates in North Wiltshire, where their early boundaries appear to have been arbitrarily cut by the later imposition of the Wansdyke in the fifth or sixth centuries AD (Bonney 1972, 170, fig. 19).

The case for extending some of these Wessex estates into prehistory has also been well argued on the grounds that some boundaries, such as those of the Wiltshire parish of Chittoe, might otherwise respect the course of a Roman road (Bonney 1972, 174–78, fig. 20; Yorke 1995, 75). While these arguments offer further encouragement to accept the earlier of the two OSL dates obtained from Wight's Whippingham/Arreton hedge-line, we shall see that the linear divisions of this type also claim powerful prehistoric analogies in other insular environments of the British Isles.

Lessons in land division from the Gaelo-Celtic fringe

An instructive analogy to the linear land division of *Vectis* may be found in some remarkable insular territories on the north-western rim of the Gaelo-Celtic world. Offshore from Ireland's Connaught coast, the Aran Islands display a system of ancient land division that has been 'fossilised' in a web of immutable stonewalls (Laheen 2010). It is here that a configuration of *baile* (*bhaile*) or 'townland' boundaries shows a marked resemblance to the north–south pattern of linear mother parishes we see in Wight.

For the islanders of Aran, each of these divisions once enclosed a sustainable landholding sufficient for the needs of a community that had been organised around a local lord or head of family. Within these units, land was further apportioned into quarters (*ceathrúna*). For the practicalities of everyday farming, each *ceathrú* was further divided into sixteen *cartrons* or *cnagaire* ('croggeries'). Ownership or tenure of the croggeries was highly dispersed in accordance with a general principle of agreed fairness.

Mary Laheen observes that where comparable systems of townlands can be examined throughout historic Ireland, their subdivision by size becomes less important than the quality of the land. As a consequence, these ancient Gaelic sub-units can vary in size according to the fertility of the terrain (Laheen 2010, 44–45). In his description of Gaelic farming in 1682, Sir Henry Piers tells how land was apportioned into units of equal value and how lots were cast to ensure fair share.

If once applied in southern Britain, such a lottery would be the very antithesis of the concept of a consolidated estate. Where inheritance was to be settled, it was common for the youngest heir to make the subdivisions and for the eldest to make first choice (Laheen 2010, 40). Here we glimpse an ancient British/Gaelic tradition of land management that could well resemble an ancient Vectensian mindset. Where vacant or unused land was available, the Irish evidence shows that practical annexations and changes of ownership might readily receive communal approval, while boundary walls and hedge-lines would remain unchanged.

On Wight, where the old long parishes cross-cut the Island's varied natural zones, the configuration of some nine or more early linear units suggests similar aspirations towards fair apportionment (Fig. 16.29). In both Aran and Wight, it is tempting to view these divisions as simple practical means of organising land use. Nevertheless, the Aran study also prompts us to recognise that the process of lottery and fair apportionment were set at the very heart of Gaelo-Celtic society, where mechanisms of ownership re-adjustment could also be ready to hand.

It appears that by the eighth or ninth century the population on Aran's Inis Meáin was already divided into principal east and west communities (Fig. 16.31; Laheen 2010, 40). With these two townlands then divided into *ceathrú* strips, the analogy with Wight becomes striking (Fig. 16.29).

When we realise that the divisions of Inis Meáin are family-based land units and that follies of human inbreeding were ever lurking in small insular societies, we can see how this island's subdivisions into *baile*, *ceathrú* and *cartrons* might offer a vital means of identifying and socially controlling the progeny of individual families. Similar precautions could be equally prudent in an early subdivision of the settled population of *Vectis*. Writing of ethnic and linguistic division within the Melanesian island of Umboi, the ethnographer Thomas Harding (1967, 173–74) describes violent confrontation and pervading disproval when a marriage is considered to be 'too close'. The size of Umboi approximates to the Isle of Wight.

Where the Irish model finds past *baile* or townland territories tied to extended family communities and their *clachan* settlements, perhaps we glimpse a means by which villa and non-villa communities could emerge within particular Romanised areas of the British Isles. The essence of *clachan* society was communal living; tied to this was the principle of an Irish 'rundale' system in which fair distribution and re-distribution of dispersed parcels of land was fundamental.

On the Aran island of Inismore, Mary Laheen (2010, 76, fig. 28) traces the dispersed estates of several present-day farms. Here, individual parcels range from 2.6 to 9 hectares. Potentially, if gathered into more centralised ownership, here are the building blocks for greater personal prosperity. On these harsh and isolated limestone islands, however, neither the social nor the physical environment has ever favoured significant change from a system that appears to be essentially prehistoric.

Across mainland Ireland, it was the social changes of the nineteenth and twentieth century that brought reconfiguration and consolidation to old landholdings of the *rundale* kind (Laheen 2010, 82). This prompts us to consider a comparable opportunity for reconfiguration, when Romanisation offered change to earlier tribal

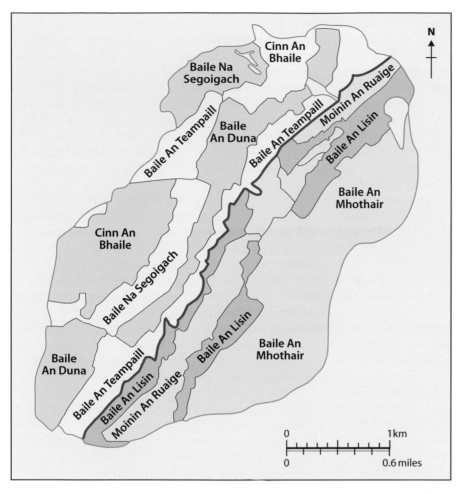

Figure 16.31. The Aran island of Inis Meáin is bisected by an ancient median boundary (red) akin to the primary east-west division of Wight. This island shows irregular ceathrúna boundaries that betray extensive alterations over time. (After Laheen 2010)

In the past, much ink and earnest debate has been expended in pursuing the elusive grail of the relict and cohesive Romano-British villa estate (Finberg 1955; Fowler 1970; Bonney 1972; Percival 1976; Yorke 1990, 8). Since this proposal was first applied to the Gloucestershire villa and parish of Withington (Finberg 1955), the quest has almost gathered a romantic appeal. Yet while we have pondered the beguiling configurations of certain ancient parishes, the archaeological jury has largely withheld its judgment. In the long parishes of Wight, we find no ready geographical concordance with the Island's generous scatter of villa and villa-like buildings; neither might we expect to do so.

In a broader European context, it now seems that many villas are best viewed simply as an array of real estate holdings that could be scattered across certain agricultural and pastoral landscapes. Their presence may be considered an optional expression of personal or family aspirational achievement. This departs from earlier perceptions of villas as imposed markers of centralised ownership and control.

systems in southern Britain. There, fresh social perspectives and some random choices to consolidate traditionally dispersed parcels of tribal lands might set some communities on the path to new landed wealth and villa construction. On the ground, however, the established boundaries provided by wall, hedge, bank or ditch might see no significant change.

Where the aisled building or 'aisled hall' appears as the principal residence at certain of our villa sites, perhaps we should consider these as 'half-way houses', where occupants had havered at the opportunity to abandon what were, in essence, *rundale* principles. In Atrebatic villas like Stroud (Petersfield) and Rapsley (Ewhurst) we see dogged adherence to communal buildings of this kind, and an outright exclusion of the type of comfortable family residence that eventually appears at Brading. Beneath the rafters of these older traditional structures, communal discussions on the working of the dispersed plots may have continued in an age-old manner.

In the northern provinces of the Empire, the choice to adopt or disregard the advantages of villa life might be prompted by a variety of geographic, social, economic or cultural considerations. Where 'villa theory' has been applied to these phenomena, we find that natural resources, transportation, regional social structures and even landscape aesthetics could all play a significant role in the presence or absence of villas (Roymans and Derks 2011, 7–11). Moreover, the diverse architecture of these buildings presents a graduated scale of comfort and status by which a successful farmer, a cosmopolitan family or a highly endowed elite might each find requisite satisfaction.

In south-eastern Britannia, we find very few countryside villas that might befit permanent residence by truly elite owners; those at Bignor and Darenth have been noted as late contenders (Taylor 2011, 182). Yet the occupants of these residences, together with any of those lesser villas with wings and corridors, might well enjoy an entire portfolio of invested incomes and real estate properties that could include the town as well as the countryside.

To these we might add diverse maritime incomes secured by a discernible train of coastal villas. These can include the buildings known at Dartford, Frindsbury, Eccles, Margate, Minster-in-Thanet, Sandwich, Folkestone, Eastbourne, Newhaven, Brighton, Pagham, Selsey, Fishbourne, Bosham, Langstone, Havant, Fareham, Bursledon, Brading and Newport (Tomalin 2006, 59–68 for complete list).

In a further array of villa sites, where the aisled house or 'aisled hall' provided the primary residence, it seems that pervading tribal or regional traditions concerning social customs, land tenure and inheritance might generate aspirations of a very different kind. Among villas of this type, Jeremy Taylor has thoughtfully drawn our attention to prestige offered by sizeable barns (Taylor 2011, 186–89). In such halls of plenty, fleece, grain, stored root crops and fodder might represent material wealth gained from all manner of dispersed landholdings. When *cornucopiae* appear on emperors' coins, such symbolism would win immediate appeal to a vast rural population whose recognition of wealth and success would never surpass the orbit of bucolic imagination. A millennium later, when those great monastic tithe barns fulfilled a comparable function, it was from a nebula of minor landholdings that most of this consumable collateral was similarly obtained.

If the lands of many Britons had long been managed in a manner generally akin to a *rundale* regime, it would be the varying social convictions of Britannia's individual tribes that would admit or resist opportunities for change. Even in the Roman homeland of Italy, where rigid centuriation was commonly applied, archaeological research now recognises 'considerable coexistence between properties of all sizes'. This, it seems, could be considered normal (Purcell 1995, 174).

In Vectensian society only a limited number of farming communities might muster sufficient agreement and perspicacity to pursue extensive re-allocation and consolidation of traditionally dispersed landholdings. Should amendments of this kind arise, they were, perhaps, a piecemeal outcome of changes induced by dowry and partible inheritance, rather than a matter of appropriation or imposition of will. At Brading and at Bowcombe, some opportune consolidation of this kind

could be achieved, but our Aran analogies suggest that a forum for agreement might permit little more than *ad hoc* improvements. Expressed in Aran terms, outcomes might barely exceed a shuffling of 'croggeries' and some opportune consolidation within *ceathrúna*. If, as we may suspect, Wight's population substantially increased during Romano-British times, then perhaps it was a relaxation of social boundaries such as marriage that eventually brought new patterns of ownership into the management of a traditionally apportioned landscape.

Today, there are no grand farms or estates on Wight, yet some very successful and wealthy landowners hold highly productive acreages dispersed across the Island. If we pitch this scenario against conjecture for cohesive Romano-British villa estates, then it now seems that tribal tradition and social conservatism probably held sway here, as it may have done across much of Britannia's villa-punctuated landscape. While we have long reached for geographical models of catchment and location to explain the siting of our villas, could it be that a principal determinant has lurked unseen within the social landscape of tribal Britain?

Despite some early displays of residential comfort on Britannia's Regnensian coastlands, no Romano-British villa has offered credible analogy with the grand estate or 'seat' of our later country gentry. Never do we find planned opulence of the kind flaunted on the northern Gallic chalklands at Warfusée-Abancourt, Estrées-sur-Noye or Lahoussée (e.g. Percival 1976, 78, fig. 20; Agache aerial archive). Elsewhere in this review, we see that the incidence of notably opulent Romano-British villas becomes even more fugitive when familiar buildings at Chedworth, Woodchester and Great Witcombe might be better viewed as cult centres or, perhaps, *fana* (Walters 2000; Walters and Rider, this volume).

Post-Roman land division and military responsibilities in the insular community of Wight

Documents issued in the reign of Edward II show that the mustering of an Island militia was the responsibility of those wealthy local landowners whose income exceeded £20. In a document of 1333 we learn that Wight landowners had to meet these levies 'in proportion to their possessions' (Worsley 1781, 35). This was a levy geared to local wealth, where each contributor was obliged to provide an appropriate body of fighting men. In effect, the food-rent levy or *tithing* system included military service and military dues. Severe fines and even land confiscations awaited prevaricators. The recruitment of local men-at-arms, and their training within particular muster zones, was essential to the well-being of the Island's elite (Worsley 1781, 35–40). The 'territorial imperative', once inherent in villa organisation, was ever alive.

In a detailed document, issued in the reign of Edward III, the tie between the military levy and Wight's ancient 'bacon-slicer' land divisions becomes explicit. In 1340 we find the Island defended by nine mustered companies each comprising 100 men (Worsley 1781, 32). By the sixteenth century, this force had been increased to ten companies, now clearly identified as '*centons*'.

With the management of each armed company overseen by a local worthy and '*Centoner*', the entire mustering arrangement bears a remarkable likeness to our early mother parish/unit divisions. We learn from another fourteenth-century document that, while this system deviated from national arrangements for local militia, on Wight it was suffered to retain its 'ancient usage' (Worsley 1781, 39). The very practicalities of this type of local conscription would have demanded that clear and unambiguous boundaries be drawn through the Island's land and population. It was these demarcations that the mother parish/land units had been able to provide.

While there is no contemporary map or delineation of the early *centon* boundaries, the families and landholdings of each of the *Centoners* are sufficiently well known to provide a realistic approximation that is tied closely to the 'tythings' of the Island (Webster, *pers. comm.*; Webster appendix map in Russell 1981; Thompson and Tomalin 2011). A simple assessment of cereal yields embodied in these 'tythings' certainly evokes analogy with the precept of the Romano-British *annona*.

In his 'notional reconstruction of Wight's tythings', drawn without prejudice to the configuration of the Island's medieval parishes, Clifford Webster's configuration comes sufficiently close to suggest that both centons and 'tythings' share a common ancestry (Fig. 16.32). Where some deviation occurs, it seems that, when the arming of civilians became necessary, certain Island families were best kept well apart!

The issue of remote ownership: some historical analogies

When we interrogate the Domesday entries for Wight, it is still possible to glimpse a little of the pre-

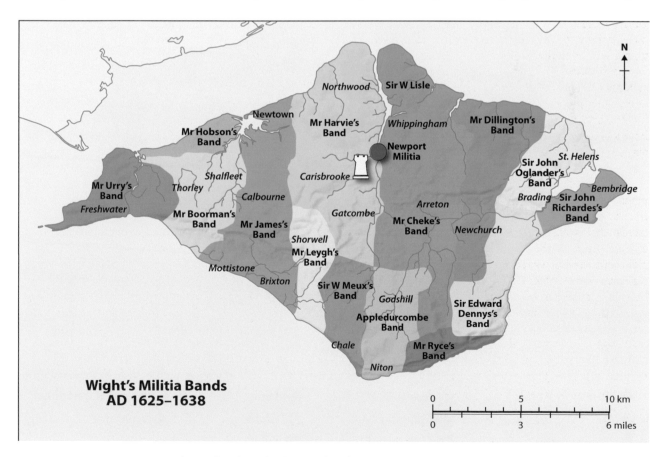

Figure 16.32. Boundaries of Wight's militia centons, based on a perceived configuration of 'tythings' and the disposition of named officers and Centoners. (After Webster, 1981 and Thompson & Tomalin 2011.)

Norman Island when, in the 'Time of King Edward', 51 individual Saxon landowners are named. There are also 27 anonymous entries that appear to be lesser ranking Islanders who presumably fell on the field at Senlac. Some of these posthumous entries for properties could concern further multiple ownerships, so their number could be considerably less than 27.

When all of these landowners are ranked by their estates, no more than 24 emerge as principal figures

holding property valued above £5 (Appendix 3, Table J). Where, at Mottistone and Gatcombe, we find reference to four 'unnamed thanes' and three 'unnamed brothers', it is tempting to believe that their very anonymity arose through remote possession and the fact that their deaths, by then, were at least some twenty years old.

Here, from the eve of 1066, is a record of the personalities and landed wealth of the Isle of Wight. Implicit in this complete list are a smaller and hidden number of

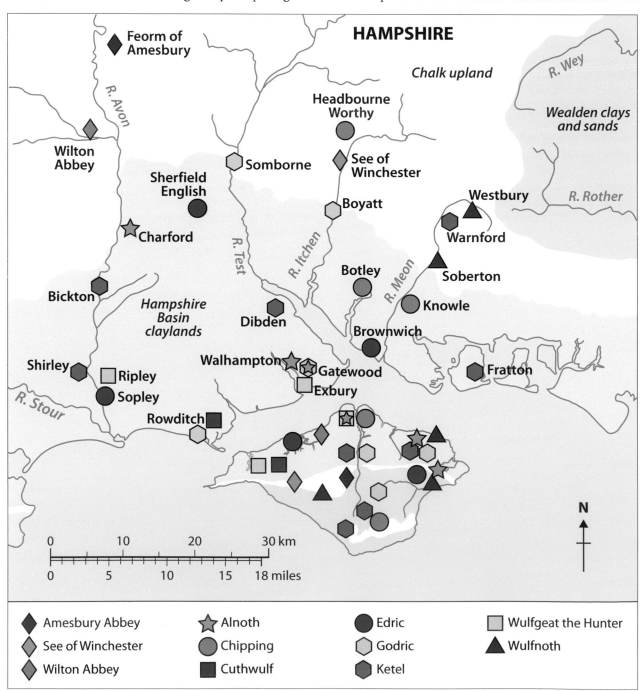

Figure 16.33. Some apparent trans-Solent landholders with estates in the Isle of Wight. These are noted in Domesday in the 'time of King Edward'.

significant residences. Perhaps these homes are not too far removed in number from the villas of the prosperous families of Roman Wight.

In the instance of Earl Tostig (or Tosti), we are certainly dealing with a principal absentee landlord capable of employing a resident steward to manage his Island interests. Other obvious non-residents are the King, Earl Godwin, Earl Harold, the Bishop of Winchester and the Abbot of Lyre. As we descend the list to the lower-rated properties, we still find landowners with substantial mainland holdings (Fig. 16.33).

A caveat must be applied here, because there ever lurk those opportunities for coincidence or repetition of other landowners of the same name. Ketel's name appears against pre-Conquest holdings in Wight at Appleford, Chale, Shide and Whitefield, as well as notably prosperous properties at Dibden, Warnford and Bickton on the Hampshire mainland.

The name Godric appears against some nine pre-Conquest properties in mainland Hampshire, including minor holdings in the New Forest. An unnamed manor in Somborne Hundred was worth £10, a sum that might identify his principal residence. On Wight, Godric is the named owner of seven properties, including valuable mills at Whitefield and Huffingford (Horringford). Back in the New Forest, he also shares holdings at Gatewood with Alnoth, who seems to be another holder of a portfolio of trans-Solent properties. This latter name is associated with Wight properties at Luton and Whitefield, where good harbourage was accessible. In the manor of Whitefield both Ketel and Godric also have recorded holdings (Fig. 16.33).

It seems that Edric, whose properties at Shalfleet and Adgestone attend Wight's natural docking points at Newtown Harbour and Bembridge Haven, was also well placed to manage trans-Solent communications. His mainland links appear to lead to a prosperous holding at Brownwich, on the east shore of Southampton Water. Another valuable Domesday mill is recorded in his possession in the valley of the Hampshire Avon at Sopley.

The name of Chipping (a.k.a. Kepping), who once owned the Wight manors of Whippingham and Stenbury, also appears against no fewer than sixteen properties on the Hampshire mainland. These include two mills at Botley (valued at £10) and three more at Headbourne Worthy (valued at £25). Such prosperity from grain and its milling may not be too far removed from those corn exports cited in Roman times by Strabo.

We do not need to pursue the Domesday list very far to see that decisions and principal activities on Anglo-Saxon Wight might often be controlled by powerful individuals with notable holdings on the mainland. This, no doubt, had been assisted by those major and brutal supplanting of earlier Island populations by the Jutes in the fifth century and by Caedwalla in Chronicle Year 686. For the organisation of Vectis in Romano-British times, we may contemplate an alternative scenario; for, arguably, much of the controlling elite may have been well embedded in the Island's indigenous population.

On Norman Thanet, the Conqueror's 'bean-counters' provide standard details of properties within the island's constituent manors of Monkton and Minster; but information on Margate, a holding of St Augustine's, Canterbury, comprises no more than a brief citing of the manorial name in Domesday's *Excerpta*. In all three manors we are denied any reference to ownerships in the 'Time of King Edward'. This deprives us of virtually any clues as to absentee ownerships that may have been held from the Kent mainland.

At the time of Domesday, Thanet was denied a clear jurisdiction of its own, being a collection of three manors all contained within the administration of the East Kent *lathe* of *Borowara* or 'Borough' (Fig. 16.34). As we see that the same *lathe* also includes Canterbury, we are bound to ponder whether this reflects a truly ancient and possibly pre-Saxon pattern of principal ownerships. Significantly, the primary division of this region into *lathes* has been generally attributed to the ancient provincial administration of the Jutish region of Kent, where it seems that at least seven *villae regali* claimed appropriate shares of the Wealden forest (Witney 1976, 124; Morris 1983, 'index of places').

Reviewing Romano-British land use by means of a Domesday yardstick

When we compare the prosperous communities of Late Saxon times with the extinct villas of *Vectis*, we find ambivalent evidence showing both continuity and discontinuity. Wealth, it seems, was still being generated on and around the Chalk, yet there had been some perceptible shifts in the pattern of settlement. In some cases, prosperity had moved away from the sites of the old villas but had remained focused within the same natural zones. In the south of the Island, in sub-zone 2a, it seems that a new area of chalkland was now being colonised in a particularly profitable manner.

In West Wight, Domesday shows that Leofing, of Coombe, held land within a few hundred metres of the

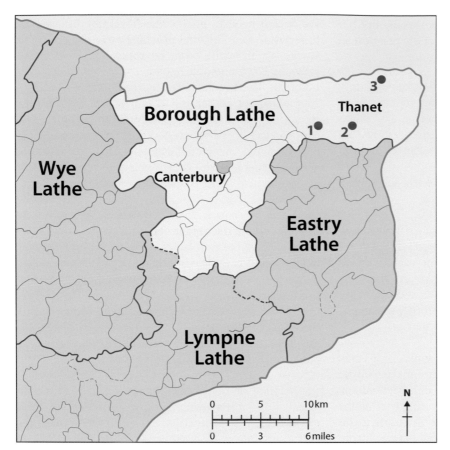

Figure 16.34. The integration of the Isle of Thanet within the Juto-Saxon lathe of 'Borough' or land of the 'Borowara'. The division of East Kent into lathes is first documented in the seventh century. Lathe boundaries are red and parish boundaries are black. Thanet's early manors of (1) Minster/Thacket, (2) Monkton and (3) Margate are also shown.

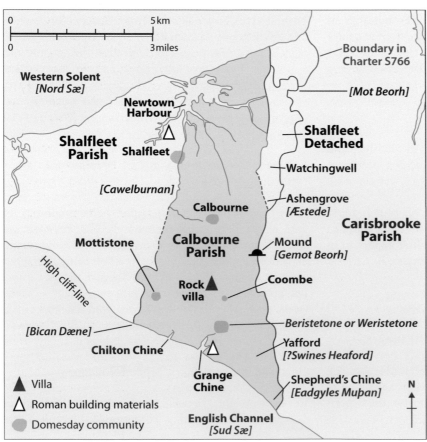

Figure 16.35. Rock villa set within the Saxon estate and mother parish of Calbourne. The Domesday communities of Coombe and Weristetone/Beristetone are its successors. Certain boundary points named in Charters S274 and S766 appear in brackets. A high southern cliff-line restricts ready access to the beach at Grange Chine. The natural harbour at Newtown is attended by an early Domesday settlement at Shalfleet.

314

old villa at Rock (Fig. 16.35). There was little prosperity here, because his tiny community was only tilling land for one plough. To sustain themselves, one of the two families had apparently harnessed the Buddlehole Brook to operate a mill (*DB*, IoW 7,18).

What happened on Rock villa's southern spread of fertile Greensand? Domesday can only offer possibilities here, and these arise at place called Weristetone (*DB*, IoW 8,5). In the time of King Edward (1066) this was a prosperous community, holding 2 hides of land that might be some 340 acres (138 ha). Four plough-teams were at work. Domesday historians suggest that miss-transcription by a Domesday scribe had changed the B into W (Kokeritz 1940, lxii; Mothersill and Jenkyns 1982, App. IoW 8,2). Similar clerical errors with B/W occur in other Domesday entries for the Island, where Wroxall became Brocheshal and Billingham became Wyllingham (Kokeritz 1940, lxii).

Correction produces 'Beristestone' as the first spelling of the familiar Island village later named Brixton and now regarded as Brighstone. This village straddled the Buddlehole Brook, just 1.6 km downstream from the villa at Rock. With a notable valuation of £5, it seems that 'B/Weristetone' may have sat on an important arable asset of the former villa estate.

In East Wight, at Arreton, in proximity to Combley Roman villa, Domesday suggests 'business as usual'. Pagan burials in a nearby hilltop round barrow at Mical Morey's Hump attest to a well-established Saxon presence. In 1086 ten plough teams were at work in the hands of ten village families and twelve further families of smallholders. All, presumably, were exploiting at least part of the old villa environs. Arreton was now a royal manor and its people were largely settled some 1.2 km south of the villa site, at a spot served by a scarp-foot spring. The village was prospering, and a stone church was maintained there by the monks of Lyre (*DB*, IoW 4).

In the neighbourhood of Brading villa, Domesday reveals a very different scene (Fig. 16.28). There was little trace of the earlier prosperity. A new pattern of settlement had emerged and several small communities had been spawned. One was sited 1 km to the north-east, at a spot destined to become Brading town (*DB*, IoW 7,7). In 1086 this tiny community comprised just four families with negligible agriculture and no more than an acre of meadow. Tradition claims that an eighth-century Saxon chapel was founded here by St Wilfred (Page 1912, 158; Margham 2000, 117). While no clear archaeological evidence of a pre-Conquest building has so far come to light, a scatter of Middle Saxon coins was recently reported within 300 m of the medieval church (T. Winch, *pers. comm.*). Pottery of this period was also recovered from a pit very close to the west front of the church (K. Trott, *pers. comm.*).

Some 500 m west of Brading villa site was the manorial holding of Adgestone. In late Saxon times, possession of this place was divided between mainland landlords Godric and Edric. Collectively, they held 1.83 virgates of land, perhaps amounting to some 55 acres (22.25 ha). There was arable land sufficient for just '1½ ploughs'. A free tenant (rated with two cows) and two smallholders were the family-heads of a very modest community that also included two slaves (*DB*, IoW 7,15 and 9,6).

A shift from the old villa to Adgestone was a logical move, for the new site offered consistent spring water. This was a distinct advantage over the villa's dependence on one or more deep wells. Over the downland hilltop, at Nunwell, three families with the help of three slaves were working a northern portion of the old villa terrain. All were settled around another spring, where they seem to have been farming about 30 acres of the zone 1 clay (Fig. 16.36).

A further entry in Domesday takes us some 1.8 km south of Brading villa to the manor of Sandham (Sandown; *DB*, IoW 13). Just before 1066, this community seems to have been farming 2 hides (perhaps about 240 acres (97 ha)) but by 1086 this had fallen to 1½ hides (possibly c. 75 acres (30 ha)). There was land for three ploughs, and just four acres of meadow. Sited on the fertile Greensand of zone 3, this should have offered a particularly productive asset to the old villa estate, but Domesday shows that this was now under-populated and under-used.

The story of weak post-Roman settlement and poor land use around Brading can be contrasted with Saxon activity in the heart of the Isle of Wight, at Bowcombe (Fig. 16.37). The high status of this community was clearly expressed during and after the sixth century AD when graves for pagan warriors were cut in the local chalk (Arnold 1982, 102). These burials include the hill that is crowned by Carisbrooke's enigmatic rectangular stronghold, now termed the 'Lower Enclosure' (Rigold 1969; Morris and Dickinson 2000). Later, near the valley floor, a Saxon church seems to have been in use for sufficient time to secure recognition in Domesday (*DB*, IoW, 1, 7; Tomalin 2002, 60).

In the environs of Carisbrooke, it is little surprise to find that King Edward the Confessor kept ownership of the desirable valley of Bowcombe) to himself. Domesday tells of a prosperous community here with land for

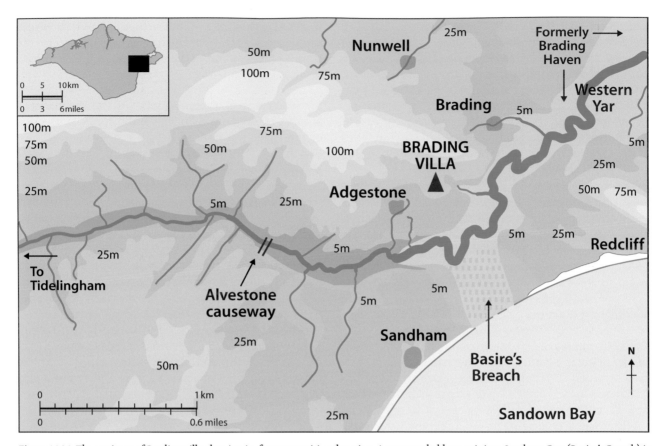

Figure 16.36. The environs of Brading villa showing its former maritime location. A suspected old sea exit into Sandown Bay (Basire's Breach) is marked, as is the Alvestone Romano-British causeway across the Eastern Yar. Saxon/medieval settlements at Adgestone, Brading Nunwell and Sandham are also named.

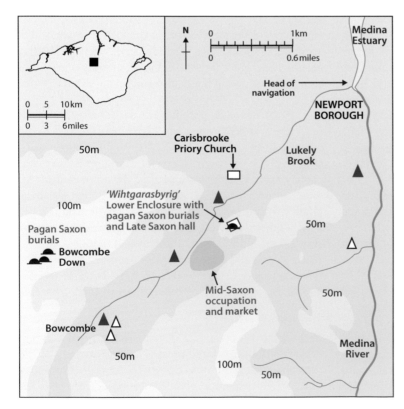

fifteen ploughs. There were also eight acres of valuable meadow, some woodland for pigs, a mill and a salt-house (*DB, IoW* 1,7). Salting, we should note, had been a practice at the neighbouring villa at Newport; while further away on the Solent coast, at Wootton Haven, there were shore-side salt kilns and evidence for Romano-British beef exports (Tomalin 2012, 260).

Boundaries of extinct land units

In north-east Wight, the Palmer's Brook hedgerow is a principal extinct boundary dividing what would otherwise appear to be a greater mother parish of Arreton. Running northward to the Solent coast

Figure 16.37. Bowcombe Valley. 'The central place' of Wight in Anglo-Saxon times. The old villa sites of the district are denoted as triangles.

at King's Quay, the brook provides the last 5.5 km of a cross-Island boundary (Figs 16.30 and 16.38, WAHL). The remaining 12 km to the southern coast is taken up by a continuous hedgerow that suffers no kinks and just one interruption. The break in the line occurs at Whitwell, where the parish boundary veers eastward to encompass the neighbouring medieval manor of Nettlecombe (Fig. 16.38). The latter is a property first mentioned in 1271. Within the bounds of this annexed estate, the course of the unit boundary is, at best, fragmentary. There is no mention of Whitwell in Domesday, and the history of the church begins in the late twelfth century when it was a chapel of the neighbouring parish of Godshill. Its progression to parish status is unclear and cannot help us, but it seems likely that the breaching of the unit boundary occurred at or after the establishment of Nettlecombe (Fig. 16.38).

In Godshill parish the course of the unit 5–6 boundary has generally fared well. The church here is a pre-Conquest foundation, gifted by William Fitz Osbern with five other Island churches before 1071. The parish completely straddles the hedgerow boundary but respects the margin of the neighbouring land units in Carisbrooke and Newchurch. Godshill is not mentioned in Domesday, probably because it was an untaxable possession of the Abbey of Lyre but, if its bounds are as early as its documented church, it seems that our long hedgerow boundary had already lost much of its significance before 1071.

If we seek to explore the meaning of this boundary then we must consider the Late Saxon history of Whippingham and Arreton. Both of these neighbouring parishes harbour pre-Conquest churches that were embodied in the Fitz Osbern gift to the French abbey of Lyre. If the terrain of these two prosperous communities was configured in the manner of the other mother parishes, then the Palmers Brook boundary is best aligned to set the two apart.

Before concluding our appraisal of these pre-Conquest land units, we must address the excessive size of the Carisbrooke mother parish (Fig. 16.38). A rough

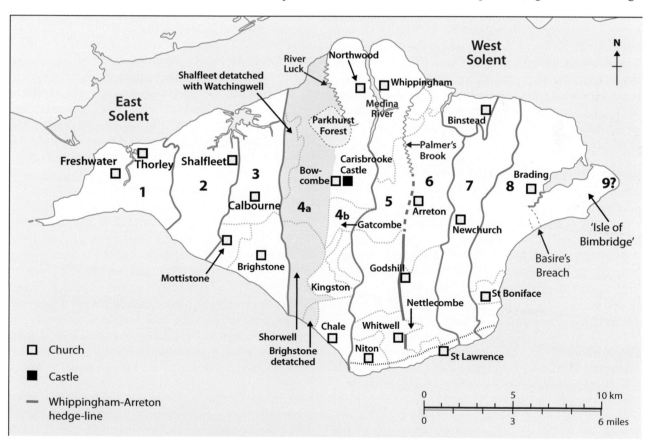

Figure 16.38. The central mother parish divisions of Anglo-Saxon Wight. Long mother parishes 2 and 3 are Shalfleet and Calbourne. Carisbrooke (4) may once have comprised Bowcombe/Watchingwell with Brighstone Detached (unit 4a). Eastern Carisbrooke with Gatcombe and Kingston daughter parishes form postulated unit 4b. Ancient combinations of the parishes of Whippingham with Whitwell, and Arreton with Godshill (units 5 and 6) share a continuous hedge-line that has largely lost its parochial identity (WAHL). The old long parishes of Newchurch (7) and Brading (8) complete Wight's linear divisions from coast to coast.

calculation indicates some 21,469 acres (8,688 ha), which is more than twice the size of any other unit. Might another median boundary be concealed here? The western boundaries of the daughter parishes of Chale, Kingston and Gatcombe offer hints that this might be so. North of Gatcombe there are no more daughters to point the way; but a short trail of consistent hedgerows leads us towards the crest of Bowcombe Down, where the summit was formerly crowned by a prominent Bronze Age round barrow with all manner of Anglo-Saxon secondary burials once interred in its setting. Pagan burials such these are a common manifestation on a boundary (Aldsworth 1978, 177, fig. 53).

From Bowcombe Down the northward course of our proposed boundary is uncertain. A route via the King's Forest of Parkhurst to the rising of the Gurnard Luck and thence to the shore of the Solent is one possibility (Fig. 16.38). David Marshall comments that a more westerly route could follow a sinuous hedge-line to join with the Rodge Brook before merging with the ancient strip tithing of Watchingwell (now Shalfleet detached). Having already noted boundary degradation at Watchingwell on or before 968, it is reasonable to suppose that a north–south median boundary within the Carisbrooke/Bowcombe unit might also have been disregarded at or before this time. If, for the sake of discussion, we accept this postulation, then Carisbrooke might lose around 10,000 acres to a former sister parish, of unit scale, on its western side. This, for convenience, we might notionally label 'Greater Shorwell' (Fig. 16.38, unit 4a).

Writing in 1982, Dom Frederick Hockey was the first to comment on the north–south configuration of Wight's ancient mother parishes. He proposed that the bold uniformity of these blocks might perhaps be attributed to Bishop Daniel (709–44) when bringing the Island under regular jurisdiction of the See of Winchester (Hockey 1982, 2). There is, however, no documentary evidence. This topic has since been carefully reviewed by John Margham, who holds the advantage of some thorough ground inspections (Margham 2003; 2006; 2007).

When we compare the post-Roman land division of *Vectis* and Thanet we find that all of these units are of substantial size. Where these can be securely recognised, these range from 2,843 ha (7,025 acres) in Shalfleet with daughter parish Brooke, to 7,133 ha (17,624 acres) in Minster-in-Thanet (Appendix 3). According to the historical accounts previously cited, it seems that the Thanet Sand of Minster parish offered the very best of Britain's fertile soils. It is here that we find just one villa, occupying this top-quality arable landscape. When we observe the relative modesty of this establishment,

we are forced to consider whether this, and perhaps the whole of Thanet's productive terrain, might be held by absentee owners. With agrarian and pastoral productivity operating smoothly, it seems that, unlike Wight, the resulting wealth and home luxuries may have accrued elsewhere.

Island markets and communication

Writing of England's medieval and Tudor economy, Sir John Clapham commented that 'it is not easy to exaggerate the importance of the export of wool in the earlier centuries, of the growing export of cloth in the later, or of the import of wine throughout' (Clapham 1957, 162).

Where might we glimpse Roman-era events such as these in the archaeological record? Surely it is in a generous scatter of Dressel 1 *amphora* fragments discarded across the Isle of Wight landscape and within its surrounding waters (Fig. 16.39, after Trott and Tomalin 2003, 166, fig. 10). From the distribution of Vectensian villas it also appears that wealth was being won both from the Island's sheep-cropped downland and from the wooded margins of its navigable creeks.

On Thanet we may conjecture a somewhat similar farming scenario, where undulating Chalk terrain could offer good upland sheep-grazing and rewarding fertility. Within the localised zone of Thanet Sand, an outstanding output of cereal crops might be sustained. Locked in the valley colluvium, there is surely a palaeoenvironmental history of the Tanatian landscape yet to be revealed.

It is when we consider the marketing and shipment of these commodities that our two island models differ. On Wight we can recognise a central marketplace in the Bowcombe valley. Here, relatively easy access could be gained to a point of shipment at the navigable head of the Medina estuary (Figs 16.23 and 16.25). Closer to this substantial inlet we find further villas at Newport (Shide) and Northwood ('Medina villa'). West of the river-mouth, a maritime villa, now lost to coastal erosion, formerly occupied a sheltered bay at Gurnard, near Cowes. Materials representing further Roman buildings are also known on this coast at Thorness Bay (Fig. 16.15).

It seems that further buildings, potentially of villa status, apparently were served by the navigable inlets offered by Newtown Harbour and the Western Yar. In most of the creeks on Wight's Solent coast we now glimpse the presence of villa communities that are well placed to exploit generous supplies of local timber suitable for shipbuilding and hence to the pursuit of ambitious voyaging in the *Oceanus Britannicus*.

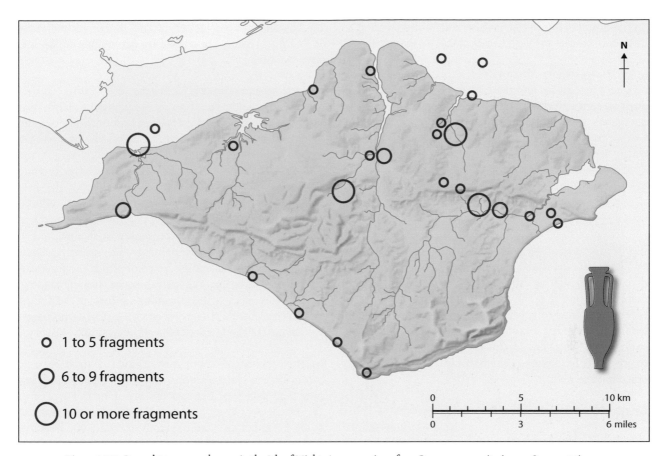

Figure 16.39. Dressel 1 type amphorae in the Isle of Wight. An expression of pro-Roman prosperity in pre-Conquest times.
(After Trott and Tomalin 2003)

In later history, we find these same activities well documented in medieval, Tudor and Stuart times when lucrative wool exports, in addition to the forays of Wightwarian privateers, are all described (Boucher James 1896, 1, 590–600; Jones and Jones 1987, 73–81). In the east of the Island, the villa at Brading attends its own substantial haven. Tudor accounts tell of a sheepskin glove industry, brewing activities, and the marketing of sheep in nearby Brading town. Unfortunately, the quayside of this struggling borough was more-often empty, and its unwelcoming seaward channel frequently silted.

On Thanet, it has been long assumed that the Wantsum Channel offered islanders their principal haven, yet we see no evidence of Tanatian villas drawing notable prosperity from such a resource. A subtle geological difference endowed Wight with a great northern clayland forest for its Romano-British and later ship-builders, but on Thanet we see no such suitable terrain, unless some of the chalkland once retained ancient stands of trees. The modest villas of Thanet also make poor comparison with the estuarine villas of the Medway, where all-important timber reserves appear to have been readily at hand.

We must also question whether the Wantsum was truly as valuable to Romano-British mariners as we have so commonly supposed. In his review of this channel's ancient physiography, Gerald Moody questions the established view that this haven served as a single landing place for the initial Claudian invasion of AD 43. The archaeological evidence for a defended beach-head and a subsequent supply base on its west bank at Richborough is well-known (Cunliffe 1968, 232–241; Manley 2002, 21–24): yet troop numbers alone would congest the Wantsum's accessible banks. An asynchronous tide and a series of accruing shingle shoals in Sandwich Bay could also create significant navigational difficulties (Moody 2008, 35–52).

Within the realm of the Cantiaci, he suggests a broader and more pragmatic scatter of landing-places in which the chalk-gap beaches of Thanet and the shallow estuarine shoreline of North Kent might be utilised to good effect (Moody 2008, 139–42). With the northern mouth of the Wantsum offering superior access over the eastern (Stonar) approach, it seems that the shipping interests of Tanatians and their various maritime visitors might naturally veer towards navigating and trafficking on the Stour to *Durovernum* (Canterbury) and piloting an upstream course through the Thames to *Londinium*.

In his study of Gallo-Roman riverine economies, Francois de Izarra recognises enduring rivalry between individual downstream riverside settlements, where ease of navigation for seafarers can be commonly overridden by a drive to intercept a greater intensity of light riverine traffic further upstream. Roman London and the ports of Rouen, Nantes and Bordeaux have all secured this desired balance, uniting an extensive network of riverine traders with the comings and goings of seafaring merchants (de Izarra 1993, 54–58).

It is in this context we see how coastal villa communities on Thanet are inevitably eclipsed by the maritime power of *Londinium*. Rather than engaging in cross-Channel merchandising, it seems that Tanatian mariners might be ever destined to service Britannia's capital city-port where much of the island's agrarian surplus was surely in demand. The *civitas* capital at *Durovernum* and military requisitions for *Rutupia* (Richborough) and might easily consume the rest.

Eventually, this becomes the shipping role of those multi-tasking 'fisherman-ploughman-farmer-sailors' described in the sixteenth century by William Camden. Here is a further reminder that, in past archaeological studies, perhaps we have been just a little too cautious in discounting the potential relevance of later economic models when seeking to explain the function and siting of such villas as those we now see in these two productive study areas.

Conclusion

In this select study of villa settings and land boundaries, I have drawn upon two exceptional Romano-British localities that have long invited attention. To what extent might these unusual insular environments be used to focus and inform our thinking on Romano-British villas as a whole? Both of these islands exclude Roman roads, *civitas* towns and conventional military installations, and in these respects, they appear atypical and unhelpful.

Yet Von Thunen's 'isolated state' (1826/1996) has long been advanced as a means of teasing out geographic truths and economic fundamentals where palimpsests of human activity might otherwise cloud our vision. It is in this role, as isolated laboratories, that our two Romano-British islands have much to offer. In both, there are still gaping archaeological lacunae to be filled. Fieldwork and reconnaissance are still urgently needed to assess the scale and intensity of non-villa communities, especially on Thanet where so much of the chalkland landscape is being so readily consumed by new construction and agri-industry.

A further impediment concerns the dating of our Vectensian and Tanatian villas. Where land was apportioned and villas established on both Thanet and Wight, it is implicit that these developments ranged over a considerable trajectory of time. On Wight, the villa sites at Brading, Combley, Newport, Clatterford and Bowcombe show activity before the close of the first century AD while on Thanet, the Abbey Farm villa at Minster claims a similarly early beginning. Moreover, in most cases, pre-Conquest occupation is also evident. It is unfortunate that the remaining villas on both islands currently offer no clear evidence of either their genesis or their termination. Yet with the exception of Brading, most Vectensian villas intimate a loss of sustained prosperity after the close of the third century. On Thanet, the demise of the Minster villa shows a similar history.

In this review of these two islands, I have focused attention on relationships between villas, land use and land division. The results are a little surprising. On Wight we have found major land units start at some 2,000 hectares and seldom exceed 5,000 hectares (Appendix 3, Table I). As postulated villa estates, these are unconvincing, yet as a means of levying *feorm*/food-rent, tax and pledges of human services they present a practicality that has won regard for at least a thousand years. A Middle to Late Saxon pedigree is offered by some informative charter boundaries, and there now arises the attractive possibility that their antiquity runs much deeper into a pre-Roman past. If a working name is now needed for these Vectensian/Wightwarian phenomena, then *levy units* may meet our need.

The absence of grand colonate villas in Britain is sufficient to suggest that there was little, if any, place for the single large consolidated personal estate among the property laws and rights that dominated the Romano-British landscape. Evidence of deployment of enslaved *coloni* as a significant agricultural workforce similarly eludes Britannia's archaeological record. Professor Rivet once reminded us that a villa's tenure pattern is not something that lends itself to excavation (Applebaum 1972, 39), yet we have since seen some courageous efforts in reconstruction.

Around the unusual fortified 'villa' at Gatcombe, Avon, a notional estate of some 5,600 hectares has been postulated, with possibly nine subsidiary 'non-villa' settlements contained within its bounds (Branigan 1977; Hingley 1989, 108, fig. 58; Smisson and Groves 2014). Nearby, in the fertile Vale of Wrington and on

Somerset's 'North Marsh', we have been shown an array of villas where each might arguably claim an estate since encapsulated within its own particular Saxon parish (Fowler and Neale 1970). Here the parish configurations are highly irregular and, at best, confusing. None of these parishes exceed 2,350 hectares, and where one (Locking) is as little as 411 hectares, we might just be tempted to postulate a consolidated home estate or 'home ground'.

It might be argued that the geographically isolated landmasses of *Vectis* and *Tanatis* provided the best opportunities for the emergence of a Romano-British colonate or large-scale personal estate. On both islands it seems that their absence may well have been dictated by an ancient ramification of minor ownerships that would ever resist consolidation. Richard Hingley (1989, 107) touches the essence of this particular British mix when commenting that 'individuals often appear to have owned numerous distinct areas of land isolated from one another and located throughout the province'. On Wight, it seems that the clustering of Roman buildings in the Bowcombe valley might fit with this conclusion.

The object of the Roman conquest of Britain had certainly been to seize and exploit valuable new resources yet, at a pragmatic level, the aim of the Pax Romana had always been the generation of wealth by the most expedient and perhaps the most sustainable means. We may also recall the comment by Dio (2.1) concerning the year AD 61, that, within two decades of the Conquest, both Claudius and Seneca had made substantial loans to leading Britons who seemed capable of yielding a good return. By 'leading Britons' we might choose to read the aristocracy found within the most responsive tribes.

Perhaps the adoption of existing boundaries and their use as 'levy units' offered the most effective way of monitoring and gathering incomes among a diaspora of Romano-British tribal and family interests. This leads us towards a different kind of villa community that, theoretically at least, might thrive within a patchwork of dispersed ownerships while holding nothing more than modest 'in-fields' at its threshold.

There are landowners in modern Wight possessing a surprising number of dispersed properties yet whose home properties are architecturally indistinguishable from the rest. We may recall, too, that the entire principle of tithe payment and the purpose of nineteenth-century 'apportionment books' was to assess each landowner not by his total holdings, but in each instance where his name appeared in the record of any particular parish. On an island fragmented by countless dispersed

landholdings, it is a system that could admirably suit the collection of *annona*. Such a system may also reflect older generic 'rundale' or *ceathrúna* type principles of fair apportionment.

An ignorance of Romano-British property law has long evoked archaeological frustration, yet most archaeologists seem agreed that a pragmatic mix of native and Roman ownerships and tenures may have best suited all (Stevens 1966, 108–9). Perhaps much of this essential framework was brokered during Claudio-Flavian times, when the brave new *civitas* market towns were under construction and native co-operation and commitment was being tempted or coerced by all manner of inducements. To obtain the most rewarding responses, these would need to be individually attuned to each tribe. Some current analogies in Afghanistan come to mind, where the disposition and co-operation of individual tribal leaders has been crucial to the interests of an occupying military force, whatever its ultimate aim might be. The Boudiccan Revolt of AD 61 is a clear example of a regionally brokered arrangement or 'accommodation' that was seriously mismanaged, while arrangements with others were apparently succeeding. From this it might be said that:

> Where lasting change in regime is sought, adversaries soften, when first they are bought.

Tacitus speaks of special rewards for T/Cogidubnus, and we may postulate other favourable inducements for further British tribes where carrots might be common and sticks seldom seen. Britannia would always be an island too far, and while Roman troops might struggle to hold a turbulent north, pacification and laissez-faire would always be the prudent rear-guard strategy among the southern population, especially after the Boudiccan disaster of AD 61.

On *Vectis*, and in the territory of the Regni, we can certainly assume handsome accommodations with indigenous tribal hierarchies. The scatter of pre-Conquest Roman ceramics in the Solent region suggests that the Pax Romana may already have been preceded by something of a 'Pax Bacchanal' (Fig. 16.39). When Suetonius (8.4.1) chalked up the island of *Vectis* among the conquests or acquisitions of Vespasian, and masons later set work to inscribe the same on those triumphal arches, was this, perhaps, a nostalgic allusion to an old cultural seduction that was already ancient history?

For effective taxation of a rural population, local flexibility is more often preferable to an imposed system of new land apportionment, where incomprehension and resistance could prove costly. We must also recognise that some potentially productive areas might eventually be held by metropolitan owners who neither desired nor exercised personal involvement in their out-of-town properties. The dearth of prosperous villas around *Londinium* is particularly striking, while *Aqua Sulis*, *Lindinis* and *Venta Belgarum* display quite the reverse. Here, explanation may owe less to locational geography and more to regionally entrenched social custom.

When, in AD 225, a 'Regulating Act' was issued to modify Caracalla's general dispensation of the rights of citizenship, it is significant that provincial governors were empowered to revert to local Celtic law to resolve unwelcome disputes. In his enticing interpretation of the tenth-century Welsh property laws of Hywel Dda, C. E. Stevens looked to the tenurial rights of *tir cyfrif* and *tir gwelyawg* to reconstruct possible Celtic landholding arrangements that may have been mirrored throughout much of Roman Britain (Stevens 1966). The resilience of native law in Britannia is confirmed by Zosimus, who records that in AD 410 the Britons promptly ejected their Roman administrators – and the 'Laws of the Romans' with them (Stevens 1966, 110).

Under the *tir cyfrif* system it appears that land was farmed from a nucleated settlement in which a gathering of various families was assembled. Where *tir gwelyawg* was applied, it seems that single extended families maintained their own land but, at death, any one internal landholding would be passed back to the entire family for redistribution. As a consequence, it appears that the system of *tir gwelyawg* worked against the inheritance and accumulation of personal capital while *tir cyfrif* engendered partible wealth that could provide for improved villas and their eventual enhancement with substantial luxuries, such mosaic floors (Stevens 1966, 123–27). From the evidence we see on *Vectis*, and at Bowcombe in particular, it seems that a system akin to *tir cyfrif* may have aided the Island's prosperity. For Tanatians, perhaps, a regime akin to *tir gwelyawg* or 'rundale' may have been their yoke.

In a corner of Britain where the Roman land-unit measurement of the *iugum* seems to have survived to become the Domesday and post-medieval measurement of the 'yoke' or *jugum,* we should not be too surprised to find that some other exceptional characteristics of Kent include an historic absence of common land and no Enclosure Acts. This, it seems, might be expected in a region where principles resembling those of *tir gwelyawg* may have been used to apportion and re-apportion its landholdings. We must, however, allow that the Juto-Saxon laws of gavelkind had since taken precedence here (Jolliffe 1962, 70–72). These had surely assisted the fragmentation of property through the partible inheritance of dispersed land, as practised by post-Roman peasant communities in this region.

Arguments for the post-Roman persistence of earlier systems of land use have frequently focused on Anglo-Saxon use of 'multiple estates' as a means of gathering income from an array of smaller and variably productive land units (e.g., Glanville Jones 1976; 1985; Bassett 1989; Brookes 2010). The role of these estates in consolidating larger lordships or kingdoms should not concern us here, but the nature of their linear components or *pays* are of particular interest where they transect an array of different habitats such as the woodlands, downlands and marshlands of East Kent (Everitt 1976; Brookes 2010, 66–69, fig. 4.1).

It seems from our accrued evidence that land use and the organisation of property levies on the island of *Vectis* may have followed an enduring pattern that was similarly suited to both Romano-Celtic and medieval needs. Behind these similarities we may also detect a common course of human behaviour within a finite geographic space, where natural resources remained largely unchanged. In Wight's medieval documents we find a number of issues that were surely common to scenarios formerly faced by the Island's Romano-British administration. From those set out by Richard Worsley (1781, 37–39), we may consider just four.

1. *A level of insular autonomy*
   The King recognises that administration of Island justice by mainland authorities is costly and better delegated to Islanders themselves. (AD 1356)

2. *Independent taxation*
   'Oppressions, extortions and injustices' are perpetrated by visiting officials to the Island. It is agreed that tax collection can be more effectively carried out when it is honestly organised and raised internally. (AD 1356)

3. *A case for a well-armed militia*
   The defence of the Island being critical to the security of Britain's Channel coast, Islanders are awarded special dispensations and subsidies to sustain an adequate resident population sufficient to resist invasion. In return, Islanders undertake to defend the Island to their full ability and not to allow their families to flee in times of threat (1352–53).

4. *A case for promoting insular maritime prowess*
   Islanders appoint three wardens who maintain a maritime watch over neighbouring waters and license the shipping of goods. In 1340 Island ships assemble in sufficient force to drive back a hostile French landing at St Helen's Point (Worsley 1781, 31).

In these events we can see that significant insular autonomy and sea power has become a pragmatic solution for the successful administration of an offshore community. We have also found that Islanders once defended their privileges and their maritime prowess with pride and vigour.

As efficient Romano-British mariners working in unified crews, we must consider whether, under the aegis of provincial military authority, pre-Roman Vectensians had once been similarly effective in maintaining a significant means of self-defence. With their homeland ever viewed as a potential steppingstone for the seaborne marauder, it seems that Vectensians, like later 'Wightwarians', would be ever bound to the leadership of their principal families, when drawn to a first line of defence. Here is a concept that may be lightly concealed within the iconography of room 12 at Brading villa, where the central figure in the maritime panel is twin-tailed Triton whose overt mastery of the sea may reflect the personality and predilections of the villa owner (Fig. 16.19).

Could it be that, in their ever-prevailing need to look to their own special defence, Wightwarians retained boundaries of a Romano-British land apportionment that could still be used to raise and control tithe payments and to provision and provide coastal militia and crews? The documentary evidence and the behaviour of Islanders in regard to 'their ancient usage' suggest that this may be so.

In the absence of firm excavated evidence, the archaeological jury will remain out. Nevertheless, the secondary message carried within the iconography of Brading's mosaics may tempt some to conclude that a prosperous coastal villa such as this might hold a central and lucrative role in assembling and shipping *annona*. Michael McCormick shows us that private investment in the building and operation of the Empire's *annona* fleets was seldom attractive when capital assets were exposed to the mercy of the winds and the seasons. Nevertheless, the offer of state subsidies, tax exemptions and generous underwriting might still make such entrepreneurial opportunities irresistible (McCormick 2002, 87–106).

In Britannia, the high yields of cereals gained on the chalklands of Wessex and Wight, and from the coastal plain of Sussex, would always make the Solent region and its *Magnus Portus* a haven for convoys and shipments. Wool and fleece for Rhineland and the soldiers of the *limes* would be similarly vital. At Brading villa, the Niedermendig quernstones and Rhenish glassware provide a helpful confirmation as to the destination of some of these sailings.

When we see the tamed Tritones and their reclining Nereids in Brading's maritime mosaic panel, the pre-occupations of our villa owner are again exposed. Perhaps a most telling symbol in this scene is the shepherd's crook in the hands of the left Triton (Fig. 16.20). With the aid of this obliging shepherd of the sea, an entire flock or convoy of ships may be safely ushered home to Brading Haven. The apparent attentions of sea-goddess Leukothea, guardian of mariners, could be equally significant (Fig. 16.20).

When, in 1296, Wight's valuable grain output was promptly shipped to support a military campaign in Scotland, we see an operation that is striking reminiscent of the *annona* system. Significantly, these supplies were loaded at Brading and in the Medina estuary (Hockey 1982, 105–8). Both are safe docking points where coastal villas formerly functioned.

In a similar requisition, in 1303, pre-shipment grain-gathering points are mentioned on the zone 3 Greensand, at Godshill and Brighstone. Of other collection points we are told nothing. It is now up to others to consider whether *Vectis* is the only instance where Romano-British levy boundaries rather than estate boundaries might still be concealed within a relict landscape that was once divided for the purpose of social and fiscal convenience.

When viewing the incidence of villas within the sealed geographic unit of an island, we are sure to question how many of such buildings have yet to be discovered. In Appendix 2, Table F we see that the intensity of villas on both *Tanatis* and *Vectis* is particular high, reducing the nominal land available per villa to no more than 9 square km on Thanet and 12 square km on Wight. On both islands it might be argued that antiquarian and archaeological activity has been sufficient to ensure a high level of villa recognition.

Comparison with results in some southern English counties shows that these intensities are not alone. In Wiltshire, current knowledge allows a space of no more than 18 square km that might be notionally allocated to each villa, simply as a means of estimating intensity. In West Sussex and Norfolk the figure is still below 30 square km, and in Surrey, Berkshire and Hampshire the notional amount of available space is still well below 40 square km per villa. In all of these counties we can see that villas were common, yet when we move to counties such as Somerset, Norfolk, East Sussex and Dorset the range of notional spacing rises markedly from 50 to 83 square km.

There are no easy explanations for these contrasts, although we will be aware that the geology and fertility of each county can greatly differ. The grouping of villas by county, rather than natural zones, admits further imprecision. Where villa intensity is evident – in Thanet, Wight, Wiltshire and West Sussex – it is notable that each displays a significant proportion of fertile chalkland in which villa development can readily occur. In Dorset however, chalkland is widespread, while the villas are relatively large yet thinly spread: a hint, perhaps, of different social and economic arrangements in the homelands of the Durotriges. Prompted by the villas of Wight and Thanet we are drawn towards a new round of locational analyses, yet this enticing avenue leads well beyond the ambit of this current study.

Envoi

Shadowed by the *Erinnyes* of academic contention, modern researchers have appeared reluctant to disclose personal perceptions of Romano-British villa society. Such reservations have done little to advance discussion or proffer analogies. When scanning glossy monthly bulletins on twentieth-century country life, we soon find that depictions of prestigious rural properties and portraits of debutante breeding stock had long served a raw Darwinian imperative. A century earlier, similar social preoccupations had been more cautiously acknowledged in Gothic fictional parody (Austen 1818). A time-hallowed sea shanty reiterates the same inflexible principle while also alluding to that unwavering seasonal tryst presented by May/*Beltine* gatherings, matings and betrothals.

> My face is my fortune, Sir, she said, all in the month of May...
> Then I cannot marry you my pretty maid, I unto her did say...

For the present writer, it seems that villa households of Britannia may have been confronted by a variety of uncompromising realities of patrilineal and matrilineal inheritance. In a later era, dilemmas of a similar kind might be found in Jane Austen's *Northanger Abbey* where we meet the raw demand to endow us with more or leave by the door! Indeed, life in some of our villas may not have been too far removed from the social and physical imbroglio so evocatively parodied in Stella Gibbons' *Cold Comfort Farm* (1932). Both characterisations remind us that, wherever the exploitation of land is organised, the 'territorial imperative' will ever hold thrall its occupants.

In his observations, of 1966, Robert Ardrey insists that here is an inherent trait of animal and human behaviour that might ever match a Darwinian drive to reproduction. In reviewing the nature of our villas perhaps we should remind ourselves that each of these buildings is a manifestation of the same dynamic: its scale, variation or embellishment reflecting no more than personal or prescribed latitudes on a path to this single fulfilment. 'There's always been Starkadders at Cold Comfort Farm.'

Acknowledgements

For hospitality and discussion on Romano-British Thanet I thank Gerald Moody and Emma Boast of the Trust for Thanet Archaeology. For their patience and editorial guidance in dealing with my interminable re-castings of this paper I am especially indebted to Kate Adcock, Anthony King and Grahame Soffe. My illustrations have been greatly improved and transposed into colour by Nich Hogben, who has also sharpened many points of discussion. Information on Abbey Farm villa at Minster-in-Thanet has been kindly provided by Keith Parfitt. Figures 1, 3, 8–24, 26, 30 and 35–39 are reproduced by courtesy of the Vectis Archaeological Trust. Figures 25, 27, 29, 33 and 37 have been sponsored by the ARA. I am most grateful to David Marshall for much stimulating discussion on our shared interest in the land boundaries of Wight.

References

Primary sources

ASC = *Anglo-Saxon Chronicle*. Trans. G. N. Garmonsway, 1953, London. Also A. Savage, 1995, London.

Bede = *Bede's Ecclesiastical history of the English Nation.* Trans by J. A. Giles, 1871. London.

DB IoW = *Domesday Book,* Hampshire. Trans. J. Morris, 1982. Phillimore, Chichester.

DB Kent = *Domesday Book,* Kent. Trans. V. Sankaran, 1983. Phillimore, Chichester.

Dio = Cassius Dio, *History.* Book LX, 19–22. Loeb Library vol. 7. Trans. 1924, since edited and presented online by Lacus Curtius. Retrieved 2020.

Ptolemy = *Geographia.* Trans. E. L. Stevenson, 1991. *Claudius Ptolemy, The Geography.* New York. Also, images retrieved online.

Suetonius = *The Twelve Caesars.* Trans. Robert Graves. Folio, London.

Secondary sources

Aldsworth, F. R. 1978 Droxford Anglo-Saxon cemetery, Soberton, Hampshire. *Proceedings of the Hampshire Field Club & Archaeological Society* 35, 93–182.

Applebaum, S. 1963 The pattern of settlement in *Roman Britain. Agricultural History Review* 11, 1–14.

Applebaum, S. 1983 A note on Ambrosius Aurelianus. *Britannia* 14, 245–46.

Applebaum, S. 1972. Roman Britain. In H. P. R. Finberg (ed.), *The agrarian history of England & Wales* II, 39. Cambridge U. P.

Ardrey, R. 1966 *The Territorial Imperative: a personal inquiry into animal origins of property and nations.* London.

Arnold, C. J. 1982 *The Anglo-Saxon Cemeteries of the Isle of Wight.* British Museum, London.

Austen, J. 1818 *Northanger Abbey.* London.

Bassett, S. R. 1989 In search of the origins of the Anglo-Saxon kingdoms. In S. R. Bassett (ed.), *The origins of the Anglo-Saxon kingdoms,* 3–27. Leicester University Press, Leicester.

Beeson, A. 1997 Achilles on Vectis: a new interpretation of a mosaic panel from Brading. *Mosaic* 24, 13–16.

Bonney, D. 1972 Early boundaries in Wessex. In P. J. Fowler (ed). *Archaeology and the Landscape,* 168–86. John Baker, London.

Boucher James, E. 1896 *The Isle of Wight: letters archaeological and historical.* H. Frowde, London.

Boys, J. 1796 *A General View of the Agriculture of Kent with observations on the means of its improvement.* Sherwood, Neely and Jones, London.

Branigan, K. 1976 *The Roman Villa in South-West England.* Moonraker Press, Bradford-on-Avon.

Brayley, E. W. 1817 *Delineations Historical and Topographical of the Isle of Thanet and the Cinque Ports.* 2 vols. Sherwood, Neely and Jones, London.

Britton, J. 1808 *The Beauties of England and Wales; or delineations topographical, historical and descriptive: Kent.* Vernor, Hood and Sharpe, London.

Brookes, S. 2010 Population ecology and multiple estate formation: the evidence from East Kent. In N. J. Higham and M. J. Ryan (eds), *The Landscape Archaeology of Anglo-Saxon England.* Boydell, Woodbridge.

Cahill, N. J. 1980 *Conquest and Colonisation on the Isle of Wight.* University of Leicester. MA Dissertation. Unpub.

Camden, W. 1586 (Latin edition) & 1695 Gibson's English edition. *Britannia, or a chorographicall description of the most flourishing kingdoms, England, Scotland and Ireland and the islands adjoining them out of the depth of antiquitie.* Andrew Heb, London, and David & Charles 1971 re-print, Newton Abbott.

Christaller, W. 1933 *Die zentralen Orte in Süddeutschland.* Gustav Fischer, Jena. For translation see C. W. Baskin 1966 *Central Places in Southern Germany.* Englewood Cliffs, New Jersey. Also P. W. English and R. C. Mayfield (eds) 1972 *Man, Space and Environment,* 601–10. Oxford University Press, Oxford.

Clapham, J. 1957 *A Concise Economic History of Britain from the Earliest Times to 1750.* Cambridge University Press, Cambridge.

Cotterill, J. 1993 Saxon raiding and the role of the Late Roman coastal forts of Britain. *Britannia* 24, 227–39.

Cunliffe B. 1968. *Fifth report on the excavations of the Roman fort at Richborough, Kent.* Research report of the Society of Antiquaries of London, no. 23. London.

De Izarra, F. 1993 *Le Fleuve et les Hommes en Gaule romaine.* Errance, Paris.

Detsicas, A. 1987 *The Cantiaci.* Alan Sutton, Gloucester.

Everitt, A. 1976 The making of the agrarian landscape in Kent. *Archaeologia Cantiana* 92, 1–31.

Finberg, H. P. R. 1955 *Roman and Saxon Withington: a study in continuity.* Leicester University Press, Leicester.

Finberg, H. P. R. 1964 *The Early Charters of Wessex.* Leicester University Press, Leicester.

Fowler P. J. and Neale, F. 1970 Fieldwork and excavation in the Butcombe area, North Somerset. *Proceedings of the University of Bristol Spelaeological Society* 12.2, 169–94. (See pp 170–80.)

Gibbons, S. D. 1932 *Cold Comfort Farm.* London.

Glover, J. 1976 *The Place-names of Kent.* Meresborough, Rainham.

Hardwick, C. 1858 *Historia Monasterii Augustini Cantuariensis by Thomas Elmham, formerly monk and Treasurer of that foundation.* Longman. London.

Hasted, E. 1800 *History and Topographical Survey of the County of Kent.* Canterbury.

Haverfield, F. J. *et al.* 'Romano-British remains' in W. Page (ed.), *Victoria County History of Kent* III, 121–22. London.

Henig, M. 2013 The mosaic pavements: their meaning and their social context. In B. Cunliffe, *The Roman Villa at Brading, Isle of Wight: the excavations of 2008–10,* 254–64. Oxford University, School of Archaeology. Monograph 77, Oxford.

Hingley, R. 1989 *Rural Settlement in Roman Britain.* Seaby, London.

Hockey, S. F. 1982 *Insula Vecta; the Isle of Wight in the Middle Ages.* Phillimore, Chichester.

Jay, L. 1990 Trust for Thanet Archaeology: excavations and evaluations 1989–1990. *Archaeologia Cantiana* 108, 237.

Johnson, S. 1976 *The Roman Forts of the Saxon shore.* Paul Elek, London.

Jolliffe, J. E. A. 1962 *Pre-Feudal England: The Jutes.* Oxford University Press, Oxford.

Jones, G. R. J. 1961 Settlement patterns in Anglo-Saxon England. *Antiquity* 35, 221–32.

Jones, H. A. 2017. The Roman villa at Minster-in-Thanet. Part 9: An architectural reconstruction. *Archaeologia Cantiana* 135, 189–208.

Jones, J. D. and Jones, J. 1987 *The Isle of Wight: an illustrated history.* Dovecote Press, Wimborne.

Kell, E. 1866 An account of the discovery of a Roman building in Gurnard Bay, Isle of Wight and its relation to the ancient British tin-trade in the Island. *Journal of the British Archaeological Association* 22, 351–68.

Kokeritz, H. 1940 *Place-names of the Isle of Wight*. Nomina Germanica 5, Uppsala.

Lacy, W. & Mullen, A. 2019. Landscape, monumentality and expression of group identities in Iron Age and Roman East Kent. *Britannia* 50, 75–108.

Laheen, M. 2010 *Drystone Walls of the Aran Islands: exploring the cultural landscape*. Collins Press, Cork.

Lewis, J. 1723 *History and Antiquities, Ecclesiastic and Civil, of the Isle of Tenet, in Kent*. London.

Margham, J. 2000 St Mary's Brading: Wilfred's church? *Proceedings of the Isle of Wight Natural History & Archaeological Society* 16, 117–35.

Margham, J. 2003 Charters, landscapes and hides in the Isle of Wight. *Landscape History* 25, 17–43.

Margham, J. 2006 The Anglo-Saxon Charter boundaries of the Isle of Wight. Part 1, West Medine. *Proceedings of the Isle of Wight Natural History & Archaeological Society* 21, 77–107.

Margham, J. 2007 The Anglo-Saxon Charter boundaries of the Isle of Wight. Part 2, East Medine. *Proceedings of the Isle of Wight Natural History & Archaeological Society* 22, 117–52.

McCormick, M. 2001 *Origins of the European Economy: communications and commerce AD 300–900*. Cambridge University Press, Cambridge.

Moody, G. 2008 *The Isle of Thanet from Prehistory to the Norman Conquest*. Tempus, Stroud.

Morris, E. L. and Dickinson, T. M. 2000 Early Saxon graves and grave goods. In C. J. Young, *Excavations at Carisbrooke Castle, Isle of Wight, 1921-1996*, 86–97. Wessex Archaeology, Salisbury.

Morris, J. 1983 *Domesday Book, Kent*. Phillimore, Chichester.

Mothersill, J. and Jenkyns, J. 1982 *Domesday Book 4. Hampshire*. Phillimore, Chichester.

Motkin, D. L. 1991 Edwin Smith and the discovery of Roman occupation in Gurnard Bay. *Proceedings of the Isle of Wight Natural History & Archaeological Society* 10, 139–47.

Muckelroy, K. 1981 Middle Bronze Age trade between Britain and Europe: a maritime perspective. *Proceedings Prehistoric Society* 47, 275–98.

Myres, J. N. L. 1989 *The English Settlements*. Oxford University Press, Oxford.

Neal, D. S. and Cosh, S. R. 2009 *Roman Mosaics of Britain, Volume III, South-East Britain, Part 1*. Society of Antiquaries of London, London. 262–80.

Oppenheim, M. 1926 Maritime history to 1688. In H. A. Doubleday (ed.). *The Victoria History of the County of Kent, volume 2*, 243–335. St Catherine Press, London.

Oulton, W. C. 1820 *Picture of Margate and its Vicinity*. Baldwin, Cradock and Joy, London.

Page, W. 1912/1973 *The Victoria History of the County of Hampshire & the Isle of Wight, Volume 5*. Constable, London. Reprint 1973 by Dawsons of Pall Mall, London.

Pearson, A. 2002 *The Roman Shore Forts: coastal defences of southern Britain*. The History Press, Stroud.

Percival, J. 1976 *The Roman Villa; an historical introduction*. Batsford, London.

Philp, B., 2005. *The Excavation of the Roman Fort at Reculver, Kent*. Kent Archaeological Rescue Unit Monograph 10. Dover.

Preston, R. E. 1983 The dynamic component of Christaller's central place theory and the theme of change in his research. *The Canadian Geographer* 27, 4–16.

Purcell, L. 1995 The Roman villa and the landscape of production. In T. J. Connell and K. Lomas (eds), *Urban Society in Roman Italy*, 151–79. University College London (UCL) Press, London.

Rigold, S. 1969 Recent investigations into the earliest defences of Carisbrooke Castle, Isle of Wight. In A. J. Taylor (ed.), *Chateau Gaillard: European castles III*, 128–38. Phillimore, London & Chichester.

Rivet, A. L. F. and Smith, C. 1979 *The Place-Names of Roman Britain*. Batsford, London.

Rollason, D. W. 1980 The date of the parish boundary of Minster-in-Thanet, Kent. *Archaeologia Cantiana* 95, 7–17.

Rollason, D. W. 1982 The Mildrith legend: a study in early medieval hagiography in England. *Midland History* 11:1, 138–49.

Roymans, N. and Derks, T., 2011 Introductory essay, in N. Roymans and T. Derks (eds.), *Villa landscapes in the North: economy, culture and lifestyles*. Amsterdam. 1–44.

Russell, P. D. D. 1981 *The Hearth Tax Returns for the Isle of Wight, 1664 to 1674*. Isle of Wight Record Series 1, Newport, IW.

Schwenninger, J.-C. 2012 OSL dating. In SLR, *Standen Heath Landfill, Isle of Wight: SLR excavation report 410.00034.00323*, 20–22. ('Grey literature' report held by the Isle of Wight Historic and Environmental Record.)

Scott, E. 1993 *A Gazetteer of Roman Villas in Britain*. Leicester University Archaeological Research Centre, Leicester.

Sewell, J. 2000 An investigation into the origin and continuity of the of the parish boundary of Carisbrooke, Isle of Wight. *Proceedings of the Hampshire Field Club & Archaeological Society* 55, 31–45.

Smisson, R. P. M. and Groves, P. 2014 Gatcombe Roman settlement: geophysical surveys 2006–2010. *Britannia* 45, 293–302.

Stevens, C. E. 1966 The social and economic aspects of rural settlement. In C. Thomas (ed.), *Rural settlement in Roman Britain*, 108–28. Council for British Archaeology (CBA) Research Report 7, London.

Taylor, P. J. 2007 Cities, world cities, networks & globalization. *GaWC Research Bulletin* 238, Globalisation and World Cities (GaWC) web release, unpaginated, Loughborough University. https://www.lboro.ac.uk/gawc/rb/rb238.html

Thompson, I. and Tomalin, D. J. 2011 The 1683 muster of Wight's parish guns. *Wight Studies* 24, 98–110.

Tomalin, D. J. 1991 Combe cluster barrows cemeteries in the Isle of Wight: a locational prediction model. *Proceedings of the Isle of Wight Natural History & Archaeological Society* 11, 85–96.

Tomalin, D. J. 2002 Wihtgarasbyrig explored. *Proceedings of the Isle of Wight Natural History & Archaeological Society* 18, 55–79.

Tomalin, D. J. 2006 Coastal villas, maritime villas. *Journal of Maritime Archaeology* 1, 29–84.

Tomalin, D. J. forthcoming *Roman Vectis: archaeology and identity in the Isle of Wight.*

Trott, K. and Tomalin, D. J. 2003 The maritime role of the island of Vectis in the British pre-Roman Iron Age. *International Journal of Nautical Archaeology* 32.2, 158–81.

Twyne, J. *c.* 1530. Cited in Brayley, 1817, vol.1, 4–5.

Von Thunen, J. H. 1826 *Der isolierte Staat in Beziehung auf Landwirtschaft und Nationalökonomie.* Translation & commentary republished by P. Hall, 1996. *Von Thunen's Isolated State.* Pergamon, Oxford.

Walters, B. 2000 Chedworth: Roman villa or sanctuary? *ARA Bulletin of the Association for Roman Archaeology* 9, 10–13.

Wilson, R. J. A. 2006 Aspects of iconography in Romano-British mosaics: the Rudston 'aquatic' scene and the Brading astronomer revisited. *Britannia* 37, 295–336.

Witney, K. P. 1976 *The Jutish Forest: a study of the Weald of Kent from AD 450 to 1380.* Athlone Press, London.

Witts, P. 2004 The Seasons mosaic at Brading: cult, culture or calendar? *Mosaic* 31, 23–32.

Witts, P. 2005 *Mosaics in Roman Britain; stories in stone.* The History Press, Stroud.

Woodward, A. B. 2002 *British Barrows. A matter of life and death.* Tempus, Stroud.

Worsley, R. 1781 *The History of the Isle of Wight.* A. Hamilton, London.

Yorke, B. 1995 *Wessex in the Early Middle Ages.* Leicester University Press, Leicester.

Young, C. J. 2000 *Excavations at Carisbrooke Castle, 1921–1996.* Wessex Archaeology for English Heritage. Salisbury.

Appendix 16.1

Table A: Vectensian villas, suspected villa sites and tile scatters plotted in Figure 16.3

		IWHER
1	Hamstead: coastal tile scatter	1261
2	Brickfields Cottage, Newtown Harbour: tegula fragments	1372
3	Saltmead: Roman tile on beach	1554
4	Thorness coast: tile scatter	2041
5	Sticelett: hypocaust tiles	1536
6	Gurnard villa (Scott IW 9)	1483
7	Cowes: coastal tile scatter at Egypt Point	1558
8	Medina villa, Northwood	5253
9	Whippingham: tile scatter	2158
10	Wootton parish: tiles and small kilns	4551
11	Seaview: tile scatter	3823
12	Thorley: tile scatter and pits exposed during pipe-laying	
13	Shalfleet: creekside occupation with scattered tiles	438
14	Watchingwell: scattered tiles and stone building materials	
15	Shalcombe: scattered building materials observed	
16	Rock villa (Scott IW 4)	277
17	Calbourne: Roman tiles reported in antiquarian account	429
18	Bowcombe building complex (Scott IW 1 and IW 2)	2024 etc

		IWHER
19	Clatterford villa: (Scott IW 7)	496
20	Carisbrooke villa (Scott IW 6)	503
21	Newport villa (Scott IW 11 and IW 12)	855
22	Shorwell parish: tile scatter	
23	Watergate (Scott IW 13)	826
24	Combley villa (Scott IW 8)	883
25	Mersley Down, Newchurch parish: tiles	
26	Mersley Farm, Newchurch: tiles	
27	Newchurch parish: tiles	
28	Brading villa (Scott IW 3)	1017
29	Yaverland: building detected in Time Team excavation	
30	Bembridge parish: tiles	
31	Chale parish: tiles	
32	Apse, Shanklin: hypocaust tiles	

Table B: Villas and suspected villas on the Isle of Thanet

A	St Mildred's Bay, Westgate: Roman foundations (Scott KE66)
B	Tivoli Park, Margate: partially excavated villa (Scott KE64)
C	Palm Bay, Margate: Roman foundations reported (Scott KE65)
D	Acol: aerial crop mark (Scott KE62)
E	East of Quex Park, near Woodchurch: aerial crop mark (Scott KE63)
F	Abbey Farm, Minster: excavated villa (Scott KE67)
G	Ebbsfleet, inshore from Pegwell Bay: several buildings identified (Moody, 2008, 147)
H	Pegwell Bay, Ramsgate: aerial crop mark of a small villa in an enclosure (Scott KE78)
I	Dumpton Gap, Ramsgate: Roman wall and artefacts lost to coastal erosion (Scott KE79)
J	Stone Gap, Broadstairs: partially excavated stone building with cellar (Moody, 2008, 145)

Table C: Additional unspecified Roman sites on the Isle of Thanet, Jones 2017

J1	Site in the vicinity of Ebbsfleet shore
J2	Site in the vicinity of Cottington Hill
J3	Site to the north of Hoo
J4	Site in the vicinity of Monkton Quarry?
J5	Site near Wantsum shore, west of St Nicholas-at-Wade
J6	Site north of St Nicholas-at-Wade
J7	Site in the vicinity of Brooks End
J8	Site in the vicinity of Lydden?
J9	Site in the vicinity of Lydden?
J10	Site in the vicinity of St Mildred's Bay

Appendix 16.2

Table D: The natural zones of Wight and Thanet

Vectis

Zone	Land area	% of land	No. of villas	% of villas
1	Northern Tertiary claylands	45%	13	36%
1a	Ria inlets (creeks)	5%	3	8%
2/2a	Chalk downland and scarp	16%	13	36%
3/3a & b	Greensand vale and clay inlier	30%	6	16%
4	Plateau of Oligocene limestone	2%	1	3%
5	Undercliff	2%	0	0%

Tanatis (with nearest Vectis zone equivalents)

Zone	Land area	% of land	No. of villas	% of villas
1a	Stonar tongue and Wantsum creeks	8%	0	0%
2	Chalkland	82%	7	87%
4	Tertiary (Thanet) Sands	10%	1	13%

Figures may not add up to 100% because of rounding

Table E: Villas and the southern chalklands

County	% chalk area	No. of villas	% villas on chalk	% villas not on chalk
Berkshire	48%	41	23 (56%)	18 (44%)
Dorset	50%	32	16 (50%)	16 (50%)
Hampshire	88%	105	88 (84%)	17 (16%)
Isle of Wight	16%	32	13 (36%)	23 (64%) (9 maritime)
Kent	50%	80	27 (34%)	53 (66%) (13 maritime)
E Sussex	18%	22	6 (27%)	16 (73%) (1 maritime)
W Sussex	30%	95	37 (39%)	58 (61%) (19 maritime)

The number of villas are guided by Scott (1993)

Table F: Known villas in southern English counties

County	Area in km²	Number of known villas	Notionally available km² per villa
Berkshire	1,300	41	32
Dorset	2,650	32	83
Gloucestershire	2,640	116	23
Hampshire	3,770	105	36
Isle of Thanet	90	10	9
Isle of Wight	380	32	12
Kent (inc. Thanet)	3,730	80	47
Norfolk	5,370	217	25
Somerset	3,450	72	47
Suffolk	3,790	28	135
Surrey	1,680	54	31
E Sussex	1,790	22	88
W Sussex	1,990	95	21
Wiltshire	3,480	189	18

Table G: Chalkland villas loosely grouped by south-coast tribal regions

Tribal region	Approx territory in km²	Approx km² of chalk	Notionally available km² chalkland per villa
Atrebatic	3,770	3,320	38
Cantiacian	3,730	1,860	69
Durotrigian	2,650	1,320	82
Regnensian	3,770	1,390	32
Vectensian	380	140	0.9

Appendix 16.3

Table H: Ecclesiastical parishes and their sizes in Thanet

	Acres	Hectares
West Thanet		
St Nicholas-at-Wade	3,660	1,481
Sarre	653	264
Monkton	2,346	949
Birchington	2,070	838
Monkton Manor total	**8,729**	**3,533**
East Thanet		
Minster	6,170	2,497
Ramsgate	3,244	1,313
Broadstairs	3,312	1,340
Margate	4,572	1,850
Stonar	798	323
Minster Manor total	**17,624**	**7,133**
THANET TOTAL	**26,353**	**10,666**

Writing before 1543, John Leland records that 'there were formerly eleven parishes and churches in this island'; four of the churches were ruinated. Hasted (1800) adds that the latter were those of Stonar, Wood (alias Woodchurch), All Saints and Sarre. The parishes of the three last churches, he explains, were united to those of Birchington and St Nicholas, so that there were then only eight parishes remaining in it, namely:

1. St Nicholas, with Sarre and All Saints annexed.
2. Monkton.
3. Minster.
4. Birchington, with Wood (*alias* Woodchurch) annexed.
5. St John, with the borough and town of Margate.
6. St Peter.
7. St Laurence, with the ville of Ramsgate.
8. Stonar.

Thanet, including Stonar, is otherwise given as a total 27,000 acres (10,926 hectares) 'comprising 3,500 (1,416 hectares) acres marsh and 23,000 (9,307 hectares) arable'.

Table I: The approximate sizes of mother parish/land units of Wight

Unit	Parish identity	Hectares
1	Freshwater with Thorley	3,002
2	Shalfleet with Brooke	2,843
3	Calbourne, with Brixton and Mottistone	3,947
4a	Part Carisbrooke with Shorwell	approx. 3,753
4b	Part Carisbrooke, with Gatcombe, Kingston, Chale and Northwood	approx. 5,129
5	Whippingham, with Whitwell, Niton, part Arreton and part Godshill	3,578
6	Part Arreton, with St Lawrence, Wootton and part Godshill	1,903
7	Newchurch	3,600
8	Brading with St Helens	4,113
9	Bembridge with Yaverland	634

Table J: Wight's principal property owners at the time of King Edward

Earl Tosti	£47	Afton, Brook, Compton Freshwater, Thorley
Earl Godwin	£29	Wroxall, Barnsley
King Edward's possession	£77.10s	Arreton, Bowcombe, Merston, Ningwood *et al.*
Edric	£20.5s	Shalfleet, Adgestone
Abbey of Lyre	£20	6 churches
Countess Gytha	£20	Wroxall
2 Free men	£17	Niton, *Abla*
See of Winchester	£16	Calbourne
Godric	£16.10s	*Hardley*, Hale, *Orham*, Pan, other Whitefield etc
Chipping	£12	Stenbury, Whippingham
Cuthwulf	£10	Wellow
4 unnamed thanes	£10	Mottistone
Alnoth	£9	Roud
Earl Harold	£8	Heasley
3 unnamed brothers	£6	Gatcombe
Wulfnoth	£7.15s	Shorwell, Sandown, Barnsley etc
Ketel	£7.7s	Chale, Shide, Appleford, Whitefield
Wulfgeat the Hunter	£5.10s	Nunwell, Luton, Wilmingham, Atherfield

17

Where did Sidonius Apollinaris live?

John Collis

Introduction

The Auvergne area of central France (Fig. 17.1) is arguably one of the best historically documented areas of western Europe in the Late Antique to Early Medieval periods. The major author of the fifth century, Sidonius Apollinaris, was bishop of Clermont-Ferrand, and passed many summers on the estate of his father-in-law, the Roman Emperor Avitus, and his writings include descriptions of life at the villa. At a slightly later date Gregory of Tours gives us further information about the area, including his famous description of the rich cornfields of the Grande Limagne. Though there is a history of topographical studies in the area (e.g. Desforges *et al.* 1970; Fournier 1962) archaeology was slow to develop, and it is only in the last twenty years that it has started to cast significant light on the period (Fizellier-Sauget 1999).

There had long been speculation on where Sidonius Apollinaris actually lived. The villa was adjacent to one of the lakes in the Massif Central, formed either in the craters of the volcanoes or in valleys blocked by lava flows. It is one of the latter, Lac Aydat or Lac d'Aydat, that is accepted by most scholars as the site of the villa. The modern name of the village, with some linguistic licence, can be derived from the name given by Sidonius Apollinaris, *Avitacum*, the estate of Avitus; names ending in *-ac* or *-at* are common in central France, and are generally assumed to derive from Roman to Early Medieval estate names, thus suggesting strong continuity of land tenure between the two periods. The clinching feature is Sidonius Apollinaris' description of the lake (*Letters* 2.2), where he describes a rock which was used as a turning point in boat races, a feature which is still to be found on the opposite side of the lake from the modern village.

The most detailed discussion of where exactly the villa lay is that by C. E. Stevens (1933). Since he wrote there have been few additional finds in the area, and none relevant to the location of the villa (Provost and Mennessier-Jouannet 1994, 22–23), but, as I am suggesting in this article, information from recent excavations elsewhere in the Auvergne may give us more clues.

La Chapelle de Pessat (Riom, Puy-de-Dôme)

During the construction of the A71 motorway from Paris to Montpellier and Beziers in 1984, the section north and east of Clermont-Ferrand was intensively field-walked revealing a couple of Neolithic, Iron Age and Roman sites at Pontcharaud and at Pâtural which were subject to major excavations (Loison *et al.* 1991; Deberge *et al.* 2007). The third major excavation in 1984 was that of Pessat where surface finds included pottery from various periods and many human bones, and aerial photography revealed a circular ditched enclosure. An emergency excavation under the direction of Bernadette Fizellier-Sauget and Jean-Michel Sauget was launched. As I had no major excavation that year, I agreed to send a team of students and Earthwatch volunteers under Duncan Hale to assist.

The site was quickly identified as La Chapelle de Pessat, a small priory dedicated to St. Martin which had been abandoned in the seventeenth/eighteenth century in favour of the less marshy new village at Pessat-Pollérande, the modern Pessat-Villeneuve. In all about 1,000 burials were excavated of an estimated 3,000, as well as the complete sequence of the priory buildings. The site lies on the northern fringe of the Grande Limagne, the large plain to the east of Clermont-Ferrand whose *terres noires* have been accumulating under marshy conditions since the Neolithic, and which, once drained, form one of the richest agricultural areas of France. Unfortunately for the archaeologist these soils do not lend themselves to stratigraphical excavation, so normally sites have to be dug in spits, and in the case of Pessat, there was also huge disturbance caused by the burials. This means that it has proved impossible to date the buildings other than in the most general terms using the evidence of the superposition and cutting of walls and burials, and comparing construction techniques and mortars. The burials are dated on the basis of their intercutting, the typology of tomb construction and a minimal number of grave goods (grave goods are confined to about ten burials). Because of the limited funding available at the time, it has proved possible only to do an anthropological study of the earliest burials and there are no C^{14} dates or other analyses available.

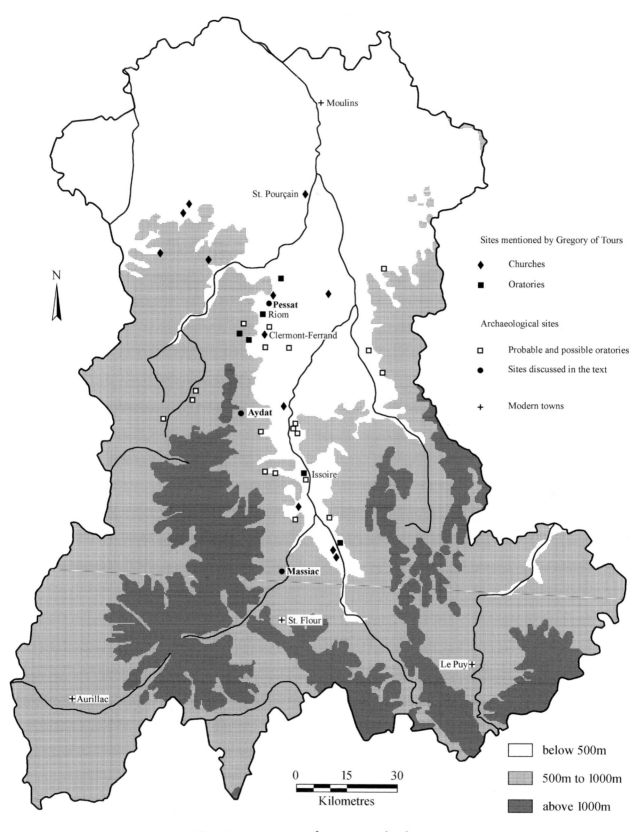

N

Sites mentioned by Gregory of Tours

◆   Churches

■   Oratories

Archaeological sites

☐   Probable and possible oratories

●   Sites discussed in the text

+   Modern towns

+ Moulins

St. Pourçain ◆

● **Pessat**
■ Riom

◆ Clermont-Ferrand

● **Aydat**

■ Issoire

● **Massiac**

+ St. Flour

Le Puy +

+ Aurillac

| 0 | 15 | 30 |

Kilometres

☐   below 500m

  500m to 1000m

  above 1000m

Figure 17.1. Location map of sites mentioned in the text.

Apart from one Late Bronze Age pit and some Late La Tène ditches and pits, the occupation starts in the Roman period with the construction of a Roman villa (Fig. 17.2). No floor levels survived intact, so there is no good dating evidence for either its construction or its abandonment. The largest room originally had an *opus signinum* floor, but none of it remained *in situ*. Fragments were found in some of the earliest graves that had cut through it, and on the basis of the good condition of these fragments, Fizellier-Sauget has suggested that in this room at least the roof had remained intact up to the time when it was turned into a mortuary chapel. She also argues that at least one other wall running north-south was still standing when the surrounding cemetery was established as four burials were aligned along it (burials 478, 598, 601 and 602).

Through preferential demolition and reconstruction of some of the walls, the Roman building was turned into a small church in the Merovingian period and an apse added to the east end (Fig. 17.3). Round the northern, western and southern sides further walls were added forming an ambulatory and porticus. The original, presumably dining, room, of the villa with its *opus signinum* floor became the chancel, and into this several burials were inserted, one in a stone sarcophagus made of local trachyandesite, a soft volcanic stone, a coffin type which is relatively common in the Massif Central. The other burials were generally in wooden coffins with the graves lined with stone or lumps of *opus signinum*. The top of the sarcophagus would have protruded above the floor surface, marked in places by a scatter of charcoal. The alignment of the burials was a mixture of south-north and east-west. One of the burials cut through the wall of the villa which would have divided the chancel from the nave, showing it had already been demolished. Similar groups of burials were found in small clusters around the church, especially in proximity to the apse, including others in stone sarcophagi, and presumably denoting family groups; 48 burials have been assigned to this phase. The only dating evidence for them was

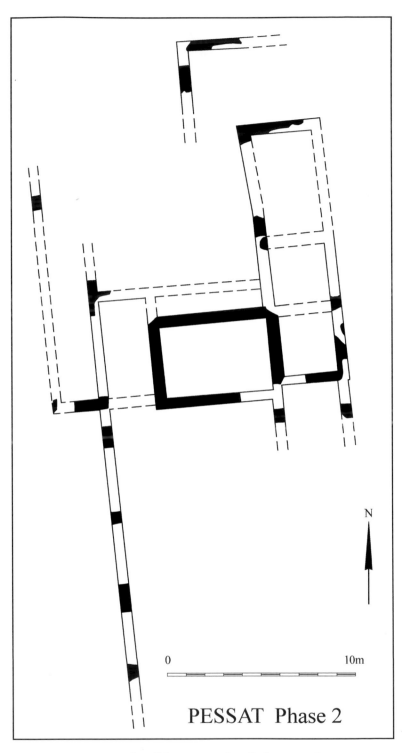

Figure 17.2. Plan of Phase 2 at La-Chapelle-de-Pessat, Riom. (After Sauget and Fizellier-Sauget 1999, Figure 3).

a double-hooked bronze tag of Merovingian type from one of the burials, and so suggests a sixth to eighth-century date. At a later date, also not closely dated but also probably in the Merovingian period, the western entrance was reconstructed with a wall with unmortared

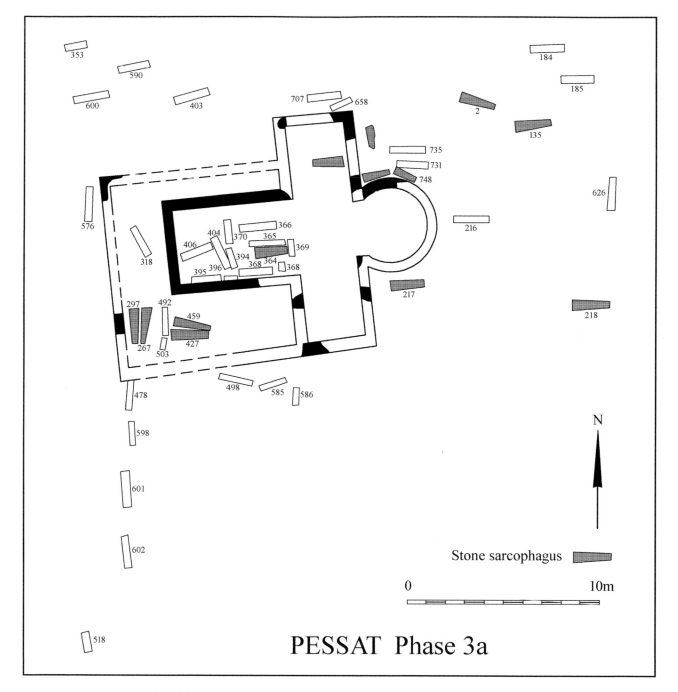

Figure 17.3. Plan of Phase 3A at La-Chapelle-de-Pessat, Riom. (After Sauget and Fizellier-Sauget 1999, Figure 4).

stone footings forming an enclosed area which included a burial in a wooden coffin (Fig. 17.4). However, there is no domestic occupation around the site, and Fizellier-Sauget argues that it falls into the category of 'private oratories', to which Gregory of Tours makes allusion, and she suggests a number of other sites in the Auvergne which would fit with this description, several of them on sites of Roman villas or which have produced Roman finds (Fig. 17.1).

The first documents mentioning the church at Pessat date to the 1190s when its dedication to St Martin is also stated. By 1296 it was under the control of the prior of St Amable at Riom and its status was a small priory. The building was reconstructed at about this time (Fig. 17.5), still using the traditional roofing of *tegulae* and *imbrices*. At a later date a dwelling was attached to the northern side; it incorporates Volvic stone, the quarry for which was not opened until the thirteenth

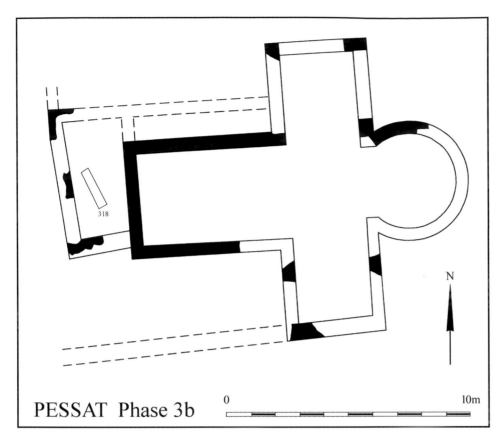

Figure 17.4. Plan of Phase 3B at La-Chapelle-de-Pessat, Riom. (After Sauget and Fizellier-Sauget 1999, Figure 5).

PESSAT Phase 3b

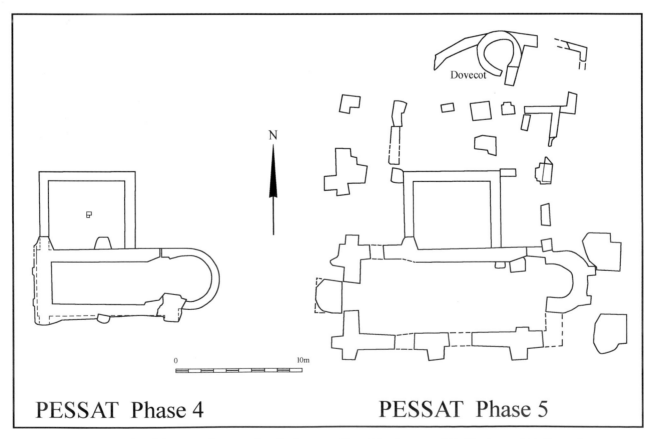

PESSAT Phase 4   PESSAT Phase 5

Figure 17.5. Plan of Phases 4 and 5 at La-Chapelle-de-Pessat, Riom. (After Sauget and Fizellier-Sauget 1999, Figure 6).

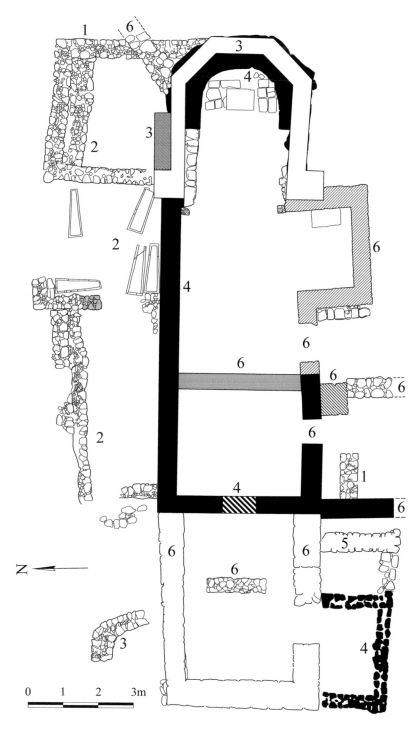

SAINT-VICTOR-DE-MASSIAC

Figure 17.6. Plan of the church of Saint-Victor-de-Massiac.
(After Tixier and Liabeuf 1984, Figure 6).

when a circular ditch was also dug enclosing the site. The building also had a bell as a bell-casting pit was discovered. Later the dwelling became an open courtyard around which were a number of domestic buildings, including a pigeon loft, a well and a possible forge. Burial intensified to the south and east of the church, with a density of burials of about seven per square metre. But from the sixteenth century the site was in decline, and by the seventeenth century a new chapel at Pessat-Pollérande was in use; there is documentary evidence in the eighteenth century that the old church was being robbed to repair the new church. The site of the old church was progressively forgotten, indeed the land was transferred to Riom in a redrawing of the parish boundaries in the late eighteenth century.

St Victor-de-Massiac (Massiac, Cantal)

The second church in the Auvergne which has been completely excavated, by Luc Tixier and René Liabeuf between 1972 and 1982, is that of St Victor which stood on a spur overlooking the modern town of Massiac (Tixier and Liabeuf 1984; Provost and Vallat 1996, 124–5; Collis 2000). With the opposing hill-top of La Madeleine which also boasts a church, it controls the entrance to the gorge of the Alagnon which flows past Blesle to Cournon where it joins the valley and the Petits Limagnes of the river Allier. There is Neolithic occupation on the spur and the outer cross-bank probably dates to this period, but there is also Hallstatt occupation at the end of the spur. In the late Roman period a smaller area was cut off by a large bank fronted by a double ditch, and it was within this enclosure, close to its entrance, that the church was built (Fig. 17.6), and, in early medieval times, a small village.

century, a date supported by the associated pottery, and there are a subterranean structure and drainage ditches as well as signs of agricultural activity on the site, suggesting a resident priest. Finally the church was increased in size, probably in the fifteenth century

The first phase of the church (Fig. 17.7a) seems to have been primarily funerary and was of high status; the masonry built building was in part faced with green marble and polished red lava, and had a tiled roof. It consisted of a nave with two rooms to the north which

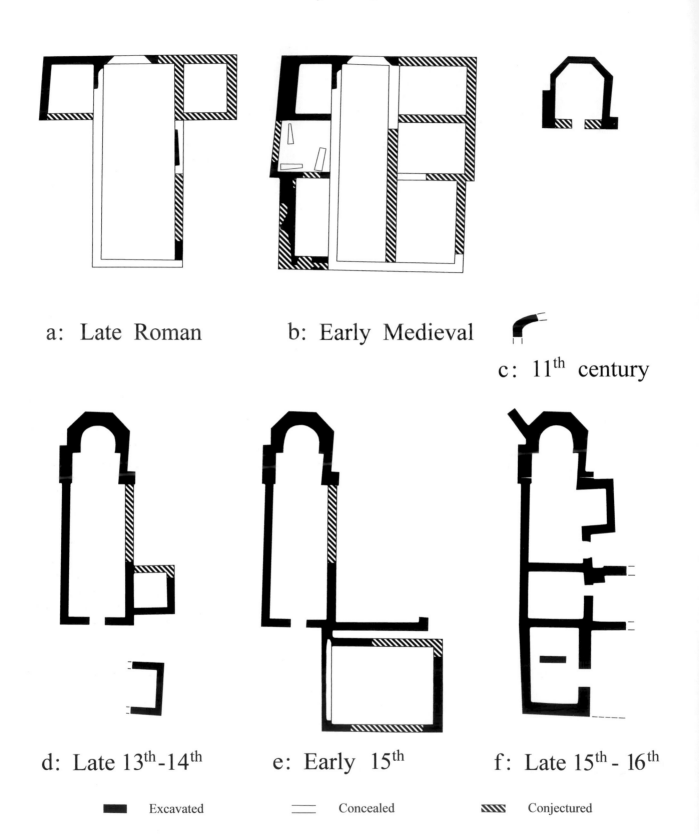

a: Late Roman   b: Early Medieval

c: 11th century

d: Late 13th-14th   e: Early 15th   f: Late 15th - 16th

■■■ Excavated   ═══ Concealed   ▨▨▨ Conjectured

SAINT-VICTOR-DE-MASSIAC

Figure 17.7. Phasing of the church of Saint-Victor-de-Massiac. (After Tixier and Liabeuf 1984, Figure 7).

the excavators suggest was mirrored by similar rooms on the southern side, but this area had been totally destroyed by more recent constructions and graves. Around the building were inhumations in graves lined with Roman *tegulae*, but these had been systematically robbed, apparently at the time of the Frankish takeover of the region. This phase is dated by the presence of 'paléochrétienne' stamped pottery. The church was also probably completely demolished as a burial from the next phase cuts though its foundations.

Sometime later, probably very soon after the desecration, the building, now certainly a church, was reconstructed, but the associated material culture was Frankish, for instance black pottery with roller-stamp decoration. The new building (Fig. 17.7b) was constructed in wood with planks inserted into stone-packed trenches. It too consisted of a nave with rooms to north and south, two of which had been used for burial. That to the north contained inhumations in stone sarcophagi, the one to the south simple inhumations. This phase lasts for several hundred years, until the late Carolingian period in the late tenth century, with the latest coins belonging to Charles the Bald (843–877) and Guillaume III (918–926). In AD 933 there is a charter in which the landowner, Giraldus and his wife Seginildis donated the property to the church at Brioude, after which the building fell into disrepair, and the manor of Ouche at the foot of the hill became the centre of activity, though St Victor continued in use as a cemetery. It was probably in the twelfth century that the old church was buried under a layer of soil, and a small polygonal chapel constructed on the site of the previous apse (Fig. 17.7c), while at the western end there was circular stone building which seems to be domestic. In a papal bull of 1185 a priory is mentioned at St Victor belonging to the Benedictine abbey at Blesle.

In 1289 the properties of Blesle were reorganised, and at St Victor this seems to relate to a clearing of the land for more intensive agriculture and the construction of field enclosures, while parts of the original church were used for dumping stone from field clearance. This agricultural expansion saw the establishment of a small village on the site and the reconstruction of what had now become the parish church (Fig. 17.7d, 17.7e). This building survived the various vicissitudes of the later medieval village (plague, possible destruction during the 100 Years War, and final desertion in the late sixteenth century due to worsening climatic and environmental conditions). In the late fifteenth century the church was rebuilt with a small lateral chapel and altar (Fig. 17.7f), apparently as a burial chapel for the lords of the manor. The priest's dwelling was finally abandoned in the seventeenth century, and by 1758 the right of baptism and burial

had passed to the nearby village of Bussac. In 1855 the church was finally demolished to provide material for the enlargement of the church at Bussac.

The wider context in the Auvergne

The two churches described here are the best documented examples in the Auvergne of continuity of Christian buildings from the Late Roman to the early modern period, despite often fundamental changes in their functions and ownership. In both cases their accessibility is due to their final abandonment in the eighteenth century, but it seems likely that similar continuity would be demonstrable under modern churches if such were possible, and it may be a characteristic of quite a number of churches in central France, though the specific nature of the original foundation may have varied. In the case of Brioude it was the sanctity of the foundation as the burial place of the martyr St. Victor which hallowed the ground, a site already mentioned by early Christian authors. In her discussion of likely early oratories, Fizellier-Sauget notes that several of the sites have produced evidence of earlier Roman occupation, and the construction of chapels and baptisteries in Roman villas is well documented in Gaul and Britain. As villas were usually the administrative centres of estates, where those estates continued to function in the early medieval period, their role as religious and especially burial centres is likely to have continued, and one wonders how many parish churches in the Auvergne have this origin. The –acum names are one indicator of continuity. The stone sarcophagi noted at both Pessat and St. Victor are common evidence of Merovingian burials, and are regularly preserved by the church and village authorities as well as being recorded by village antiquaries; the Auvergne also has a number of more elaborate Late Antique decorated sarcophagi.

The circular enclosure which surrounds the site at Pessat is also a common feature in the topographical layout of villages in the Grande Limagne, marking the historical core of the village, though usually only visible as property boundaries or streets. In many cases, though not all, the church lies in the centre of these enclosures, as in the case of Lussat or St. Beauzire, but it may also include a high status lay building as at Lussat. But in other cases the space is occupied by normal houses forming a circle around an open space, as at Aulnat, which may have been used as a market or for other communal activities. In some cases this central area is raised above the surrounding land, suggesting a defensive role in some cases. Thus the sequence found at Pessat may be fairly typical. The use of archaeology to explore village origins is still relatively undeveloped in central France, but these examples suggest its great potential.

Figure 17.8. View overlooking the village and church of Aydat and their relationship to the lake.

Aydat

Sidonius Apollinaris is perhaps the iconic author for the western empire in the fifth and sixth centuries. As the civil administrative structure started crumbling the church increasingly took over some of its roles. Sidonius, for instance, as bishop of Clermont, took a leading role in organising the defence against the Visigothic attack, and himself went to Rome to negotiate with the senate, and also to Toulouse where the Visigothic royal family with which he had many personal ties was based. Of all the villa sites in the Auvergne, *Avitacum* is one of the most likely to have had an administrative and religious role. Standing outside the apse at the east end of the twelfth-century church, despite some silting up of the lake over the past 1,500 years, it is easy to imagine the view Sidonius may have had from his villa (Fig. 17.8). On all the evidence, I would be very surprised if excavation in and around the church were not to reveal the original villa.

Dedication

This article was originally intended to be included in the Festschrift for Martin Biddle, but could not be finished in time to meet the deadline. Belatedly I offer the paper (completed in 2015) to him, and in memory of the two Scandinavian girls who shared a room on the Winchester excavation in 1964, Birthe Kjølbye-Biddle and Sissel Sødring Collis.

References

Ancient sources

Sidonius Apollinaris, *Letters* = Anderson, W. B. 1936 (ed. and trans.) *Poems and Letters of Sidonius Apollinaris.* Loeb Edition, Harvard University Press, Cambridge, Mass.

Modern sources

Collis J. R. 2000 *The Hill-Fort Study Group: visit to Burgundy and the Auvergne, April 15th – 19th 2000.* Hill-Fort Study Group, Oxford.

Deberge, Y., Collis, J. and Dunkley, J. 2007 *Clermont-Ferrand – Le Pâtural (Puy-de-Dôme). Evolution d'un établissement agricole gaulois (IIIe–IIe s. avant J.-C.) en Limagne d'Auvergne.* Documents d'Archéologie en Rhône-Alpes et en Auvergne 30, Lyon.

Desforges, E., Fournier, G., P. F., Hatt, J. J. and Imberdis, F. 1970 *Nouvelles Recherches sur les Origines de Clermont-Ferrand.* Institut d'Etudes du Massif Central, Clermont–Ferrand.

Fizellier-Sauget, B. (ed.) 1999 *L'Auvergne de Sidoine Apollinaire à Grégoire de Tours: Histoire et Archéologie.* Actes des XIIIèmes Journées internationales d'Archéologie Mérovingienne, Clermont-Ferrand 3-6 octobre 1991. Université de Clermont-Ferrand II, Clermont-Ferrand.

Fournier, G. 1962 *Le peuplement rural Basse Auvergne durant le haut Moyen âge*. Paris.

Loison, G., Collis, J. and Guichard, V. 1991 Les pratiques funéraires en Auvergne à la fin du Second Age du Fer: nouvelles données. *Revue Archéologique du Centre de la France* 30, 97–111.

Provost, M. and Mennessier–Jouannet, C. 1994b *Carte Archéologique de la Gaule: 63/2 Le Puy-de-Dôme*. Fondation Maison des Sciences de l'Homme, Paris.

Provost, M. and Vallat, P. 1996 *Carte Archéologique de la Gaule: 15 Cantal*. Fondation Maison des Sciences de l'Homme, Paris.

Sauget, B. and J.-M. 1986 *Archéologie et Autoroute: La Chapelle de Pessat*. Ville de Riom, Musée de Francisque Mandet, Riom.

Sauget, J.-M. and Fizellier-Sauget, B. 1999 La "Chapelle de Pessat": exemple de l'évolution d'une paroisse rurale en Basse Auvergne depuis le haut moyen-âge. In B. Fizellier-Sauget (ed.), *L'Auvergne de Sidoine Apollinaire à Grégoire de Tours: Histoire et Archéologie,* 301-306. Actes des XIIIèmes Journées internationales d'Archéologie Mérovingienne, Clermont-Ferrand 3-6 octobre 1991. Université de Clermont-Ferrand II, Clermont-Ferrand.

Stevens, C. E. 1933 *Sidonius Apollinaris and his Age*. The Clarendon Press, Oxford.

Tixier, L. and Liabeuf, R. 1984 Aménagements et constructions sur le plateau de Saint-Victor-de-Massiac (Cantal) de la protohistoire au XVIe siècle: essai d'interprétation stratigraphique et chronologique. *Archéologie médiévale* 14, 221–257.

18

From Roman villa to medieval village at the Mola di Monte Gelato, Lazio, Italy

Anthony C. King

In memory of the late
Tim Potter (1944-2000)
An inspiring mentor and archaeologist

Excavations at the Mola di Monte Gelato, near Mazzano Romano, c. 40 km north of Rome, took place 1986-90, under the direction of the late Tim Potter (British Museum) and the author (Potter and King 1997). The result was a striking sequence spanning the Roman Imperial period to the twelfth century, commencing with a well-appointed villa, then a late Roman farm or village with, crucially, a fourth-century church attached to it, progressing after a probable gap in the seventh century to a papal reorganization of the site into a church-based *domusculta* (estate) with a dispersed village-like settlement around it. This continued from the ninth to the eleventh century, when the settlement was abandoned, apart from a nearby fortified site and the water mill (*mola*), in favour of the more defendable village of Mazzano. This paper is a review of the site's significance, in the light of recent scholarship since the excavation report was published in 1997.

Background

John Ward-Perkins and others believed that in southern Etruria at least, classical farming units survived up to c. AD 900, the decisive break coming with the rise of local lords and nobles who were to create their own citadels of power (Kahane *et al.* 1968, 165; Wickham 1978a; see Potter 1979, 155ff). His thesis was supported by the abundant evidence for the papal *domuscultae*. These were a series of estates created by the Popes in the vicinity of the city of Rome. The earliest was built up in the 750s by Pope Zacharias, and in southern Etruria, we know from the *Liber Pontificalis* (I.501-2) that, about 780, Pope Hadrian I took estates of his own and others that he bought from other landowners, to make up the *domusculta* of *Capracorum* (Partner 1966, 74-6). Ward-Perkins also argued that the evidence from Santa Cornelia, identified with *Capracorum* (see Christie and Daniels 1991; Christie 1992), together with the occurrence of the distinctive early medieval

glazed pottery, Forum ware or *ceramica a vetrina pesante*, on villa sites explored in the South Etruria Survey (see Potter 1979, 1-14; Patterson 2004; Keay *et al.* 2020; Witcher 2020a, for background to this project and its methodology), amply supported his view of a classical agrarian system persisting well into the Middle Ages. The survival of classical estate names in documents and inscriptions, like that of AD 871 from Civita Castellana with its many references to *fundi,* also seemed to support his view (see Marazzi 1997).

The problem, though, was that the late Roman sites in part of the survey area, the Ager Faliscus, could in no instance be shown to have been occupied into the early medieval period. Two key types of pottery were involved, one being the Forum ware alluded to above and the other late Roman African Red Slip ware. The former, thought to have been in production from about AD 750, was identified on no villa site, while the African Red Slip ware found in the area rarely dated after about AD 500 (see Gilkes *et al.* 1999, 269). There was thus a gap between the apparent ending of the villas in the Ager Faliscus and start of the early medieval settlements of nearly two centuries. Only excavation on key sites would fill this chronological hiatus.

Two early medieval sites in the region, Mazzano Romano and Ponte Nepesino, were accordingly investigated in 1971 and 1982 respectively (Potter 1972; Cameron *et al.* 1984). Although both yielded fascinating and important results, including finds of Forum ware, neither could be taken earlier than the ninth century, or perhaps the late eighth century (as discussed by Patterson 2020b, 258-9). This approach to the problem did not appear to be filling the gap, and so it was decided to look at the problem from another direction, namely by exploring a Roman site with known late material on it, i.e. fifth-sixth century pottery. In this way it should be possible to establish when the site was finally abandoned.

The Site

The Mola di Monte Gelato seemed an obvious choice. The site is situated some 40 km north of Rome, beside the River Treia (Figs 18.1 and 18.2; see also updated distribution maps of the region in Patterson *et al.* 2020). In antiquity it was connected with the main road to Rome by a country road, paved in all probability in the first century AD, as the subsequent excavation was to show. Prodigious quantities of surface finds were recorded by the British School survey, dating to the late Republican and Imperial periods, and in addition there was a small castle site, Il Castellaccio, overlooking the valley, and a twelfth-century mill tower and adjacent defensive tower, probably of 16th-century date. The juxtaposition of the castle and the late Roman villa-like complex is particularly interesting, being one of a number of such instances in the Ager Faliscus (Potter 1979, 165): it is almost as though there was a move from one to the other.

The site has been known from 1875, when Coppi excavated a chapel or church somewhere near the river. It had *a cappuccina* burials (re-using Roman roof tiles) and was presumed to be of early Christian date. This led the great Italian historian, Giuseppe Tomassetti (1882) to some very interesting conclusions linking the site to the *domusculta* of *Capracorum*, resulting from a study of the relevant documents. A century later, in 1983, road-widening activities at the site exposed late Roman and apparently early medieval remains, which the Soprintendenza alle Antichità took to be Coppi's chapel, since there were also tile burials. This was the spur to set up an excavation under the auspices of the British Museum, with extensive help from the British School at Rome, the British Academy, the Comune of Campagnano di Roma, the Society of Antiquaries, the Roman Society and King Alfred's College (now University of Winchester). Many in the excavation team came from King Alfred's College or the British Museum, with

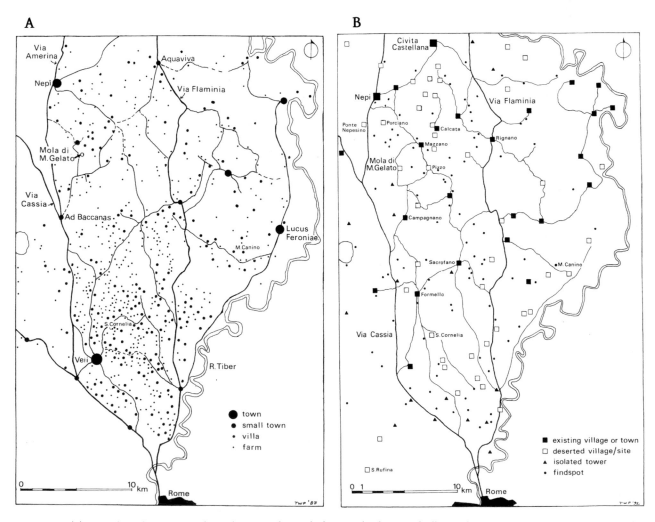

Figure 18.1. (A) Map of South Etruria in the early Imperial period, showing the density of villas in the survey area between the River Tiber and the Via Cassia, other settlements and Roman roads. (B) Map of South Etruria in the medieval period, showing Mola di Monte Gelato, other settlements and the roads in use in this period. (From Potter and King 1997, Figs 2 and 3)

343

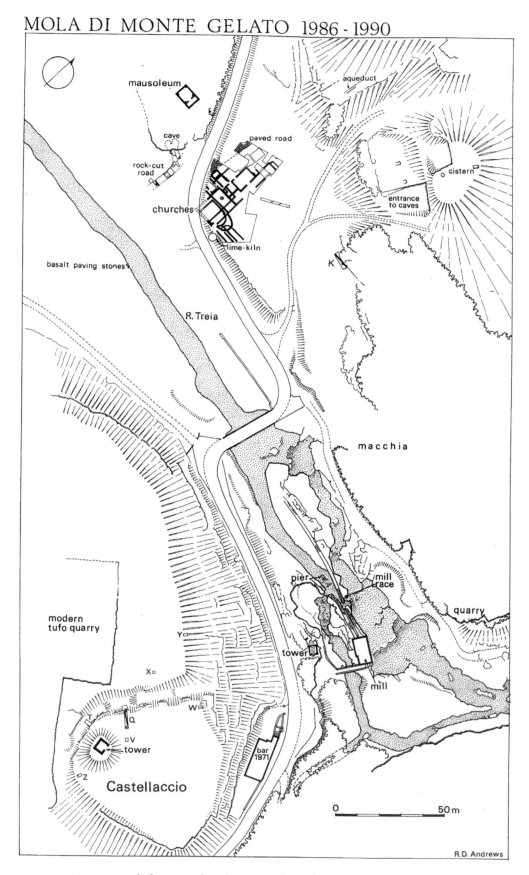

Figure 18.2. Mola di Monte Gelato: the excavated sites. (From Potter and King 1997, Fig. 4)

additional help from volunteers from various British universities and excavation units, and Italian students. The final excavation report was published in 1997, and the summary of the sequence that follows is a shortened version of the conclusions (Potter and King 1997, 421-8) with, in addition, some new suggestions for the use of the site in the late Roman period.

Villa to Farmstead: the Imperial and Late Antique site sequence (Fig. 18.3)

The early Imperial villa

The first buildings were laid out in the Augustan period, the choice of position no doubt influenced by the beauty of the setting. The waterfalls, in particular, make this one of the most delightful places in the Treia valley, a point that will not have been lost upon a Roman owner who was clearly conscious of the merits of ostentatious display. Moreover, the site had the advantage of easy accessibility to *Veii*, c. 20 km to the south (to the south of Formello and Santa Cornelia on Fig. 18.1) and to Rome itself: the urban market being a factor of enduring significance for much of the site's history. It was one of a large number of new sites established in the region in the early imperial period (Witcher 2020b, fig. 4.8).

The Augustan complex was ornate, and would be classified as a large villa in the descriptive methodology used by the South Etruria Survey (Witcher 2020b, 151). Although relatively little of its plan could be recovered, it had an imposing façade, embellished by fine architectural elements. Within were rooms floored in mosaic and with painted wall-plaster; a courtyard with a pool and clumps of trees; marble statuary (one from a *nymphaeum*) and other elements, such as a *labrum* from a fountain (Claridge 1997). No *pars rustica* was discovered, although there would have been ample space for it.

The question of the identity of the owner may here be relevant (Fig. 18.4). A tomb monument of the Valerii (recovered from the late Roman limekiln) was, to judge from its size and preservation, probably erected nearby, and may record the name of the first owner, namely C. Valerius Faustus. As *magister* of the *Augustales* of *Veii* (a title likely to be of Augustan date), he would have been an important local official, and his profession, a cattle merchant, included some very rich people (Gilliver 1990). He is precisely the sort of *nouveau riche* freedman who would have wished to construct for himself an elegant country residence (see Witcher 2020b, 119-20, 160-1). And certainly, as a *mercator bovarius,* we could expect him to have provided his villa with a *pars rustica.*

In the years after AD 100, the original entrance was blocked off by the construction of a simple, linear bath house. Beside it ran the road, now paved with *selce* blocks, and two cisterns were built to provide the water. By about AD 130, a fishpond by the portico had been partly filled in, and had presumably gone out of use. In this deposit were pottery wasters, and a new type of wine *amphora*, of local production (Arthur 1997; Witcher 2020b, 180, 183, 187). The quality of the refuse requires emphasis, especially the glass (Price 1997), while pottery graffiti attest the presence of literate Greeks, presumably slaves (Murray *et al.* 1991). Likewise, the bones of delicacies such as dormice attest a high standard of living (King 1997). The elegant temple-tomb of perhaps c. AD 150, situated on the far side of the road, and in splendid and prominent isolation on a ridge, must surely have been the burial place of the villa's still-rich owners (DeLaine 1997).

Within a century, however, we see changes that were to mark the demise of the early imperial villa. Features such as the fishpond and cisterns were obliterated with dumps of refuse in the late second-early third centuries (Roberts 1997, groups 2 and 3). Moreover, these features contained architectural and decorative elements, such as a broken *labrum,* showing that the surrounding buildings were largely demolished. Certainly, we cannot argue for a process of gradual decay, and the finds show that the inhabitants were prosperous to the last (see Witcher 2020b, 203-6). No structures of the early third-mid fourth centuries were identified, with the possible exception of a tile floor in a small 'lobby' room. There was also a virtual absence of third-century pottery, even in residual contexts, and also of glass. There were only six coins of the mid to late third century, and two of the earlier part of the fourth century, all either in late Roman deposits, or unstratified (Hobbs 1997).

The Late Roman settlement (Fig. 18.5)

The very different character of the community that reoccupied the site c. AD 350 is manifested both by the architecture and the finds. Although many of the old wall lines were followed, sometimes incorporating still-upstanding *opus reticulatum* from the Augustan villa, the new work was relatively crude and variable in style. There was no detectable use of mosaic or wall-plaster, and timber was widely employed for partitions and other features. In short, these buildings would seem to have been essentially utilitarian in purpose (see Patterson 2020a, 229).

The courtyard was apparently retained as such in this period, but the portico was blocked in, creating one or

Mola di Monte Gelato 1986-90: phases

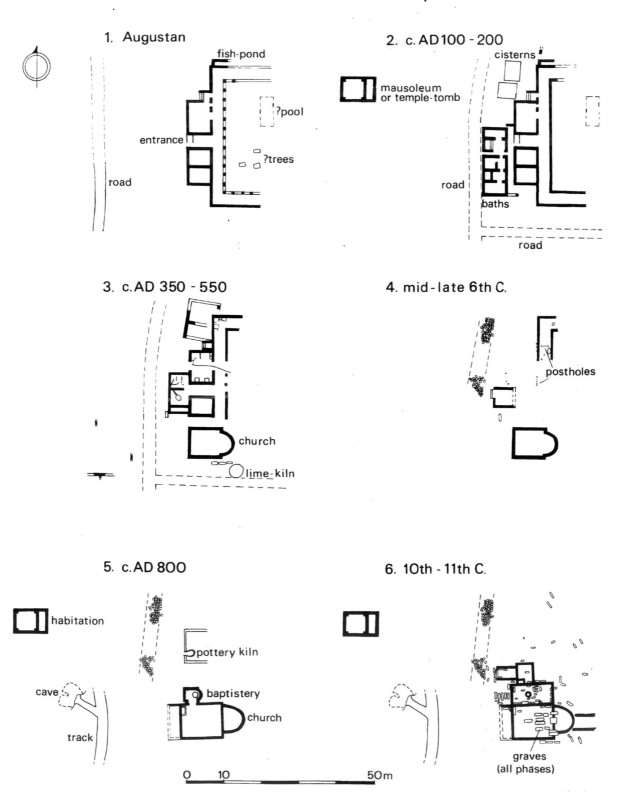

Figure 18.3. Mola di Monte Gelato: phase plan of the excavations, excluding the Castellaccio site. (From Potter and King 1997, Fig.12)

Figure 18.4. Mola di Monte Gelato: head of C. Valerius Zetus from the tomb monument, found broken up in the late Roman lime kiln.

more rooms. In the north-west corner were some curious wooden structures, tentatively interpreted as storage bins, for agricultural produce (Fig. 18.6). Nearby, a large room of the villa was rebuilt, partly as a stable (or byre), with wooden stalls and drains, and partly as a workshop. Here, there was a hearth with bronze-casting waste, and two rock-cut squarish pits, against a wall. In one were substantial quantities of second-century glass; these could represent scavenging in earlier deposits with the intention of recycling (Munro 2011). There was another workshop, also with metalworking hearths, constructed on the site of the baths (Fig. 18.7; Barba 2017, fig. 2). In the next room was a second stable (or byre), again with timber stalls and drains. Iron tools from the area included a metalworking hammer, and instruments for carpentry; some of the iron may have been collected together for recycling. Other artisan activities included the carving of bone and in all probability the production of wool and hides.

Another industrial activity was the production of lime in a kiln of substantially larger dimensions than normal (Fig.

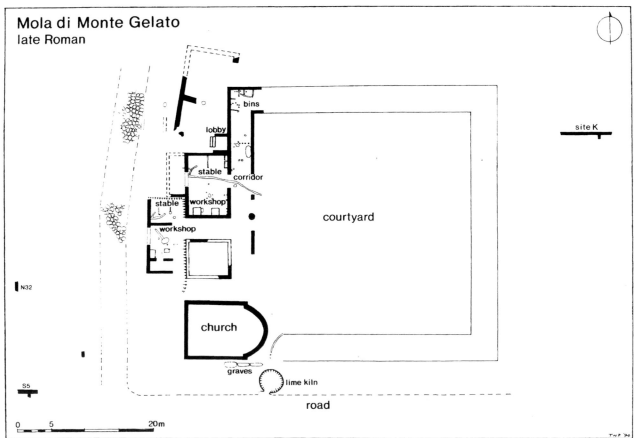

Figure 18.5. Mola di Monte Gelato: plan of late Roman features of phases 3 and 4. (From Potter and King 1997, Fig. 38)

347

Figure 18.6. Mola di Monte Gelato: north-west corner of the courtyard portico, showing slots and post-holes for probable grain bins dug into the early Imperial floor. The fish-pool infilled in the second century is visible in the background (with vertical scale).

Figure 18.7. Mola di Monte Gelato: early Imperial rooms reused in the late Roman period as workshops, with a channelled furnace visible in the central room.

*Figure 18.8. Mola di Monte Gelato: excavation of a piece of
early Imperial sculpture in the lime kiln.*

We can also suggest that the settlement was considerably enlarged in the late Roman period. Buildings of the fifth-sixth centuries were encountered on both the eastern and western margins of the site. There was also a new structure over the former cisterns. The establishment of a more village-like community may be implied by this, with a reasonable population. Even so, the small quantities of African red slip ware and imported amphorae do not support the idea of any great affluence: rather, this was the home to relatively impoverished farmers and artisans, quite conceivably tenants or even slaves.

The presence of dated Christian tombstones of AD 361 and later, from the nineteenth-century excavations at the site and from nearby (Fiocchi Nicolai 1988, 235), and more significantly, the addition of a small church to the settlement, at a date that cannot be closely assigned, but could be c. AD 400, suggest, however, other explanations (see Patterson 2020a, 238-40). Given the site's later importance as an ecclesiastical centre, and the benefactions made by Constantine to the Church, of land in the vicinity of *Veii* and Nepi (Marazzi 1997), the hypothesis can be put forward that it may have become papal property in the late Roman period (Patterson 2020a, 226; Fiocchi Nicolai 2007, 114-7). Indeed, consideration should be given to the idea that it could have been a monastic foundation. The picture of craftworking at the site would be consistent with this. Furthermore, literary sources commonly record an association between monasteries and water mills from an early date, and the likelihood is that the present mill at the Mola represents the successor to earlier ones, exploiting the advantageous configuration of the river at this point (see Barnish 1995, 135). The presence of female skeletons in the graves of this period would not be an impediment to this interpretation, since wives and other female relatives could be included in monastic foundations (Barnish 1995, 134). The late Roman settlement at San Vincenzo (Hodges 1997, 47-58) has many similarities, and it is discussion of that site as a possible monastic estate-centre that allows for a similar suggestion to be made for Monte Gelato.

18.8). There will have been no shortage of marble in the vicinity, whether from tombs or ruinous villas, and there was a ready market for lime in Rome. Agricultural produce may also have been transported to the city (see Patterson 2020a, 245, 250-1). While animal husbandry reverted to the traditional sheep/goat economy of the region, the plant remains point to the cultivation of wheat and barley, as well as millet, oats, lentils, horse-beans, peas and olives (Giorgi 1997). There is no way of determining how much of a surplus there was (if indeed any); but the recovery of 24 late Roman coins of the fourth-fifth centuries (Hobbs 1997) is an indication of some participation in wider markets (see Barnish 1995).

The fifth and first half of the sixth centuries saw a gradual decline in many parts of the site. The wooden bins and the limekiln went out of use by c. AD 400, and hearths began to build up over the mortar floors. There is an image of a gradual degeneration into a state of squalor. The latest imported vessel to reach Monte Gelato is unlikely to be much later than c. AD 520, and the few amphorae also do not post-date the early sixth century. Four coins take occupation down to at least c. AD 550, about which time substantial falls of roofs and walls occurred, never to be cleared away. Thereafter, traces of structures are confined to some post-holes, and the latest 'Roman' presence is a burial, assignable from a ceramic vessel (Roberts 1997, group 8, no. 187) and radiocarbon dating (BM-2862: cal AD 565-635) to the late sixth or early seventh century. Thereafter, for nearly 200 years, a human presence is essentially undetectable. Thus, the picture of decay and then demise, around the mid-sixth century, conforms remarkably closely with both San Vincenzo al Volturno, in Isernia (Hodges 1997) and San Giovanni di Ruoti, near Potenza (Small and Buck 1994), although this should be set against evidence from the nearby Farfa area in the Sabina Tiberina, where ceramics suggest activity continuing into the seventh century and later (Gilkes *et al.* 1999). Looming over the site sequence outlined above are historical events associated with the arrival of the Lombards, towards the end of the sixth century, in the region to the north of Rome (Patterson 2020b, 252-7). It could easily be the case that Monte Gelato's decline and virtual abandonment at this period may be due to political instability and military disruption. However, no direct trace of this can be seen at the site, so interpretation along these lines must remain speculative.

Farmstead to Village: the medieval site sequence

The domusculta of Capracorum

The construction of a new, larger and elaborately decorated church, c. AD 800, with a conjoined baptistery (Figs 18.9 and 18.10), can be safely ascribed to the period of the *domusculta* of *Capracorum* and, on documentary evidence, Monte Gelato can be regarded as one of its estate-centres (Potter and King 1997, 5-6; see Wickham 1978b, 174; Patterson 2020c, 274-80, 282, 287-9, 293, 296, Fig. 7.4). It is perhaps puzzling that, apart from a possible perimeter wall with a structure against it, no other major buildings were encountered. Reused Roman features, like the temple-tomb, and rock-cut caves (Fig. 18.11) apparently sufficed. But the animal bones (once again with pig predominant, echoing the earlier animal economy; see King 1997 and De Grossi Mazorin 2020, 635-6) and the plant remains correspond with

references to the produce of the *domusculta,* while a pottery kiln (Fig. 18.12), making wares exactly paralleled in Rome (Patterson 1997), probably provided transport containers for these foodstuffs. The maintenance of the Roman paved road was evidently of importance, and many of the blocks were relaid around this time.

The extensive early medieval cemetery, and analysis of the human remains (Conheeney 1997), suggest that there was a normal population of men, women and children (Fig. 18.13), with a clear hierarchy: the more elaborate graves clustered in or around the church and baptistery, while beneath the altar were two primary burials, which on radiocarbon dating (BM-2861: cal AD 545-630) must have been interred as relics and may have been the remains of holy men or saints. There were a few grave offerings, but little use of coffins. In general, the mode of burial was disorderly, propinquity to the ecclesiastical buildings (*ad sanctos*) being the prime concern. Study of the bones shows that this was a hard-working peasant population (including those buried in high-status' graves, and both men and women), with features indicating family links: the adjacent graves of two apparently related individuals, both accompanied by Roman coins, in pagan tradition, is here especially noteworthy. We infer that, between the foundation of the *domusculta* and the abandonment of the site some three centuries later, c. AD 1100, the community became ever more parochial and conservative, isolated from the outside world. The recovery of but a single medieval coin, of AD 884-5, is perhaps symptomatic of this.

The abandonment of the pottery kiln, in the mid- (or possibly late) ninth century may mark the demise of the *domusculta* (see Patterson 2020c, 283, 298). At Monte Gelato, it is not possible to say much about events between the late ninth century and the beginning of the eleventh century. Although there is some pottery of this period, only the sequence over the bath house suggests unbroken occupation. On the other hand, many decorative elements in the church, including a very fine probable altar screen with the Agnus Dei (Osborne 1994; 1997), remained to be broken up c. AD 1000, and burials seem to have been made continuously: on balance, therefore, it seems that the site remained in use over this time, albeit in a decaying state.

The rebuilding of c. AD 1000, and the decline and end of the site

In the late tenth or early eleventh century, the baptistery was rebuilt on a much larger scale, with a rather grand font (Gilkes and Potter 1997); and other rooms were added to the north of the baptistery, including an entrance.

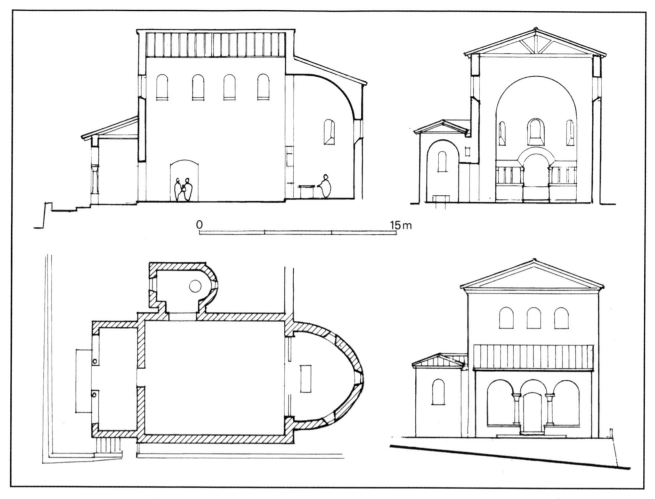

Figure 18.9. Mola di Monte Gelato: reconstructed plan and elevations of the church and baptistery, c. AD 800.
(Drawing by Sheila Gibson, from Potter and King 1997, Fig. 73)

Although the work was relatively crude, and there is no surviving evidence for embellishment, the importance of the ecclesiastical complex would seem to have been strongly reaffirmed.

It was a short-lived revival. Around the beginning of the twelfth century the buildings were systematically demolished, and the materials carted away. Occupation also ceased in the rock-cut cave and in the temple-tomb, and the impression is of a systematic and orderly evacuation. Indeed, some of the more important graves were emptied of the bones, and then reconstructed, which may well reflect the fact that the place was not forgotten. Burials continued to be made for a time, including those of children placed in graves cut into or across the demolished wall footings in the baptistery. Moreover, in the church a foundation was constructed, probably to support a wayside shrine or some other form of commemorative monument, such as a cross. Continued veneration of

Figure 18.10. Mola di Monte Gelato:
part of a chancel screen or iconostasis
from the church of c. AD 800.

Figure 18.11. Mola di Monte Gelato: cave adjacent to the main excavated site, with evidence of ninth-century occupation.

Figure 18.12. Mola di Monte Gelato: ninth-century pottery kiln positioned in the south-west corner of an abandoned late Roman room, itself adapted from the early Imperial villa. A section of fallen masonry is visible in the foreground.

Figure 18.13. Mola di Monte Gelato: infant skeleton from the baptistery area.

this long-lived focus of Christian worship and interment was clearly considered a matter of considerable consequence.

The population very likely moved to the nearby castle site of Castellaccio (identifiable as *castrum Capracorum* from a *bulla* of 1053; Tomassetti 1883, 137ff.). The occurrence at the castle of some eleventh-century pottery and, overwhelmingly, of twelfth-century material, tends to support this conclusion. Whether this was an enforced move to the castle, c. 250 m north-east, or a voluntary decision to abandon an unprotectable location, is not known. The very limited excavations at Castellaccio (where heavy tree cover restricted trenching) revealed the remains of a masonry curtain wall, with a building constructed behind it (Wilkinson 1997). The dearth of refuse implies a relatively small community, and the pottery evidence shows that Castellaccio was not occupied much after the end of the twelfth century. A migration to Mazzano, which has traditionally included the Mola di Monte Gelato within its sphere of influence, is more than likely. Only the twelfth-century mill continued in use, exploiting its advantageous position on the river, and protected, it would seem, by militia based in an adjoining tower (Fedeli Bernardini 1997).

Conclusion

What has the excavation contributed to the Ward-Perkins hypothesis of continuity of the farming system? A notable feature of the sequence as a whole is the continuity of the alignment generated by the road and early buildings alongside it. This is enhanced by the extensive rebuilding of walls on earlier footings. Obviously, it is tempting to see continuity of occupation in this sequence, but we must ask ourselves how far the changes and rebuildings might represent ruptures in the occupation of the site. This particularly applies to the evidence for decline and possible hiatus in the seventh century.

While Monte Gelato has not demonstrated that Ward-Perkins was right, neither has it proved him wrong, since any postulated gap need not have been very long, and the revival of the site as a *domusculta* centre may well have been linked with the re-establishment of traditional farming in the area. The excavations have clearly shown the importance of the church site as a focus for the local early medieval community, thus providing some element of continuity in the religious sphere, if not so clearly in the realm of agriculture and economics. As Francovich and Hodges (2003, 84-102) have argued, however, the *domuscultae* and monastic settlements such as San Vincenzo al Volturno (Hodges 1997), together

with other ninth-century churches on Roman sites, such as Le Mura di Santo Stefano, Anguillara (Van der Noort and Whitehouse 1992, 152; 2009) were relatively short-lived attempts at ecclesiastical land management, which were eventually overtaken by the rise of villages, and more importantly, hill-top settlements (*castelli*) under seigneurial control (see Hubert 2000, 589; Valenti 2016; Patterson 2020b, 257-8; 2020c, 287-9, 301, Fig. 7.4). The decline of papal control at Monte Gelato after the ninth century preceded the move to the Castellaccio and then, presumably, to Mazzano, which was a pre-existing defensive settlement of the type that was to dominate central Italy for much of the Middle Ages (Fig. 18.14; Messineo and Carbonara 1993, 85-94).

The earlier transition from villa to 'village' in the late Roman period is, arguably, of greater significance to this volume. At Monte Gelato, the medium-sized villa of the early Empire goes into decline and probable abandonment in the third century. This corresponds with similar down-turns at other villas, notably Settefinestre in Etruria (Carandini 1985), and has been linked with both the relative up-swing in the economic fortunes of the provinces as opposed to Italy and to a decline in slave-dependent villa economies (see Rathbone 1983; Wickham 1994, ch. 1) during the third century. The establishment of the farming settlement at Monte Gelato in the fourth century is of some interest in this context, as it is apparent from survey statistics that many early Imperial sites in central Italy did not continue into the late Roman period (Potter 1979, 140; Patterson 2020a).

In the final excavation report (Potter and King 1997, 423-4; see above) we suggested that the late Roman establishment may have been strongly linked to the Church, perhaps even monastic in nature (see Barnish 1995). Equally, the building of a small church by c. AD 400 at the site may imply an ordinary farm or *fundus* owned by a Christian, such as the wealthy Melania, who is said to have had 62 settlements or estates near Rome, each with some 400 slaves who farmed the land (*Vita S. Melaniae Junioris* (Latin) 18; Jones 1973, 793; Clark 1984). The lack of wealth at Monte Gelato during this period suggests an absentee owner, and an estate devoted to production, the fruits of which were enjoyed elsewhere. This interpretation would fit with the model of aristocratic interest in Christianisation, and consequent development of churches on their rural estates, probably in conjunction with ecclesiastical oversight (Chavarria Arnau 2006; 2010; Castiglia 2018, 223-4).

A third possibility can also be suggested, that late Roman Monte Gelato was a peasant settlement reusing a former villa site that had been abandoned a century or

Figure 18.14. The hill-town of Calcata, on a promontory overlooking the River Treia a few kilometres downstream of Monte Gelato and Mazzano. It is a typical example of a medieval defended settlement in South Etruria. (Photo: A. C. King)

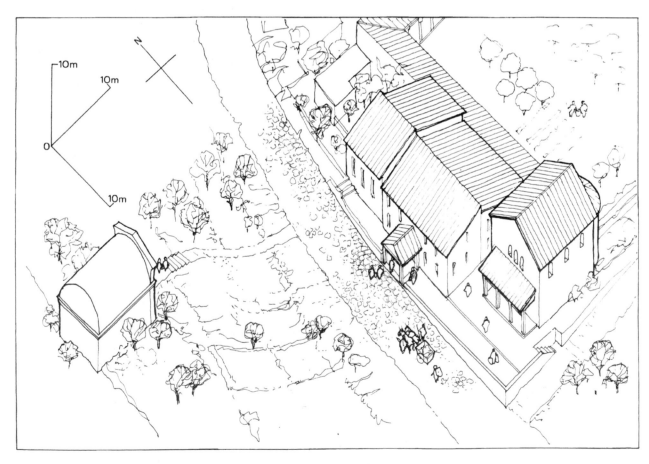

Figure 18.15. Mola di Monte Gelato: a reconstruction of the late Roman settlement, phase 3. (Drawing by Sheila Gibson, from Potter and King 1997, Fig. 70)

so earlier (Patterson 2020a, 242; see Hodges 2021; Bowes 2021). The nature of the settlement (Fig. 18.15) with a relatively low level of material culture, probably nearer self-sufficiency than regular surplus production, would support this, and the church may suggest a genuine focus for a village community of the late fourth to sixth centuries, with a proto-parish (*pieve*) organisation (see Pergola 1999). If this was the case, the Christianisation of the site may be the result of the inhabitants' desire for a place of worship, rather than the imposition of a church by an aristocratic owner or patron, or by ecclesiastical authorities (see Bowes 2007; Castiglia 2018, 245-6). Wickham (1994, 113-5) and Francovich and Hodges (2003, 109-10) have argued that the late Roman period was a time of opportunity for the peasantry, and the establishment of villages such as Monte Gelato and Torrita di Siena in Tuscany (Francovich and Hodges 2003, 49-51) on the sites of villas makes them 'prototypes of a medieval settlement form' (Francovich and Hodges 2003, 108).

The eventual decline of the late Roman settlement at Monte Gelato may have been the result of rural insecurity as much as anything else. The sixth-century Lombard advance made the northern territory of Rome difficult to occupy safely by the seventh century (Wickham 1981, 64-5; Patterson *et al.* 2004, 18-28; Patterson 2020b, 252-7), and it was not until the papal initiative of the *domuscultae* that Monte Gelato and other settlements revived.

Acknowledgements

This paper was prepared for a volume arising from a conference held in 2005, entitled 'From Villa to Village. Continuity and change', hosted by the Upper Nene Archaeological Society at Northampton, UK. Regrettably, the proposed volume was not published, and therefore the editors kindly agreed to place the paper in this volume. At the same time, the Tiber Valley Project and other recent research have led to new perspectives on the Monte Gelato site, which have been incorporated and duly acknowledged throughout this paper.

References

Ancient sources

Liber Pontificalis = Davis, R. 2000 (ed. and trans.) *The Book of Pontiffs.* 2nd edition, Liverpool University Press, Liverpool.

Vita S. Melaniae Junioris = Clark, E. A. 1984 (ed. and trans.) *The Life of Melania the Younger.* Edwin Mellen Press, New York.

Modern sources

Arthur, P. 1997 The Roman commercial amphorae. In Potter and King 1997, 299-316.

Barba, A. C. 2017 Metalworking in the 'Post-Classical' phases of Roman villas in Italy (5th-7th centuries AD). *Mélanges de l'Ecole Française de Rome – Moyen Age* 129.2, online edition https://journals.openedition.org/mefrm/3692 or https://doi.org/10.4000/mefrm.3692

Barnish, S. J. B. 1995 Christians and countrymen at San Vincenzo, c. AD 400-550. In Hodges, R. (ed.), *San Vincenzo al Volturno 2: the 1980-86 excavations part II.* Archaeological Monograph of the British School at Rome 9, 131-7, London.

Bowes, K. 2007 'Christianization' and the rural home. *Journal of Early Christian Studies* 15, 143-70.

Bowes, K. 2021 (ed.) *The Roman Peasant Project 2009-2014. Excavating the Roman rural poor.* Penn Press, Philadelphia.

Cameron, F. *et al.* 1984 Il castello di Ponte Nepesino e il confine settentrionale del ducato di Roma. *Archeologia Medievale* 11, 63-147.

Carandini, A. (ed) 1985 *Settefinestre. una villa schiavistica nell'Etruria romana.* Panini, Modena.

Castiglia, G. 2018 Rural churches and settlements in late-antique and Early Medieval Tuscany. *Journal of Roman Archaeology* 31, 223-47.

Chavarria Arnau, A. 2006 Aristocracias tardoantiguas y cristianización del territorio (siglos IV-V): ¿otro mito historiografico? *Rivista di Archeologia Cristiana* 82, 201-30.

Chavarria Arnau, A. 2010 Churches and villas in the 5th century: reflections on Italian archaeological data. In Delogu, P. and Gasparri, S. (ed.), *Le Trasformazioni del V secolo. L'Italia, i barbari e l'Occidente romano,* 639-62. Brepols Publishers, Turnhout.

Christie, N. 1992 Papal *domuscultae*: the case of Santa Cornelia. In Herring, E., Whitehouse, R. and Wilkins, J. (ed.), *Papers of the Fourth Conference of Italian Archaeology, 4, New Developments in Italian Archaeology, part 2,* 155-63. Accordia Research Centre, London.

Christie, N. and Daniels, C. M. 1991 Santa Cornelia: the excavation of an early medieval estate and a medieval monastery. In Christie, N. (ed.), *Three South Etrurian Churches.* Archaeological Monograph of the British School at Rome 4, 1-209, London.

Claridge, A. 1997 Marble sculpture, objects and veneer of the Roman period. In Potter and King 1997, 207-16.

Clark, E. A. 1984 *The Life of Melania the Younger.* E. Mellen Press, New York.

Conheeney, J. 1997 The human bone. In Potter and King 1997, 118-80.

De Grossi Mazzorin, J. 2020 L'archeozoologia dei contesti religiosi della tarda antichità e dell'alto medioevo.

In Castiglia, G. and Pergola, P. (ed.), Instrumentum Domesticum. *Archeologia cristiana, temi, metodologie e cultura materiale della tarda antichità e dell'alto medioevo, Vol. 1*, 635-53. Sussidi allo Studio delle Antichità Cristiane 29, Pontificio Istituto di Archeologia Cristiana, Vatican City.

DeLaine, J. 1997 The temple-tomb or mausoleum. In Potter and King 1997, 42-5.

Fedeli Bernardini, F. 1997 La Torre o sia Nova Mola: il mulino di Montegelato. In Potter and King 1997, 188-200.

Fiocchi Nicolai, V. 1988 *I Cimiteri Paleocristiani del Lazio: I. Etruria Meridionale.* Pontificio Istituto di Archeologia Cristiana, Vatican City.

Fiocchi Nicolai, V. 2007 Il ruolo dell'evergetismo aristocratico nella costruzione degli edifici di culto cristiani nell'hinterland di Roma. In Brogiolo, G. P. (ed.), *Archeologia e società tra tardo antico e alto medioevo. 12° Seminario sul Tardo Antico e l'Alto Medioevo, Padova, 29 settembre–1 ottobre 2005*, 107-126. Società Archeologica, Mantua.

Francovich, R. and Hodges, R. 2003 *Villa to Village. The transformation of the Roman countryside in Italy, c. 400-1000.* Duckworth, London.

Gilkes, O., King, A. and French, A. 1999 From villa to village: ceramics and Late Antique settlement in the Sabina Tiberina. *Archeologia Medievale* 26, 269-77.

Gilkes, O. and Potter, T. W. 1997 The baptisteries. In Potter and King 1997, 84-91.

Gilliver, C. M. 1990 A *mercator bovarius* from Veii in a new inscription from the Mola di Monte Gelato. *Papers of the British School at Rome* 58, 193-6.

Giorgi, J. 1997 The charred plant remains. In Potter and King 1997, 407-11.

Hobbs, R. 1997 The coins. In Potter and King 1997, 236-41.

Hodges, R. 1997 *Light in the Dark Ages. The rise and fall of San Vincenzo al Volturno.* Duckworth, London.

Hodges, R. 2021 Review of Patterson *et al.* 2020. *Bryn Mawr Classical Review* 2021.03.24 (online). https://bmcr.brynmawr.edu/2021/2021.03.24/ [accessed March 2021]

Hubert, Ét. 2000 L'*incastellamento* dans le Latium: Remarques à propos de fouilles récentes. *Annales. Histoire, Sciences Sociales* 55.3, 583-99.

Jones, A. H. M. 1973 *The Later Roman Empire, 284-602.* Blackwell, Oxford.

Kahane, A., Murray-Threipland, L. and Ward-Perkins, J. B. 1968 The Ager Veientanus north and east of Veii. *Papers of the British School at Rome* 36, 1-218.

Keay, S., Millett, M. and Smith, C. 2020 The Tiber Valley Project: an introduction. In Patterson *et al.* 2020, 1-8.

King, A. C. 1997 Mammal, reptile and amphibian bones. In Potter and King 1997, 383-403.

Marazzi, F. 1997 Il *Patrimonium Tusciae* della Chiesa Romana tra VI e X secolo: note sulle sue pertinenze fondarie. In Potter and King 1997, 412-20.

Messineo, G. and Carbonara, A. 1993 *Via Flaminia.* Libreria dello Stato, Rome.

Munro, B. 2011 Approaching architectural recycling in Roman and Late Roman villas. In Mladenović, D. and Russell, B. (ed.), *TRAC 2010: Proceedings of the Twentieth Annual Theoretical Roman Archaeology Conference, Oxford 2010*, 76–88. Oxbow Books, Oxford.

Murray, O. *et al.* 1991 A 'stork-vase' from the Mola di Monte Gelato. *Papers of the British School at Rome* 59, 177-95.

Osborne, J. 1994 A Carolingian *Agnus Dei* relief from Mola di Monte Gelato, near Rome. *Gesta* 33.2, 73-8.

Osborne, J. 1997 The early medieval sculpture. In Potter and King 1997, 217-28.

Partner, P. 1966 Notes on the lands of the Roman Church in the Early Middle Ages. *Papers of the British School at Rome* 34, 68-78.

Patterson, H. 1997 The early medieval and medieval pottery. In Potter and King 1997, 366-83.

Patterson, H. 2004 Introduction. In Patterson, H. (ed.), *Bridging the Tiber. Approaches to regional archaeology in the Middle Tiber Valley.* Archaeological Monograph of the British School at Rome 13, London.

Patterson, H. 2020a The late antique landscapes of the middle Tiber valley: the mid-third to mid-sixth centuries AD. In Patterson *et al.* 2020, 208-51.

Patterson, H. 2020b The end of the Roman unity: the Tiber valley in the late sixth to seventh centuries AD. In Patterson *et al.* 2020, 252-73.

Patterson, H. 2020c The middle Tiber valley in the eighth and ninth centuries AD. In Patterson *et al.* 2020, 274-301.

Patterson, H., Di Giuseppe, H. and Witcher, R. 2001 Three South Etrurian 'crises': first results of the Tiber Valley Project. *Papers of the British School at Rome* 72, 1-36.

Patterson, H., Witcher, R. and Di Giuseppe, H. 2020 (ed.) *The Changing Landscapes of Rome's Northern Hinterland. The British School at Rome's Tiber Valley Project.* Archaeopress Roman Archaeology 70, Oxford.

Pergola, P. (ed.) 1999 *Alle Origini della Parrocchia Rurale (IV-VIII sec.).* Pontificio Istituto di Archeologia, Vatican City.

Potter, T. W. 1972 Excavations in the medieval centre of Mazzano Romano. *Papers of the British School at Rome* 40, 135-45.

Potter, T. W. 1979 *The Changing Landscape of South Etruria.* Elek, London.

Potter, T. W. and King, A. C. 1997 *Excavations at the Mola di Monte Gelato: a Roman and medieval settlement in South Etruria.* Archaeological Monograph of the British School at Rome 11, London.

Price, J. 1997 The glass. In Potter and King 1997, 265-86.

Rathbone, D. W. 1983 The slave mode of production in Italy. *Journal of Roman Studies* 73, 160-8.

Roberts, P. 1997 The Roman pottery. In Potter and King 1997, 316-58.

Small, A. M. and Buck, R. J. 1994 *The Excavations of San Giovanni di Ruoti I. The villas and their environment.* University of Toronto Press, Toronto.

Tomassetti, G. 1882 Della Campagna romana nel medio evo. *Archivio della Società Romana di Storia Patria* 5, 67-156.

Tomassetti, G. 1883 Della Campagna romana nel medio evo (cont.). *Archivio della Società Romana di Storia Patria* 6, 173-222.

Valenti, M. 2016 Fortified settlements of the 8th to 10th Centuries. Italy and the case of Tuscany. In Christie, N. and Herold, H. (ed.), *Fortified Settlements in Early Medieval Europe. Defended communities of the 8th-10th centuries*, 289-301. Oxbow Books, Oxford.

Van der Noort, R. and Whitehouse, D. 1992 Le Mura di Santo Stefano, Anguillara, revisited. In Herring, E., Whitehouse, R. and Wilkins, J. (ed.), *Papers of the Fourth Conference of Italian Archaeology, 4, New Developments in Italian Archaeology, part 2*, 147-53. Accordia Research Centre, London.

Van der Noort, R. and Whitehouse, D. 2009 Excavations at Le Mura di Santo Stefano, Anguillara Sabazia. *Papers of the British School at Rome* 77, 159-223.

Wickham. C. 1978a Historical aspects of medieval South Etruria. In Blake, H., Potter T. W. and Whitehouse, D. B. (ed.), *Papers in Italian Archaeology I.* British Archaeological Reports (BAR) Supplementary Series 41, 373-90, Oxford.

Wickham, C. 1978b Historical and topographical notes on early medieval South Etruria (part one). *Papers of the British School at Rome* 46, 132-79.

Wickham. C. 1981 *Early Medieval Italy: central power and local society 400-1000.* Macmillan, London.

Wickham, C. 1994 *Land and Power. Studies in Italian and European social history, 400-1200.* British School at Rome, London.

Wilkinson, D. 1997 Excavations at Castellaccio, 1990. In Potter and King 1997, 170-88.

Witcher, R. 2020a The middle Tiber valley: history of studies and project methodologies. In Patterson *et al.* 2020, 9-73.

Witcher, R. 2020b The early and mid-imperial landscapes of the middle Tiber valley (*c.* 50 BC – AD 250). In Patterson *et al.* 2020, 117-207.

Index

Compiled by A. C. King and K. Adcock